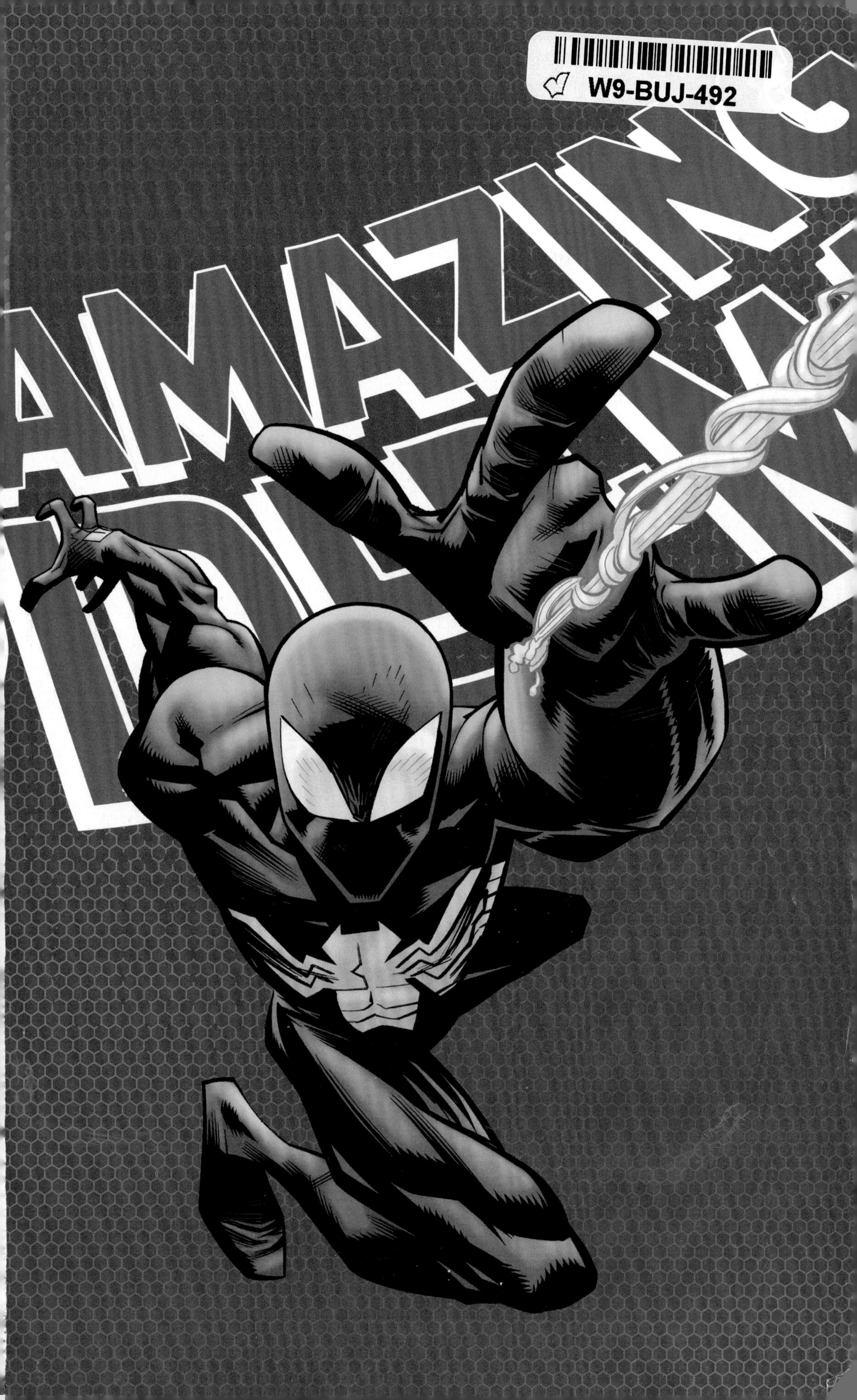

After leaving a tense dinner with Curt Conners' family in their underground home – teenaged Billy resents his father for making him hide his reptilian appearance – Peter Parker ran into an even more tense situation! Mercenaries Taskmaster and Black Ant had chased Aleksei Sytsevich (Rhino) right into the restaurant where May Parker was eating! As the building collapsed, Spider-Man protected Aunt May rather than save Aleksei from capture, knowing the decision would haunt him.

He doesn't yet know that Rhino was delivered to Kraven the Hunter. When Kraven hasn't been attacking poachers and their guides in his African territory, Sergei Kravinoff has been working with Arcade on a mysterious venture – with their sights set on a launch site a little closer to home...

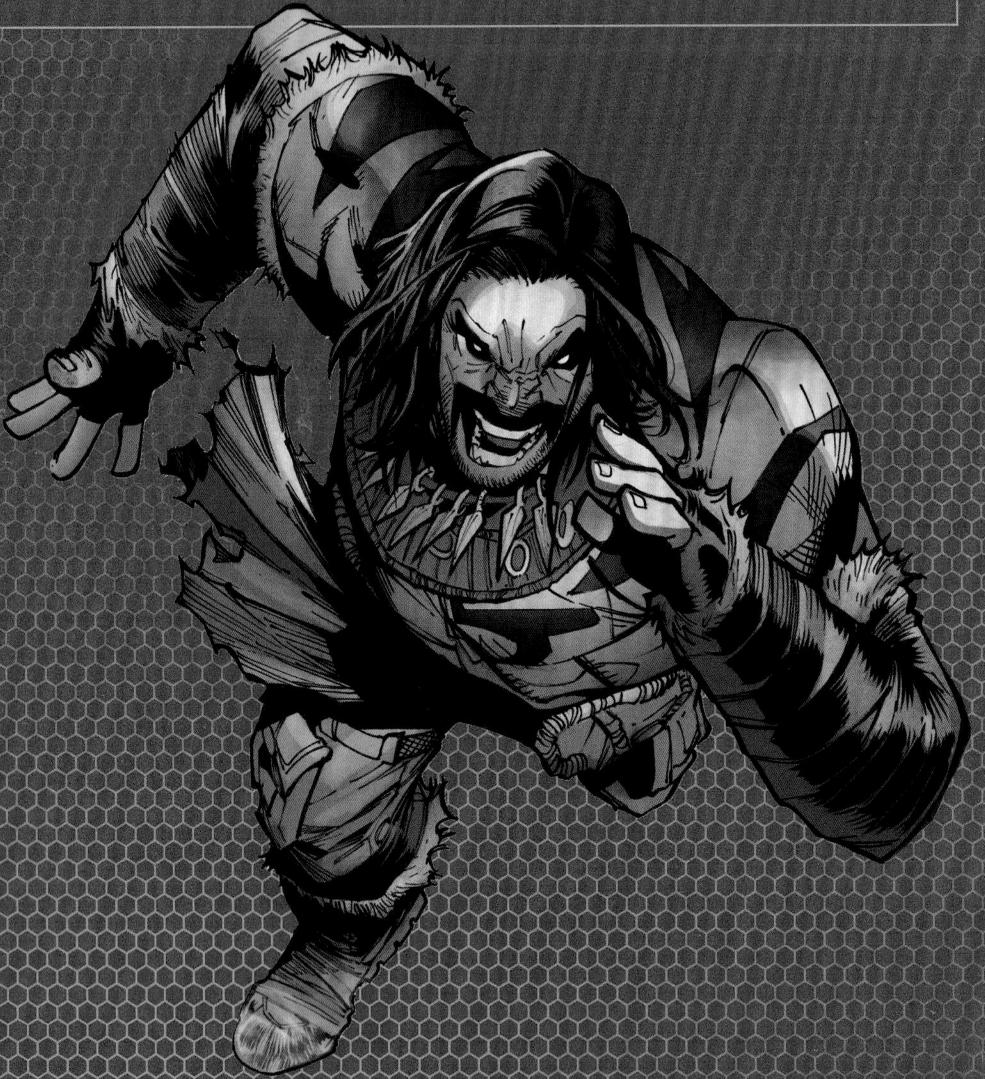

SPIDER-MAN CREATED BY STAN LEE & STEVE DITKO

COLLECTION EDITOR JENNIFER GRÜNWALD • ASSISTANT EDITOR CAITLIN O'CONNELL
ASSOCIATE MANAGING EDITOR KATERI WOODY • EDITOR, SPECIAL PROJECTS MARK D. BEAZLEY
VP PRODUCTION & SPECIAL PROJECTS JEFF YOUNGQUIST • BOOK DESIGNER JAY BOWEN

SVP PRINT, SALES & MARKETING DAVID GABRIEL • DIRECTOR, LICENSED PUBLISHING SVEN LARSEN
EDITOR IN CHIEF C.B. CEBULSKI • CHIEF CREATIVE OFFICER JOE QUESADA
PRESIDENT DAN BUCKLEY • EXECUTIVE PRODUCER ALAN FINE

AMAZING SPIDER-MAN: HUNTED. Contains material originally published in magazine form as AMAZING SPIDER-MAN #16-23, #16.HU and #18.HU-20.HU. First printing 2019. ISBN 978-1-302-91434-9. Published by MARVEL WORLDWIDE, INC., a subsidiary of MARVEL ENTERTAINMENT, LLC. OFFICE OF PUBLICATION: 135 West 50th Street, New York, NY 10020. © 2019 MARVEL No similarity between any of the names, characters, persons, and/or institutions in this magazine with those of any living or dead person or institution is intended, and any such similarity which may exist is purely coincidental. **Printed in Canada.** DAN BUCKLEY, President, Marvel Entertainment; JOHN NEE, Publisher; JOE QUESADA, Chief Creative Officer; TOM BREVOORT, SVP of Publishing; DAVID BOGART, Associate Publisher & SVP of Talent Affairs; DAVID GABRIEL, SVP of Sales & Marketing, Publishing; JEFF YOUNGQUIST, VP of Production & Special Projects; DAN CARR, Executive Director of Publishing Technology; ALEX MORALES, Director of Publishing Operations; DAN EDINGTON, Managing Editor; SUSAN CRESPI, Production Manager; STAN LEE, Chairman Emeritus. For information regarding advertising in Marvel Comics or on Marvel.com, please contact Vit DeBellis, Custom Solutions & Integrated Advertising Manager, at vdebellis@marvel.com. For Marvel subscription inquiries, please call 888-511-5480. **Manufactured between 6/21/2019 and 7/23/2019 by SOLISCO PRINTERS, SCOTT, QC, CANADA.**

10 9 8 7 6 5 4 3 2 1

the AMAZING SPIDER-MAN

HUNTED

WRITER NICK SPENCER

AMAZING SPIDER-MAN #16
PENCILERS RYAN OTTLEY
& ALBERTO ALBURQUERQUE
INKERS CLIFF RATHBURN
& ALBERTO ALBURQUERQUE
COLOR ARTISTS LAURA MARTIN,
BRIAN REBER & CARLOS LOPEZ
COVER ART CULLY HAMNER & JUSTIN PONSOR

AMAZING SPIDER-MAN #16.HU
ARTIST IBAN COELLO
COLOR ARTIST EDGAR DELGADO
COVER ART GREG LAND & JUSTIN PONSOR

AMAZING SPIDER-MAN #17-18, #20 & #22
PENCILER HUMBERTO RAMOS
INKERS VICTOR OLAZABA WITH
HUMBERTO RAMOS (#22)
COLOR ARTISTS EDGAR DELGADO (#17)
& ERICK ARCINIEGA (#18, #20)
COVER ART HUMBERTO RAMOS
& EDGAR DELGADO

AMAZING SPIDER-MAN #18.HU
ARTIST KEN LASHLEY
COLOR ARTIST ERICK ARCINIEGA
COVER ART GREG LAND & FRANK D'ARMATA

AMAZING SPIDER-MAN #19 & #21
PENCILER GERARDO SANDOVAL
INKERS GERARDO SANDOVAL
WITH VICTOR NAVA (#21)
COLOR ARTISTS EDGAR DELGADO
& ERICK ARCINIEGA
COVER ART HUMBERTO RAMOS
& EDGAR DELGADO

AMAZING SPIDER-MAN #19.HU
PENCILER CHRIS BACHALO
INKERS WAYNE FAUCHER, LIVESAY,
JAIME MENDOZA, VICTOR OLAZABA,
TIM TOWNSEND & AL VEY
COLOR ARTIST ERICK ARCINIEGA
COVER ART GREG LAND & FRANK D'ARMATA

AMAZING SPIDER-MAN #20.HU
PENCILER CORY SMITH
INKER MARK MORALES
COLOR ARTIST ERICK ARCINIEGA
"MOTHER" ARTIST TYLER CROOK
"MOTHER" COLOR ARTIST JIM CAMPBELL
COVER ART GREG LAND & FRANK D'ARMATA

AMAZING SPIDER-MAN #23
PENCILER RYAN OTTLEY
INKER CLIFF RATHBURN
COLOR ARTIST NATHAN FAIRBAIRN
COVER ART RYAN OTTLEY & NATHAN FAIRBAIRN

LETTERER VC's JOE CARAMAGNA
ASSISTANT EDITOR KATHLEEN WISNESKI
EDITOR NICK LOWE

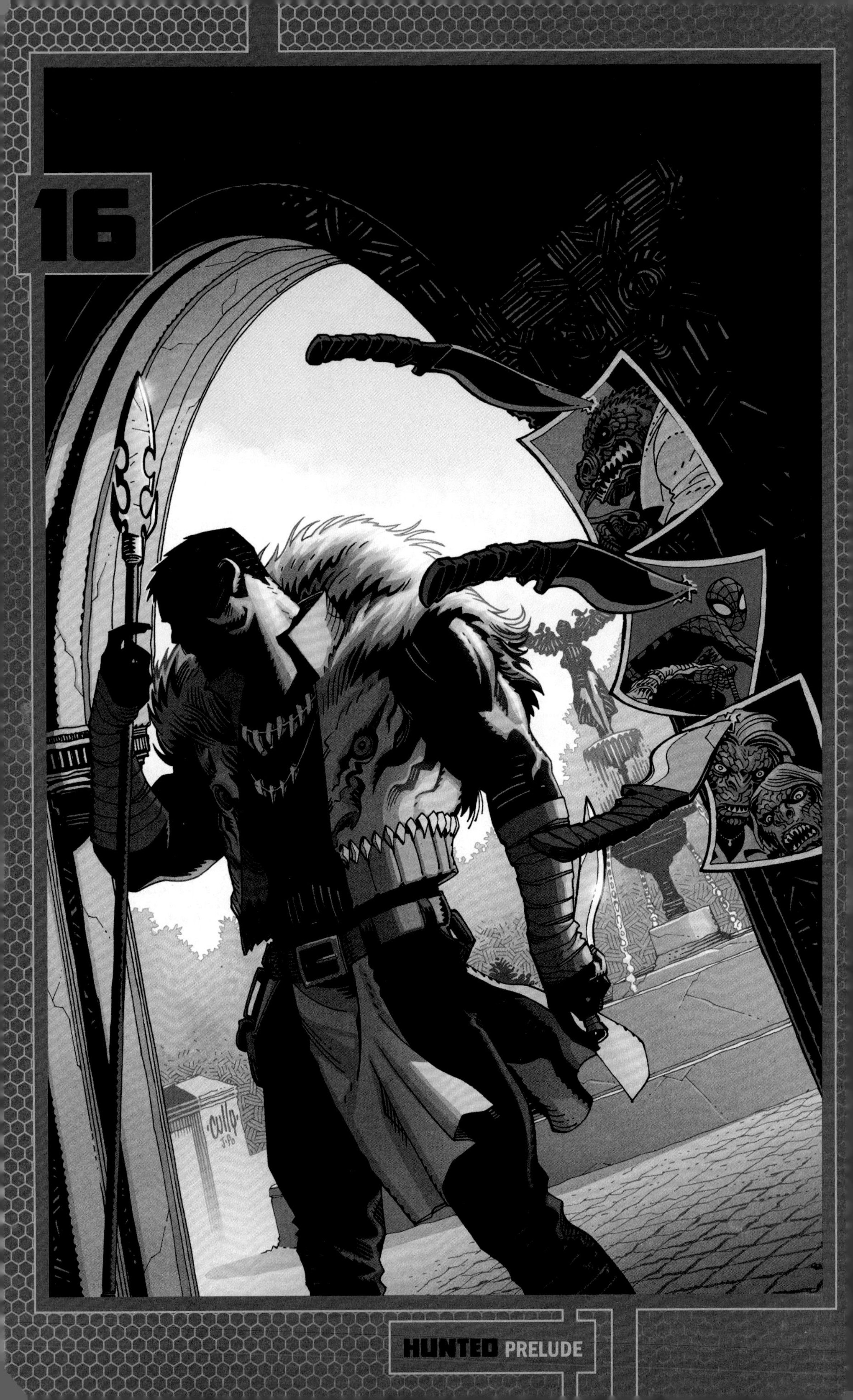
16
HUNTED PRELUDE

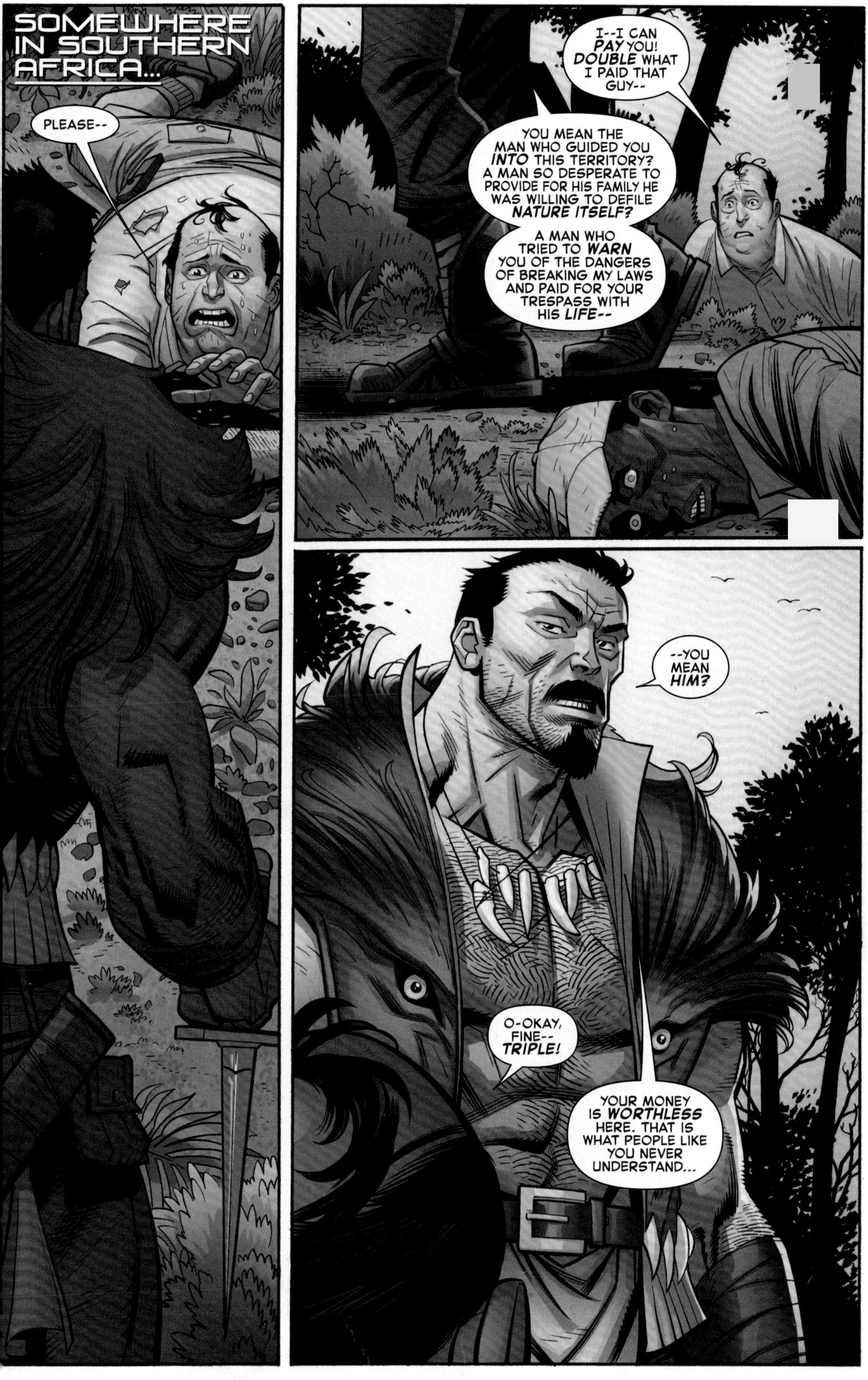
SOMEWHERE IN SOUTHERN AFRICA...
PLEASE--
I--I CAN PAY YOU! DOUBLE WHAT I PAID THAT GUY--
YOU MEAN THE MAN WHO GUIDED YOU INTO THIS TERRITORY? A MAN SO DESPERATE TO PROVIDE FOR HIS FAMILY HE WAS WILLING TO DEFILE NATURE ITSELF?
A MAN WHO TRIED TO WARN YOU OF THE DANGERS OF BREAKING MY LAWS AND PAID FOR YOUR TRESPASS WITH HIS LIFE--
--YOU MEAN HIM?
O-OKAY, FINE--TRIPLE!
YOUR MONEY IS WORTHLESS HERE. THAT IS WHAT PEOPLE LIKE YOU NEVER UNDERSTAND...

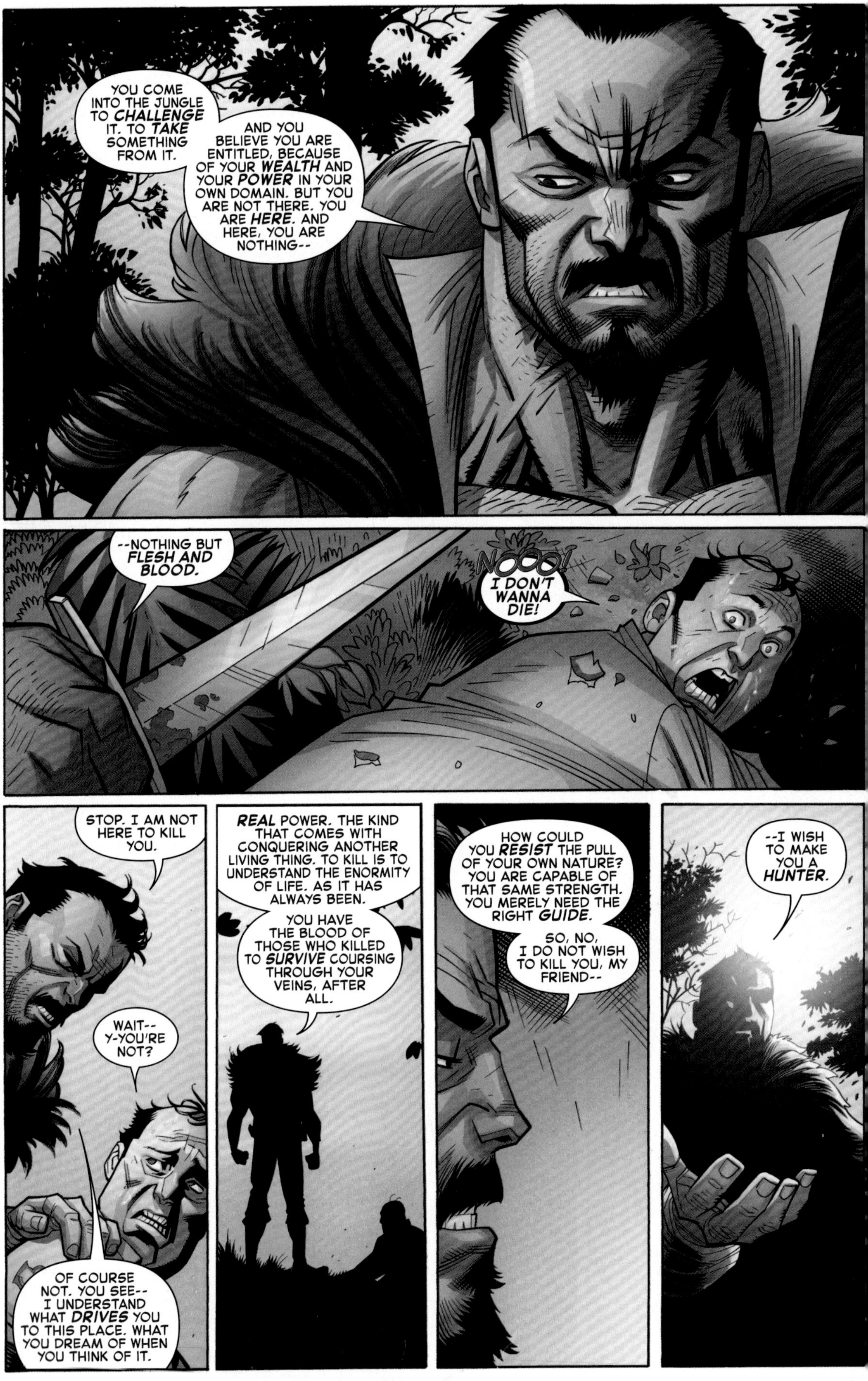
YOU COME INTO THE JUNGLE TO CHALLENGE IT. TO TAKE SOMETHING FROM IT.
AND YOU BELIEVE YOU ARE ENTITLED, BECAUSE OF YOUR WEALTH AND YOUR POWER IN YOUR OWN DOMAIN. BUT YOU ARE NOT THERE. YOU ARE HERE. AND HERE, YOU ARE NOTHING--
--NOTHING BUT FLESH AND BLOOD.
NOOO! I DON'T WANNA DIE!
STOP. I AM NOT HERE TO KILL YOU.
WAIT-- Y-YOU'RE NOT?
OF COURSE NOT. YOU SEE-- I UNDERSTAND WHAT DRIVES YOU TO THIS PLACE. WHAT YOU DREAM OF WHEN YOU THINK OF IT.
REAL POWER. THE KIND THAT COMES WITH CONQUERING ANOTHER LIVING THING. TO KILL IS TO UNDERSTAND THE ENORMITY OF LIFE. AS IT HAS ALWAYS BEEN.
YOU HAVE THE BLOOD OF THOSE WHO KILLED TO SURVIVE COURSING THROUGH YOUR VEINS, AFTER ALL.
HOW COULD YOU RESIST THE PULL OF YOUR OWN NATURE? YOU ARE CAPABLE OF THAT SAME STRENGTH. YOU MERELY NEED THE RIGHT GUIDE.
SO, NO, I DO NOT WISH TO KILL YOU, MY FRIEND--
--I WISH TO MAKE YOU A HUNTER.

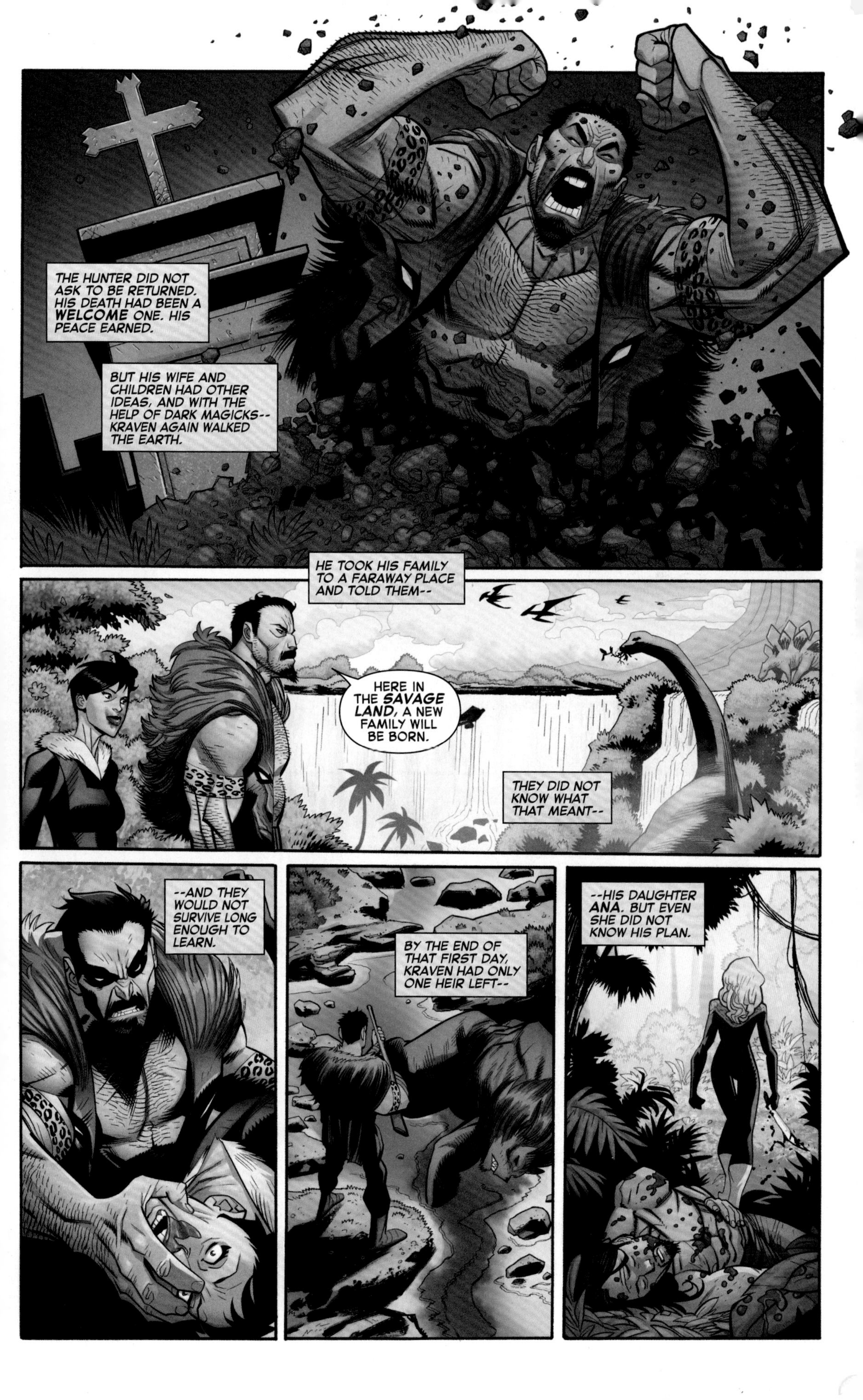
THE HUNTER DID NOT ASK TO BE RETURNED. HIS DEATH HAD BEEN A WELCOME ONE. HIS PEACE EARNED.
BUT HIS WIFE AND CHILDREN HAD OTHER IDEAS, AND WITH THE HELP OF DARK MAGICKS-- KRAVEN AGAIN WALKED THE EARTH.
HE TOOK HIS FAMILY TO A FARAWAY PLACE AND TOLD THEM--
HERE IN THE SAVAGE LAND, A NEW FAMILY WILL BE BORN.
THEY DID NOT KNOW WHAT THAT MEANT--
--AND THEY WOULD NOT SURVIVE LONG ENOUGH TO LEARN.
BY THE END OF THAT FIRST DAY, KRAVEN HAD ONLY ONE HEIR LEFT--
--HIS DAUGHTER ANA. BUT EVEN SHE DID NOT KNOW HIS PLAN.

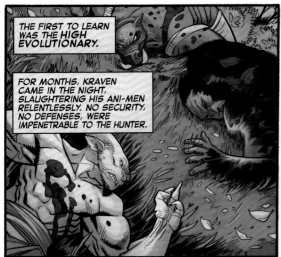

THE FIRST TO LEARN WAS THE **HIGH EVOLUTIONARY.**

FOR MONTHS, KRAVEN CAME IN THE NIGHT, SLAUGHTERING HIS ANI-MEN RELENTLESSLY. NO SECURITY, NO DEFENSES, WERE IMPENETRABLE TO THE HUNTER.

SEEING HIS BELOVED CREATIONS DIE OVER AND OVER, UNABLE TO WITHSTAND ANY MORE **HEARTBREAK,** THE HIGH EVOLUTIONARY RELENTED--

PLEASE! WHATEVER IT IS YOU WANT FROM ME, MAKE IT KNOWN! **SHOW YOURSELF!**

HE GAVE KRAVEN WHAT HE WANTED--

--SONS.

THIS WAS THE NEW FAMILY THE HUNTER HAD PROMISED--

--ONE MADE IN HIS OWN IMAGE.

PERFECT CLONES OF THEIR FATHER, EACH ONE. EIGHTY-SEVEN ALTOGETHER.

ENTIRELY HUMAN, BUT DESIGNED TO AGE INTO ADULTHOOD AT AN ACCELERATED PACE. TIME WAS OF THE ESSENCE, AFTER ALL.

WHEN HIS ONLY DAUGHTER LEARNED THE TRUTH, SHE LEFT IN DISGUST.

THIS IS A **DISGRACE!** A DISHONOR TO OUR HOUSE, FATHER! IF YOU ARE TO DO THIS--

--THEN I **RENOUNCE OUR NAME!** I WILL BE A KRAVINOFF **NO LONGER!**

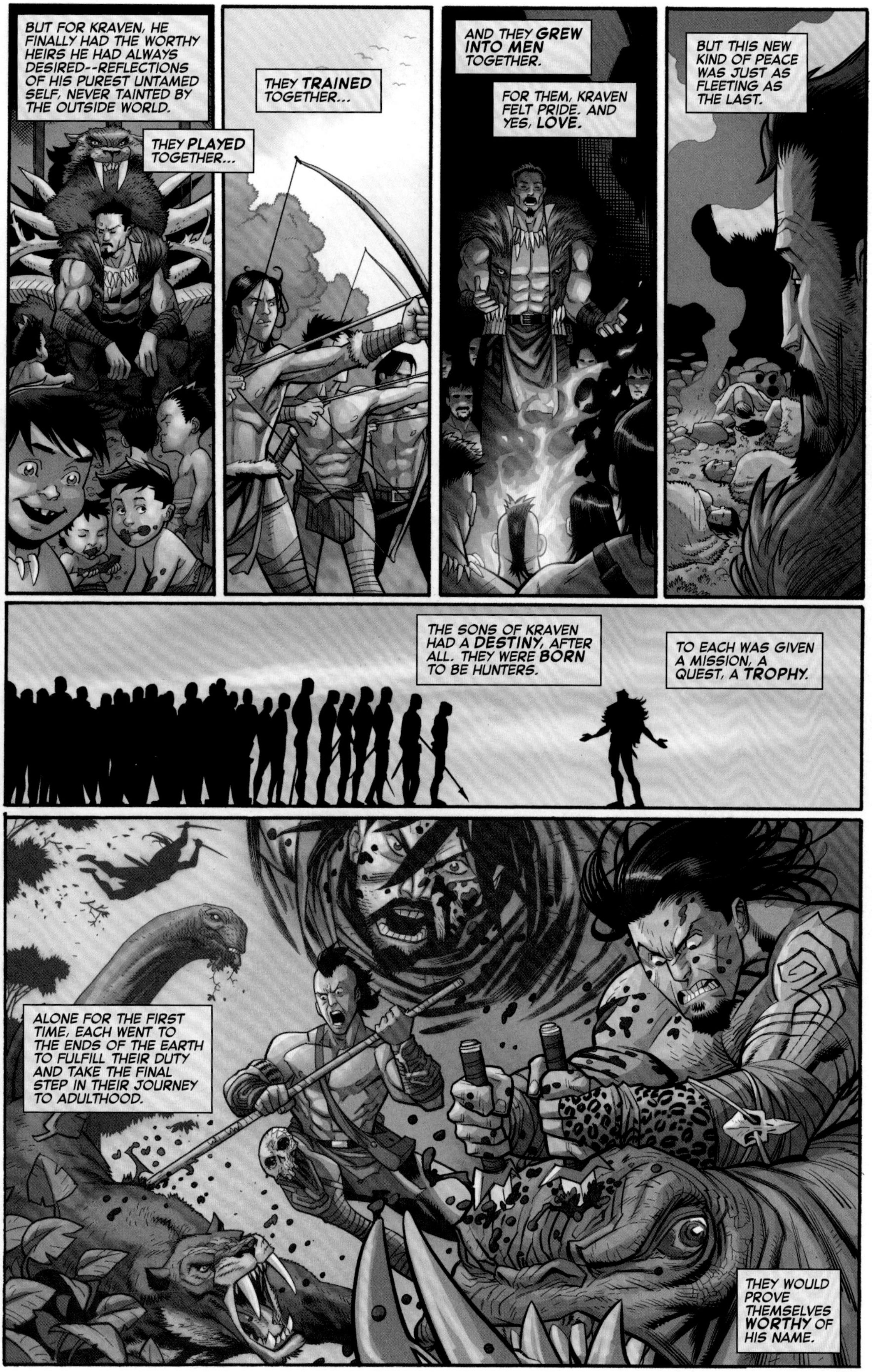
BUT FOR KRAVEN, HE FINALLY HAD THE WORTHY HEIRS HE HAD ALWAYS DESIRED--REFLECTIONS OF HIS PUREST UNTAMED SELF, NEVER TAINTED BY THE OUTSIDE WORLD.
THEY PLAYED TOGETHER...
THEY TRAINED TOGETHER...
AND THEY GREW INTO MEN TOGETHER.
FOR THEM, KRAVEN FELT PRIDE. AND YES, LOVE.
BUT THIS NEW KIND OF PEACE WAS JUST AS FLEETING AS THE LAST.
THE SONS OF KRAVEN HAD A DESTINY, AFTER ALL. THEY WERE BORN TO BE HUNTERS.
TO EACH WAS GIVEN A MISSION, A QUEST, A TROPHY.
ALONE FOR THE FIRST TIME, EACH WENT TO THE ENDS OF THE EARTH TO FULFILL THEIR DUTY AND TAKE THE FINAL STEP IN THEIR JOURNEY TO ADULTHOOD.
THEY WOULD PROVE THEMSELVES WORTHY OF HIS NAME.

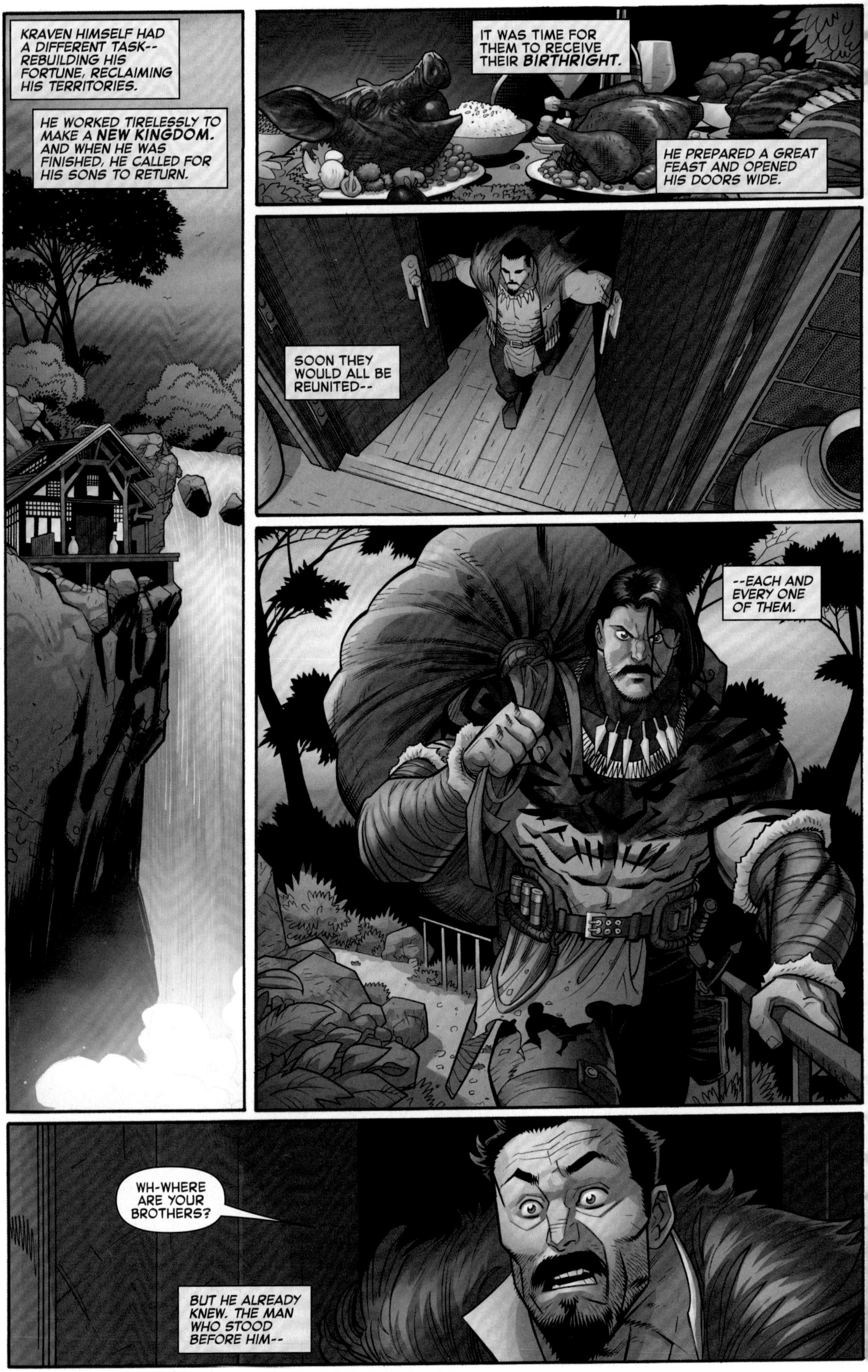
KRAVEN HIMSELF HAD A DIFFERENT TASK-- REBUILDING HIS FORTUNE, RECLAIMING HIS TERRITORIES.
HE WORKED TIRELESSLY TO MAKE A NEW KINGDOM. AND WHEN HE WAS FINISHED, HE CALLED FOR HIS SONS TO RETURN.
IT WAS TIME FOR THEM TO RECEIVE THEIR BIRTHRIGHT.
HE PREPARED A GREAT FEAST AND OPENED HIS DOORS WIDE.
SOON THEY WOULD ALL BE REUNITED--
--EACH AND EVERY ONE OF THEM.
WH-WHERE ARE YOUR BROTHERS?
BUT HE ALREADY KNEW. THE MAN WHO STOOD BEFORE HIM--

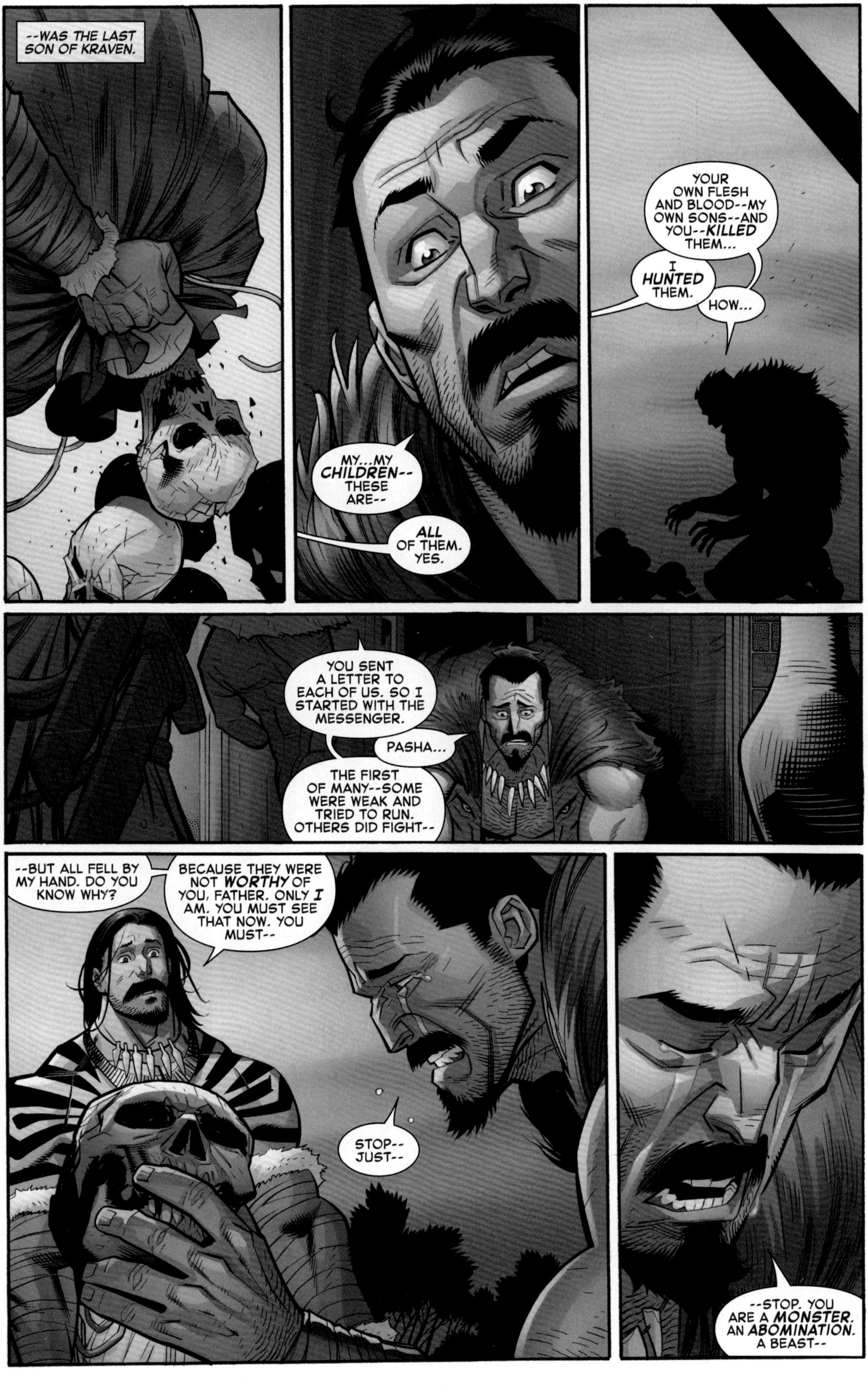
--WAS THE LAST SON OF KRAVEN.
MY...MY CHILDREN--THESE ARE--
ALL OF THEM. YES.
YOUR OWN FLESH AND BLOOD--MY OWN SONS--AND YOU--KILLED THEM...
I HUNTED THEM.
HOW...
YOU SENT A LETTER TO EACH OF US. SO I STARTED WITH THE MESSENGER.
PASHA...
THE FIRST OF MANY--SOME WERE WEAK AND TRIED TO RUN. OTHERS DID FIGHT--
--BUT ALL FELL BY MY HAND. DO YOU KNOW WHY?
BECAUSE THEY WERE NOT WORTHY OF YOU, FATHER. ONLY I AM. YOU MUST SEE THAT NOW. YOU MUST--
STOP--JUST--
--STOP. YOU ARE A MONSTER. AN ABOMINATION. A BEAST--

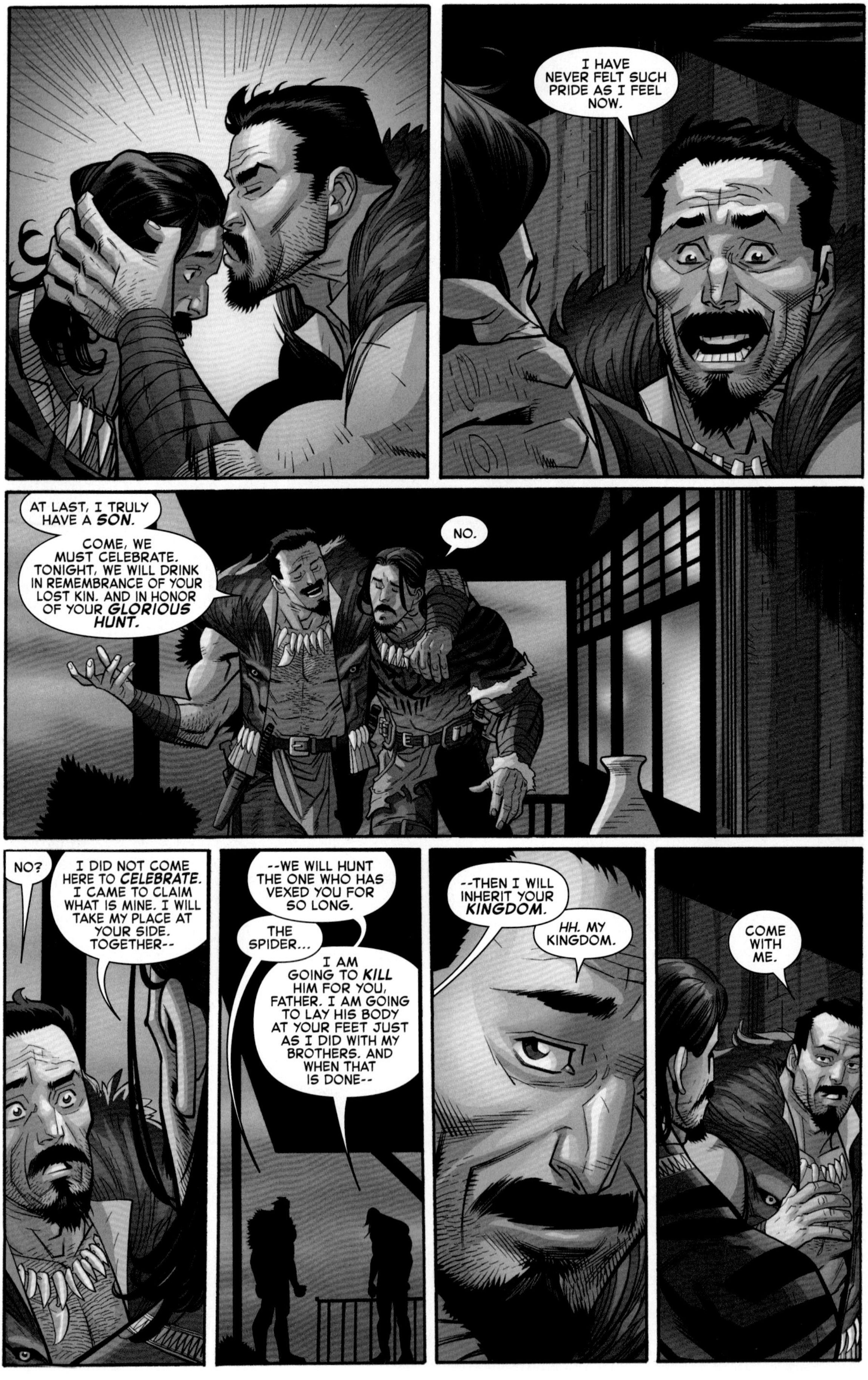
I HAVE NEVER FELT SUCH PRIDE AS I FEEL NOW.
AT LAST, I TRULY HAVE A SON.
COME, WE MUST CELEBRATE. TONIGHT, WE WILL DRINK IN REMEMBRANCE OF YOUR LOST KIN. AND IN HONOR OF YOUR GLORIOUS HUNT.
NO.
NO?
I DID NOT COME HERE TO CELEBRATE. I CAME TO CLAIM WHAT IS MINE. I WILL TAKE MY PLACE AT YOUR SIDE. TOGETHER--
--WE WILL HUNT THE ONE WHO HAS VEXED YOU FOR SO LONG.
THE SPIDER...
I AM GOING TO KILL HIM FOR YOU, FATHER. I AM GOING TO LAY HIS BODY AT YOUR FEET JUST AS I DID WITH MY BROTHERS. AND WHEN THAT IS DONE--
--THEN I WILL INHERIT YOUR KINGDOM.
HH. MY KINGDOM.
COME WITH ME.

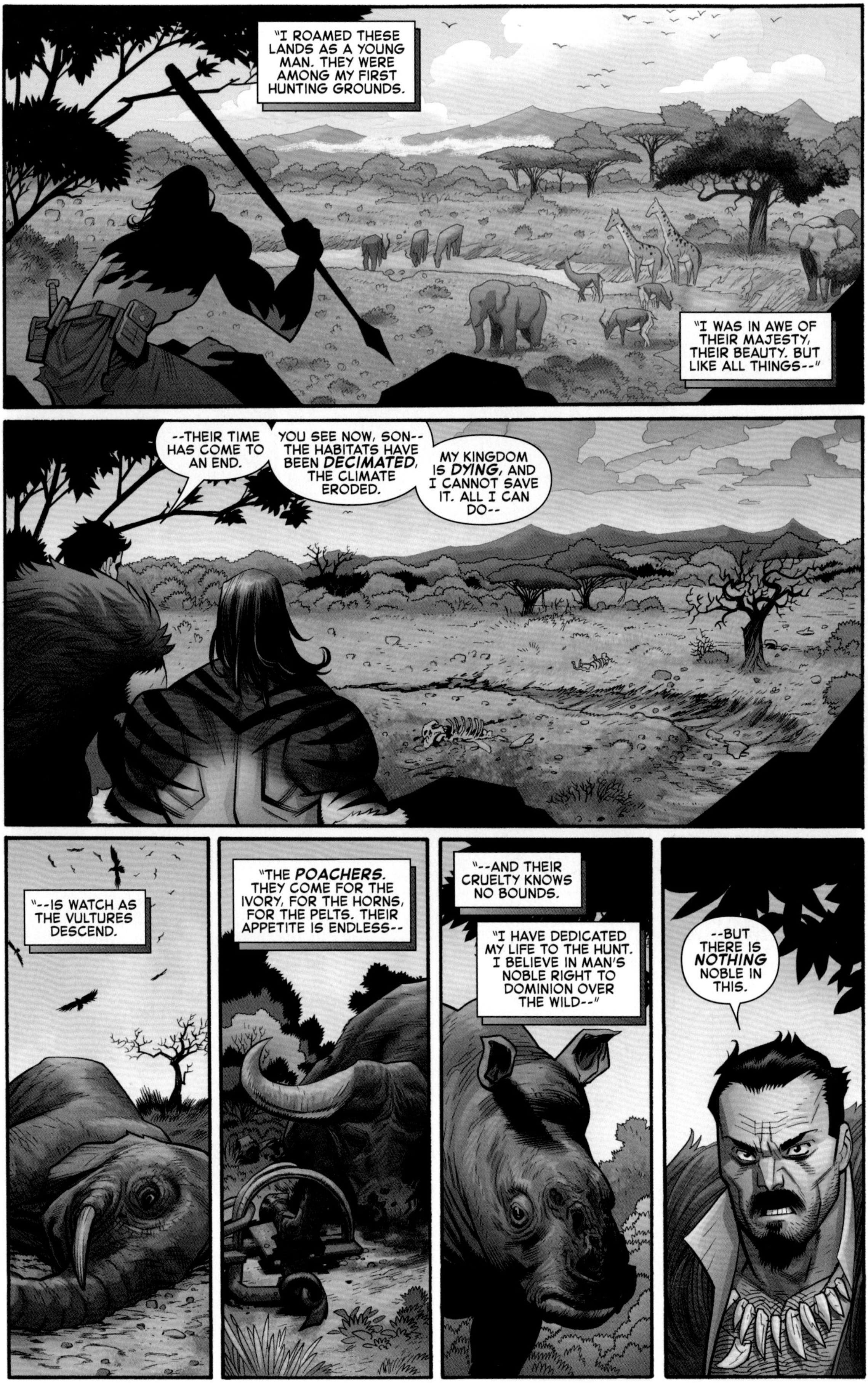
"I ROAMED THESE LANDS AS A YOUNG MAN. THEY WERE AMONG MY FIRST HUNTING GROUNDS.
"I WAS IN AWE OF THEIR MAJESTY, THEIR BEAUTY. BUT LIKE ALL THINGS--"
--THEIR TIME HAS COME TO AN END.
YOU SEE NOW, SON-- THE HABITATS HAVE BEEN DECIMATED, THE CLIMATE ERODED.
MY KINGDOM IS DYING, AND I CANNOT SAVE IT. ALL I CAN DO--
"--IS WATCH AS THE VULTURES DESCEND.
"THE POACHERS. THEY COME FOR THE IVORY, FOR THE HORNS, FOR THE PELTS. THEIR APPETITE IS ENDLESS--
"--AND THEIR CRUELTY KNOWS NO BOUNDS.
"I HAVE DEDICATED MY LIFE TO THE HUNT. I BELIEVE IN MAN'S NOBLE RIGHT TO DOMINION OVER THE WILD--"
--BUT THERE IS NOTHING NOBLE IN THIS.

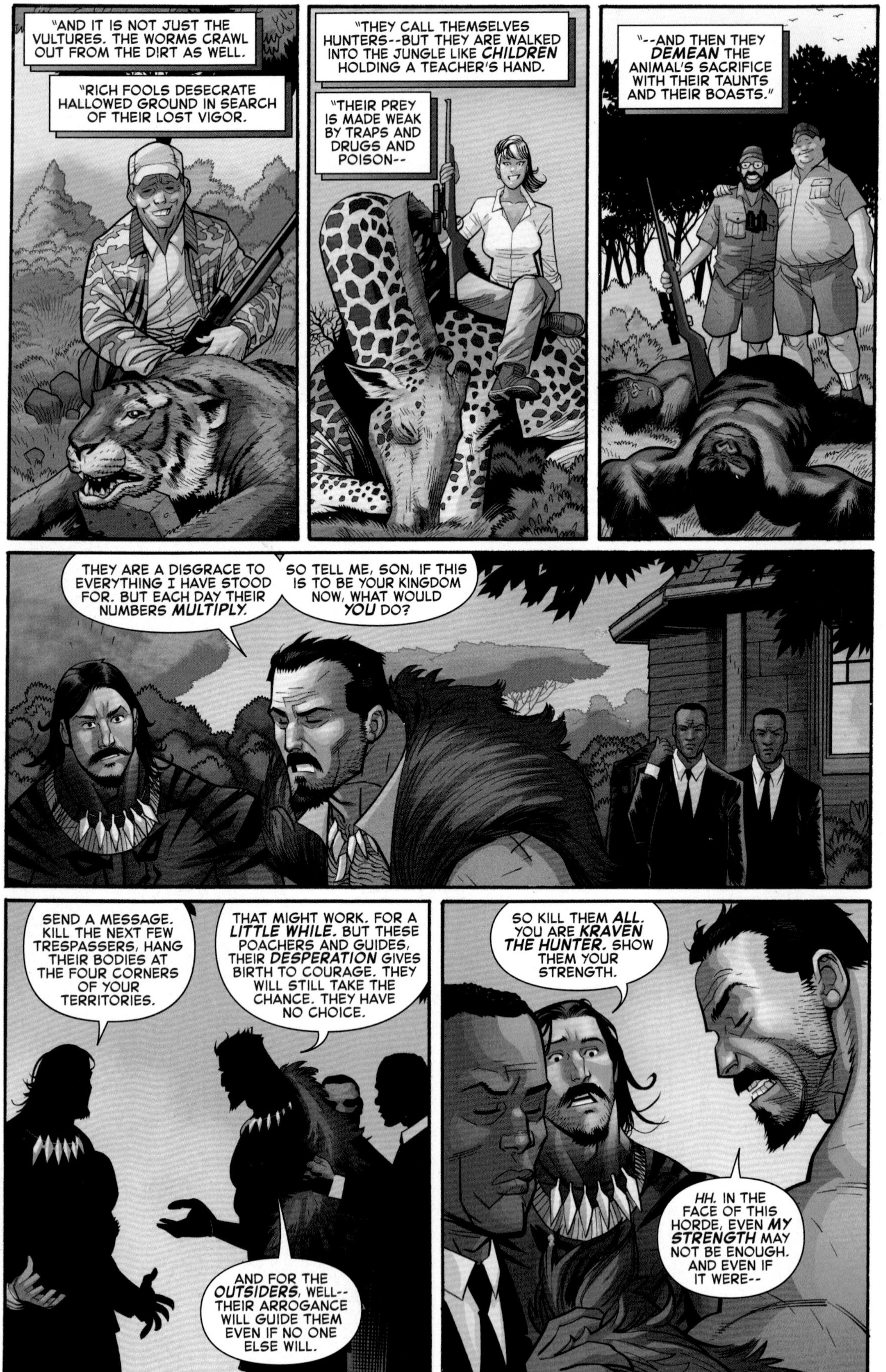
"AND IT IS NOT JUST THE VULTURES. THE WORMS CRAWL OUT FROM THE DIRT AS WELL.
"RICH FOOLS DESECRATE HALLOWED GROUND IN SEARCH OF THEIR LOST VIGOR.
"THEY CALL THEMSELVES HUNTERS--BUT THEY ARE WALKED INTO THE JUNGLE LIKE CHILDREN HOLDING A TEACHER'S HAND.
"THEIR PREY IS MADE WEAK BY TRAPS AND DRUGS AND POISON--
"--AND THEN THEY DEMEAN THE ANIMAL'S SACRIFICE WITH THEIR TAUNTS AND THEIR BOASTS."
THEY ARE A DISGRACE TO EVERYTHING I HAVE STOOD FOR. BUT EACH DAY THEIR NUMBERS MULTIPLY.
SO TELL ME, SON, IF THIS IS TO BE YOUR KINGDOM NOW, WHAT WOULD YOU DO?
SEND A MESSAGE. KILL THE NEXT FEW TRESPASSERS, HANG THEIR BODIES AT THE FOUR CORNERS OF YOUR TERRITORIES.
THAT MIGHT WORK. FOR A LITTLE WHILE. BUT THESE POACHERS AND GUIDES, THEIR DESPERATION GIVES BIRTH TO COURAGE. THEY WILL STILL TAKE THE CHANCE. THEY HAVE NO CHOICE.
AND FOR THE OUTSIDERS, WELL-- THEIR ARROGANCE WILL GUIDE THEM EVEN IF NO ONE ELSE WILL.
SO KILL THEM ALL. YOU ARE KRAVEN THE HUNTER. SHOW THEM YOUR STRENGTH.
HH. IN THE FACE OF THIS HORDE, EVEN MY STRENGTH MAY NOT BE ENOUGH. AND EVEN IF IT WERE--

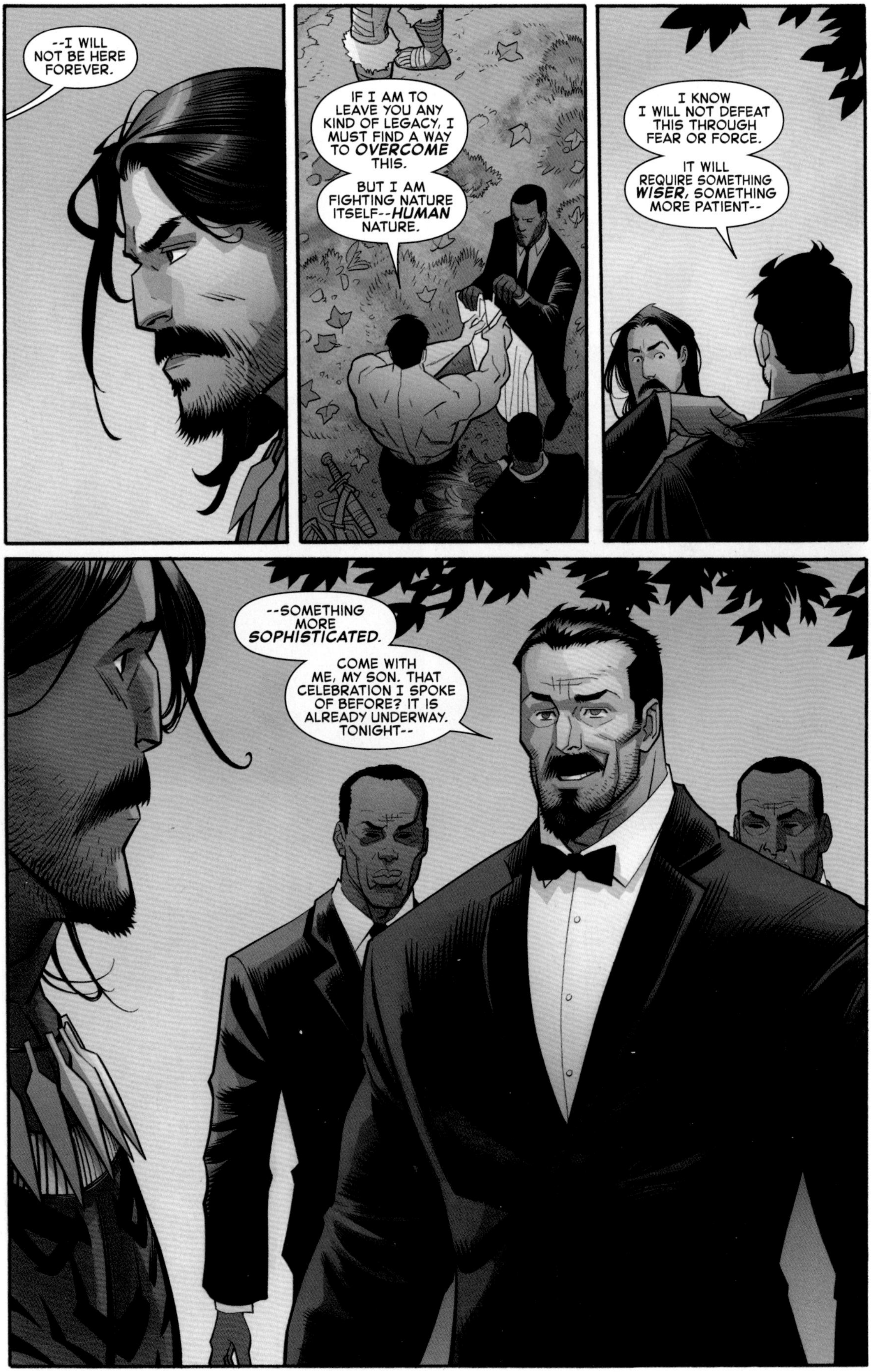
--I WILL NOT BE HERE FOREVER.
IF I AM TO LEAVE YOU ANY KIND OF LEGACY, I MUST FIND A WAY TO OVERCOME THIS.
BUT I AM FIGHTING NATURE ITSELF--HUMAN NATURE.
I KNOW I WILL NOT DEFEAT THIS THROUGH FEAR OR FORCE.
IT WILL REQUIRE SOMETHING WISER, SOMETHING MORE PATIENT--
--SOMETHING MORE SOPHISTICATED.
COME WITH ME, MY SON. THAT CELEBRATION I SPOKE OF BEFORE? IT IS ALREADY UNDERWAY. TONIGHT--

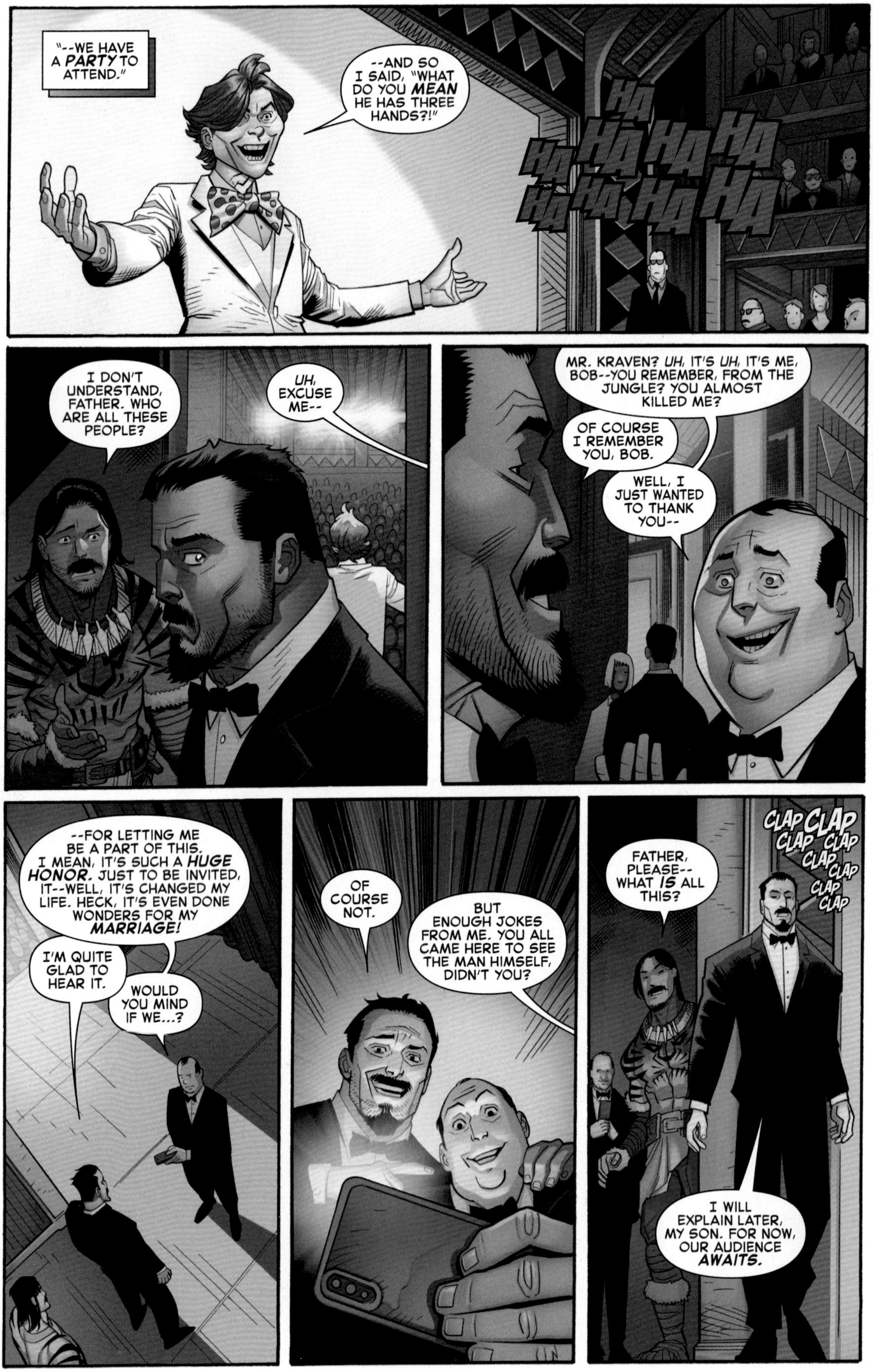
"--WE HAVE A PARTY TO ATTEND."
--AND SO I SAID, "WHAT DO YOU MEAN HE HAS THREE HANDS?!"
HA HA HA HA HA HA HA HA HA HA
I DON'T UNDERSTAND, FATHER. WHO ARE ALL THESE PEOPLE?
UH, EXCUSE ME--
MR. KRAVEN? UH, IT'S UH, IT'S ME, BOB--YOU REMEMBER, FROM THE JUNGLE? YOU ALMOST KILLED ME?
OF COURSE I REMEMBER YOU, BOB.
WELL, I JUST WANTED TO THANK YOU--
--FOR LETTING ME BE A PART OF THIS. I MEAN, IT'S SUCH A HUGE HONOR. JUST TO BE INVITED, IT--WELL, IT'S CHANGED MY LIFE. HECK, IT'S EVEN DONE WONDERS FOR MY MARRIAGE!
I'M QUITE GLAD TO HEAR IT.
WOULD YOU MIND IF WE...?
OF COURSE NOT.
BUT ENOUGH JOKES FROM ME. YOU ALL CAME HERE TO SEE THE MAN HIMSELF, DIDN'T YOU?
CLAP CLAP CLAP CLAP CLAP CLAP CLAP CLAP
FATHER, PLEASE--WHAT IS ALL THIS?
I WILL EXPLAIN LATER, MY SON. FOR NOW, OUR AUDIENCE AWAITS.

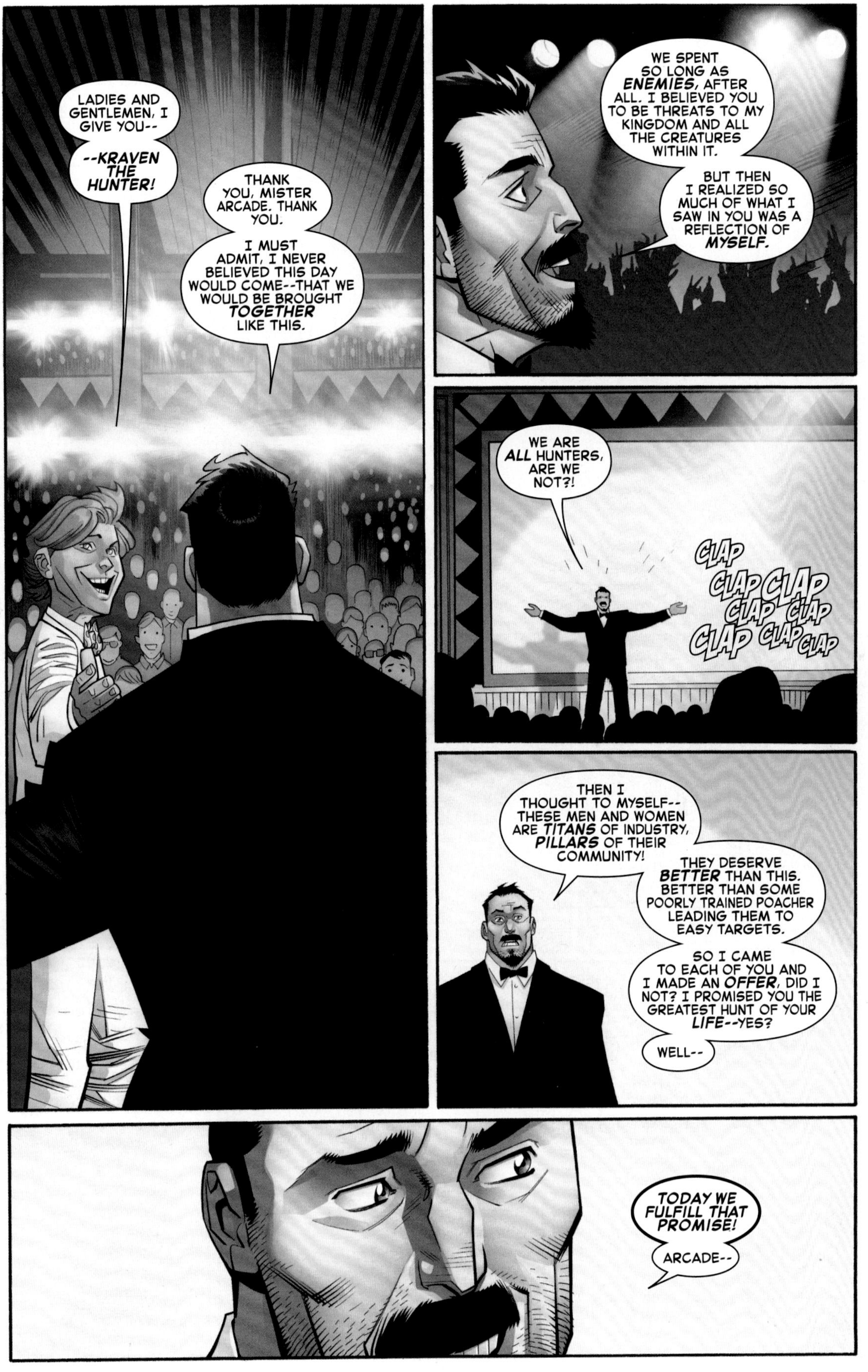

LADIES AND GENTLEMEN, I GIVE YOU--
--KRAVEN THE HUNTER!
THANK YOU, MISTER ARCADE. THANK YOU.
I MUST ADMIT, I NEVER BELIEVED THIS DAY WOULD COME--THAT WE WOULD BE BROUGHT TOGETHER LIKE THIS.
WE SPENT SO LONG AS ENEMIES, AFTER ALL. I BELIEVED YOU TO BE THREATS TO MY KINGDOM AND ALL THE CREATURES WITHIN IT.
BUT THEN I REALIZED SO MUCH OF WHAT I SAW IN YOU WAS A REFLECTION OF MYSELF.
WE ARE ALL HUNTERS, ARE WE NOT?!
CLAP
CLAP CLAP
CLAP CLAP
CLAP CLAP CLAP
THEN I THOUGHT TO MYSELF--THESE MEN AND WOMEN ARE TITANS OF INDUSTRY, PILLARS OF THEIR COMMUNITY!
THEY DESERVE BETTER THAN THIS. BETTER THAN SOME POORLY TRAINED POACHER LEADING THEM TO EASY TARGETS.
SO I CAME TO EACH OF YOU AND I MADE AN OFFER, DID I NOT? I PROMISED YOU THE GREATEST HUNT OF YOUR LIFE--YES?
WELL--
TODAY WE FULFILL THAT PROMISE!
ARCADE--

--SHOW THESE WARRIORS THE GAME WE HAVE PREPARED FOR THEM!

YOU GOT IT, BOSS! GATHER 'ROUND, FOLKS, AND FEAST YOUR EYES ON SOME OF THE DEADLIEST CREATURES EVER TO ROAM THE EARTH! WE CALL THEM--

--THE SAVAGE SIX!

THE VICIOUS *VULTURE!*

THE SADISTIC *SCORPION!*

THE TERRIFYING *TARANTULA!*

THE STUPENDOUS *STEGRON!*

THE CUNNING *KING COBRA!*

AND JUST ADDED--THE RAMPAGING *RHINO!*

BUT THIS IS JUST THE BEGINNING...

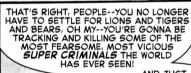

THAT'S RIGHT, PEOPLE--YOU NO LONGER HAVE TO SETTLE FOR LIONS AND TIGERS AND BEARS, OH MY--YOU'RE GONNA BE TRACKING AND KILLING SOME OF THE MOST FEARSOME, MOST VICIOUS *SUPER CRIMINALS* THE WORLD HAS EVER SEEN!

AND JUST WAIT UNTIL YOU SEE *WHERE* YOU'LL BE DOING ALL THAT KILLING--CHARTER JETS ARE LINED UP ON THE RUNWAY WAITING TO TAKE YOU TO ONE OF THE WORLD'S MOST EXOTIC LOCALES!

AND I WILL BE WITH YOU *EVERY* STEP OF THE WAY, MY FRIENDS AND FELLOW GAMESMEN.

THIS IS WHAT YOU HAVE *WAITED* FOR! THIS IS WHAT YOU HAVE *PAID* FOR! THIS IS THE MOMENT YOU WILL TELL YOUR CHILDREN AND YOUR GRANDCHILDREN ABOUT!

THE *GRAND HUNT* IS UPON US!

YEAH! WOOO!

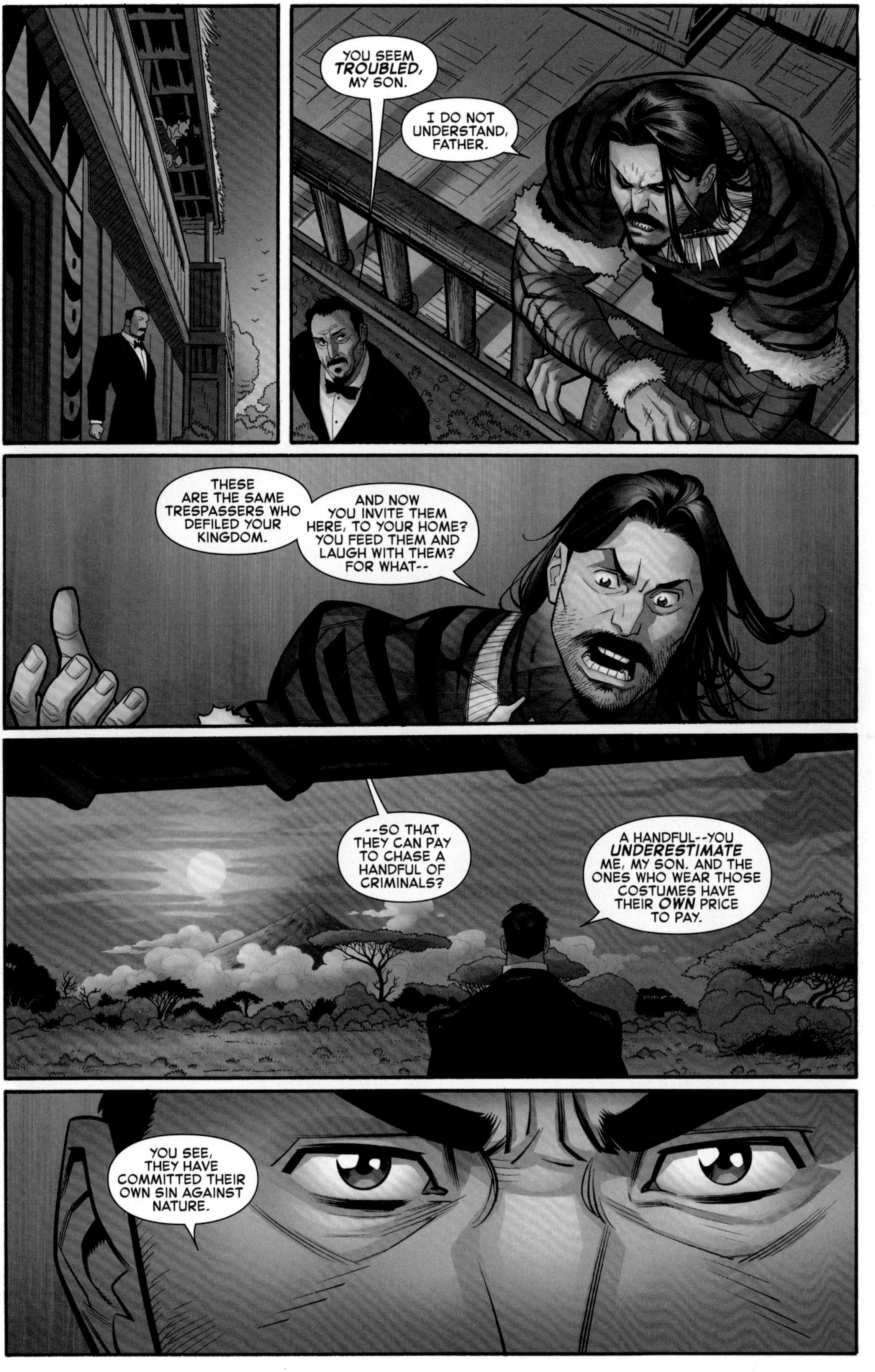

YOU SEEM *TROUBLED*, MY SON.
I DO NOT UNDERSTAND, FATHER.
THESE ARE THE SAME TRESPASSERS WHO DEFILED YOUR KINGDOM.
AND NOW YOU INVITE THEM HERE, TO YOUR HOME? YOU FEED THEM AND LAUGH WITH THEM? FOR WHAT--
--SO THAT THEY CAN PAY TO CHASE A HANDFUL OF CRIMINALS?
A HANDFUL--YOU *UNDERESTIMATE* ME, MY SON. AND THE ONES WHO WEAR THOSE COSTUMES HAVE THEIR *OWN* PRICE TO PAY.
YOU SEE, THEY HAVE COMMITTED THEIR OWN SIN AGAINST NATURE.

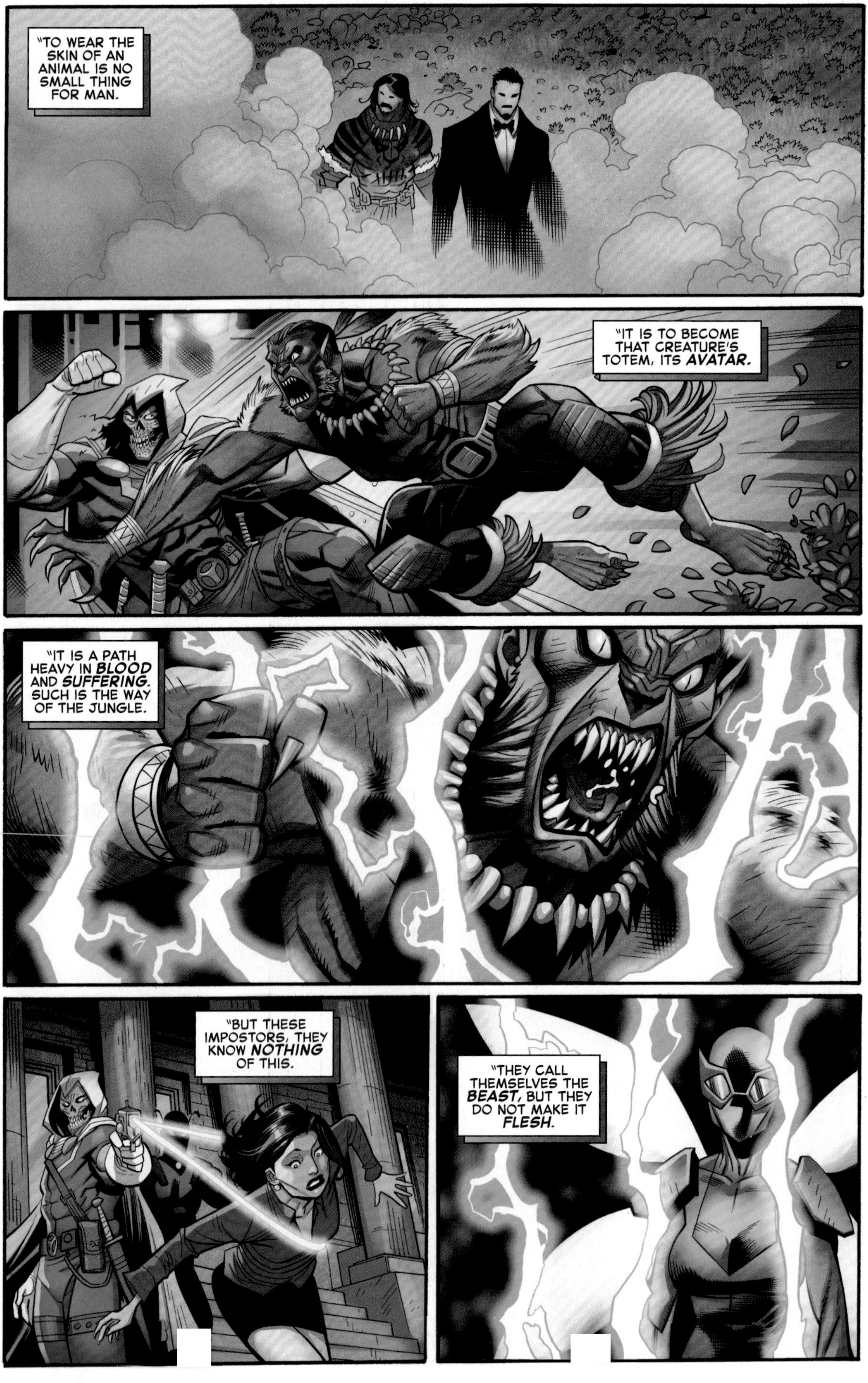
"TO WEAR THE SKIN OF AN ANIMAL IS NO SMALL THING FOR MAN.
"IT IS TO BECOME THAT CREATURE'S TOTEM, ITS *AVATAR.*
"IT IS A PATH HEAVY IN *BLOOD* AND *SUFFERING.* SUCH IS THE WAY OF THE JUNGLE.
"BUT THESE IMPOSTORS, THEY KNOW *NOTHING* OF THIS.
"THEY CALL THEMSELVES THE *BEAST,* BUT THEY DO NOT MAKE IT *FLESH.*

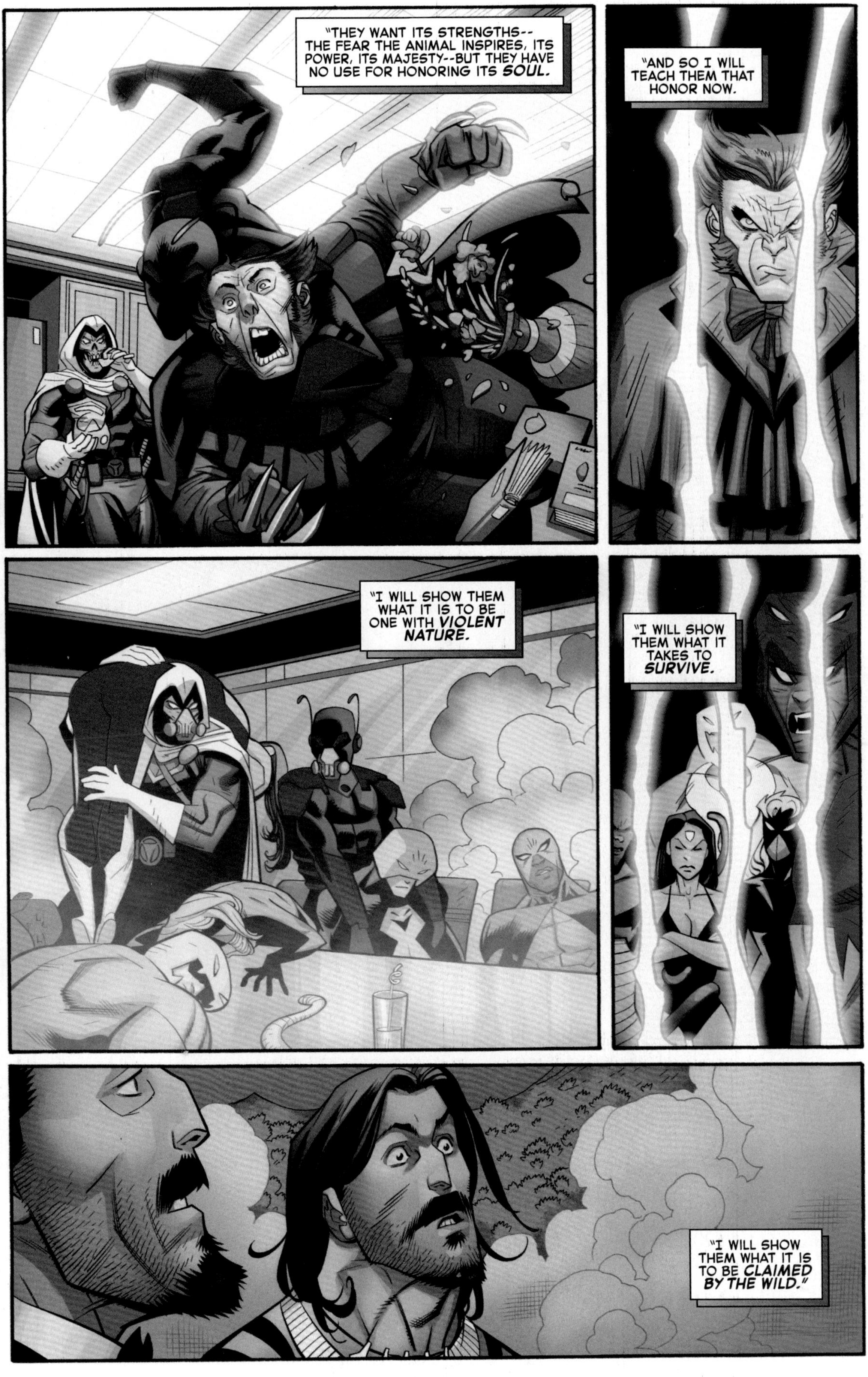
"THEY WANT ITS STRENGTHS-- THE FEAR THE ANIMAL INSPIRES, ITS POWER, ITS MAJESTY--BUT THEY HAVE NO USE FOR HONORING ITS SOUL.
"AND SO I WILL TEACH THEM THAT HONOR NOW.
"I WILL SHOW THEM WHAT IT IS TO BE ONE WITH VIOLENT NATURE.
"I WILL SHOW THEM WHAT IT TAKES TO SURVIVE.
"I WILL SHOW THEM WHAT IT IS TO BE CLAIMED BY THE WILD."

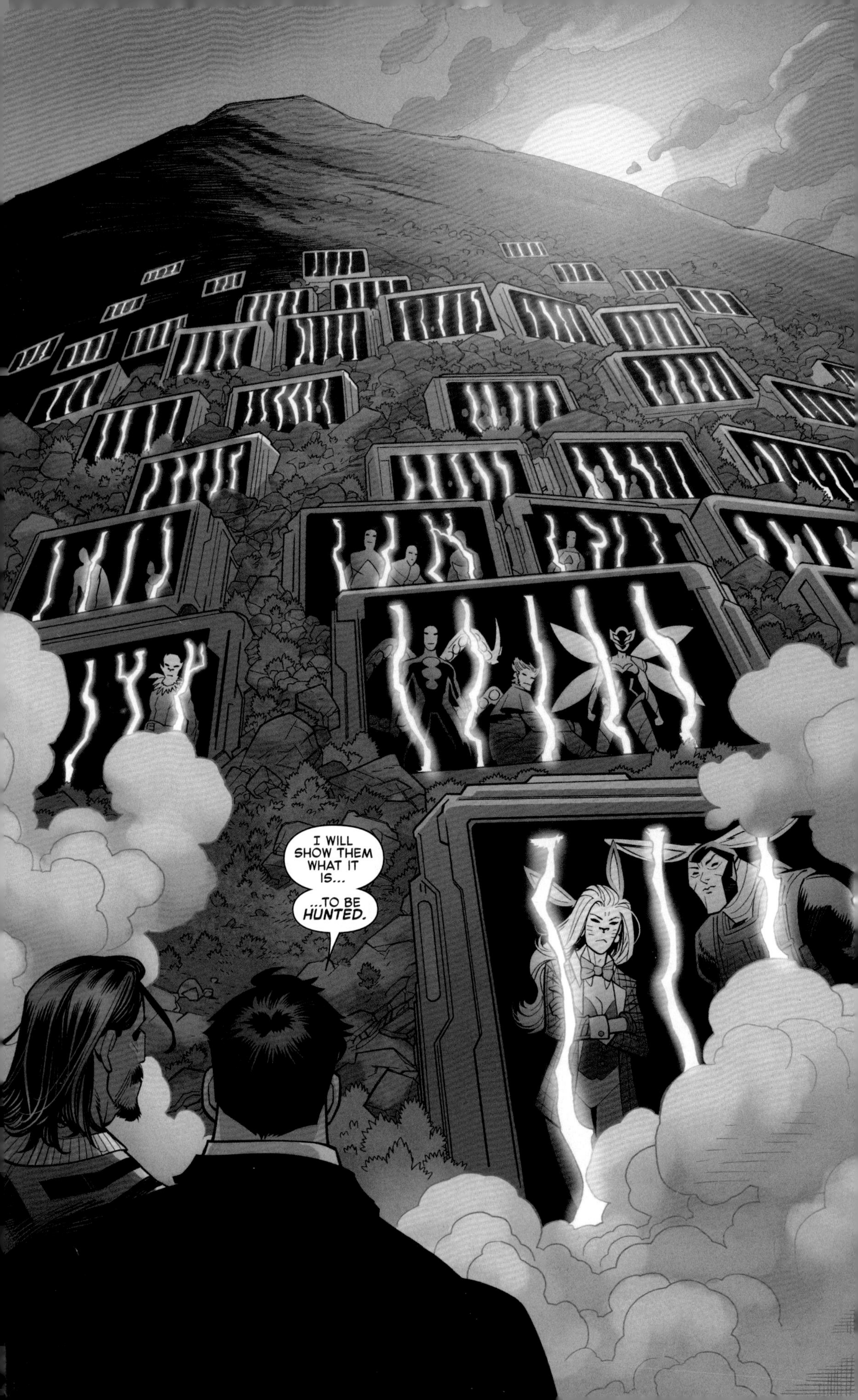
I WILL SHOW THEM WHAT IT IS...
...TO BE HUNTED.

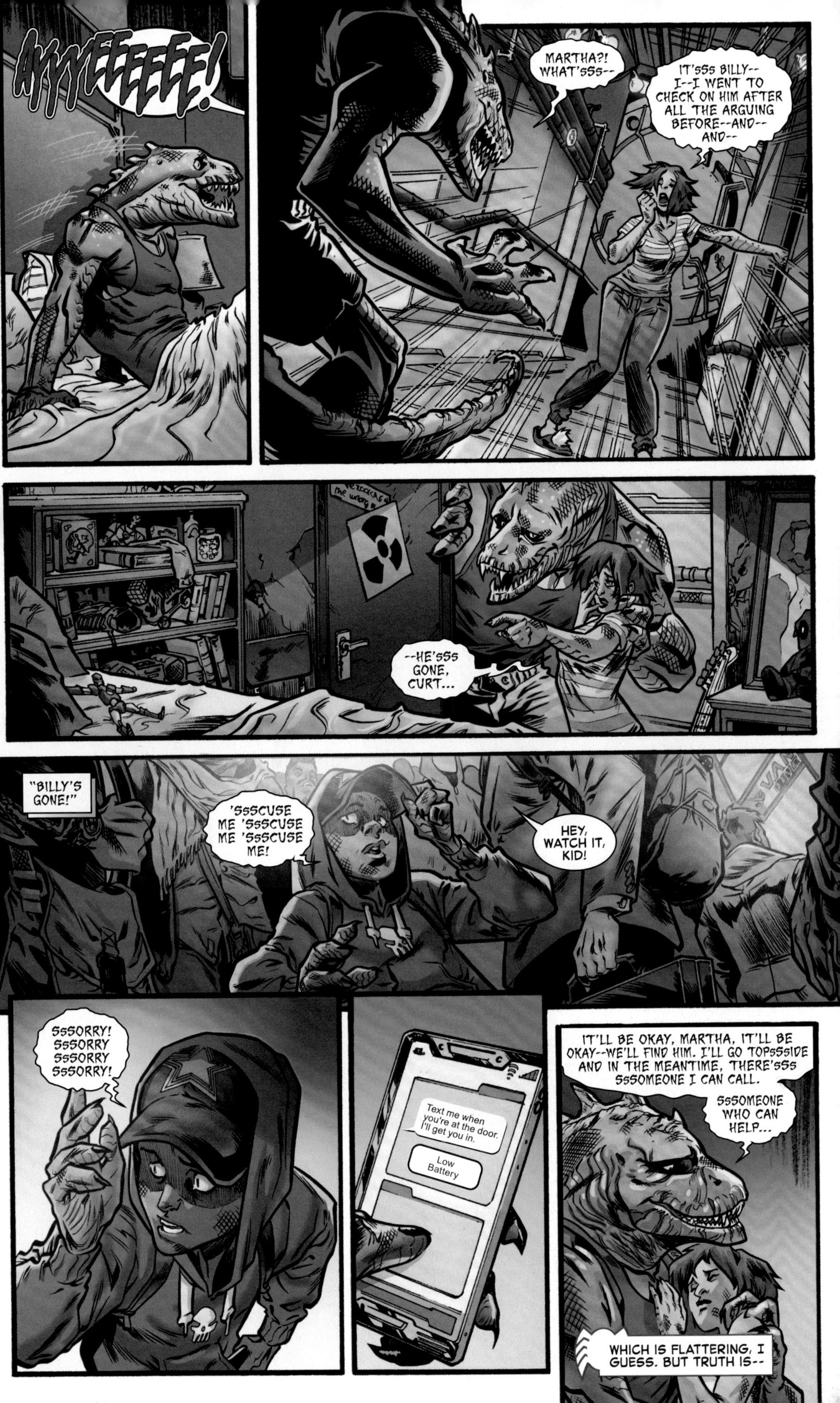
AYYYEEEEEEE!
MARTHA?! WHAT'SSS--
IT'SSS BILLY-- I--I WENT TO CHECK ON HIM AFTER ALL THE ARGUING BEFORE--AND-- AND--
--HE'SSS GONE, CURT...
"BILLY'S GONE!"
'SSSCUSE ME 'SSSCUSE ME 'SSSCUSE ME!
HEY, WATCH IT, KID!
SSSORRY! SSSORRY SSSORRY SSSORRY!
Text me when you're at the door. I'll get you in.
Low Battery
IT'LL BE OKAY, MARTHA, IT'LL BE OKAY--WE'LL FIND HIM. I'LL GO TOPSSSIDE AND IN THE MEANTIME, THERE'SSS SSSOMEONE I CAN CALL.
SSSOMEONE WHO CAN HELP...
WHICH IS FLATTERING, I GUESS. BUT TRUTH IS--

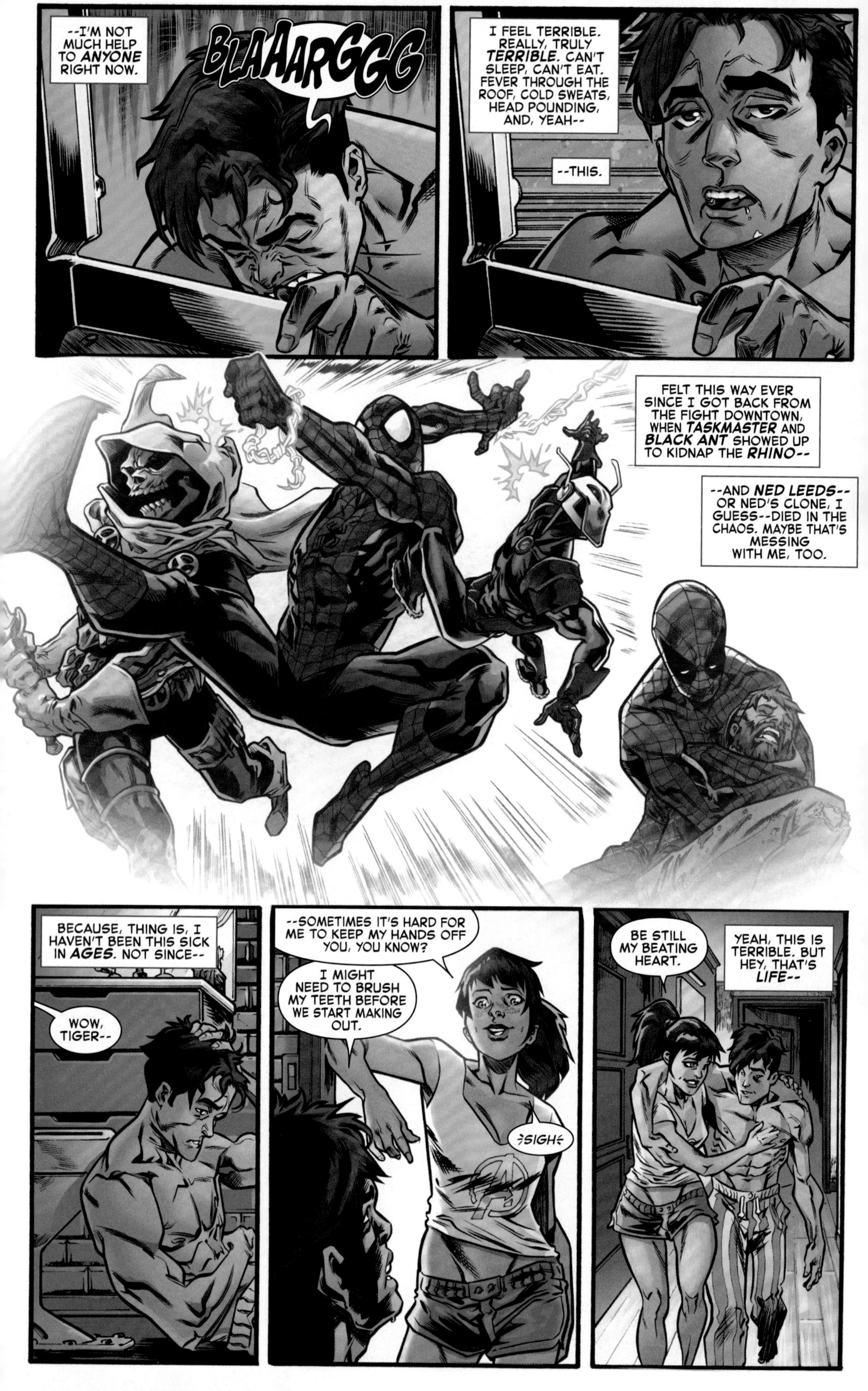
--I'M NOT MUCH HELP TO ANYONE RIGHT NOW.
BLAAARGGG
I FEEL TERRIBLE. REALLY, TRULY TERRIBLE. CAN'T SLEEP, CAN'T EAT. FEVER THROUGH THE ROOF, COLD SWEATS, HEAD POUNDING, AND, YEAH--
--THIS.
FELT THIS WAY EVER SINCE I GOT BACK FROM THE FIGHT DOWNTOWN, WHEN TASKMASTER AND BLACK ANT SHOWED UP TO KIDNAP THE RHINO--
--AND NED LEEDS--OR NED'S CLONE, I GUESS--DIED IN THE CHAOS. MAYBE THAT'S MESSING WITH ME, TOO.
BECAUSE, THING IS, I HAVEN'T BEEN THIS SICK IN AGES. NOT SINCE--
WOW, TIGER--
--SOMETIMES IT'S HARD FOR ME TO KEEP MY HANDS OFF YOU, YOU KNOW?
I MIGHT NEED TO BRUSH MY TEETH BEFORE WE START MAKING OUT.
SIGH
BE STILL MY BEATING HEART.
YEAH, THIS IS TERRIBLE. BUT HEY, THAT'S LIFE--

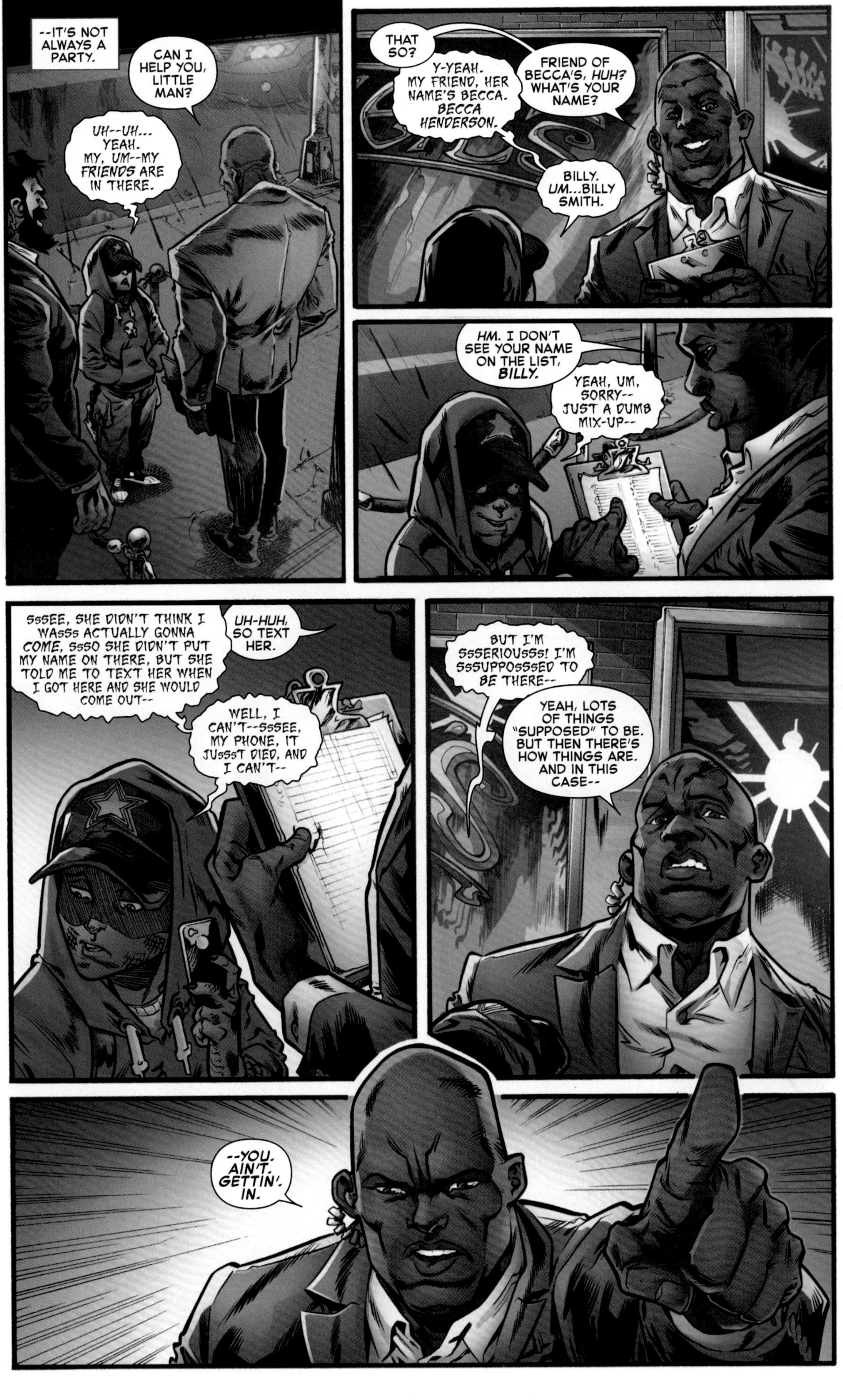
--IT'S NOT ALWAYS A PARTY.
CAN I HELP YOU, LITTLE MAN?
UH--UH... YEAH. MY, UM--MY FRIENDS ARE IN THERE.
THAT SO?
Y-YEAH. MY FRIEND, HER NAME'S BECCA. BECCA HENDERSON.
FRIEND OF BECCA'S, HUH? WHAT'S YOUR NAME?
BILLY. UM...BILLY SMITH.
HM. I DON'T SEE YOUR NAME ON THE LIST, BILLY.
YEAH, UM, SORRY-- JUST A DUMB MIX-UP--
SsSEE, SHE DIDN'T THINK I WAsSs ACTUALLY GONNA COME, SsSO SHE DIDN'T PUT MY NAME ON THERE, BUT SHE TOLD ME TO TEXT HER WHEN I GOT HERE AND SHE WOULD COME OUT--
UH-HUH, SO TEXT HER.
WELL, I CAN'T--SsSEE, MY PHONE, IT JUSsST DIED, AND I CAN'T--
BUT I'M SsSERIOUSsS! I'M SsSUPPOSsSED TO BE THERE--
YEAH, LOTS OF THINGS "SUPPOSED" TO BE. BUT THEN THERE'S HOW THINGS ARE. AND IN THIS CASE--
--YOU. AIN'T. GETTIN'. IN.

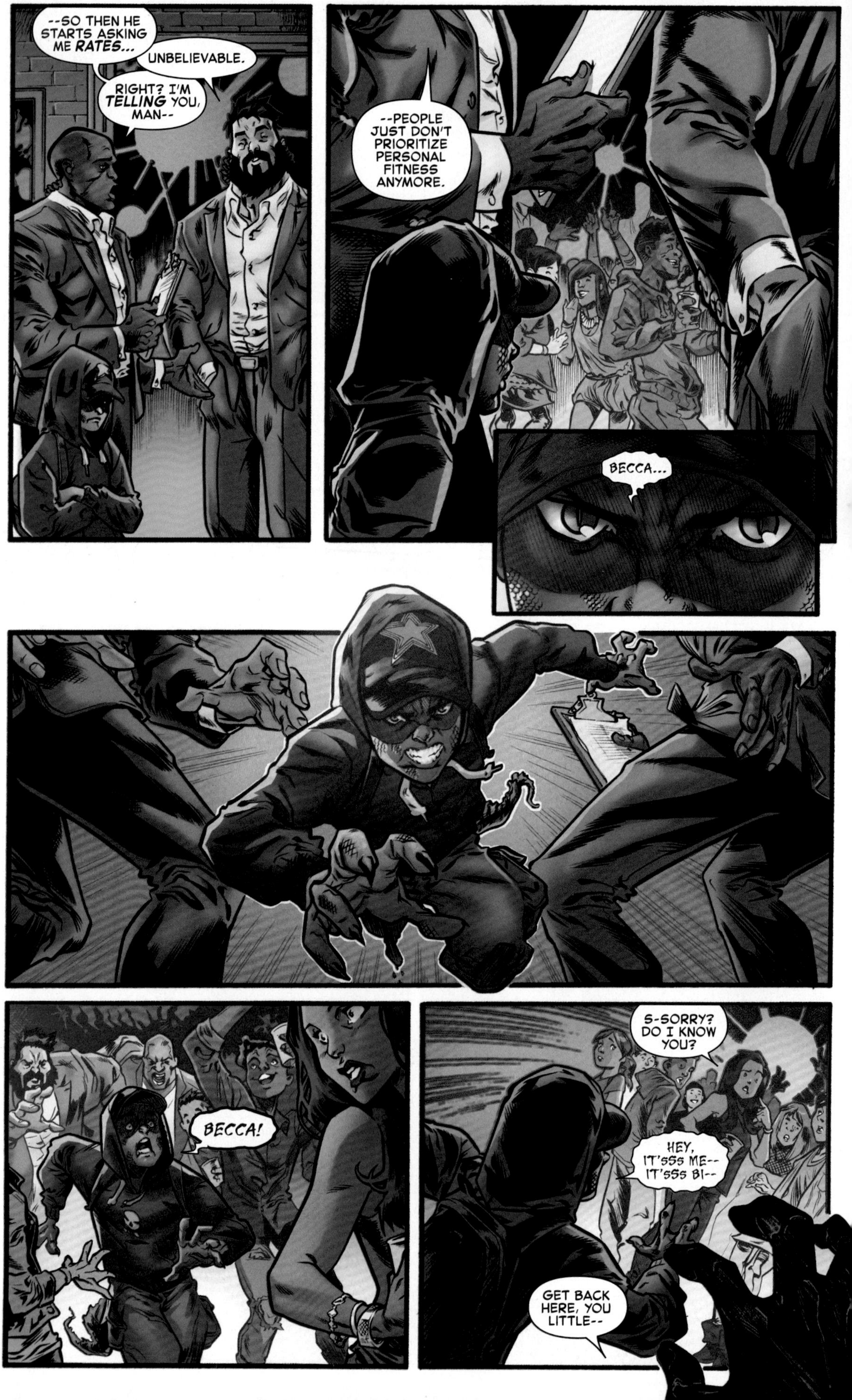
--SO THEN HE STARTS ASKING ME RATES...
UNBELIEVABLE.
RIGHT? I'M TELLING YOU, MAN--
--PEOPLE JUST DON'T PRIORITIZE PERSONAL FITNESS ANYMORE.
BECCA...
BECCA!
S-SORRY? DO I KNOW YOU?
HEY, IT'SSS ME-- IT'SSS BI--
GET BACK HERE, YOU LITTLE--

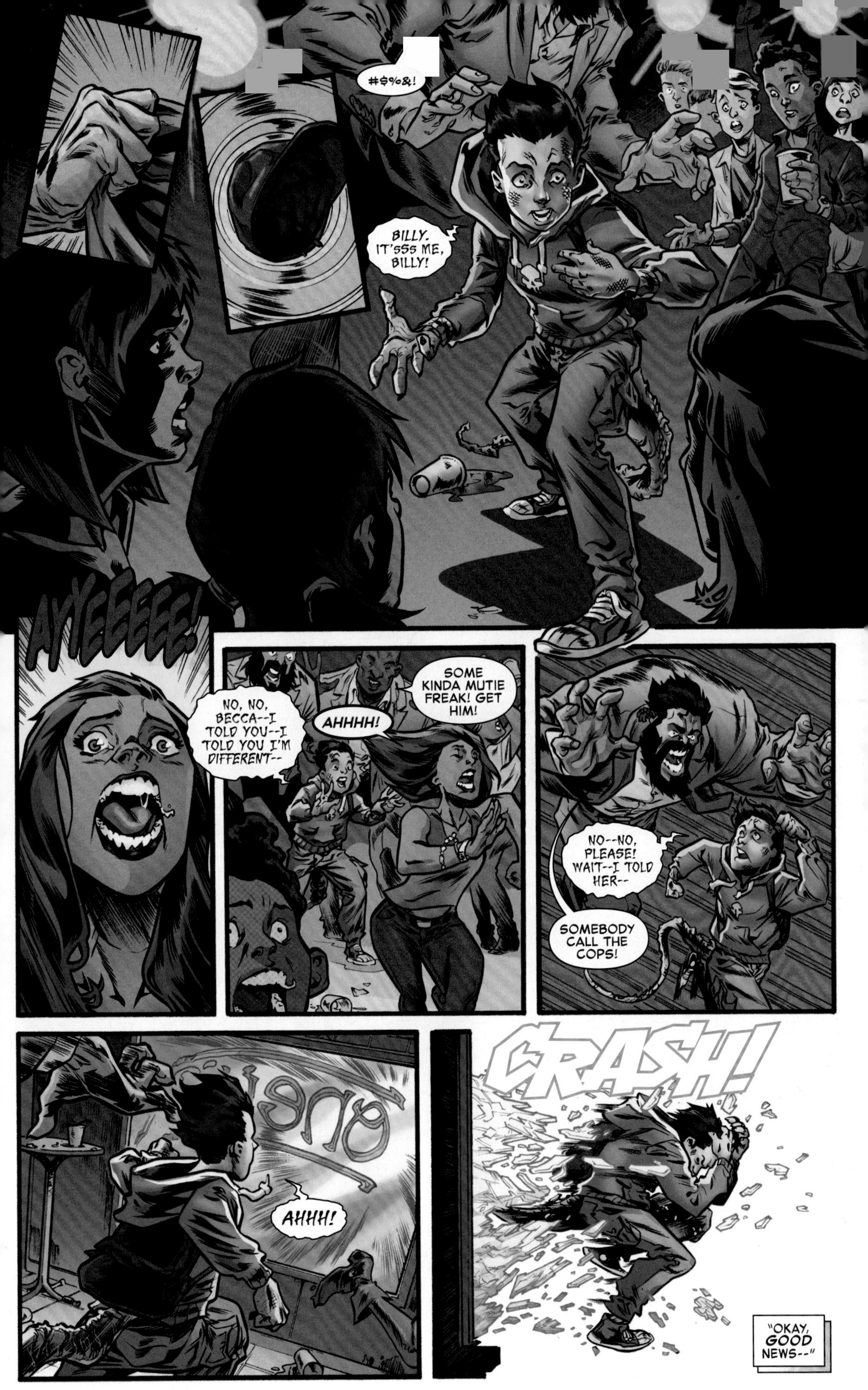
#$%&!
BILLY. IT'SSS ME, BILLY!
AYEEEEE!
NO, NO, BECCA--I TOLD YOU--I TOLD YOU I'M DIFFERENT--
AHHHH!
SOME KINDA MUTIE FREAK! GET HIM!
NO--NO, PLEASE! WAIT--I TOLD HER--
SOMEBODY CALL THE COPS!
AHHH!
CRASH!
"OKAY, GOOD NEWS--"

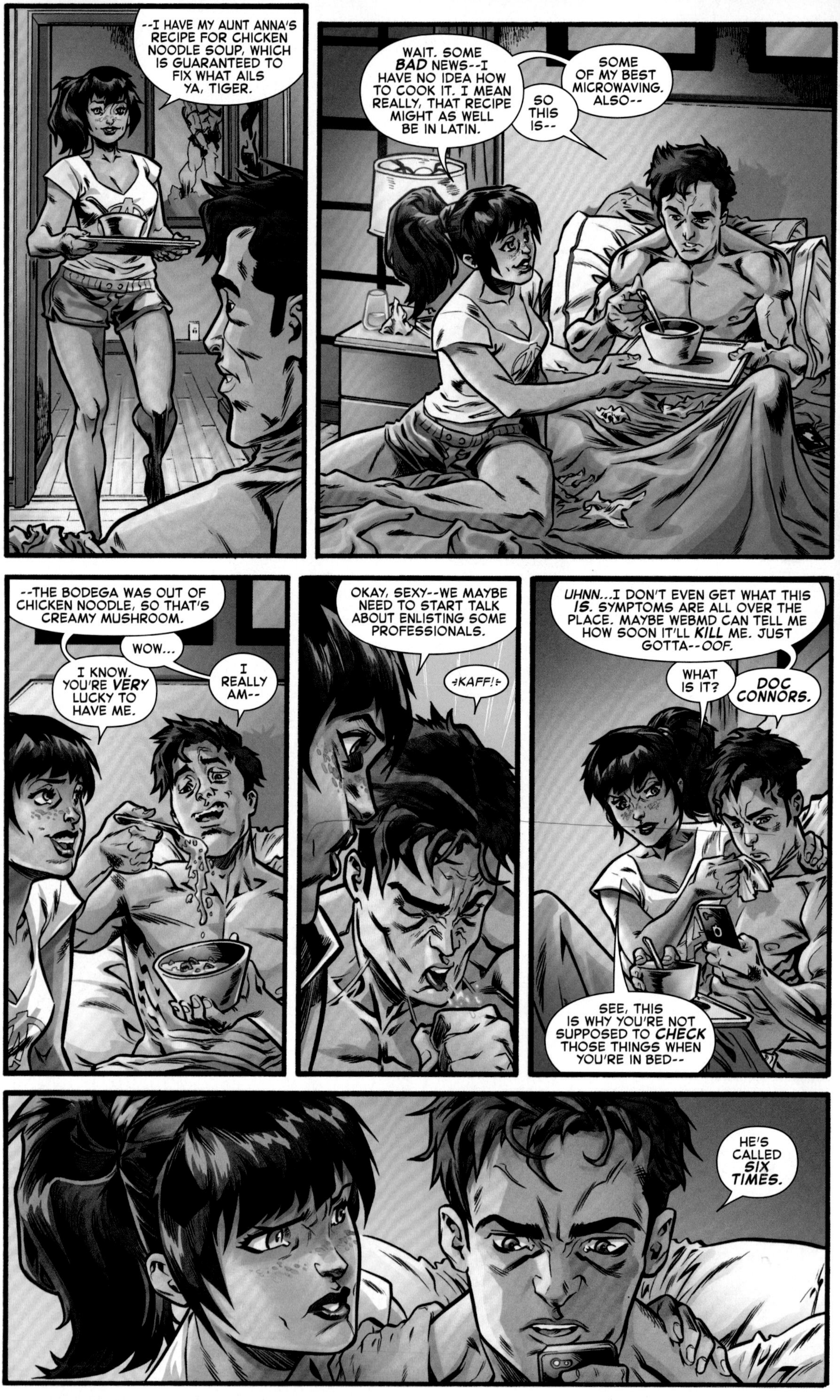
--I HAVE MY AUNT ANNA'S RECIPE FOR CHICKEN NOODLE SOUP, WHICH IS GUARANTEED TO FIX WHAT AILS YA, TIGER.
WAIT. SOME BAD NEWS--I HAVE NO IDEA HOW TO COOK IT. I MEAN REALLY, THAT RECIPE MIGHT AS WELL BE IN LATIN.
SO THIS IS--
SOME OF MY BEST MICROWAVING. ALSO--
--THE BODEGA WAS OUT OF CHICKEN NOODLE, SO THAT'S CREAMY MUSHROOM.
WOW...
I KNOW. YOU'RE VERY LUCKY TO HAVE ME.
I REALLY AM--
OKAY, SEXY--WE MAYBE NEED TO START TALK ABOUT ENLISTING SOME PROFESSIONALS.
KAFF!
UHNN...I DON'T EVEN GET WHAT THIS IS. SYMPTOMS ARE ALL OVER THE PLACE. MAYBE WEBMD CAN TELL ME HOW SOON IT'LL KILL ME. JUST GOTTA--OOF.
WHAT IS IT?
DOC CONNORS.
SEE, THIS IS WHY YOU'RE NOT SUPPOSED TO CHECK THOSE THINGS WHEN YOU'RE IN BED--
HE'S CALLED SIX TIMES.

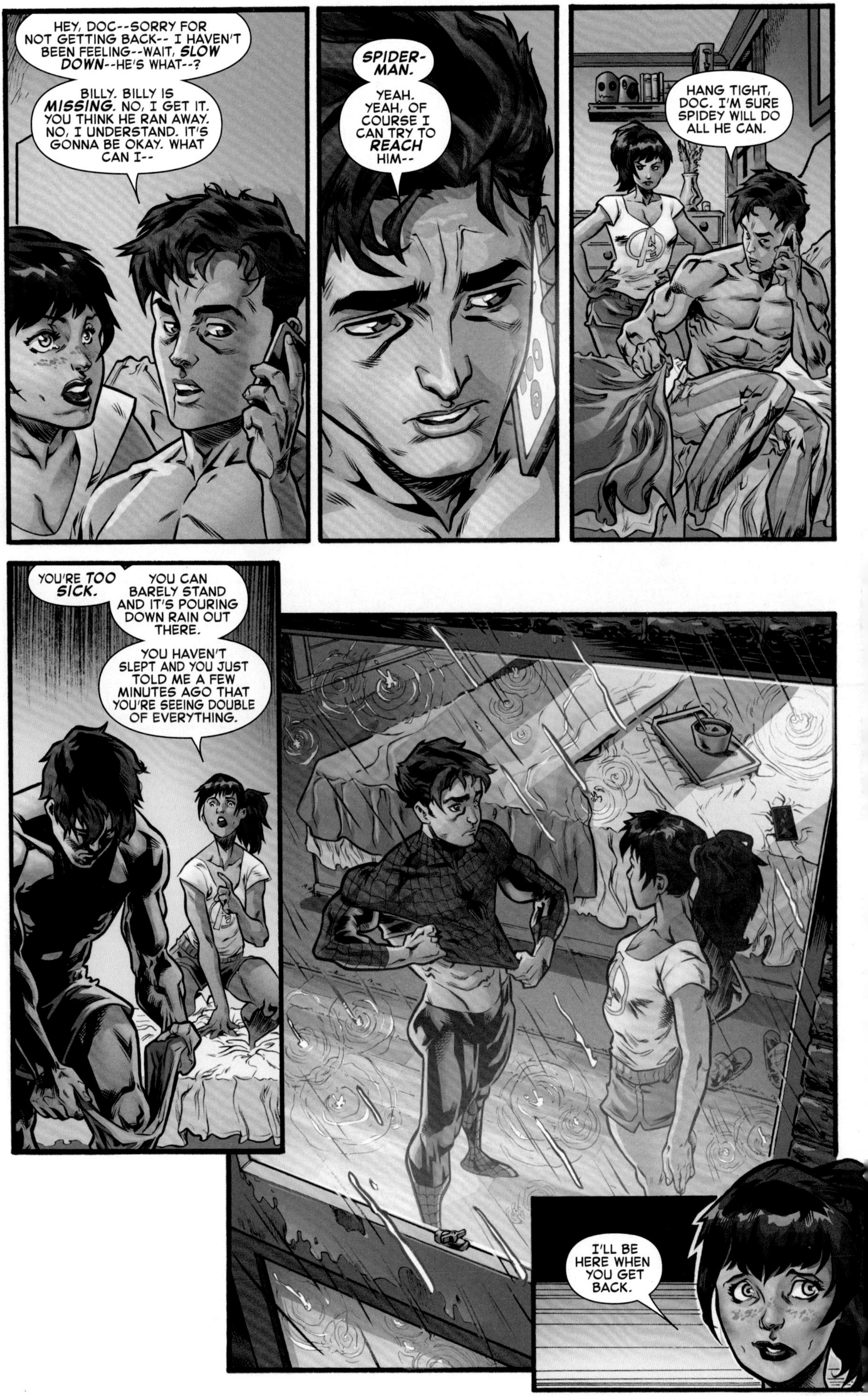
HEY, DOC--SORRY FOR NOT GETTING BACK-- I HAVEN'T BEEN FEELING--WAIT, SLOW DOWN--HE'S WHAT--?
BILLY. BILLY IS MISSING. NO, I GET IT. YOU THINK HE RAN AWAY. NO, I UNDERSTAND. IT'S GONNA BE OKAY. WHAT CAN I--
SPIDER-MAN.
YEAH. YEAH, OF COURSE I CAN TRY TO REACH HIM--
HANG TIGHT, DOC. I'M SURE SPIDEY WILL DO ALL HE CAN.
YOU'RE TOO SICK.
YOU CAN BARELY STAND AND IT'S POURING DOWN RAIN OUT THERE.
YOU HAVEN'T SLEPT AND YOU JUST TOLD ME A FEW MINUTES AGO THAT YOU'RE SEEING DOUBLE OF EVERYTHING.
I'LL BE HERE WHEN YOU GET BACK.

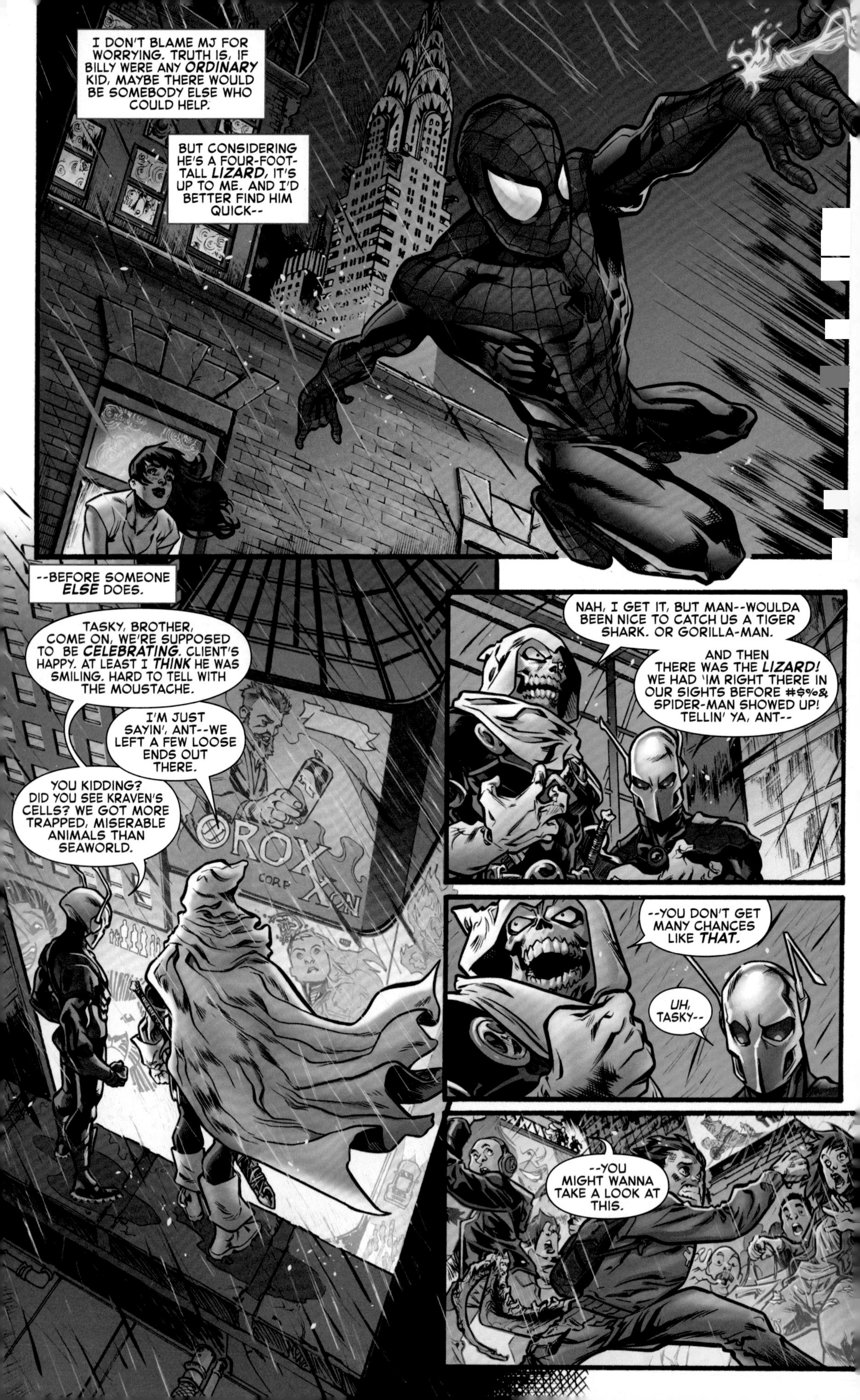
I DON'T BLAME MJ FOR WORRYING. TRUTH IS, IF BILLY WERE ANY ORDINARY KID, MAYBE THERE WOULD BE SOMEBODY ELSE WHO COULD HELP.
BUT CONSIDERING HE'S A FOUR-FOOT-TALL LIZARD, IT'S UP TO ME. AND I'D BETTER FIND HIM QUICK--
--BEFORE SOMEONE ELSE DOES.
TASKY, BROTHER, COME ON, WE'RE SUPPOSED TO BE CELEBRATING. CLIENT'S HAPPY. AT LEAST I THINK HE WAS SMILING. HARD TO TELL WITH THE MOUSTACHE.
I'M JUST SAYIN', ANT--WE LEFT A FEW LOOSE ENDS OUT THERE.
YOU KIDDING? DID YOU SEE KRAVEN'S CELLS? WE GOT MORE TRAPPED, MISERABLE ANIMALS THAN SEAWORLD.
ROXXON
CORP
NAH, I GET IT, BUT MAN--WOULDA BEEN NICE TO CATCH US A TIGER SHARK. OR GORILLA-MAN.
AND THEN THERE WAS THE LIZARD! WE HAD 'IM RIGHT THERE IN OUR SIGHTS BEFORE #$%& SPIDER-MAN SHOWED UP! TELLIN' YA, ANT--
--YOU DON'T GET MANY CHANCES LIKE THAT.
UH, TASKY--
--YOU MIGHT WANNA TAKE A LOOK AT THIS.

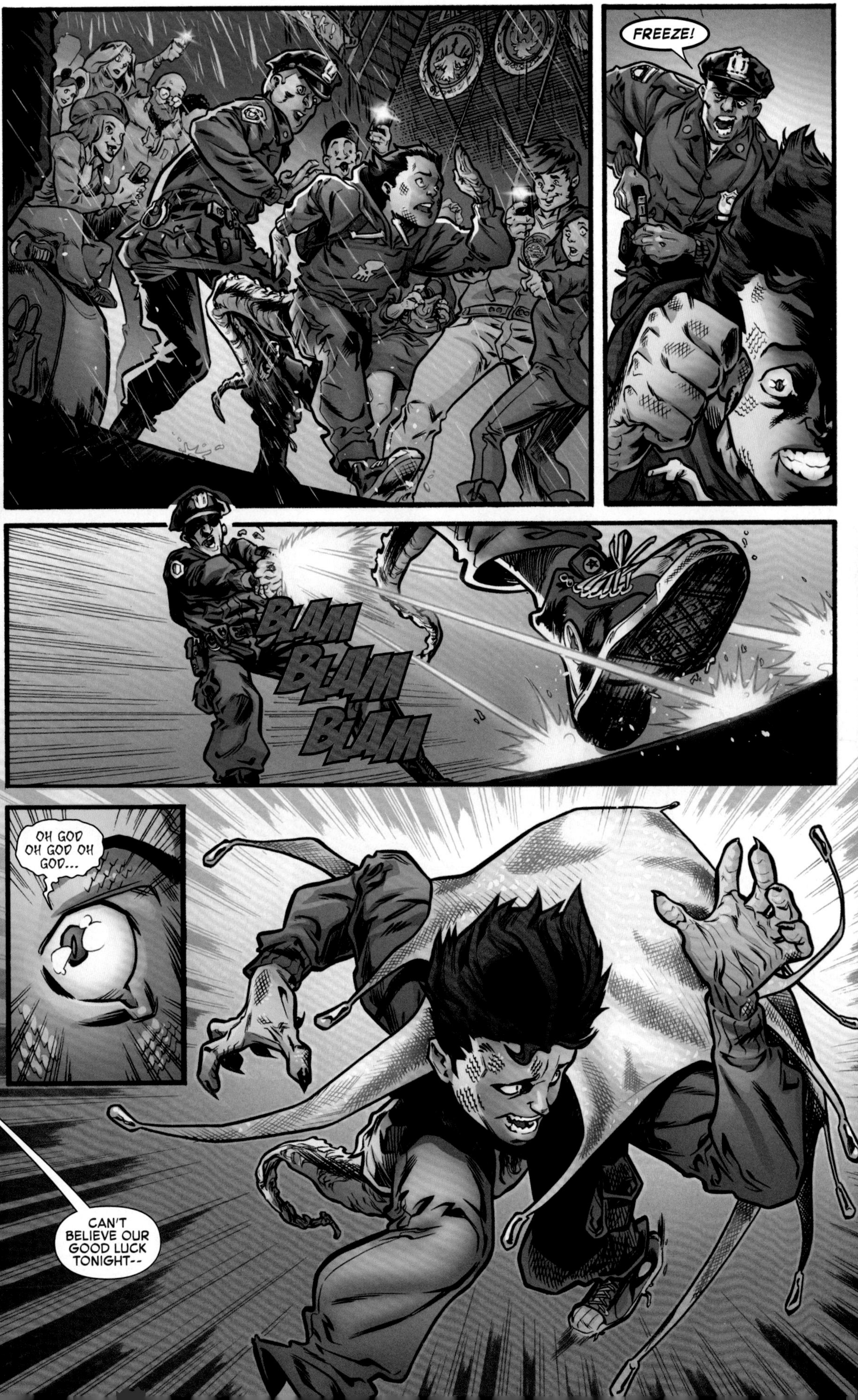
FREEZE!
BLAM
BLAM
BLAM
OH GOD OH GOD OH GOD...
CAN'T BELIEVE OUR GOOD LUCK TONIGHT--

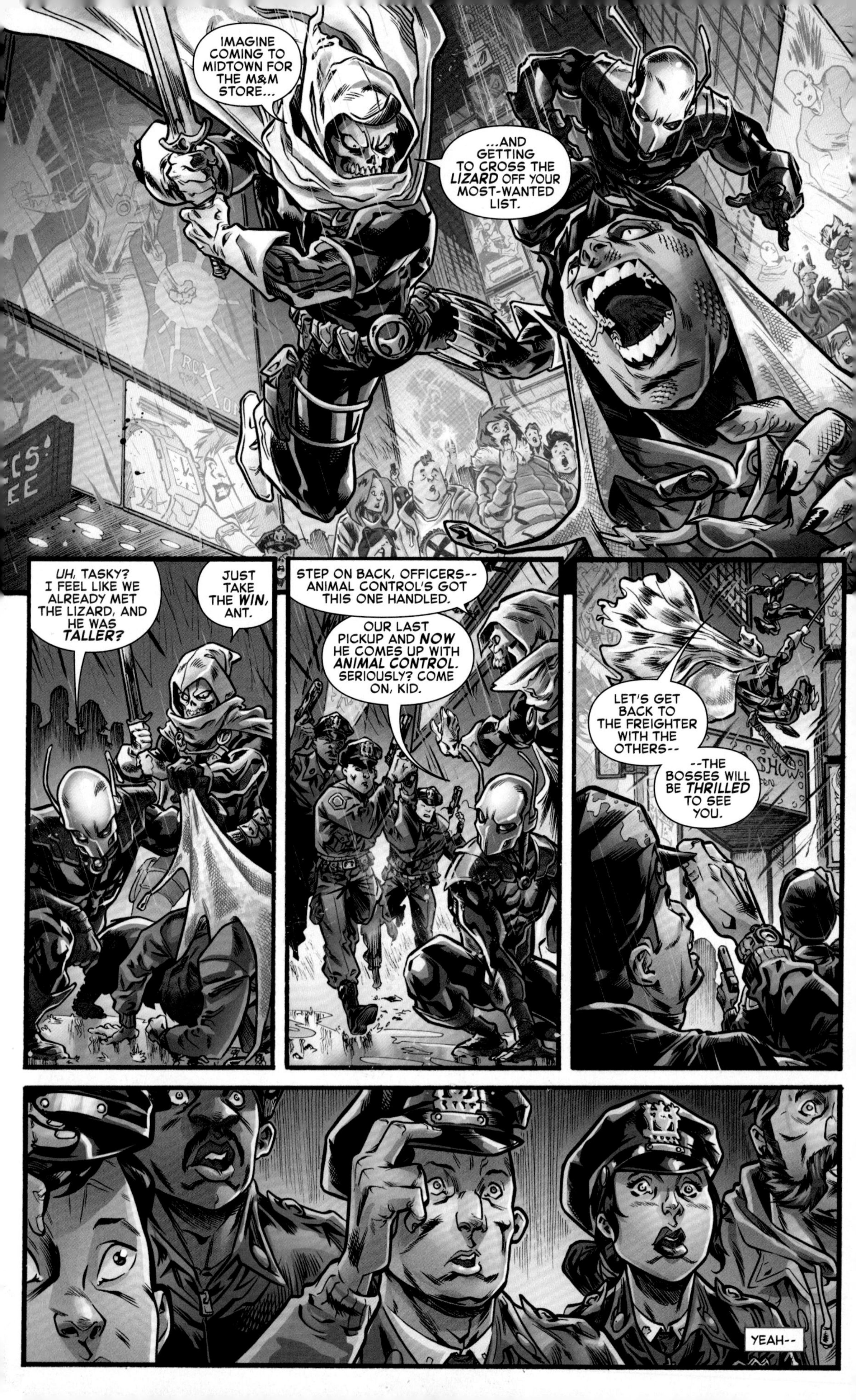
IMAGINE COMING TO MIDTOWN FOR THE M&M STORE...
...AND GETTING TO CROSS THE LIZARD OFF YOUR MOST-WANTED LIST.
UH, TASKY? I FEEL LIKE WE ALREADY MET THE LIZARD, AND HE WAS TALLER?
JUST TAKE THE WIN, ANT.
STEP ON BACK, OFFICERS-- ANIMAL CONTROL'S GOT THIS ONE HANDLED.
OUR LAST PICKUP AND NOW HE COMES UP WITH ANIMAL CONTROL. SERIOUSLY? COME ON, KID.
LET'S GET BACK TO THE FREIGHTER WITH THE OTHERS--
--THE BOSSES WILL BE THRILLED TO SEE YOU.
YEAH--

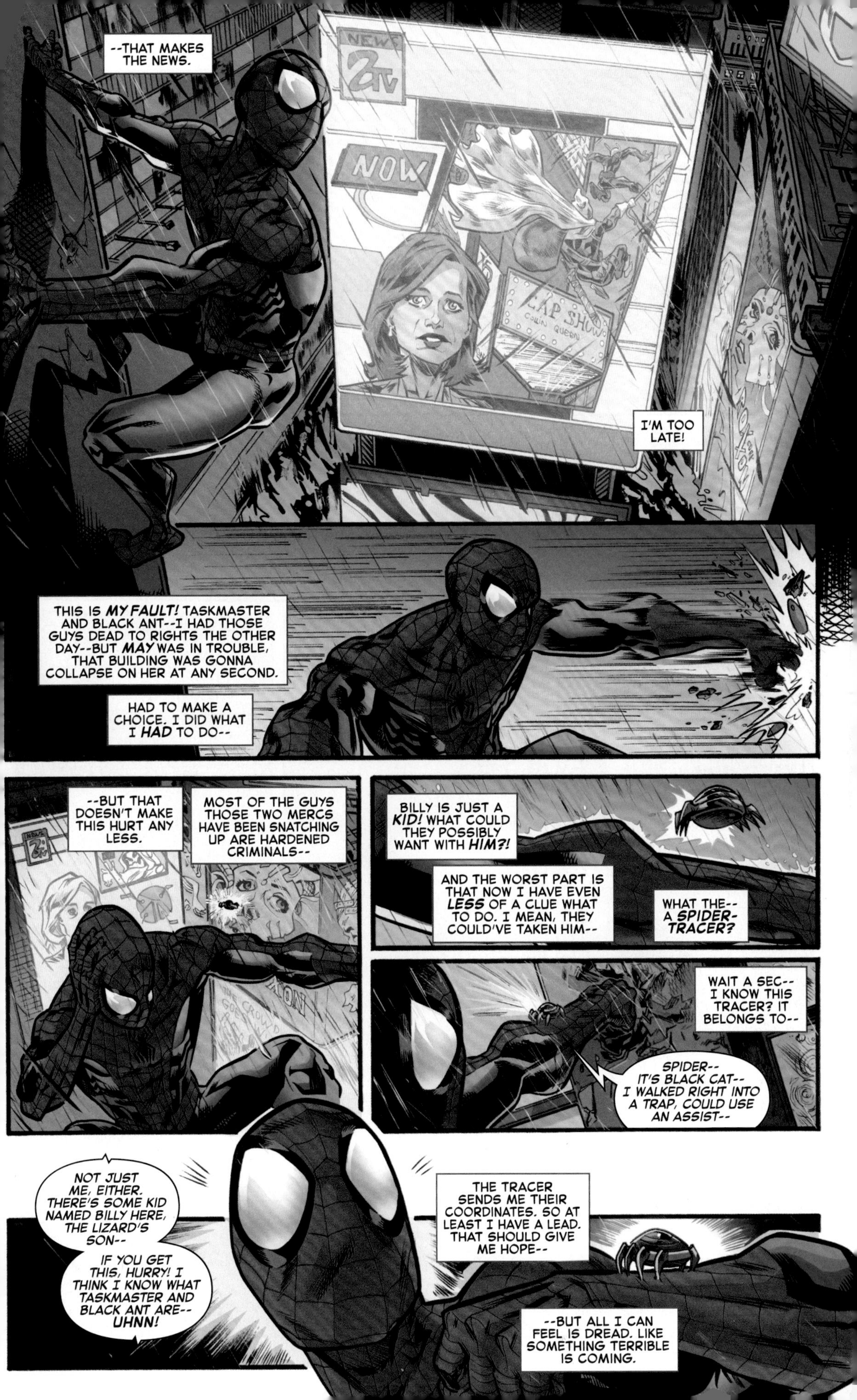

--THAT MAKES THE NEWS.
NEWS 2 TV
NOW
I'M TOO LATE!
THIS IS MY FAULT! TASKMASTER AND BLACK ANT--I HAD THOSE GUYS DEAD TO RIGHTS THE OTHER DAY--BUT MAY WAS IN TROUBLE, THAT BUILDING WAS GONNA COLLAPSE ON HER AT ANY SECOND.
HAD TO MAKE A CHOICE. I DID WHAT I HAD TO DO--
--BUT THAT DOESN'T MAKE THIS HURT ANY LESS.
MOST OF THE GUYS THOSE TWO MERCS HAVE BEEN SNATCHING UP ARE HARDENED CRIMINALS--
BILLY IS JUST A KID! WHAT COULD THEY POSSIBLY WANT WITH HIM?!
AND THE WORST PART IS THAT NOW I HAVE EVEN LESS OF A CLUE WHAT TO DO. I MEAN, THEY COULD'VE TAKEN HIM--
WHAT THE-- A SPIDER-TRACER?
WAIT A SEC-- I KNOW THIS TRACER? IT BELONGS TO--
SPIDER-- IT'S BLACK CAT-- I WALKED RIGHT INTO A TRAP, COULD USE AN ASSIST--
NOT JUST ME, EITHER. THERE'S SOME KID NAMED BILLY HERE, THE LIZARD'S SON--
IF YOU GET THIS, HURRY! I THINK I KNOW WHAT TASKMASTER AND BLACK ANT ARE-- UHNN!
THE TRACER SENDS ME THEIR COORDINATES. SO AT LEAST I HAVE A LEAD. THAT SHOULD GIVE ME HOPE--
--BUT ALL I CAN FEEL IS DREAD. LIKE SOMETHING TERRIBLE IS COMING.

GOOD EVENING, AND WELCOME TO THE PLAZA HOTEL, MR...?

CADE. R. CADE.

WELL, IT'S WONDERFUL TO HAVE YOU STAYING WITH US, MISTER CADE. I SEE YOU HAVE A RATHER LARGE GROUP RESERVATION-- WILL YOU BE NEEDING HELP WITH YOUR THINGS?

HMM? OH--

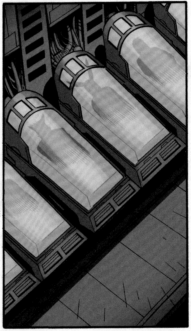

--OH YES, WE BROUGHT *LOTS* AND *LOTS* OF THINGS...

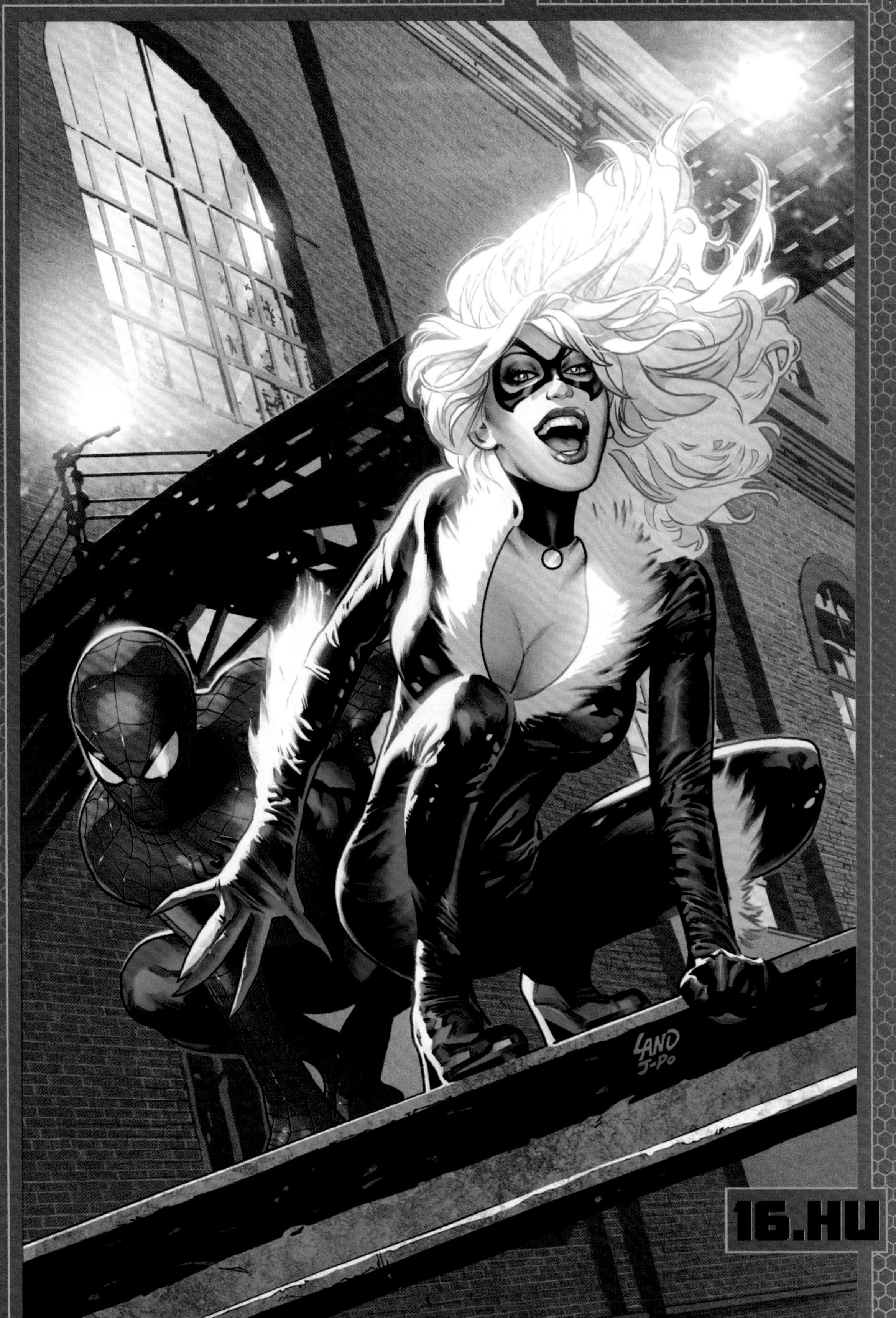
16.HU

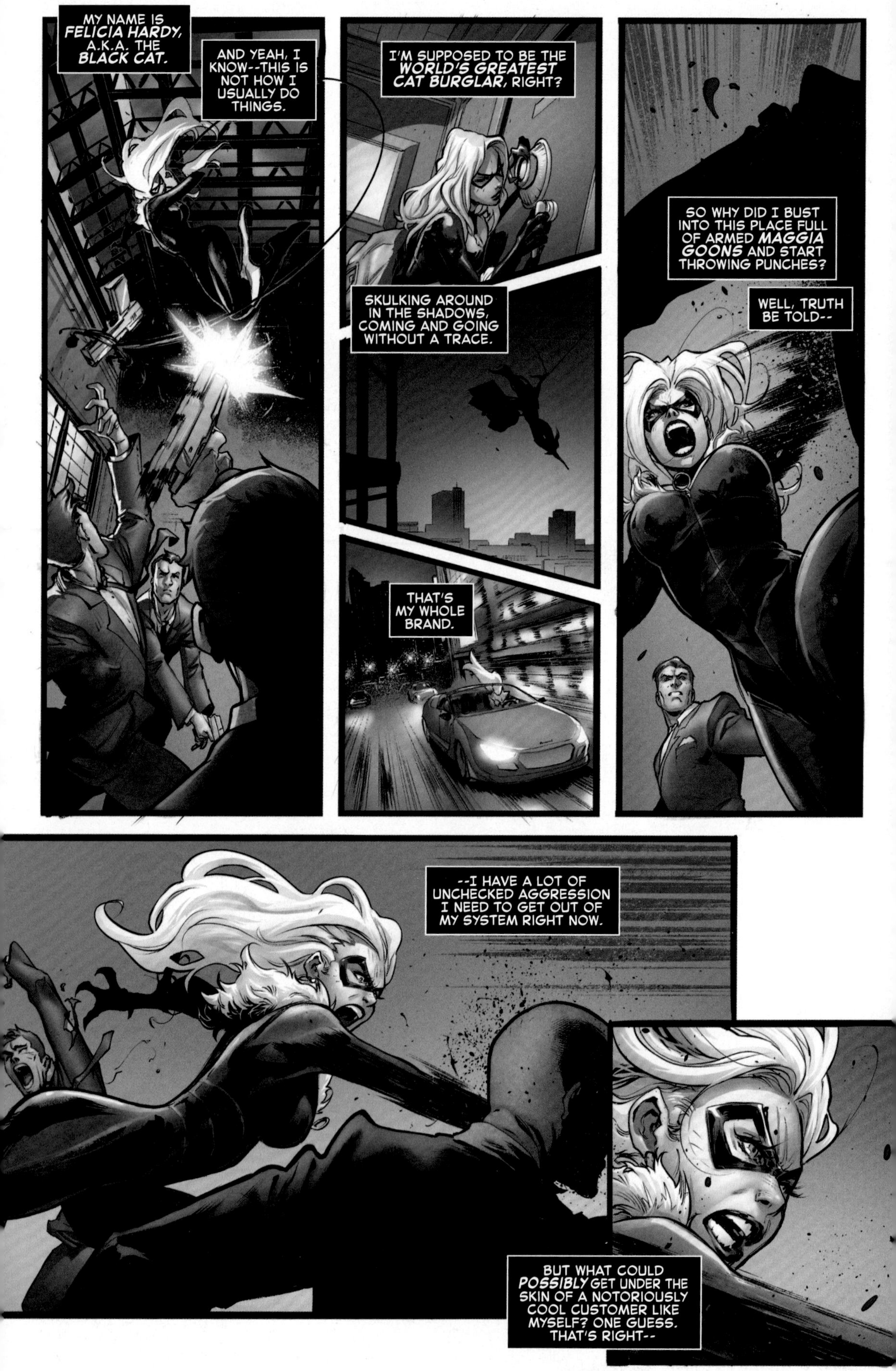
MY NAME IS FELICIA HARDY, A.K.A. THE BLACK CAT.
AND YEAH, I KNOW--THIS IS NOT HOW I USUALLY DO THINGS.
I'M SUPPOSED TO BE THE WORLD'S GREATEST CAT BURGLAR, RIGHT?
SKULKING AROUND IN THE SHADOWS, COMING AND GOING WITHOUT A TRACE.
THAT'S MY WHOLE BRAND.
SO WHY DID I BUST INTO THIS PLACE FULL OF ARMED MAGGIA GOONS AND START THROWING PUNCHES?
WELL, TRUTH BE TOLD--
--I HAVE A LOT OF UNCHECKED AGGRESSION I NEED TO GET OUT OF MY SYSTEM RIGHT NOW.
BUT WHAT COULD POSSIBLY GET UNDER THE SKIN OF A NOTORIOUSLY COOL CUSTOMER LIKE MYSELF? ONE GUESS. THAT'S RIGHT--

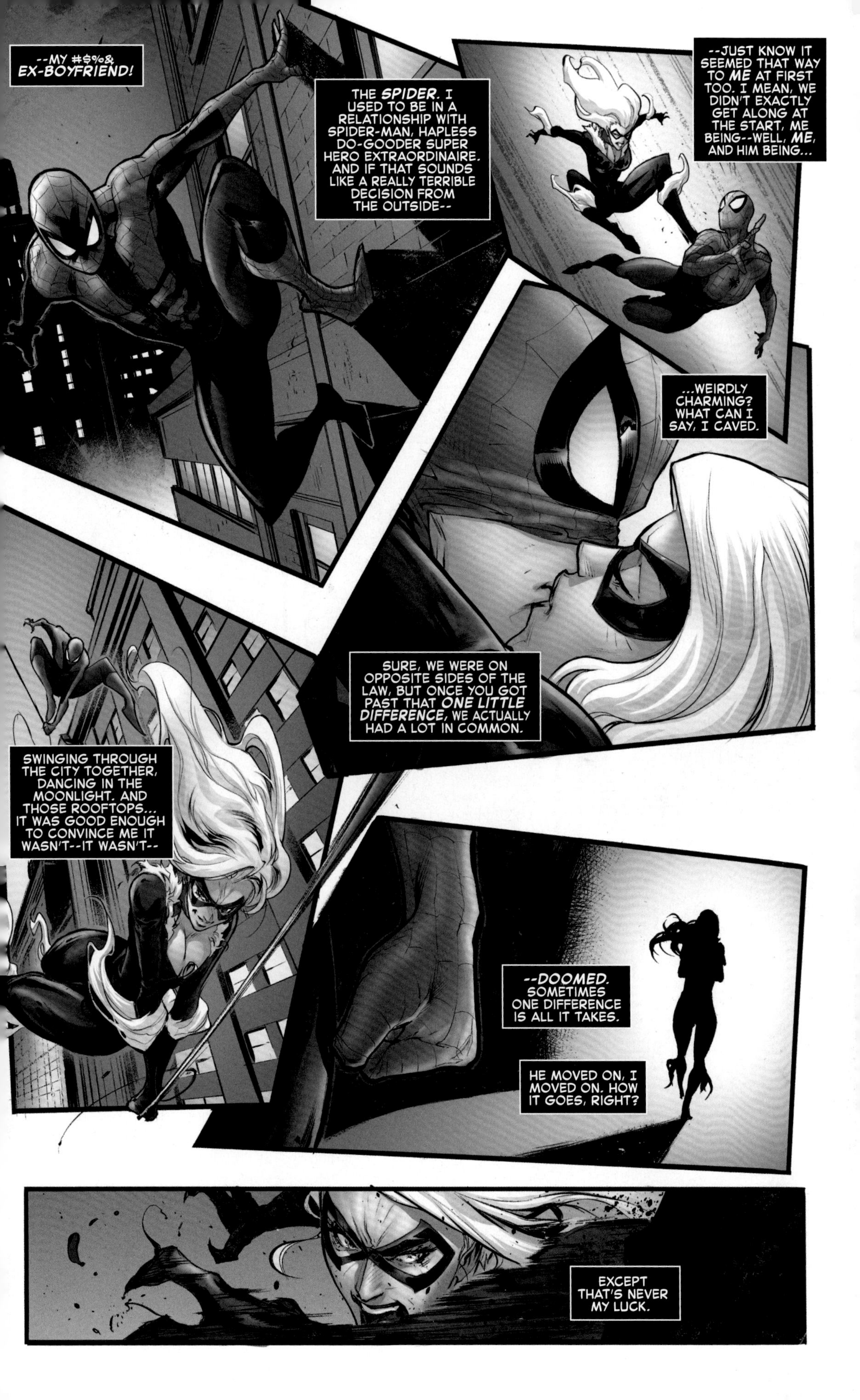
--MY #$%& EX-BOYFRIEND!
THE SPIDER. I USED TO BE IN A RELATIONSHIP WITH SPIDER-MAN, HAPLESS DO-GOODER SUPER HERO EXTRAORDINAIRE. AND IF THAT SOUNDS LIKE A REALLY TERRIBLE DECISION FROM THE OUTSIDE--
--JUST KNOW IT SEEMED THAT WAY TO ME AT FIRST TOO. I MEAN, WE DIDN'T EXACTLY GET ALONG AT THE START, ME BEING--WELL, ME, AND HIM BEING...
...WEIRDLY CHARMING? WHAT CAN I SAY, I CAVED.
SURE, WE WERE ON OPPOSITE SIDES OF THE LAW, BUT ONCE YOU GOT PAST THAT ONE LITTLE DIFFERENCE, WE ACTUALLY HAD A LOT IN COMMON.
SWINGING THROUGH THE CITY TOGETHER, DANCING IN THE MOONLIGHT. AND THOSE ROOFTOPS... IT WAS GOOD ENOUGH TO CONVINCE ME IT WASN'T--IT WASN'T--
--DOOMED. SOMETIMES ONE DIFFERENCE IS ALL IT TAKES.
HE MOVED ON, I MOVED ON. HOW IT GOES, RIGHT?
EXCEPT THAT'S NEVER MY LUCK.

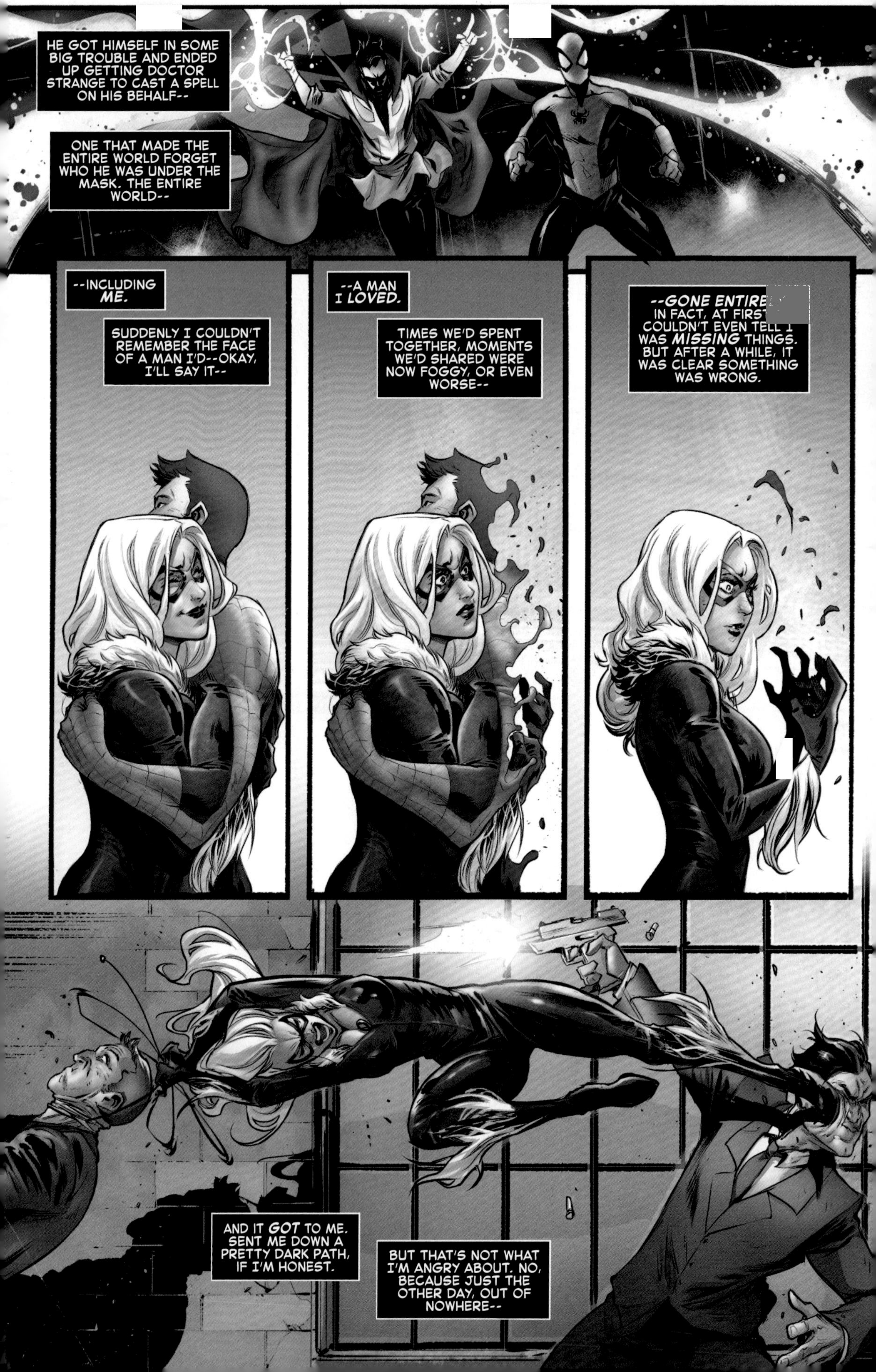
HE GOT HIMSELF IN SOME BIG TROUBLE AND ENDED UP GETTING DOCTOR STRANGE TO CAST A SPELL ON HIS BEHALF--
ONE THAT MADE THE ENTIRE WORLD FORGET WHO HE WAS UNDER THE MASK. THE ENTIRE WORLD--
--INCLUDING *ME.*
SUDDENLY I COULDN'T REMEMBER THE FACE OF A MAN I'D--OKAY, I'LL SAY IT--
--A MAN I *LOVED.*
TIMES WE'D SPENT TOGETHER, MOMENTS WE'D SHARED WERE NOW FOGGY, OR EVEN WORSE--
--GONE ENTIRE
IN FACT, AT FIRS
COULDN'T EVEN TELL I WAS *MISSING* THINGS. BUT AFTER A WHILE, IT WAS CLEAR SOMETHING WAS WRONG.
AND IT *GOT* TO ME. SENT ME DOWN A PRETTY DARK PATH, IF I'M HONEST.
BUT THAT'S NOT WHAT I'M ANGRY ABOUT. NO, BECAUSE JUST THE OTHER DAY, OUT OF NOWHERE--

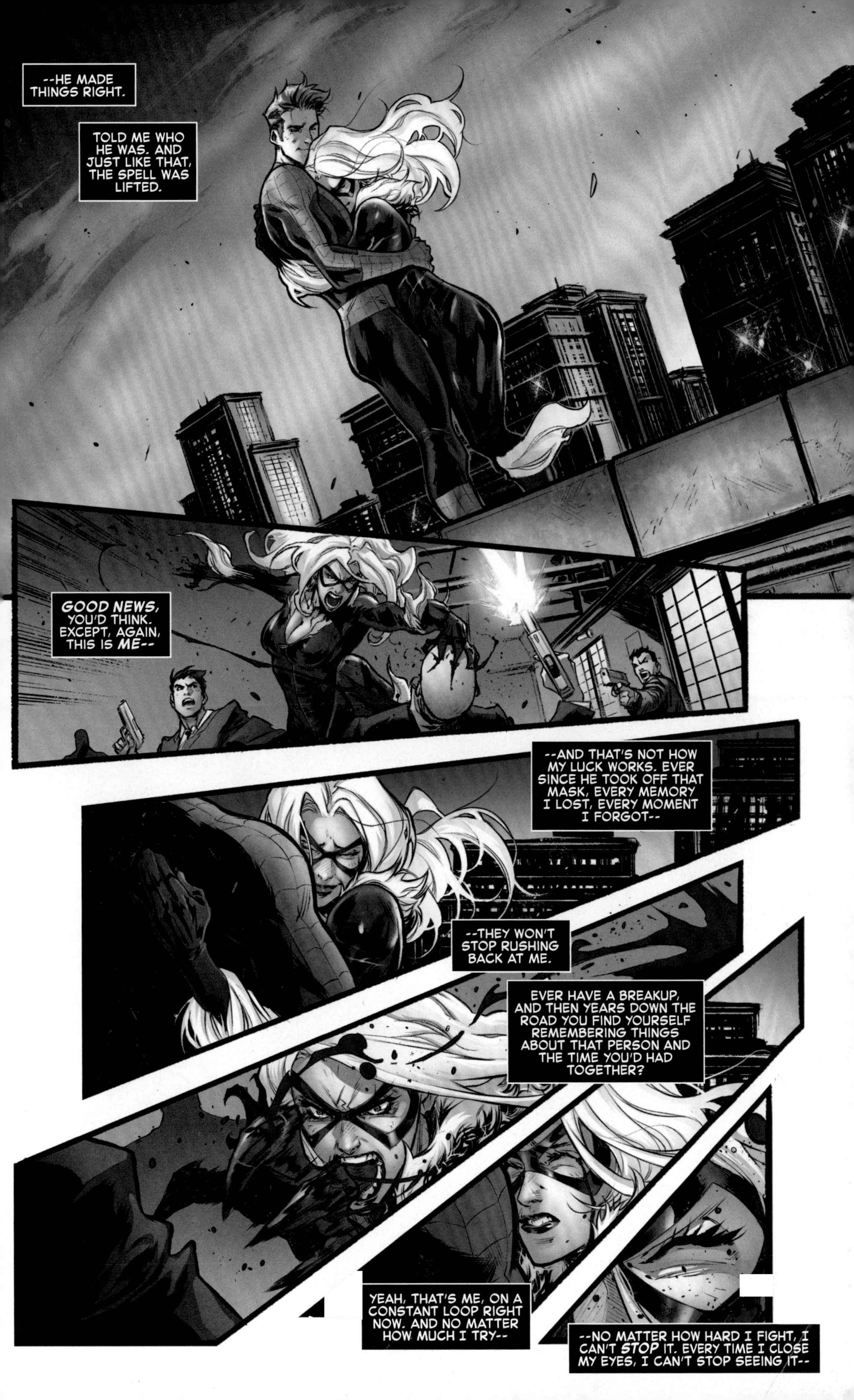
--HE MADE THINGS RIGHT.
TOLD ME WHO HE WAS. AND JUST LIKE THAT, THE SPELL WAS LIFTED.
GOOD NEWS, YOU'D THINK. EXCEPT, AGAIN, THIS IS ME--
--AND THAT'S NOT HOW MY LUCK WORKS. EVER SINCE HE TOOK OFF THAT MASK, EVERY MEMORY I LOST, EVERY MOMENT I FORGOT--
--THEY WON'T STOP RUSHING BACK AT ME.
EVER HAVE A BREAKUP, AND THEN YEARS DOWN THE ROAD YOU FIND YOURSELF REMEMBERING THINGS ABOUT THAT PERSON AND THE TIME YOU'D HAD TOGETHER?
YEAH, THAT'S ME, ON A CONSTANT LOOP RIGHT NOW. AND NO MATTER HOW MUCH I TRY--
--NO MATTER HOW HARD I FIGHT, I CAN'T STOP IT. EVERY TIME I CLOSE MY EYES, I CAN'T STOP SEEING IT--

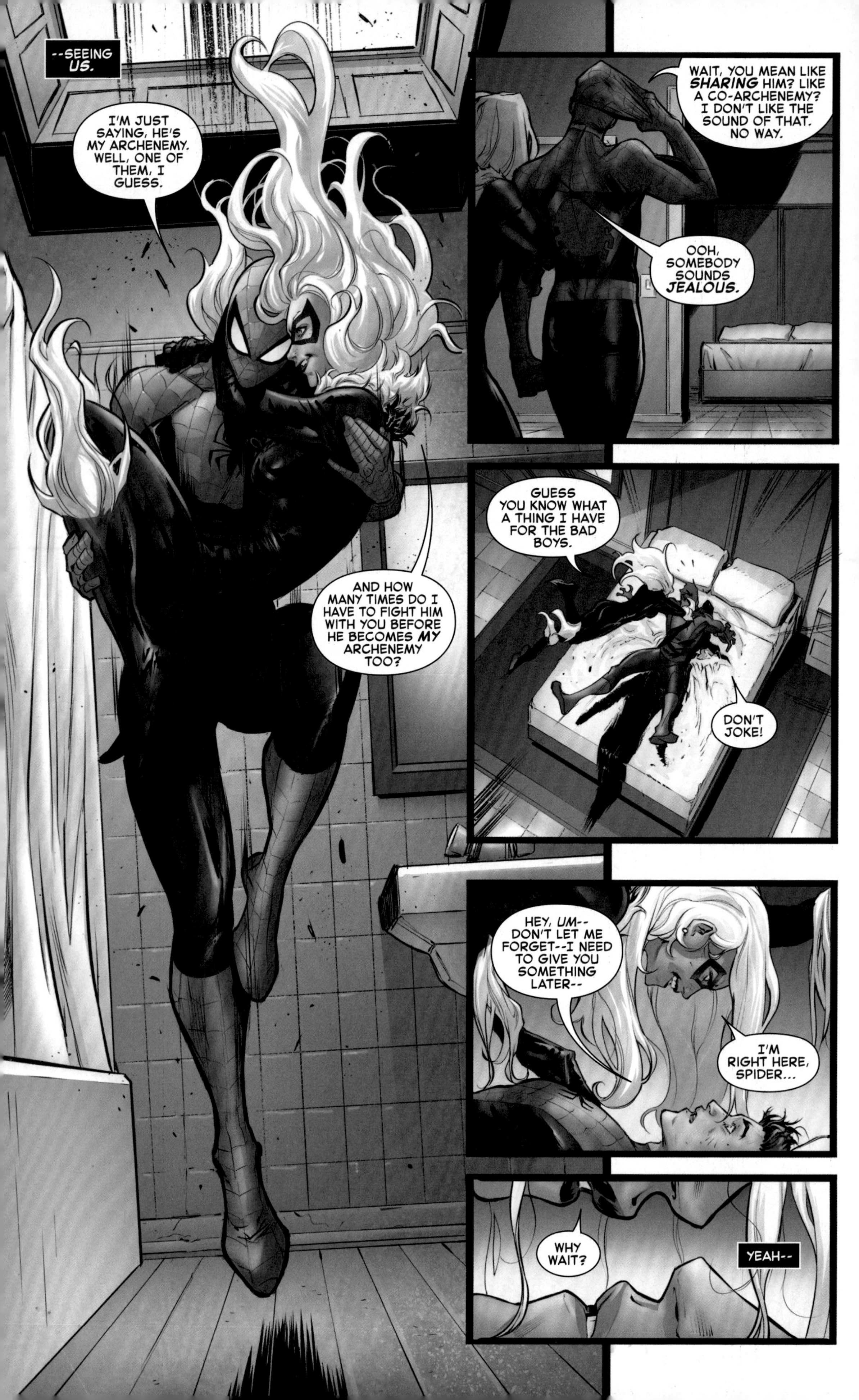
--SEEING *US.*
I'M JUST SAYING, HE'S MY ARCHENEMY. WELL, ONE OF THEM, I GUESS.
AND HOW MANY TIMES DO I HAVE TO FIGHT HIM WITH YOU BEFORE HE BECOMES *MY* ARCHENEMY TOO?
WAIT, YOU MEAN LIKE *SHARING* HIM? LIKE A CO-ARCHENEMY? I DON'T LIKE THE SOUND OF THAT. NO WAY.
OOH, SOMEBODY SOUNDS *JEALOUS.*
GUESS YOU KNOW WHAT A THING I HAVE FOR THE BAD BOYS.
DON'T JOKE!
HEY, *UM*--DON'T LET ME FORGET--I NEED TO GIVE YOU SOMETHING LATER--
I'M RIGHT HERE, SPIDER...
WHY WAIT?
YEAH--

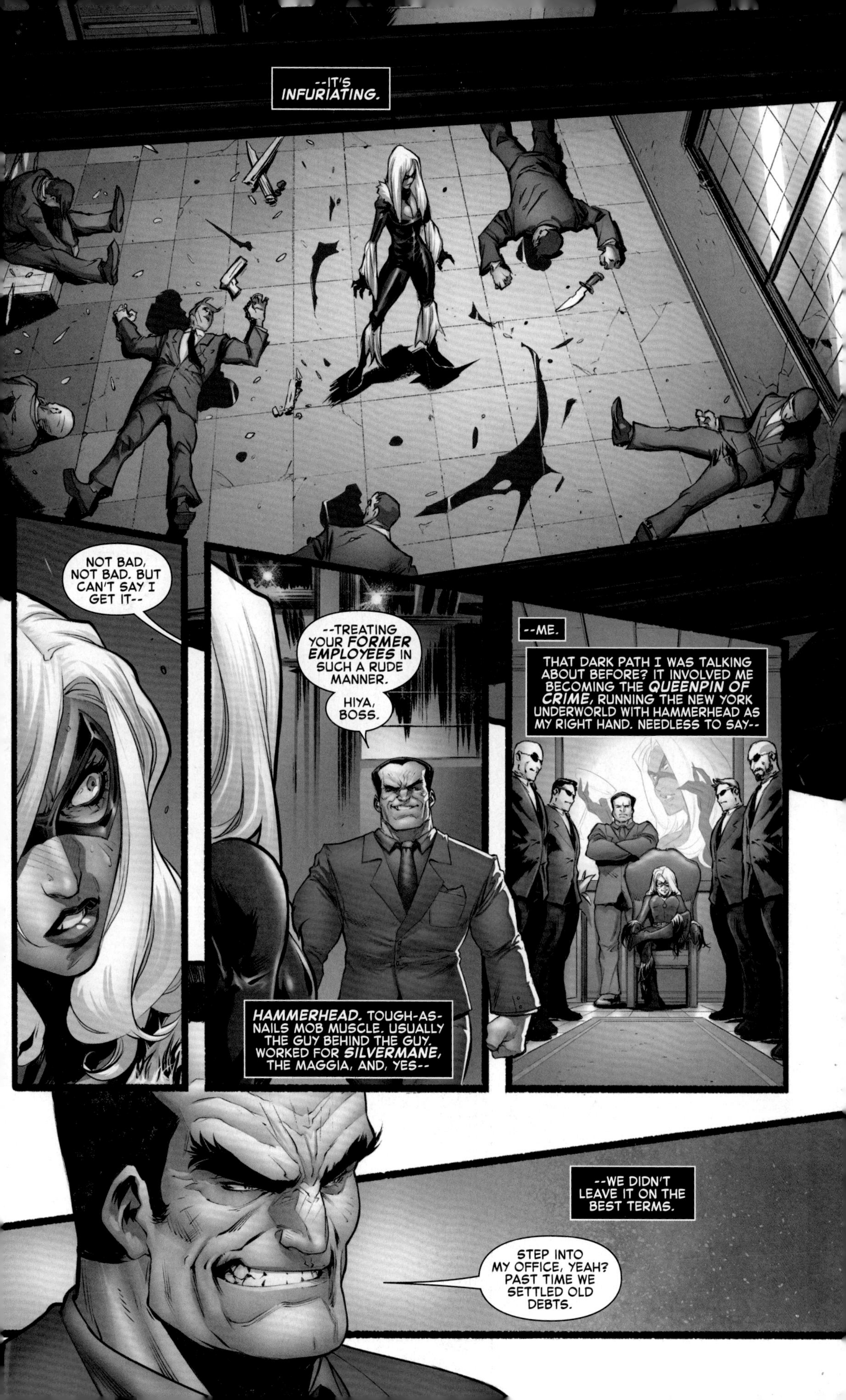
--IT'S INFURIATING.
NOT BAD, NOT BAD. BUT CAN'T SAY I GET IT--
--TREATING YOUR FORMER EMPLOYEES IN SUCH A RUDE MANNER.
HIYA, BOSS.
HAMMERHEAD. TOUGH-AS-NAILS MOB MUSCLE. USUALLY THE GUY BEHIND THE GUY. WORKED FOR SILVERMANE, THE MAGGIA, AND, YES--
--ME.
THAT DARK PATH I WAS TALKING ABOUT BEFORE? IT INVOLVED ME BECOMING THE QUEENPIN OF CRIME, RUNNING THE NEW YORK UNDERWORLD WITH HAMMERHEAD AS MY RIGHT HAND. NEEDLESS TO SAY--
--WE DIDN'T LEAVE IT ON THE BEST TERMS.
STEP INTO MY OFFICE, YEAH? PAST TIME WE SETTLED OLD DEBTS.

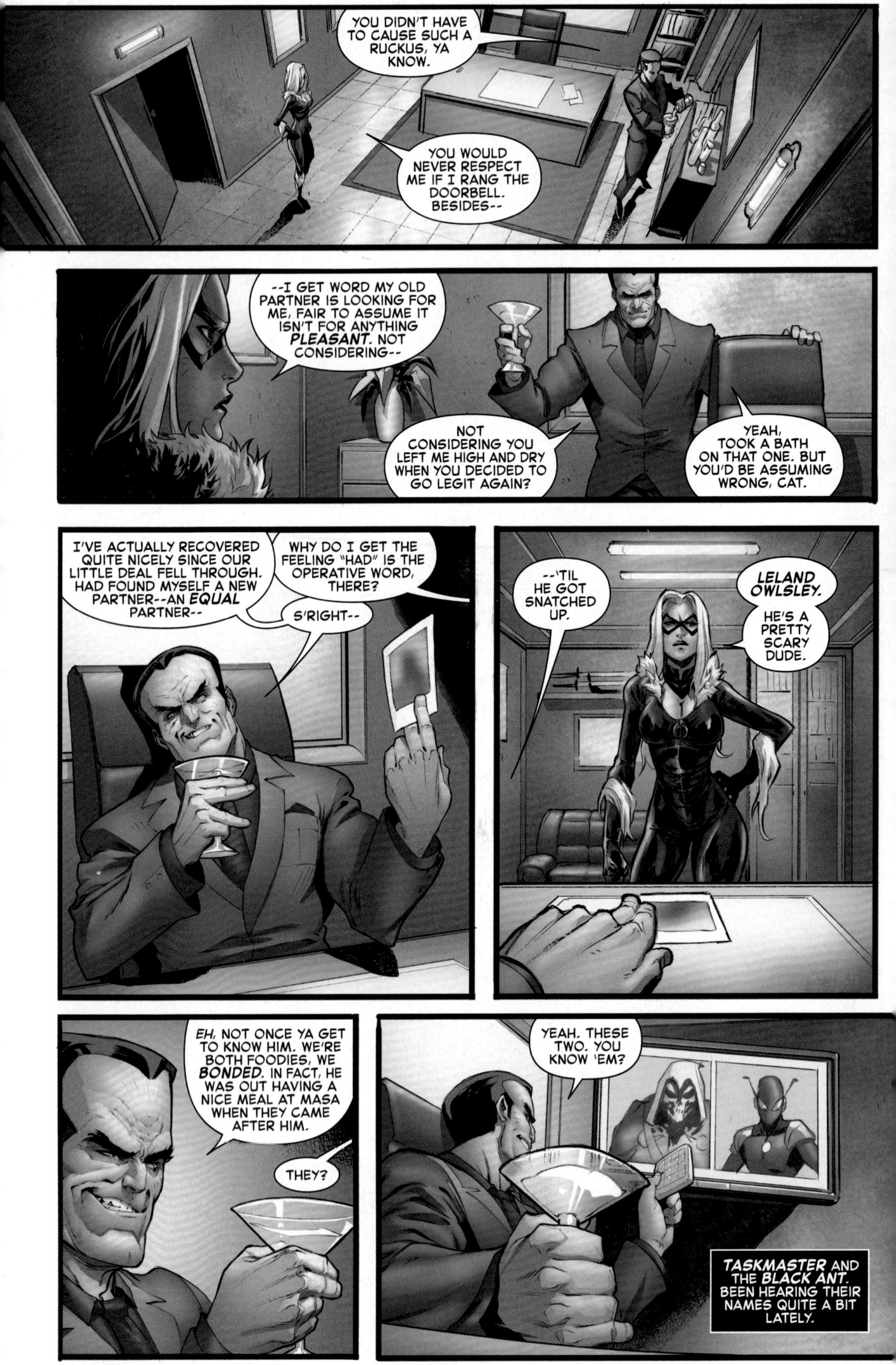
YOU DIDN'T HAVE TO CAUSE SUCH A RUCKUS, YA KNOW.
YOU WOULD NEVER RESPECT ME IF I RANG THE DOORBELL. BESIDES--
--I GET WORD MY OLD PARTNER IS LOOKING FOR ME, FAIR TO ASSUME IT ISN'T FOR ANYTHING PLEASANT. NOT CONSIDERING--
NOT CONSIDERING YOU LEFT ME HIGH AND DRY WHEN YOU DECIDED TO GO LEGIT AGAIN?
YEAH, TOOK A BATH ON THAT ONE. BUT YOU'D BE ASSUMING WRONG, CAT.
I'VE ACTUALLY RECOVERED QUITE NICELY SINCE OUR LITTLE DEAL FELL THROUGH. HAD FOUND MYSELF A NEW PARTNER--AN EQUAL PARTNER--
WHY DO I GET THE FEELING "HAD" IS THE OPERATIVE WORD, THERE?
S'RIGHT--
--'TIL HE GOT SNATCHED UP.
LELAND OWLSLEY.
HE'S A PRETTY SCARY DUDE.
EH, NOT ONCE YA GET TO KNOW HIM. WE'RE BOTH FOODIES, WE BONDED. IN FACT, HE WAS OUT HAVING A NICE MEAL AT MASA WHEN THEY CAME AFTER HIM.
THEY?
YEAH. THESE TWO. YOU KNOW 'EM?
TASKMASTER AND THE BLACK ANT. BEEN HEARING THEIR NAMES QUITE A BIT LATELY.

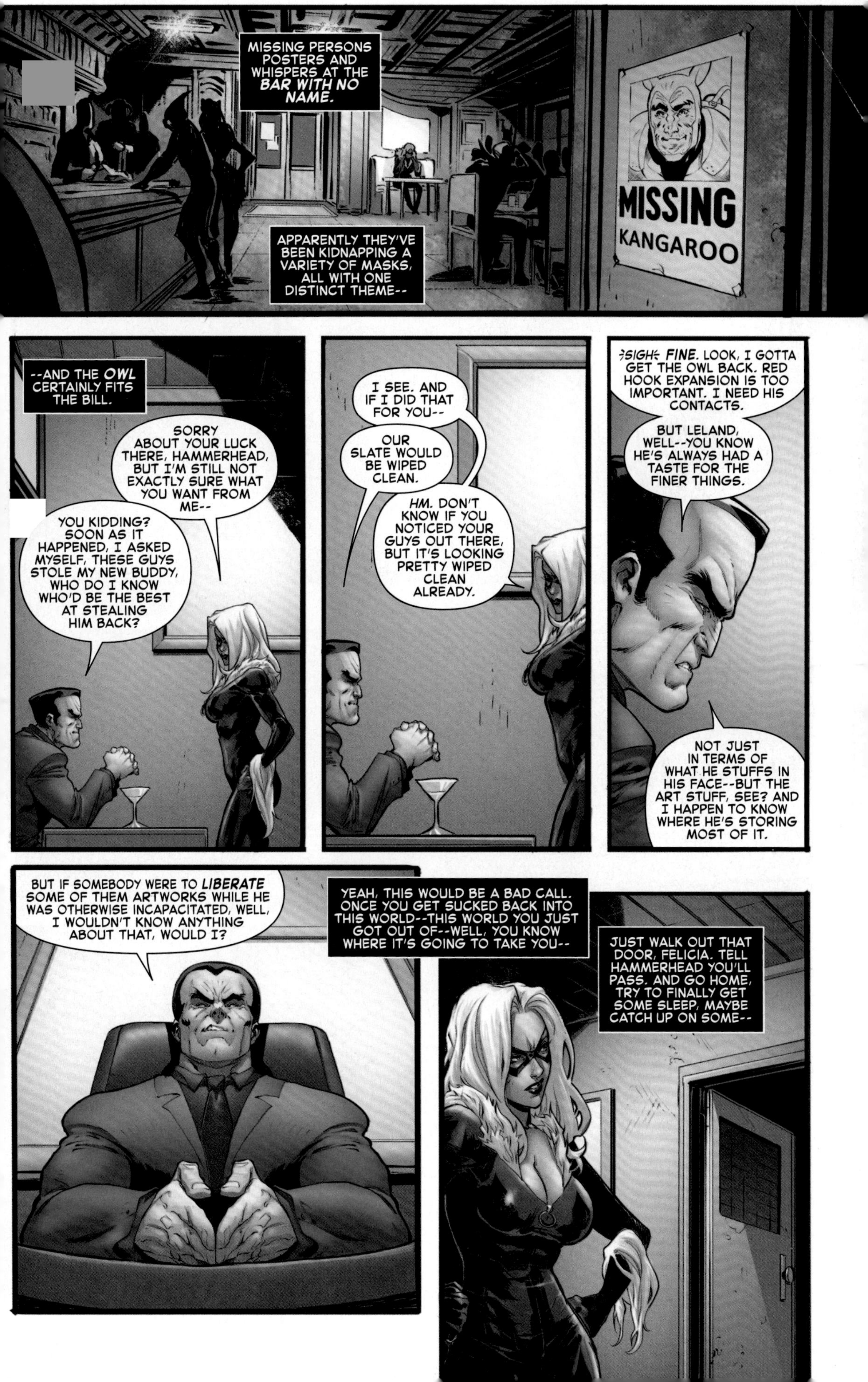

MISSING PERSONS POSTERS AND WHISPERS AT THE *BAR WITH NO NAME.*
MISSING
KANGAROO
APPARENTLY THEY'VE BEEN KIDNAPPING A VARIETY OF MASKS, ALL WITH ONE DISTINCT THEME--
--AND THE *OWL* CERTAINLY FITS THE BILL.
SORRY ABOUT YOUR LUCK THERE, HAMMERHEAD, BUT I'M STILL NOT EXACTLY SURE WHAT YOU WANT FROM ME--
YOU KIDDING? SOON AS IT HAPPENED, I ASKED MYSELF, THESE GUYS STOLE MY NEW BUDDY, WHO DO I KNOW WHO'D BE THE BEST AT STEALING HIM BACK?
I SEE. AND IF I DID THAT FOR YOU--
OUR SLATE WOULD BE WIPED CLEAN.
HM. DON'T KNOW IF YOU NOTICED YOUR GUYS OUT THERE, BUT IT'S LOOKING PRETTY WIPED CLEAN ALREADY.
SIGH *FINE.* LOOK, I GOTTA GET THE OWL BACK. RED HOOK EXPANSION IS TOO IMPORTANT. I NEED HIS CONTACTS.
BUT LELAND, WELL--YOU KNOW HE'S ALWAYS HAD A TASTE FOR THE FINER THINGS.
NOT JUST IN TERMS OF WHAT HE STUFFS IN HIS FACE--BUT THE ART STUFF, SEE? AND I HAPPEN TO KNOW WHERE HE'S STORING MOST OF IT.
BUT IF SOMEBODY WERE TO *LIBERATE* SOME OF THEM ARTWORKS WHILE HE WAS OTHERWISE INCAPACITATED, WELL, I WOULDN'T KNOW ANYTHING ABOUT THAT, WOULD I?
YEAH, THIS WOULD BE A BAD CALL. ONCE YOU GET SUCKED BACK INTO THIS WORLD--THIS WORLD YOU JUST GOT OUT OF--WELL, YOU KNOW WHERE IT'S GOING TO TAKE YOU--
JUST WALK OUT THAT DOOR, FELICIA. TELL HAMMERHEAD YOU'LL PASS. AND GO HOME, TRY TO FINALLY GET SOME SLEEP, MAYBE CATCH UP ON SOME--

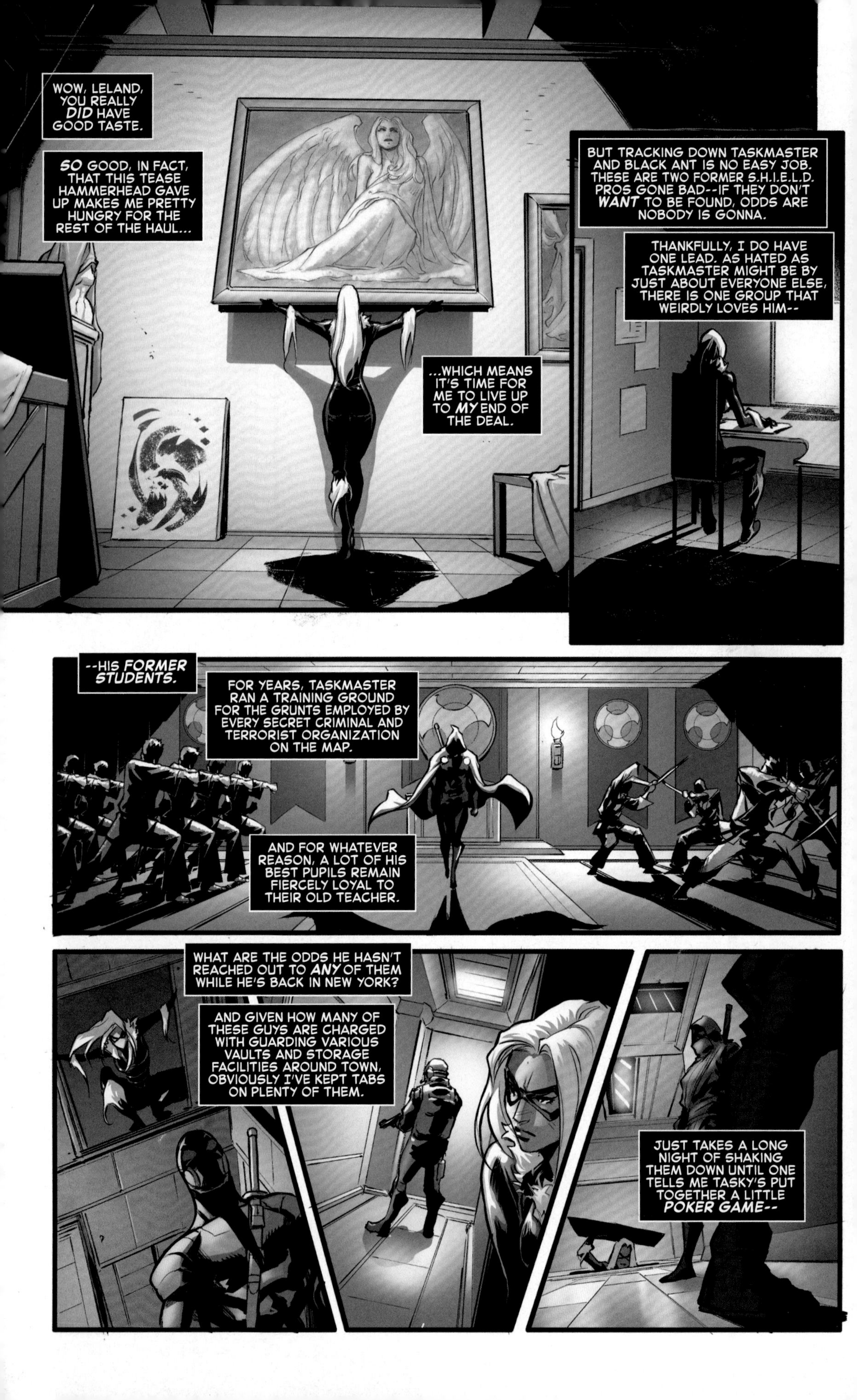
WOW, LELAND, YOU REALLY DID HAVE GOOD TASTE.
SO GOOD, IN FACT, THAT THIS TEASE HAMMERHEAD GAVE UP MAKES ME PRETTY HUNGRY FOR THE REST OF THE HAUL...
...WHICH MEANS IT'S TIME FOR ME TO LIVE UP TO MY END OF THE DEAL.
BUT TRACKING DOWN TASKMASTER AND BLACK ANT IS NO EASY JOB. THESE ARE TWO FORMER S.H.I.E.L.D. PROS GONE BAD--IF THEY DON'T WANT TO BE FOUND, ODDS ARE NOBODY IS GONNA.
THANKFULLY, I DO HAVE ONE LEAD. AS HATED AS TASKMASTER MIGHT BE BY JUST ABOUT EVERYONE ELSE, THERE IS ONE GROUP THAT WEIRDLY LOVES HIM--
--HIS FORMER STUDENTS.
FOR YEARS, TASKMASTER RAN A TRAINING GROUND FOR THE GRUNTS EMPLOYED BY EVERY SECRET CRIMINAL AND TERRORIST ORGANIZATION ON THE MAP.
AND FOR WHATEVER REASON, A LOT OF HIS BEST PUPILS REMAIN FIERCELY LOYAL TO THEIR OLD TEACHER.
WHAT ARE THE ODDS HE HASN'T REACHED OUT TO ANY OF THEM WHILE HE'S BACK IN NEW YORK?
AND GIVEN HOW MANY OF THESE GUYS ARE CHARGED WITH GUARDING VARIOUS VAULTS AND STORAGE FACILITIES AROUND TOWN, OBVIOUSLY I'VE KEPT TABS ON PLENTY OF THEM.
JUST TAKES A LONG NIGHT OF SHAKING THEM DOWN UNTIL ONE TELLS ME TASKY'S PUT TOGETHER A LITTLE POKER GAME--

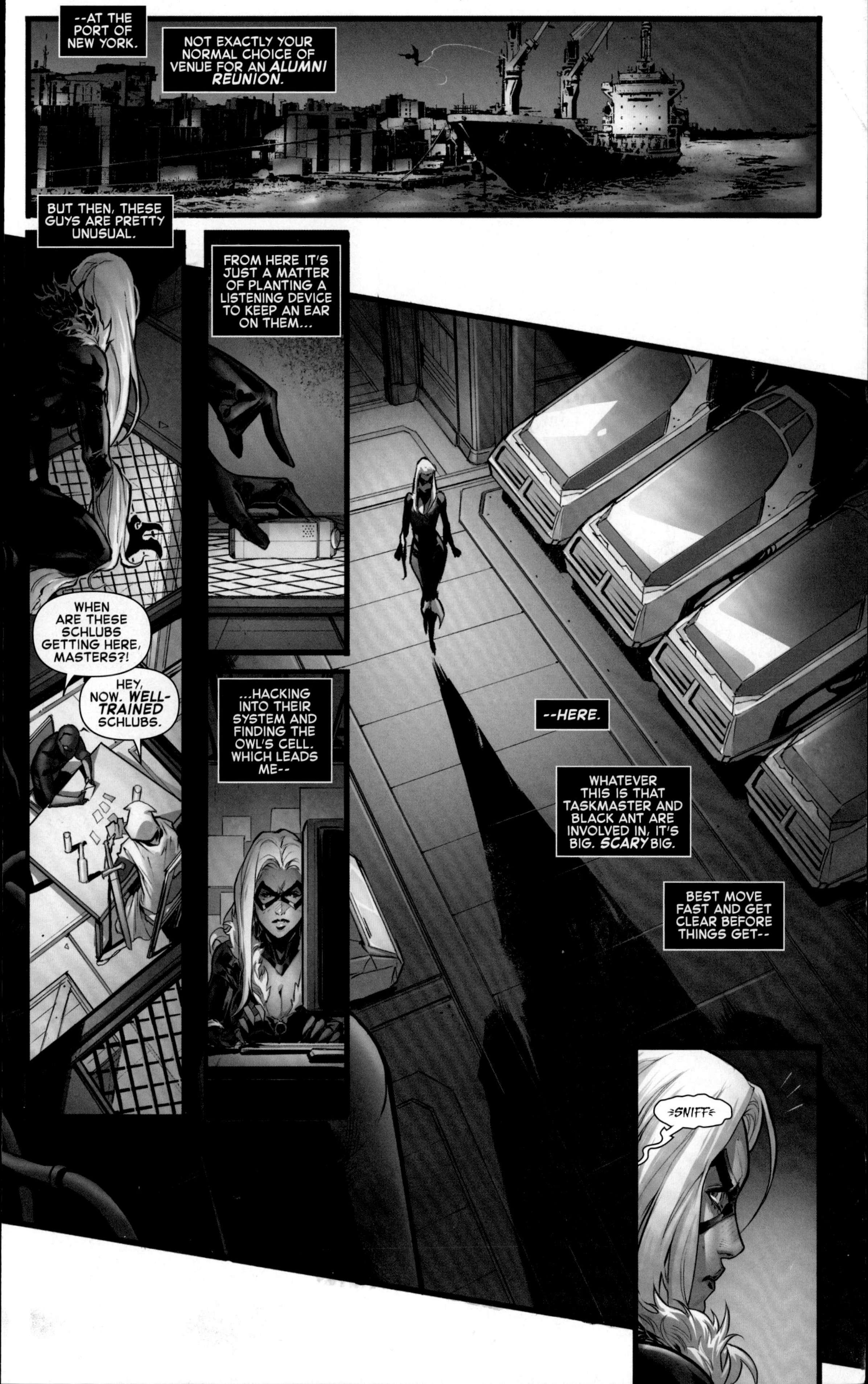
--AT THE PORT OF NEW YORK.
NOT EXACTLY YOUR NORMAL CHOICE OF VENUE FOR AN ALUMNI REUNION.
BUT THEN, THESE GUYS ARE PRETTY UNUSUAL.
WHEN ARE THESE SCHLUBS GETTING HERE, MASTERS?!
HEY, NOW. WELL-TRAINED SCHLUBS.
FROM HERE IT'S JUST A MATTER OF PLANTING A LISTENING DEVICE TO KEEP AN EAR ON THEM...
...HACKING INTO THEIR SYSTEM AND FINDING THE OWL'S CELL. WHICH LEADS ME--
--HERE.
WHATEVER THIS IS THAT TASKMASTER AND BLACK ANT ARE INVOLVED IN, IT'S BIG. SCARY BIG.
BEST MOVE FAST AND GET CLEAR BEFORE THINGS GET--
SNIFF

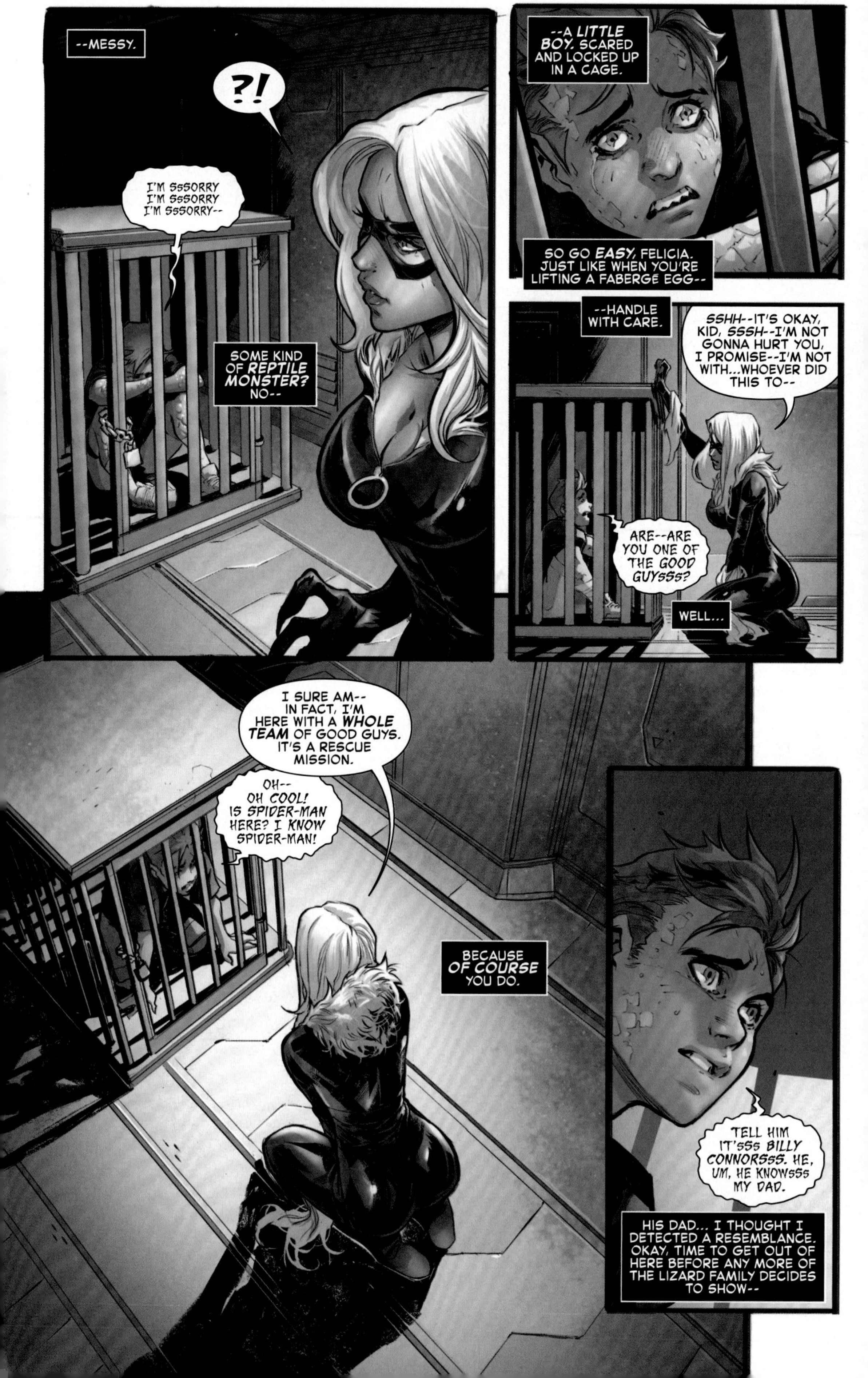
--MESSY.
?!
I'M SsSORRY I'M SsSORRY I'M SsSORRY--
SOME KIND OF REPTILE MONSTER? NO--
--A LITTLE BOY. SCARED AND LOCKED UP IN A CAGE.
SO GO EASY, FELICIA. JUST LIKE WHEN YOU'RE LIFTING A FABERGÉ EGG--
--HANDLE WITH CARE.
SSHH--IT'S OKAY, KID, SSSH--I'M NOT GONNA HURT YOU, I PROMISE--I'M NOT WITH...WHOEVER DID THIS TO--
ARE--ARE YOU ONE OF THE GOOD GUYSSS?
WELL...
I SURE AM-- IN FACT, I'M HERE WITH A WHOLE TEAM OF GOOD GUYS. IT'S A RESCUE MISSION.
OH-- OH COOL! IS SPIDER-MAN HERE? I KNOW SPIDER-MAN!
BECAUSE OF COURSE YOU DO.
TELL HIM IT'SSS BILLY CONNORSSS. HE, UM, HE KNOWSSS MY DAD.
HIS DAD... I THOUGHT I DETECTED A RESEMBLANCE. OKAY, TIME TO GET OUT OF HERE BEFORE ANY MORE OF THE LIZARD FAMILY DECIDES TO SHOW--

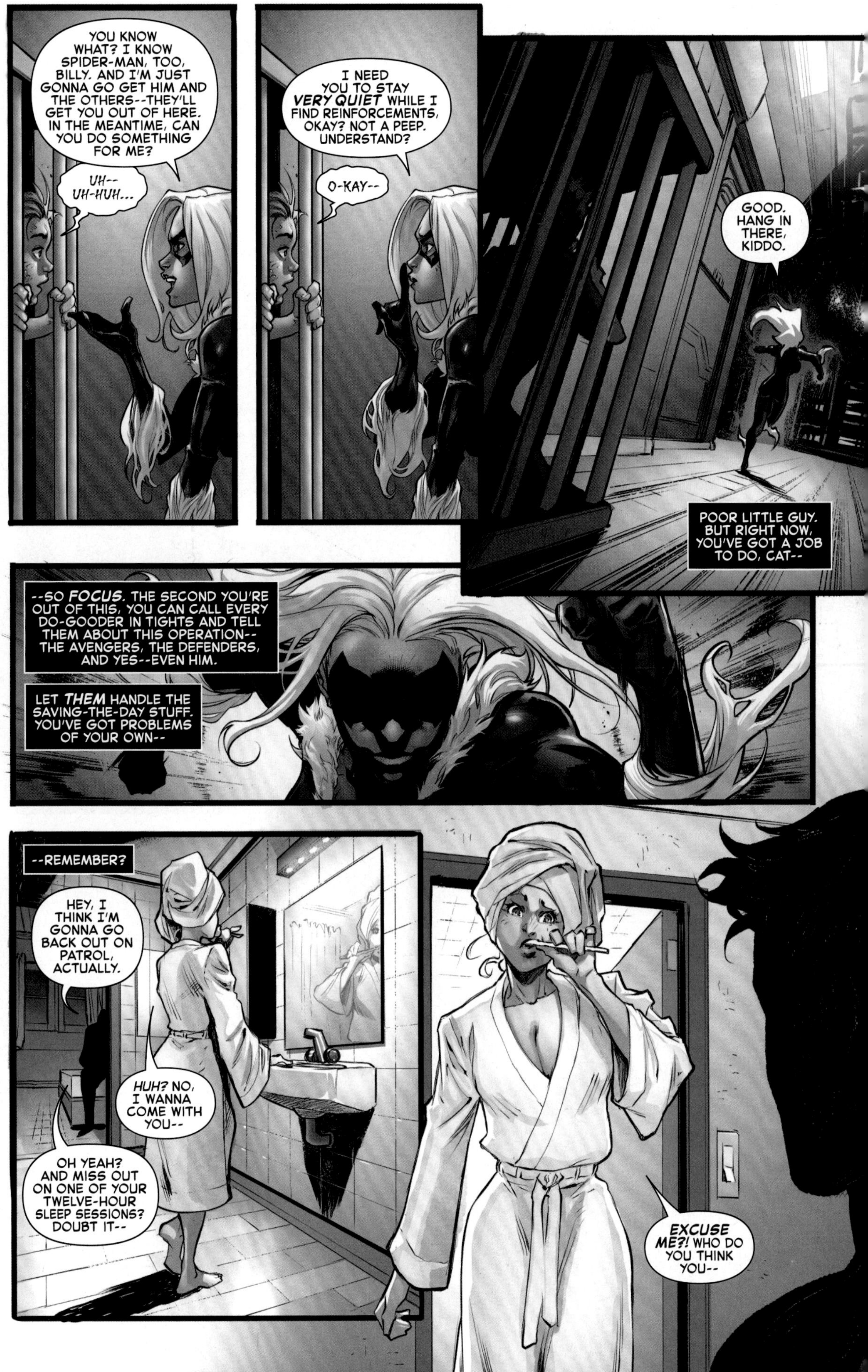
YOU KNOW WHAT? I KNOW SPIDER-MAN, TOO, BILLY. AND I'M JUST GONNA GO GET HIM AND THE OTHERS--THEY'LL GET YOU OUT OF HERE. IN THE MEANTIME, CAN YOU DO SOMETHING FOR ME?
UH-- UH-HUH...
I NEED YOU TO STAY VERY QUIET WHILE I FIND REINFORCEMENTS, OKAY? NOT A PEEP. UNDERSTAND?
O-KAY--
GOOD. HANG IN THERE, KIDDO.
POOR LITTLE GUY. BUT RIGHT NOW, YOU'VE GOT A JOB TO DO, CAT--
--SO FOCUS. THE SECOND YOU'RE OUT OF THIS, YOU CAN CALL EVERY DO-GOODER IN TIGHTS AND TELL THEM ABOUT THIS OPERATION-- THE AVENGERS, THE DEFENDERS, AND YES--EVEN HIM.
LET THEM HANDLE THE SAVING-THE-DAY STUFF. YOU'VE GOT PROBLEMS OF YOUR OWN--
--REMEMBER?
HEY, I THINK I'M GONNA GO BACK OUT ON PATROL, ACTUALLY.
HUH? NO, I WANNA COME WITH YOU--
OH YEAH? AND MISS OUT ON ONE OF YOUR TWELVE-HOUR SLEEP SESSIONS? DOUBT IT--
EXCUSE ME?! WHO DO YOU THINK YOU--

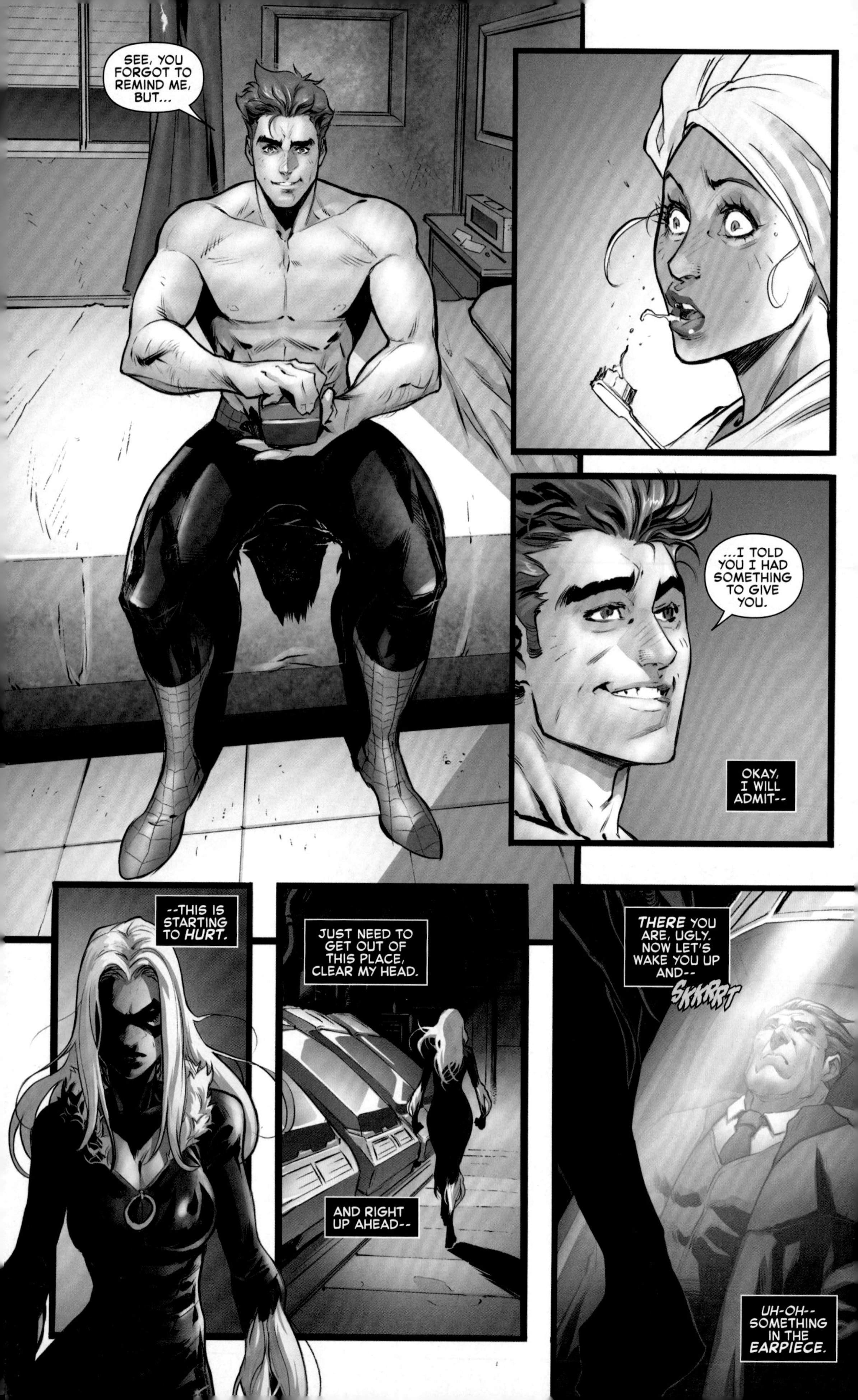
SEE, YOU FORGOT TO REMIND ME, BUT...
...I TOLD YOU I HAD SOMETHING TO GIVE YOU.
OKAY, I WILL ADMIT--
--THIS IS STARTING TO *HURT.*
JUST NEED TO GET OUT OF THIS PLACE, CLEAR MY HEAD.
AND RIGHT UP AHEAD--
THERE YOU ARE, UGLY. NOW LET'S WAKE YOU UP AND--
SKKRRT
UH-OH--SOMETHING IN THE *EARPIECE.*

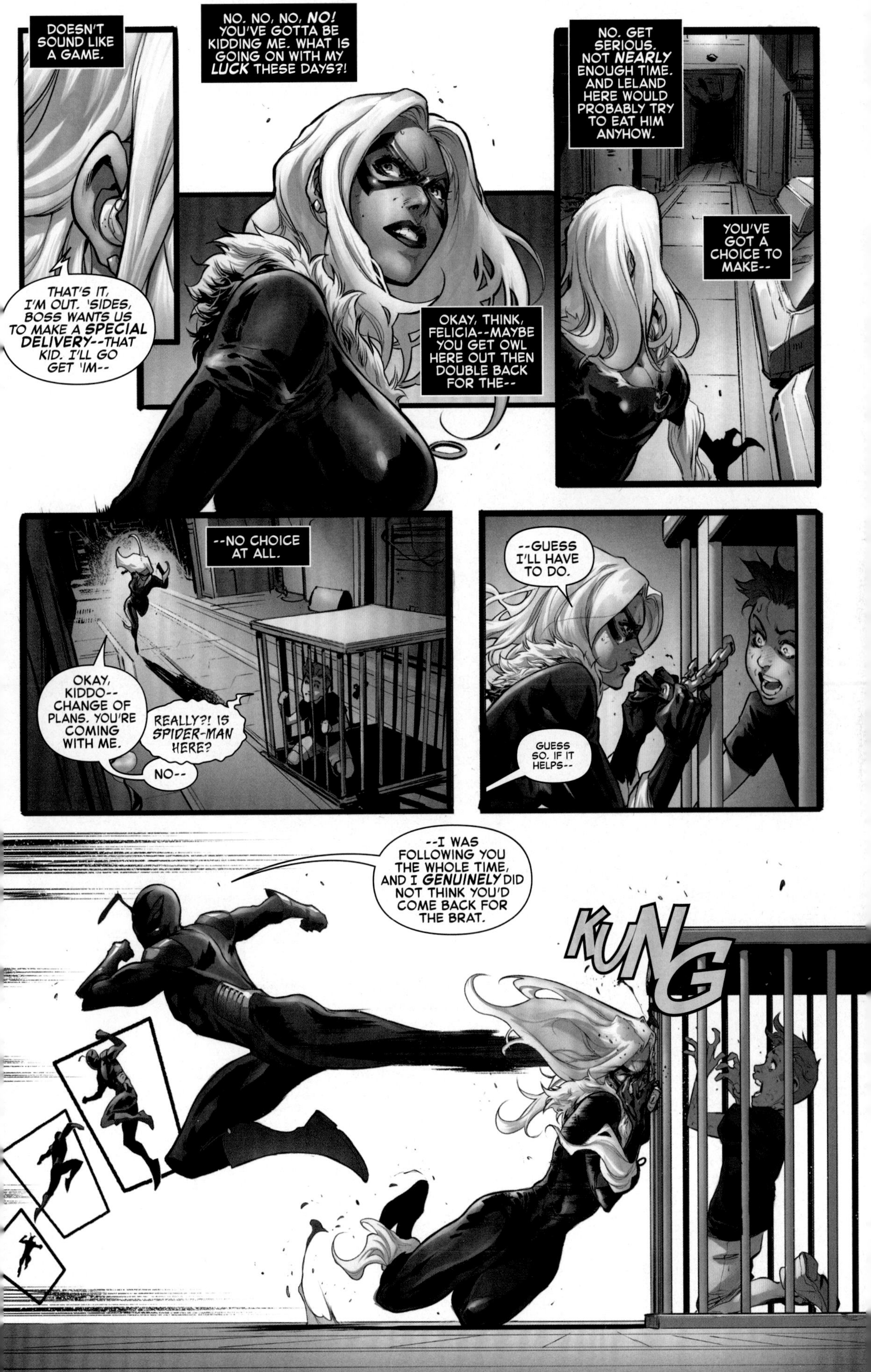
DOESN'T SOUND LIKE A GAME.
THAT'S IT, I'M OUT. 'SIDES, BOSS WANTS US TO MAKE A SPECIAL DELIVERY--THAT KID. I'LL GO GET 'IM--
NO. NO, NO, NO! YOU'VE GOTTA BE KIDDING ME. WHAT IS GOING ON WITH MY LUCK THESE DAYS?!
OKAY, THINK, FELICIA--MAYBE YOU GET OWL HERE OUT THEN DOUBLE BACK FOR THE--
NO. GET SERIOUS. NOT NEARLY ENOUGH TIME. AND LELAND HERE WOULD PROBABLY TRY TO EAT HIM ANYHOW.
YOU'VE GOT A CHOICE TO MAKE--
--NO CHOICE AT ALL.
OKAY, KIDDO--CHANGE OF PLANS. YOU'RE COMING WITH ME.
REALLY?! IS SPIDER-MAN HERE?
NO--
--GUESS I'LL HAVE TO DO.
GUESS SO. IF IT HELPS--
--I WAS FOLLOWING YOU THE WHOLE TIME, AND I GENUINELY DID NOT THINK YOU'D COME BACK FOR THE BRAT.
KUNG

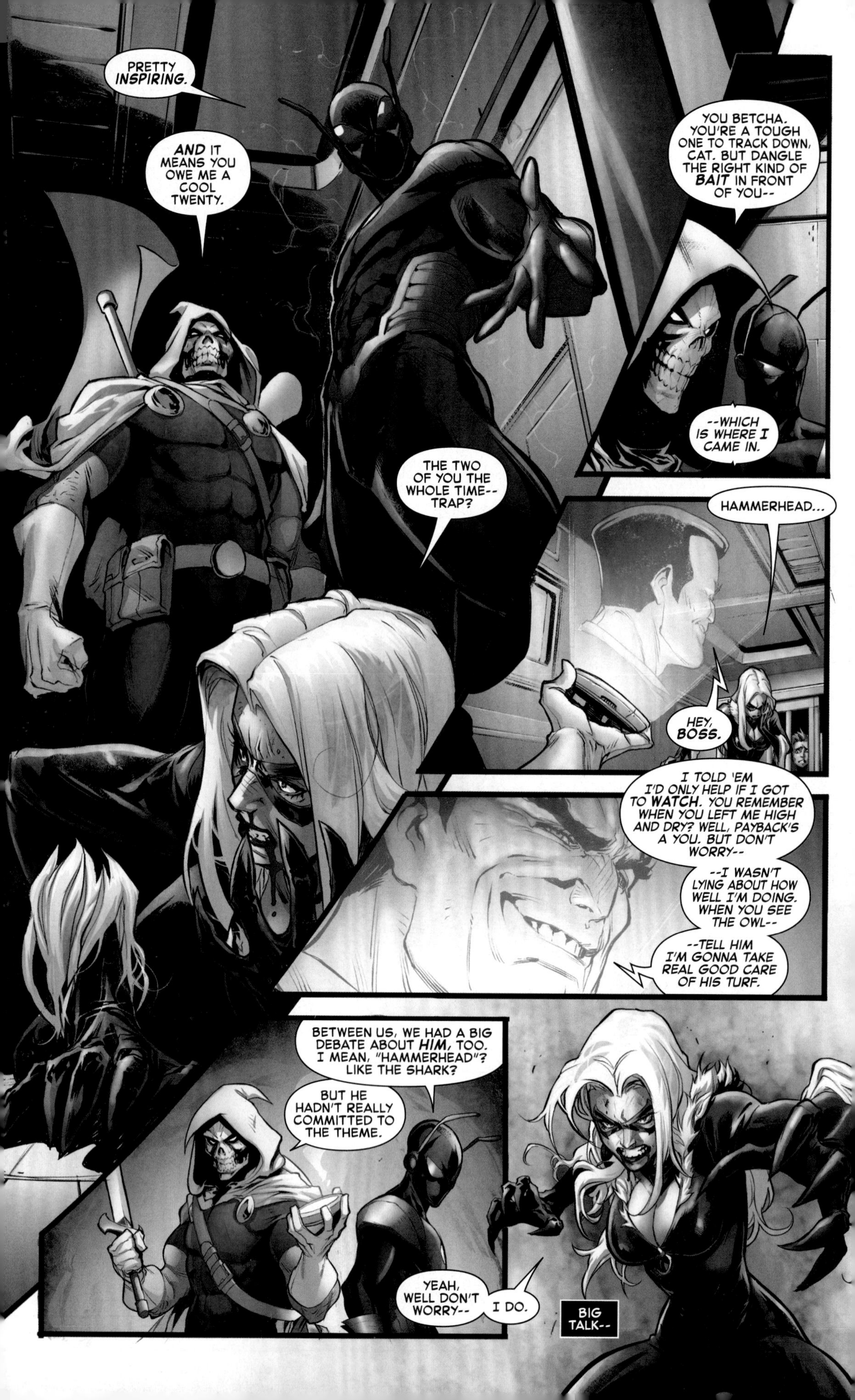
PRETTY INSPIRING.
AND IT MEANS YOU OWE ME A COOL TWENTY.
YOU BETCHA. YOU'RE A TOUGH ONE TO TRACK DOWN, CAT. BUT DANGLE THE RIGHT KIND OF BAIT IN FRONT OF YOU--
--WHICH IS WHERE I CAME IN.
THE TWO OF YOU THE WHOLE TIME-- TRAP?
HAMMERHEAD...
HEY, BOSS.
I TOLD 'EM I'D ONLY HELP IF I GOT TO WATCH. YOU REMEMBER WHEN YOU LEFT ME HIGH AND DRY? WELL, PAYBACK'S A YOU. BUT DON'T WORRY--
--I WASN'T LYING ABOUT HOW WELL I'M DOING. WHEN YOU SEE THE OWL--
--TELL HIM I'M GONNA TAKE REAL GOOD CARE OF HIS TURF.
BETWEEN US, WE HAD A BIG DEBATE ABOUT HIM, TOO. I MEAN, "HAMMERHEAD"? LIKE THE SHARK?
BUT HE HADN'T REALLY COMMITTED TO THE THEME.
YEAH, WELL DON'T WORRY--
I DO.
BIG TALK--

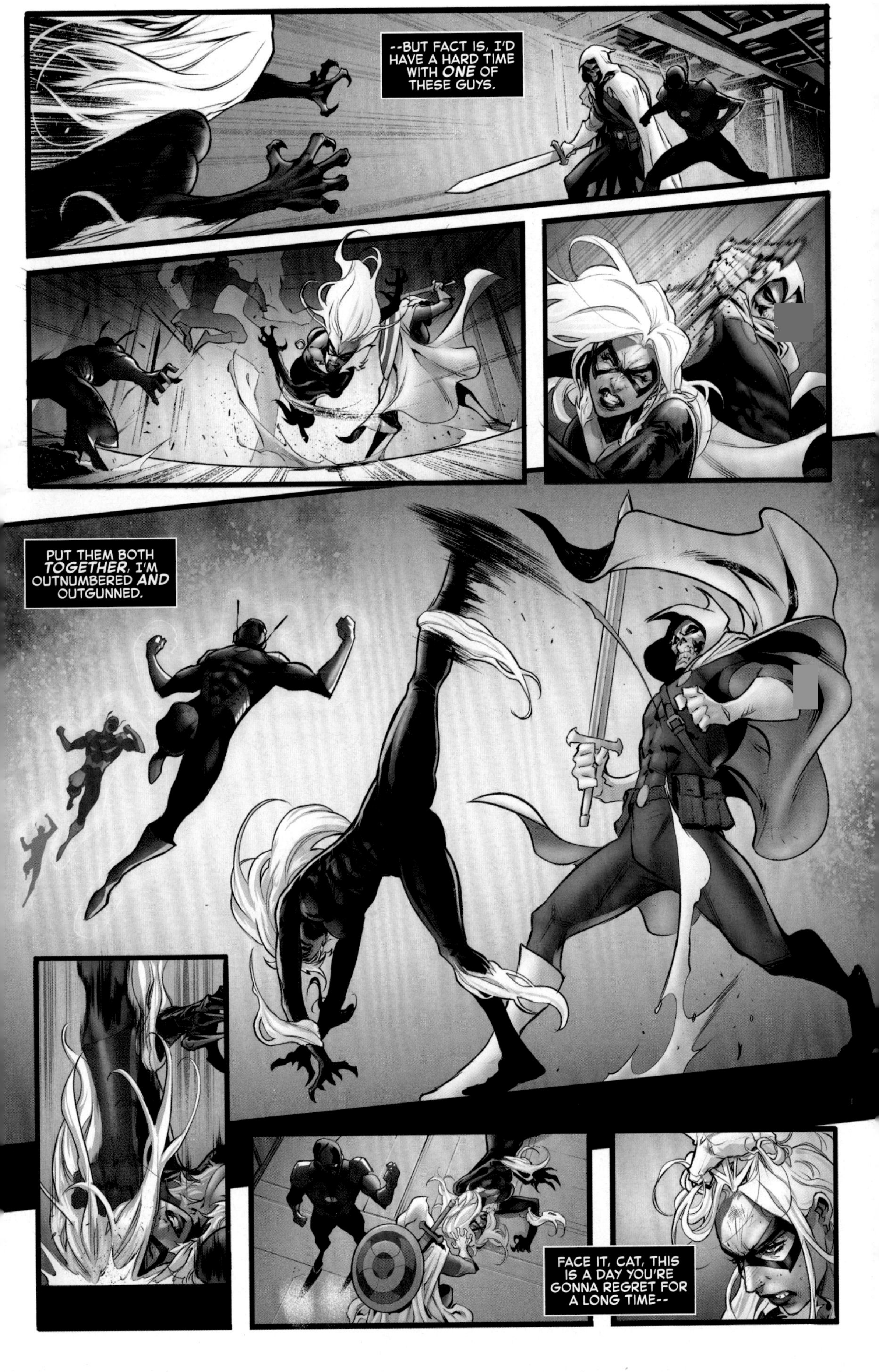
--BUT FACT IS, I'D HAVE A HARD TIME WITH ONE OF THESE GUYS.
PUT THEM BOTH TOGETHER, I'M OUTNUMBERED AND OUTGUNNED.
FACE IT, CAT, THIS IS A DAY YOU'RE GONNA REGRET FOR A LONG TIME--

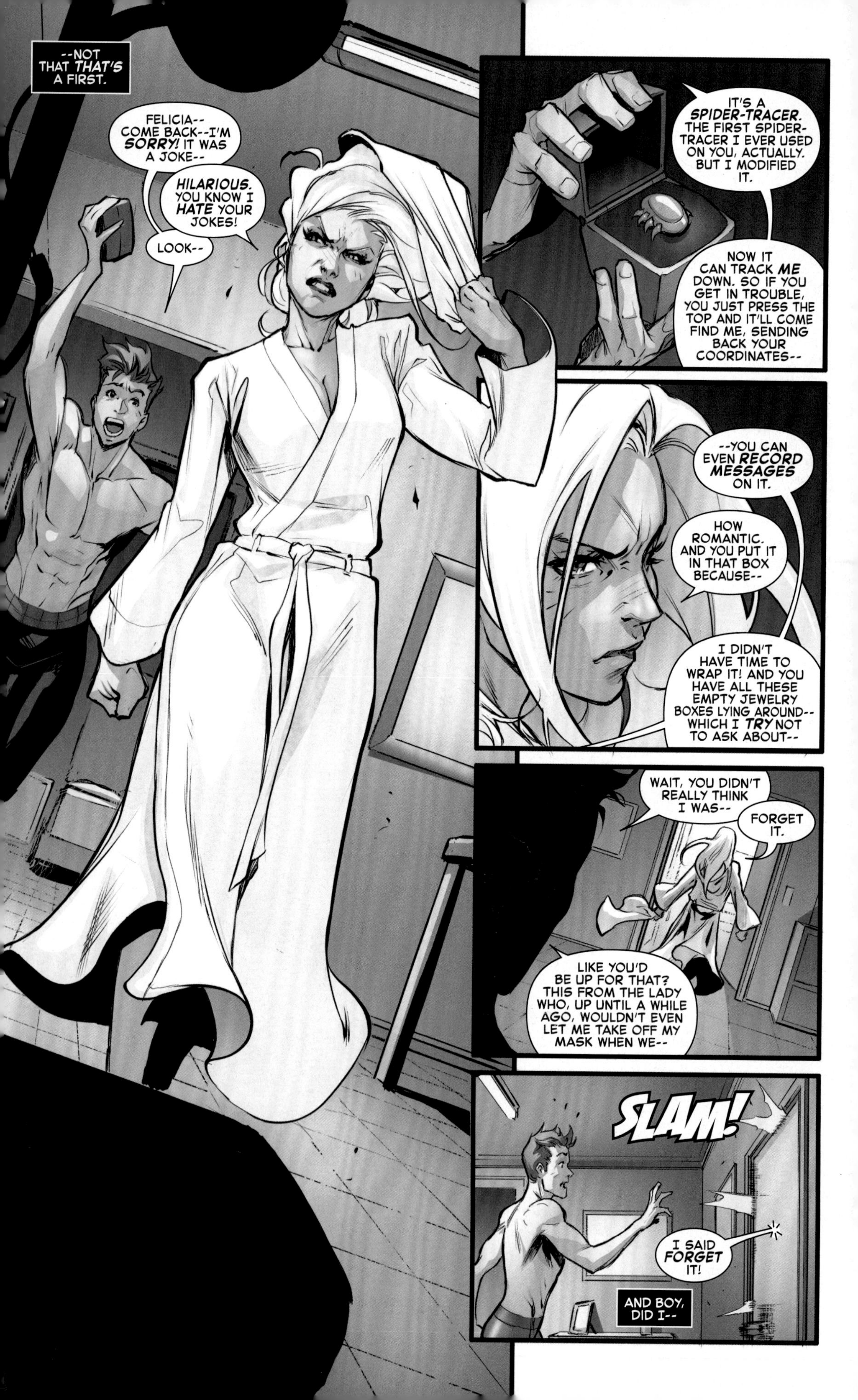
--NOT THAT THAT'S A FIRST.
FELICIA-- COME BACK--I'M SORRY! IT WAS A JOKE--
HILARIOUS. YOU KNOW I HATE YOUR JOKES!
LOOK--
IT'S A SPIDER-TRACER. THE FIRST SPIDER-TRACER I EVER USED ON YOU, ACTUALLY. BUT I MODIFIED IT.
NOW IT CAN TRACK ME DOWN. SO IF YOU GET IN TROUBLE, YOU JUST PRESS THE TOP AND IT'LL COME FIND ME, SENDING BACK YOUR COORDINATES--
--YOU CAN EVEN RECORD MESSAGES ON IT.
HOW ROMANTIC. AND YOU PUT IT IN THAT BOX BECAUSE--
I DIDN'T HAVE TIME TO WRAP IT! AND YOU HAVE ALL THESE EMPTY JEWELRY BOXES LYING AROUND--WHICH I TRY NOT TO ASK ABOUT--
WAIT, YOU DIDN'T REALLY THINK I WAS--
FORGET IT.
LIKE YOU'D BE UP FOR THAT? THIS FROM THE LADY WHO, UP UNTIL A WHILE AGO, WOULDN'T EVEN LET ME TAKE OFF MY MASK WHEN WE--
SLAM!
I SAID FORGET IT!
AND BOY, DID I--

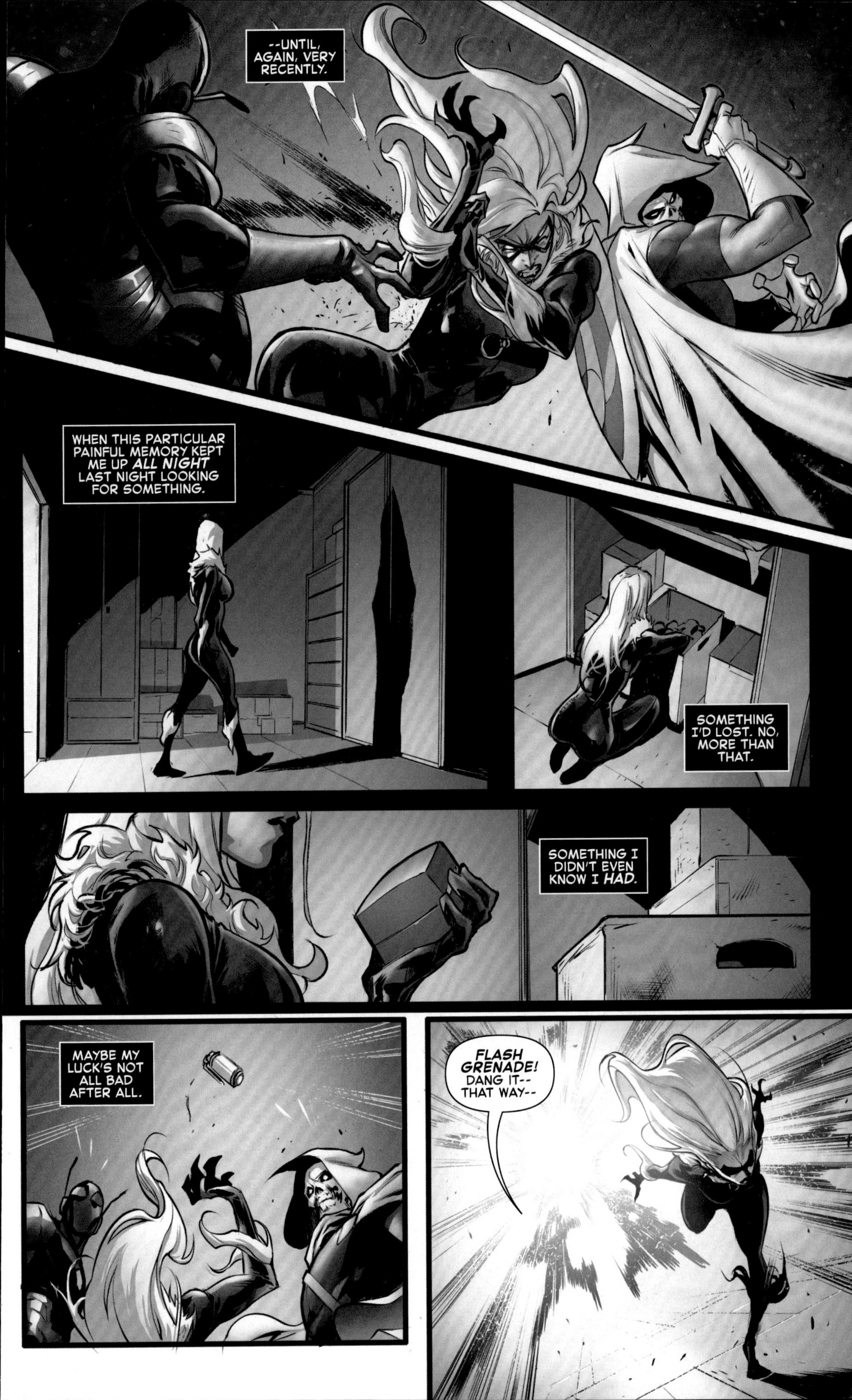
--UNTIL, AGAIN, VERY RECENTLY.
WHEN THIS PARTICULAR PAINFUL MEMORY KEPT ME UP ALL NIGHT LAST NIGHT LOOKING FOR SOMETHING.
SOMETHING I'D LOST. NO, MORE THAN THAT.
SOMETHING I DIDN'T EVEN KNOW I HAD.
MAYBE MY LUCK'S NOT ALL BAD AFTER ALL.
FLASH GRENADE! DANG IT-- THAT WAY--

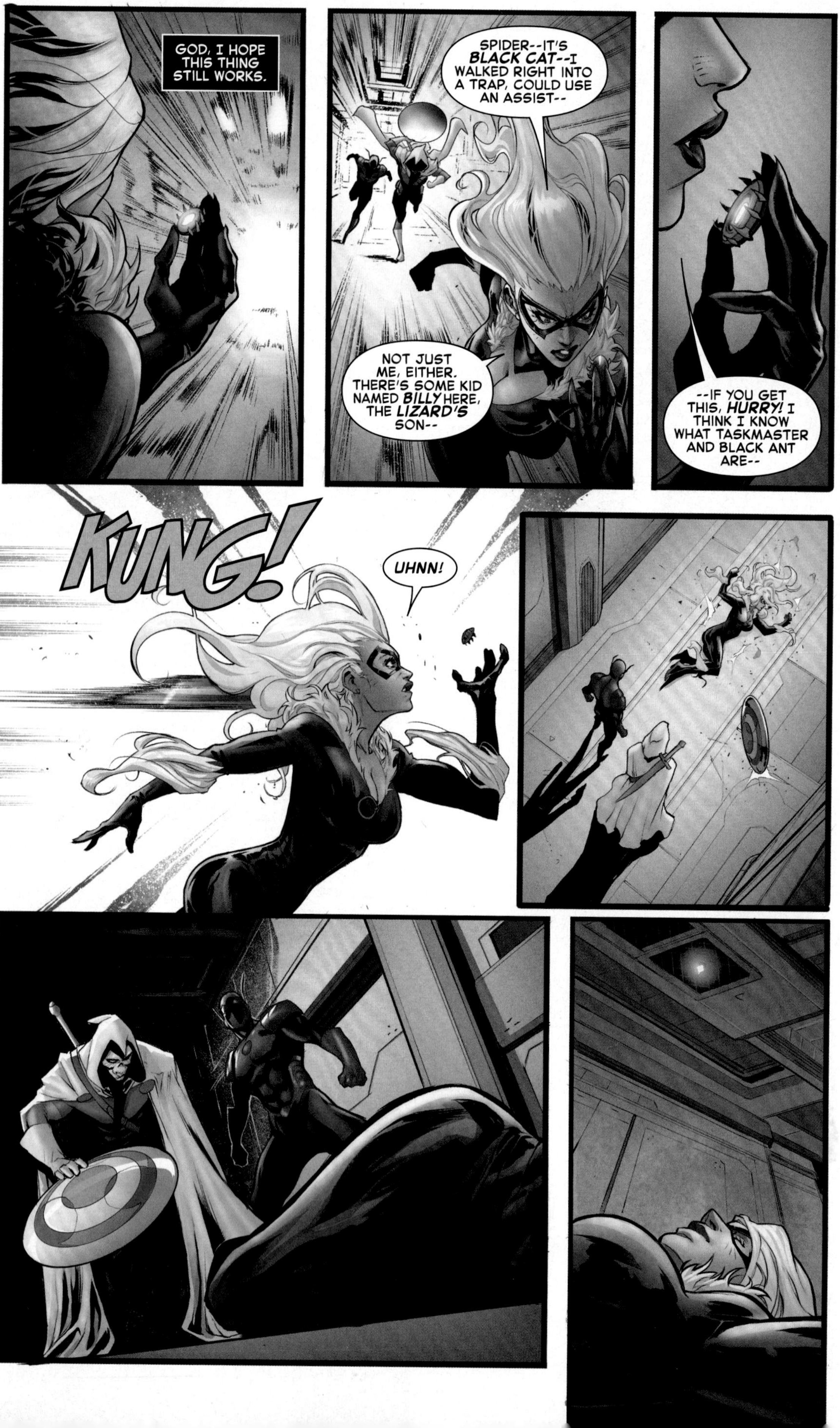
GOD, I HOPE THIS THING STILL WORKS.
SPIDER--IT'S BLACK CAT--I WALKED RIGHT INTO A TRAP, COULD USE AN ASSIST--
NOT JUST ME, EITHER. THERE'S SOME KID NAMED BILLY HERE, THE LIZARD'S SON--
--IF YOU GET THIS, HURRY! I THINK I KNOW WHAT TASKMASTER AND BLACK ANT ARE--
KUNG!
UHNN!

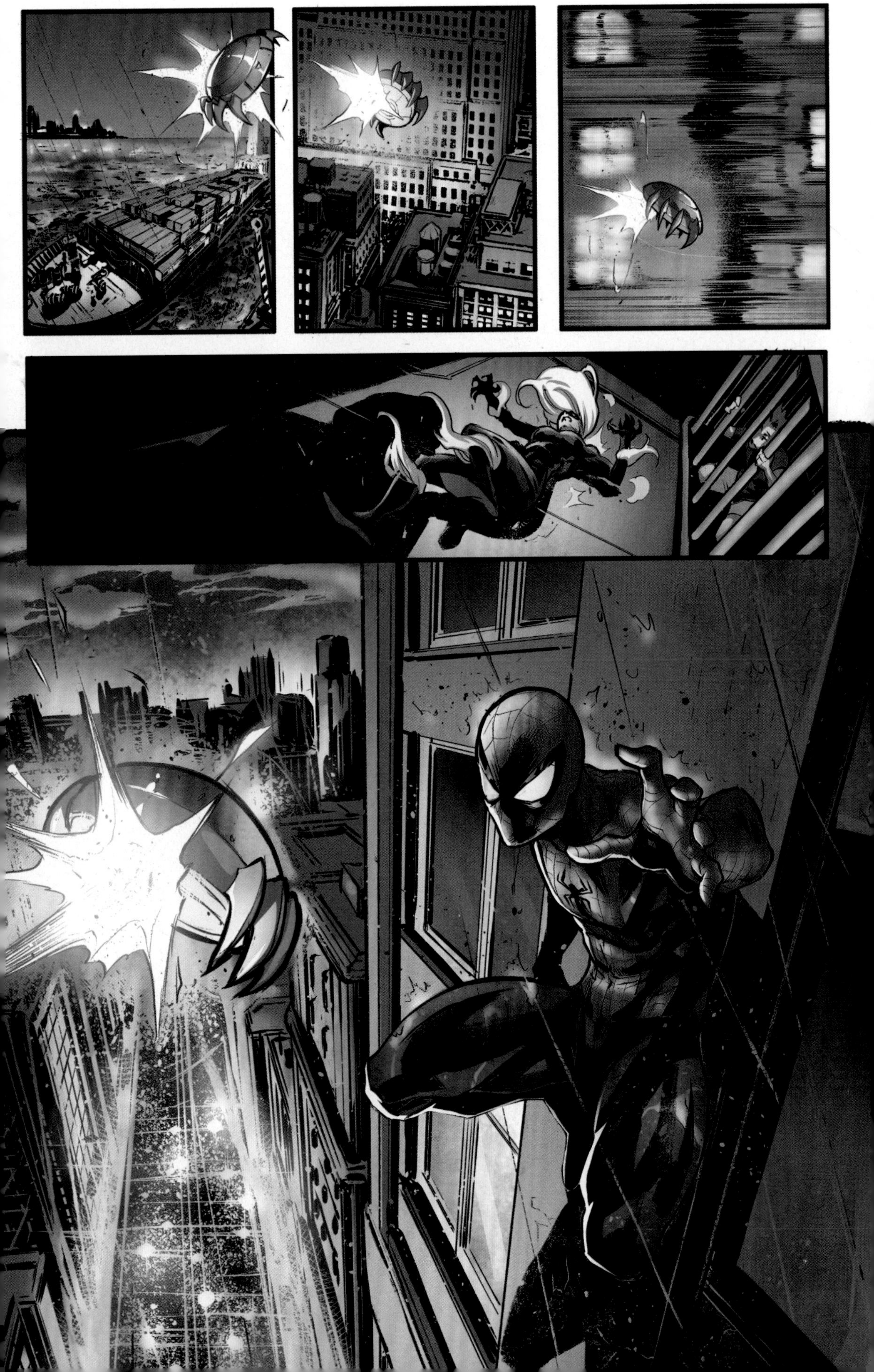

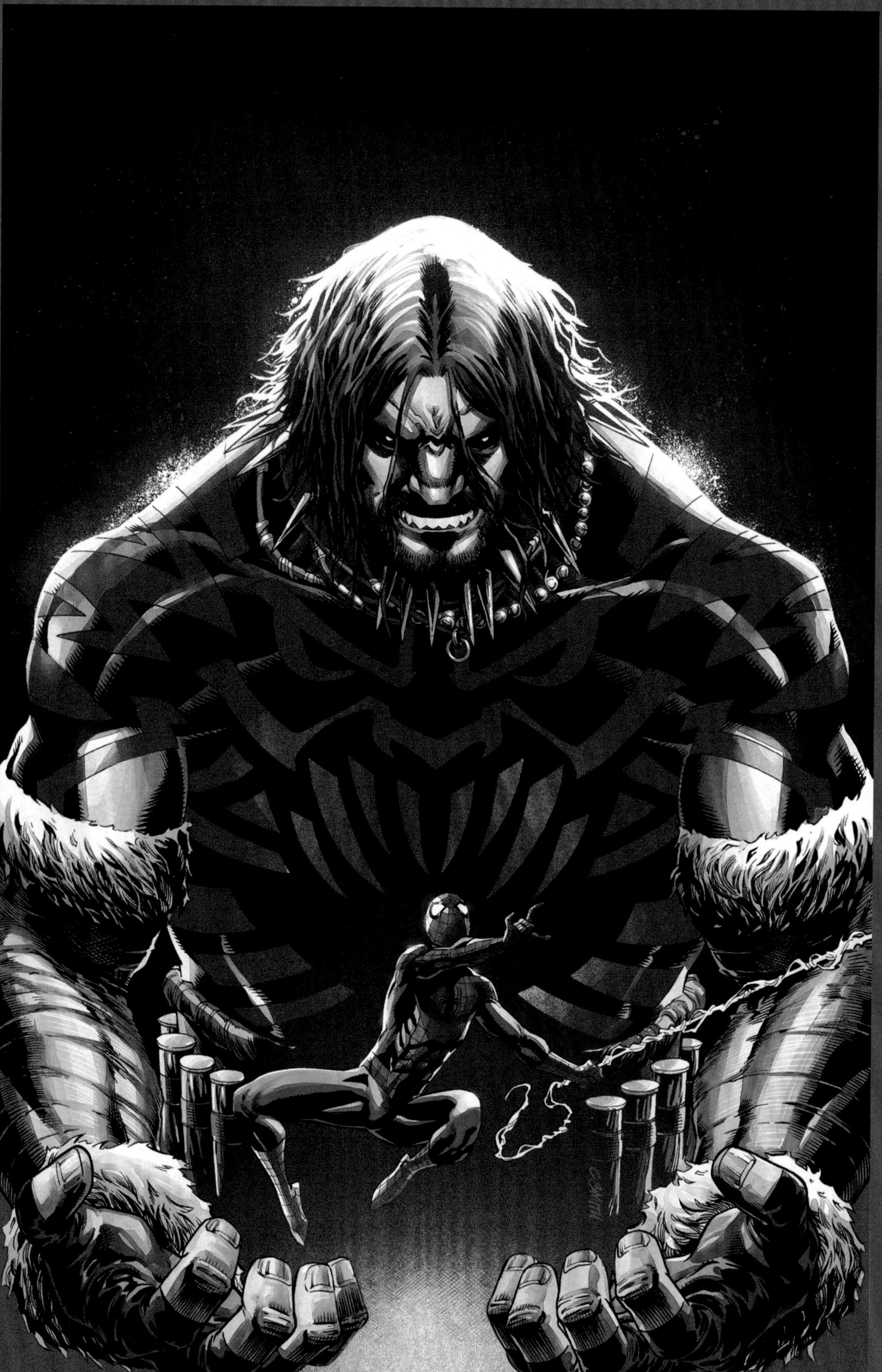

#17 VARIANT BY CORY SMITH & ANDRES MOSSA

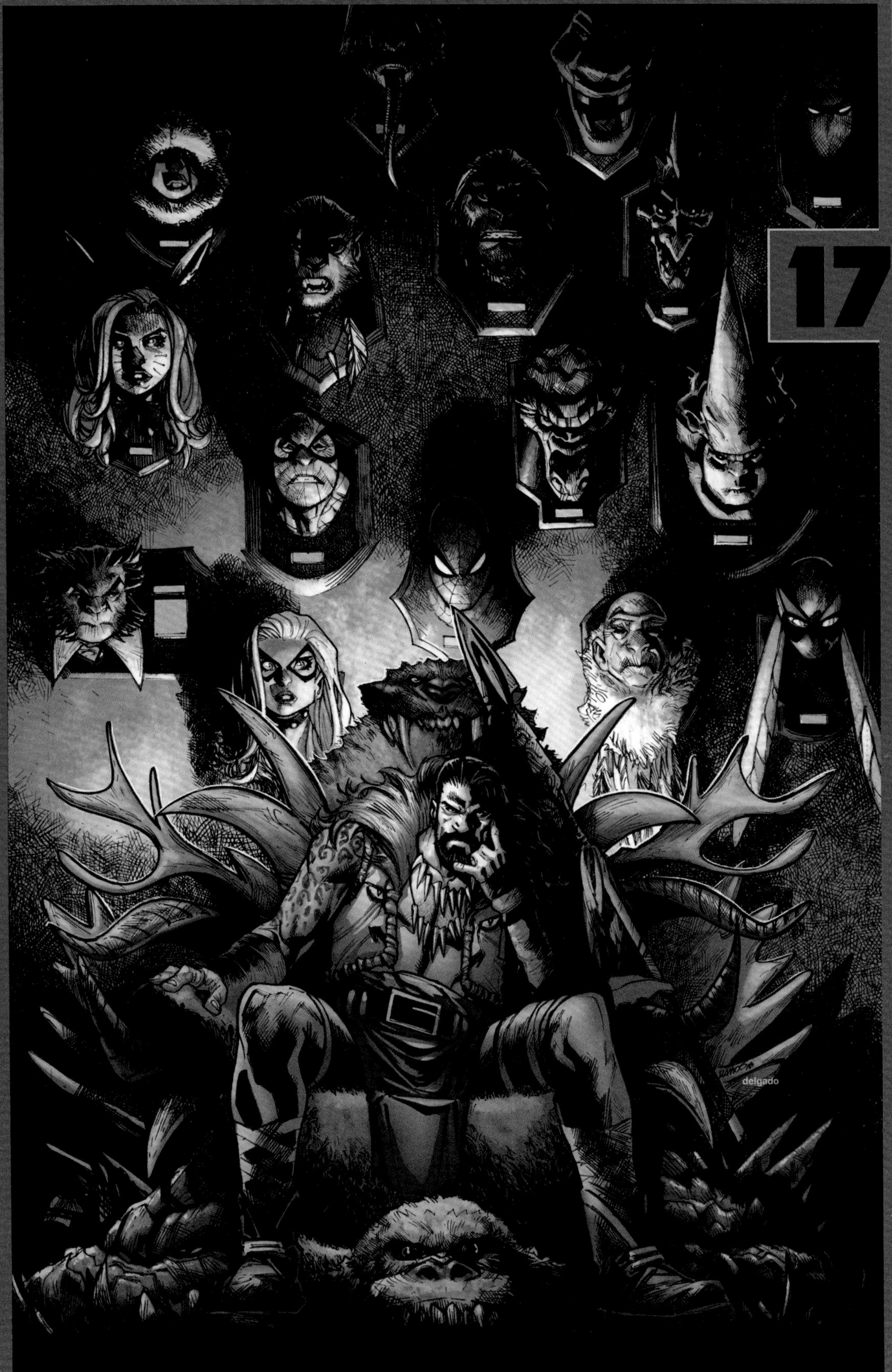
delgado

17

HUNTED PART 1

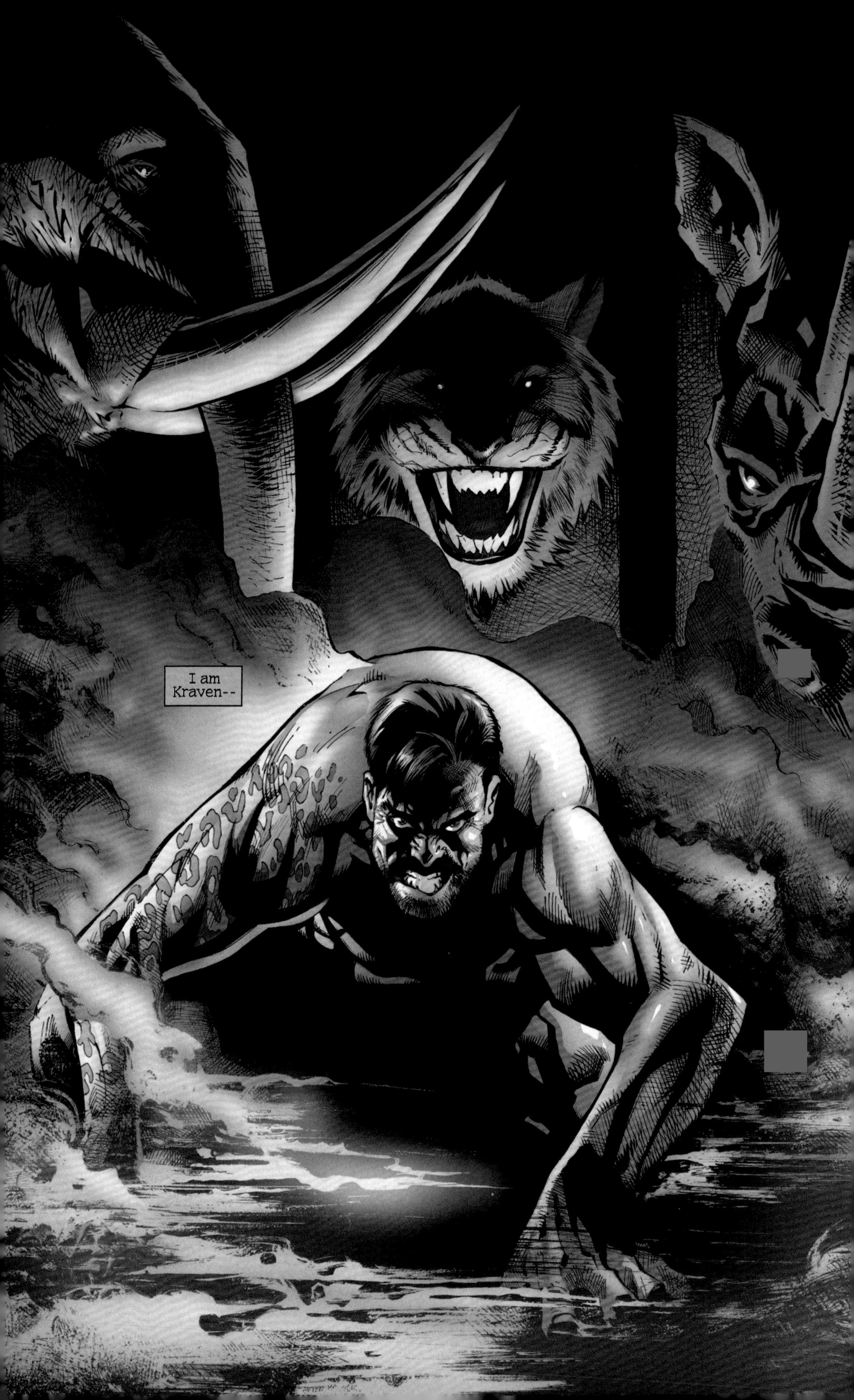
I am Kraven--

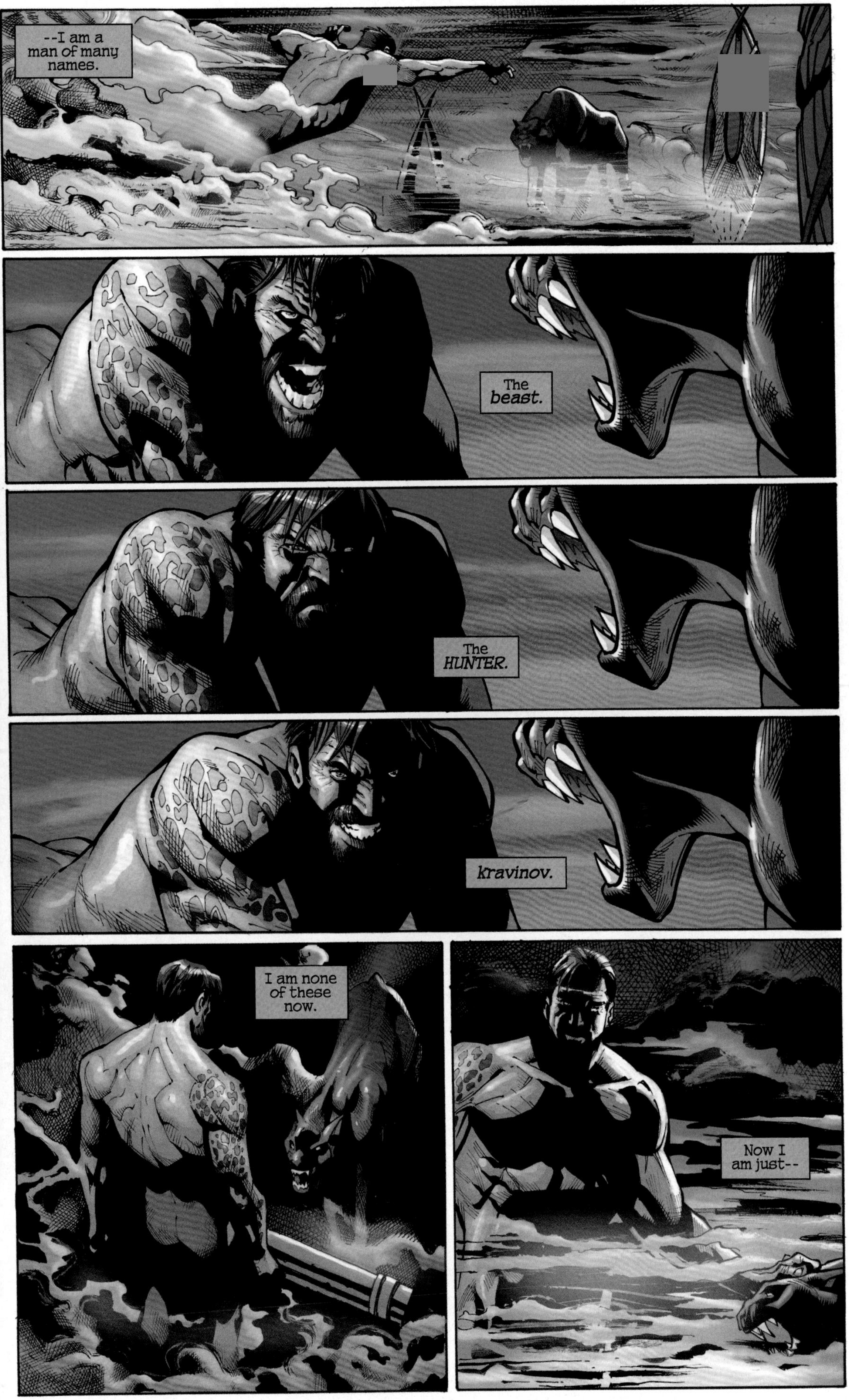
--I am a man of many names.
The *beast.*
The *HUNTER.*
kravinov.
I am none of these now.
Now I am just--

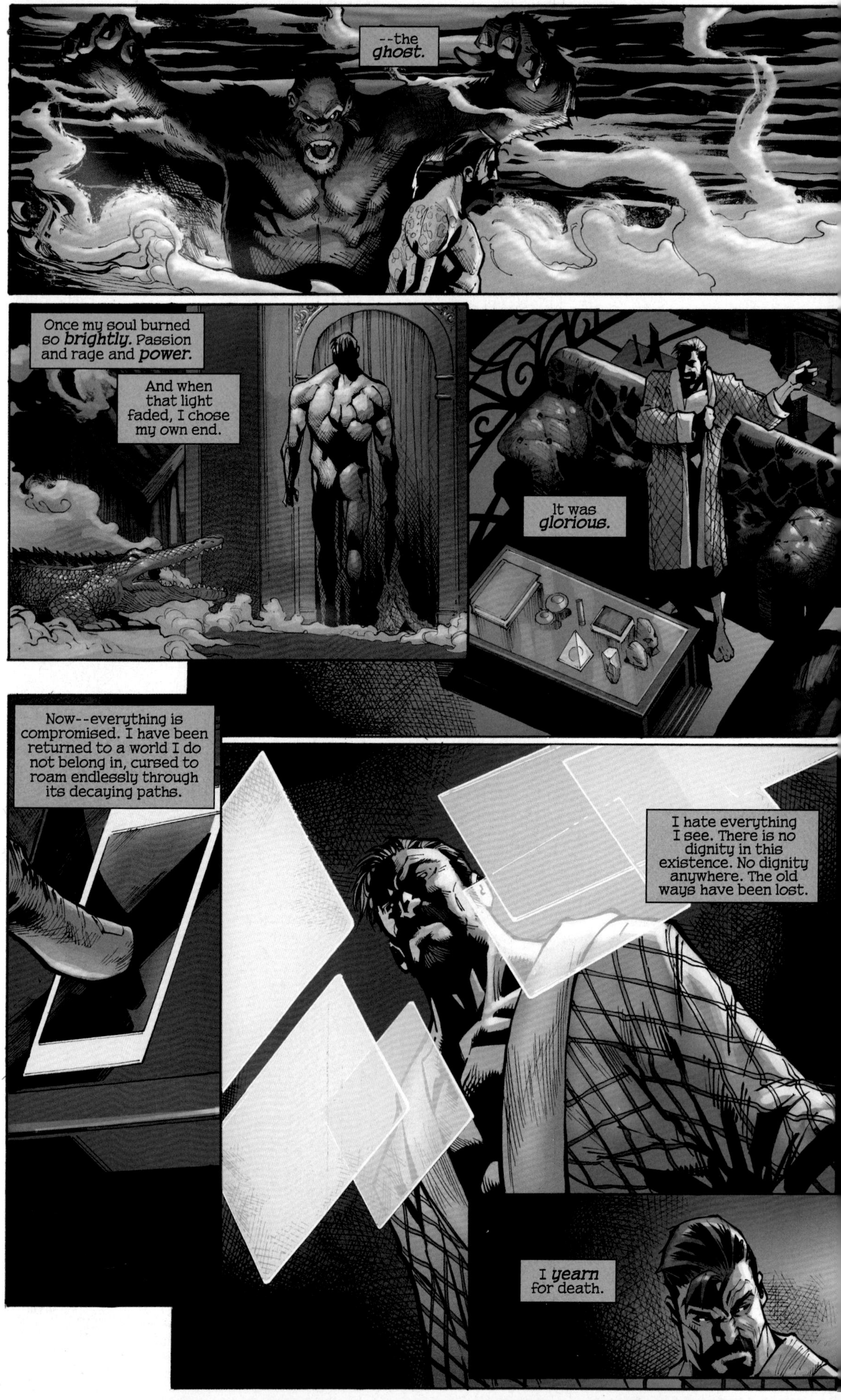
--the ghost.
Once my soul burned so brightly. Passion and rage and power.
And when that light faded, I chose my own end.
It was glorious.
Now--everything is compromised. I have been returned to a world I do not belong in, cursed to roam endlessly through its decaying paths.
I hate everything I see. There is no dignity in this existence. No dignity anywhere. The old ways have been lost.
I yearn for death.

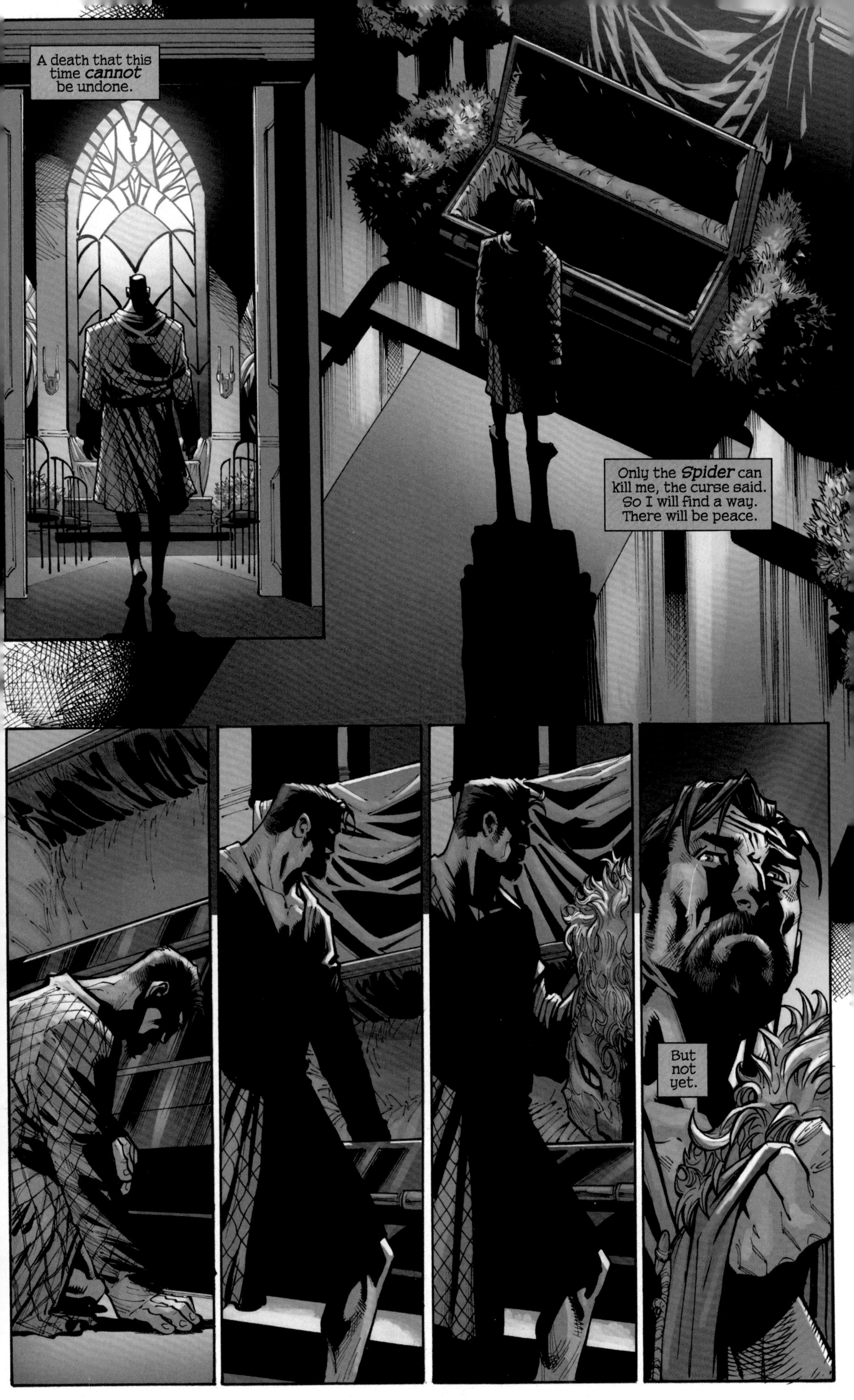
A death that this time *cannot* be undone.
Only the *Spider* can kill me, the curse said. So I will find a way. There will be peace.
But not yet.

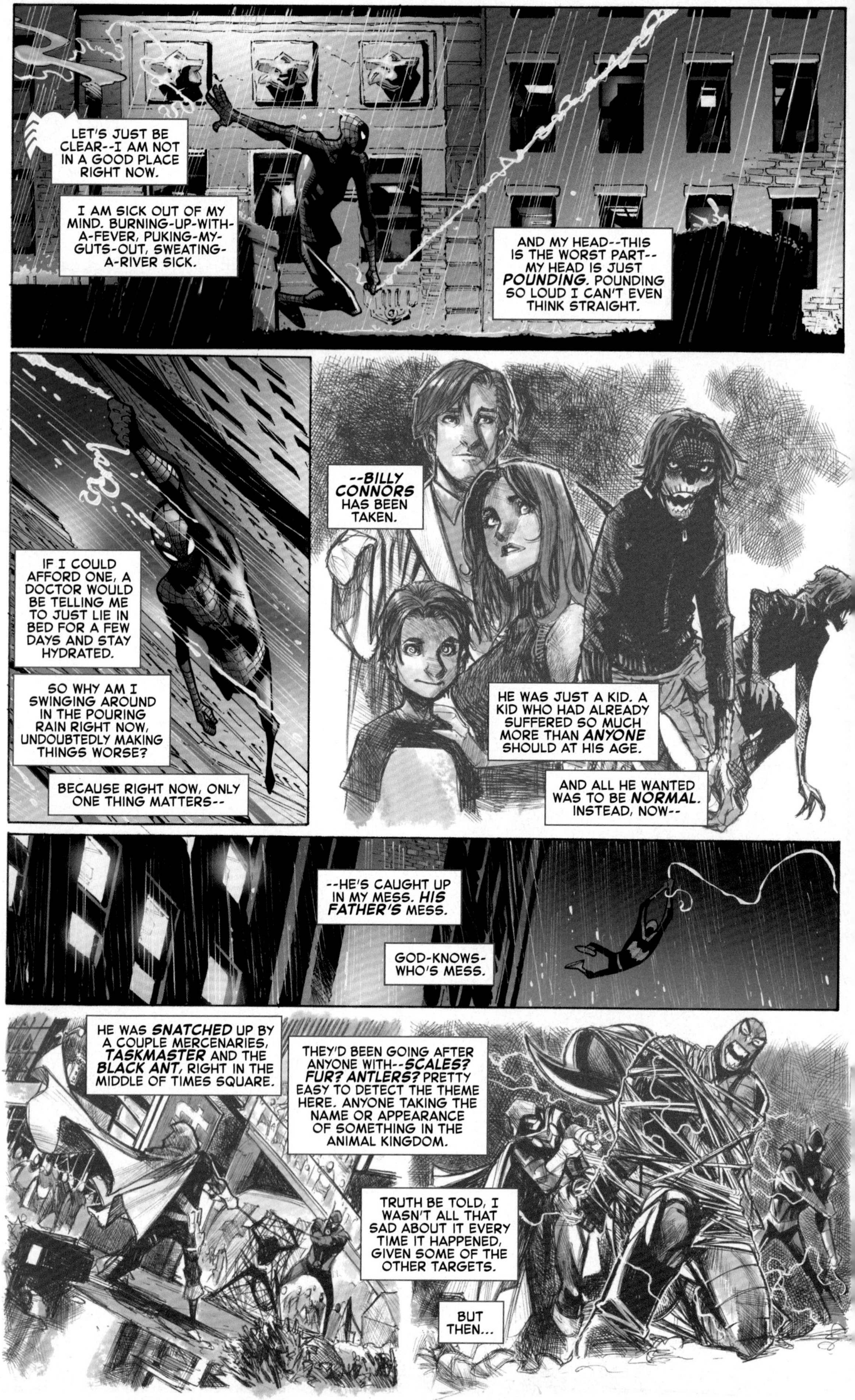
LET'S JUST BE CLEAR--I AM NOT IN A GOOD PLACE RIGHT NOW.
I AM SICK OUT OF MY MIND. BURNING-UP-WITH-A-FEVER, PUKING-MY-GUTS-OUT, SWEATING-A-RIVER SICK.
AND MY HEAD--THIS IS THE WORST PART--MY HEAD IS JUST POUNDING. POUNDING SO LOUD I CAN'T EVEN THINK STRAIGHT.
IF I COULD AFFORD ONE, A DOCTOR WOULD BE TELLING ME TO JUST LIE IN BED FOR A FEW DAYS AND STAY HYDRATED.
SO WHY AM I SWINGING AROUND IN THE POURING RAIN RIGHT NOW, UNDOUBTEDLY MAKING THINGS WORSE?
BECAUSE RIGHT NOW, ONLY ONE THING MATTERS--
--BILLY CONNORS HAS BEEN TAKEN.
HE WAS JUST A KID. A KID WHO HAD ALREADY SUFFERED SO MUCH MORE THAN ANYONE SHOULD AT HIS AGE.
AND ALL HE WANTED WAS TO BE NORMAL. INSTEAD, NOW--
--HE'S CAUGHT UP IN MY MESS. HIS FATHER'S MESS.
GOD-KNOWS-WHO'S MESS.
HE WAS SNATCHED UP BY A COUPLE MERCENARIES, TASKMASTER AND THE BLACK ANT, RIGHT IN THE MIDDLE OF TIMES SQUARE.
THEY'D BEEN GOING AFTER ANYONE WITH--SCALES? FUR? ANTLERS? PRETTY EASY TO DETECT THE THEME HERE. ANYONE TAKING THE NAME OR APPEARANCE OF SOMETHING IN THE ANIMAL KINGDOM.
TRUTH BE TOLD, I WASN'T ALL THAT SAD ABOUT IT EVERY TIME IT HAPPENED, GIVEN SOME OF THE OTHER TARGETS.
BUT THEN...

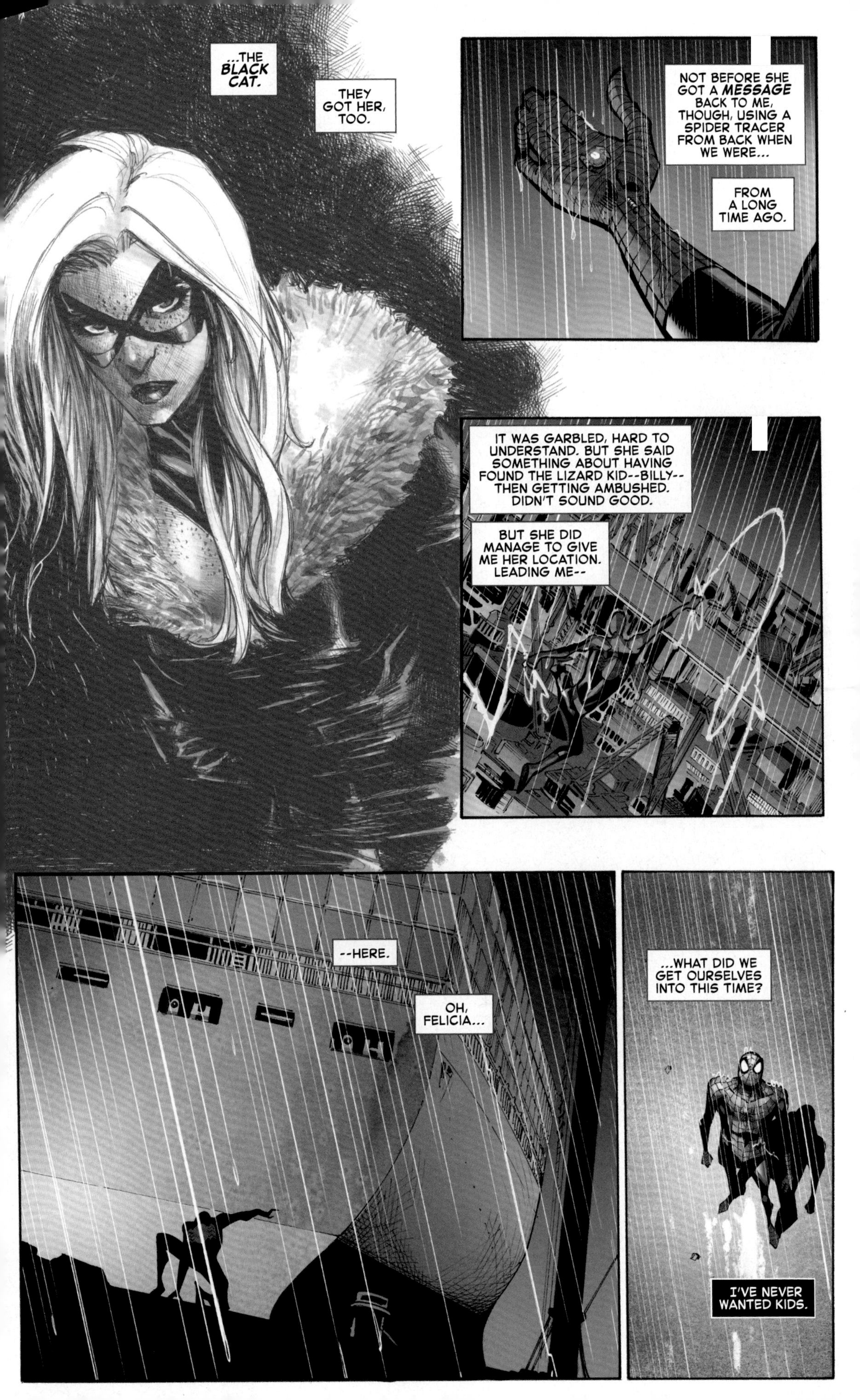
...THE BLACK CAT.
THEY GOT HER, TOO.
NOT BEFORE SHE GOT A MESSAGE BACK TO ME, THOUGH, USING A SPIDER TRACER FROM BACK WHEN WE WERE...
FROM A LONG TIME AGO.
IT WAS GARBLED, HARD TO UNDERSTAND. BUT SHE SAID SOMETHING ABOUT HAVING FOUND THE LIZARD KID--BILLY--THEN GETTING AMBUSHED. DIDN'T SOUND GOOD.
BUT SHE DID MANAGE TO GIVE ME HER LOCATION. LEADING ME--
--HERE.
OH, FELICIA...
...WHAT DID WE GET OURSELVES INTO THIS TIME?
I'VE NEVER WANTED KIDS.

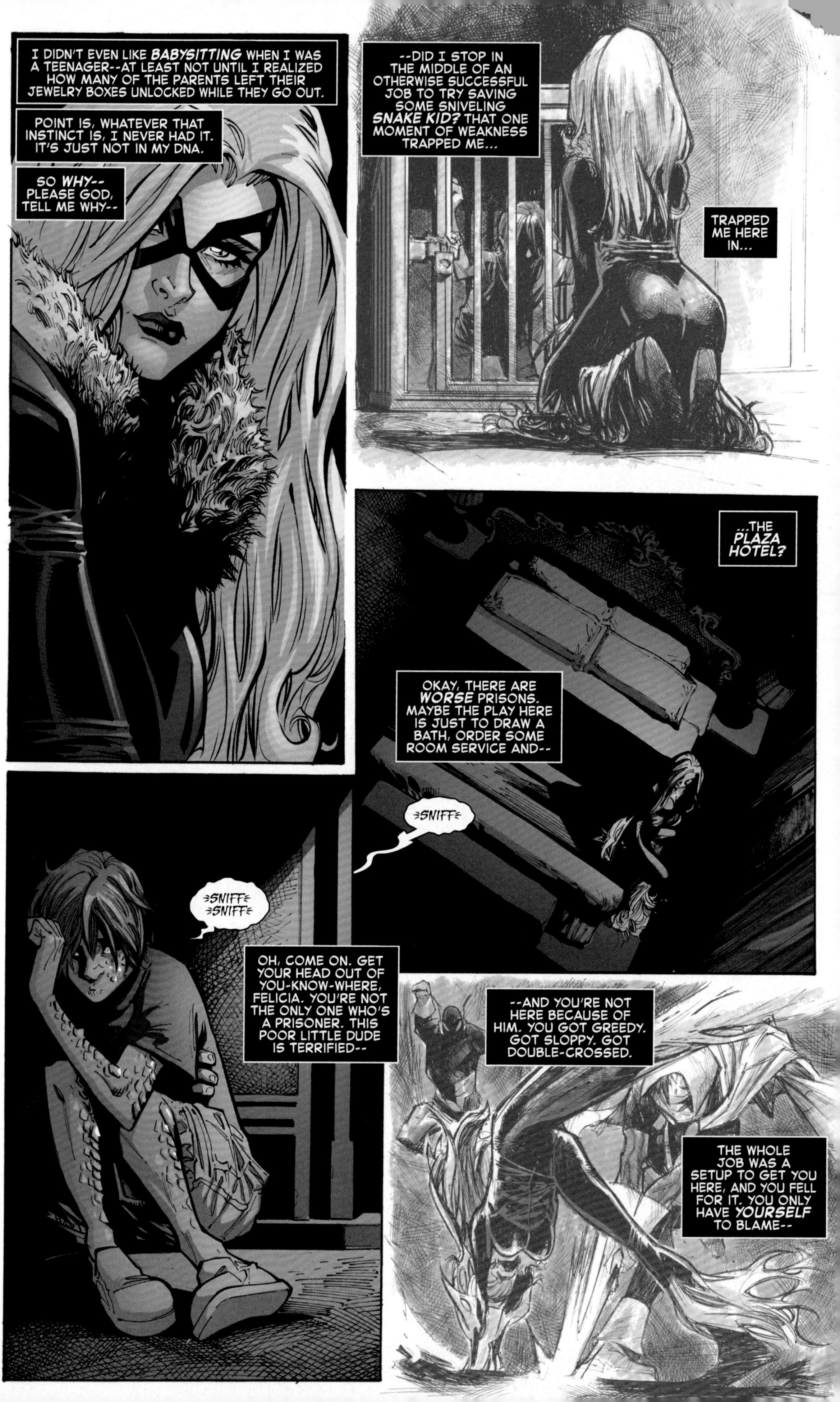

I DIDN'T EVEN LIKE BABYSITTING WHEN I WAS A TEENAGER--AT LEAST NOT UNTIL I REALIZED HOW MANY OF THE PARENTS LEFT THEIR JEWELRY BOXES UNLOCKED WHILE THEY GO OUT.
POINT IS, WHATEVER THAT INSTINCT IS, I NEVER HAD IT. IT'S JUST NOT IN MY DNA.
SO WHY-- PLEASE GOD, TELL ME WHY--
--DID I STOP IN THE MIDDLE OF AN OTHERWISE SUCCESSFUL JOB TO TRY SAVING SOME SNIVELING SNAKE KID? THAT ONE MOMENT OF WEAKNESS TRAPPED ME...
TRAPPED ME HERE IN...
...THE PLAZA HOTEL?
OKAY, THERE ARE WORSE PRISONS. MAYBE THE PLAY HERE IS JUST TO DRAW A BATH, ORDER SOME ROOM SERVICE AND--
SNIFF
SNIFF SNIFF
OH, COME ON. GET YOUR HEAD OUT OF YOU-KNOW-WHERE, FELICIA. YOU'RE NOT THE ONLY ONE WHO'S A PRISONER. THIS POOR LITTLE DUDE IS TERRIFIED--
--AND YOU'RE NOT HERE BECAUSE OF HIM. YOU GOT GREEDY. GOT SLOPPY. GOT DOUBLE-CROSSED.
THE WHOLE JOB WAS A SETUP TO GET YOU HERE, AND YOU FELL FOR IT. YOU ONLY HAVE YOURSELF TO BLAME--

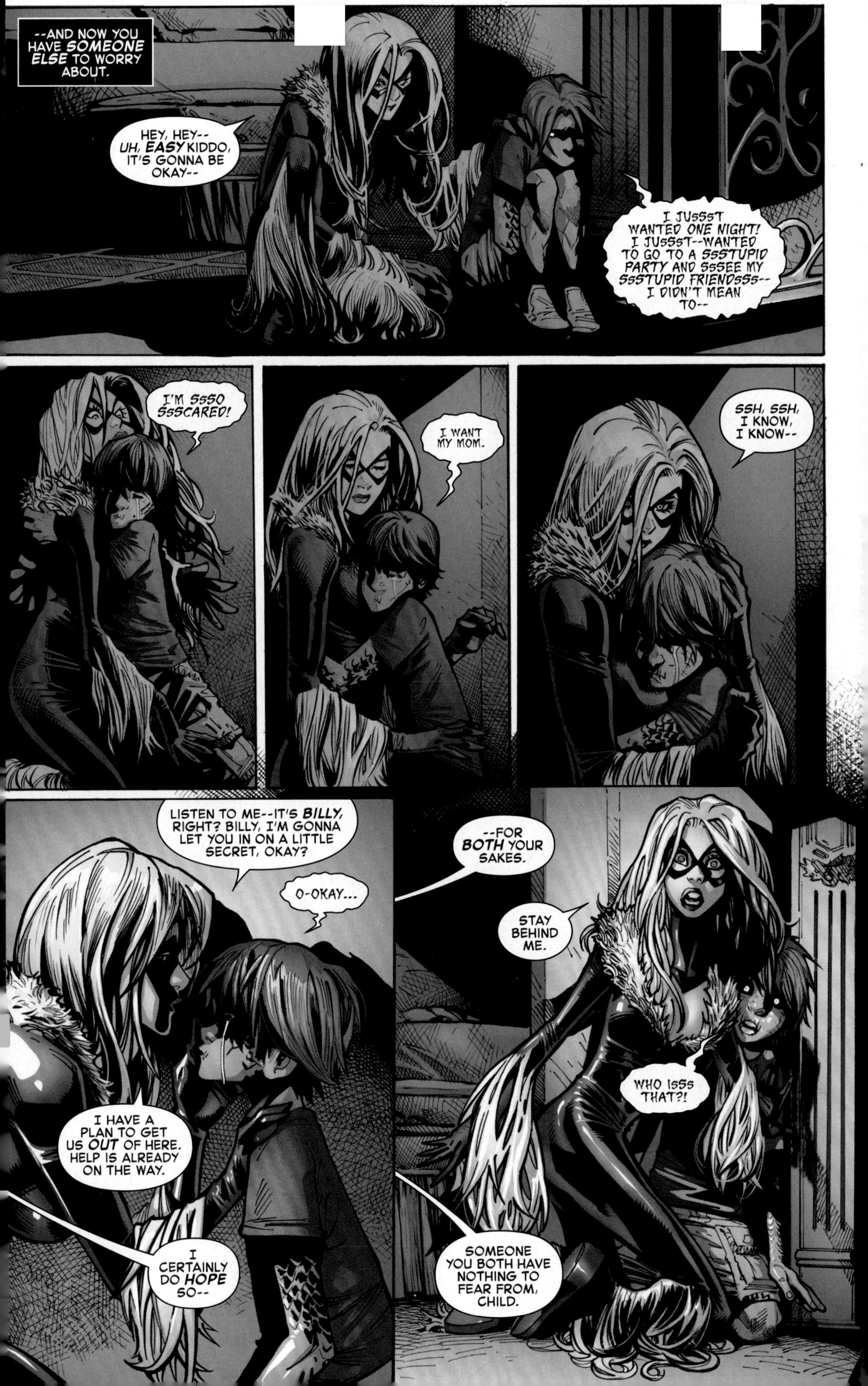
--AND NOW YOU HAVE SOMEONE ELSE TO WORRY ABOUT.
HEY, HEY-- UH, EASY KIDDO, IT'S GONNA BE OKAY--
I JUSSST WANTED ONE NIGHT! I JUSSST--WANTED TO GO TO A SSSTUPID PARTY AND SSSEE MY SSSTUPID FRIENDSSS-- I DIDN'T MEAN TO--
I'M SSSO SSSCARED!
I WANT MY MOM.
SSH, SSH, I KNOW, I KNOW--
LISTEN TO ME--IT'S BILLY, RIGHT? BILLY, I'M GONNA LET YOU IN ON A LITTLE SECRET, OKAY?
O-OKAY...
I HAVE A PLAN TO GET US OUT OF HERE. HELP IS ALREADY ON THE WAY.
I CERTAINLY DO HOPE SO--
--FOR BOTH YOUR SAKES.
STAY BEHIND ME.
WHO ISSS THAT?!
SOMEONE YOU BOTH HAVE NOTHING TO FEAR FROM, CHILD.

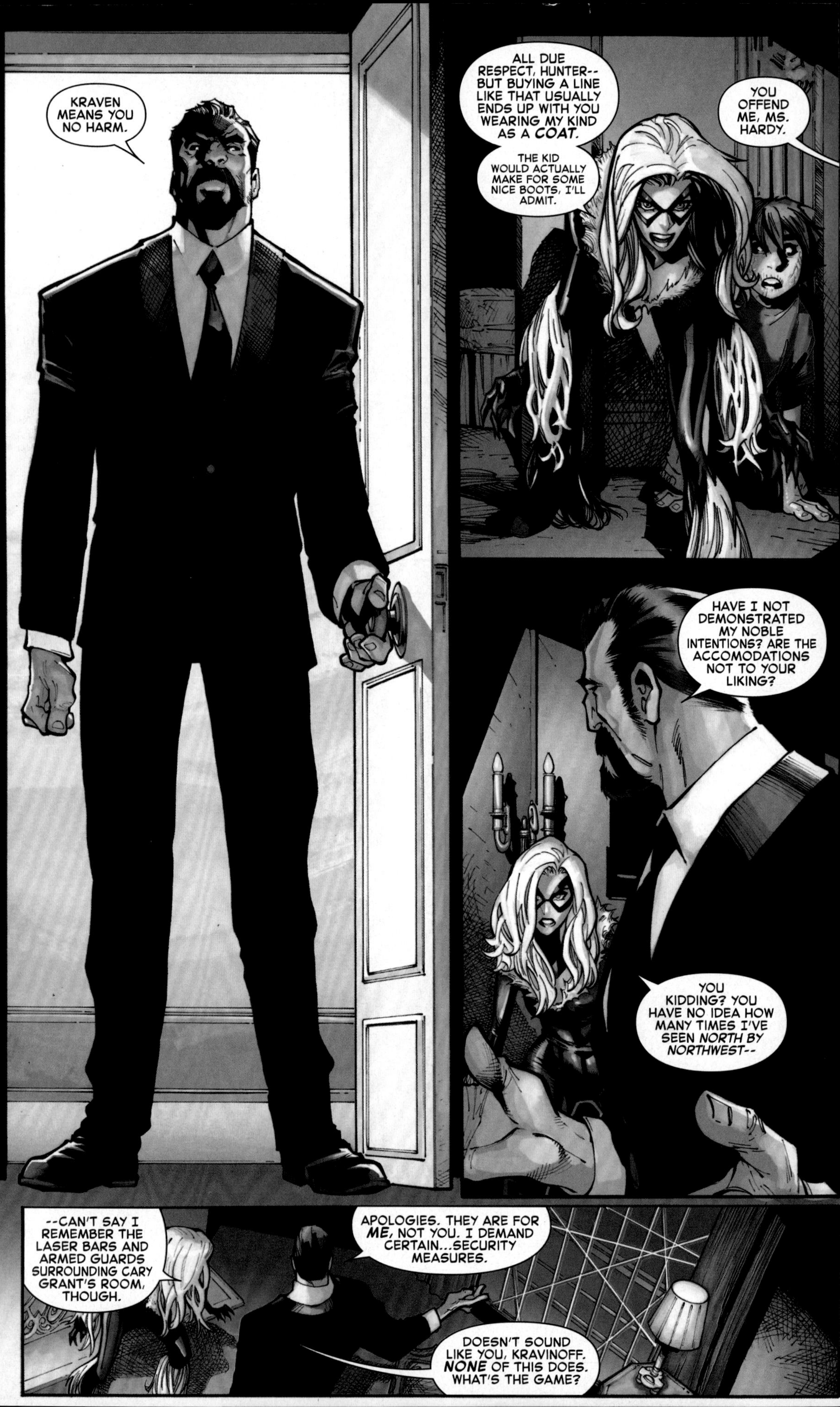
KRAVEN MEANS YOU NO HARM.
ALL DUE RESPECT, HUNTER--BUT BUYING A LINE LIKE THAT USUALLY ENDS UP WITH YOU WEARING MY KIND AS A COAT.
THE KID WOULD ACTUALLY MAKE FOR SOME NICE BOOTS, I'LL ADMIT.
YOU OFFEND ME, MS. HARDY.
HAVE I NOT DEMONSTRATED MY NOBLE INTENTIONS? ARE THE ACCOMODATIONS NOT TO YOUR LIKING?
YOU KIDDING? YOU HAVE NO IDEA HOW MANY TIMES I'VE SEEN NORTH BY NORTHWEST--
--CAN'T SAY I REMEMBER THE LASER BARS AND ARMED GUARDS SURROUNDING CARY GRANT'S ROOM, THOUGH.
APOLOGIES. THEY ARE FOR ME, NOT YOU. I DEMAND CERTAIN...SECURITY MEASURES.
DOESN'T SOUND LIKE YOU, KRAVINOFF. NONE OF THIS DOES. WHAT'S THE GAME?

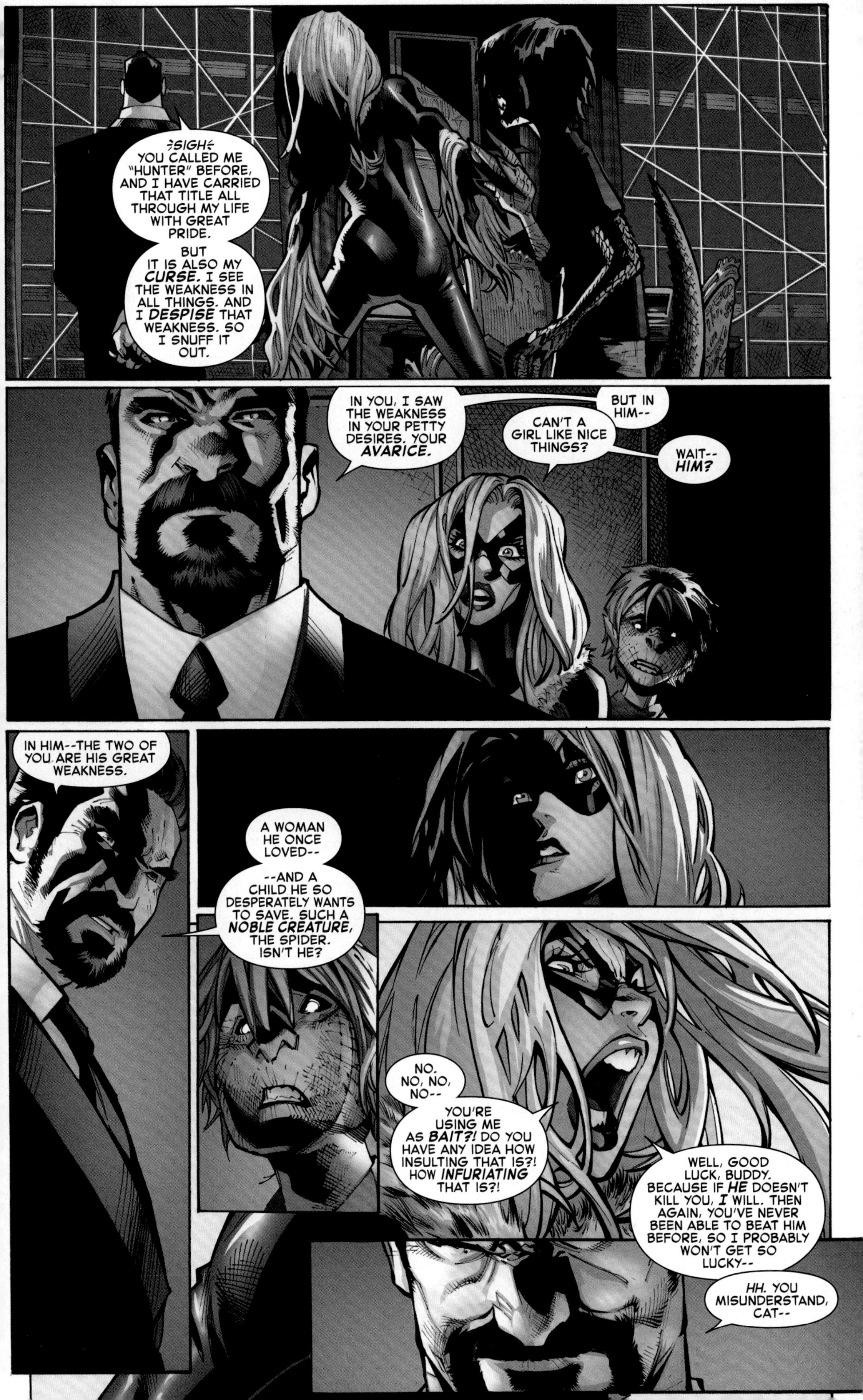

⁓SIGH⁓ YOU CALLED ME "HUNTER" BEFORE, AND I HAVE CARRIED THAT TITLE ALL THROUGH MY LIFE WITH GREAT PRIDE.
BUT IT IS ALSO MY CURSE. I SEE THE WEAKNESS IN ALL THINGS. AND I DESPISE THAT WEAKNESS. SO I SNUFF IT OUT.
IN YOU, I SAW THE WEAKNESS IN YOUR PETTY DESIRES. YOUR AVARICE.
CAN'T A GIRL LIKE NICE THINGS?
BUT IN HIM--
WAIT-- HIM?
IN HIM--THE TWO OF YOU ARE HIS GREAT WEAKNESS.
A WOMAN HE ONCE LOVED--
--AND A CHILD HE SO DESPERATELY WANTS TO SAVE. SUCH A NOBLE CREATURE, THE SPIDER. ISN'T HE?
NO. NO, NO, NO--
YOU'RE USING ME AS BAIT?! DO YOU HAVE ANY IDEA HOW INSULTING THAT IS?! HOW INFURIATING THAT IS?!
WELL, GOOD LUCK, BUDDY. BECAUSE IF HE DOESN'T KILL YOU, I WILL. THEN AGAIN, YOU'VE NEVER BEEN ABLE TO BEAT HIM BEFORE, SO I PROBABLY WON'T GET SO LUCKY--
HH. YOU MISUNDERSTAND, CAT--

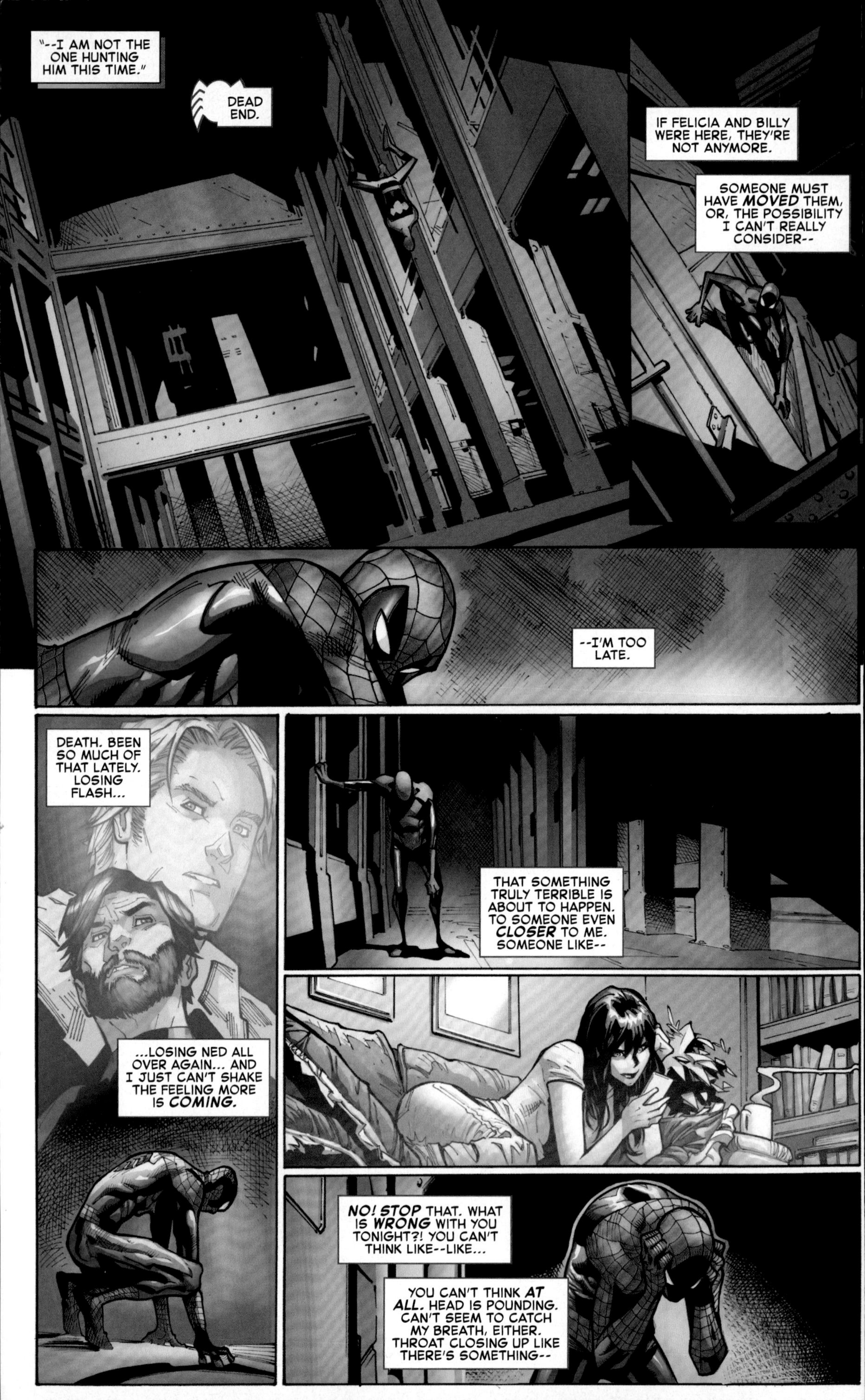
"--I AM NOT THE ONE HUNTING HIM THIS TIME."
DEAD END.
IF FELICIA AND BILLY WERE HERE, THEY'RE NOT ANYMORE.
SOMEONE MUST HAVE MOVED THEM, OR, THE POSSIBILITY I CAN'T REALLY CONSIDER--
--I'M TOO LATE.
DEATH. BEEN SO MUCH OF THAT LATELY. LOSING FLASH...
...LOSING NED ALL OVER AGAIN... AND I JUST CAN'T SHAKE THE FEELING MORE IS COMING.
THAT SOMETHING TRULY TERRIBLE IS ABOUT TO HAPPEN. TO SOMEONE EVEN CLOSER TO ME. SOMEONE LIKE--
NO! STOP THAT. WHAT IS WRONG WITH YOU TONIGHT?! YOU CAN'T THINK LIKE--LIKE...
YOU CAN'T THINK AT ALL. HEAD IS POUNDING. CAN'T SEEM TO CATCH MY BREATH, EITHER. THROAT CLOSING UP LIKE THERE'S SOMETHING--

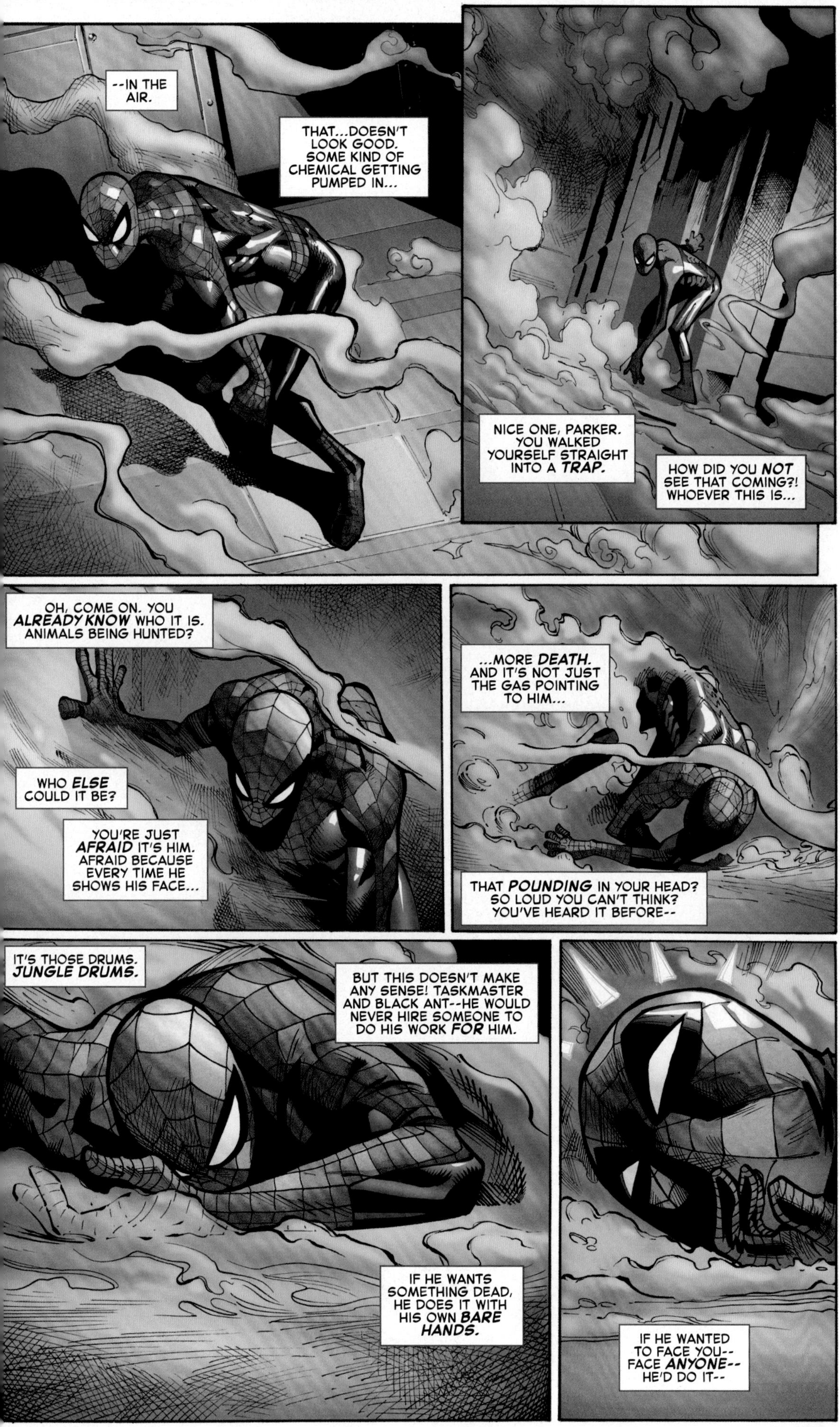
--IN THE AIR.
THAT...DOESN'T LOOK GOOD. SOME KIND OF CHEMICAL GETTING PUMPED IN...
NICE ONE, PARKER. YOU WALKED YOURSELF STRAIGHT INTO A TRAP.
HOW DID YOU NOT SEE THAT COMING?! WHOEVER THIS IS...
OH, COME ON. YOU ALREADY KNOW WHO IT IS. ANIMALS BEING HUNTED?
WHO ELSE COULD IT BE?
YOU'RE JUST AFRAID IT'S HIM. AFRAID BECAUSE EVERY TIME HE SHOWS HIS FACE...
...MORE DEATH. AND IT'S NOT JUST THE GAS POINTING TO HIM...
THAT POUNDING IN YOUR HEAD? SO LOUD YOU CAN'T THINK? YOU'VE HEARD IT BEFORE--
IT'S THOSE DRUMS. JUNGLE DRUMS.
BUT THIS DOESN'T MAKE ANY SENSE! TASKMASTER AND BLACK ANT--HE WOULD NEVER HIRE SOMEONE TO DO HIS WORK FOR HIM.
IF HE WANTS SOMETHING DEAD, HE DOES IT WITH HIS OWN BARE HANDS.
IF HE WANTED TO FACE YOU-- FACE ANYONE-- HE'D DO IT--

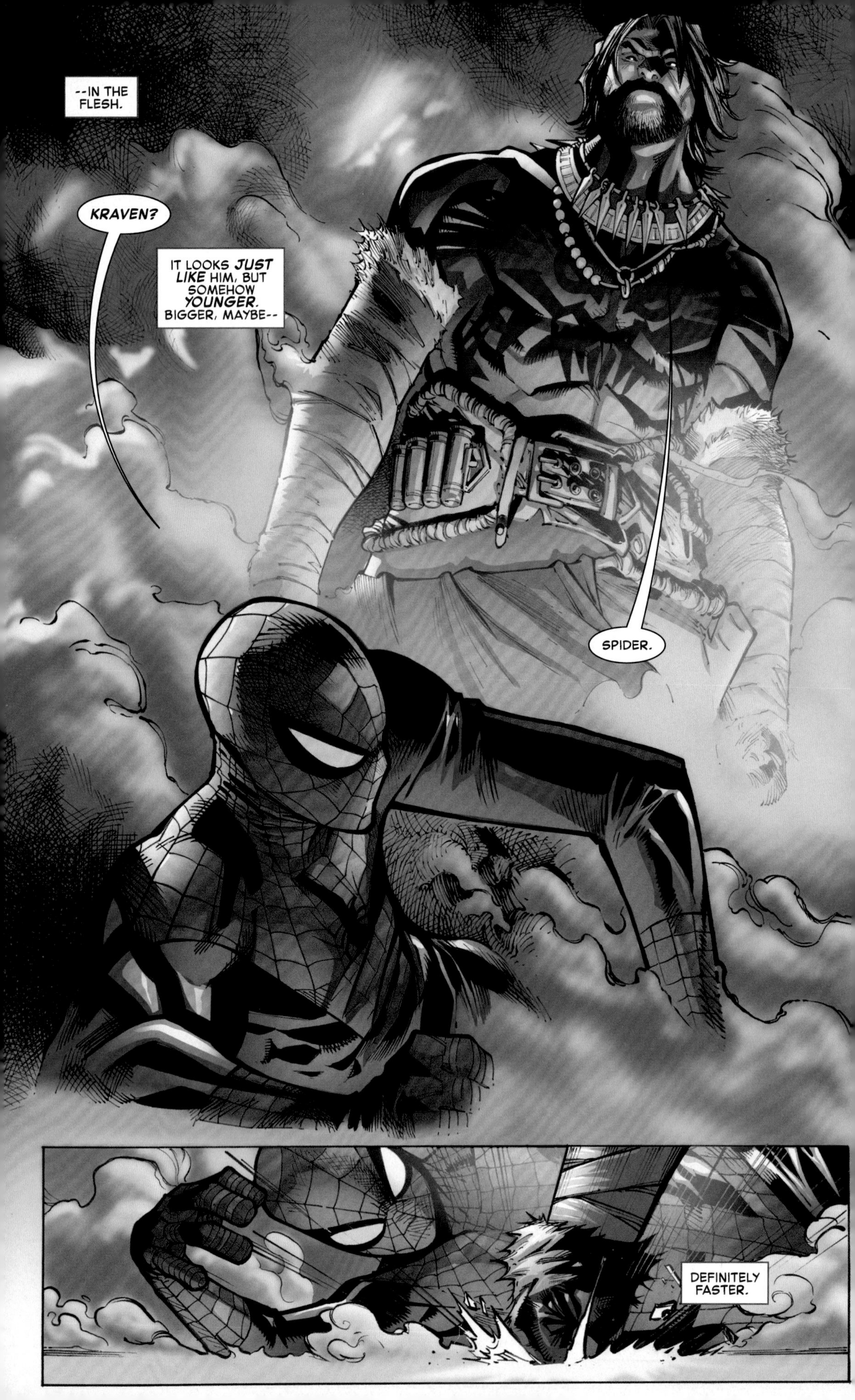
--IN THE FLESH.
KRAVEN?
IT LOOKS JUST LIKE HIM, BUT SOMEHOW YOUNGER. BIGGER, MAYBE--
SPIDER.
DEFINITELY FASTER.

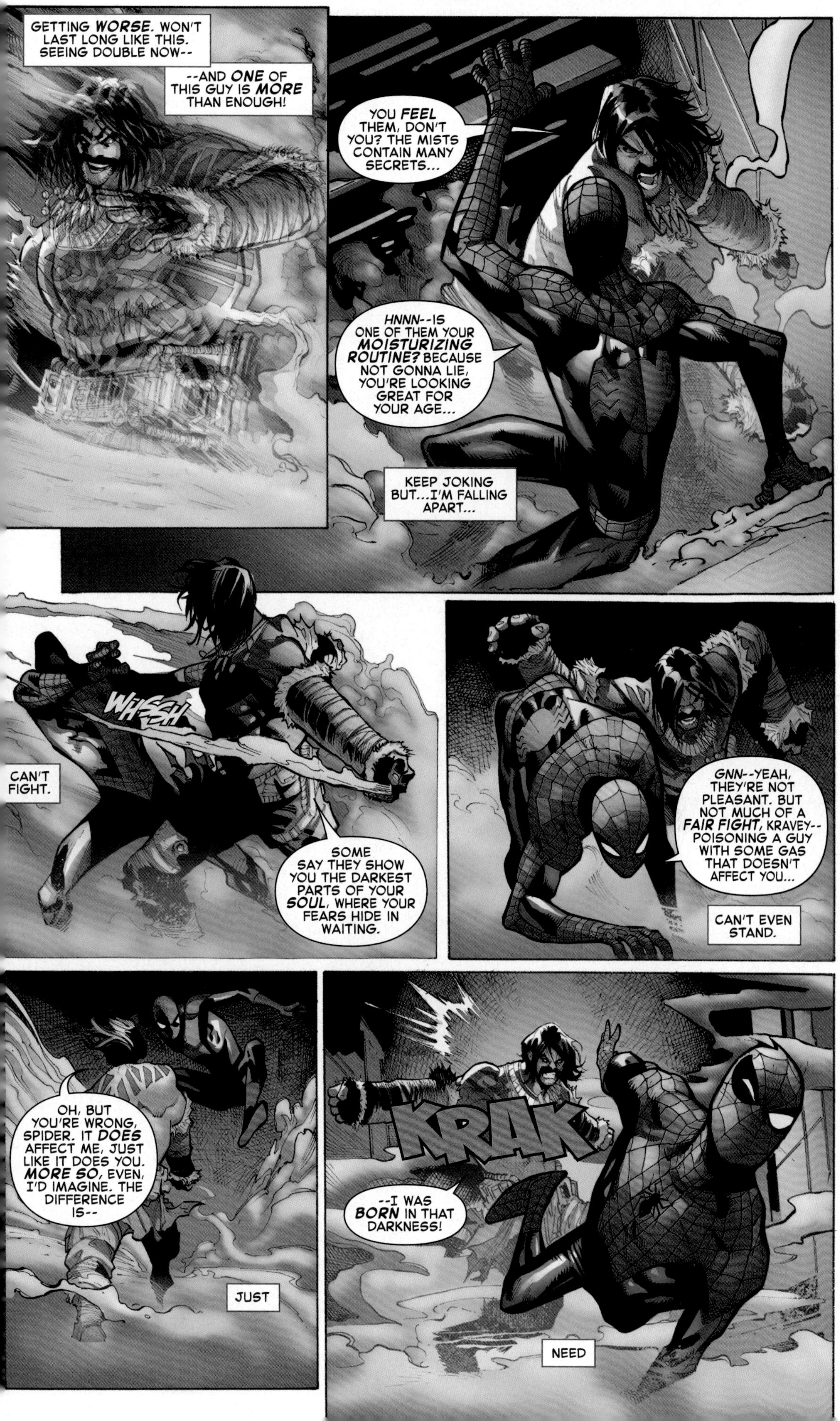
GETTING WORSE. WON'T LAST LONG LIKE THIS. SEEING DOUBLE NOW--
--AND ONE OF THIS GUY IS MORE THAN ENOUGH!
YOU FEEL THEM, DON'T YOU? THE MISTS CONTAIN MANY SECRETS...
HNNN--IS ONE OF THEM YOUR MOISTURIZING ROUTINE? BECAUSE NOT GONNA LIE, YOU'RE LOOKING GREAT FOR YOUR AGE...
KEEP JOKING BUT...I'M FALLING APART...
WHSSH
CAN'T FIGHT.
SOME SAY THEY SHOW YOU THE DARKEST PARTS OF YOUR SOUL, WHERE YOUR FEARS HIDE IN WAITING.
GNN--YEAH, THEY'RE NOT PLEASANT. BUT NOT MUCH OF A FAIR FIGHT, KRAVEY--POISONING A GUY WITH SOME GAS THAT DOESN'T AFFECT YOU...
CAN'T EVEN STAND.
OH, BUT YOU'RE WRONG, SPIDER. IT DOES AFFECT ME, JUST LIKE IT DOES YOU. MORE SO, EVEN, I'D IMAGINE. THE DIFFERENCE IS--
JUST
KRAK
--I WAS BORN IN THAT DARKNESS!
NEED

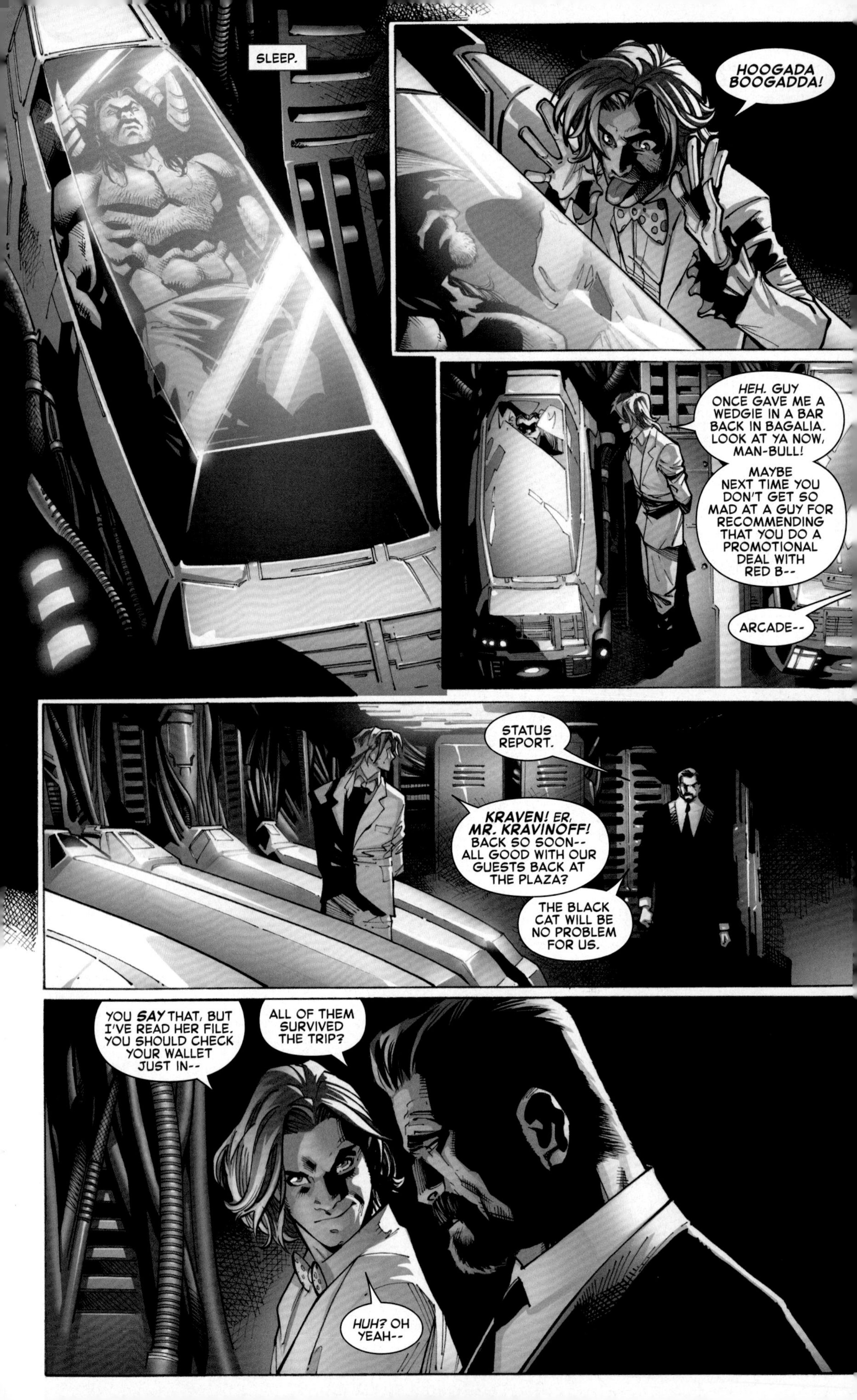
SLEEP.
HOOGADA BOOGADDA!
HEH. GUY ONCE GAVE ME A WEDGIE IN A BAR BACK IN BAGALIA. LOOK AT YA NOW, MAN-BULL!
MAYBE NEXT TIME YOU DON'T GET SO MAD AT A GUY FOR RECOMMENDING THAT YOU DO A PROMOTIONAL DEAL WITH RED B--
ARCADE--
STATUS REPORT.
KRAVEN! ER, MR. KRAVINOFF! BACK SO SOON-- ALL GOOD WITH OUR GUESTS BACK AT THE PLAZA?
THE BLACK CAT WILL BE NO PROBLEM FOR US.
YOU SAY THAT, BUT I'VE READ HER FILE. YOU SHOULD CHECK YOUR WALLET JUST IN--
ALL OF THEM SURVIVED THE TRIP?
HUH? OH YEAH--

SQUID'S A LITTLE WORSE FOR WEAR, BUT YEAH--WAS JUST DOING A DIAGNOSTIC CHECK-SLASH-TAUNTING SESSION WITH THE LOT. ALL ALIVE AND KICKING IN CRYOGENIC FREEZE, BOSS.

HNN. GOOD. AND THE **SHIELD?**

JUST WAITING TO GO ONLINE. WHICH BRINGS ME TO AN UNCOMFORTABLE SUBJECT--

WE'VE SECURED THE AREA. YOUR MEN HAVE SWEPT FOR CIVILIANS AND ARE READY TO "REDIRECT" THEM ON A MOMENT'S NOTICE.

BUT I WOULDN'T WAIT TOO MANY MORE MOMENTS TO GIVE **NOTICE,** IF YOU FOLLOW ME. OUR BOYS IN THE BALLROOM--

"--THEY'RE GETTING A LITTLE **RESTLESS.**"

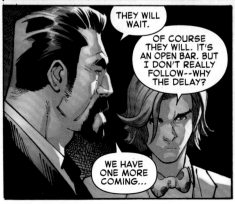

THEY WILL WAIT.

OF COURSE THEY WILL. IT'S AN OPEN BAR. BUT I DON'T REALLY FOLLOW--WHY THE DELAY?

WE HAVE ONE MORE COMING...

...ONE LAST **TROPHY** TO COLLECT.

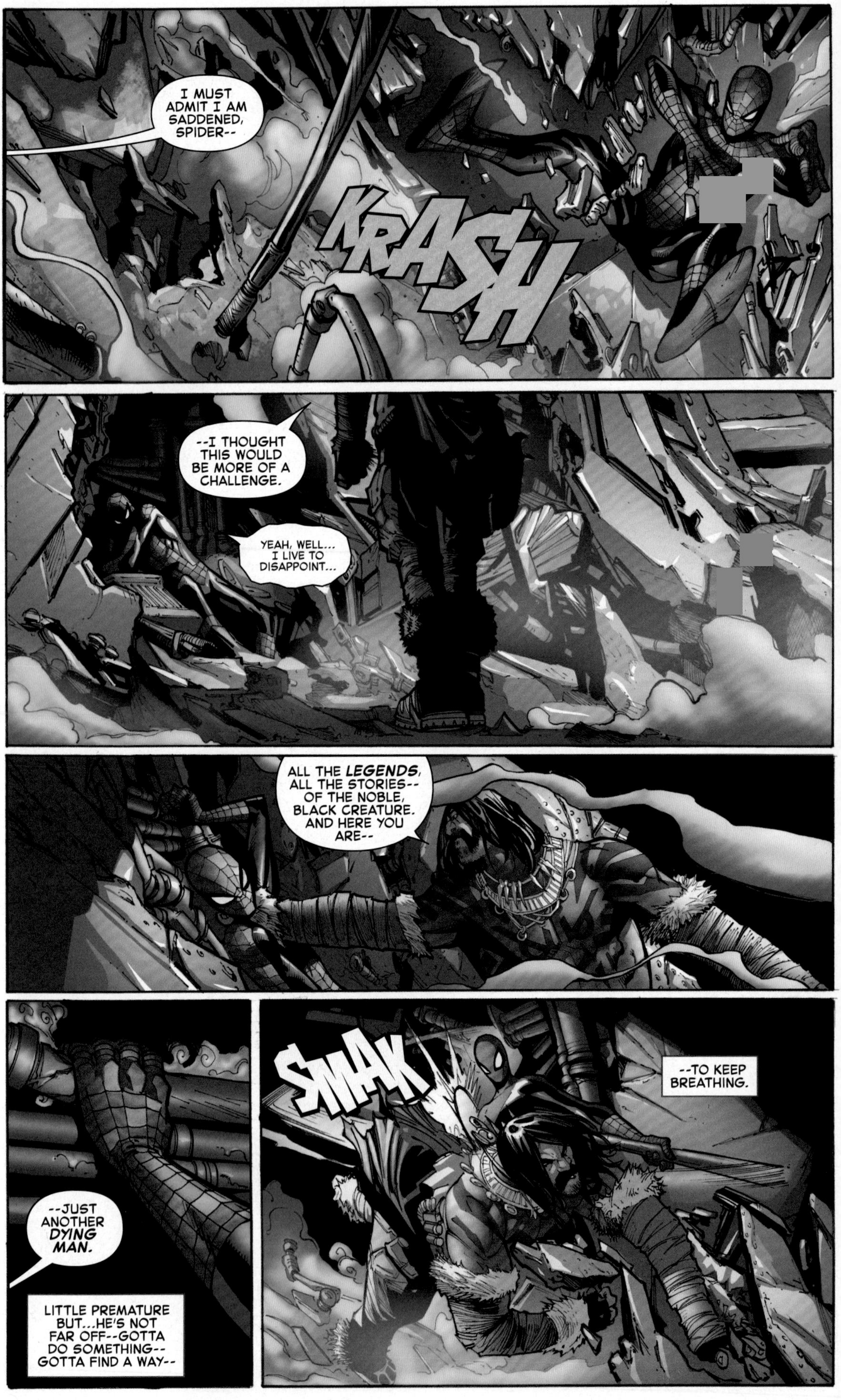
I MUST ADMIT I AM SADDENED, SPIDER--
KRASH
--I THOUGHT THIS WOULD BE MORE OF A CHALLENGE.
YEAH, WELL... I LIVE TO DISAPPOINT...
ALL THE LEGENDS, ALL THE STORIES-- OF THE NOBLE, BLACK CREATURE. AND HERE YOU ARE--
--JUST ANOTHER DYING MAN.
LITTLE PREMATURE BUT...HE'S NOT FAR OFF--GOTTA DO SOMETHING-- GOTTA FIND A WAY--
SMAK
--TO KEEP BREATHING.

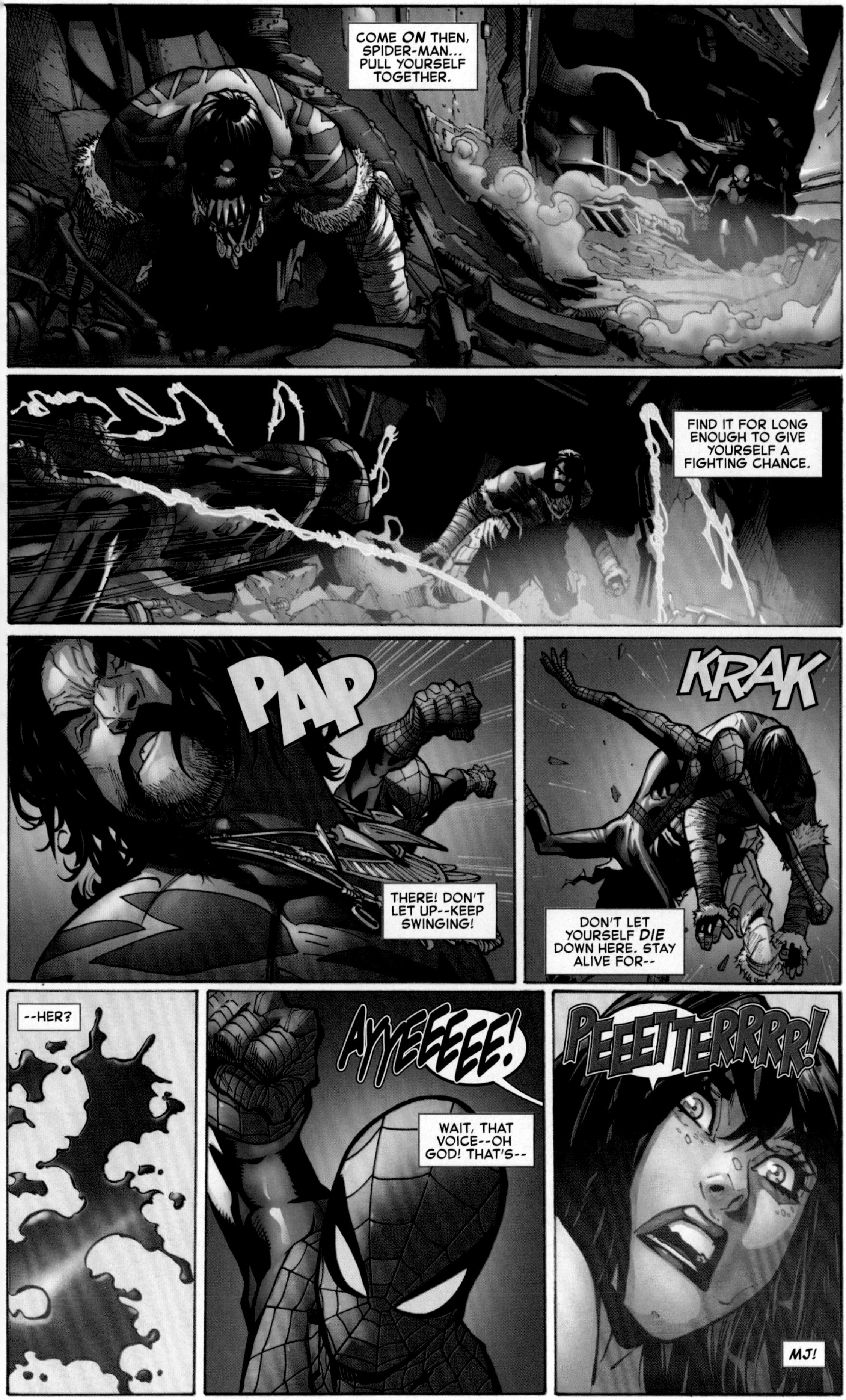
COME ON THEN, SPIDER-MAN... PULL YOURSELF TOGETHER.
FIND IT FOR LONG ENOUGH TO GIVE YOURSELF A FIGHTING CHANCE.
PAP
THERE! DON'T LET UP--KEEP SWINGING!
KRAK
DON'T LET YOURSELF DIE DOWN HERE. STAY ALIVE FOR--
--HER?
AYYEEEEE!
WAIT, THAT VOICE--OH GOD! THAT'S--
PEEEETTERRRR!
MJ!

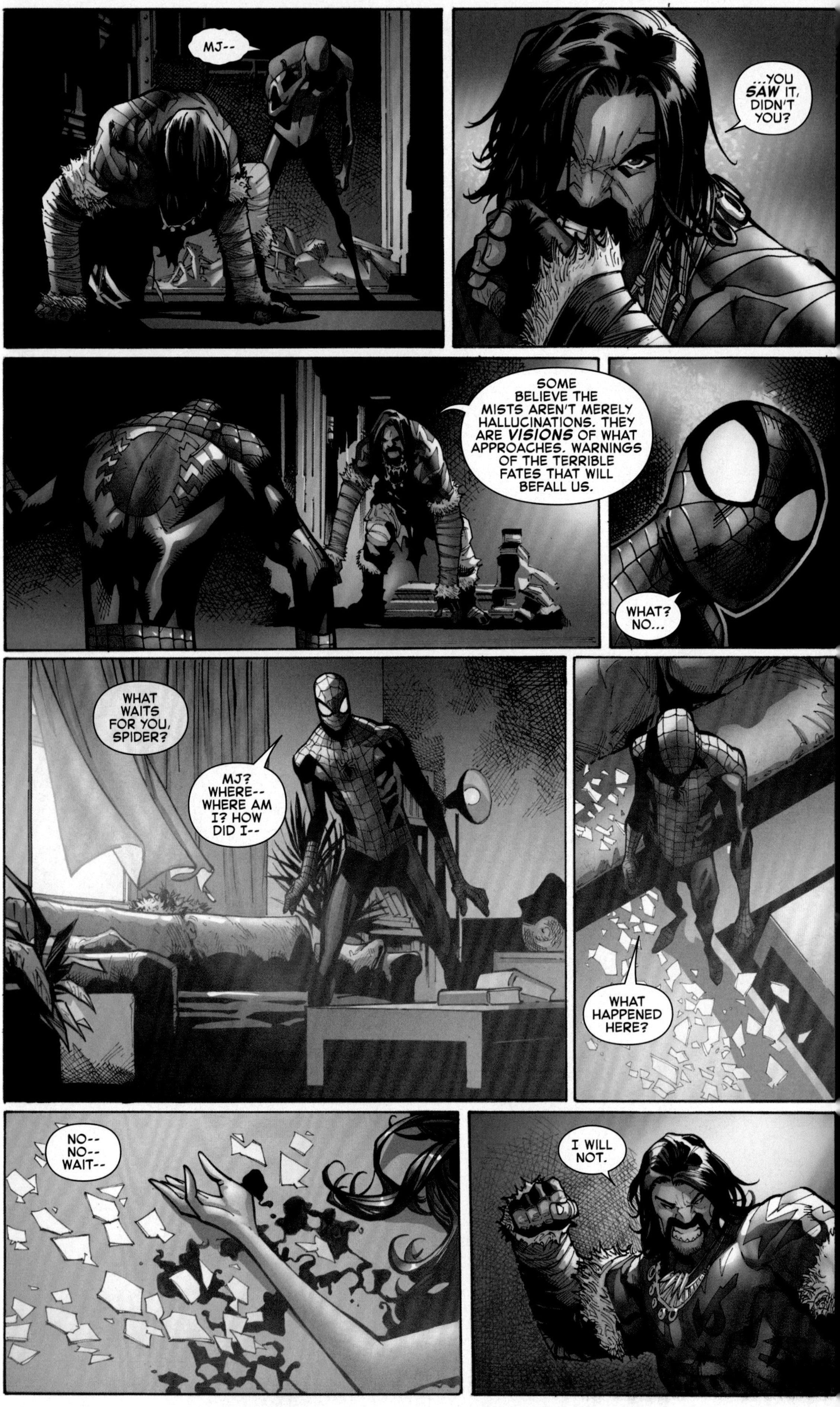
MJ--
...YOU SAW IT, DIDN'T YOU?
SOME BELIEVE THE MISTS AREN'T MERELY HALLUCINATIONS. THEY ARE VISIONS OF WHAT APPROACHES. WARNINGS OF THE TERRIBLE FATES THAT WILL BEFALL US.
WHAT? NO...
WHAT WAITS FOR YOU, SPIDER?
MJ? WHERE-- WHERE AM I? HOW DID I--
WHAT HAPPENED HERE?
NO-- NO-- WAIT--
I WILL NOT.

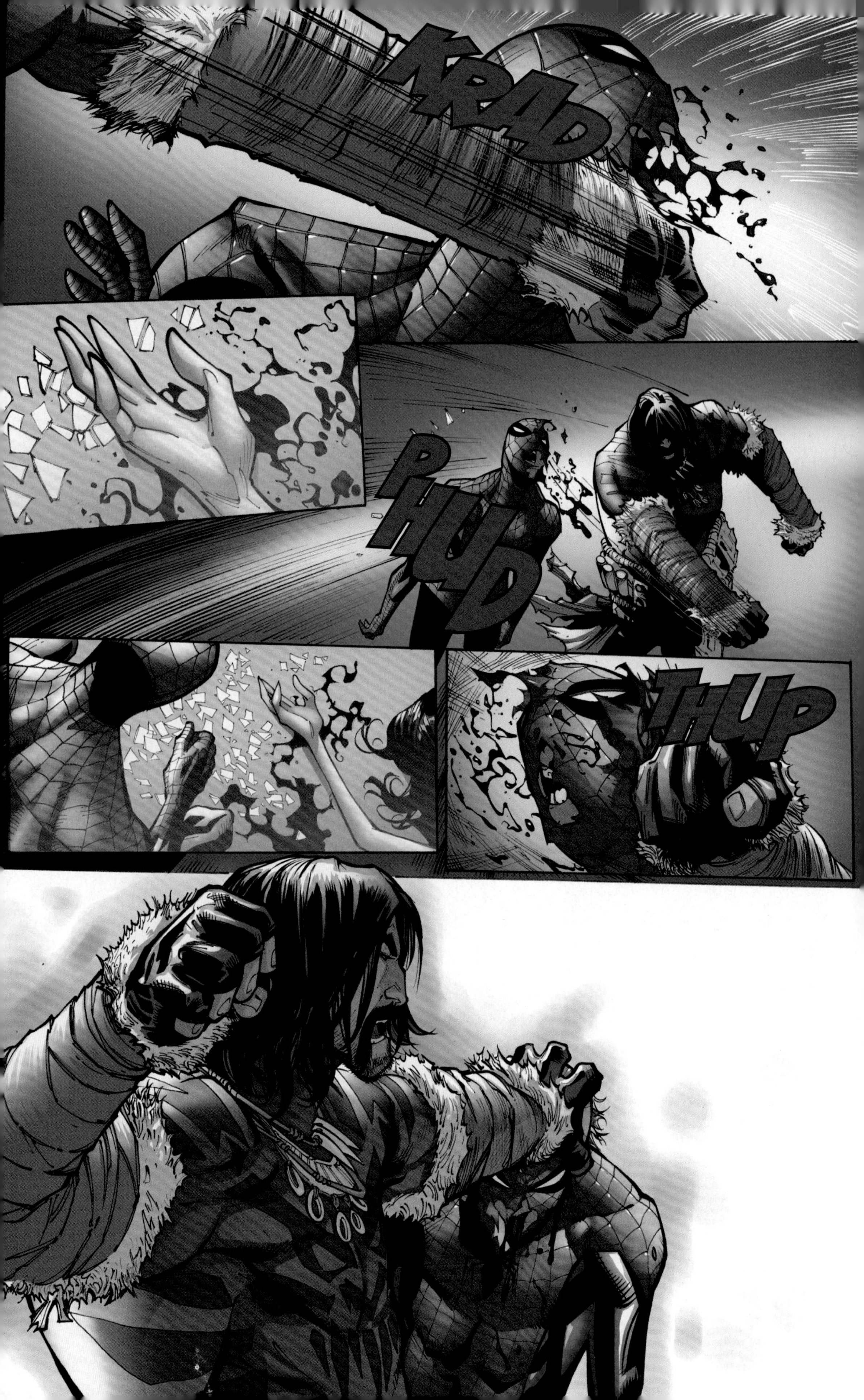
KRAD
PHUD
THUP

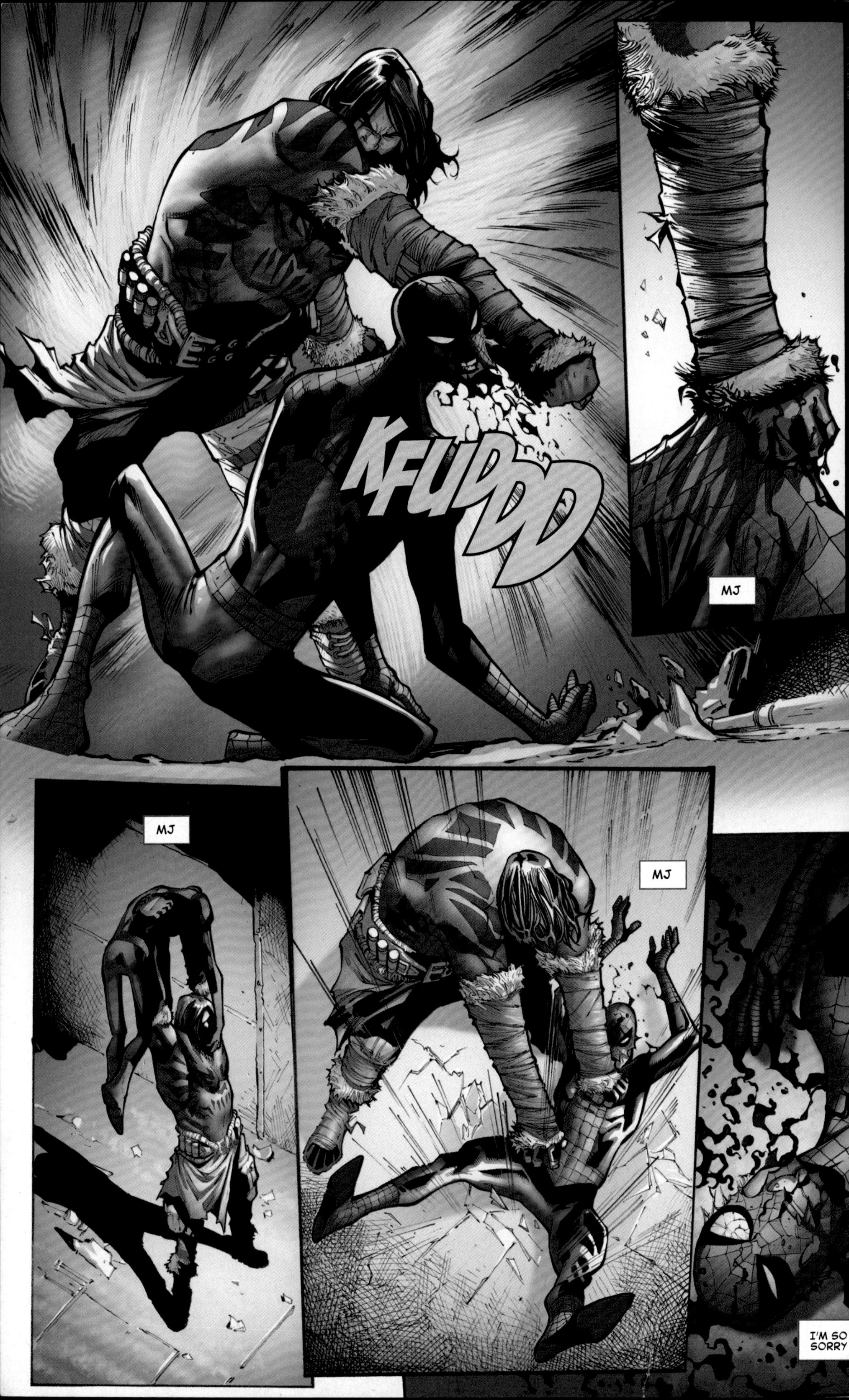
KFUDDD
MJ
MJ
MJ
I'M SO
SORRY

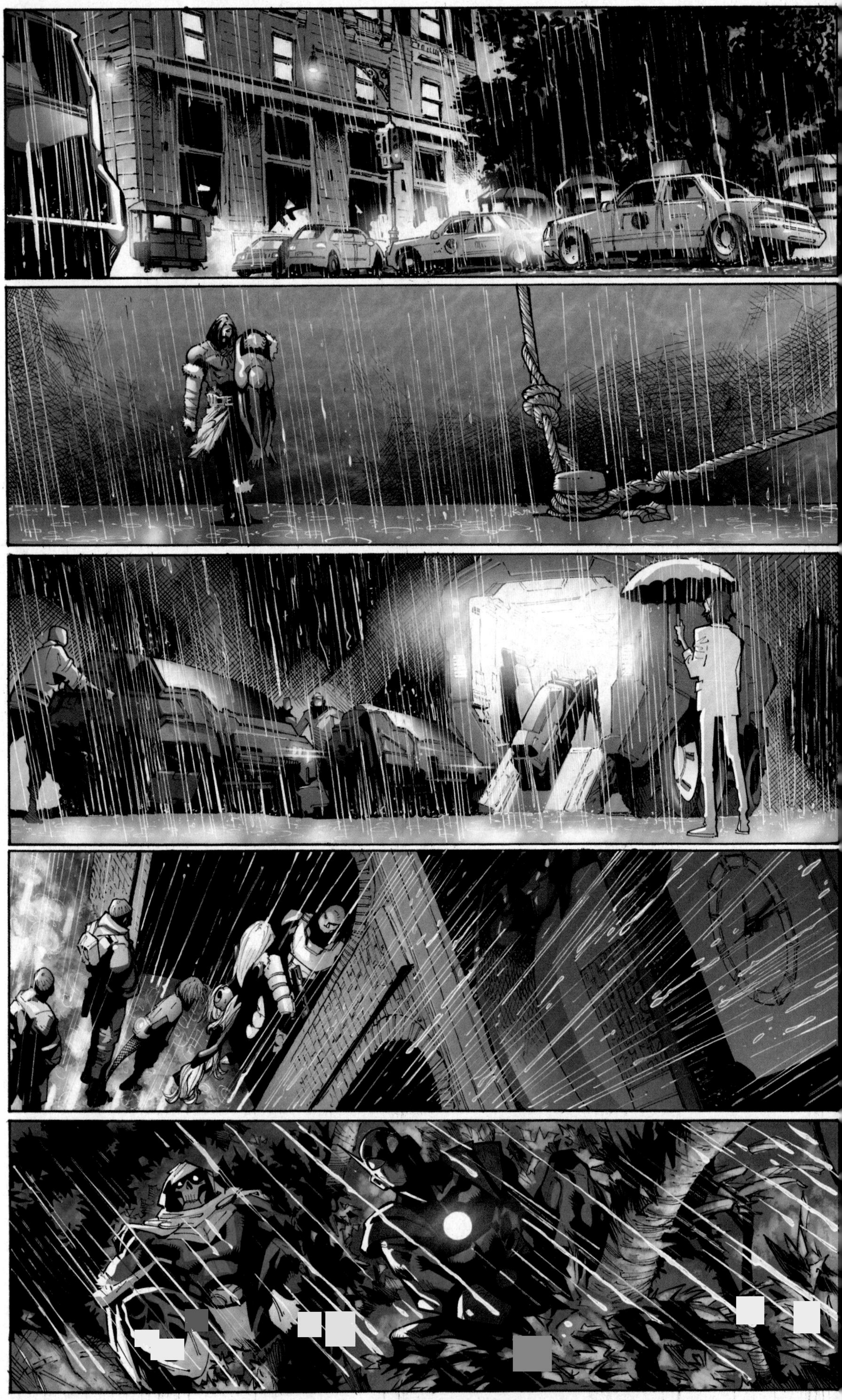

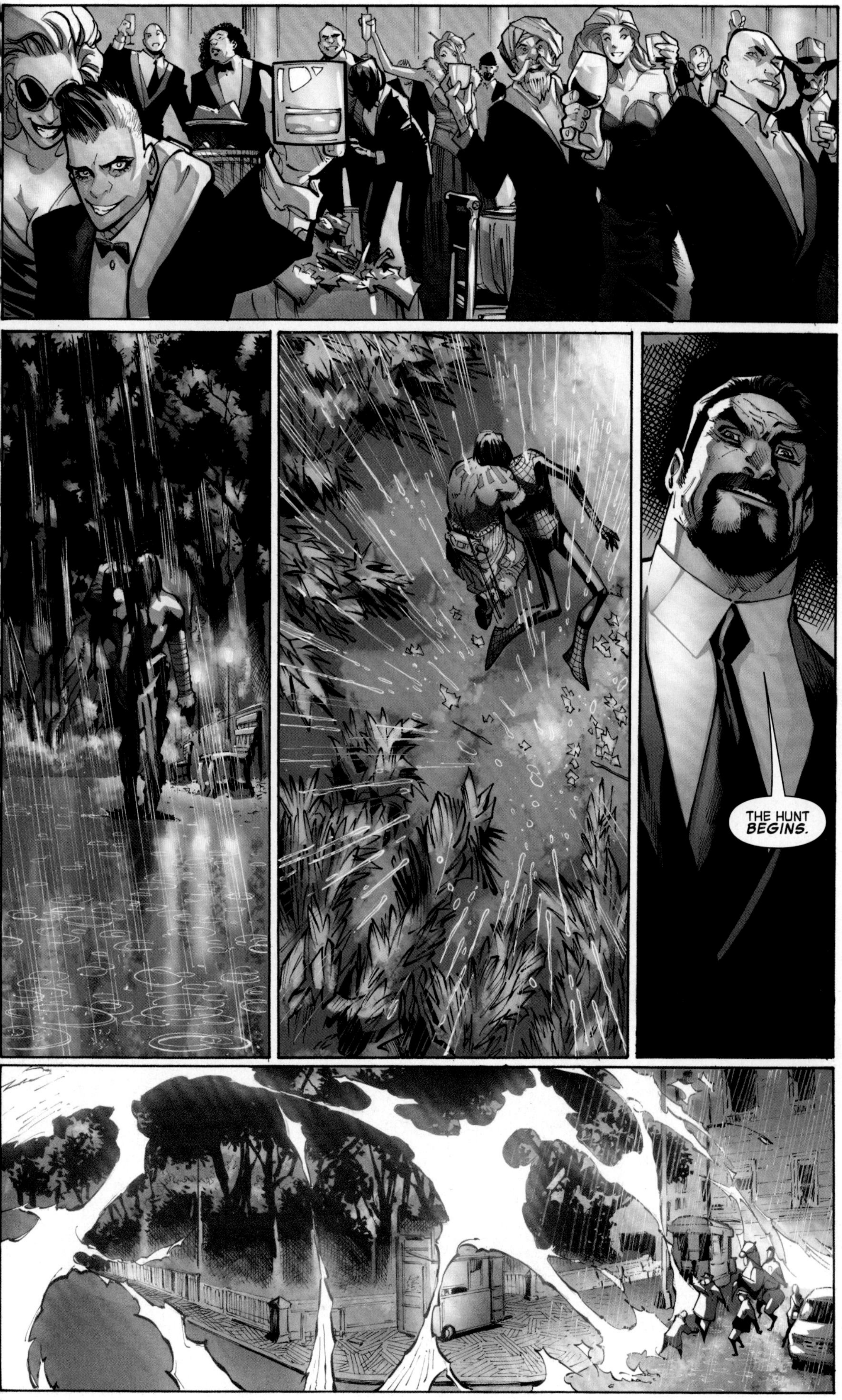
THE HUNT BEGINS.

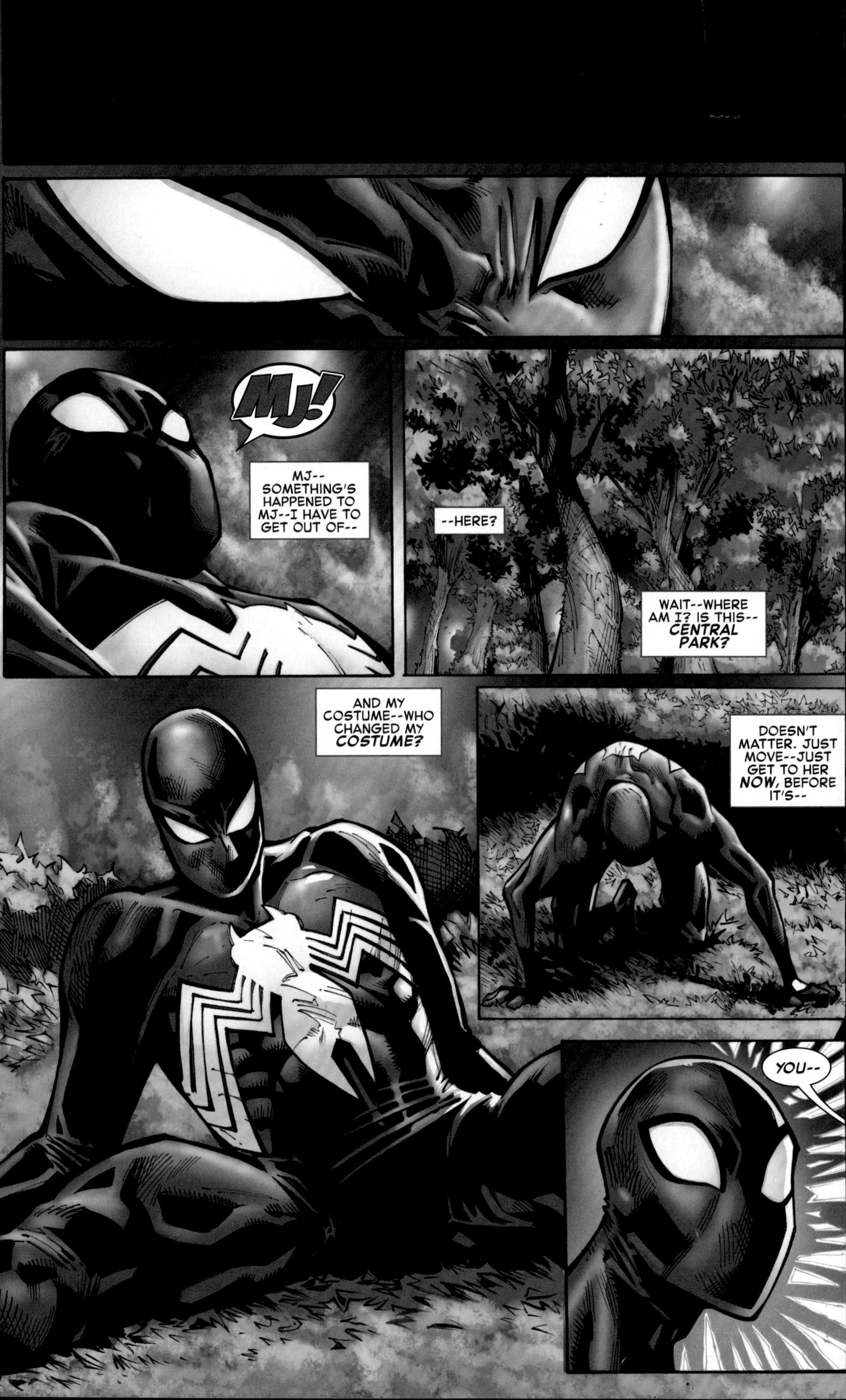
MJ!
MJ-- SOMETHING'S HAPPENED TO MJ--I HAVE TO GET OUT OF--
--HERE?
WAIT--WHERE AM I? IS THIS-- CENTRAL PARK?
AND MY COSTUME--WHO CHANGED MY COSTUME?
DOESN'T MATTER. JUST MOVE--JUST GET TO HER NOW, BEFORE IT'S--
YOU--

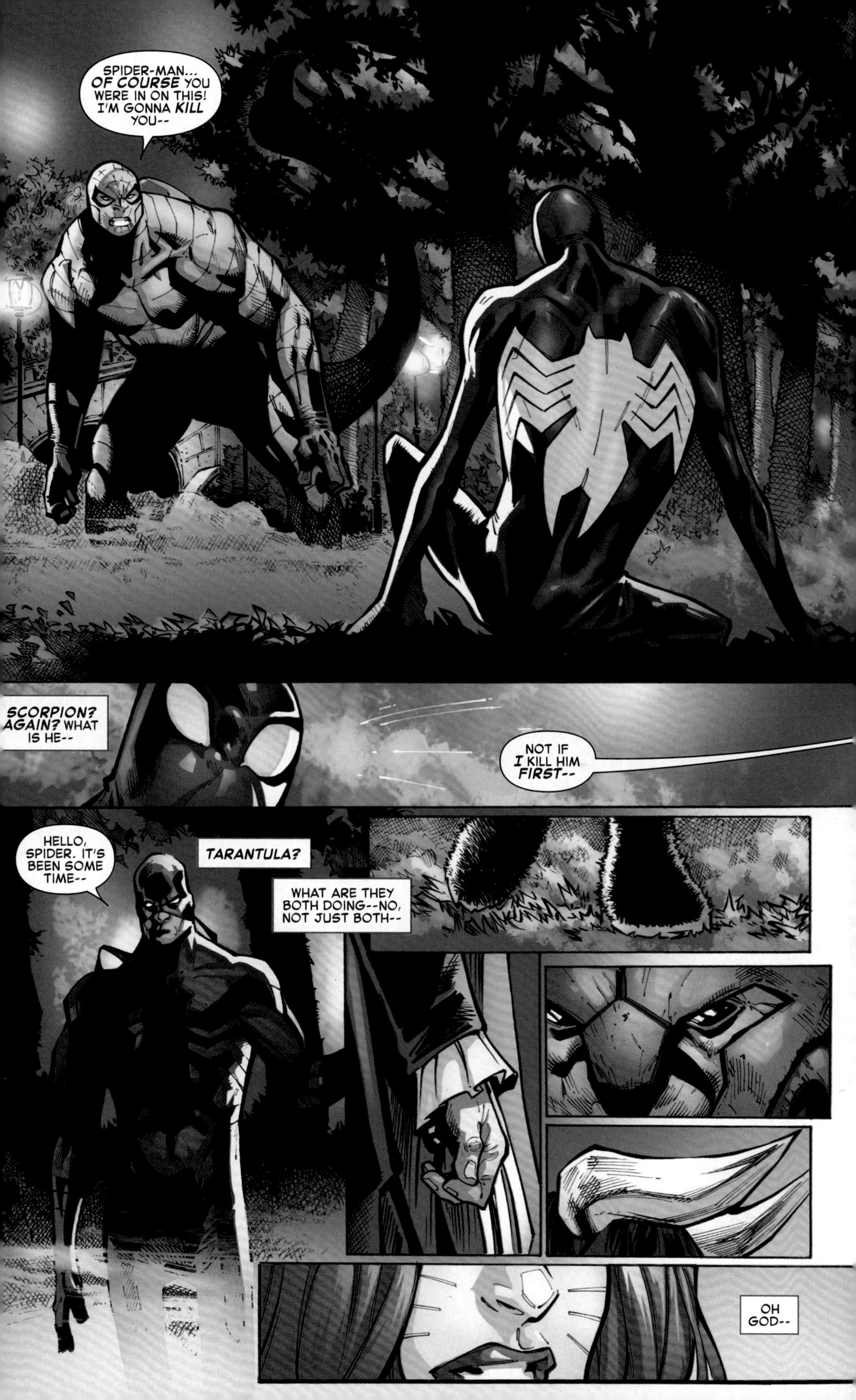
SPIDER-MAN... OF COURSE YOU WERE IN ON THIS! I'M GONNA KILL YOU--
SCORPION? AGAIN? WHAT IS HE--
NOT IF I KILL HIM FIRST--
HELLO, SPIDER. IT'S BEEN SOME TIME--
TARANTULA?
WHAT ARE THEY BOTH DOING--NO, NOT JUST BOTH--
OH GOD--

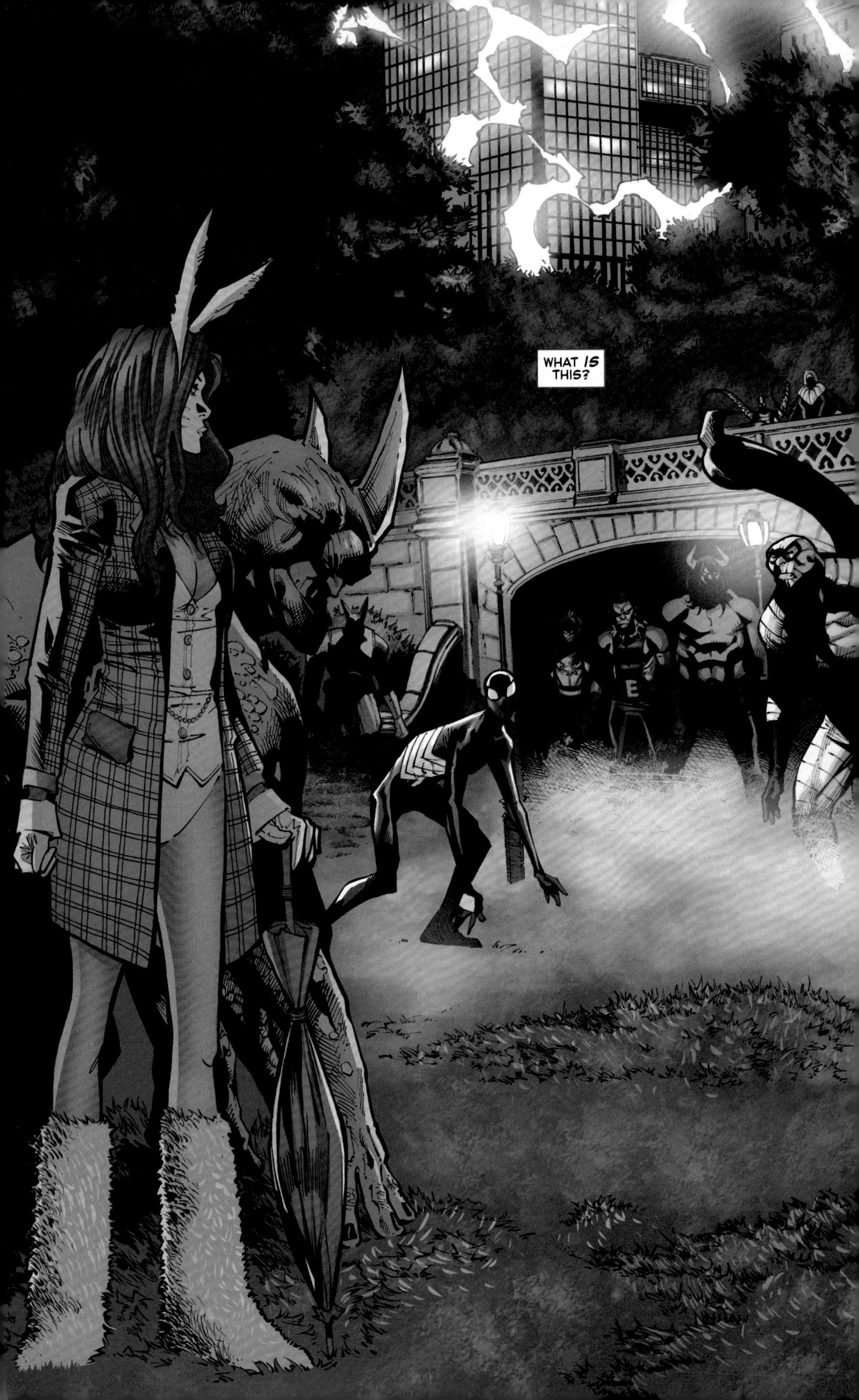
WHAT IS THIS?

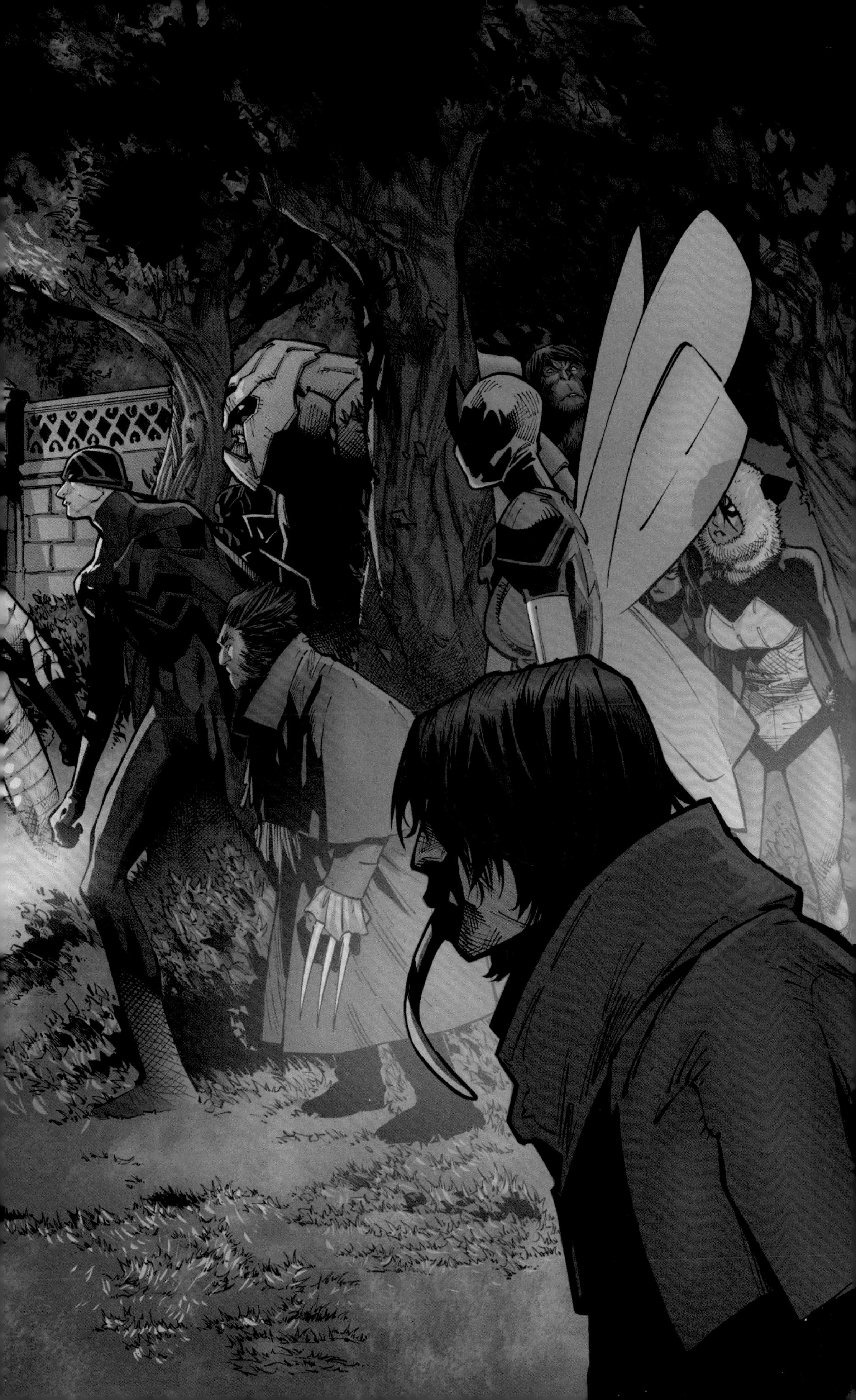

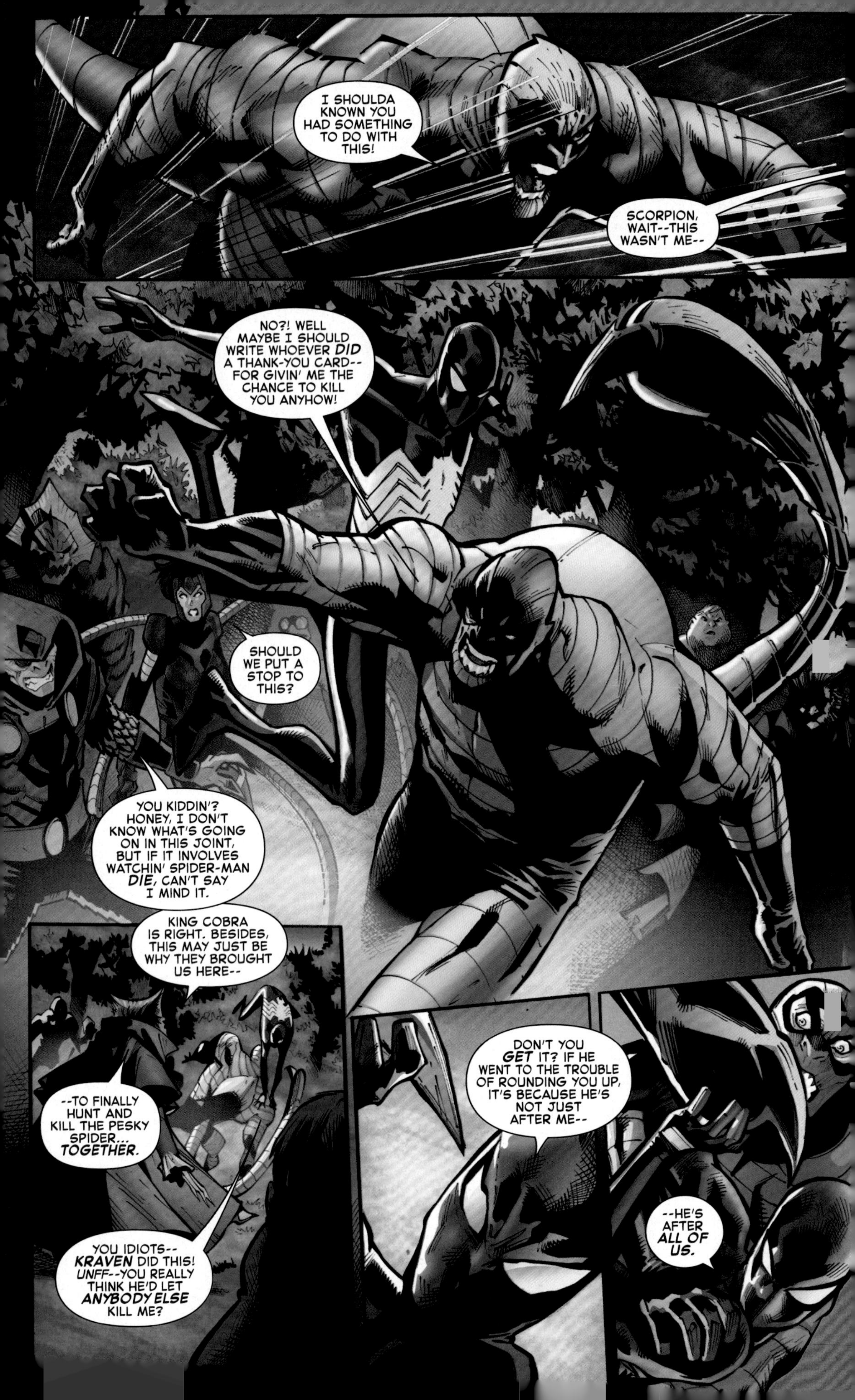

I SHOULDA KNOWN YOU HAD SOMETHING TO DO WITH THIS!
SCORPION, WAIT--THIS WASN'T ME--
NO?! WELL MAYBE I SHOULD WRITE WHOEVER *DID* A THANK-YOU CARD--FOR GIVIN' ME THE CHANCE TO KILL YOU ANYHOW!
SHOULD WE PUT A STOP TO THIS?
YOU KIDDIN'? HONEY, I DON'T KNOW WHAT'S GOING ON IN THIS JOINT, BUT IF IT INVOLVES WATCHIN' SPIDER-MAN *DIE*, CAN'T SAY I MIND IT.
KING COBRA IS RIGHT. BESIDES, THIS MAY JUST BE WHY THEY BROUGHT US HERE--
--TO FINALLY HUNT AND KILL THE PESKY SPIDER... ***TOGETHER.***
YOU IDIOTS--***KRAVEN*** DID THIS! *UNFF*--YOU REALLY THINK HE'D LET ***ANYBODY ELSE*** KILL ME?
DON'T YOU ***GET*** IT? IF HE WENT TO THE TROUBLE OF ROUNDING YOU UP, IT'S BECAUSE HE'S NOT JUST AFTER ME--
--HE'S AFTER ***ALL OF US.***

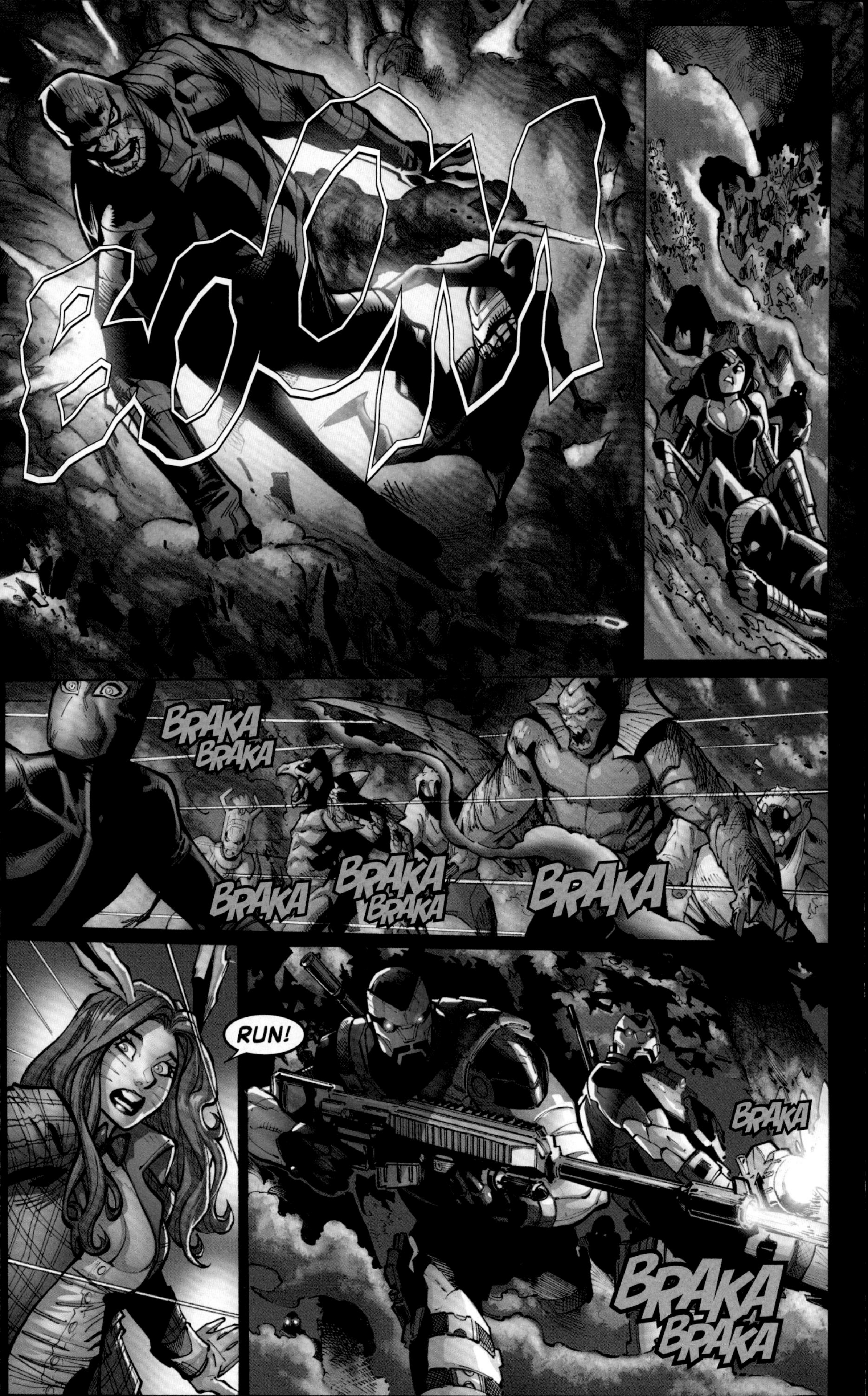
BOOM
BRAKA BRAKA
BRAKA
BRAKA BRAKA
BRAKA
RUN!
BRAKA
BRAKA BRAKA

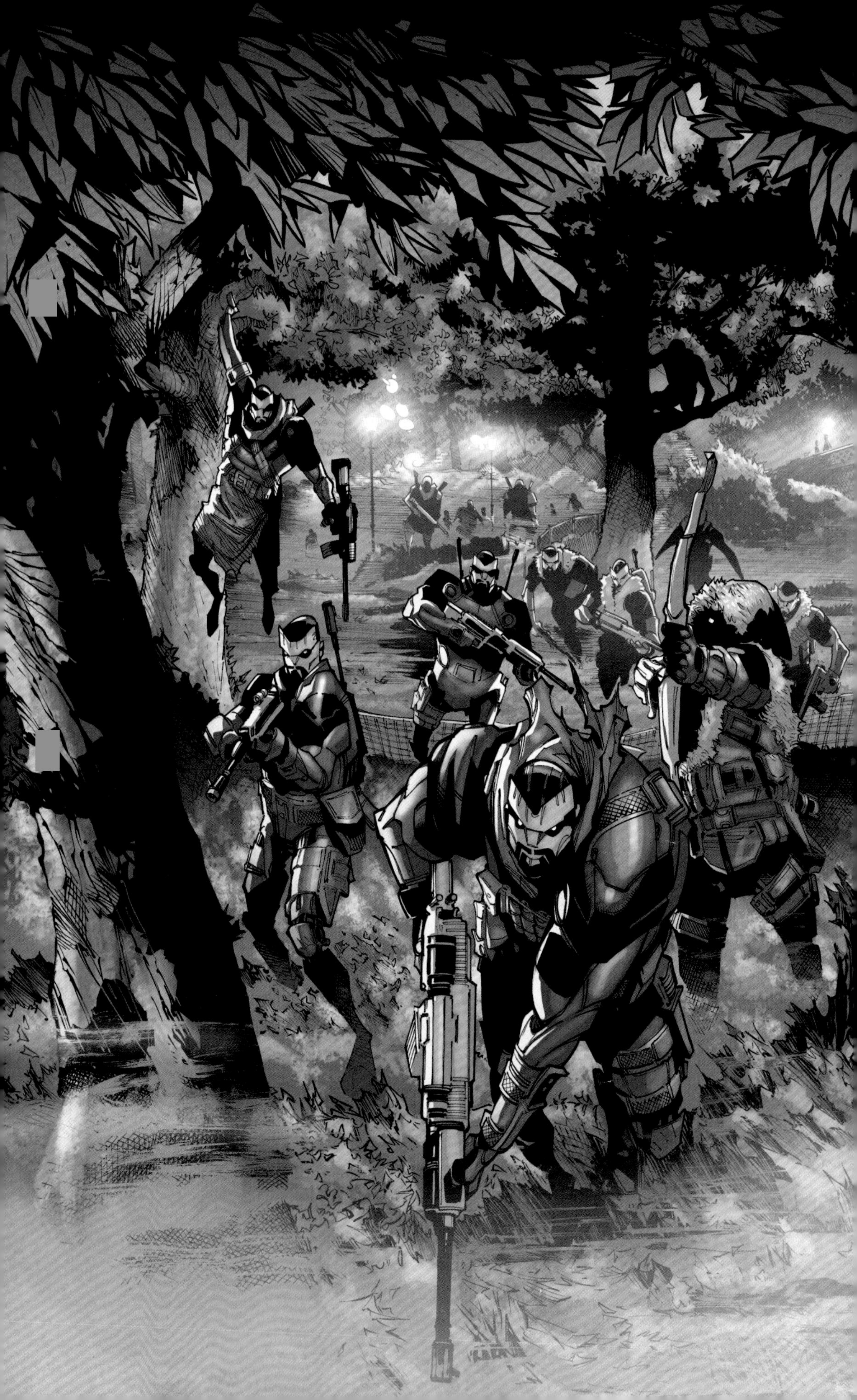

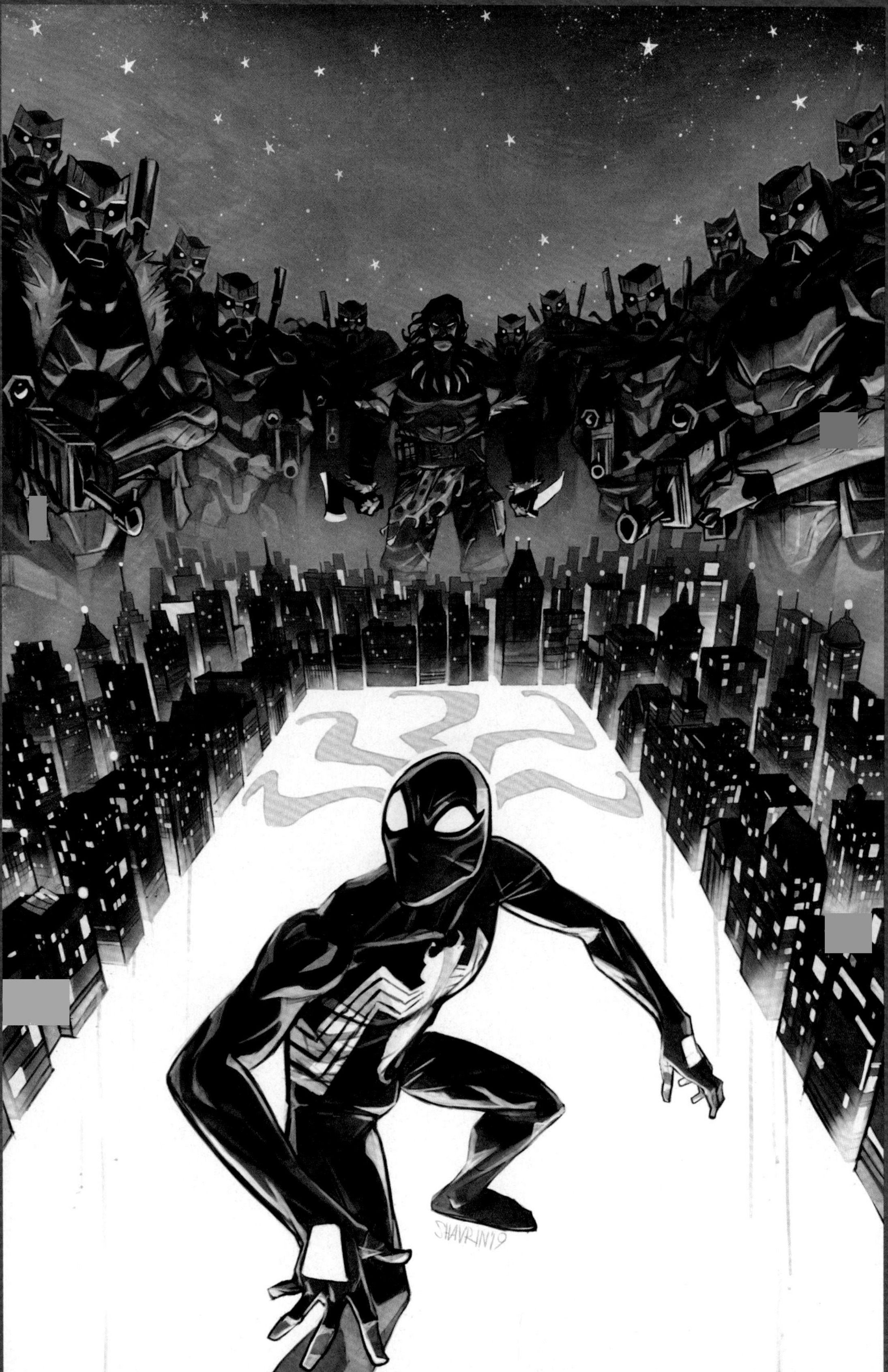
SHAVRIN19

#18 VARIANT BY IVAN SHAVRIN

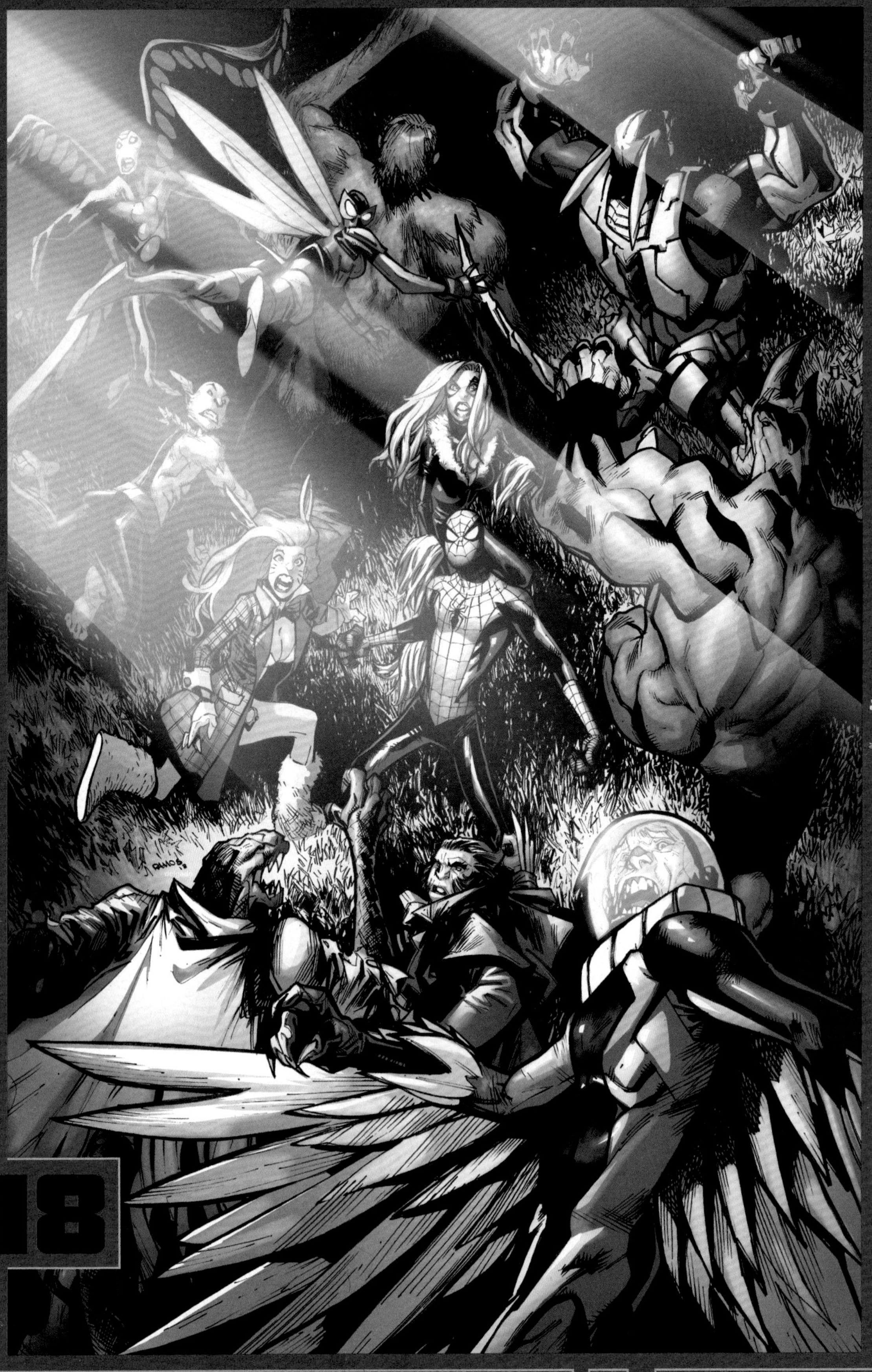

18

HUNTED PART 2

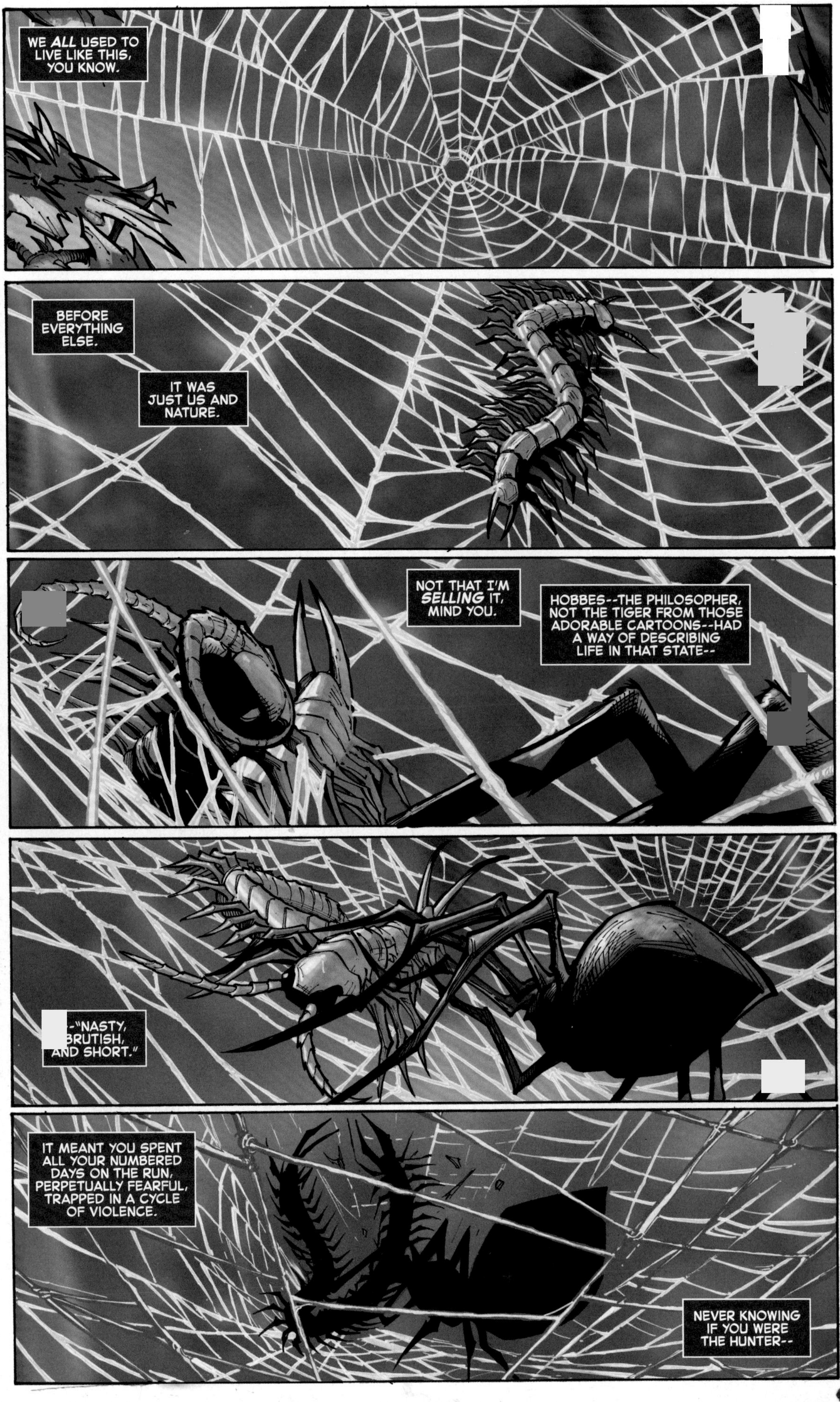
WE ALL USED TO LIVE LIKE THIS, YOU KNOW.
BEFORE EVERYTHING ELSE.
IT WAS JUST US AND NATURE.
NOT THAT I'M SELLING IT, MIND YOU.
HOBBES--THE PHILOSOPHER, NOT THE TIGER FROM THOSE ADORABLE CARTOONS--HAD A WAY OF DESCRIBING LIFE IN THAT STATE--
-"NASTY, BRUTISH, AND SHORT."
IT MEANT YOU SPENT ALL YOUR NUMBERED DAYS ON THE RUN, PERPETUALLY FEARFUL, TRAPPED IN A CYCLE OF VIOLENCE.
NEVER KNOWING IF YOU WERE THE HUNTER--

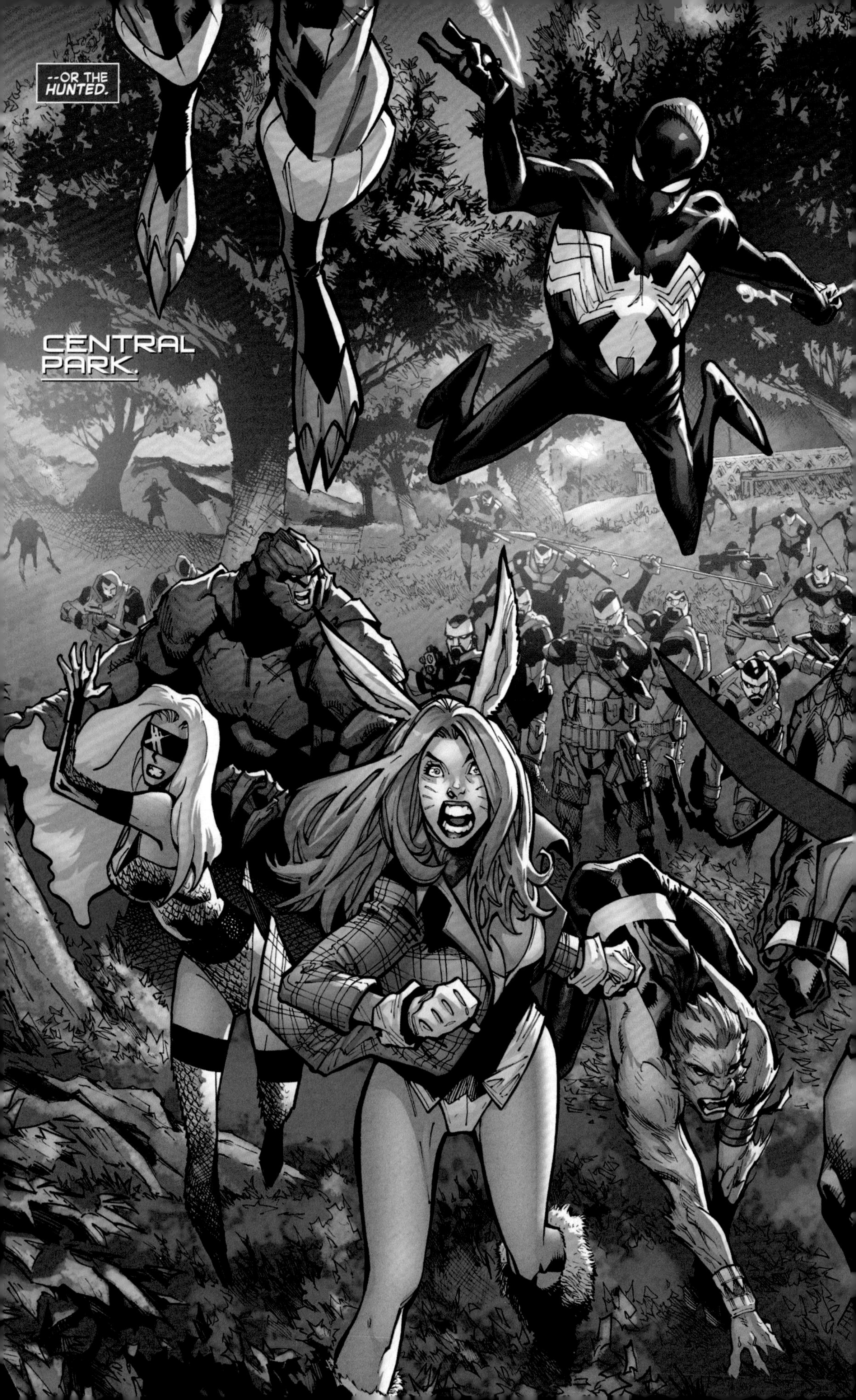
--OR THE HUNTED.
CENTRAL PARK.

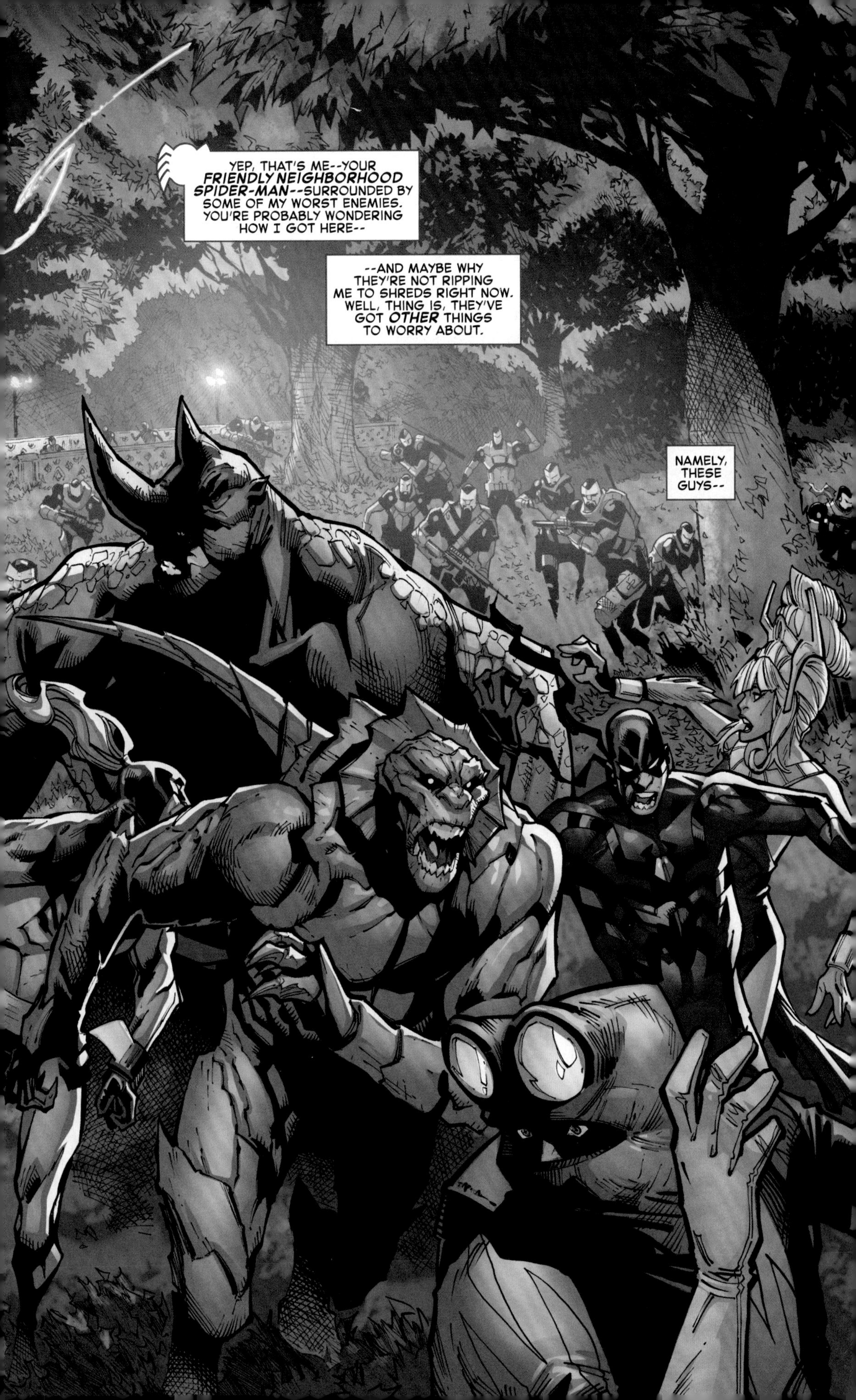
YEP, THAT'S ME--YOUR FRIENDLY NEIGHBORHOOD SPIDER-MAN--SURROUNDED BY SOME OF MY WORST ENEMIES. YOU'RE PROBABLY WONDERING HOW I GOT HERE--
--AND MAYBE WHY THEY'RE NOT RIPPING ME TO SHREDS RIGHT NOW. WELL, THING IS, THEY'VE GOT OTHER THINGS TO WORRY ABOUT.
NAMELY, THESE GUYS--

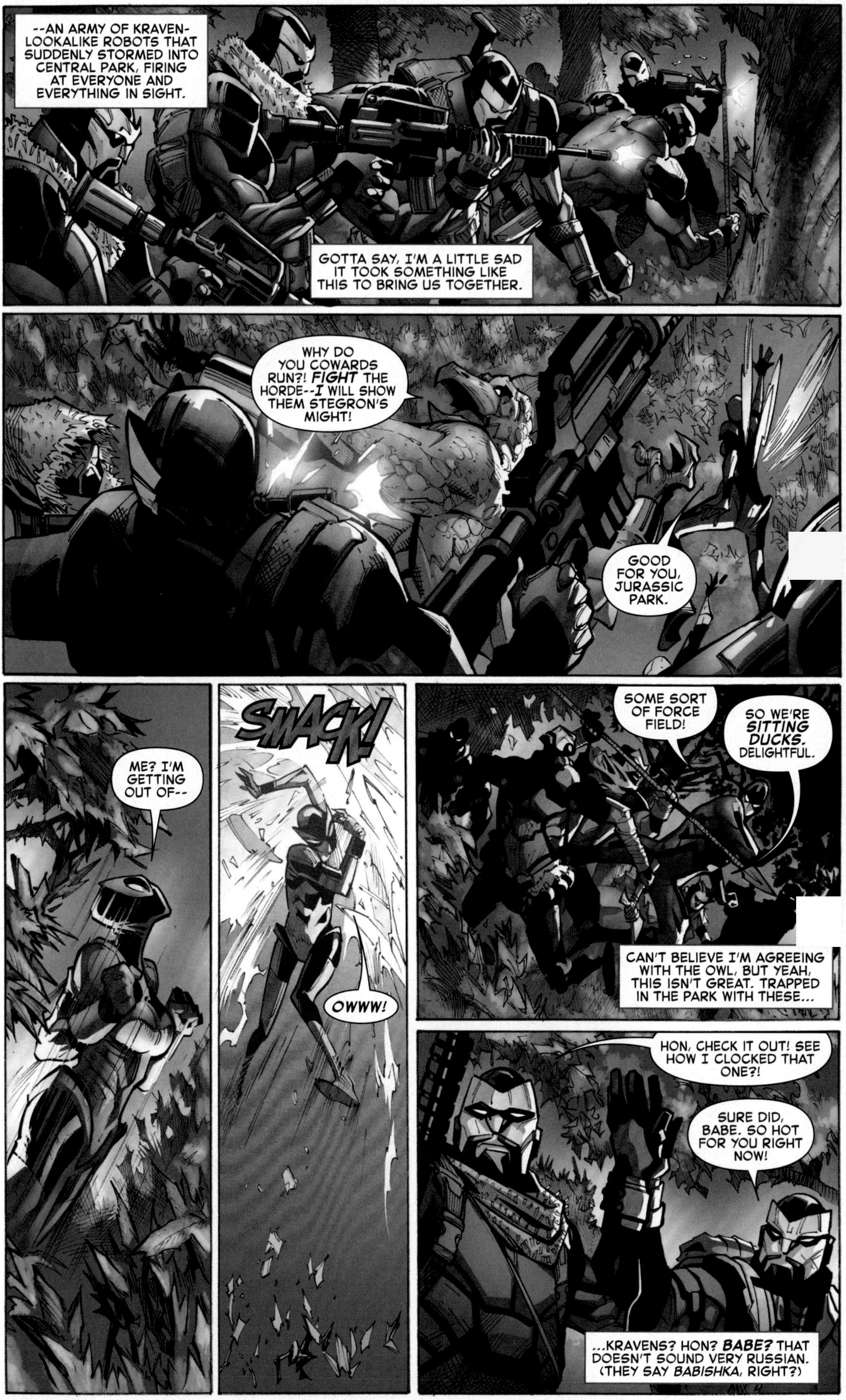
--AN ARMY OF KRAVEN-LOOKALIKE ROBOTS THAT SUDDENLY STORMED INTO CENTRAL PARK, FIRING AT EVERYONE AND EVERYTHING IN SIGHT.
GOTTA SAY, I'M A LITTLE SAD IT TOOK SOMETHING LIKE THIS TO BRING US TOGETHER.
WHY DO YOU COWARDS RUN?! FIGHT THE HORDE--I WILL SHOW THEM STEGRON'S MIGHT!
GOOD FOR YOU, JURASSIC PARK.
ME? I'M GETTING OUT OF--
SMACK!
OWWW!
SOME SORT OF FORCE FIELD!
SO WE'RE SITTING DUCKS. DELIGHTFUL.
CAN'T BELIEVE I'M AGREEING WITH THE OWL, BUT YEAH, THIS ISN'T GREAT. TRAPPED IN THE PARK WITH THESE...
HON, CHECK IT OUT! SEE HOW I CLOCKED THAT ONE?!
SURE DID, BABE. SO HOT FOR YOU RIGHT NOW!
...KRAVENS? HON? BABE? THAT DOESN'T SOUND VERY RUSSIAN. (THEY SAY BABISHKA, RIGHT?)

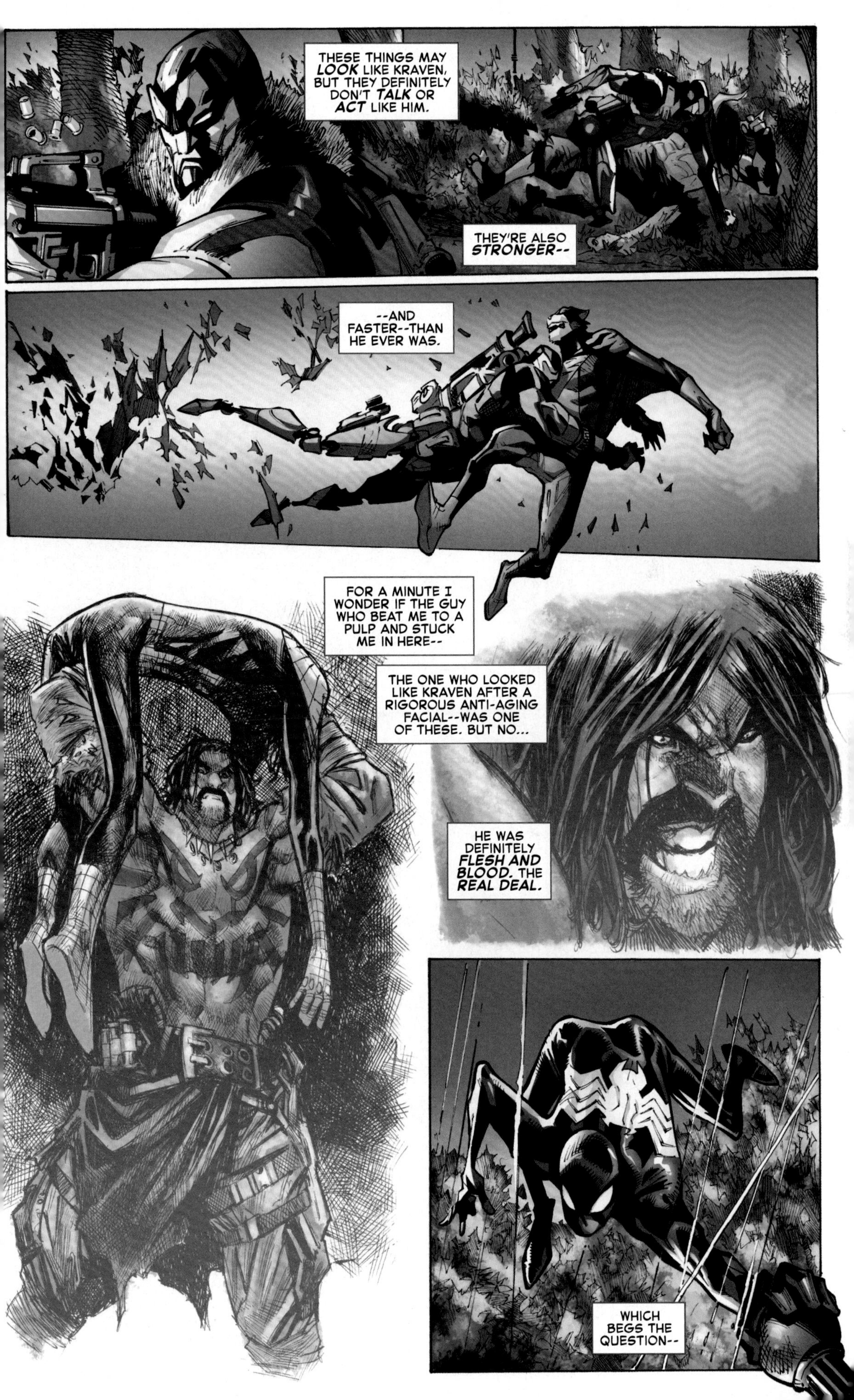
THESE THINGS MAY LOOK LIKE KRAVEN, BUT THEY DEFINITELY DON'T TALK OR ACT LIKE HIM.
THEY'RE ALSO STRONGER--
--AND FASTER--THAN HE EVER WAS.
FOR A MINUTE I WONDER IF THE GUY WHO BEAT ME TO A PULP AND STUCK ME IN HERE--
THE ONE WHO LOOKED LIKE KRAVEN AFTER A RIGOROUS ANTI-AGING FACIAL--WAS ONE OF THESE. BUT NO...
HE WAS DEFINITELY FLESH AND BLOOD. THE REAL DEAL.
WHICH BEGS THE QUESTION--

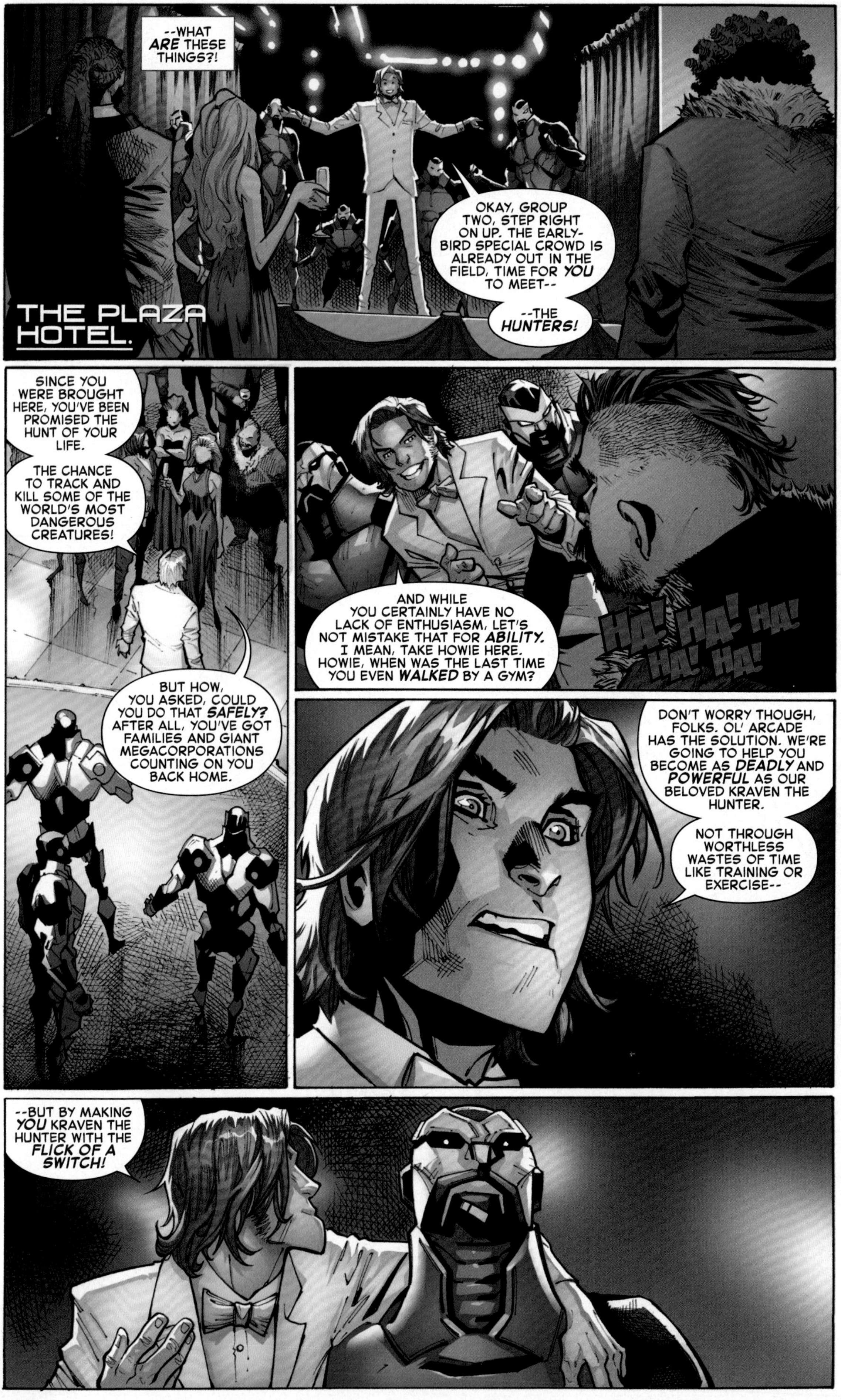
--WHAT ARE THESE THINGS?!
OKAY, GROUP TWO, STEP RIGHT ON UP. THE EARLY-BIRD SPECIAL CROWD IS ALREADY OUT IN THE FIELD, TIME FOR YOU TO MEET--
THE PLAZA HOTEL.
--THE HUNTERS!
SINCE YOU WERE BROUGHT HERE, YOU'VE BEEN PROMISED THE HUNT OF YOUR LIFE.
THE CHANCE TO TRACK AND KILL SOME OF THE WORLD'S MOST DANGEROUS CREATURES!
AND WHILE YOU CERTAINLY HAVE NO LACK OF ENTHUSIASM, LET'S NOT MISTAKE THAT FOR ABILITY. I MEAN, TAKE HOWIE HERE. HOWIE, WHEN WAS THE LAST TIME YOU EVEN WALKED BY A GYM?
HA! HA! HA! HA! HA!
BUT HOW, YOU ASKED, COULD YOU DO THAT SAFELY? AFTER ALL, YOU'VE GOT FAMILIES AND GIANT MEGACORPORATIONS COUNTING ON YOU BACK HOME.
DON'T WORRY THOUGH, FOLKS. OL' ARCADE HAS THE SOLUTION. WE'RE GOING TO HELP YOU BECOME AS DEADLY AND POWERFUL AS OUR BELOVED KRAVEN THE HUNTER.
NOT THROUGH WORTHLESS WASTES OF TIME LIKE TRAINING OR EXERCISE--
--BUT BY MAKING YOU KRAVEN THE HUNTER WITH THE FLICK OF A SWITCH!

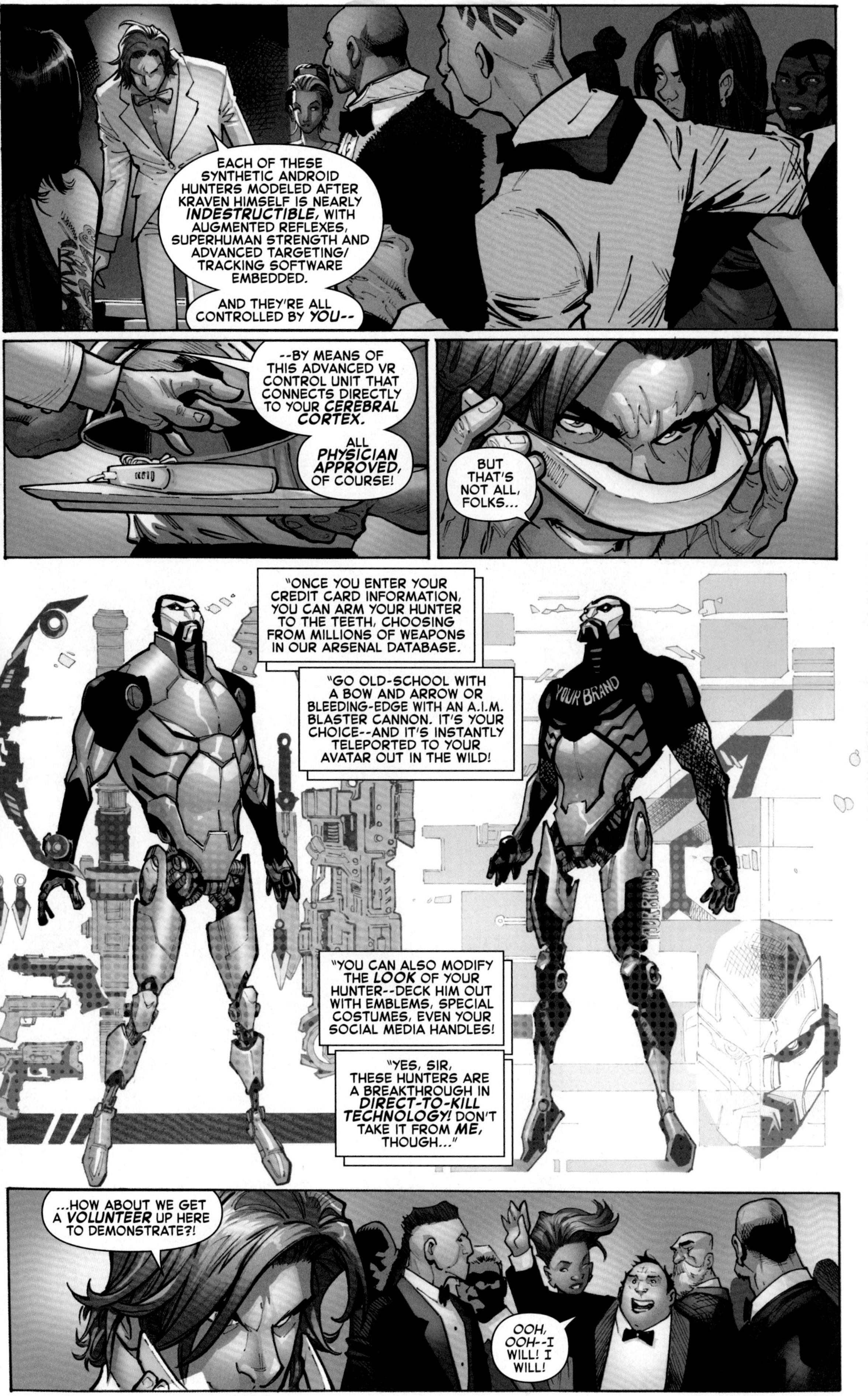
EACH OF THESE SYNTHETIC ANDROID HUNTERS MODELED AFTER KRAVEN HIMSELF IS NEARLY INDESTRUCTIBLE, WITH AUGMENTED REFLEXES, SUPERHUMAN STRENGTH AND ADVANCED TARGETING/ TRACKING SOFTWARE EMBEDDED.
AND THEY'RE ALL CONTROLLED BY YOU--
--BY MEANS OF THIS ADVANCED VR CONTROL UNIT THAT CONNECTS DIRECTLY TO YOUR CEREBRAL CORTEX.
ALL PHYSICIAN APPROVED, OF COURSE!
BUT THAT'S NOT ALL, FOLKS...
"ONCE YOU ENTER YOUR CREDIT CARD INFORMATION, YOU CAN ARM YOUR HUNTER TO THE TEETH, CHOOSING FROM MILLIONS OF WEAPONS IN OUR ARSENAL DATABASE.
"GO OLD-SCHOOL WITH A BOW AND ARROW OR BLEEDING-EDGE WITH AN A.I.M. BLASTER CANNON. IT'S YOUR CHOICE--AND IT'S INSTANTLY TELEPORTED TO YOUR AVATAR OUT IN THE WILD!
YOUR BRAND
YOUR BRAND
"YOU CAN ALSO MODIFY THE LOOK OF YOUR HUNTER--DECK HIM OUT WITH EMBLEMS, SPECIAL COSTUMES, EVEN YOUR SOCIAL MEDIA HANDLES!
"YES, SIR, THESE HUNTERS ARE A BREAKTHROUGH IN DIRECT-TO-KILL TECHNOLOGY! DON'T TAKE IT FROM ME, THOUGH..."
...HOW ABOUT WE GET A VOLUNTEER UP HERE TO DEMONSTRATE?!
OOH, OOH--I WILL! I WILL!

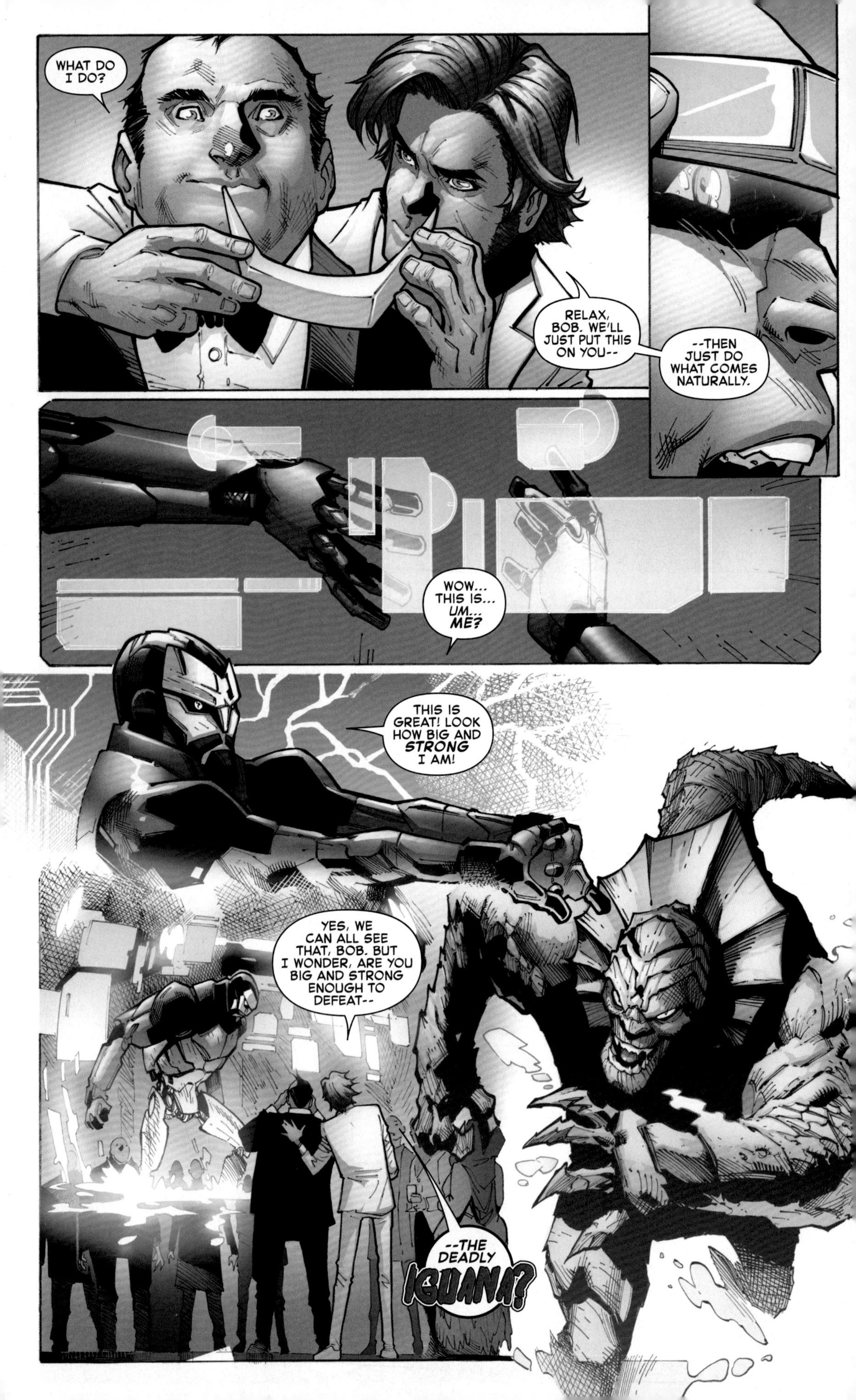
WHAT DO I DO?
RELAX, BOB. WE'LL JUST PUT THIS ON YOU--
--THEN JUST DO WHAT COMES NATURALLY.
WOW... THIS IS... UM... ME?
THIS IS GREAT! LOOK HOW BIG AND STRONG I AM!
YES, WE CAN ALL SEE THAT, BOB. BUT I WONDER, ARE YOU BIG AND STRONG ENOUGH TO DEFEAT--
--THE DEADLY IGUANA?

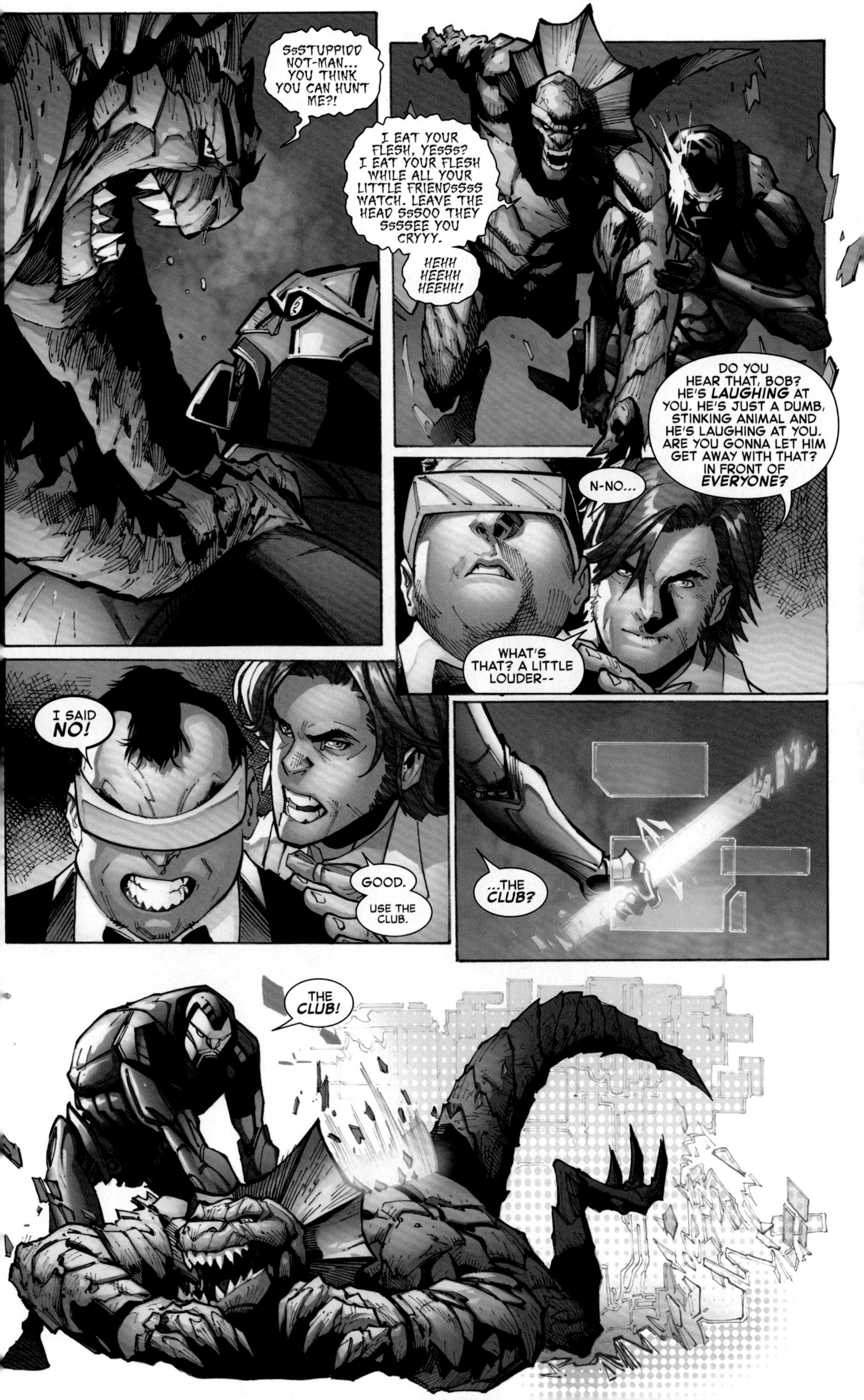
SsSTUPPIDD NOT-MAN... YOU THINK YOU CAN HUNT ME?!
I EAT YOUR FLESH, YESSS? I EAT YOUR FLESH WHILE ALL YOUR LITTLE FRIENDSSSS WATCH. LEAVE THE HEAD SSSOO THEY SSSSEE YOU CRYYY.
HEHH HEEHH HEEHH!
DO YOU HEAR THAT, BOB? HE'S LAUGHING AT YOU. HE'S JUST A DUMB, STINKING ANIMAL AND HE'S LAUGHING AT YOU. ARE YOU GONNA LET HIM GET AWAY WITH THAT? IN FRONT OF EVERYONE?
N-NO...
WHAT'S THAT? A LITTLE LOUDER--
I SAID NO!
GOOD.
USE THE CLUB.
...THE CLUB?
THE CLUB!

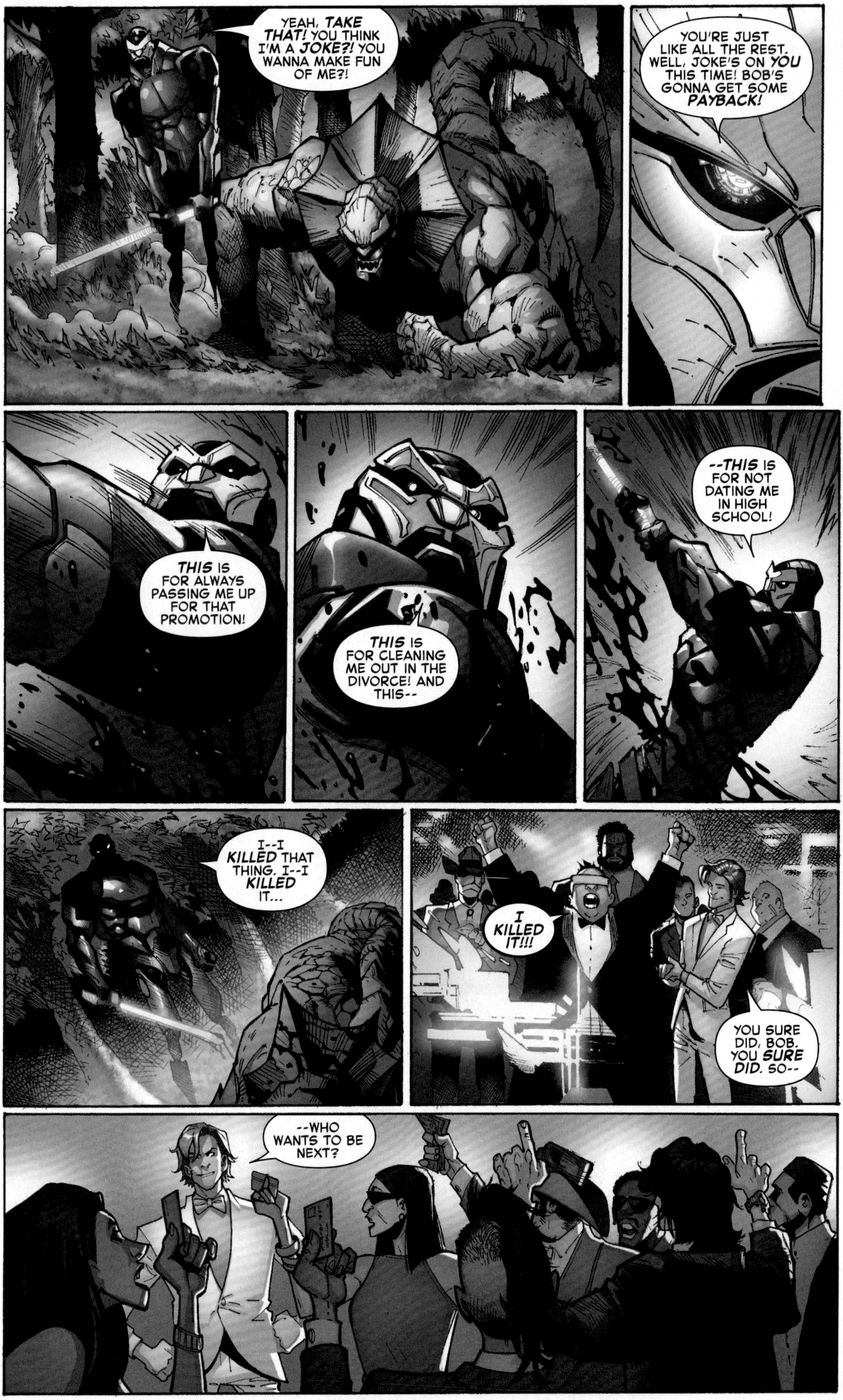

YEAH, TAKE THAT! YOU THINK I'M A JOKE?! YOU WANNA MAKE FUN OF ME?!
YOU'RE JUST LIKE ALL THE REST. WELL, JOKE'S ON YOU THIS TIME! BOB'S GONNA GET SOME PAYBACK!
THIS IS FOR ALWAYS PASSING ME UP FOR THAT PROMOTION!
THIS IS FOR CLEANING ME OUT IN THE DIVORCE! AND THIS--
--THIS IS FOR NOT DATING ME IN HIGH SCHOOL!
I--I KILLED THAT THING. I--I KILLED IT...
I KILLED IT!!!
YOU SURE DID, BOB. YOU SURE DID. SO--
--WHO WANTS TO BE NEXT?

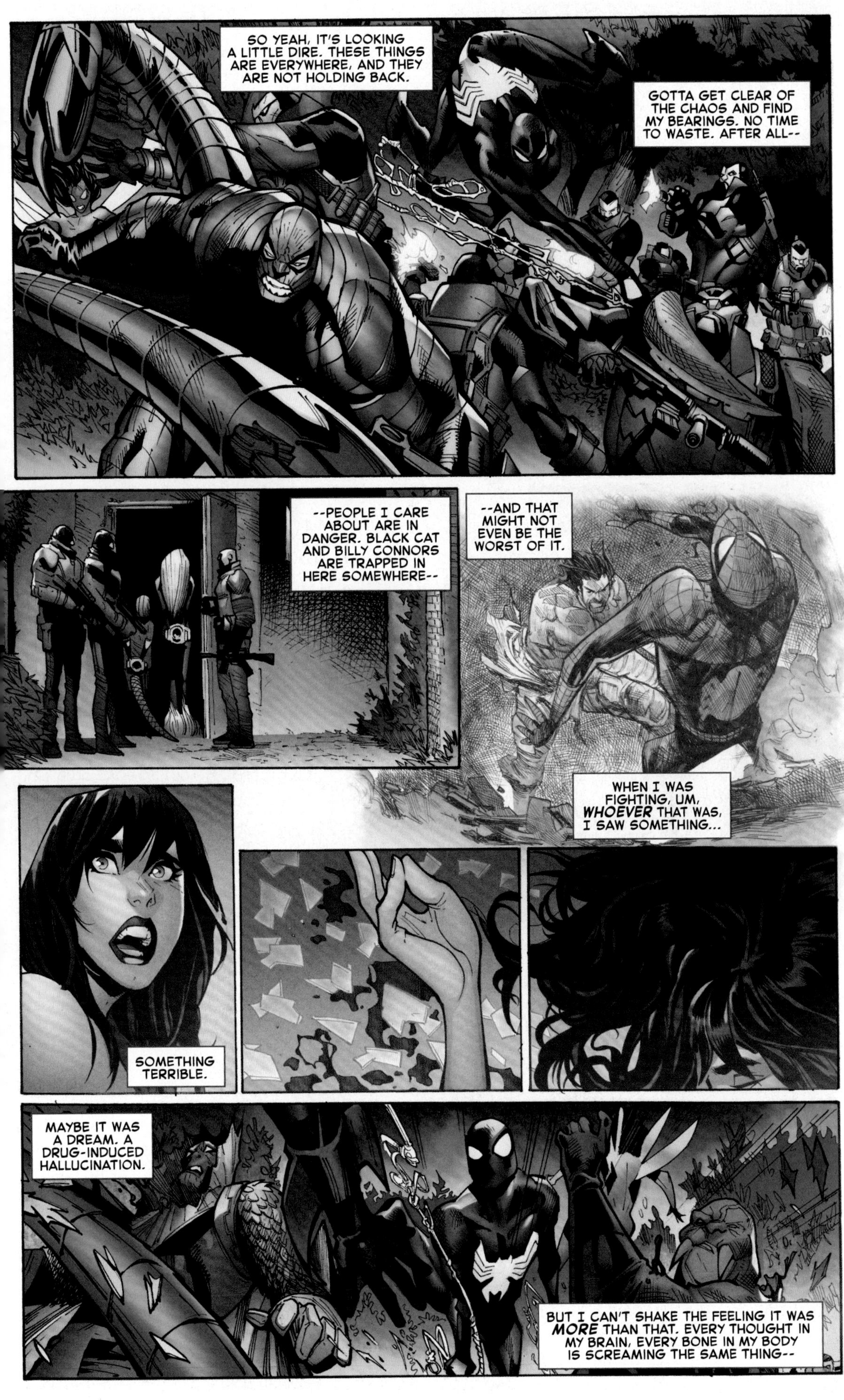

SO YEAH, IT'S LOOKING A LITTLE DIRE. THESE THINGS ARE EVERYWHERE, AND THEY ARE NOT HOLDING BACK.
GOTTA GET CLEAR OF THE CHAOS AND FIND MY BEARINGS. NO TIME TO WASTE. AFTER ALL--
--PEOPLE I CARE ABOUT ARE IN DANGER. BLACK CAT AND BILLY CONNORS ARE TRAPPED IN HERE SOMEWHERE--
--AND THAT MIGHT NOT EVEN BE THE WORST OF IT.
WHEN I WAS FIGHTING, UM, *WHOEVER* THAT WAS, I SAW SOMETHING...
SOMETHING TERRIBLE.
MAYBE IT WAS A DREAM. A DRUG-INDUCED HALLUCINATION.
BUT I CAN'T SHAKE THE FEELING IT WAS *MORE* THAN THAT. EVERY THOUGHT IN MY BRAIN, EVERY BONE IN MY BODY IS SCREAMING THE SAME THING--

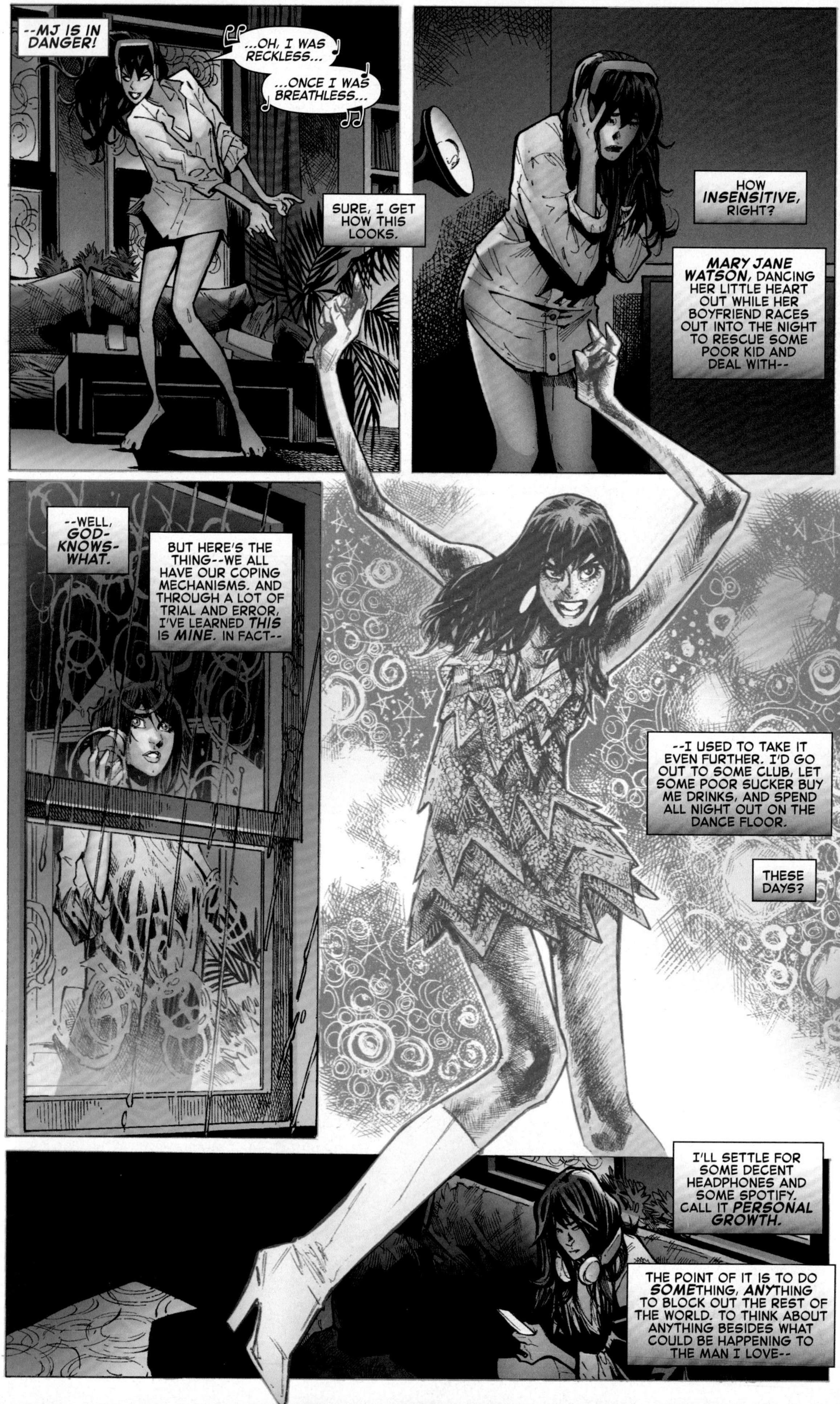

--MJ IS IN DANGER!
...OH, I WAS RECKLESS...
...ONCE I WAS BREATHLESS...
SURE, I GET HOW THIS LOOKS.
HOW INSENSITIVE, RIGHT?
MARY JANE WATSON, DANCING HER LITTLE HEART OUT WHILE HER BOYFRIEND RACES OUT INTO THE NIGHT TO RESCUE SOME POOR KID AND DEAL WITH--
--WELL, GOD-KNOWS-WHAT.
BUT HERE'S THE THING--WE ALL HAVE OUR COPING MECHANISMS. AND THROUGH A LOT OF TRIAL AND ERROR, I'VE LEARNED THIS IS MINE. IN FACT--
--I USED TO TAKE IT EVEN FURTHER. I'D GO OUT TO SOME CLUB, LET SOME POOR SUCKER BUY ME DRINKS, AND SPEND ALL NIGHT OUT ON THE DANCE FLOOR.
THESE DAYS?
I'LL SETTLE FOR SOME DECENT HEADPHONES AND SOME SPOTIFY. CALL IT PERSONAL GROWTH.
THE POINT OF IT IS TO DO SOMETHING, ANYTHING TO BLOCK OUT THE REST OF THE WORLD. TO THINK ABOUT ANYTHING BESIDES WHAT COULD BE HAPPENING TO THE MAN I LOVE--

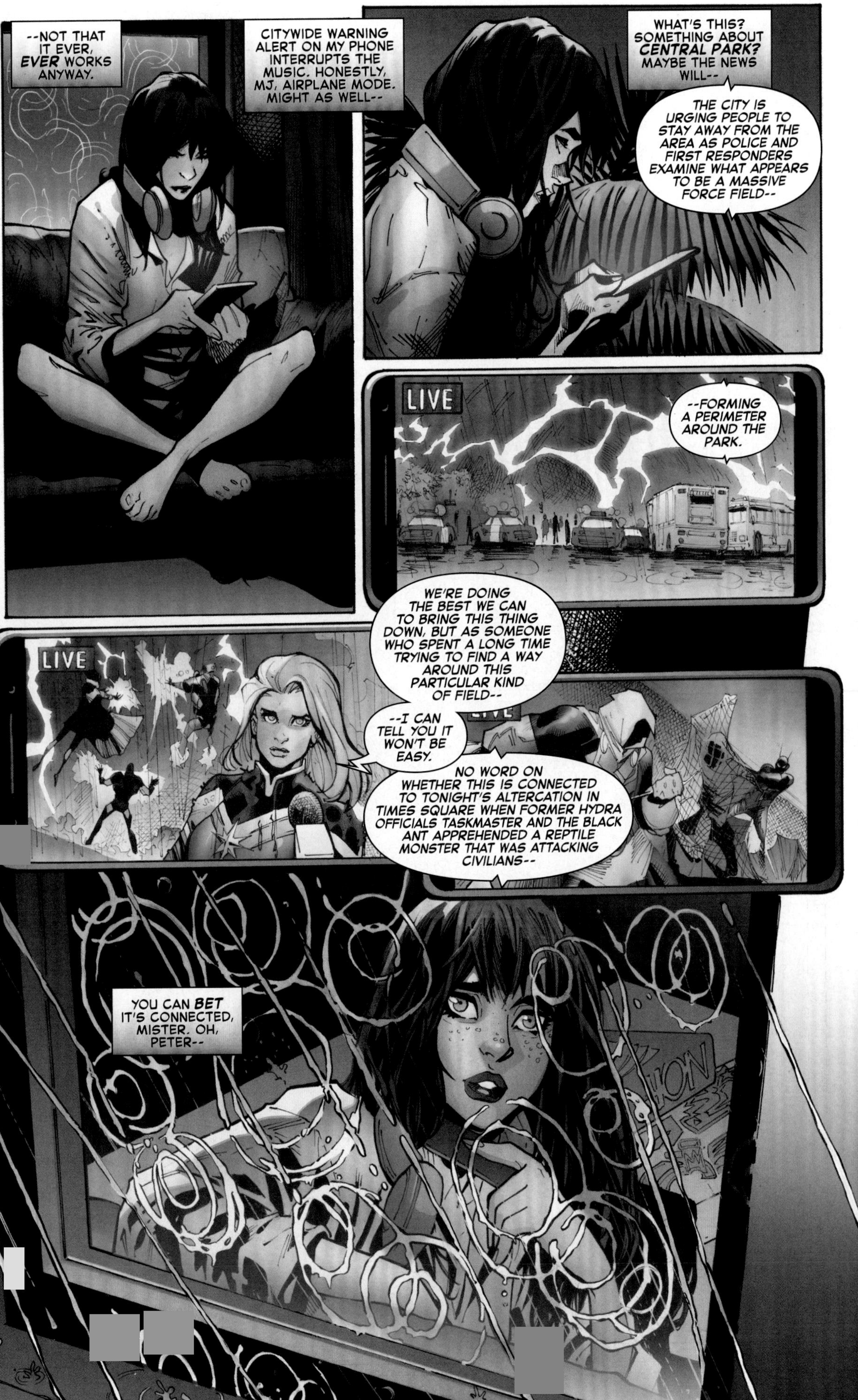
--NOT THAT IT EVER, **EVER** WORKS ANYWAY.
CITYWIDE WARNING ALERT ON MY PHONE INTERRUPTS THE MUSIC. HONESTLY, MJ, AIRPLANE MODE. MIGHT AS WELL--
WHAT'S THIS? SOMETHING ABOUT **CENTRAL PARK?** MAYBE THE NEWS WILL--
THE CITY IS URGING PEOPLE TO STAY AWAY FROM THE AREA AS POLICE AND FIRST RESPONDERS EXAMINE WHAT APPEARS TO BE A MASSIVE FORCE FIELD--
LIVE
--FORMING A PERIMETER AROUND THE PARK.
WE'RE DOING THE BEST WE CAN TO BRING THIS THING DOWN, BUT AS SOMEONE WHO SPENT A LONG TIME TRYING TO FIND A WAY AROUND THIS PARTICULAR KIND OF FIELD--
LIVE
--I CAN TELL YOU IT WON'T BE EASY.
NO WORD ON WHETHER THIS IS CONNECTED TO TONIGHT'S ALTERCATION IN TIMES SQUARE WHEN FORMER HYDRA OFFICIALS TASKMASTER AND THE BLACK ANT APPREHENDED A REPTILE MONSTER THAT WAS ATTACKING CIVILIANS--
YOU CAN **BET** IT'S CONNECTED, MISTER. OH, PETER--

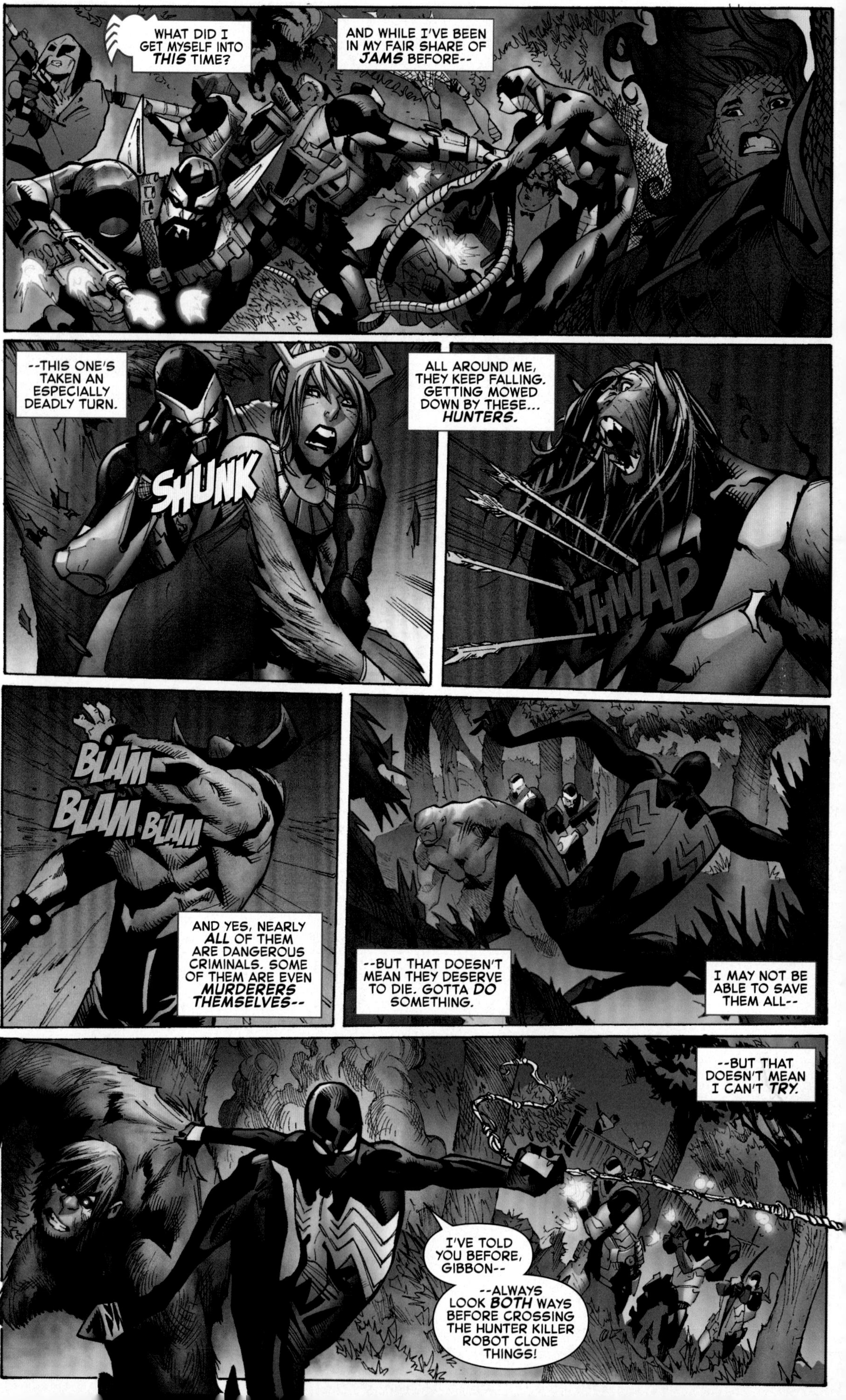
WHAT DID I GET MYSELF INTO THIS TIME?
AND WHILE I'VE BEEN IN MY FAIR SHARE OF JAMS BEFORE--
--THIS ONE'S TAKEN AN ESPECIALLY DEADLY TURN.
SHUNK
ALL AROUND ME, THEY KEEP FALLING. GETTING MOWED DOWN BY THESE... HUNTERS.
THWAP
BLAM BLAM BLAM
AND YES, NEARLY ALL OF THEM ARE DANGEROUS CRIMINALS. SOME OF THEM ARE EVEN MURDERERS THEMSELVES--
--BUT THAT DOESN'T MEAN THEY DESERVE TO DIE. GOTTA DO SOMETHING.
I MAY NOT BE ABLE TO SAVE THEM ALL--
--BUT THAT DOESN'T MEAN I CAN'T TRY.
I'VE TOLD YOU BEFORE, GIBBON--
--ALWAYS LOOK BOTH WAYS BEFORE CROSSING THE HUNTER KILLER ROBOT CLONE THINGS!

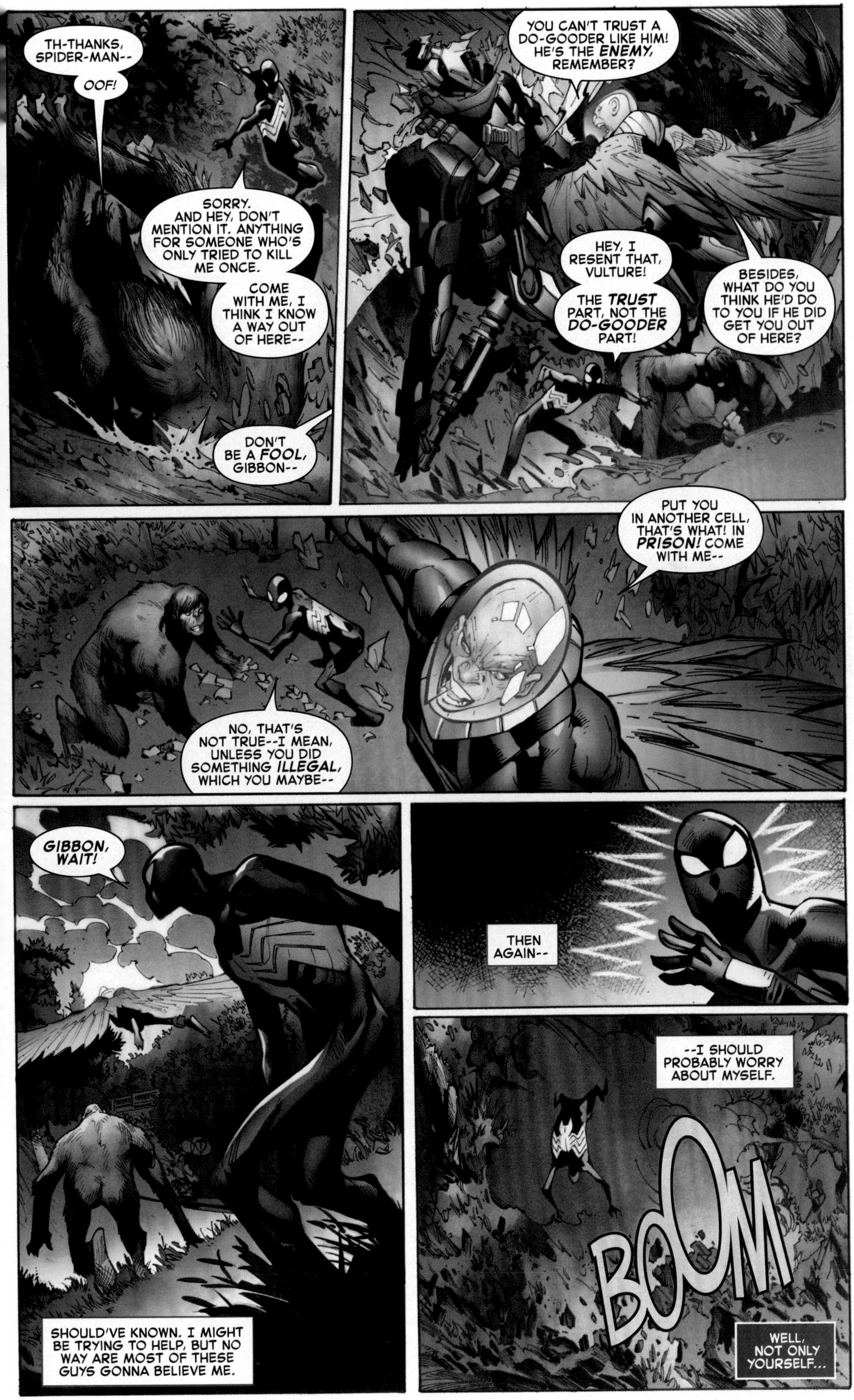
TH-THANKS, SPIDER-MAN--
OOF!
SORRY. AND HEY, DON'T MENTION IT. ANYTHING FOR SOMEONE WHO'S ONLY TRIED TO KILL ME ONCE.
COME WITH ME, I THINK I KNOW A WAY OUT OF HERE--
DON'T BE A FOOL, GIBBON--
YOU CAN'T TRUST A DO-GOODER LIKE HIM! HE'S THE ENEMY, REMEMBER?
HEY, I RESENT THAT, VULTURE!
THE TRUST PART, NOT THE DO-GOODER PART!
BESIDES, WHAT DO YOU THINK HE'D DO TO YOU IF HE DID GET YOU OUT OF HERE?
PUT YOU IN ANOTHER CELL, THAT'S WHAT! IN PRISON! COME WITH ME--
NO, THAT'S NOT TRUE--I MEAN, UNLESS YOU DID SOMETHING ILLEGAL, WHICH YOU MAYBE--
GIBBON, WAIT!
SHOULD'VE KNOWN. I MIGHT BE TRYING TO HELP, BUT NO WAY ARE MOST OF THESE GUYS GONNA BELIEVE ME.
THEN AGAIN--
--I SHOULD PROBABLY WORRY ABOUT MYSELF.
BOOM
WELL, NOT ONLY YOURSELF...

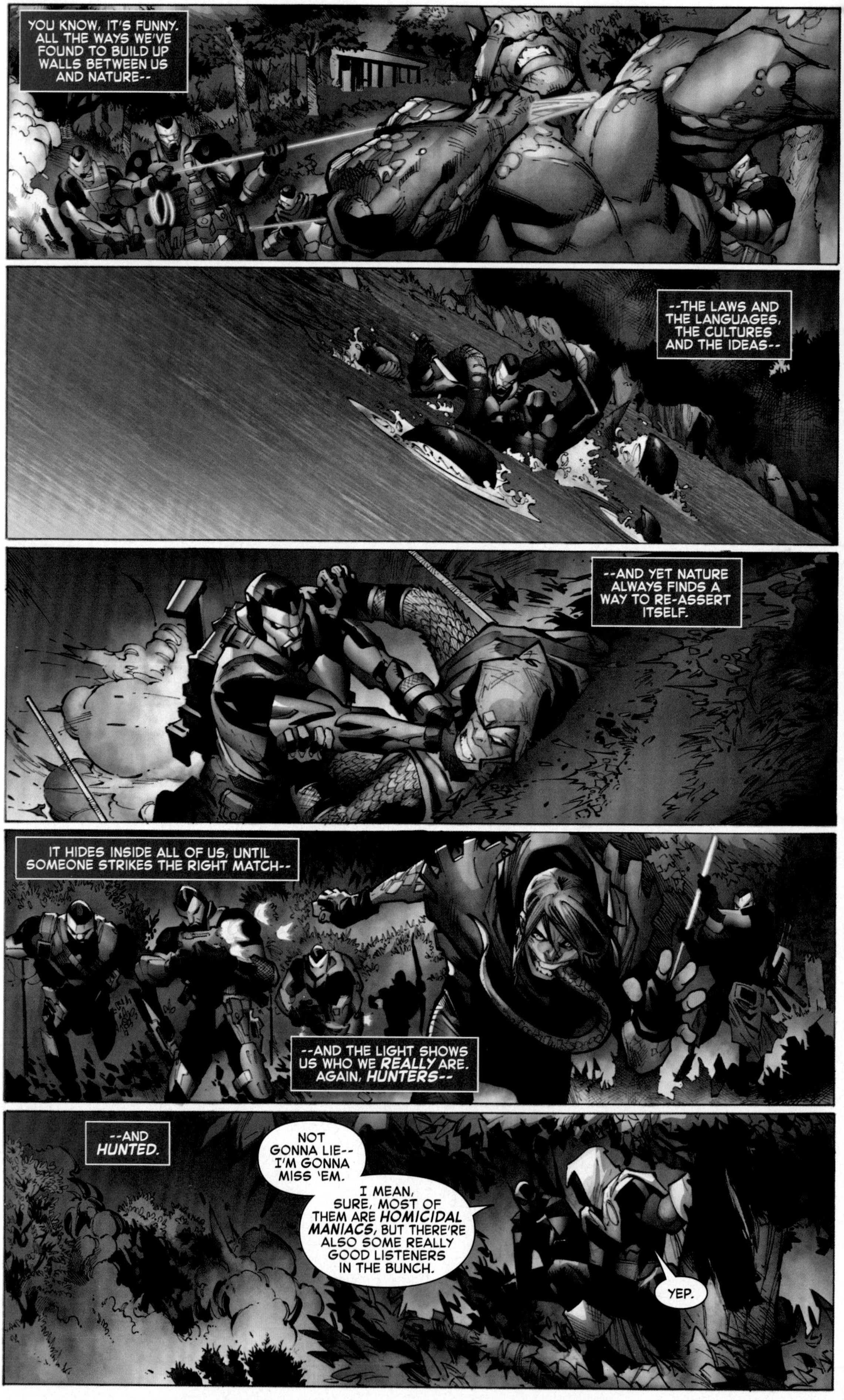
YOU KNOW, IT'S FUNNY. ALL THE WAYS WE'VE FOUND TO BUILD UP WALLS BETWEEN US AND NATURE--
--THE LAWS AND THE LANGUAGES, THE CULTURES AND THE IDEAS--
--AND YET NATURE ALWAYS FINDS A WAY TO RE-ASSERT ITSELF.
IT HIDES INSIDE ALL OF US, UNTIL SOMEONE STRIKES THE RIGHT MATCH--
--AND THE LIGHT SHOWS US WHO WE REALLY ARE. AGAIN, HUNTERS--
--AND HUNTED.
NOT GONNA LIE-- I'M GONNA MISS 'EM.
I MEAN, SURE, MOST OF THEM ARE HOMICIDAL MANIACS, BUT THERE'RE ALSO SOME REALLY GOOD LISTENERS IN THE BUNCH.
YEP.

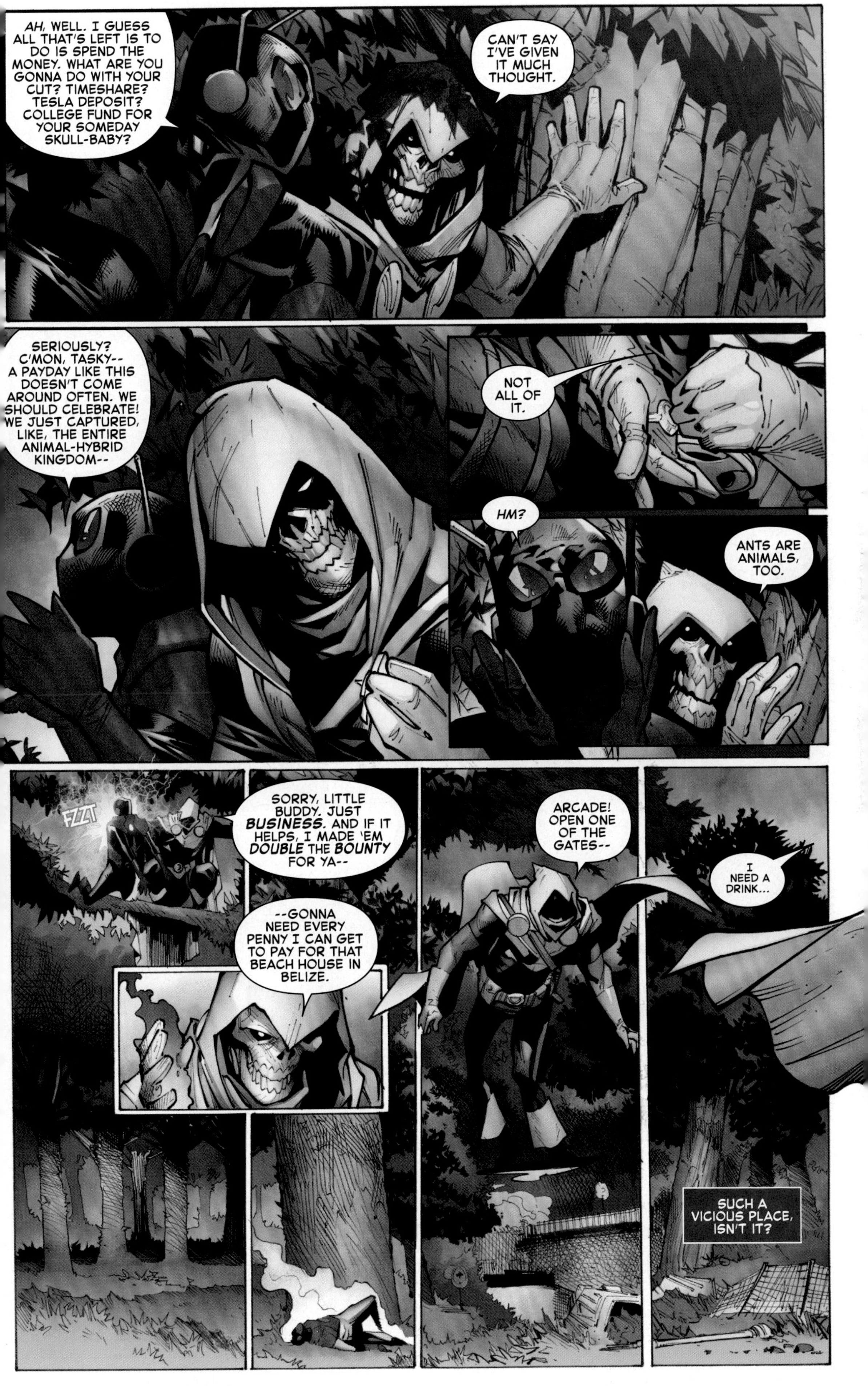
AH, WELL. I GUESS ALL THAT'S LEFT IS TO DO IS SPEND THE MONEY. WHAT ARE YOU GONNA DO WITH YOUR CUT? TIMESHARE? TESLA DEPOSIT? COLLEGE FUND FOR YOUR SOMEDAY SKULL-BABY?
CAN'T SAY I'VE GIVEN IT MUCH THOUGHT.
SERIOUSLY? C'MON, TASKY-- A PAYDAY LIKE THIS DOESN'T COME AROUND OFTEN. WE SHOULD CELEBRATE! WE JUST CAPTURED, LIKE, THE ENTIRE ANIMAL-HYBRID KINGDOM--
NOT ALL OF IT.
HM?
ANTS ARE ANIMALS, TOO.
FZZT
SORRY, LITTLE BUDDY. JUST BUSINESS. AND IF IT HELPS, I MADE 'EM DOUBLE THE BOUNTY FOR YA--
--GONNA NEED EVERY PENNY I CAN GET TO PAY FOR THAT BEACH HOUSE IN BELIZE.
ARCADE! OPEN ONE OF THE GATES--
I NEED A DRINK...
SUCH A VICIOUS PLACE, ISN'T IT?

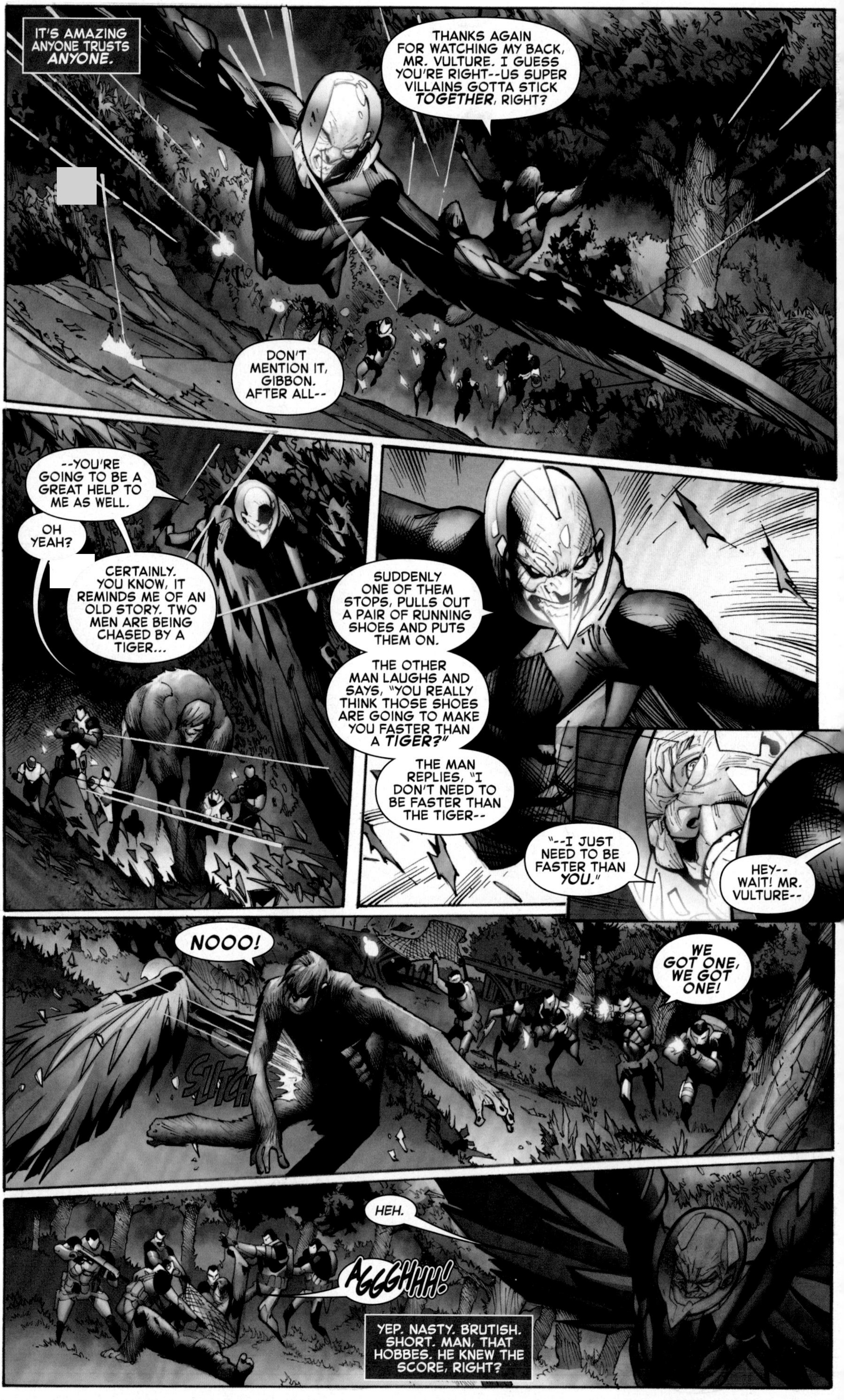
IT'S AMAZING ANYONE TRUSTS ANYONE.
THANKS AGAIN FOR WATCHING MY BACK, MR. VULTURE. I GUESS YOU'RE RIGHT--US SUPER VILLAINS GOTTA STICK TOGETHER, RIGHT?
DON'T MENTION IT, GIBBON. AFTER ALL--
--YOU'RE GOING TO BE A GREAT HELP TO ME AS WELL.
OH YEAH?
CERTAINLY. YOU KNOW, IT REMINDS ME OF AN OLD STORY. TWO MEN ARE BEING CHASED BY A TIGER...
SUDDENLY ONE OF THEM STOPS, PULLS OUT A PAIR OF RUNNING SHOES AND PUTS THEM ON.
THE OTHER MAN LAUGHS AND SAYS, "YOU REALLY THINK THOSE SHOES ARE GOING TO MAKE YOU FASTER THAN A TIGER?"
THE MAN REPLIES, "I DON'T NEED TO BE FASTER THAN THE TIGER--
"--I JUST NEED TO BE FASTER THAN YOU."
HEY-- WAIT! MR. VULTURE--
NOOO!
SLITCH
WE GOT ONE, WE GOT ONE!
HEH.
AGGGHHH!
YEP. NASTY. BRUTISH. SHORT. MAN, THAT HOBBES. HE KNEW THE SCORE, RIGHT?

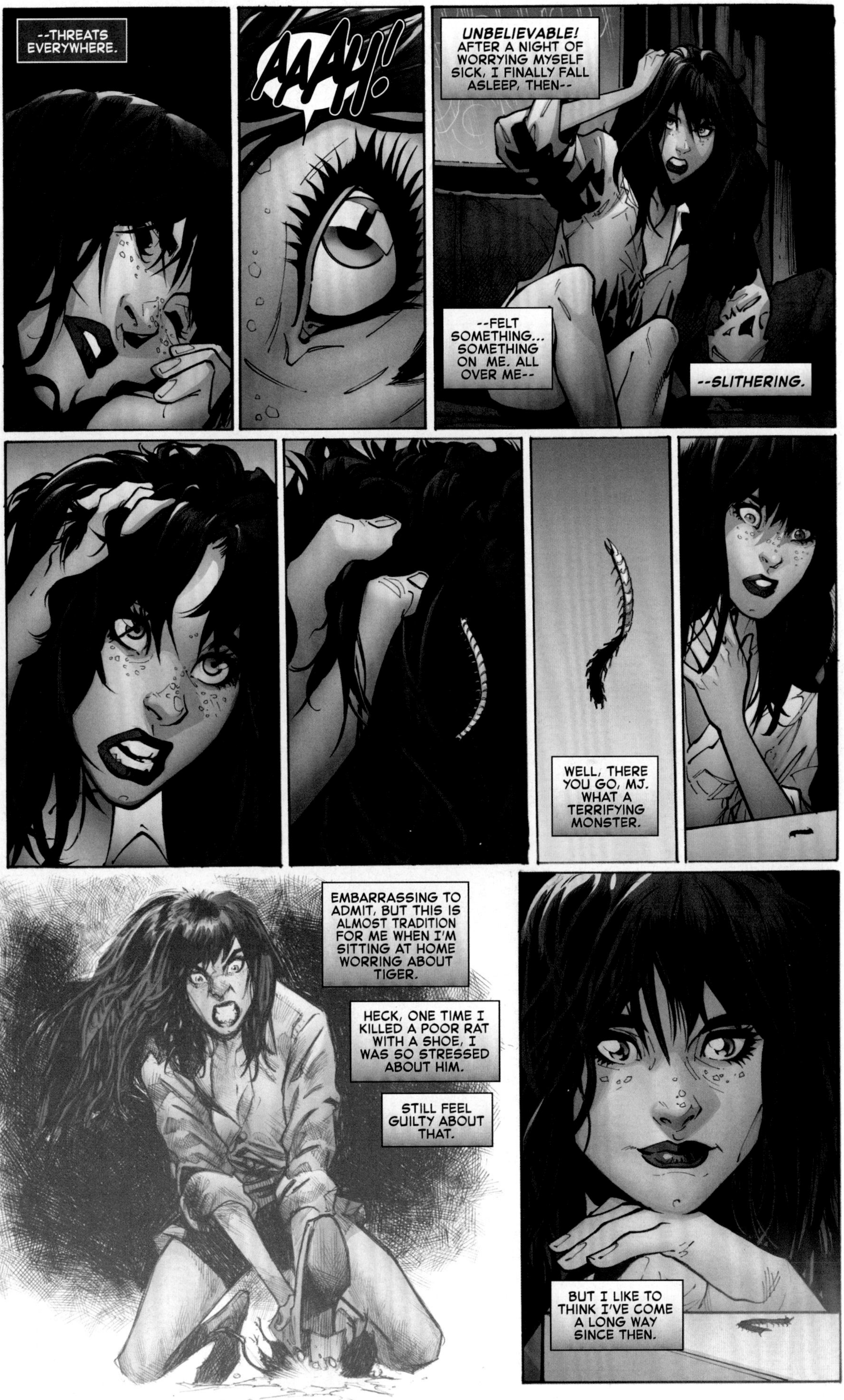
--THREATS EVERYWHERE.
AAAH!
UNBELIEVABLE! AFTER A NIGHT OF WORRYING MYSELF SICK, I FINALLY FALL ASLEEP, THEN--
--FELT SOMETHING... SOMETHING ON ME. ALL OVER ME--
--SLITHERING.
WELL, THERE YOU GO, MJ. WHAT A TERRIFYING MONSTER.
EMBARRASSING TO ADMIT, BUT THIS IS ALMOST TRADITION FOR ME WHEN I'M SITTING AT HOME WORRING ABOUT TIGER.
HECK, ONE TIME I KILLED A POOR RAT WITH A SHOE, I WAS SO STRESSED ABOUT HIM.
STILL FEEL GUILTY ABOUT THAT.
BUT I LIKE TO THINK I'VE COME A LONG WAY SINCE THEN.

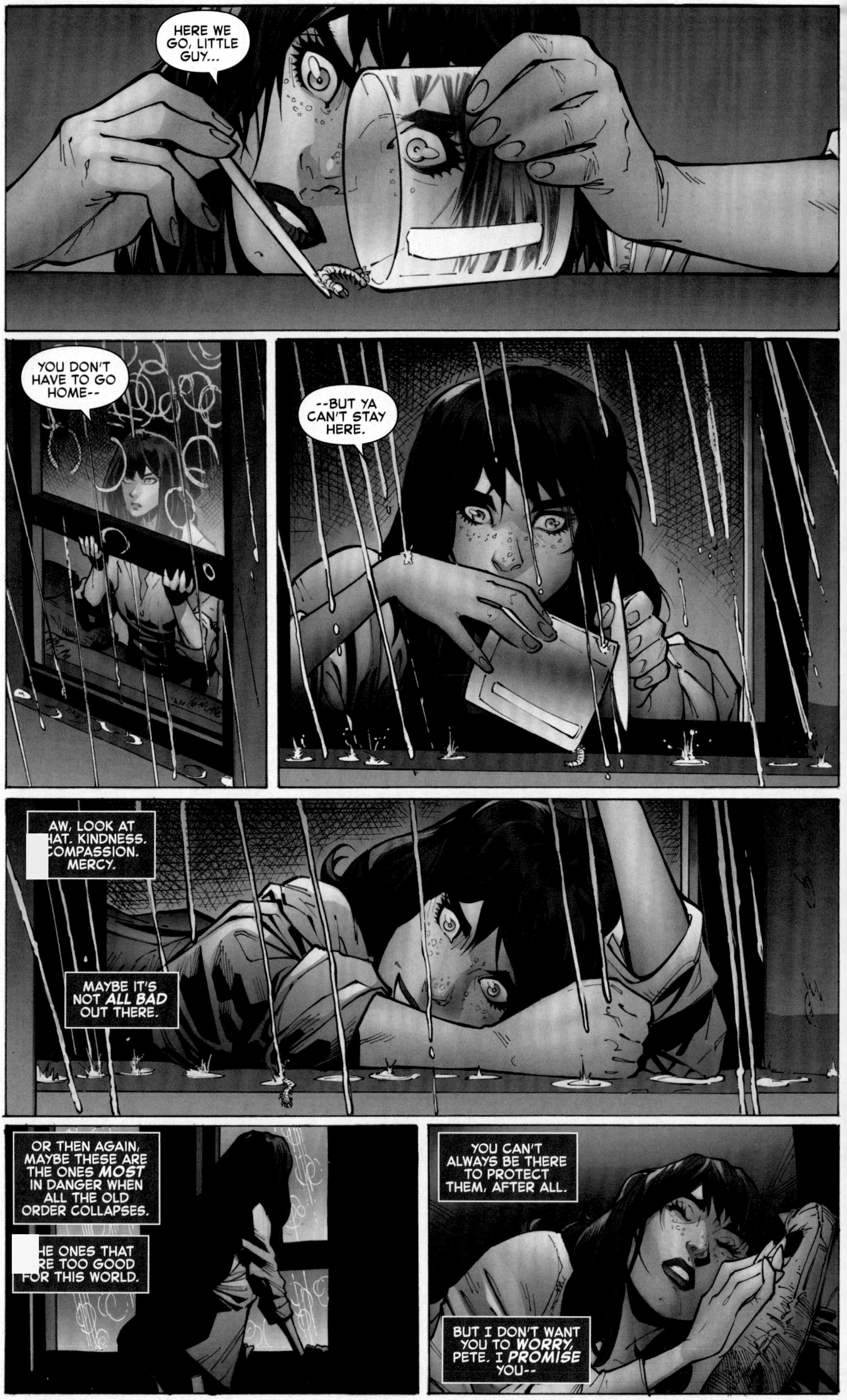
HERE WE GO, LITTLE GUY...
YOU DON'T HAVE TO GO HOME--
--BUT YA CAN'T STAY HERE.
AW, LOOK AT HAT. KINDNESS. COMPASSION. MERCY.
MAYBE IT'S NOT ALL BAD OUT THERE.
OR THEN AGAIN, MAYBE THESE ARE THE ONES MOST IN DANGER WHEN ALL THE OLD ORDER COLLAPSES.
HE ONES THAT RE TOO GOOD FOR THIS WORLD.
YOU CAN'T ALWAYS BE THERE TO PROTECT THEM, AFTER ALL.
BUT I DON'T WANT YOU TO WORRY, PETE. I PROMISE YOU--

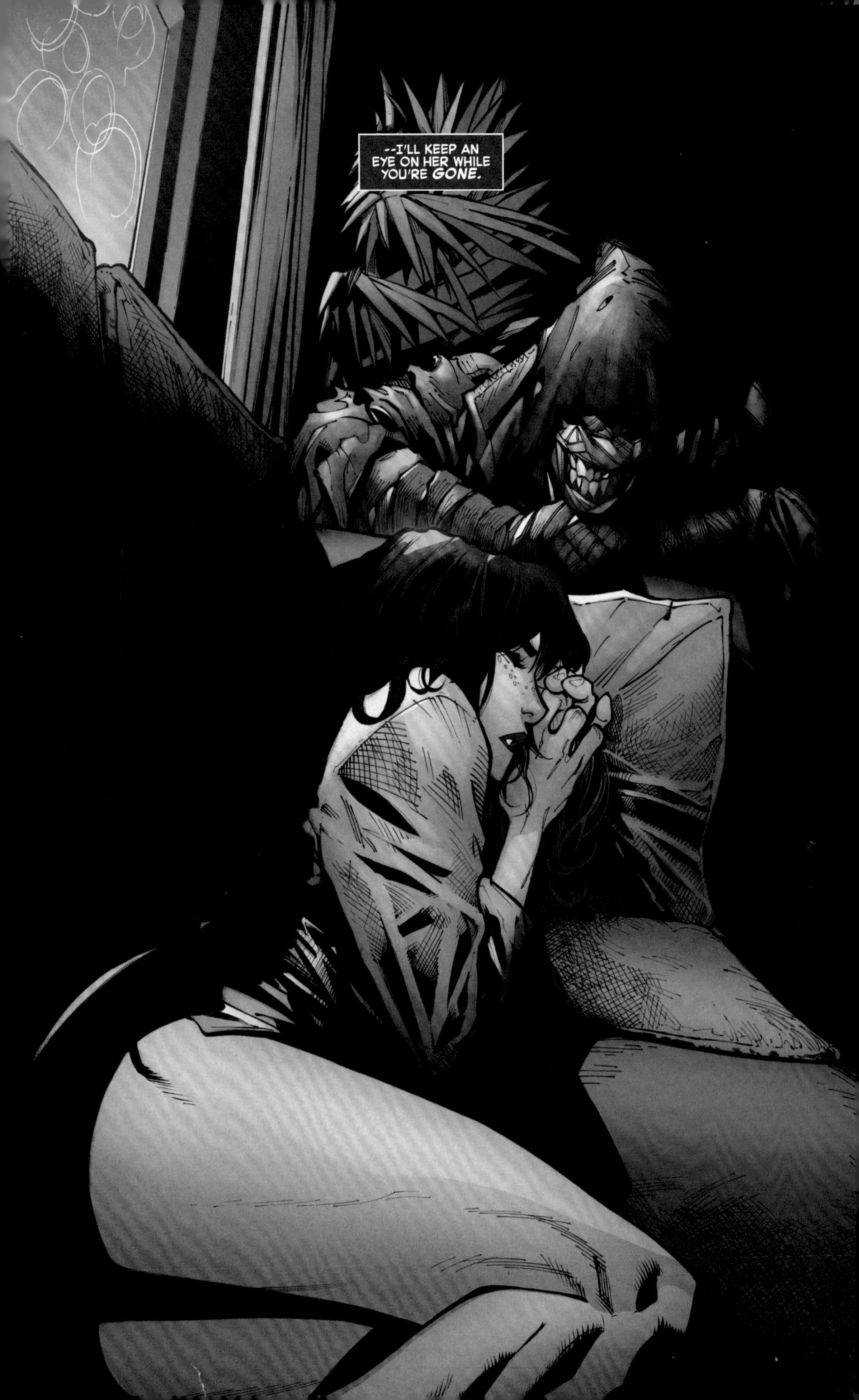
--I'LL KEEP AN EYE ON HER WHILE YOU'RE GONE.

13.HU

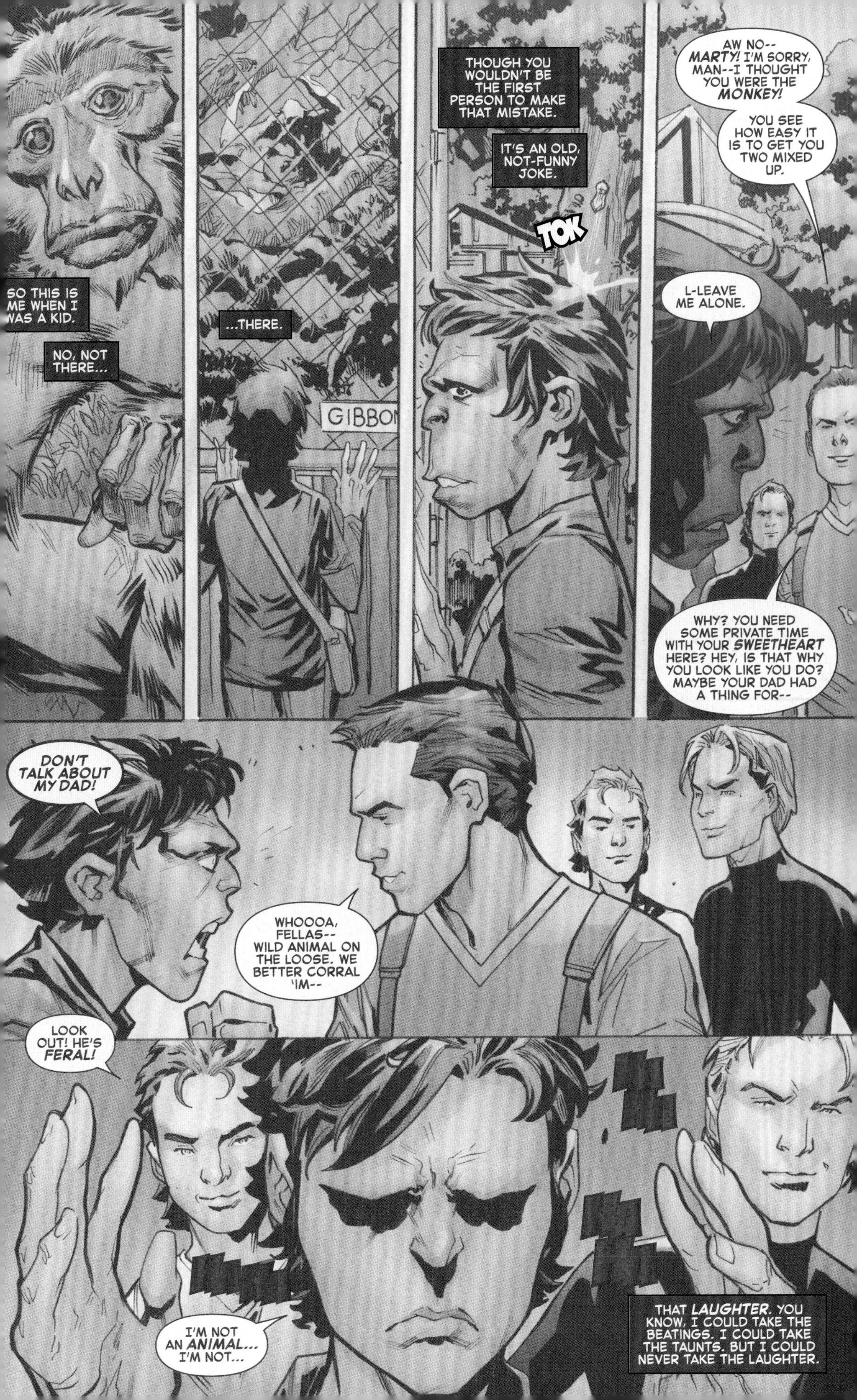

SO THIS IS ME WHEN I WAS A KID.
NO, NOT THERE...
...THERE.
GIBBON
THOUGH YOU WOULDN'T BE THE FIRST PERSON TO MAKE THAT MISTAKE.
IT'S AN OLD, NOT-FUNNY JOKE.
TOK
AW NO-- MARTY! I'M SORRY, MAN--I THOUGHT YOU WERE THE MONKEY!
YOU SEE HOW EASY IT IS TO GET YOU TWO MIXED UP.
L-LEAVE ME ALONE.
WHY? YOU NEED SOME PRIVATE TIME WITH YOUR SWEETHEART HERE? HEY, IS THAT WHY YOU LOOK LIKE YOU DO? MAYBE YOUR DAD HAD A THING FOR--
DON'T TALK ABOUT MY DAD!
WHOOOA, FELLAS-- WILD ANIMAL ON THE LOOSE. WE BETTER CORRAL 'IM--
LOOK OUT! HE'S FERAL!
I'M NOT AN ANIMAL... I'M NOT...
THAT LAUGHTER. YOU KNOW, I COULD TAKE THE BEATINGS. I COULD TAKE THE TAUNTS. BUT I COULD NEVER TAKE THE LAUGHTER.

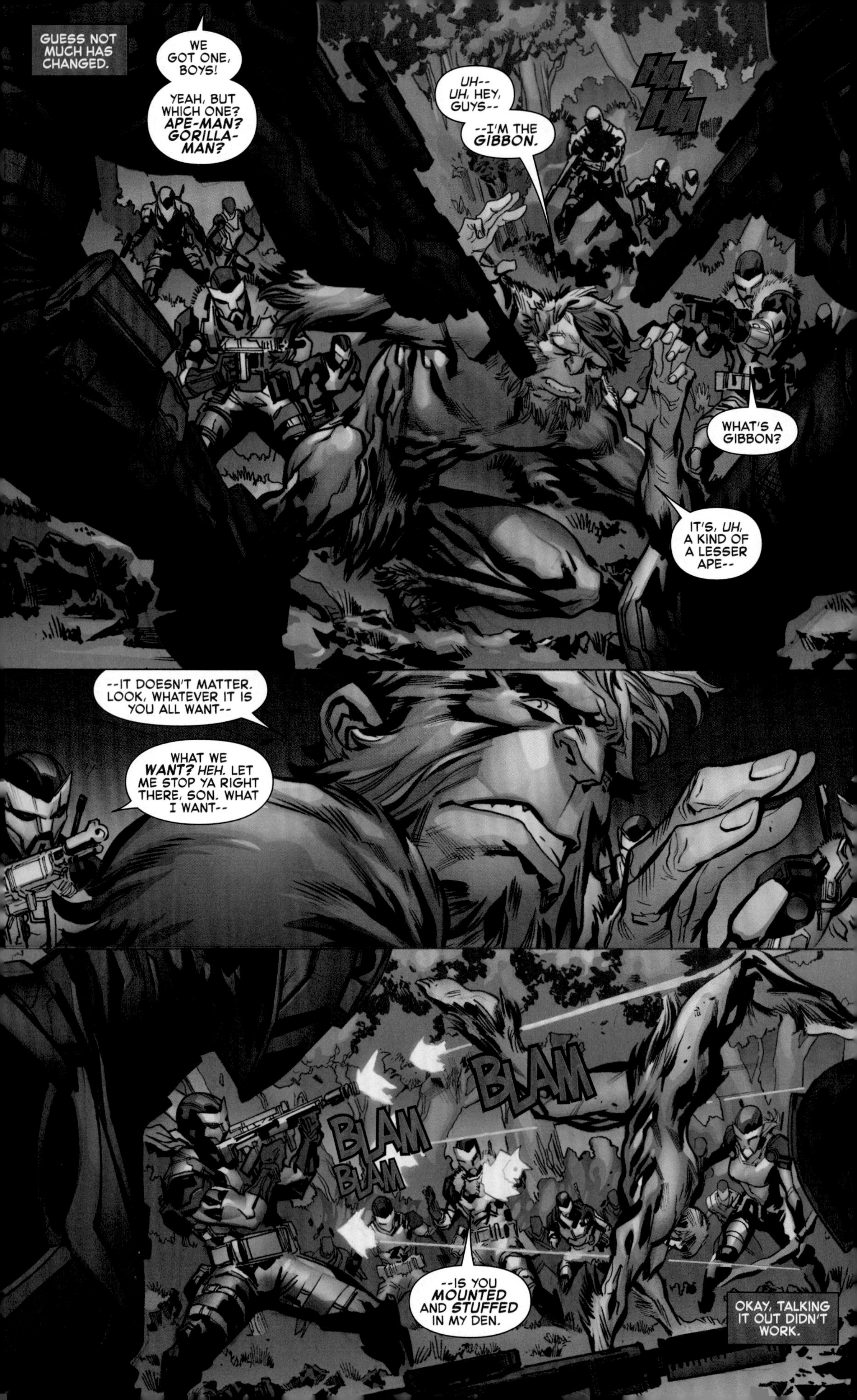

GUESS NOT MUCH HAS CHANGED.
WE GOT ONE, BOYS!
YEAH, BUT WHICH ONE? *APE-MAN? GORILLA-MAN?*
UH-- *UH*, HEY, GUYS--
--I'M THE *GIBBON.*
WHAT'S A GIBBON?
IT'S, *UH*, A KIND OF A LESSER APE--
--IT DOESN'T MATTER. LOOK, WHATEVER IT IS YOU ALL WANT--
WHAT WE *WANT? HEH.* LET ME STOP YA RIGHT THERE, SON. WHAT I WANT--
BLAM
BLAM
BLAM
--IS YOU *MOUNTED* AND *STUFFED* IN MY DEN.
OKAY, TALKING IT OUT DIDN'T WORK.

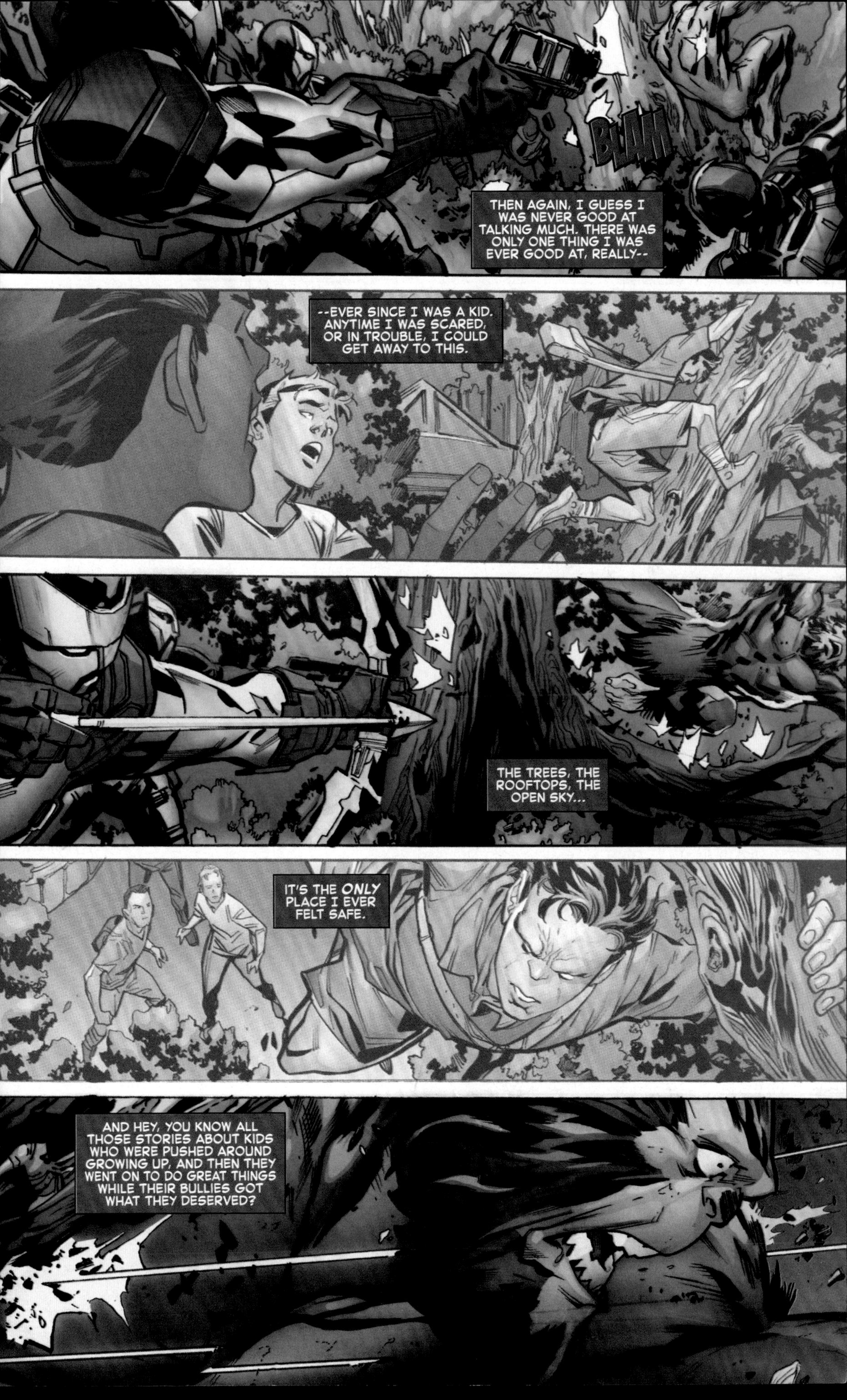
BLAM
THEN AGAIN, I GUESS I WAS NEVER GOOD AT TALKING MUCH. THERE WAS ONLY ONE THING I WAS EVER GOOD AT, REALLY--
--EVER SINCE I WAS A KID. ANYTIME I WAS SCARED, OR IN TROUBLE, I COULD GET AWAY TO THIS.
THE TREES, THE ROOFTOPS, THE OPEN SKY...
IT'S THE *ONLY* PLACE I EVER FELT SAFE.
AND HEY, YOU KNOW ALL THOSE STORIES ABOUT KIDS WHO WERE PUSHED AROUND GROWING UP, AND THEN THEY WENT ON TO DO GREAT THINGS WHILE THEIR BULLIES GOT WHAT THEY DESERVED?

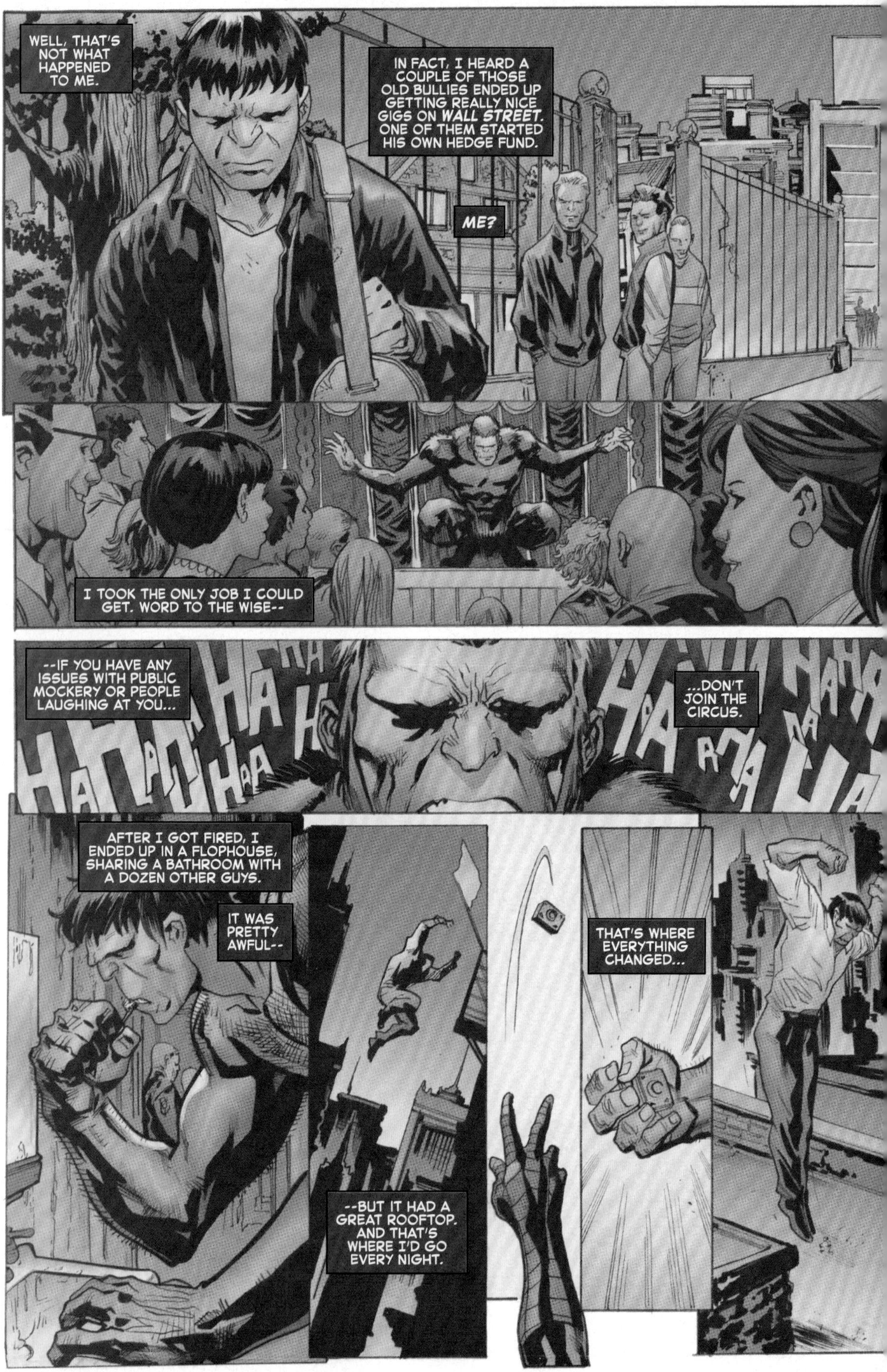
WELL, THAT'S NOT WHAT HAPPENED TO ME.
IN FACT, I HEARD A COUPLE OF THOSE OLD BULLIES ENDED UP GETTING REALLY NICE GIGS ON WALL STREET. ONE OF THEM STARTED HIS OWN HEDGE FUND.
ME?
I TOOK THE ONLY JOB I COULD GET. WORD TO THE WISE--
--IF YOU HAVE ANY ISSUES WITH PUBLIC MOCKERY OR PEOPLE LAUGHING AT YOU...
...DON'T JOIN THE CIRCUS.
AFTER I GOT FIRED, I ENDED UP IN A FLOPHOUSE, SHARING A BATHROOM WITH A DOZEN OTHER GUYS.
IT WAS PRETTY AWFUL--
--BUT IT HAD A GREAT ROOFTOP. AND THAT'S WHERE I'D GO EVERY NIGHT.
THAT'S WHERE EVERYTHING CHANGED...

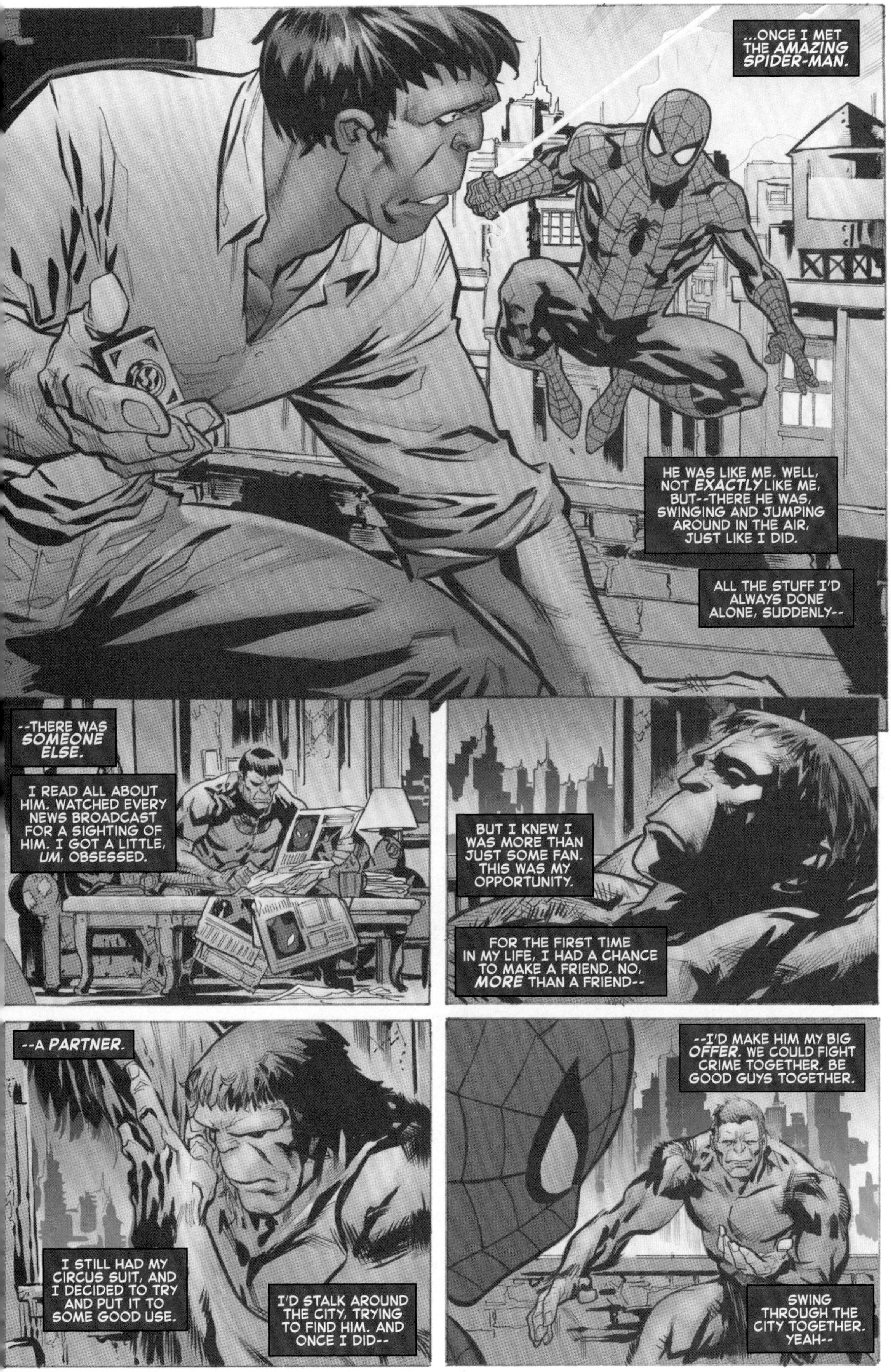
...ONCE I MET THE AMAZING SPIDER-MAN.
HE WAS LIKE ME. WELL, NOT EXACTLY LIKE ME, BUT--THERE HE WAS, SWINGING AND JUMPING AROUND IN THE AIR, JUST LIKE I DID.
ALL THE STUFF I'D ALWAYS DONE ALONE, SUDDENLY--
--THERE WAS SOMEONE ELSE.
I READ ALL ABOUT HIM. WATCHED EVERY NEWS BROADCAST FOR A SIGHTING OF HIM. I GOT A LITTLE, UM, OBSESSED.
BUT I KNEW I WAS MORE THAN JUST SOME FAN. THIS WAS MY OPPORTUNITY.
FOR THE FIRST TIME IN MY LIFE, I HAD A CHANCE TO MAKE A FRIEND. NO, MORE THAN A FRIEND--
--A PARTNER.
I STILL HAD MY CIRCUS SUIT, AND I DECIDED TO TRY AND PUT IT TO SOME GOOD USE.
I'D STALK AROUND THE CITY, TRYING TO FIND HIM. AND ONCE I DID--
--I'D MAKE HIM MY BIG OFFER. WE COULD FIGHT CRIME TOGETHER. BE GOOD GUYS TOGETHER.
SWING THROUGH THE CITY TOGETHER. YEAH--

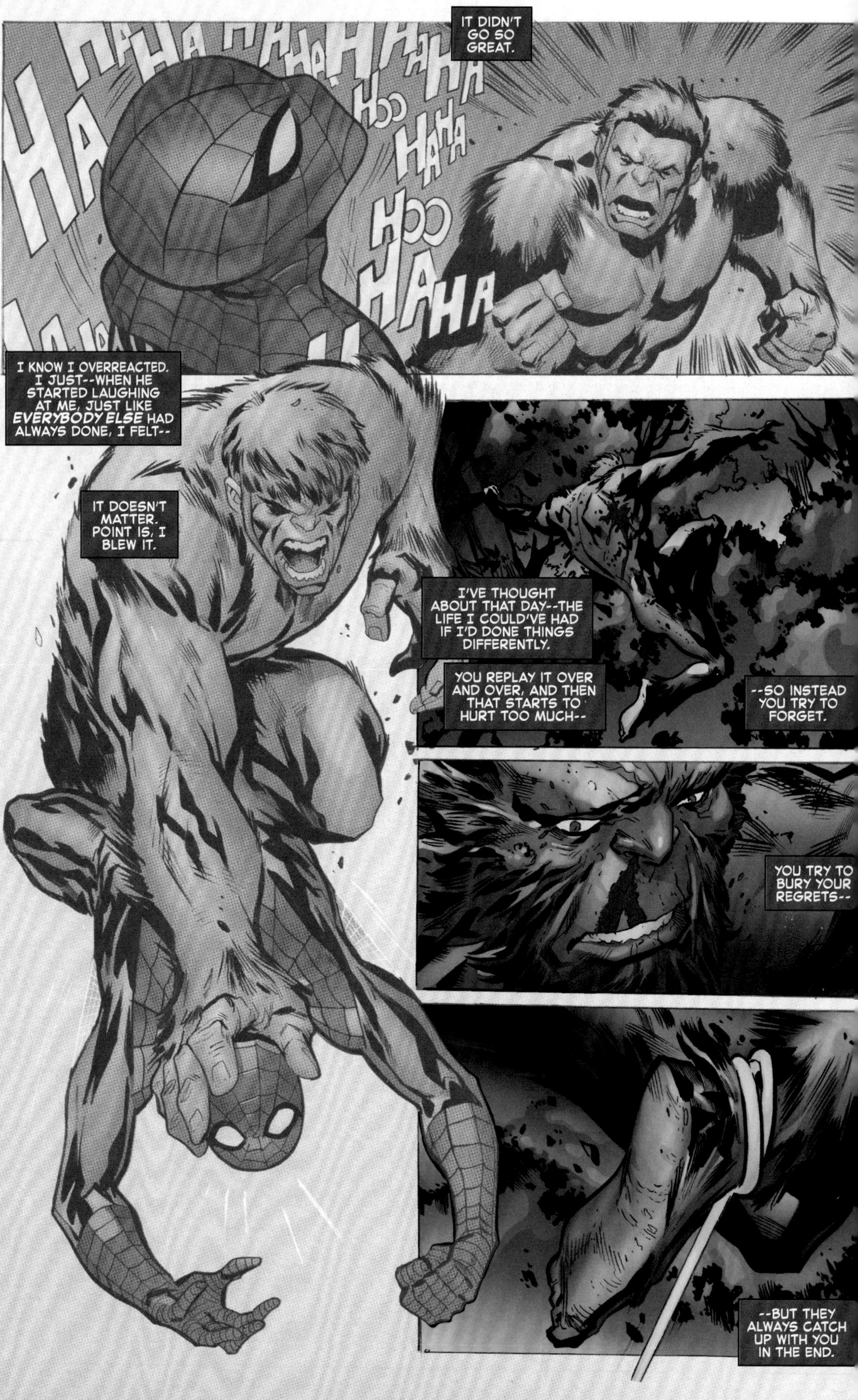
IT DIDN'T GO SO GREAT.
HA HA HA HA HA HA HA HA HA HA HOO HA HA HOO HA HA HA
I KNOW I OVERREACTED. I JUST--WHEN HE STARTED LAUGHING AT ME, JUST LIKE EVERYBODY ELSE HAD ALWAYS DONE, I FELT--
IT DOESN'T MATTER. POINT IS, I BLEW IT.
I'VE THOUGHT ABOUT THAT DAY--THE LIFE I COULD'VE HAD IF I'D DONE THINGS DIFFERENTLY.
YOU REPLAY IT OVER AND OVER, AND THEN THAT STARTS TO HURT TOO MUCH--
--SO INSTEAD YOU TRY TO FORGET.
YOU TRY TO BURY YOUR REGRETS--
--BUT THEY ALWAYS CATCH UP WITH YOU IN THE END.

GOT 'IM!

SWEET! DON'T LET HIM GET AWAY AGAIN!

THAT FACE-- I *KNOW* THAT FACE. IT LOOKS LIKE--

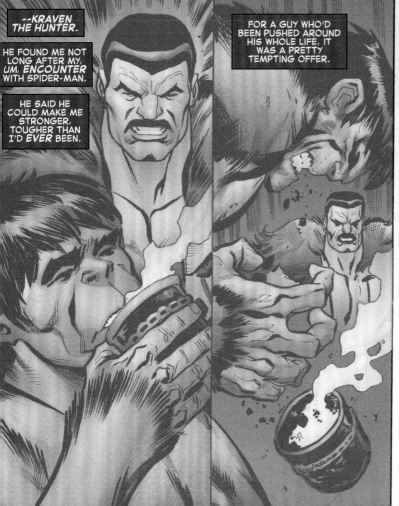

--KRAVEN THE HUNTER.

HE FOUND ME NOT LONG AFTER MY, UM, *ENCOUNTER* WITH SPIDER-MAN.

HE SAID HE COULD MAKE ME STRONGER, TOUGHER THAN I'D *EVER* BEEN.

FOR A GUY WHO'D BEEN PUSHED AROUND HIS WHOLE LIFE, IT WAS A PRETTY TEMPTING OFFER.

BUT ALL I CAN REMEMBER ABOUT DRINKING THAT POTION IS HOW MUCH IT HURT.

AND HOW IT TURNED ME INTO AN EVEN BIGGER FREAK. I DIDN'T NEED THE CIRCUS SUIT ANYMORE--

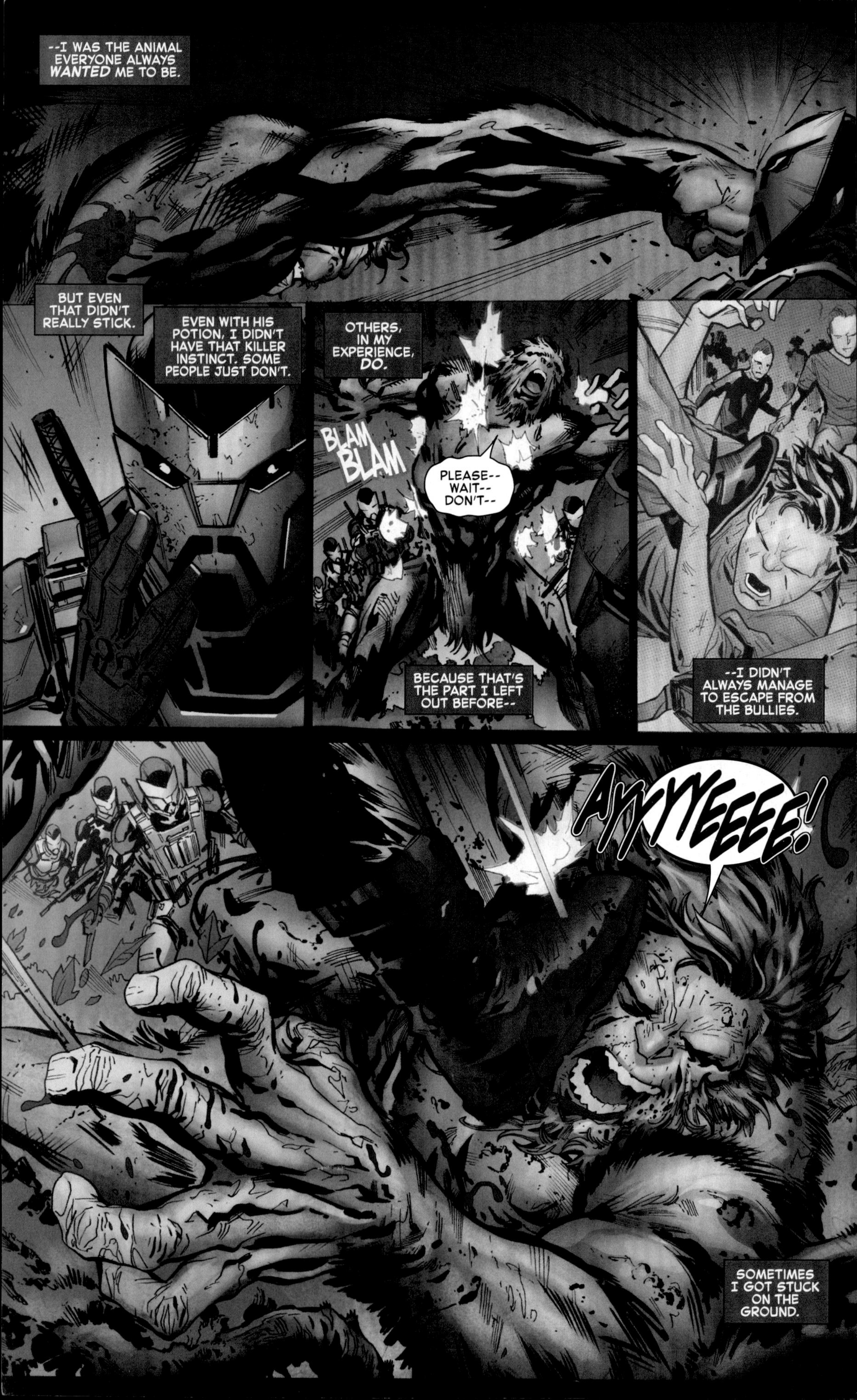
--I WAS THE ANIMAL EVERYONE ALWAYS *WANTED* ME TO BE.
BUT EVEN THAT DIDN'T REALLY STICK.
EVEN WITH HIS POTION, I DIDN'T HAVE THAT KILLER INSTINCT. SOME PEOPLE JUST DON'T.
OTHERS, IN MY EXPERIENCE, *DO*.
BLAM BLAM
PLEASE-- WAIT-- DON'T--
BECAUSE THAT'S THE PART I LEFT OUT BEFORE--
--I DIDN'T ALWAYS MANAGE TO ESCAPE FROM THE BULLIES.
AYYYEEEE!
SOMETIMES I GOT STUCK ON THE GROUND.

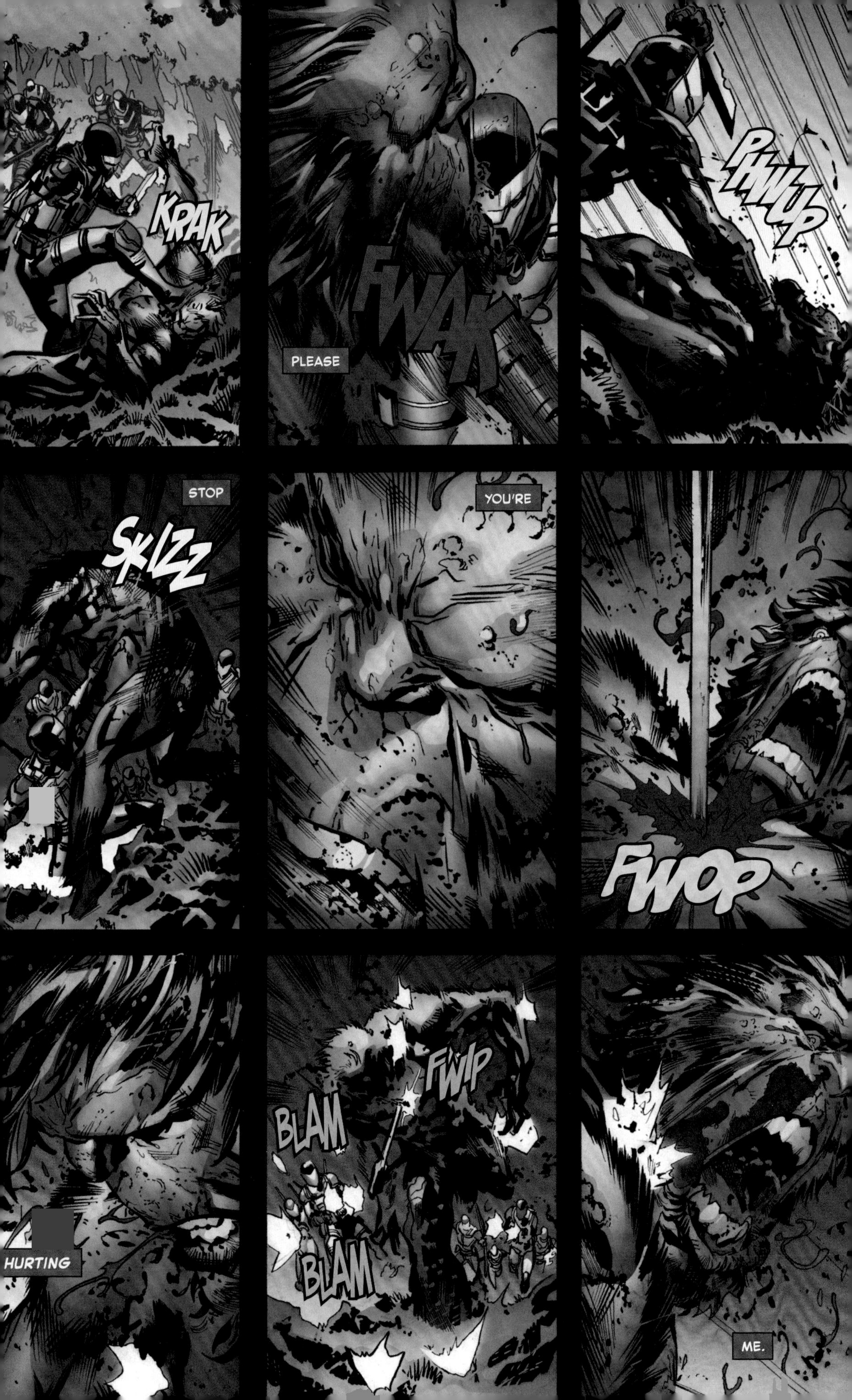
KRAK
PLEASE
FWAK
PHWUP
STOP
SKIZZ
YOU'RE
FWOP
HURTING
FWIP
BLAM
BLAM
ME.

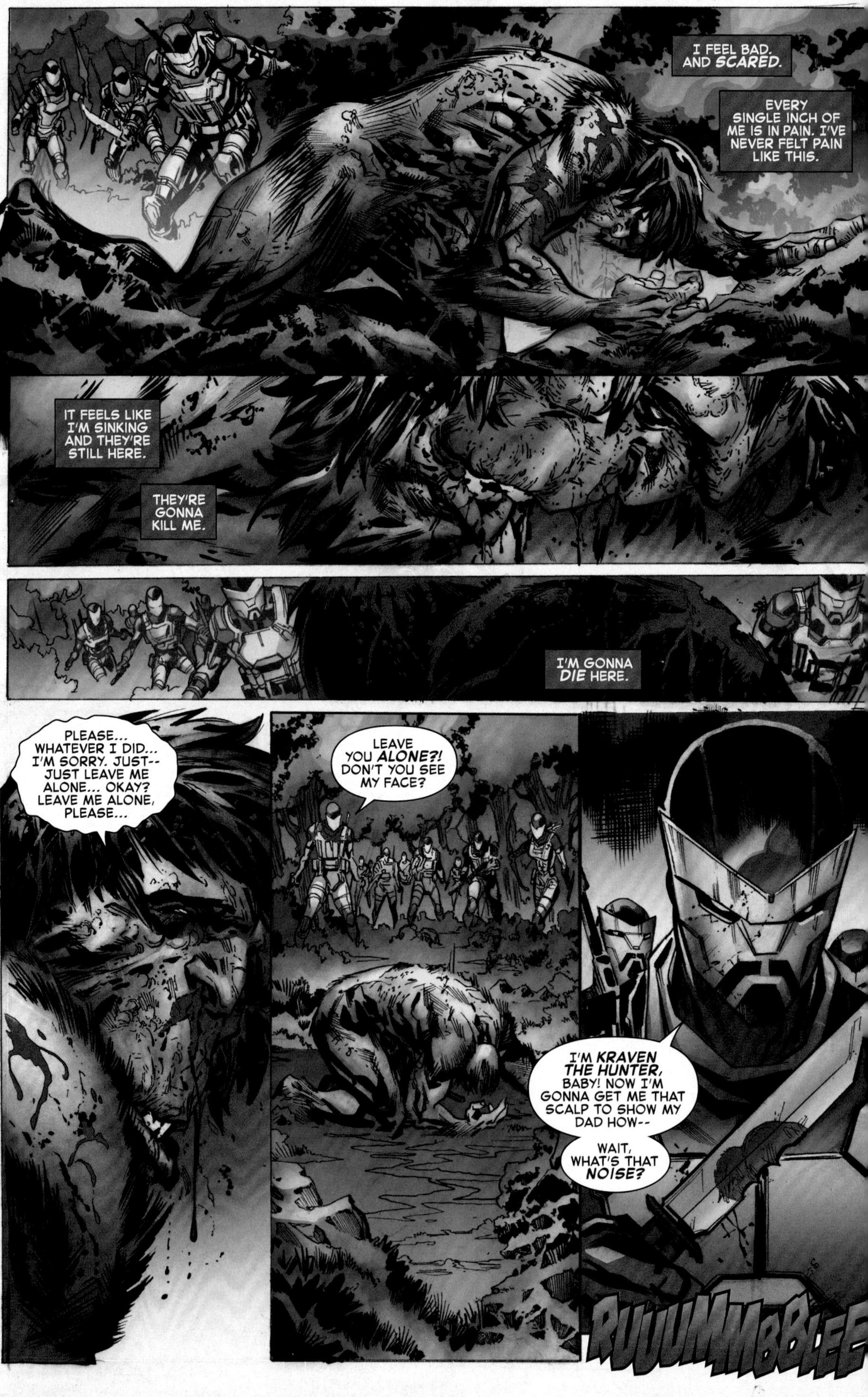

I FEEL BAD. AND SCARED.
EVERY SINGLE INCH OF ME IS IN PAIN. I'VE NEVER FELT PAIN LIKE THIS.
IT FEELS LIKE I'M SINKING AND THEY'RE STILL HERE.
THEY'RE GONNA KILL ME.
I'M GONNA DIE HERE.
PLEASE... WHATEVER I DID... I'M SORRY. JUST--JUST LEAVE ME ALONE... OKAY? LEAVE ME ALONE, PLEASE...
LEAVE YOU ALONE?! DON'T YOU SEE MY FACE?
I'M KRAVEN THE HUNTER, BABY! NOW I'M GONNA GET ME THAT SCALP TO SHOW MY DAD HOW--
WAIT, WHAT'S THAT NOISE?
RUUUMMBBLEE

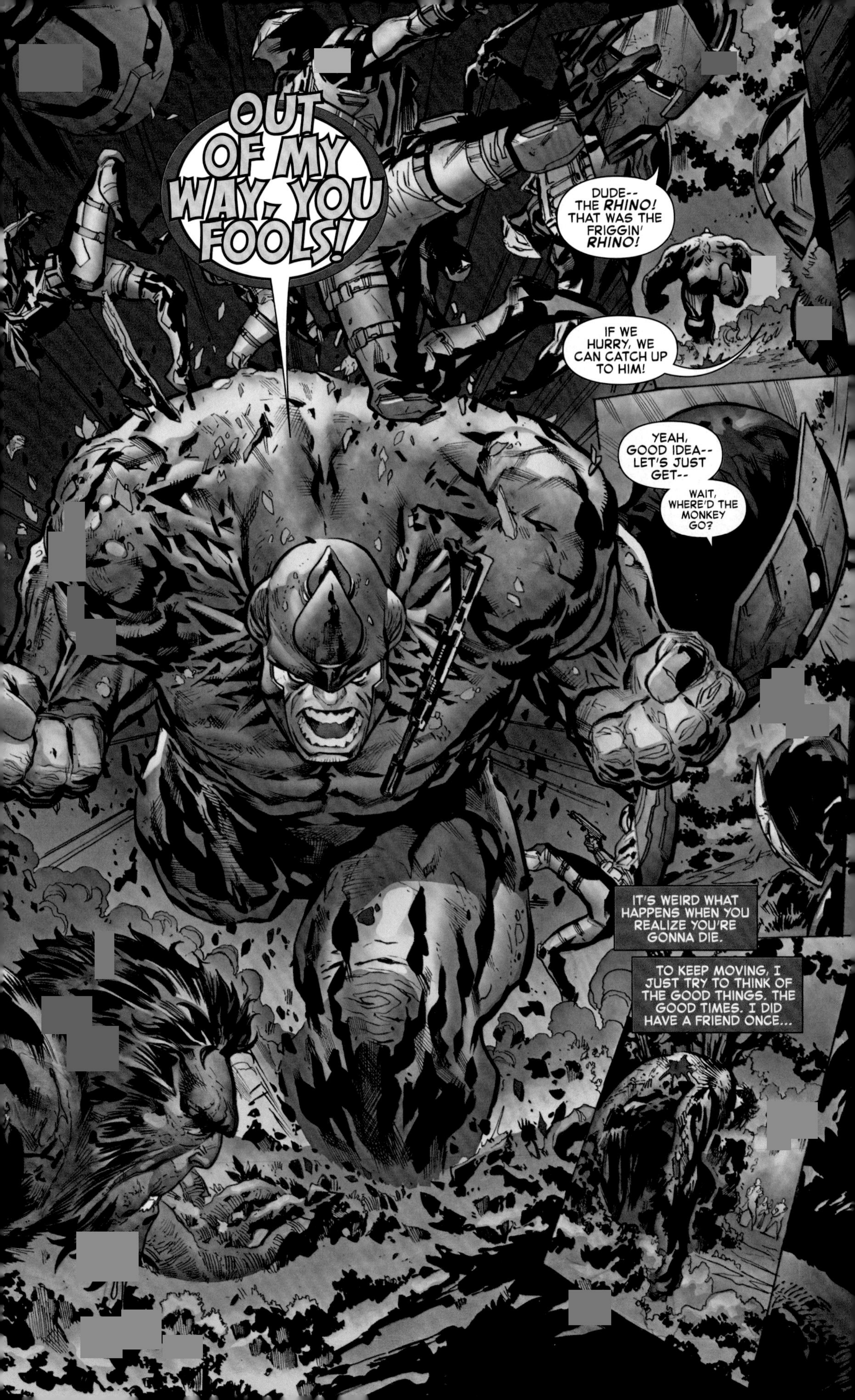
OUT OF MY WAY, YOU FOOLS!
DUDE-- THE *RHINO!* THAT WAS THE FRIGGIN' *RHINO!*
IF WE HURRY, WE CAN CATCH UP TO HIM!
YEAH, GOOD IDEA-- LET'S JUST GET--
WAIT, WHERE'D THE MONKEY GO?
IT'S WEIRD WHAT HAPPENS WHEN YOU REALIZE YOU'RE GONNA DIE.
TO KEEP MOVING, I JUST TRY TO THINK OF THE GOOD THINGS. THE GOOD TIMES. I DID HAVE A FRIEND ONCE...

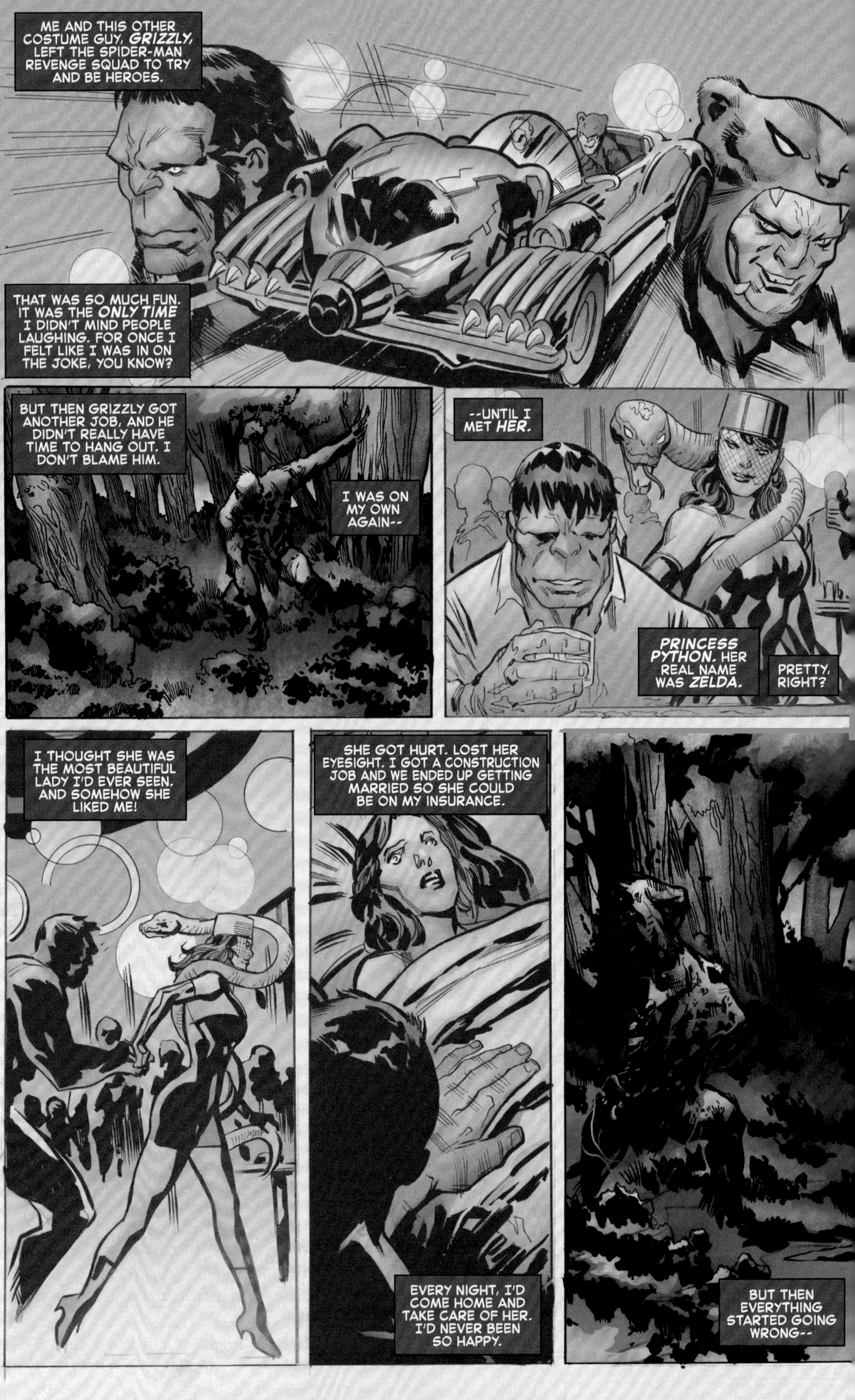

ME AND THIS OTHER COSTUME GUY, GRIZZLY, LEFT THE SPIDER-MAN REVENGE SQUAD TO TRY AND BE HEROES.
THAT WAS SO MUCH FUN. IT WAS THE ONLY TIME I DIDN'T MIND PEOPLE LAUGHING. FOR ONCE I FELT LIKE I WAS IN ON THE JOKE, YOU KNOW?
BUT THEN GRIZZLY GOT ANOTHER JOB, AND HE DIDN'T REALLY HAVE TIME TO HANG OUT. I DON'T BLAME HIM.
I WAS ON MY OWN AGAIN--
--UNTIL I MET HER.
PRINCESS PYTHON. HER REAL NAME WAS ZELDA.
PRETTY, RIGHT?
I THOUGHT SHE WAS THE MOST BEAUTIFUL LADY I'D EVER SEEN. AND SOMEHOW SHE LIKED ME!
SHE GOT HURT. LOST HER EYESIGHT. I GOT A CONSTRUCTION JOB AND WE ENDED UP GETTING MARRIED SO SHE COULD BE ON MY INSURANCE.
EVERY NIGHT, I'D COME HOME AND TAKE CARE OF HER. I'D NEVER BEEN SO HAPPY.
BUT THEN EVERYTHING STARTED GOING WRONG--

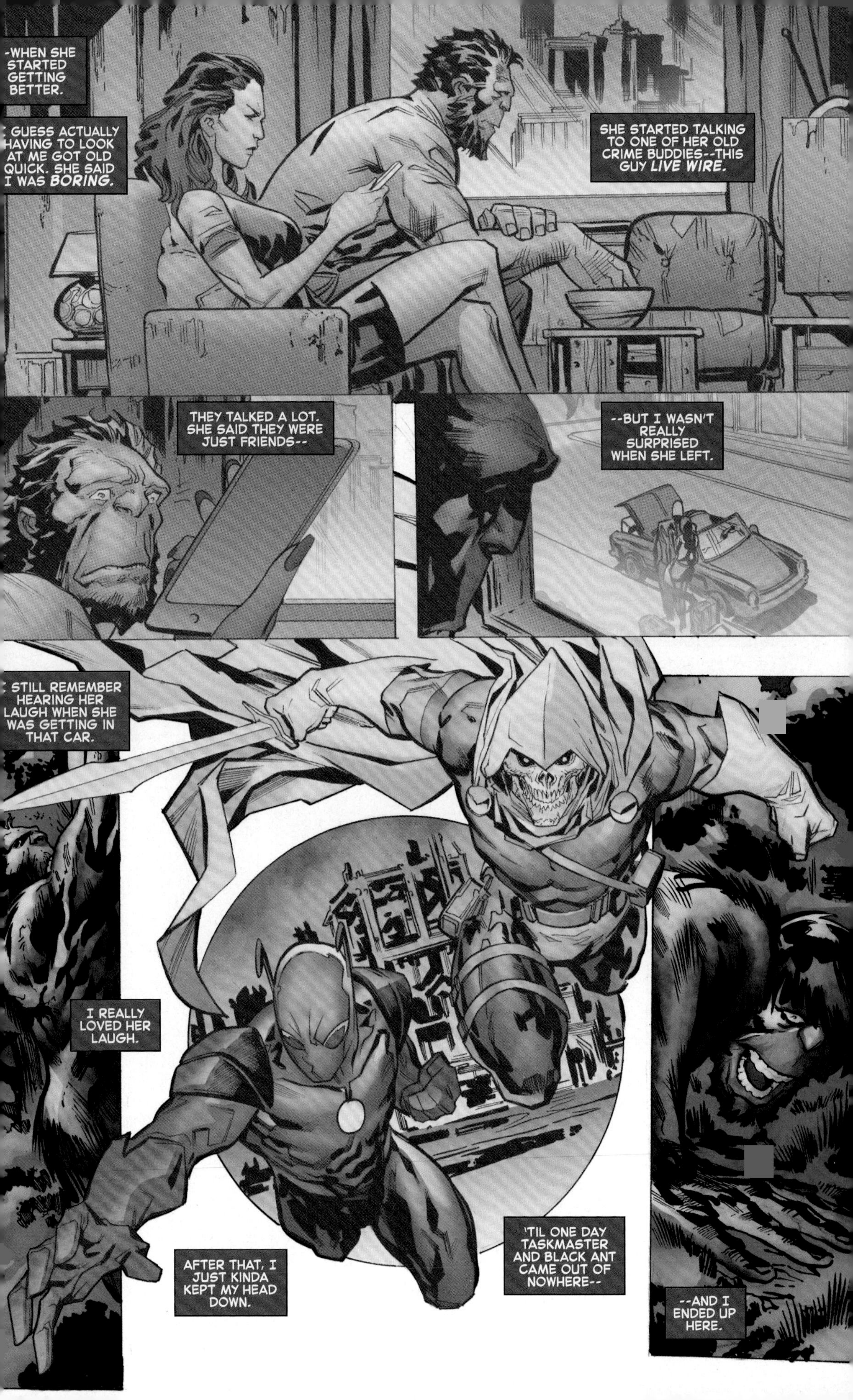
-WHEN SHE STARTED GETTING BETTER.
I GUESS ACTUALLY HAVING TO LOOK AT ME GOT OLD QUICK. SHE SAID I WAS BORING.
SHE STARTED TALKING TO ONE OF HER OLD CRIME BUDDIES--THIS GUY LIVE WIRE.
THEY TALKED A LOT. SHE SAID THEY WERE JUST FRIENDS--
--BUT I WASN'T REALLY SURPRISED WHEN SHE LEFT.
I STILL REMEMBER HEARING HER LAUGH WHEN SHE WAS GETTING IN THAT CAR.
I REALLY LOVED HER LAUGH.
AFTER THAT, I JUST KINDA KEPT MY HEAD DOWN.
'TIL ONE DAY TASKMASTER AND BLACK ANT CAME OUT OF NOWHERE--
--AND I ENDED UP HERE.

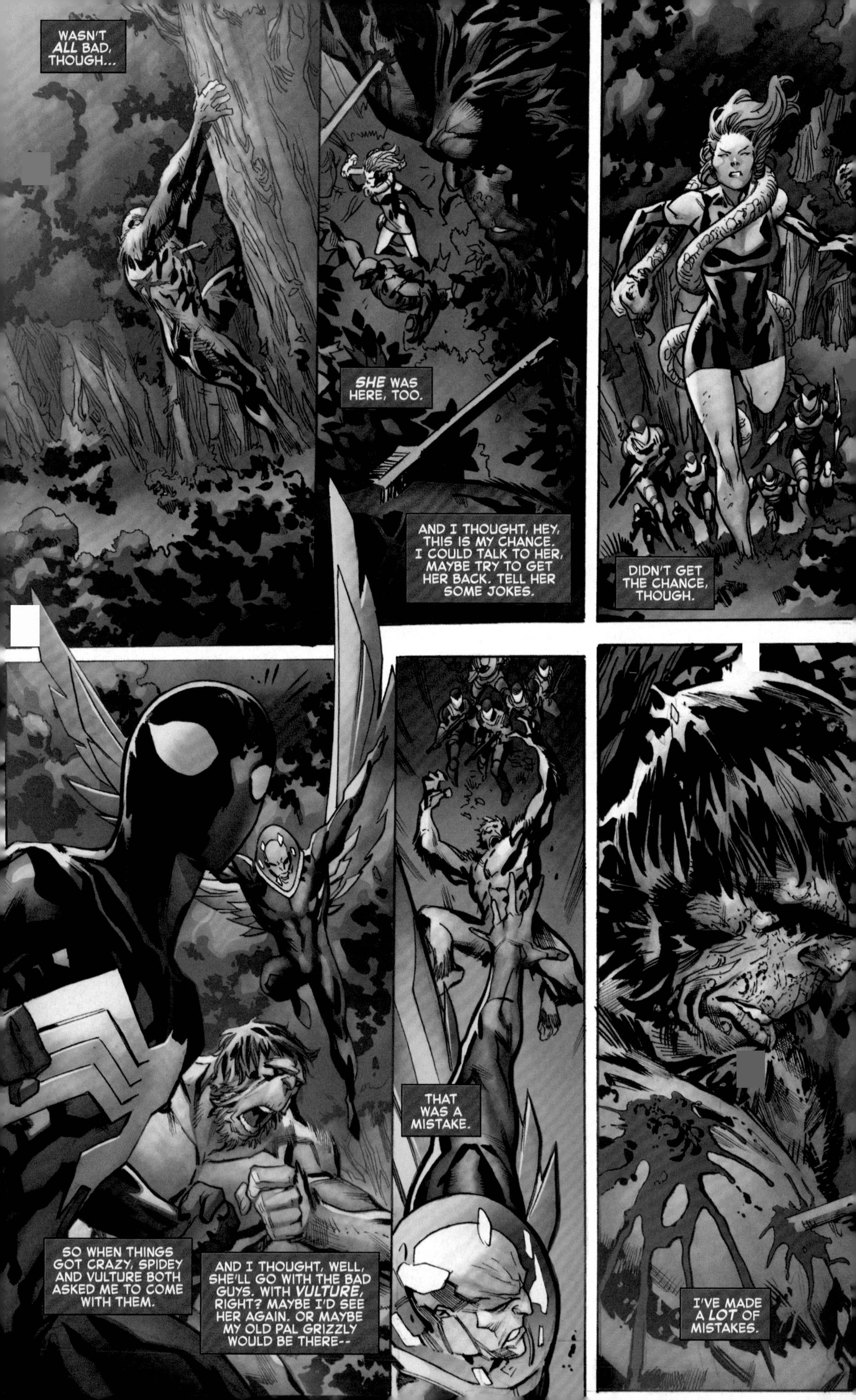
WASN'T ALL BAD, THOUGH...
SHE WAS HERE, TOO.
AND I THOUGHT, HEY, THIS IS MY CHANCE. I COULD TALK TO HER, MAYBE TRY TO GET HER BACK. TELL HER SOME JOKES.
DIDN'T GET THE CHANCE, THOUGH.
SO WHEN THINGS GOT CRAZY, SPIDEY AND VULTURE BOTH ASKED ME TO COME WITH THEM.
AND I THOUGHT, WELL, SHE'LL GO WITH THE BAD GUYS. WITH VULTURE, RIGHT? MAYBE I'D SEE HER AGAIN. OR MAYBE MY OLD PAL GRIZZLY WOULD BE THERE--
THAT WAS A MISTAKE.
I'VE MADE A LOT OF MISTAKES.

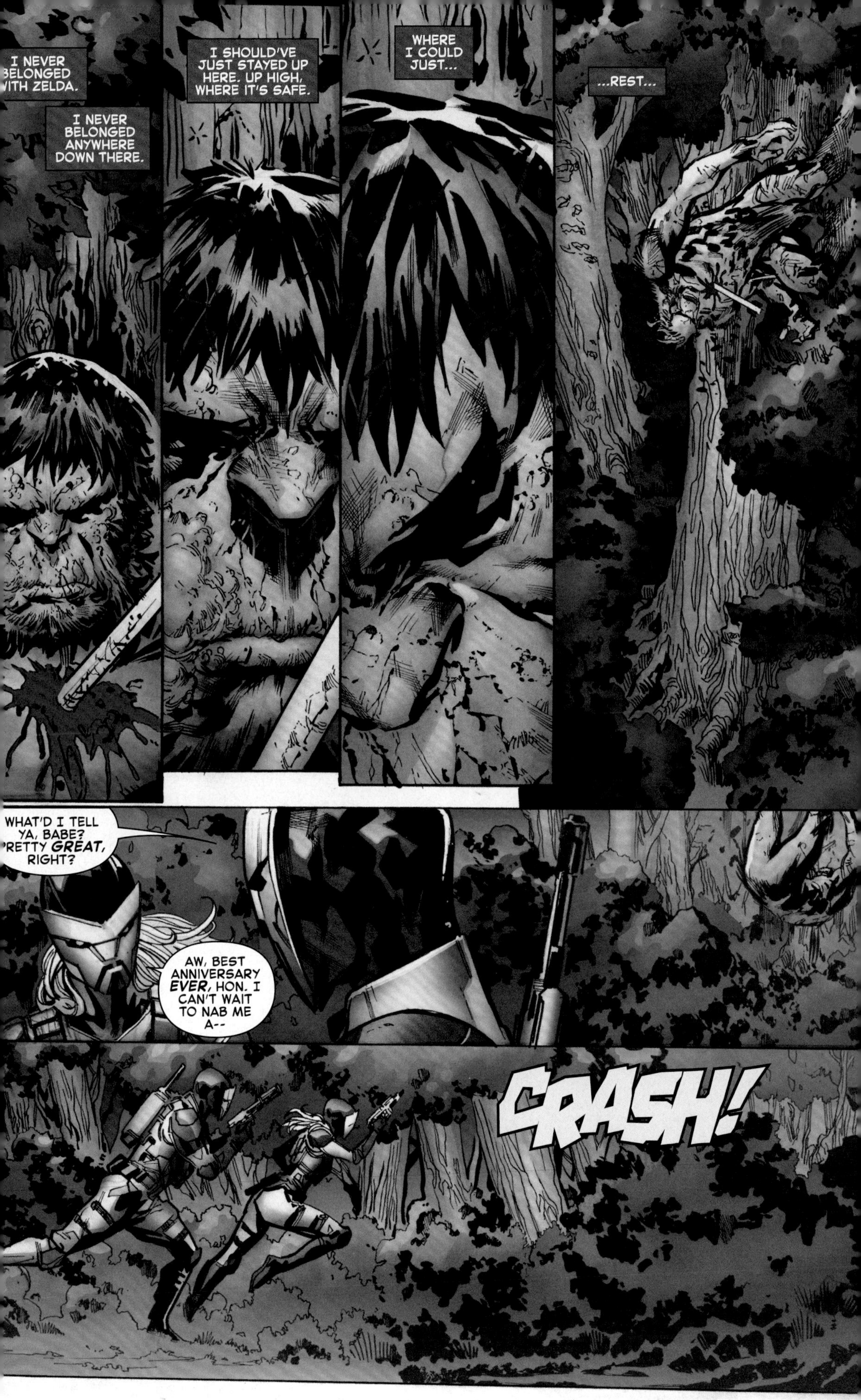
I NEVER BELONGED WITH ZELDA.
I NEVER BELONGED ANYWHERE DOWN THERE.
I SHOULD'VE JUST STAYED UP HERE. UP HIGH, WHERE IT'S SAFE.
WHERE I COULD JUST...
...REST...
WHAT'D I TELL YA, BABE? PRETTY GREAT, RIGHT?
AW, BEST ANNIVERSARY EVER, HON. I CAN'T WAIT TO NAB ME A--
CRASH!

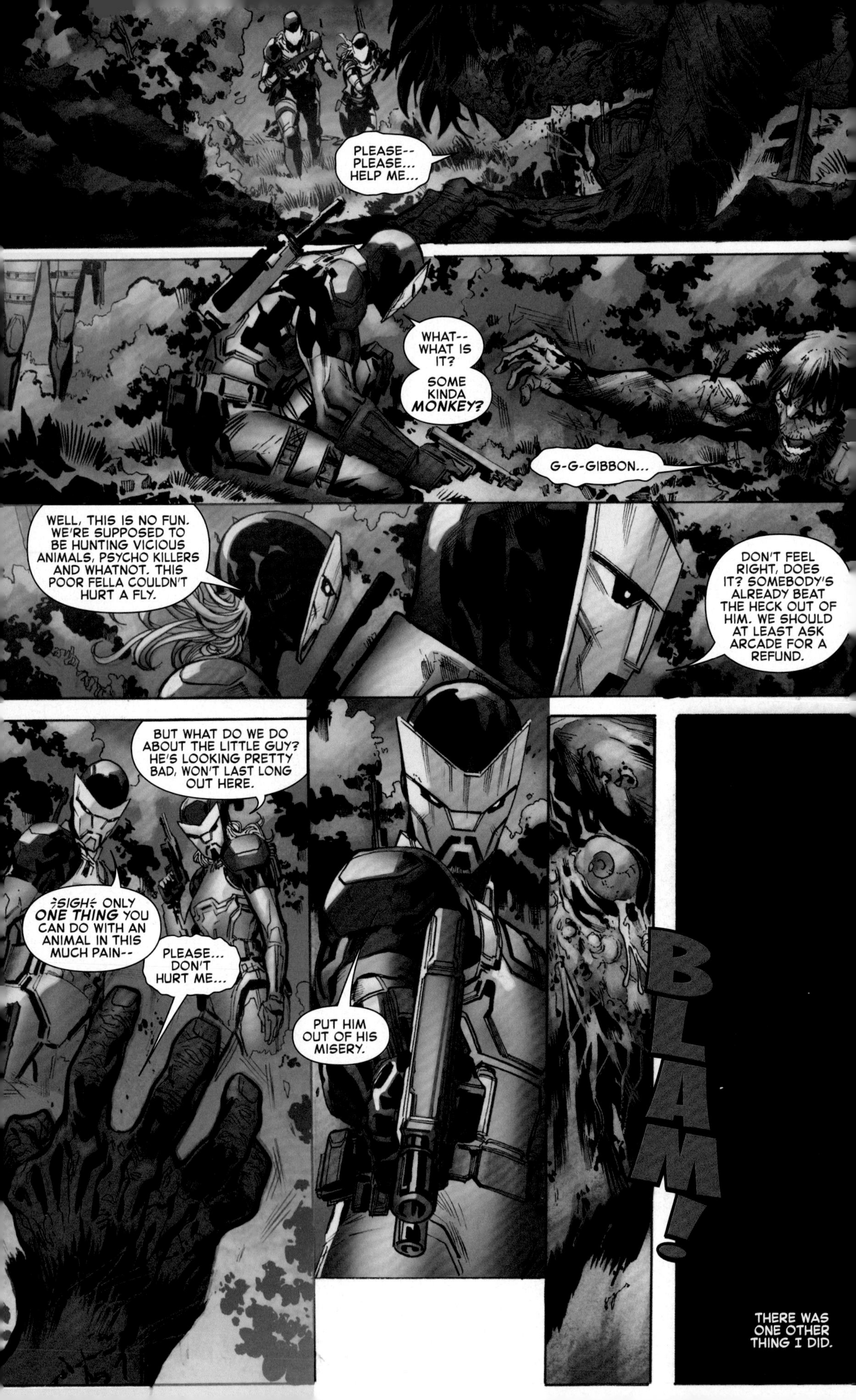
PLEASE--
PLEASE...
HELP ME...
WHAT--
WHAT IS
IT?
SOME
KINDA
MONKEY?
G-G-GIBBON...
WELL, THIS IS NO FUN. WE'RE SUPPOSED TO BE HUNTING VICIOUS ANIMALS, PSYCHO KILLERS AND WHATNOT. THIS POOR FELLA COULDN'T HURT A FLY.
DON'T FEEL RIGHT, DOES IT? SOMEBODY'S ALREADY BEAT THE HECK OUT OF HIM. WE SHOULD AT LEAST ASK ARCADE FOR A REFUND.
BUT WHAT DO WE DO ABOUT THE LITTLE GUY? HE'S LOOKING PRETTY BAD, WON'T LAST LONG OUT HERE.
SIGH ONLY *ONE THING* YOU CAN DO WITH AN ANIMAL IN THIS MUCH PAIN--
PLEASE... DON'T HURT ME...
PUT HIM OUT OF HIS MISERY.
BLAM!
THERE WAS ONE OTHER THING I DID.

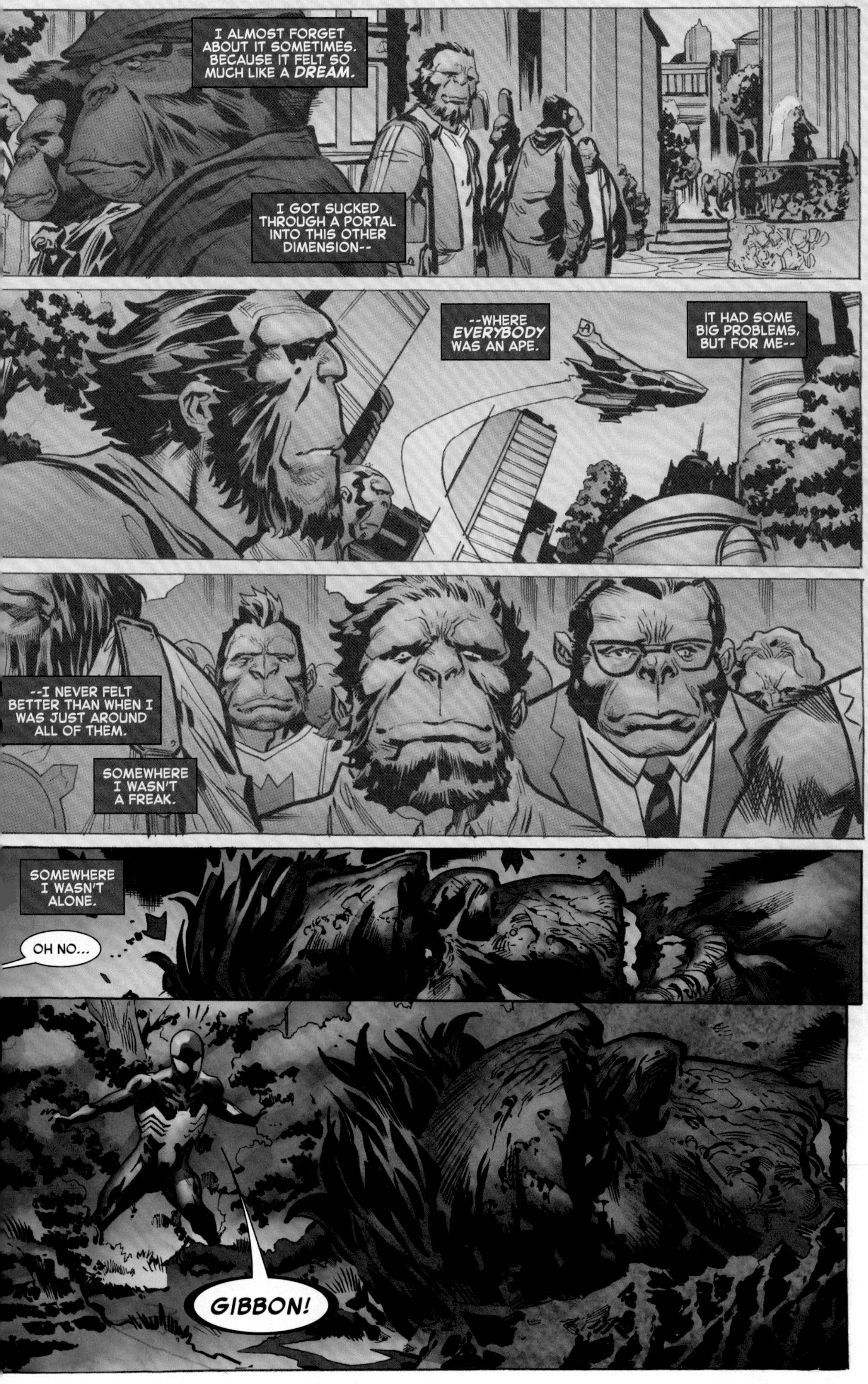
I ALMOST FORGET ABOUT IT SOMETIMES. BECAUSE IT FELT SO MUCH LIKE A DREAM.
I GOT SUCKED THROUGH A PORTAL INTO THIS OTHER DIMENSION--
--WHERE EVERYBODY WAS AN APE.
IT HAD SOME BIG PROBLEMS, BUT FOR ME--
--I NEVER FELT BETTER THAN WHEN I WAS JUST AROUND ALL OF THEM.
SOMEWHERE I WASN'T A FREAK.
SOMEWHERE I WASN'T ALONE.
OH NO...
GIBBON!

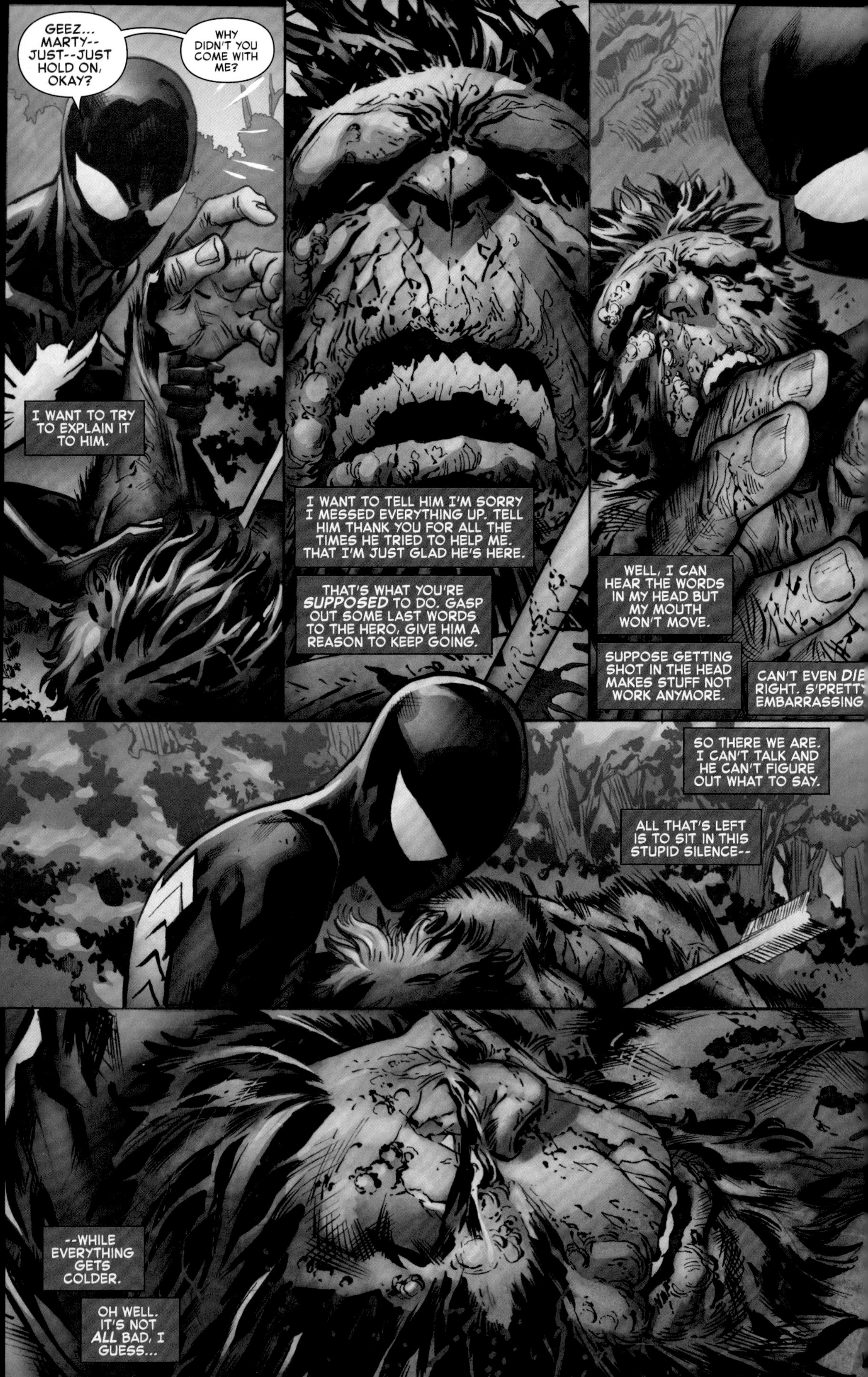

GEEZ... MARTY-- JUST--JUST HOLD ON, OKAY?
WHY DIDN'T YOU COME WITH ME?
I WANT TO TRY TO EXPLAIN IT TO HIM.
I WANT TO TELL HIM I'M SORRY I MESSED EVERYTHING UP. TELL HIM THANK YOU FOR ALL THE TIMES HE TRIED TO HELP ME. THAT I'M JUST GLAD HE'S HERE.
THAT'S WHAT YOU'RE *SUPPOSED* TO DO. GASP OUT SOME LAST WORDS TO THE HERO, GIVE HIM A REASON TO KEEP GOING.
WELL, I CAN HEAR THE WORDS IN MY HEAD BUT MY MOUTH WON'T MOVE.
SUPPOSE GETTING SHOT IN THE HEAD MAKES STUFF NOT WORK ANYMORE.
CAN'T EVEN *DIE* RIGHT. S'PRETTY EMBARRASSING
SO THERE WE ARE. I CAN'T TALK AND HE CAN'T FIGURE OUT WHAT TO SAY.
ALL THAT'S LEFT IS TO SIT IN THIS STUPID SILENCE--
--WHILE EVERYTHING GETS COLDER.
OH WELL. IT'S NOT *ALL* BAD, I GUESS...

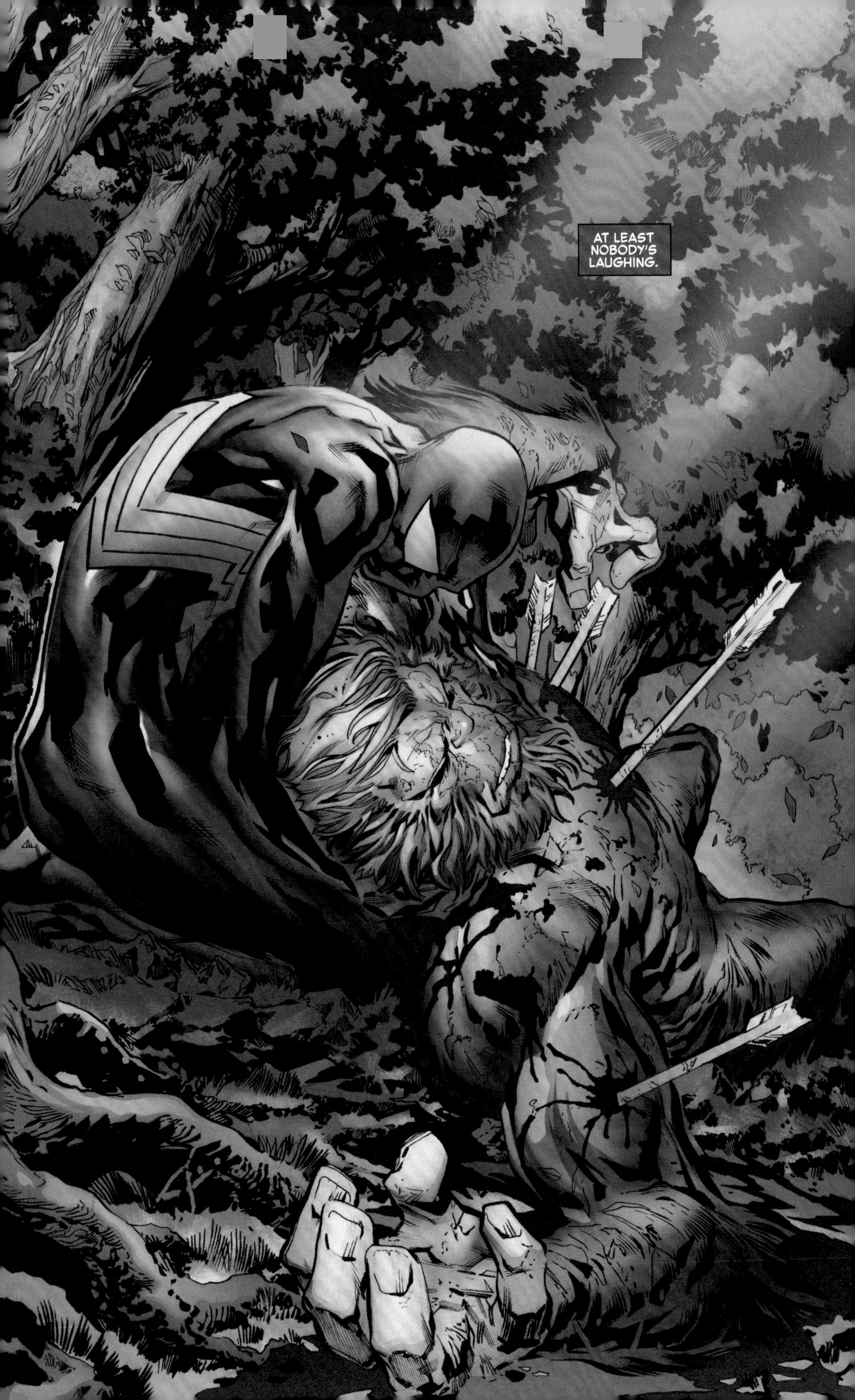
AT LEAST NOBODY'S LAUGHING.

19

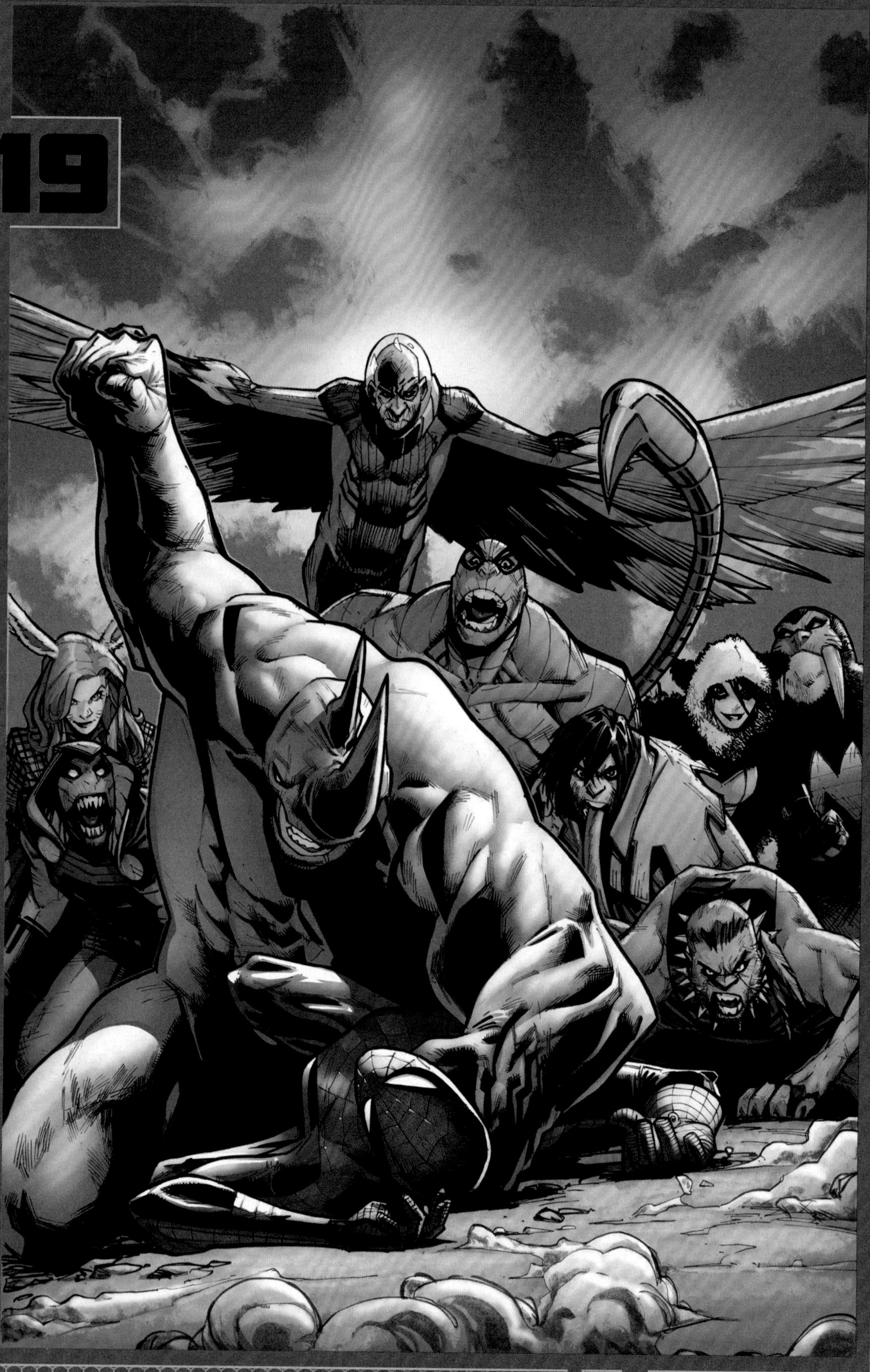

HUNTED PART 3

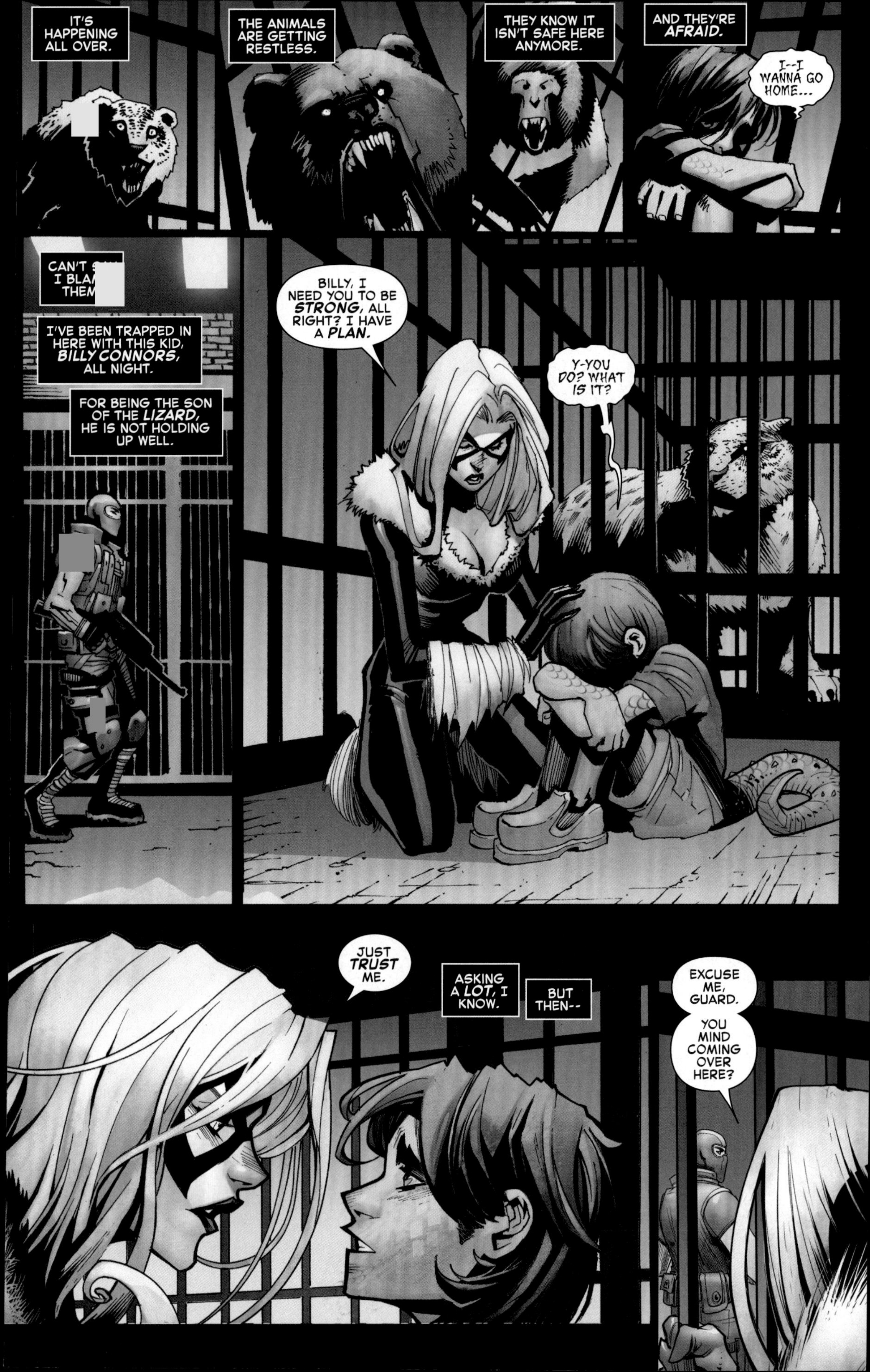

IT'S HAPPENING ALL OVER.
THE ANIMALS ARE GETTING RESTLESS.
THEY KNOW IT ISN'T SAFE HERE ANYMORE.
AND THEY'RE *AFRAID.*
I--I WANNA GO HOME...
CAN'T S I BLAM THEM
I'VE BEEN TRAPPED IN HERE WITH THIS KID, *BILLY CONNORS,* ALL NIGHT.
FOR BEING THE SON OF THE *LIZARD,* HE IS NOT HOLDING UP WELL.
BILLY, I NEED YOU TO BE *STRONG,* ALL RIGHT? I HAVE A *PLAN.*
Y-YOU *DO?* WHAT *IS* IT?
JUST *TRUST* ME.
ASKING A *LOT,* I KNOW.
BUT THEN--
EXCUSE ME, GUARD.
YOU MIND COMING OVER HERE?

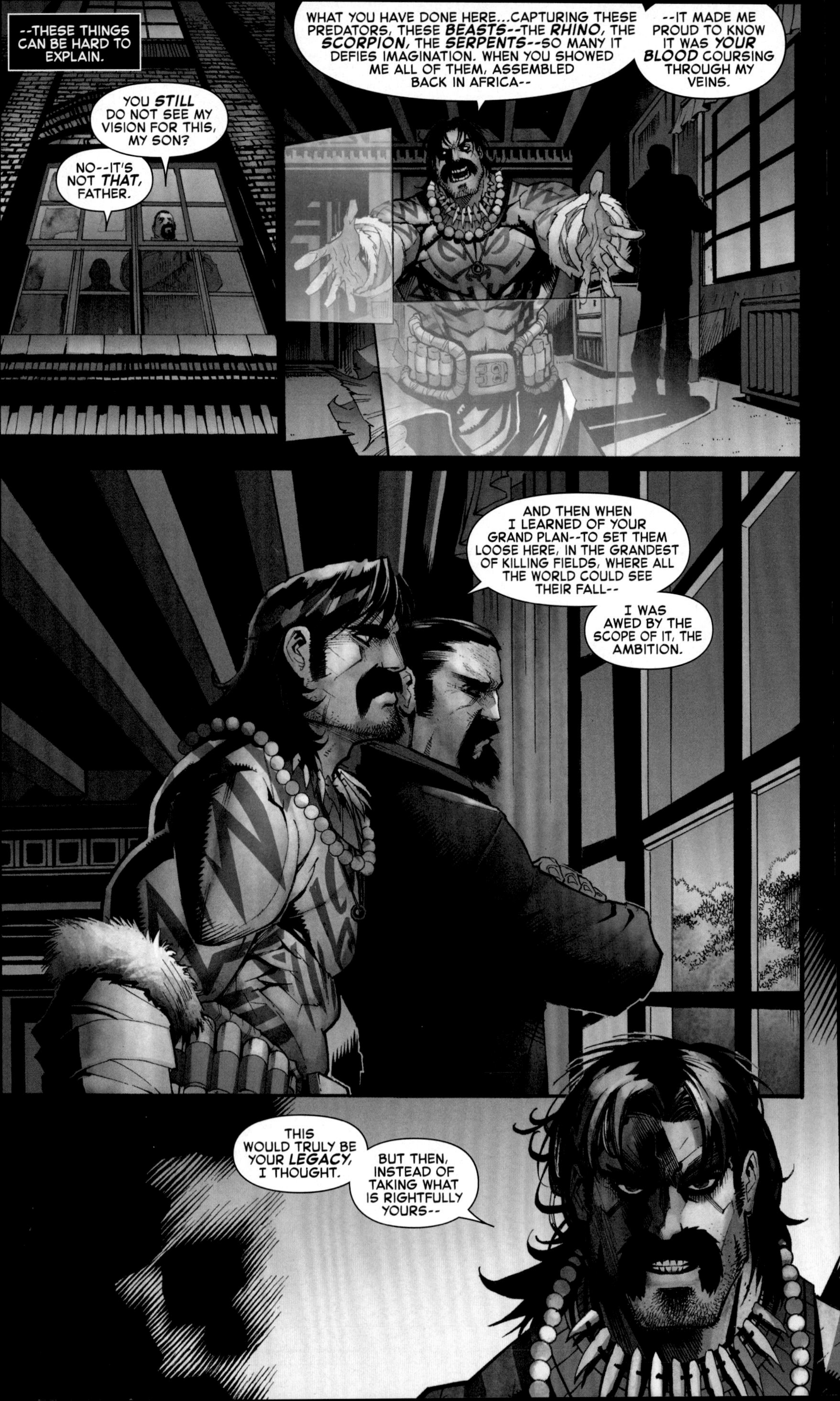
--THESE THINGS CAN BE HARD TO EXPLAIN.
YOU STILL DO NOT SEE MY VISION FOR THIS, MY SON?
NO--IT'S NOT THAT, FATHER.
WHAT YOU HAVE DONE HERE...CAPTURING THESE PREDATORS, THESE BEASTS--THE RHINO, THE SCORPION, THE SERPENTS--SO MANY IT DEFIES IMAGINATION. WHEN YOU SHOWED ME ALL OF THEM, ASSEMBLED BACK IN AFRICA--
--IT MADE ME PROUD TO KNOW IT WAS YOUR BLOOD COURSING THROUGH MY VEINS.
AND THEN WHEN I LEARNED OF YOUR GRAND PLAN--TO SET THEM LOOSE HERE, IN THE GRANDEST OF KILLING FIELDS, WHERE ALL THE WORLD COULD SEE THEIR FALL--
I WAS AWED BY THE SCOPE OF IT, THE AMBITION.
THIS WOULD TRULY BE YOUR LEGACY, I THOUGHT.
BUT THEN, INSTEAD OF TAKING WHAT IS RIGHTFULLY YOURS--

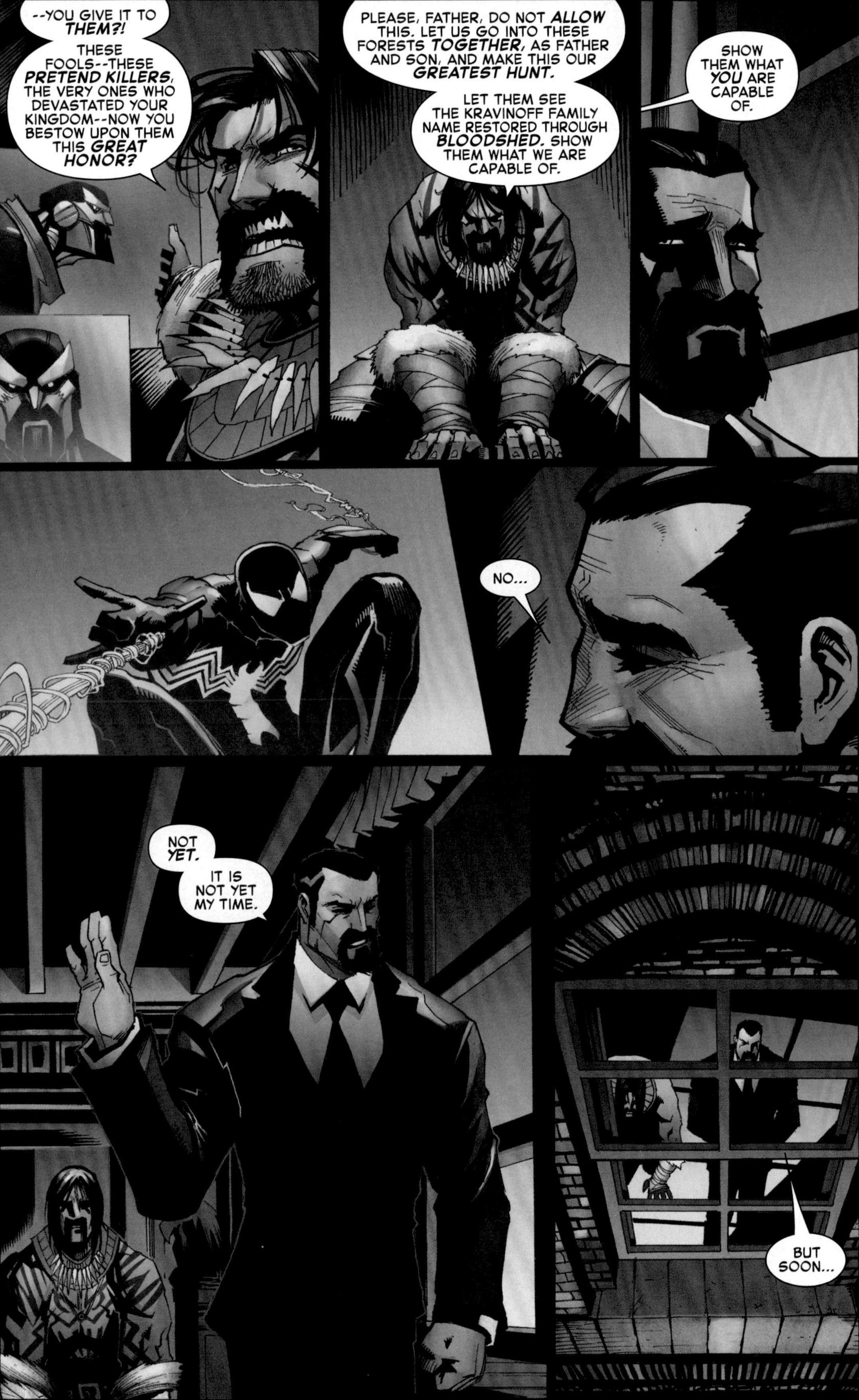
--YOU GIVE IT TO THEM?!
THESE FOOLS--THESE PRETEND KILLERS, THE VERY ONES WHO DEVASTATED YOUR KINGDOM--NOW YOU BESTOW UPON THEM THIS GREAT HONOR?
PLEASE, FATHER, DO NOT ALLOW THIS. LET US GO INTO THESE FORESTS TOGETHER, AS FATHER AND SON, AND MAKE THIS OUR GREATEST HUNT.
LET THEM SEE THE KRAVINOFF FAMILY NAME RESTORED THROUGH BLOODSHED. SHOW THEM WHAT WE ARE CAPABLE OF.
SHOW THEM WHAT YOU ARE CAPABLE OF.
NO...
NOT YET.
IT IS NOT YET MY TIME.
BUT SOON...

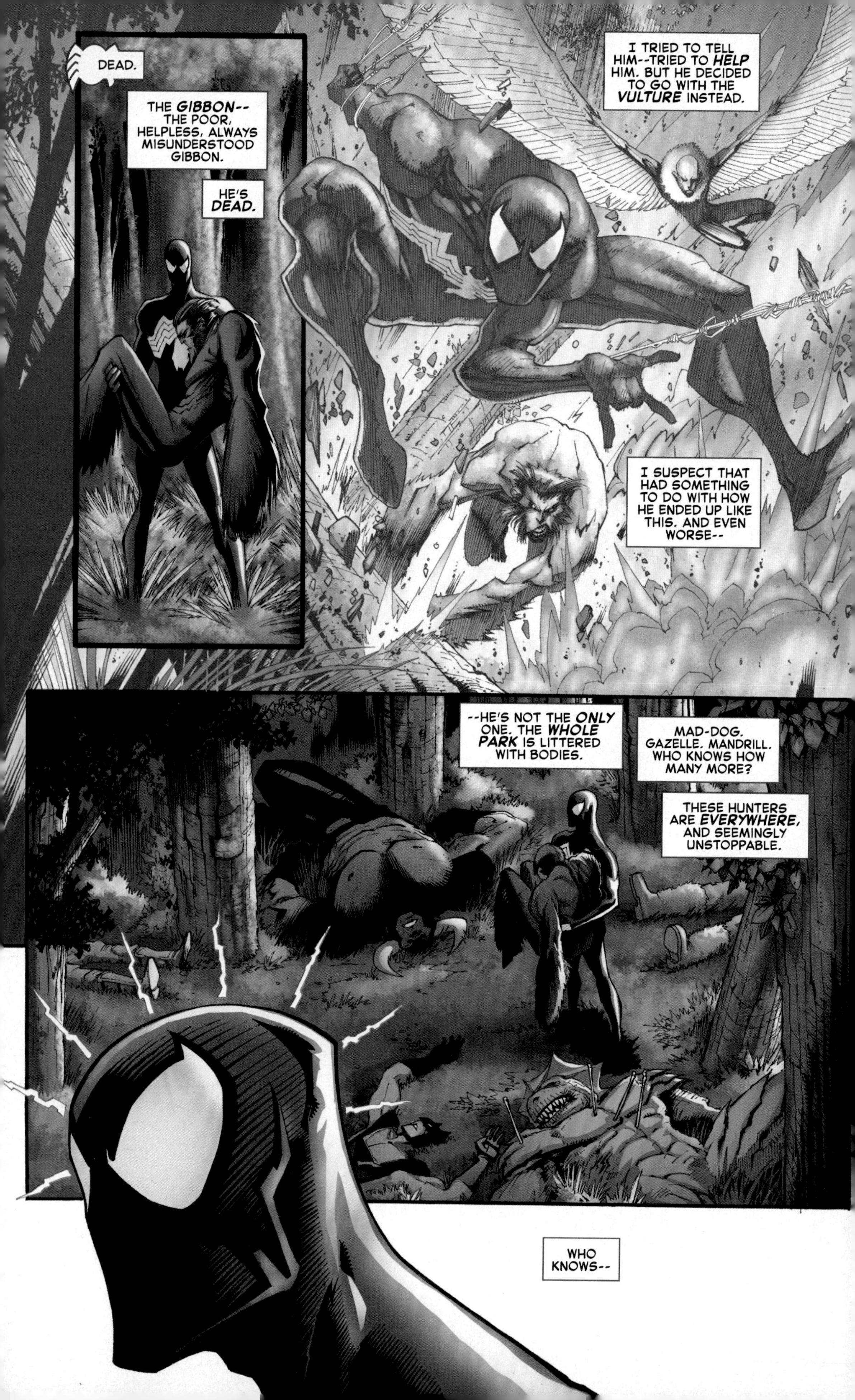

DEAD.
THE GIBBON--
THE POOR, HELPLESS, ALWAYS MISUNDERSTOOD GIBBON.
HE'S DEAD.
I TRIED TO TELL HIM--TRIED TO HELP HIM. BUT HE DECIDED TO GO WITH THE VULTURE INSTEAD.
I SUSPECT THAT HAD SOMETHING TO DO WITH HOW HE ENDED UP LIKE THIS. AND EVEN WORSE--
--HE'S NOT THE ONLY ONE. THE WHOLE PARK IS LITTERED WITH BODIES.
MAD-DOG. GAZELLE. MANDRILL. WHO KNOWS HOW MANY MORE?
THESE HUNTERS ARE EVERYWHERE, AND SEEMINGLY UNSTOPPABLE.
WHO KNOWS--

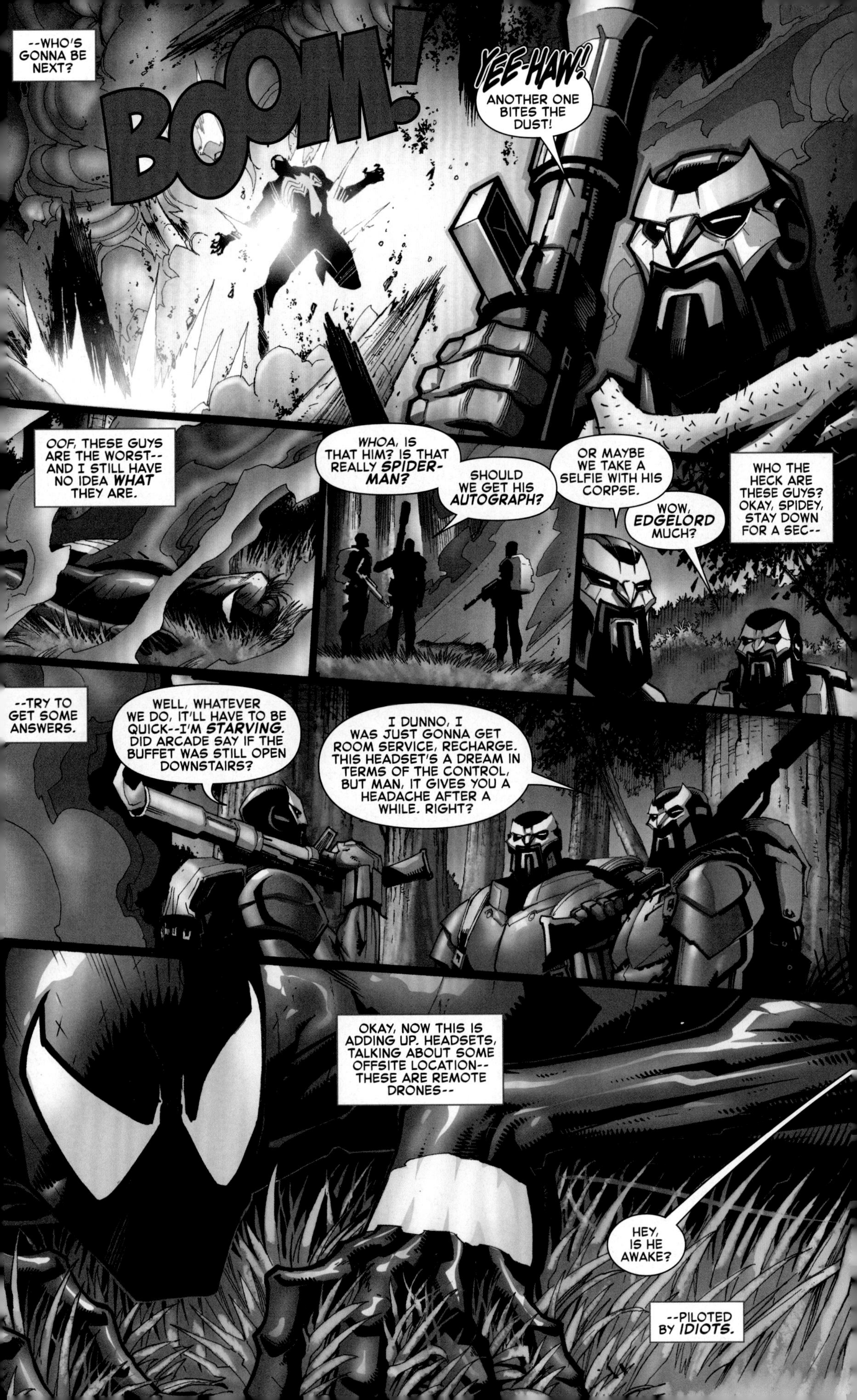
--WHO'S GONNA BE NEXT?
BOOM!
YEE-HAW! ANOTHER ONE BITES THE DUST!
OOF, THESE GUYS ARE THE WORST--AND I STILL HAVE NO IDEA WHAT THEY ARE.
WHOA, IS THAT HIM? IS THAT REALLY SPIDER-MAN?
SHOULD WE GET HIS AUTOGRAPH?
OR MAYBE WE TAKE A SELFIE WITH HIS CORPSE.
WOW, EDGELORD MUCH?
WHO THE HECK ARE THESE GUYS? OKAY, SPIDEY, STAY DOWN FOR A SEC--
--TRY TO GET SOME ANSWERS.
WELL, WHATEVER WE DO, IT'LL HAVE TO BE QUICK--I'M STARVING. DID ARCADE SAY IF THE BUFFET WAS STILL OPEN DOWNSTAIRS?
I DUNNO, I WAS JUST GONNA GET ROOM SERVICE, RECHARGE. THIS HEADSET'S A DREAM IN TERMS OF THE CONTROL, BUT MAN, IT GIVES YOU A HEADACHE AFTER A WHILE. RIGHT?
OKAY, NOW THIS IS ADDING UP. HEADSETS, TALKING ABOUT SOME OFFSITE LOCATION--THESE ARE REMOTE DRONES--
HEY, IS HE AWAKE?
--PILOTED BY IDIOTS.

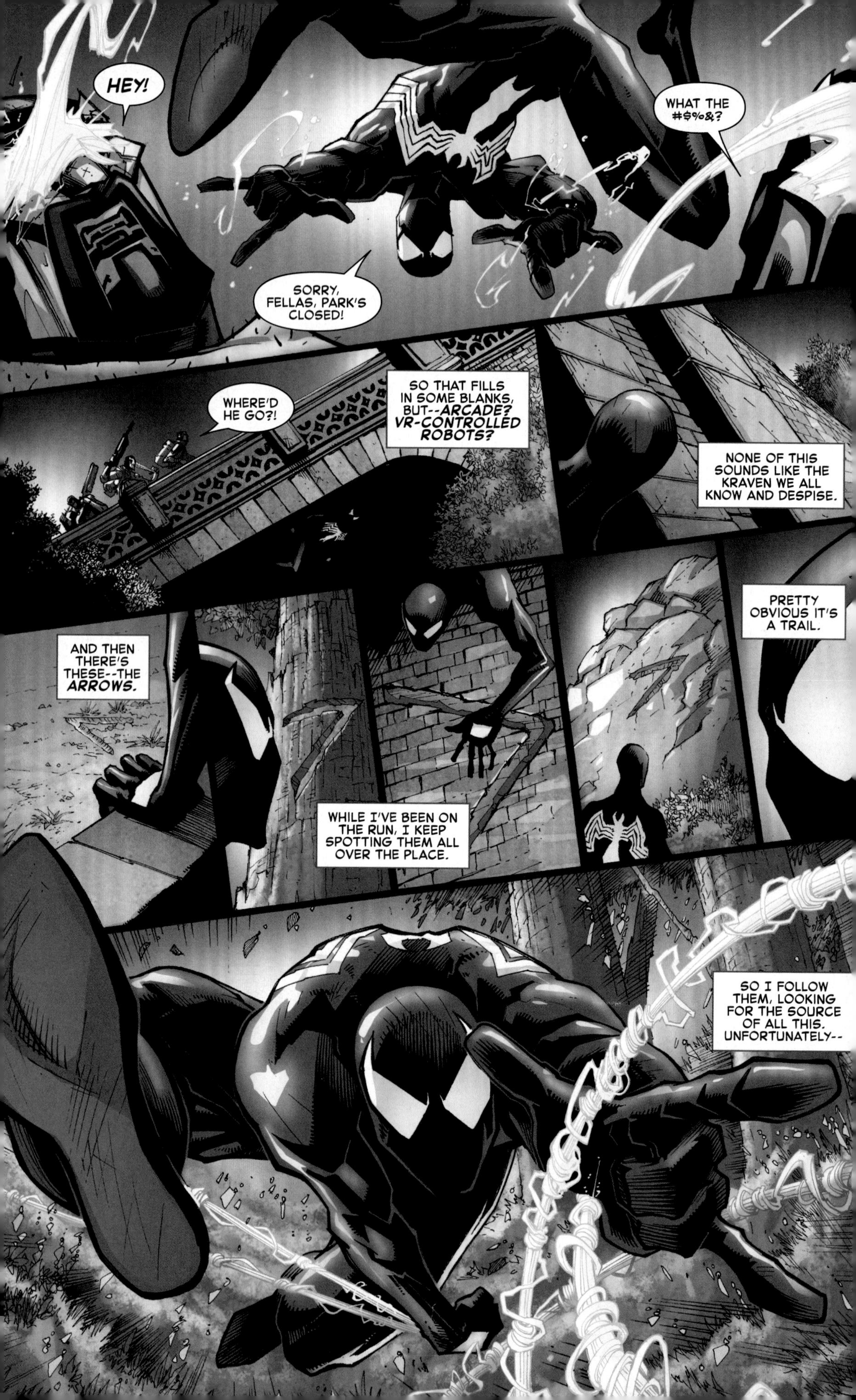
HEY!
WHAT THE #$%&?
SORRY, FELLAS, PARK'S CLOSED!
WHERE'D HE GO?!
SO THAT FILLS IN SOME BLANKS, BUT--ARCADE? VR-CONTROLLED ROBOTS?
NONE OF THIS SOUNDS LIKE THE KRAVEN WE ALL KNOW AND DESPISE.
AND THEN THERE'S THESE--THE ARROWS.
WHILE I'VE BEEN ON THE RUN, I KEEP SPOTTING THEM ALL OVER THE PLACE.
PRETTY OBVIOUS IT'S A TRAIL.
SO I FOLLOW THEM, LOOKING FOR THE SOURCE OF ALL THIS. UNFORTUNATELY--

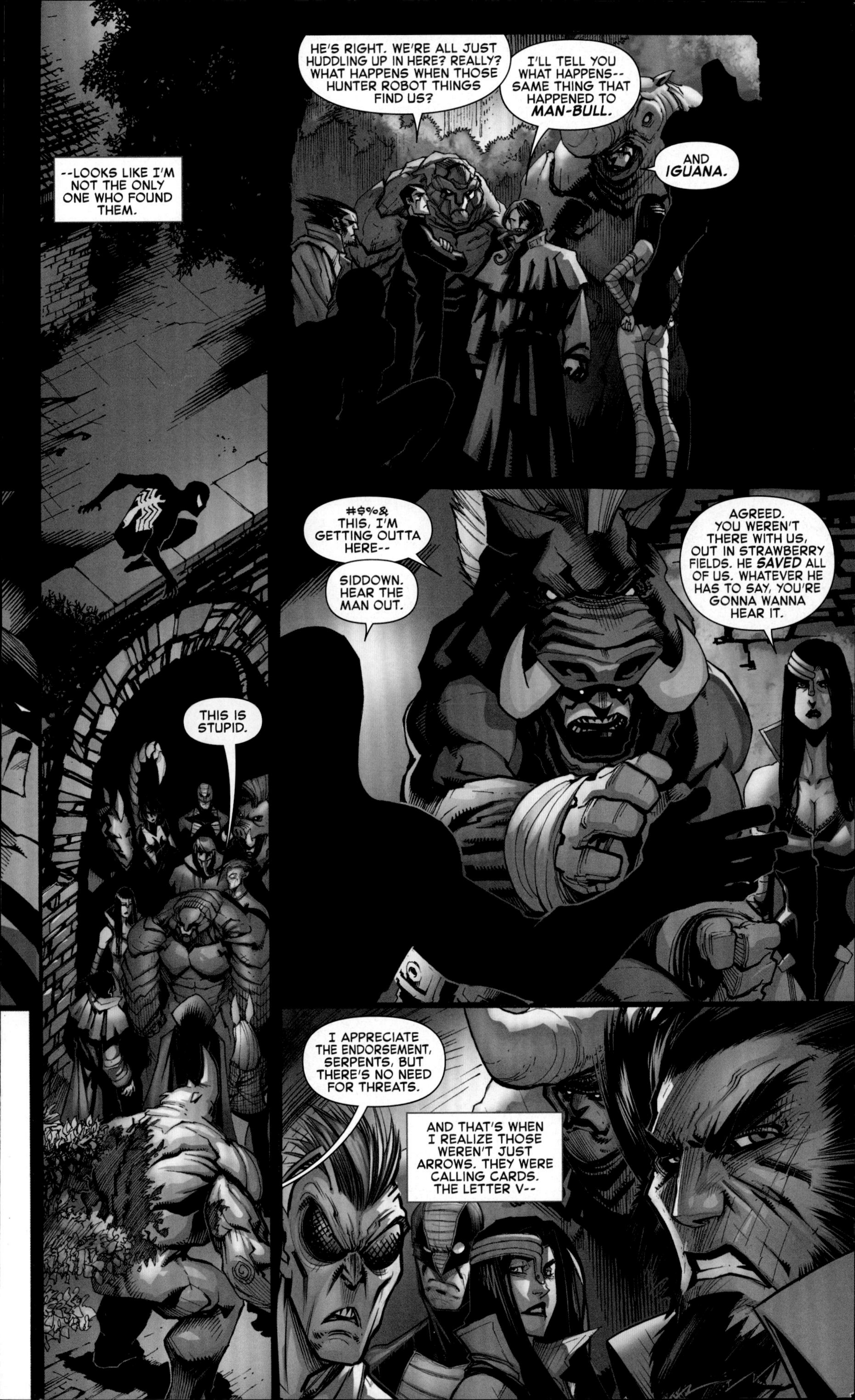
--LOOKS LIKE I'M NOT THE ONLY ONE WHO FOUND THEM.
HE'S RIGHT. WE'RE ALL JUST HUDDLING UP IN HERE? REALLY? WHAT HAPPENS WHEN THOSE HUNTER ROBOT THINGS FIND US?
I'LL TELL YOU WHAT HAPPENS-- SAME THING THAT HAPPENED TO MAN-BULL.
AND IGUANA.
THIS IS STUPID.
#$%& THIS, I'M GETTING OUTTA HERE--
SIDDOWN. HEAR THE MAN OUT.
AGREED. YOU WEREN'T THERE WITH US, OUT IN STRAWBERRY FIELDS. HE SAVED ALL OF US. WHATEVER HE HAS TO SAY, YOU'RE GONNA WANNA HEAR IT.
I APPRECIATE THE ENDORSEMENT, SERPENTS, BUT THERE'S NO NEED FOR THREATS.
AND THAT'S WHEN I REALIZE THOSE WEREN'T JUST ARROWS. THEY WERE CALLING CARDS. THE LETTER V--

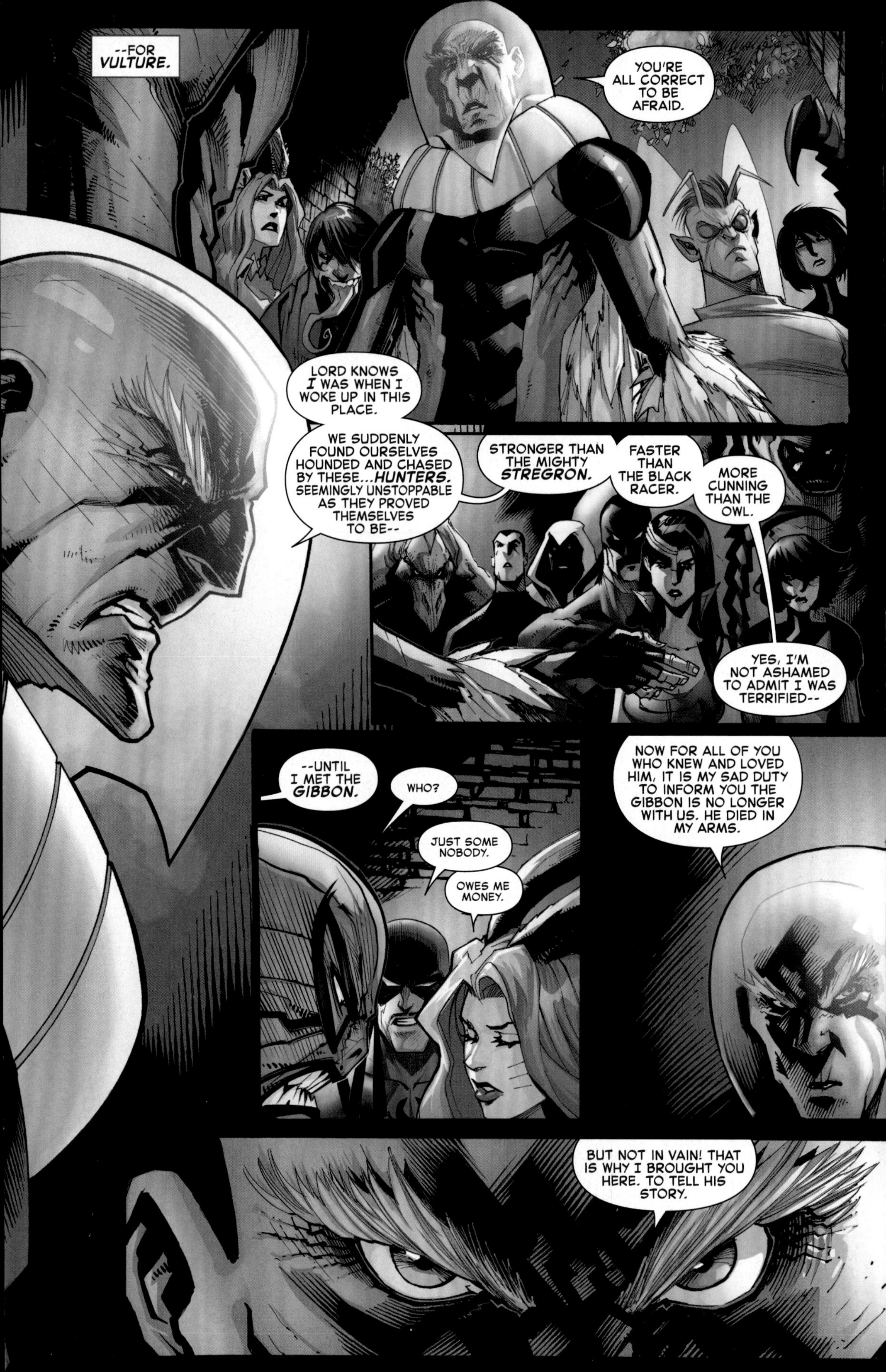
--FOR VULTURE.
YOU'RE ALL CORRECT TO BE AFRAID.
LORD KNOWS I WAS WHEN I WOKE UP IN THIS PLACE.
WE SUDDENLY FOUND OURSELVES HOUNDED AND CHASED BY THESE... HUNTERS. SEEMINGLY UNSTOPPABLE AS THEY PROVED THEMSELVES TO BE--
STRONGER THAN THE MIGHTY STREGRON.
FASTER THAN THE BLACK RACER.
MORE CUNNING THAN THE OWL.
YES, I'M NOT ASHAMED TO ADMIT I WAS TERRIFIED--
--UNTIL I MET THE GIBBON.
WHO?
JUST SOME NOBODY.
OWES ME MONEY.
NOW FOR ALL OF YOU WHO KNEW AND LOVED HIM, IT IS MY SAD DUTY TO INFORM YOU THE GIBBON IS NO LONGER WITH US. HE DIED IN MY ARMS.
BUT NOT IN VAIN! THAT IS WHY I BROUGHT YOU HERE. TO TELL HIS STORY.

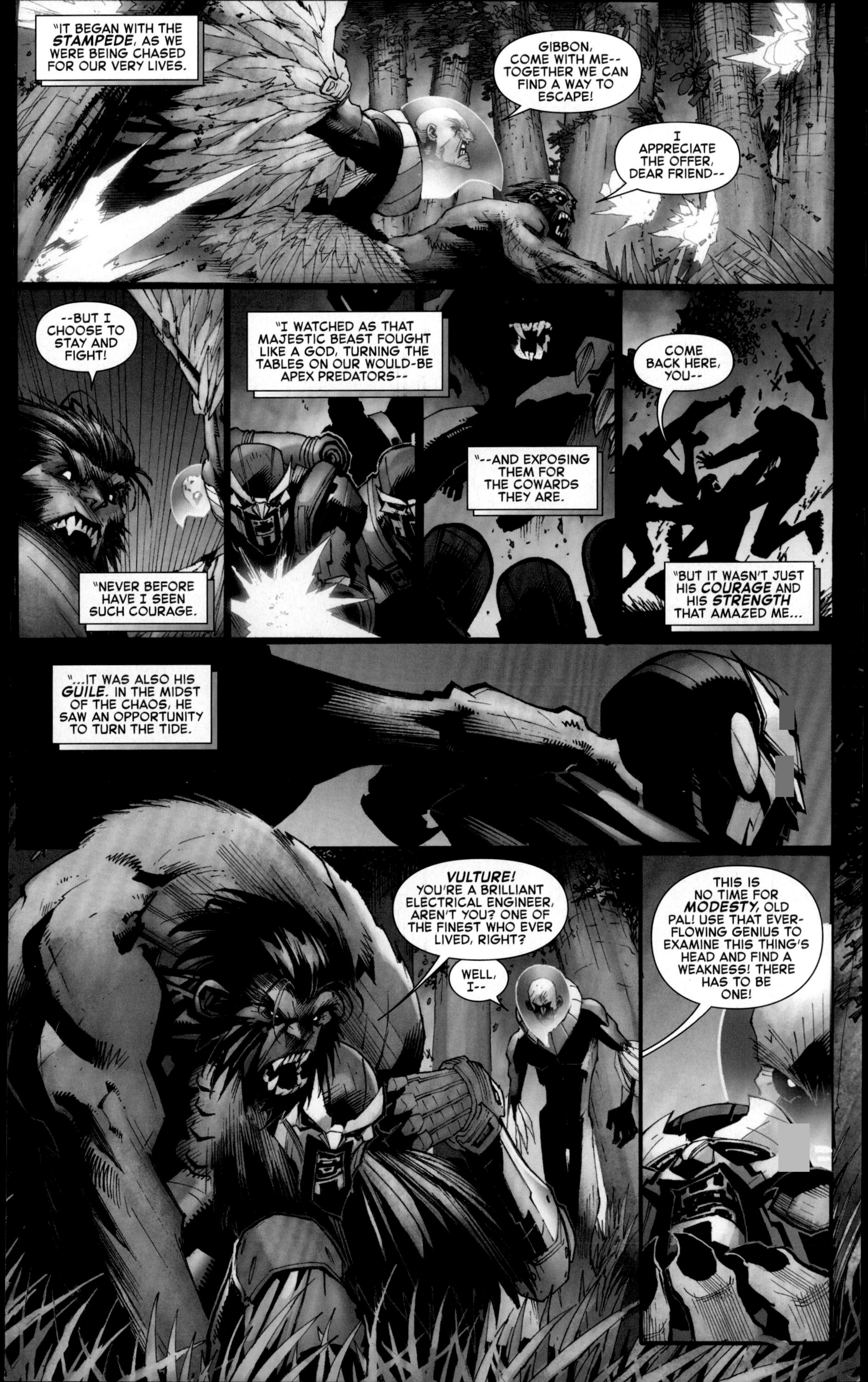
"IT BEGAN WITH THE STAMPEDE, AS WE WERE BEING CHASED FOR OUR VERY LIVES.
GIBBON, COME WITH ME-- TOGETHER WE CAN FIND A WAY TO ESCAPE!
I APPRECIATE THE OFFER, DEAR FRIEND--
--BUT I CHOOSE TO STAY AND FIGHT!
"NEVER BEFORE HAVE I SEEN SUCH COURAGE.
"I WATCHED AS THAT MAJESTIC BEAST FOUGHT LIKE A GOD, TURNING THE TABLES ON OUR WOULD-BE APEX PREDATORS--
"--AND EXPOSING THEM FOR THE COWARDS THEY ARE.
COME BACK HERE, YOU--
"BUT IT WASN'T JUST HIS COURAGE AND HIS STRENGTH THAT AMAZED ME...
"...IT WAS ALSO HIS GUILE. IN THE MIDST OF THE CHAOS, HE SAW AN OPPORTUNITY TO TURN THE TIDE.
VULTURE! YOU'RE A BRILLIANT ELECTRICAL ENGINEER, AREN'T YOU? ONE OF THE FINEST WHO EVER LIVED, RIGHT?
WELL, I--
THIS IS NO TIME FOR MODESTY, OLD PAL! USE THAT EVER-FLOWING GENIUS TO EXAMINE THIS THING'S HEAD AND FIND A WEAKNESS! THERE HAS TO BE ONE!

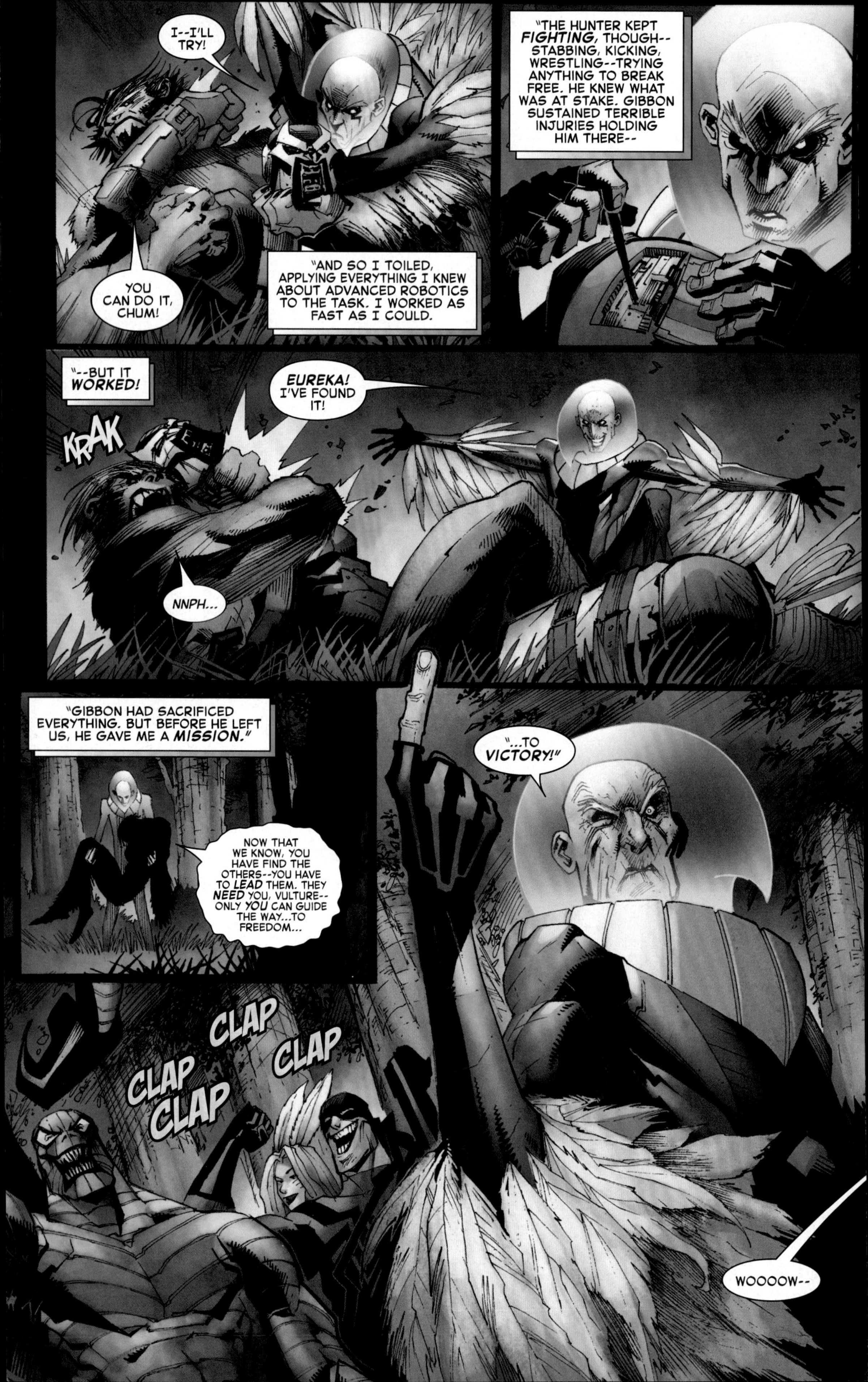

I--I'LL TRY!
YOU CAN DO IT, CHUM!
"AND SO I TOILED, APPLYING EVERYTHING I KNEW ABOUT ADVANCED ROBOTICS TO THE TASK. I WORKED AS FAST AS I COULD.
"THE HUNTER KEPT FIGHTING, THOUGH--STABBING, KICKING, WRESTLING--TRYING ANYTHING TO BREAK FREE. HE KNEW WHAT WAS AT STAKE. GIBBON SUSTAINED TERRIBLE INJURIES HOLDING HIM THERE--
"--BUT IT WORKED!
EUREKA! I'VE FOUND IT!
KRAK
NNPH...
"GIBBON HAD SACRIFICED EVERYTHING. BUT BEFORE HE LEFT US, HE GAVE ME A MISSION."
NOW THAT WE KNOW, YOU HAVE FIND THE OTHERS--YOU HAVE TO LEAD THEM. THEY NEED YOU, VULTURE--ONLY YOU CAN GUIDE THE WAY...TO FREEDOM...
"...TO VICTORY!"
CLAP CLAP CLAP CLAP
WOOOOW--

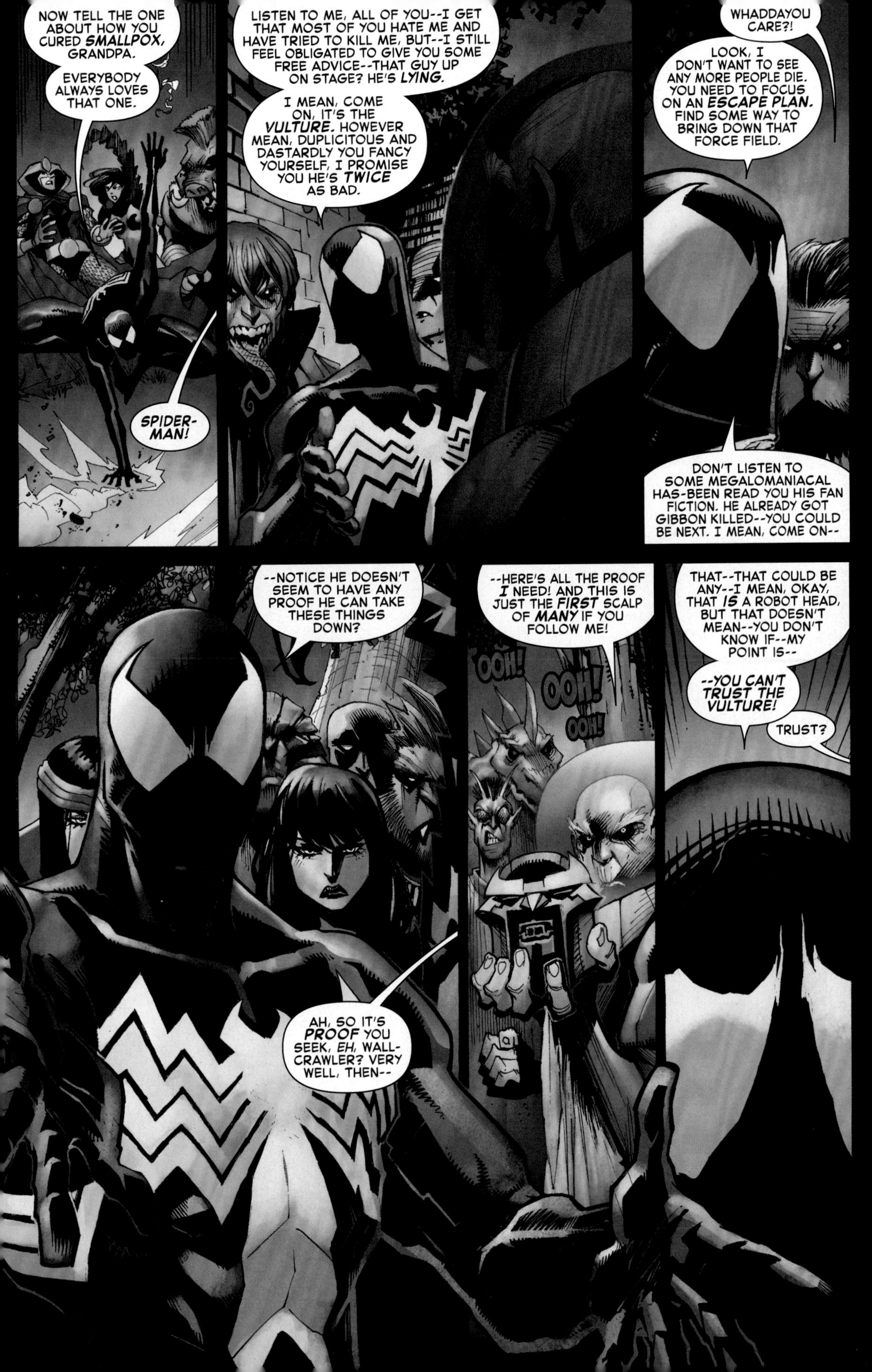
NOW TELL THE ONE ABOUT HOW YOU CURED SMALLPOX, GRANDPA.
EVERYBODY ALWAYS LOVES THAT ONE.
SPIDER-MAN!
LISTEN TO ME, ALL OF YOU--I GET THAT MOST OF YOU HATE ME AND HAVE TRIED TO KILL ME, BUT--I STILL FEEL OBLIGATED TO GIVE YOU SOME FREE ADVICE--THAT GUY UP ON STAGE? HE'S LYING.
I MEAN, COME ON, IT'S THE VULTURE. HOWEVER MEAN, DUPLICITOUS AND DASTARDLY YOU FANCY YOURSELF, I PROMISE YOU HE'S TWICE AS BAD.
WHADDAYOU CARE?!
LOOK, I DON'T WANT TO SEE ANY MORE PEOPLE DIE. YOU NEED TO FOCUS ON AN ESCAPE PLAN. FIND SOME WAY TO BRING DOWN THAT FORCE FIELD.
DON'T LISTEN TO SOME MEGALOMANIACAL HAS-BEEN READ YOU HIS FAN FICTION. HE ALREADY GOT GIBBON KILLED--YOU COULD BE NEXT. I MEAN, COME ON--
--NOTICE HE DOESN'T SEEM TO HAVE ANY PROOF HE CAN TAKE THESE THINGS DOWN?
AH, SO IT'S PROOF YOU SEEK, EH, WALL-CRAWLER? VERY WELL, THEN--
--HERE'S ALL THE PROOF I NEED! AND THIS IS JUST THE FIRST SCALP OF MANY IF YOU FOLLOW ME!
OOH!
OOH!
OOH!
THAT--THAT COULD BE ANY--I MEAN, OKAY, THAT IS A ROBOT HEAD, BUT THAT DOESN'T MEAN--YOU DON'T KNOW IF--MY POINT IS--
--YOU CAN'T TRUST THE VULTURE!
TRUST?

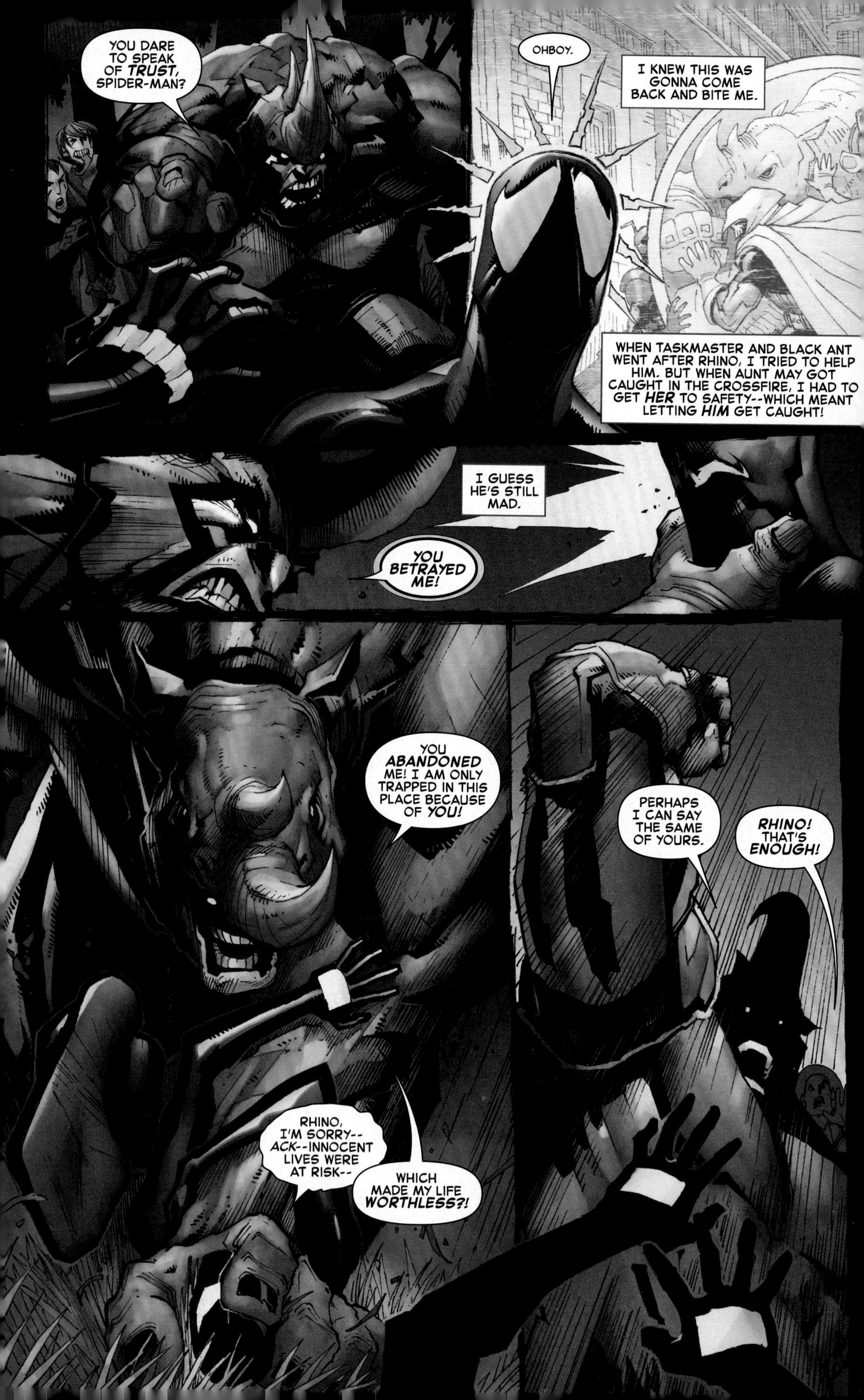
YOU DARE TO SPEAK OF TRUST, SPIDER-MAN?
OHBOY.
I KNEW THIS WAS GONNA COME BACK AND BITE ME.
WHEN TASKMASTER AND BLACK ANT WENT AFTER RHINO, I TRIED TO HELP HIM. BUT WHEN AUNT MAY GOT CAUGHT IN THE CROSSFIRE, I HAD TO GET HER TO SAFETY--WHICH MEANT LETTING HIM GET CAUGHT!
I GUESS HE'S STILL MAD.
YOU BETRAYED ME!
YOU ABANDONED ME! I AM ONLY TRAPPED IN THIS PLACE BECAUSE OF YOU!
RHINO, I'M SORRY--ACK--INNOCENT LIVES WERE AT RISK--
WHICH MADE MY LIFE WORTHLESS?!
PERHAPS I CAN SAY THE SAME OF YOURS.
RHINO! THAT'S ENOUGH!

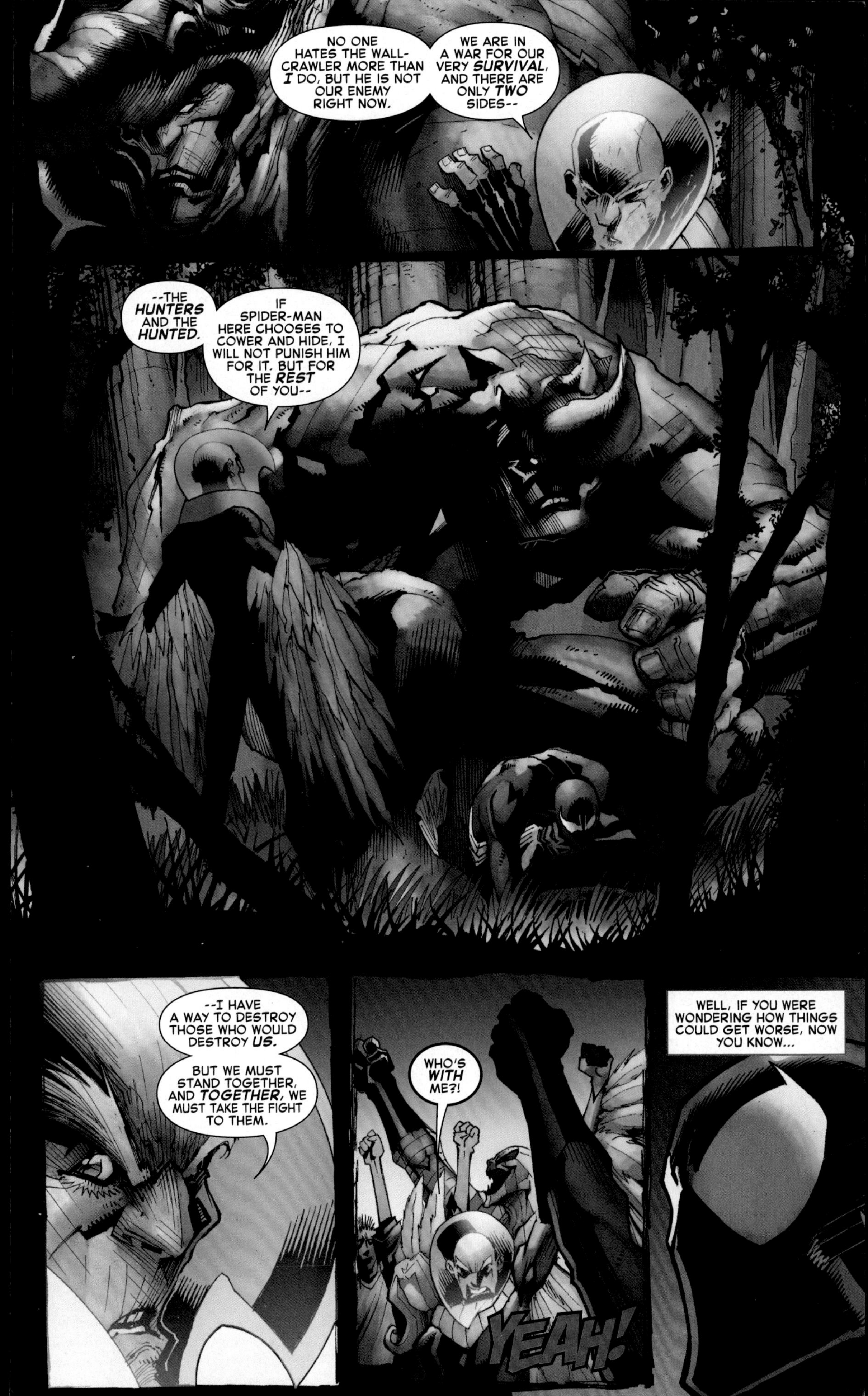
NO ONE HATES THE WALL-CRAWLER MORE THAN I DO, BUT HE IS NOT OUR ENEMY RIGHT NOW.
WE ARE IN A WAR FOR OUR VERY SURVIVAL, AND THERE ARE ONLY TWO SIDES--
--THE HUNTERS AND THE HUNTED.
IF SPIDER-MAN HERE CHOOSES TO COWER AND HIDE, I WILL NOT PUNISH HIM FOR IT. BUT FOR THE REST OF YOU--
--I HAVE A WAY TO DESTROY THOSE WHO WOULD DESTROY US.
BUT WE MUST STAND TOGETHER, AND TOGETHER, WE MUST TAKE THE FIGHT TO THEM.
WHO'S WITH ME?!
YEAH!
WELL, IF YOU WERE WONDERING HOW THINGS COULD GET WORSE, NOW YOU KNOW...

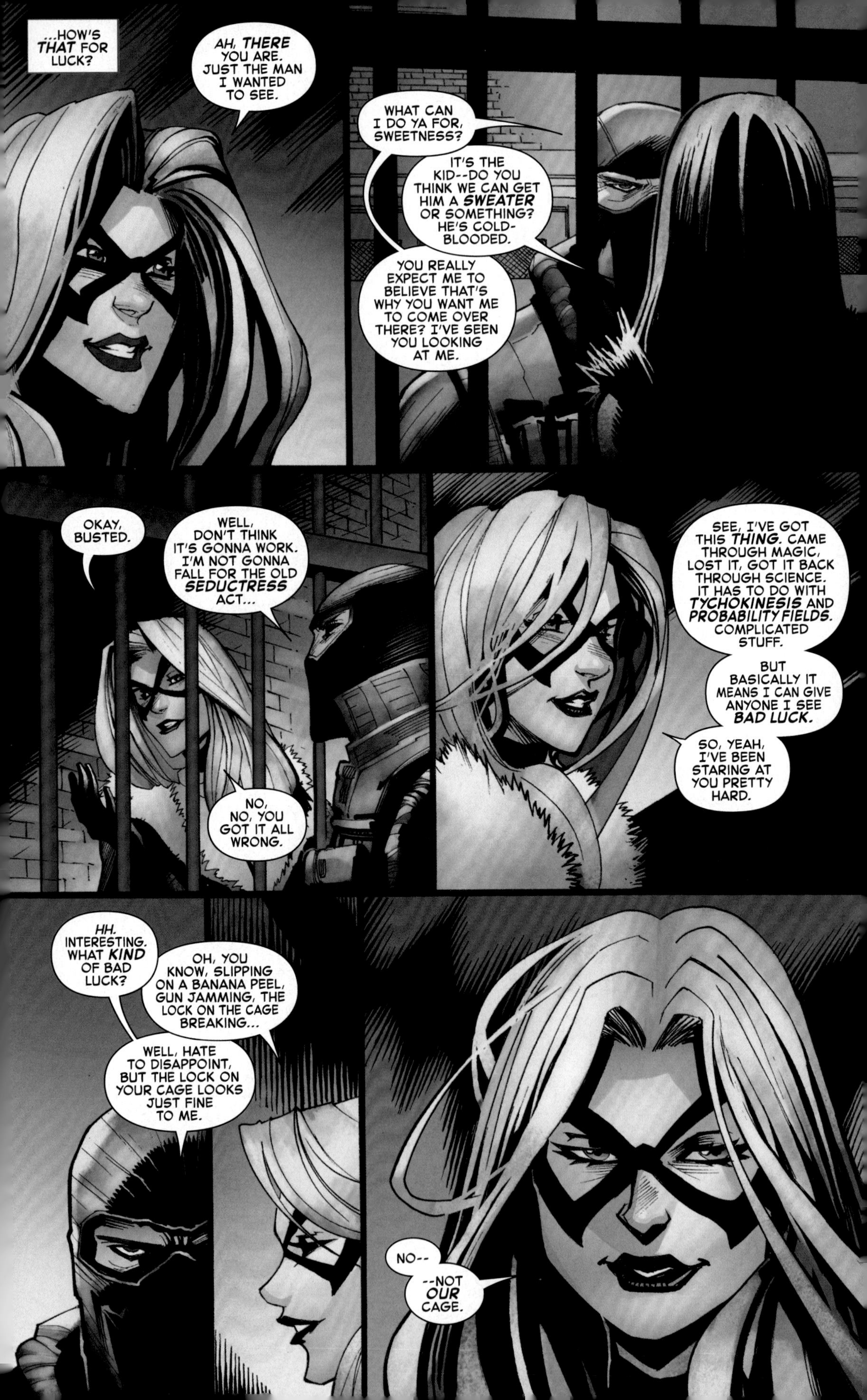

...HOW'S THAT FOR LUCK?
AH, THERE YOU ARE. JUST THE MAN I WANTED TO SEE.
WHAT CAN I DO YA FOR, SWEETNESS?
IT'S THE KID--DO YOU THINK WE CAN GET HIM A SWEATER OR SOMETHING? HE'S COLD-BLOODED.
YOU REALLY EXPECT ME TO BELIEVE THAT'S WHY YOU WANT ME TO COME OVER THERE? I'VE SEEN YOU LOOKING AT ME.
OKAY, BUSTED.
WELL, DON'T THINK IT'S GONNA WORK. I'M NOT GONNA FALL FOR THE OLD SEDUCTRESS ACT...
NO, NO, YOU GOT IT ALL WRONG.
SEE, I'VE GOT THIS THING. CAME THROUGH MAGIC, LOST IT, GOT IT BACK THROUGH SCIENCE. IT HAS TO DO WITH TYCHOKINESIS AND PROBABILITY FIELDS. COMPLICATED STUFF.
BUT BASICALLY IT MEANS I CAN GIVE ANYONE I SEE BAD LUCK.
SO, YEAH, I'VE BEEN STARING AT YOU PRETTY HARD.
HH. INTERESTING. WHAT KIND OF BAD LUCK?
OH, YOU KNOW, SLIPPING ON A BANANA PEEL, GUN JAMMING, THE LOCK ON THE CAGE BREAKING...
WELL, HATE TO DISAPPOINT, BUT THE LOCK ON YOUR CAGE LOOKS JUST FINE TO ME.
NO--
--NOT OUR CAGE.

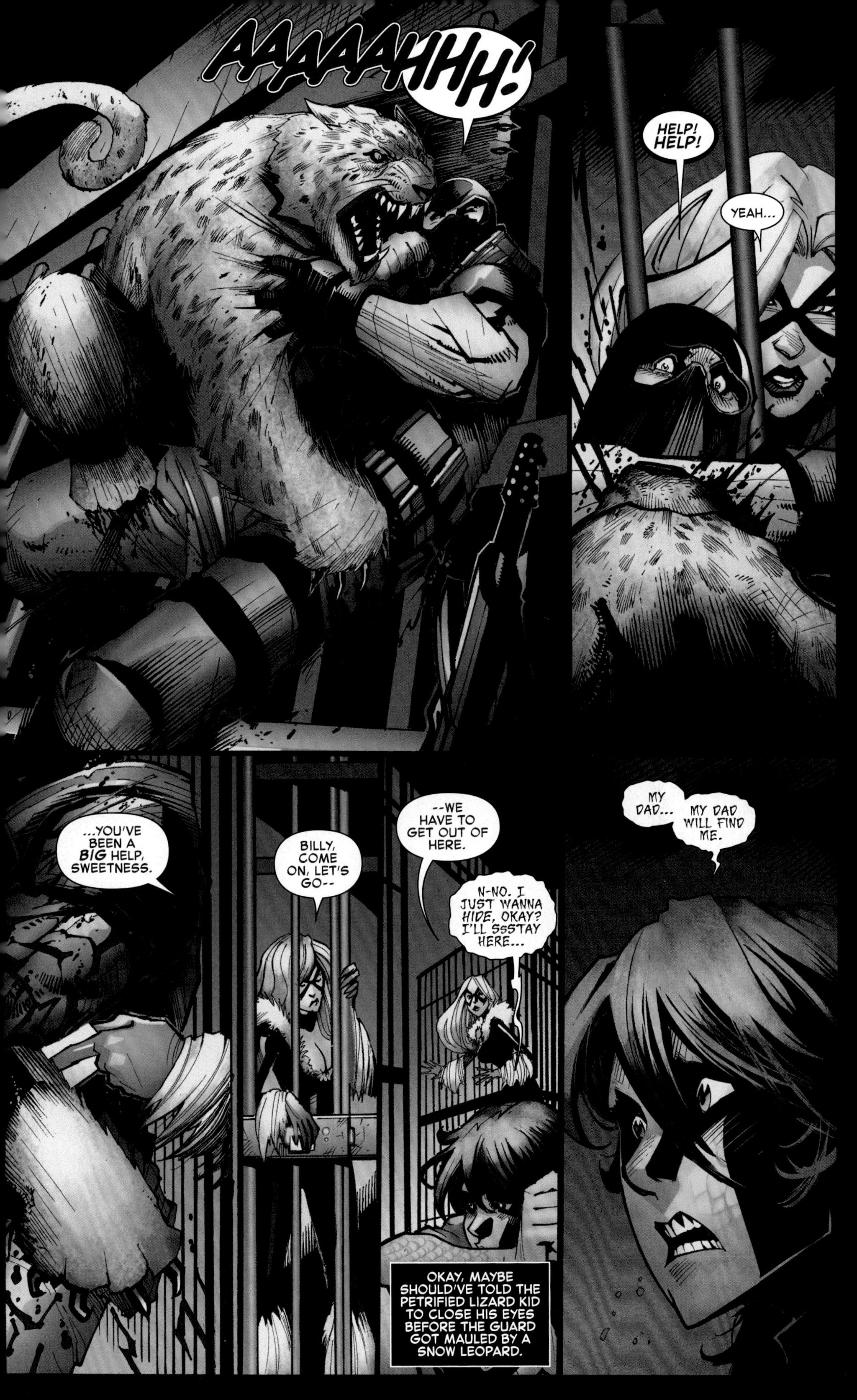
AAAAAHHH!
HELP! HELP!
YEAH...
...YOU'VE BEEN A BIG HELP, SWEETNESS.
BILLY, COME ON, LET'S GO--
--WE HAVE TO GET OUT OF HERE.
N-NO. I JUST WANNA HIDE, OKAY? I'LL SSSTAY HERE...
OKAY, MAYBE SHOULD'VE TOLD THE PETRIFIED LIZARD KID TO CLOSE HIS EYES BEFORE THE GUARD GOT MAULED BY A SNOW LEOPARD.
MY DAD...
MY DAD WILL FIND ME.

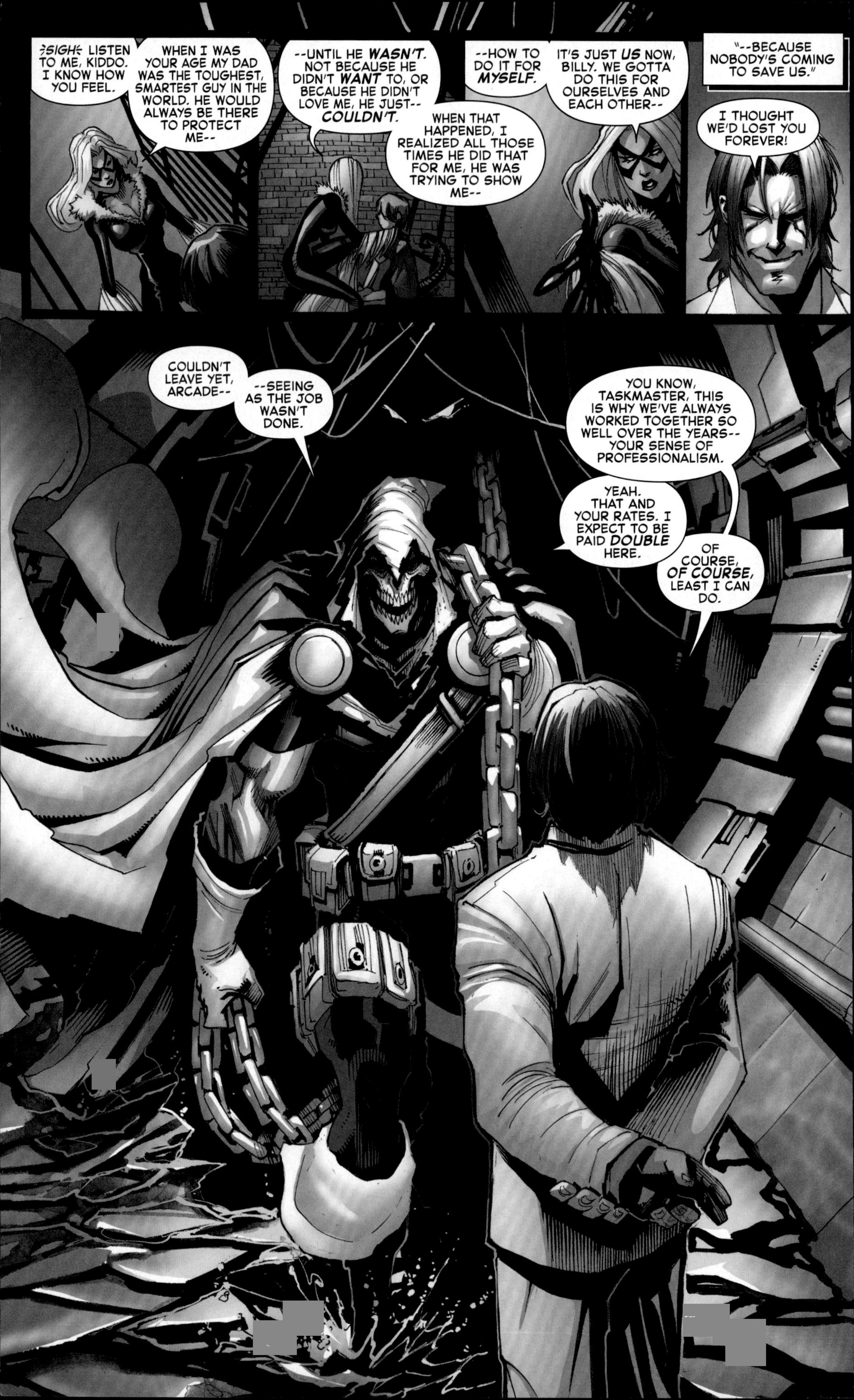
SIGH LISTEN TO ME, KIDDO. I KNOW HOW YOU FEEL.
WHEN I WAS YOUR AGE MY DAD WAS THE TOUGHEST, SMARTEST GUY IN THE WORLD. HE WOULD ALWAYS BE THERE TO PROTECT ME--
--UNTIL HE WASN'T. NOT BECAUSE HE DIDN'T WANT TO, OR BECAUSE HE DIDN'T LOVE ME, HE JUST-- COULDN'T.
WHEN THAT HAPPENED, I REALIZED ALL THOSE TIMES HE DID THAT FOR ME, HE WAS TRYING TO SHOW ME--
--HOW TO DO IT FOR MYSELF.
IT'S JUST US NOW, BILLY. WE GOTTA DO THIS FOR OURSELVES AND EACH OTHER--
"--BECAUSE NOBODY'S COMING TO SAVE US."
I THOUGHT WE'D LOST YOU FOREVER!
COULDN'T LEAVE YET, ARCADE--
--SEEING AS THE JOB WASN'T DONE.
YOU KNOW, TASKMASTER, THIS IS WHY WE'VE ALWAYS WORKED TOGETHER SO WELL OVER THE YEARS-- YOUR SENSE OF PROFESSIONALISM.
YEAH. THAT AND YOUR RATES. I EXPECT TO BE PAID DOUBLE HERE.
OF COURSE, OF COURSE, LEAST I CAN DO.

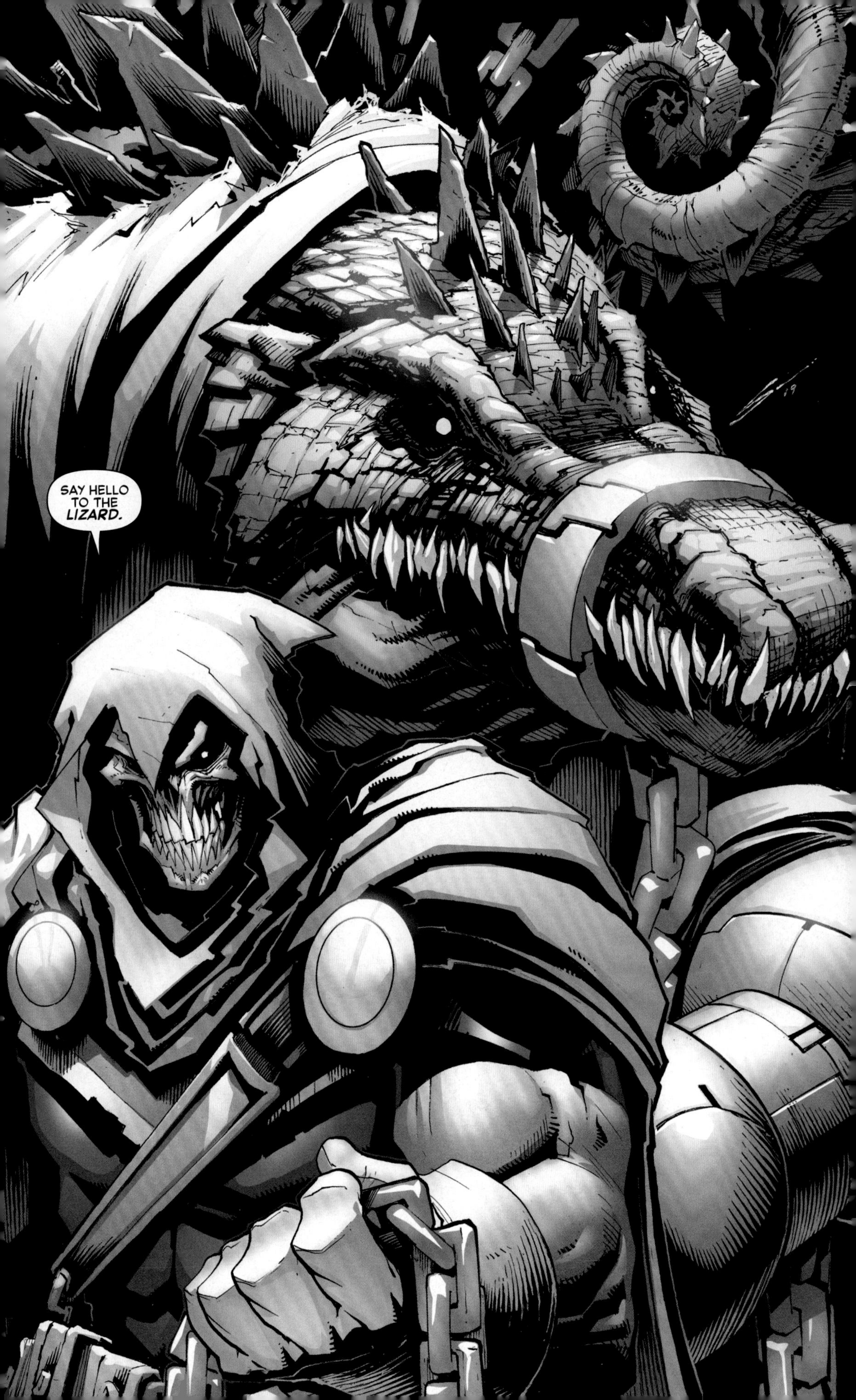
SAY HELLO TO THE LIZARD.

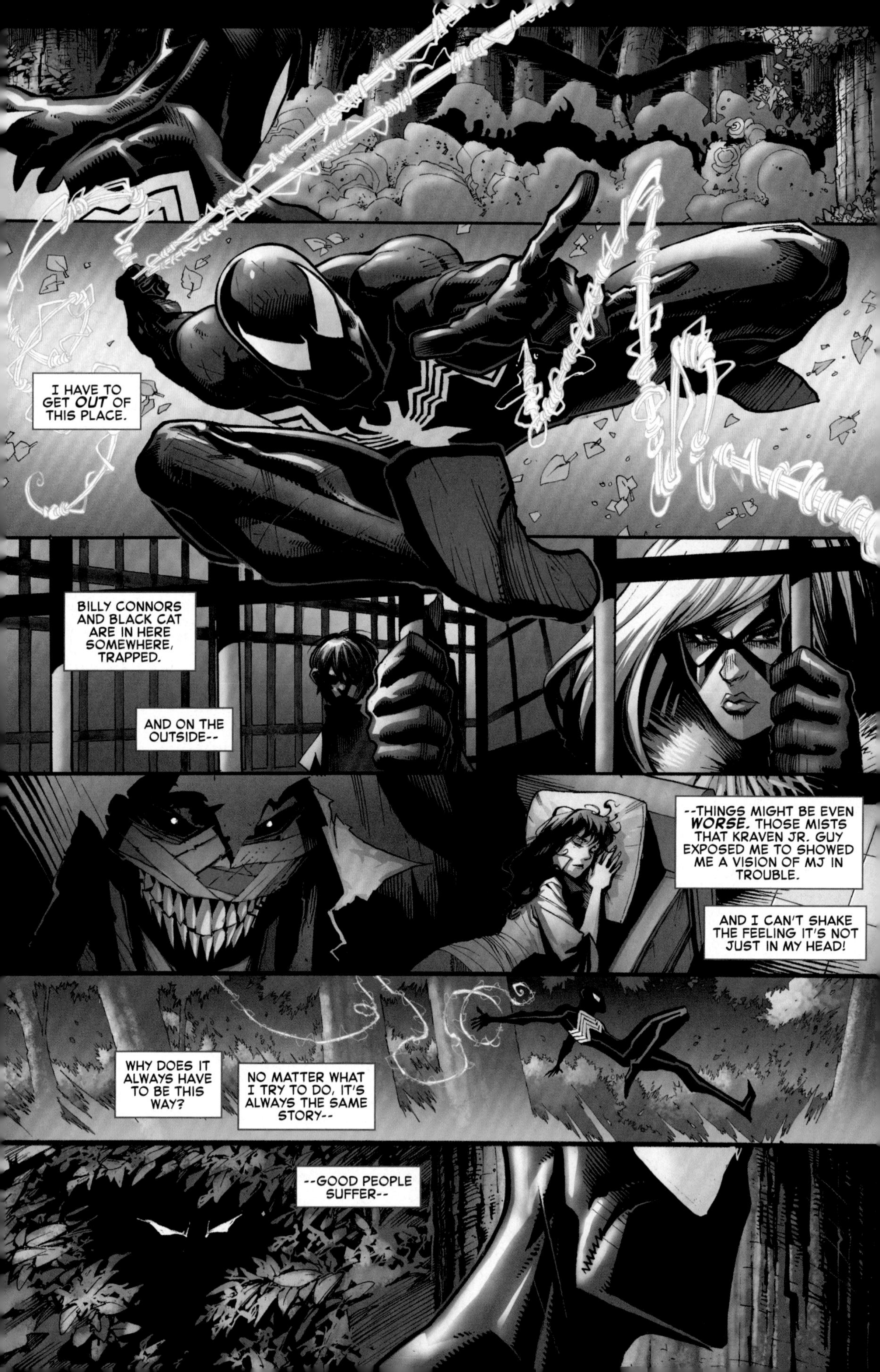
I HAVE TO GET OUT OF THIS PLACE.
BILLY CONNORS AND BLACK CAT ARE IN HERE SOMEWHERE, TRAPPED.
AND ON THE OUTSIDE--
--THINGS MIGHT BE EVEN WORSE. THOSE MISTS THAT KRAVEN JR. GUY EXPOSED ME TO SHOWED ME A VISION OF MJ IN TROUBLE.
AND I CAN'T SHAKE THE FEELING IT'S NOT JUST IN MY HEAD!
WHY DOES IT ALWAYS HAVE TO BE THIS WAY?
NO MATTER WHAT I TRY TO DO, IT'S ALWAYS THE SAME STORY--
--GOOD PEOPLE SUFFER--

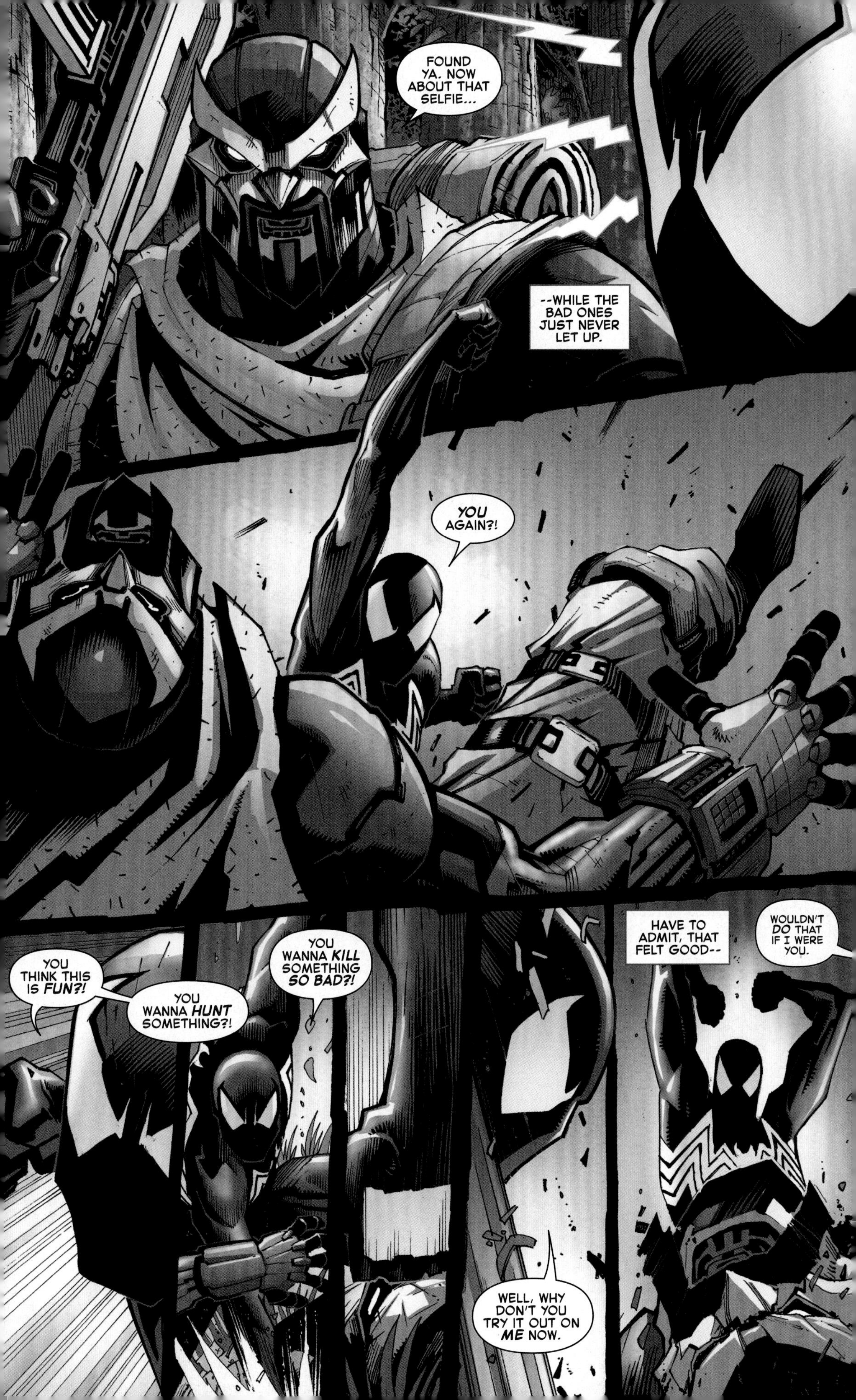
FOUND YA. NOW ABOUT THAT SELFIE...
--WHILE THE BAD ONES JUST NEVER LET UP.
YOU AGAIN?!
YOU THINK THIS IS FUN?!
YOU WANNA HUNT SOMETHING?!
YOU WANNA KILL SOMETHING SO BAD?!
WELL, WHY DON'T YOU TRY IT OUT ON ME NOW.
HAVE TO ADMIT, THAT FELT GOOD--
WOULDN'T DO THAT IF I WERE YOU.

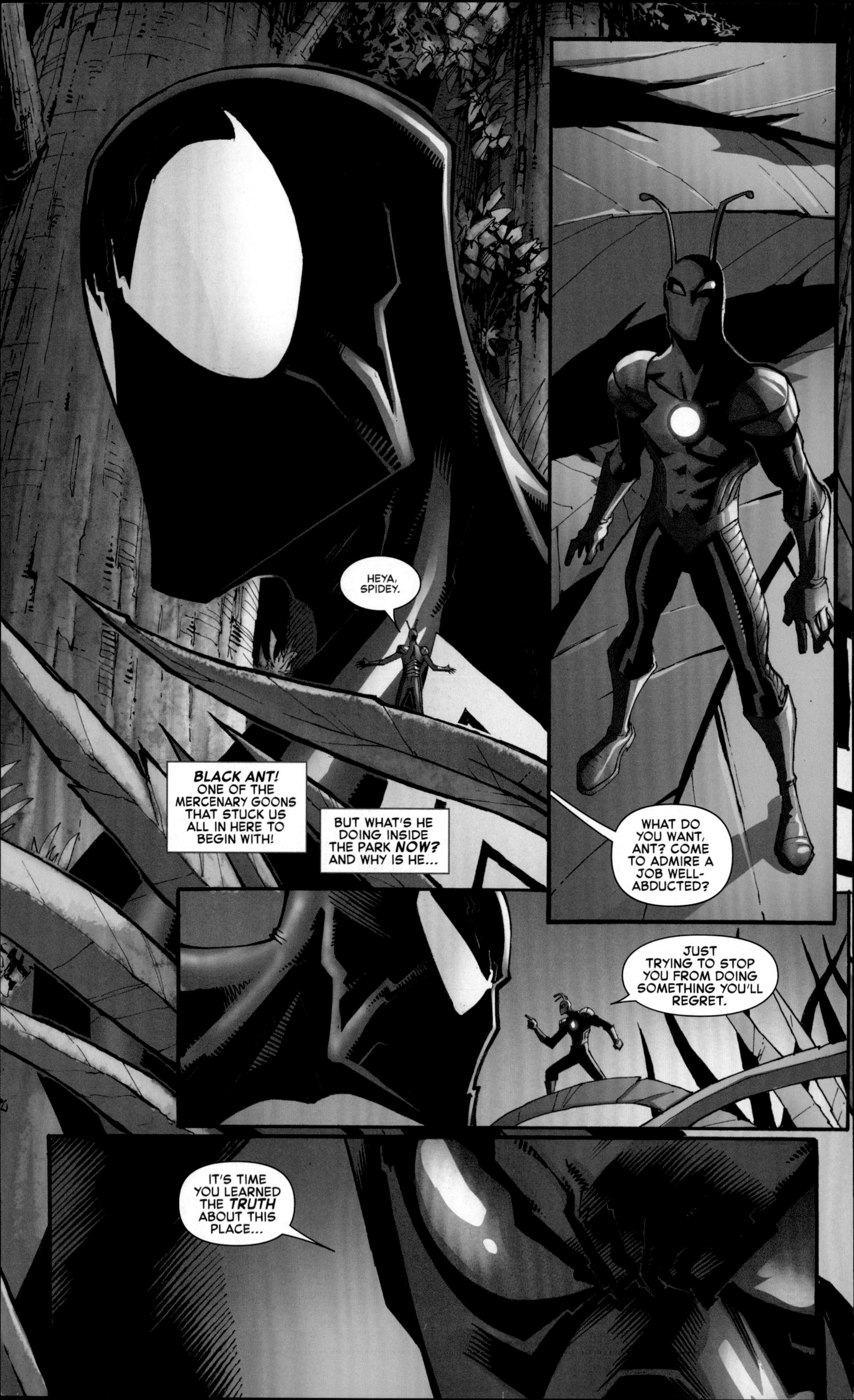
HEYA, SPIDEY.
WHAT DO YOU WANT, ANT? COME TO ADMIRE A JOB WELL-ABDUCTED?
BLACK ANT! ONE OF THE MERCENARY GOONS THAT STUCK US ALL IN HERE TO BEGIN WITH!
BUT WHAT'S HE DOING INSIDE THE PARK NOW? AND WHY IS HE...
JUST TRYING TO STOP YOU FROM DOING SOMETHING YOU'LL REGRET.
IT'S TIME YOU LEARNED THE TRUTH ABOUT THIS PLACE...

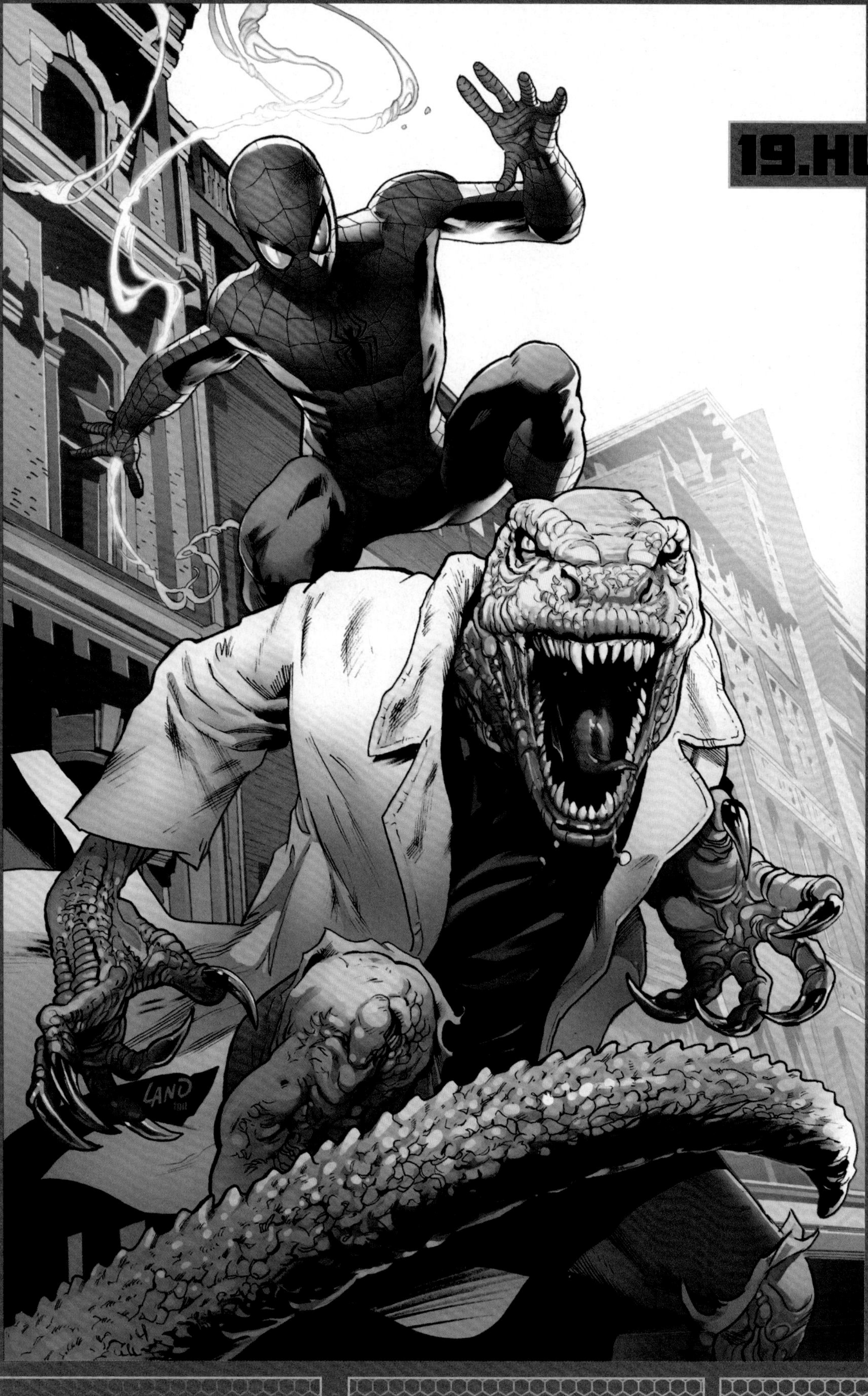

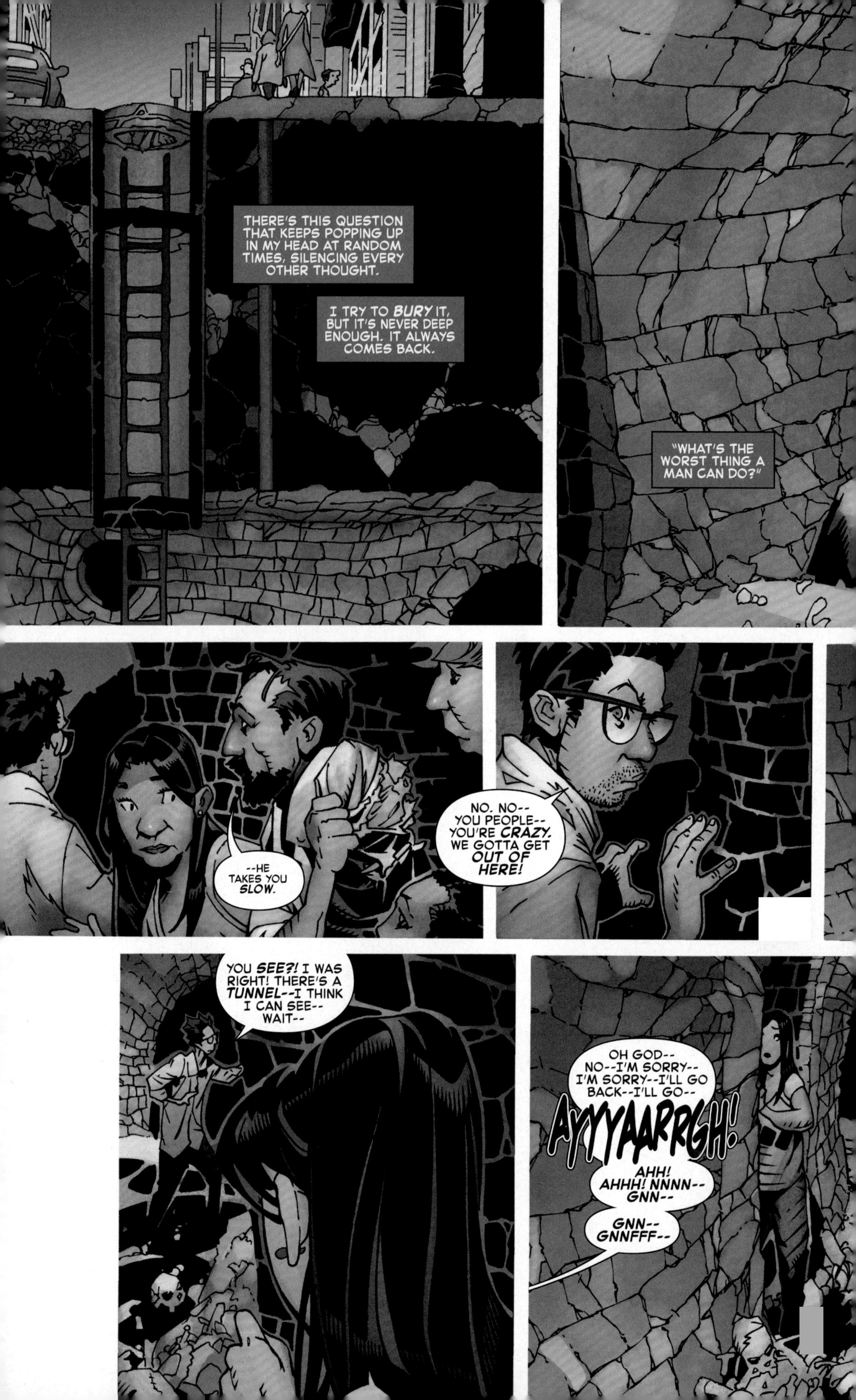

THERE'S THIS QUESTION THAT KEEPS POPPING UP IN MY HEAD AT RANDOM TIMES, SILENCING EVERY OTHER THOUGHT.
I TRY TO BURY IT, BUT IT'S NEVER DEEP ENOUGH. IT ALWAYS COMES BACK.
"WHAT'S THE WORST THING A MAN CAN DO?"
--HE TAKES YOU SLOW.
NO. NO--YOU PEOPLE--YOU'RE CRAZY. WE GOTTA GET OUT OF HERE!
YOU SEE?! I WAS RIGHT! THERE'S A TUNNEL--I THINK I CAN SEE--WAIT--
OH GOD--NO--I'M SORRY--I'M SORRY--I'LL GO BACK--I'LL GO--
AYYYAARRGH!
AHH! AHHH! NNNN--GNN--
GNN--GNNFFF--

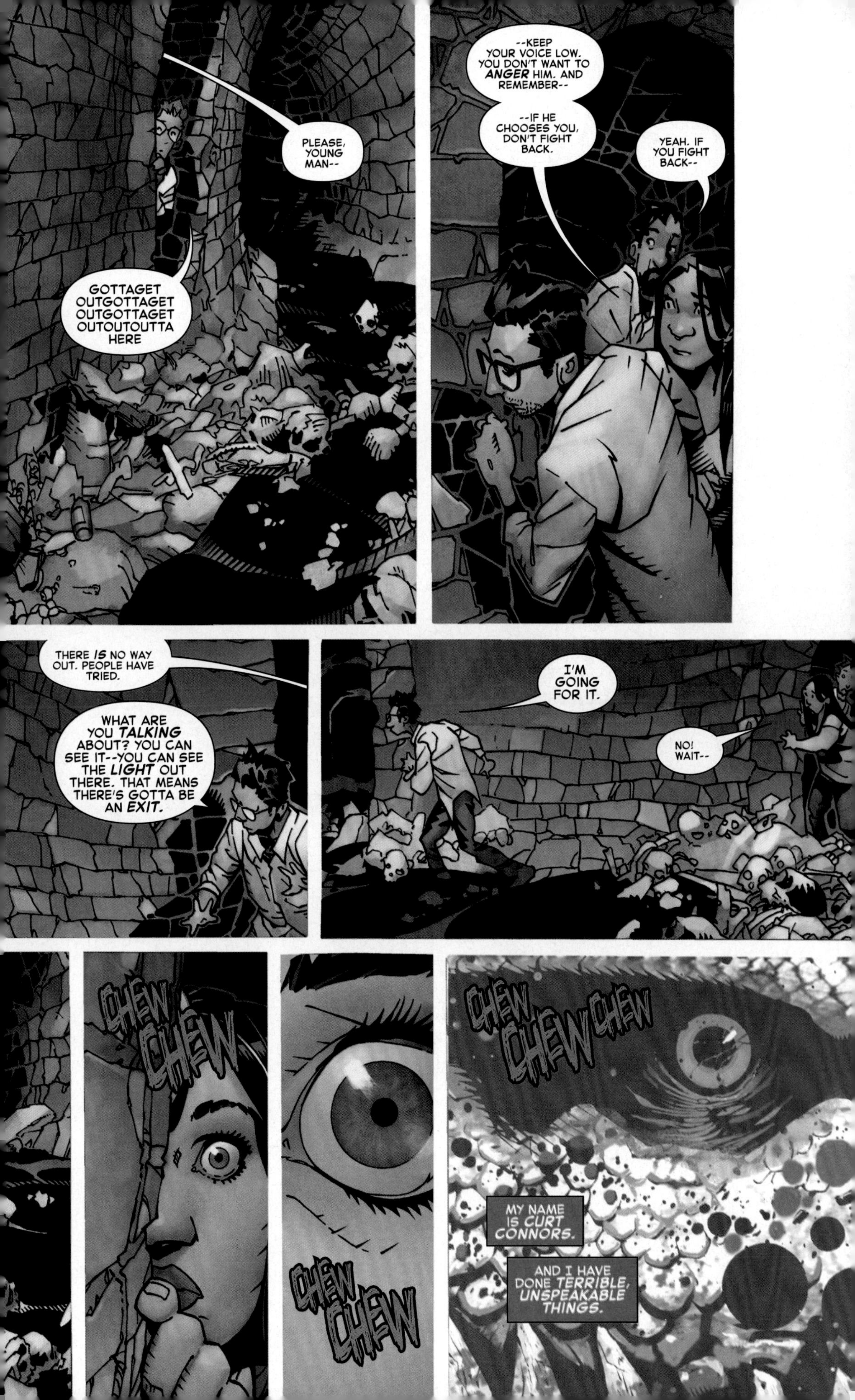
PLEASE, YOUNG MAN--
GOTTAGET OUTGOTTAGET OUTGOTTAGET OUTOUTOUTTA HERE
--KEEP YOUR VOICE LOW. YOU DON'T WANT TO ANGER HIM. AND REMEMBER--
--IF HE CHOOSES YOU, DON'T FIGHT BACK.
YEAH. IF YOU FIGHT BACK--
THERE IS NO WAY OUT. PEOPLE HAVE TRIED.
WHAT ARE YOU TALKING ABOUT? YOU CAN SEE IT--YOU CAN SEE THE LIGHT OUT THERE. THAT MEANS THERE'S GOTTA BE AN EXIT.
I'M GOING FOR IT.
NO! WAIT--
CHEW CHEW
CHEW CHEW
CHEW CHEW CHEW
MY NAME IS CURT CONNORS.
AND I HAVE DONE TERRIBLE, UNSPEAKABLE THINGS.

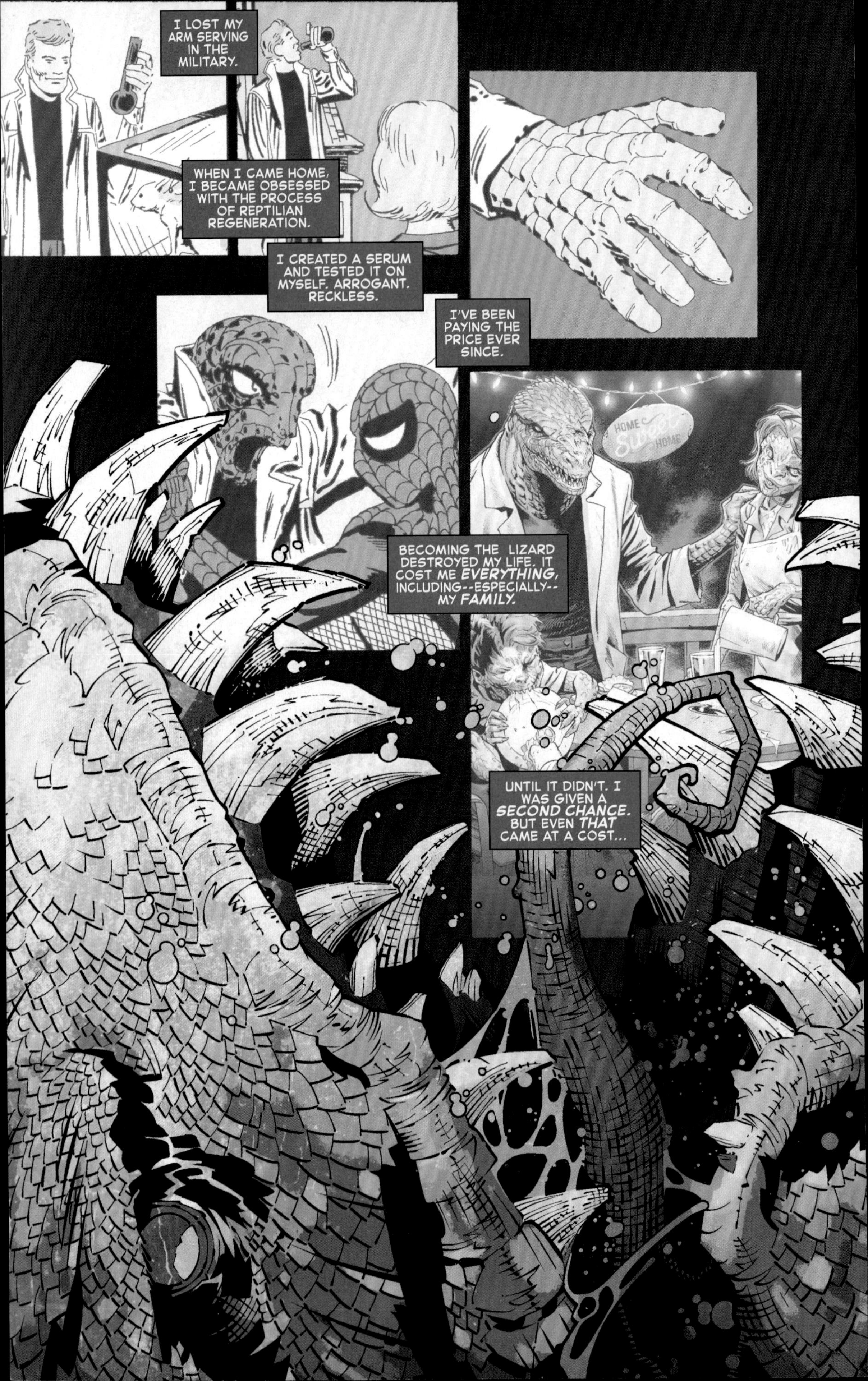
I LOST MY ARM SERVING IN THE MILITARY.
WHEN I CAME HOME, I BECAME OBSESSED WITH THE PROCESS OF REPTILIAN REGENERATION.
I CREATED A SERUM AND TESTED IT ON MYSELF. ARROGANT. RECKLESS.
I'VE BEEN PAYING THE PRICE EVER SINCE.
HOME Sweet HOME
BECOMING THE LIZARD DESTROYED MY LIFE. IT COST ME *EVERYTHING,* INCLUDING--ESPECIALLY--MY *FAMILY.*
UNTIL IT DIDN'T. I WAS GIVEN A *SECOND CHANCE.* BUT EVEN *THAT* CAME AT A COST...

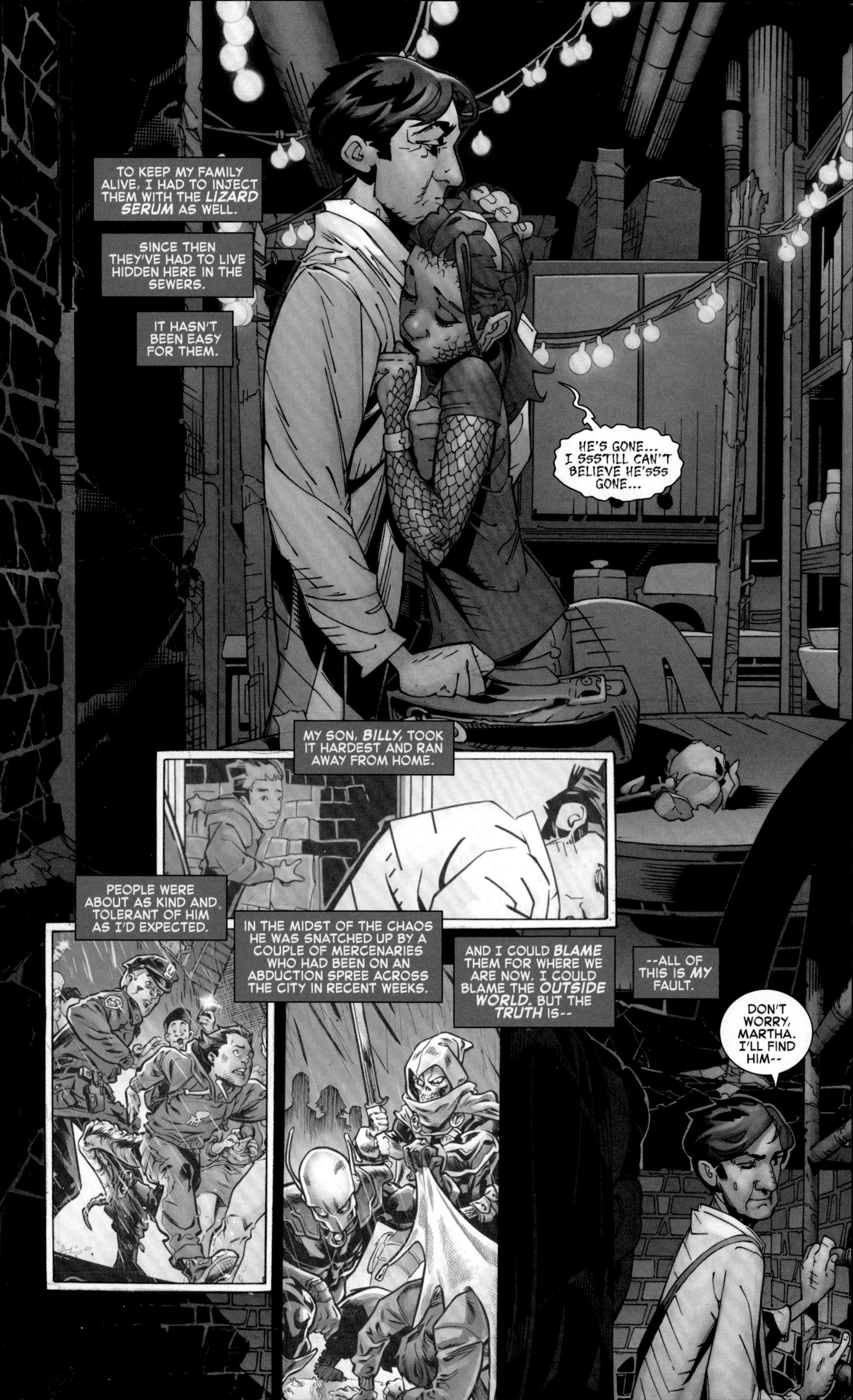

TO KEEP MY FAMILY ALIVE, I HAD TO INJECT THEM WITH THE LIZARD SERUM AS WELL.
SINCE THEN THEY'VE HAD TO LIVE HIDDEN HERE IN THE SEWERS.
IT HASN'T BEEN EASY FOR THEM.
HE'S GONE... I SSSTILL CAN'T BELIEVE HE'SSS GONE...
MY SON, BILLY, TOOK IT HARDEST AND RAN AWAY FROM HOME.
PEOPLE WERE ABOUT AS KIND AND TOLERANT OF HIM AS I'D EXPECTED.
IN THE MIDST OF THE CHAOS HE WAS SNATCHED UP BY A COUPLE OF MERCENARIES WHO HAD BEEN ON AN ABDUCTION SPREE ACROSS THE CITY IN RECENT WEEKS.
AND I COULD BLAME THEM FOR WHERE WE ARE NOW. I COULD BLAME THE OUTSIDE WORLD. BUT THE TRUTH IS--
--ALL OF THIS IS MY FAULT.
DON'T WORRY, MARTHA. I'LL FIND HIM--

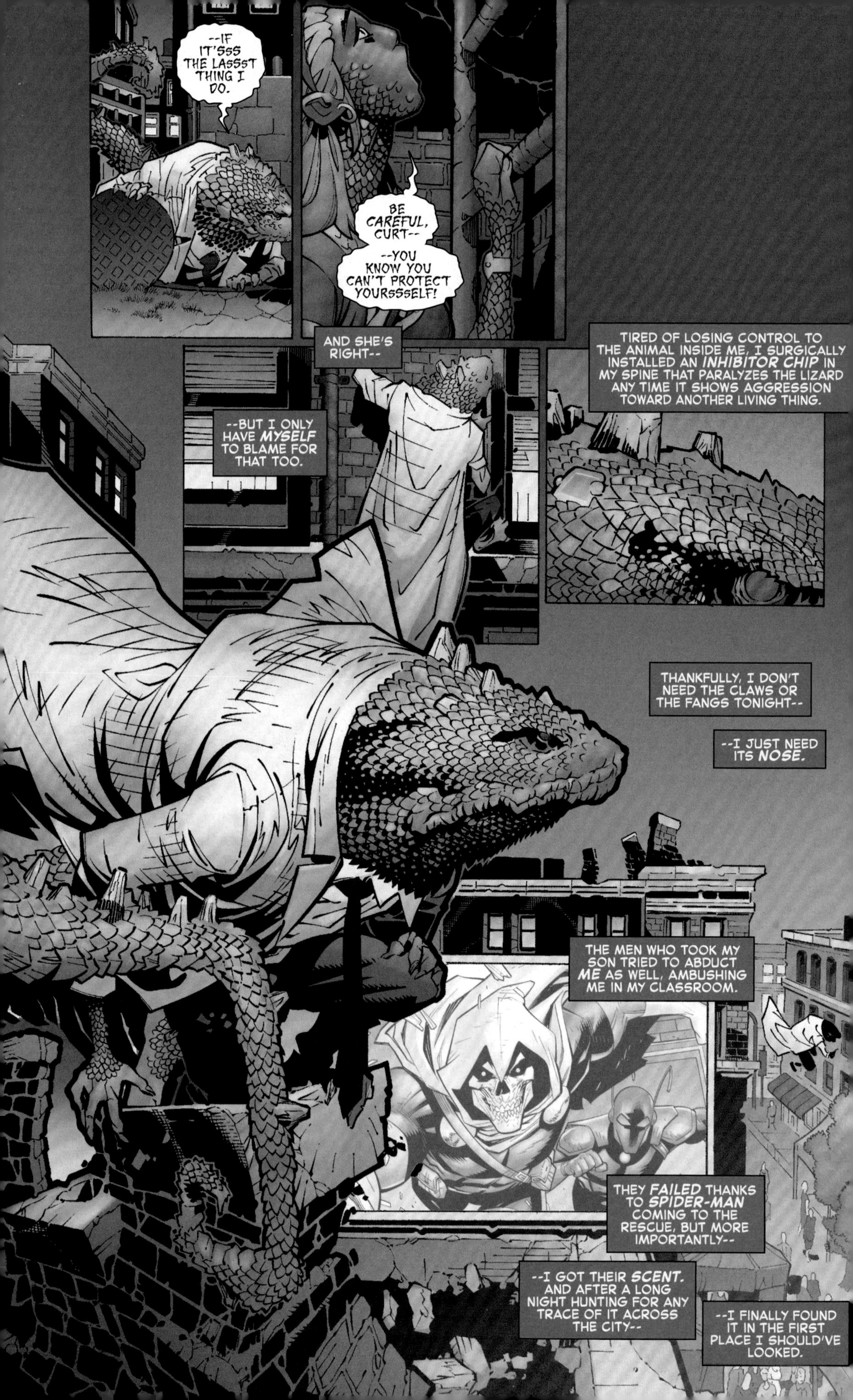
--IF IT'SSS THE LASSST THING I DO.
BE CAREFUL, CURT--
--YOU KNOW YOU CAN'T PROTECT YOURSSSELF!
AND SHE'S RIGHT--
--BUT I ONLY HAVE MYSELF TO BLAME FOR THAT TOO.
TIRED OF LOSING CONTROL TO THE ANIMAL INSIDE ME, I SURGICALLY INSTALLED AN INHIBITOR CHIP IN MY SPINE THAT PARALYZES THE LIZARD ANY TIME IT SHOWS AGGRESSION TOWARD ANOTHER LIVING THING.
THANKFULLY, I DON'T NEED THE CLAWS OR THE FANGS TONIGHT--
--I JUST NEED ITS NOSE.
THE MEN WHO TOOK MY SON TRIED TO ABDUCT ME AS WELL, AMBUSHING ME IN MY CLASSROOM.
THEY FAILED THANKS TO SPIDER-MAN COMING TO THE RESCUE, BUT MORE IMPORTANTLY--
--I GOT THEIR SCENT. AND AFTER A LONG NIGHT HUNTING FOR ANY TRACE OF IT ACROSS THE CITY--
--I FINALLY FOUND IT IN THE FIRST PLACE I SHOULD'VE LOOKED.

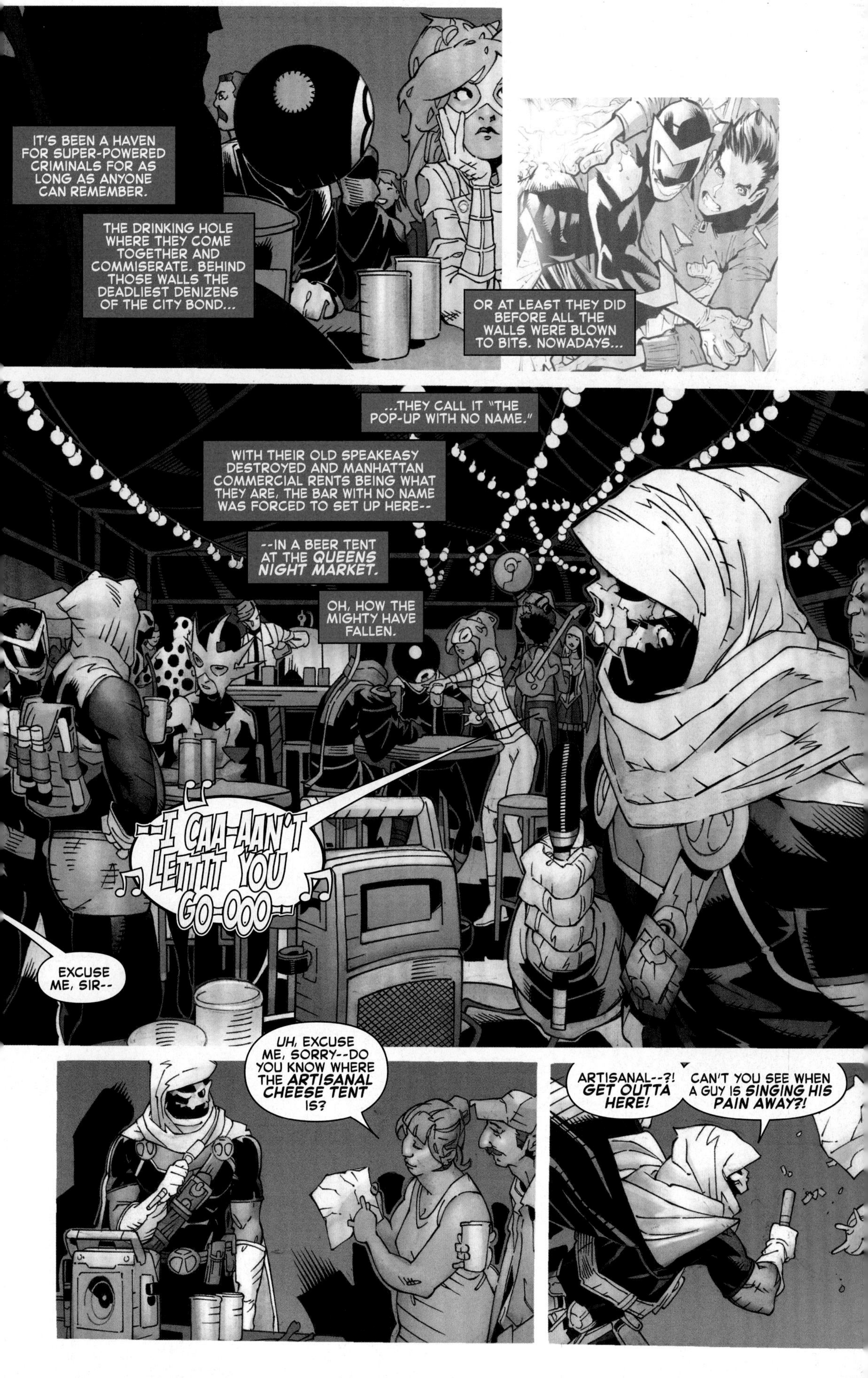
IT'S BEEN A HAVEN FOR SUPER-POWERED CRIMINALS FOR AS LONG AS ANYONE CAN REMEMBER.
THE DRINKING HOLE WHERE THEY COME TOGETHER AND COMMISERATE. BEHIND THOSE WALLS THE DEADLIEST DENIZENS OF THE CITY BOND...
OR AT LEAST THEY DID BEFORE ALL THE WALLS WERE BLOWN TO BITS. NOWADAYS...
...THEY CALL IT "THE POP-UP WITH NO NAME."
WITH THEIR OLD SPEAKEASY DESTROYED AND MANHATTAN COMMERCIAL RENTS BEING WHAT THEY ARE, THE BAR WITH NO NAME WAS FORCED TO SET UP HERE--
--IN A BEER TENT AT THE *QUEENS NIGHT MARKET.*
OH, HOW THE MIGHTY HAVE FALLEN.
--I CAA-AAN'T LETTTT YOU GO-OOO--
EXCUSE ME, SIR--
UH, EXCUSE ME, SORRY--DO YOU KNOW WHERE THE ***ARTISANAL CHEESE TENT*** IS?
ARTISANAL--?! ***GET OUTTA HERE!***
CAN'T YOU SEE WHEN A GUY IS ***SINGING HIS PAIN AWAY?!***

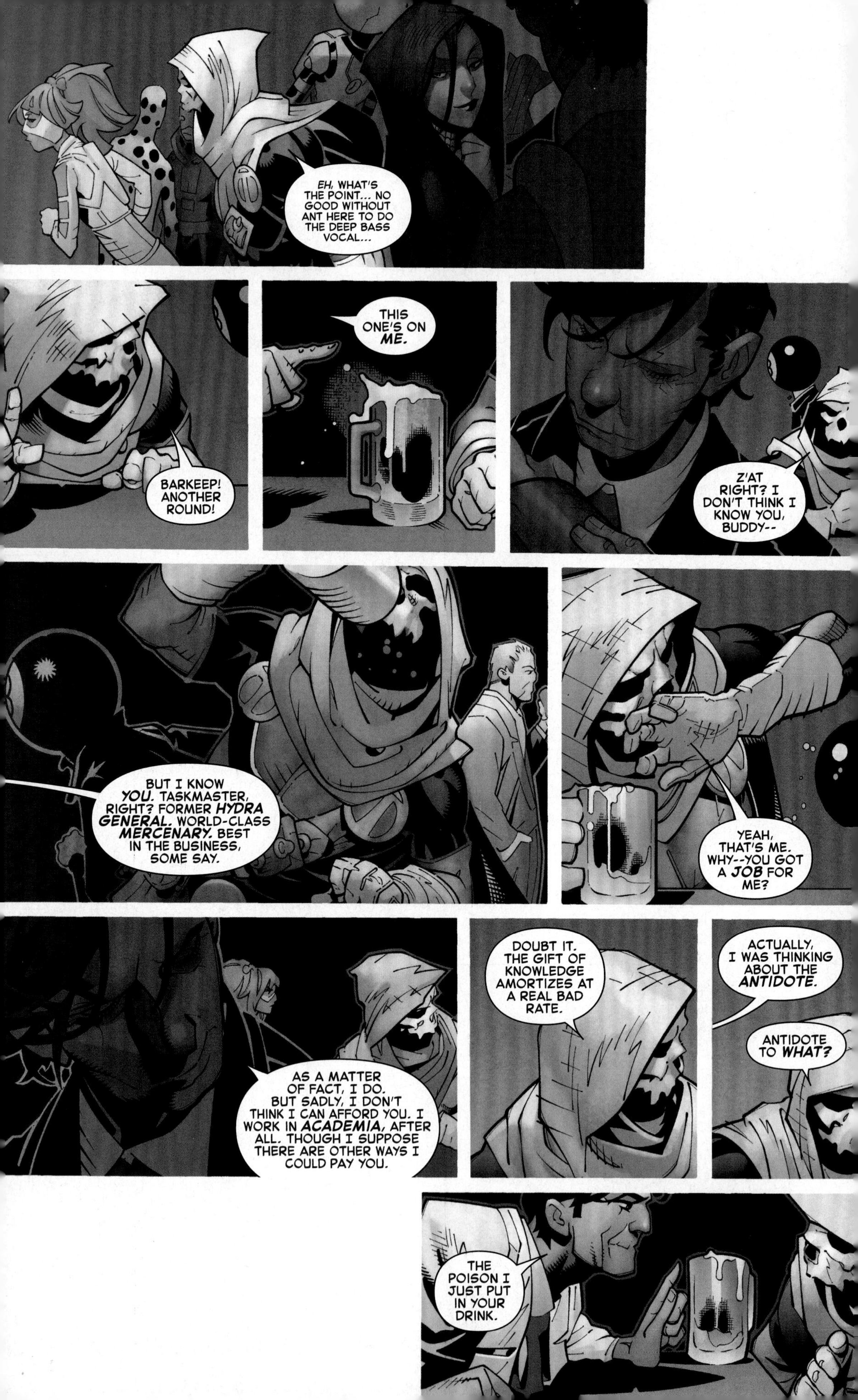
EH, WHAT'S THE POINT... NO GOOD WITHOUT ANT HERE TO DO THE DEEP BASS VOCAL...
BARKEEP! ANOTHER ROUND!
THIS ONE'S ON ME.
Z'AT RIGHT? I DON'T THINK I KNOW YOU, BUDDY--
BUT I KNOW YOU. TASKMASTER, RIGHT? FORMER HYDRA GENERAL. WORLD-CLASS MERCENARY. BEST IN THE BUSINESS, SOME SAY.
YEAH, THAT'S ME. WHY--YOU GOT A JOB FOR ME?
AS A MATTER OF FACT, I DO. BUT SADLY, I DON'T THINK I CAN AFFORD YOU. I WORK IN ACADEMIA, AFTER ALL. THOUGH I SUPPOSE THERE ARE OTHER WAYS I COULD PAY YOU.
DOUBT IT. THE GIFT OF KNOWLEDGE AMORTIZES AT A REAL BAD RATE.
ACTUALLY, I WAS THINKING ABOUT THE ANTIDOTE.
ANTIDOTE TO WHAT?
THE POISON I JUST PUT IN YOUR DRINK.

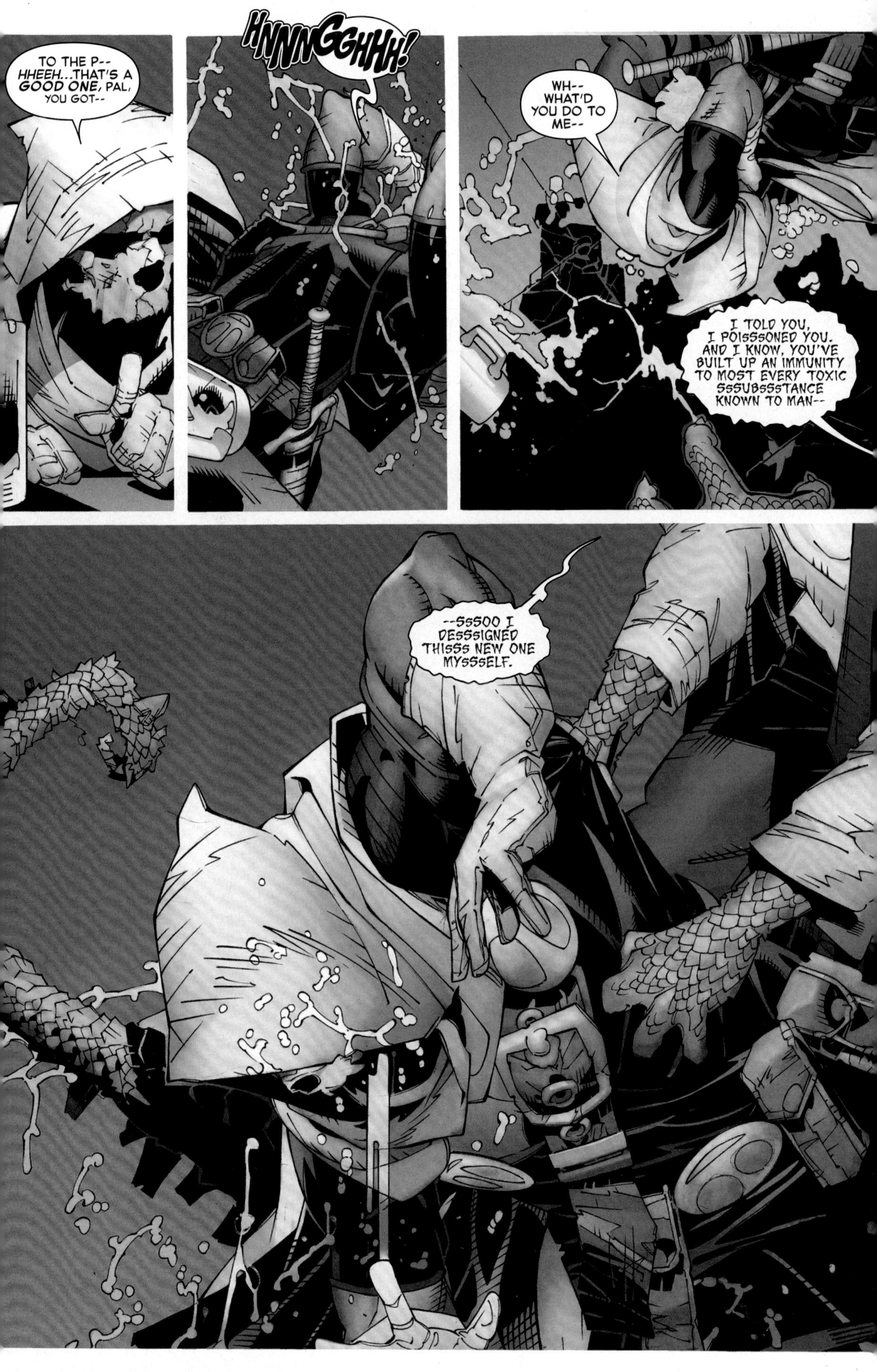
TO THE P--
HHEEH...THAT'S A GOOD ONE, PAL, YOU GOT--
HNNNGGHHH!
WH-- WHAT'D YOU DO TO ME--
I TOLD YOU, I POISSSONED YOU. AND I KNOW, YOU'VE BUILT UP AN IMMUNITY TO MOST EVERY TOXIC SSSUBSSSTANCE KNOWN TO MAN--
--SSSOO I DESSSIGNED THISSS NEW ONE MYSSSELF.

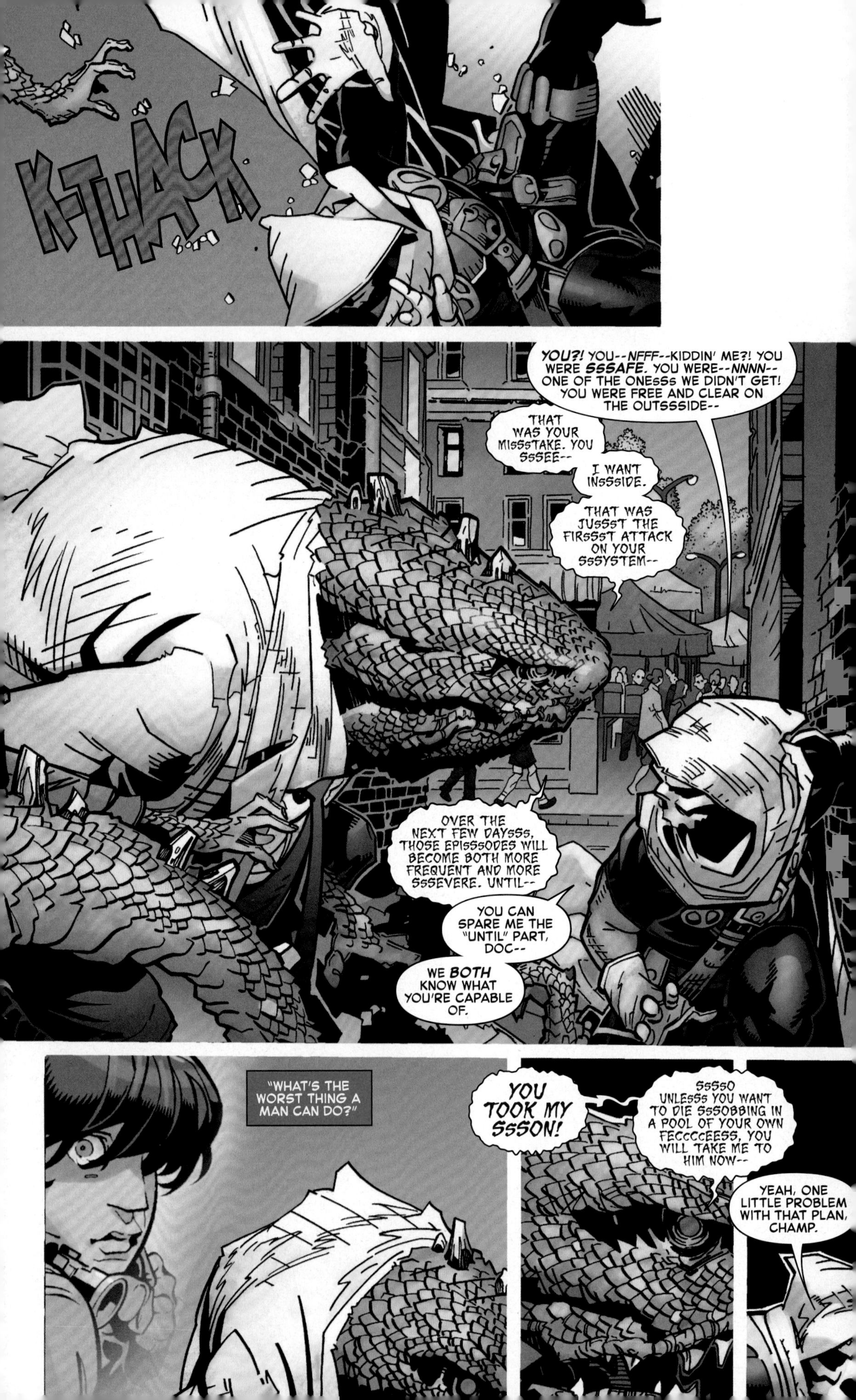
K-THACK
YOU?! YOU--NFFF--KIDDIN' ME?! YOU WERE SSSAFE. YOU WERE--NNNN--ONE OF THE ONESsS WE DIDN'T GET! YOU WERE FREE AND CLEAR ON THE OUTSSSIDE--
THAT WAS YOUR MISSSTAKE. YOU SSSEE--
I WANT INSSSIDE.
THAT WAS JUSSST THE FIRSSST ATTACK ON YOUR SSSYSTEM--
OVER THE NEXT FEW DAYSSS, THOSE EPISSSODES WILL BECOME BOTH MORE FREQUENT AND MORE SSSEVERE. UNTIL--
YOU CAN SPARE ME THE "UNTIL" PART, DOC--
WE BOTH KNOW WHAT YOU'RE CAPABLE OF.
"WHAT'S THE WORST THING A MAN CAN DO?"
YOU TOOK MY SSSON!
SSSSO UNLESSS YOU WANT TO DIE SSSOBBING IN A POOL OF YOUR OWN FECCCCEESS, YOU WILL TAKE ME TO HIM NOW--
YEAH, ONE LITTLE PROBLEM WITH THAT PLAN, CHAMP.

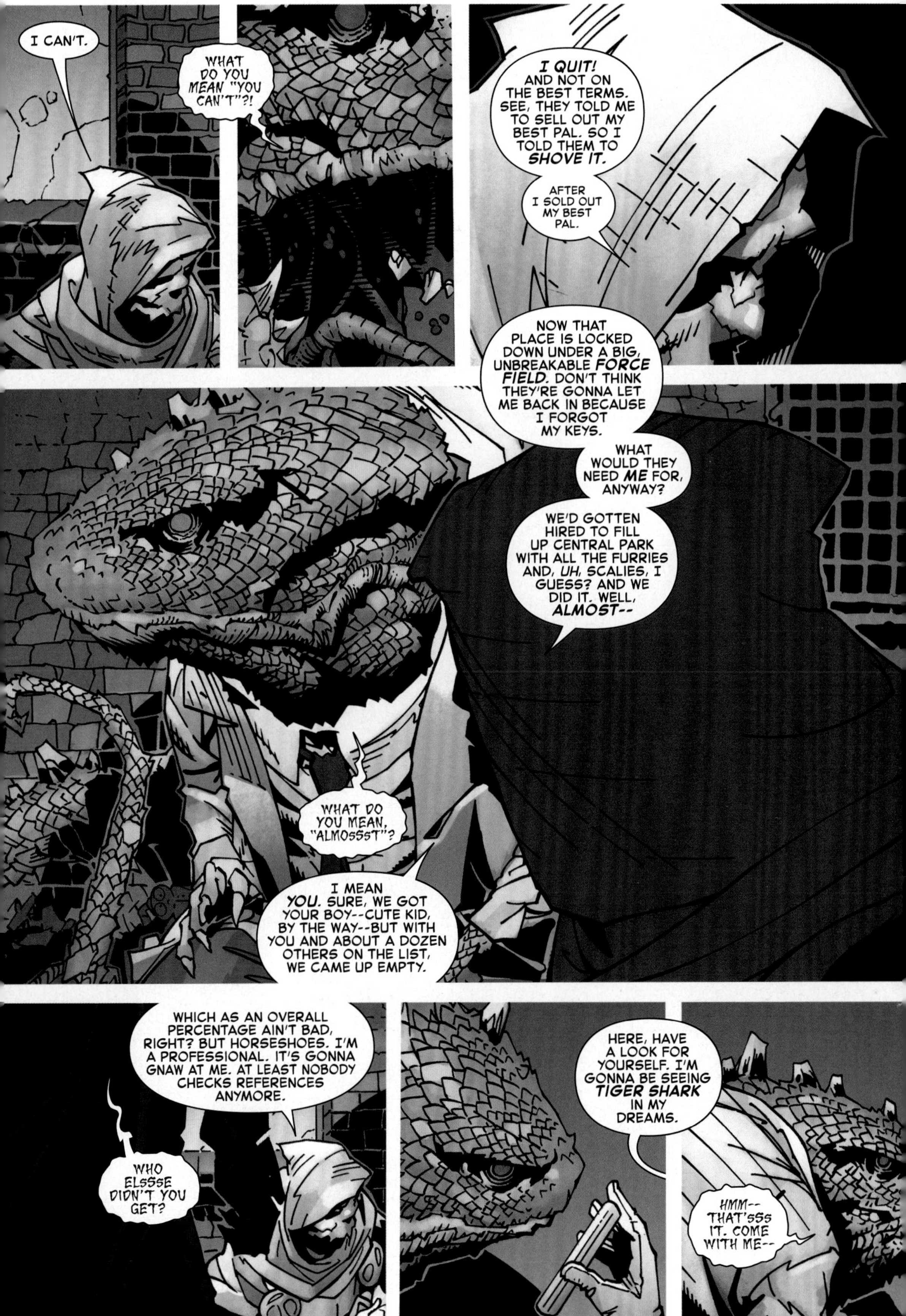

I CAN'T.
WHAT DO YOU MEAN "YOU CAN'T"?!
I QUIT! AND NOT ON THE BEST TERMS. SEE, THEY TOLD ME TO SELL OUT MY BEST PAL. SO I TOLD THEM TO SHOVE IT.
AFTER I SOLD OUT MY BEST PAL.
NOW THAT PLACE IS LOCKED DOWN UNDER A BIG, UNBREAKABLE FORCE FIELD. DON'T THINK THEY'RE GONNA LET ME BACK IN BECAUSE I FORGOT MY KEYS.
WHAT WOULD THEY NEED ME FOR, ANYWAY?
WE'D GOTTEN HIRED TO FILL UP CENTRAL PARK WITH ALL THE FURRIES AND, UH, SCALIES, I GUESS? AND WE DID IT. WELL, ALMOST--
WHAT DO YOU MEAN, "ALMOSSST"?
I MEAN YOU. SURE, WE GOT YOUR BOY--CUTE KID, BY THE WAY--BUT WITH YOU AND ABOUT A DOZEN OTHERS ON THE LIST, WE CAME UP EMPTY.
WHICH AS AN OVERALL PERCENTAGE AIN'T BAD, RIGHT? BUT HORSESHOES. I'M A PROFESSIONAL. IT'S GONNA GNAW AT ME. AT LEAST NOBODY CHECKS REFERENCES ANYMORE.
WHO ELSSSE DIDN'T YOU GET?
HERE, HAVE A LOOK FOR YOURSELF. I'M GONNA BE SEEING TIGER SHARK IN MY DREAMS.
HMM--THAT'SSS IT. COME WITH ME--

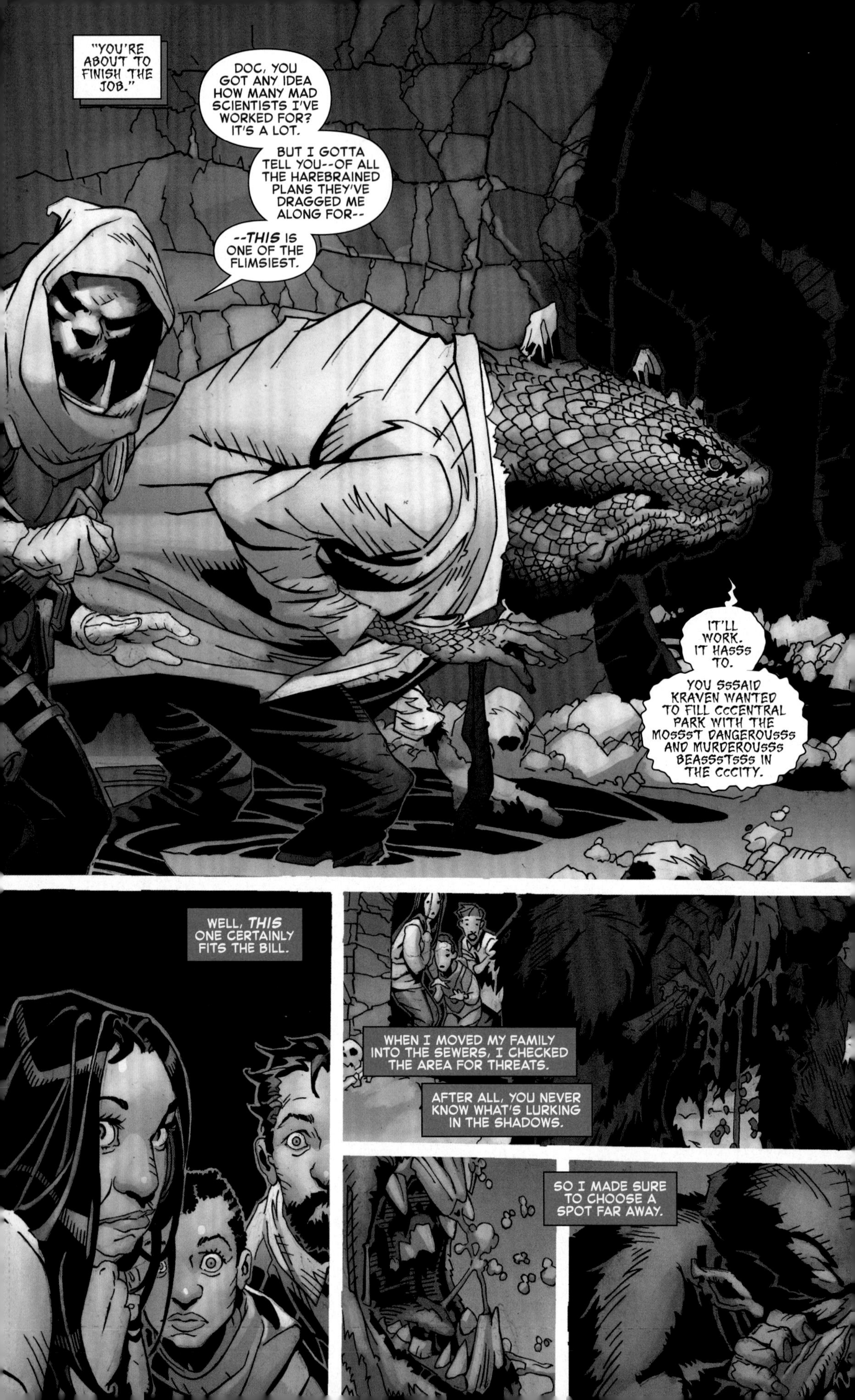
"YOU'RE ABOUT TO FINISH THE JOB."
DOC, YOU GOT ANY IDEA HOW MANY MAD SCIENTISTS I'VE WORKED FOR? IT'S A LOT.
BUT I GOTTA TELL YOU--OF ALL THE HAREBRAINED PLANS THEY'VE DRAGGED ME ALONG FOR--
--THIS IS ONE OF THE FLIMSIEST.
IT'LL WORK. IT HASSS TO.
YOU SSSAID KRAVEN WANTED TO FILL CCCENTRAL PARK WITH THE MOSSST DANGEROUSSS AND MURDEROUSSS BEASSSTSSS IN THE CCCITY.
WELL, THIS ONE CERTAINLY FITS THE BILL.
WHEN I MOVED MY FAMILY INTO THE SEWERS, I CHECKED THE AREA FOR THREATS.
AFTER ALL, YOU NEVER KNOW WHAT'S LURKING IN THE SHADOWS.
SO I MADE SURE TO CHOOSE A SPOT FAR AWAY.

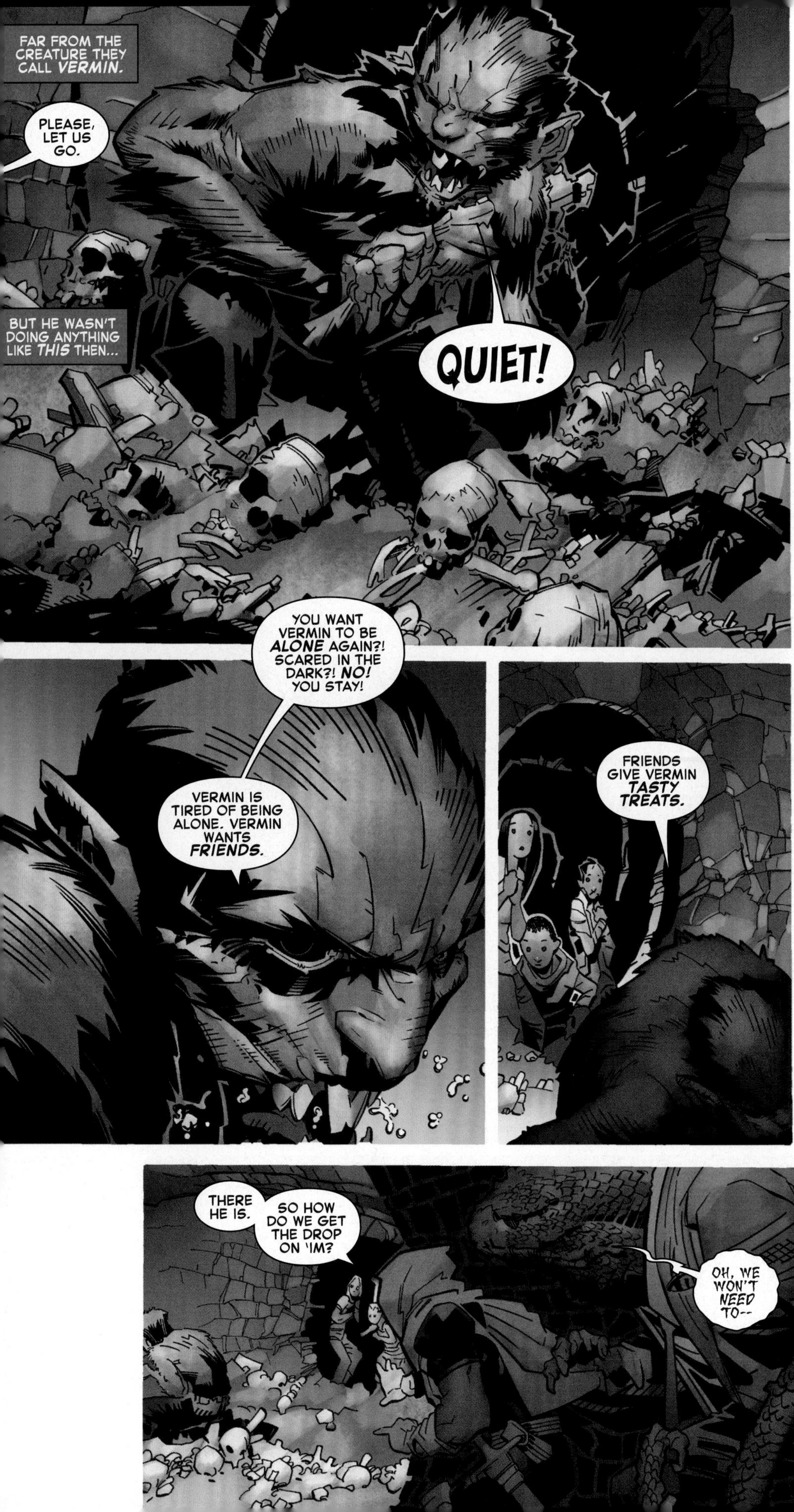
FAR FROM THE CREATURE THEY CALL VERMIN.
PLEASE, LET US GO.
BUT HE WASN'T DOING ANYTHING LIKE THIS THEN...
QUIET!
YOU WANT VERMIN TO BE ALONE AGAIN?! SCARED IN THE DARK?! NO! YOU STAY!
VERMIN IS TIRED OF BEING ALONE. VERMIN WANTS FRIENDS.
FRIENDS GIVE VERMIN TASTY TREATS.
THERE HE IS.
SO HOW DO WE GET THE DROP ON 'IM?
OH, WE WON'T NEED TO--

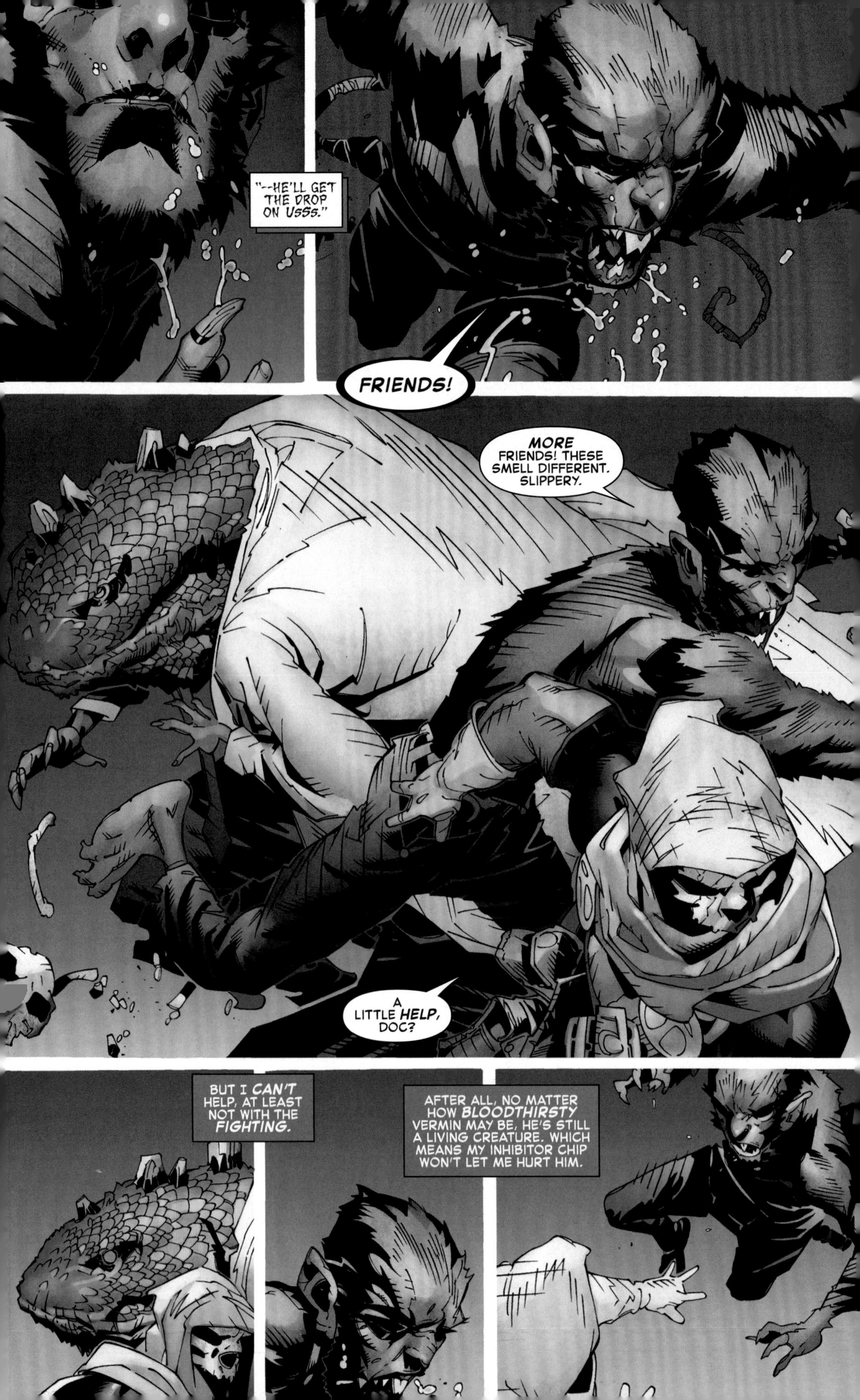
"--HE'LL GET THE DROP ON USSS."
FRIENDS!
MORE FRIENDS! THESE SMELL DIFFERENT. SLIPPERY.
A LITTLE HELP, DOC?
BUT I CAN'T HELP, AT LEAST NOT WITH THE FIGHTING.
AFTER ALL, NO MATTER HOW BLOODTHIRSTY VERMIN MAY BE, HE'S STILL A LIVING CREATURE. WHICH MEANS MY INHIBITOR CHIP WON'T LET ME HURT HIM.

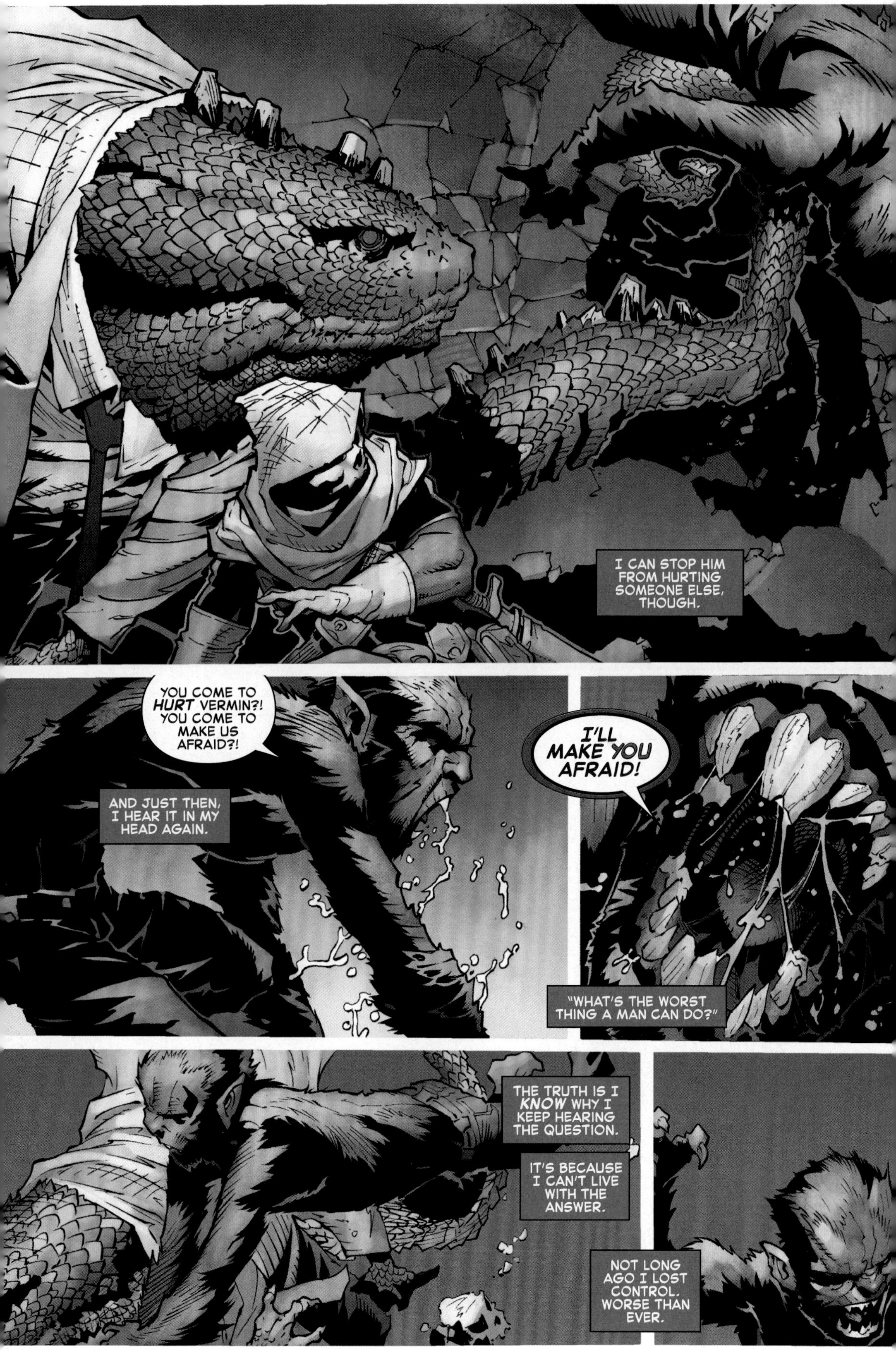
I CAN STOP HIM FROM HURTING SOMEONE ELSE, THOUGH.
YOU COME TO HURT VERMIN?! YOU COME TO MAKE US AFRAID?!
AND JUST THEN, I HEAR IT IN MY HEAD AGAIN.
I'LL MAKE YOU AFRAID!
"WHAT'S THE WORST THING A MAN CAN DO?"
THE TRUTH IS I KNOW WHY I KEEP HEARING THE QUESTION.
IT'S BECAUSE I CAN'T LIVE WITH THE ANSWER.
NOT LONG AGO I LOST CONTROL. WORSE THAN EVER.

THE MONSTER TOOK ME OVER. AND I VANISHED.

I BECAME NOTHING BUT REPTILE. NOTHING BUT LIZARD.

LIZARDS DO NOT RAISE THEIR YOUNG.

LIZARDS DO NOT CARE FOR THEIR YOUNG.

"WHAT'S THE WORST THING A MAN CAN DO?"

BILLY DIED. BY THE LIZARD'S HAND.

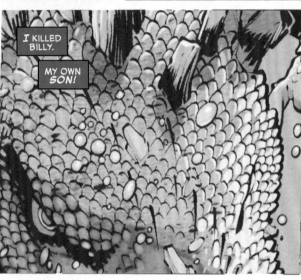

I KILLED BILLY.

MY OWN SON!

HE'S STILL PAYING FOR YOUR MISTAKES.

HE'S STILL SUFFERING BECAUSE OF YOU!

ARE YOU GOING TO FAIL HIM AGAIN?!

HURT HIS OWN CHILD.

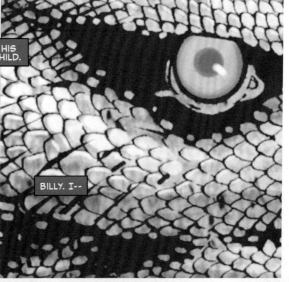

BILLY. I--

I *DESERVE* THIS. I DESERVE--

BUT WHAT DOES *HE* DESERVE?

HE CAME BACK. THEY BROUGHT HIM BACK TO LIFE.

IS IT *REALLY* HIM?

YOU GET TO TRY AGAIN. GET TO PRETEND IT NEVER HAPPENED. EVERYONE GETS TO PRETEND IT NEVER HAPPENED. (BUT IT DID.)

ARE YOU GOING TO LET HIM *DIE* AGAIN, YOU MONSTER?!

NO!

THUD

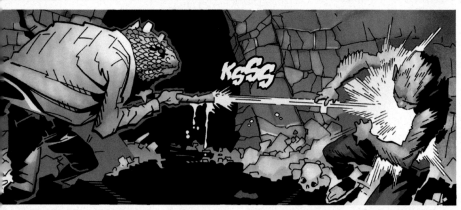

KSSS

TANK

NOW WHAT?

FIRST, WE FREE THE PEOPLE THE CREATURE TRAPPED DOWN HERE. TRY TO DO A LITTLE GOOD.

IT DOESN'T COME CLOSE TO EVENING UP MY SCORE IN LIFE, BUT IT'S *SOMETHING.*

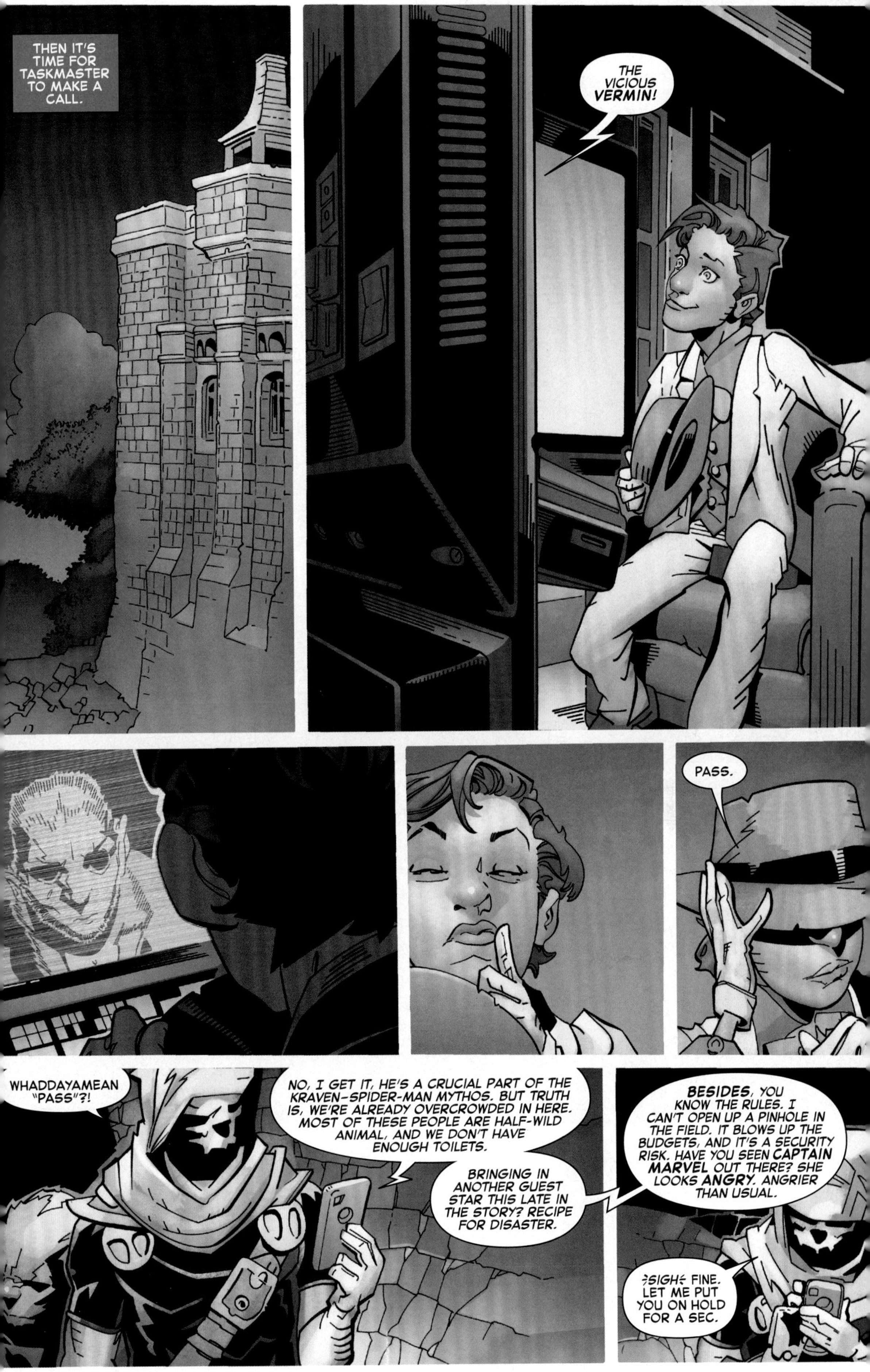
THEN IT'S TIME FOR TASKMASTER TO MAKE A CALL.
THE VICIOUS VERMIN!
PASS.
WHADDAYAMEAN "PASS"?!
NO, I GET IT, HE'S A CRUCIAL PART OF THE KRAVEN-SPIDER-MAN MYTHOS. BUT TRUTH IS, WE'RE ALREADY OVERCROWDED IN HERE. MOST OF THESE PEOPLE ARE HALF-WILD ANIMAL, AND WE DON'T HAVE ENOUGH TOILETS.
BRINGING IN ANOTHER GUEST STAR THIS LATE IN THE STORY? RECIPE FOR DISASTER.
BESIDES, YOU KNOW THE RULES. I CAN'T OPEN UP A PINHOLE IN THE FIELD. IT BLOWS UP THE BUDGETS, AND IT'S A SECURITY RISK. HAVE YOU SEEN CAPTAIN MARVEL OUT THERE? SHE LOOKS ANGRY. ANGRIER THAN USUAL.
⇒SIGH⇐ FINE. LET ME PUT YOU ON HOLD FOR A SEC.

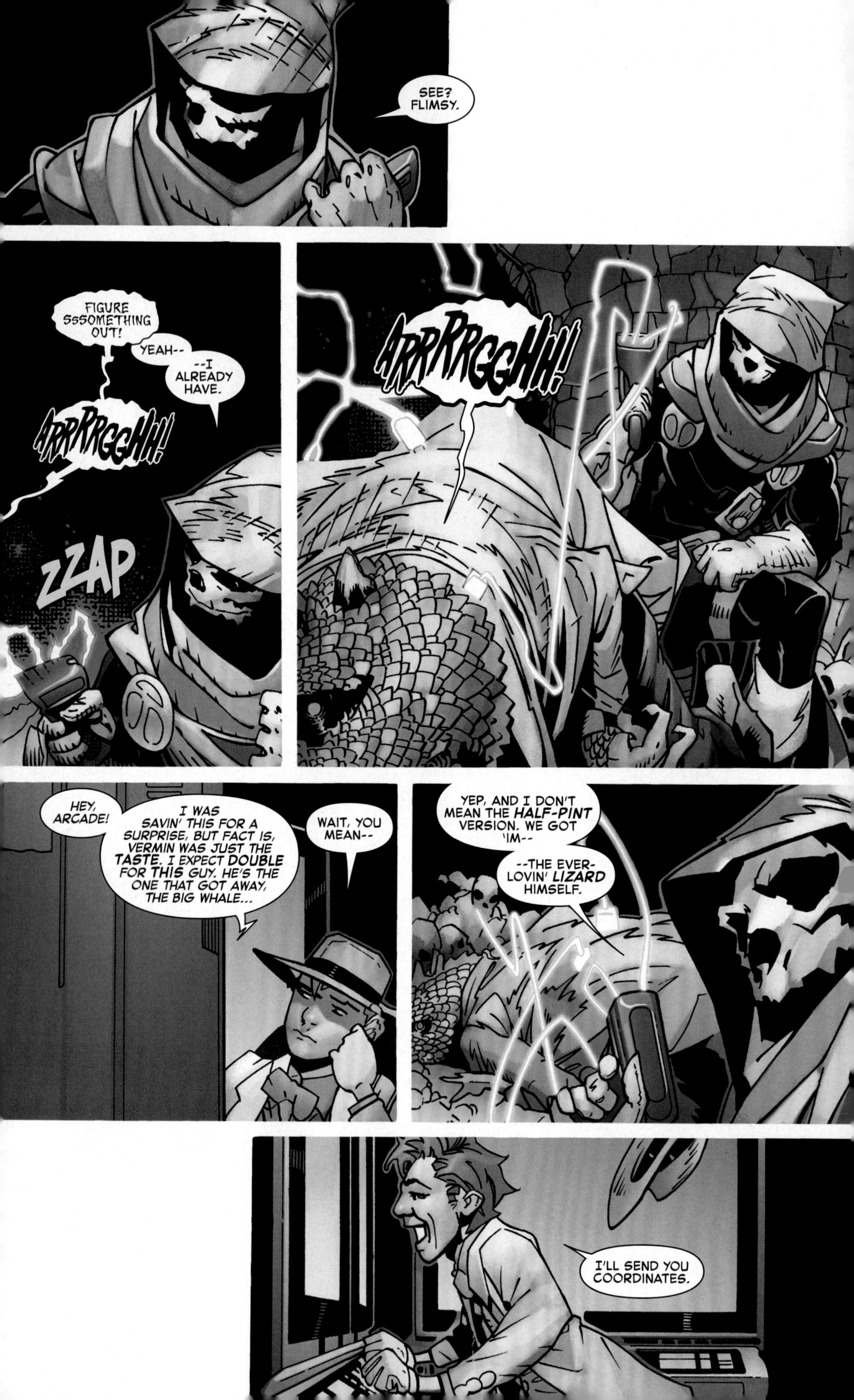
SEE? FLIMSY.
FIGURE SssOMETHING OUT!
YEAH--
--I ALREADY HAVE.
ARRRRGGHH!
ZZAP
ARRRRGGHH!
HEY, ARCADE!
I WAS SAVIN' THIS FOR A SURPRISE, BUT FACT IS, VERMIN WAS JUST THE TASTE. I EXPECT DOUBLE FOR THIS GUY. HE'S THE ONE THAT GOT AWAY, THE BIG WHALE...
WAIT, YOU MEAN--
YEP, AND I DON'T MEAN THE HALF-PINT VERSION. WE GOT 'IM--
--THE EVER-LOVIN' LIZARD HIMSELF.
I'LL SEND YOU COORDINATES.

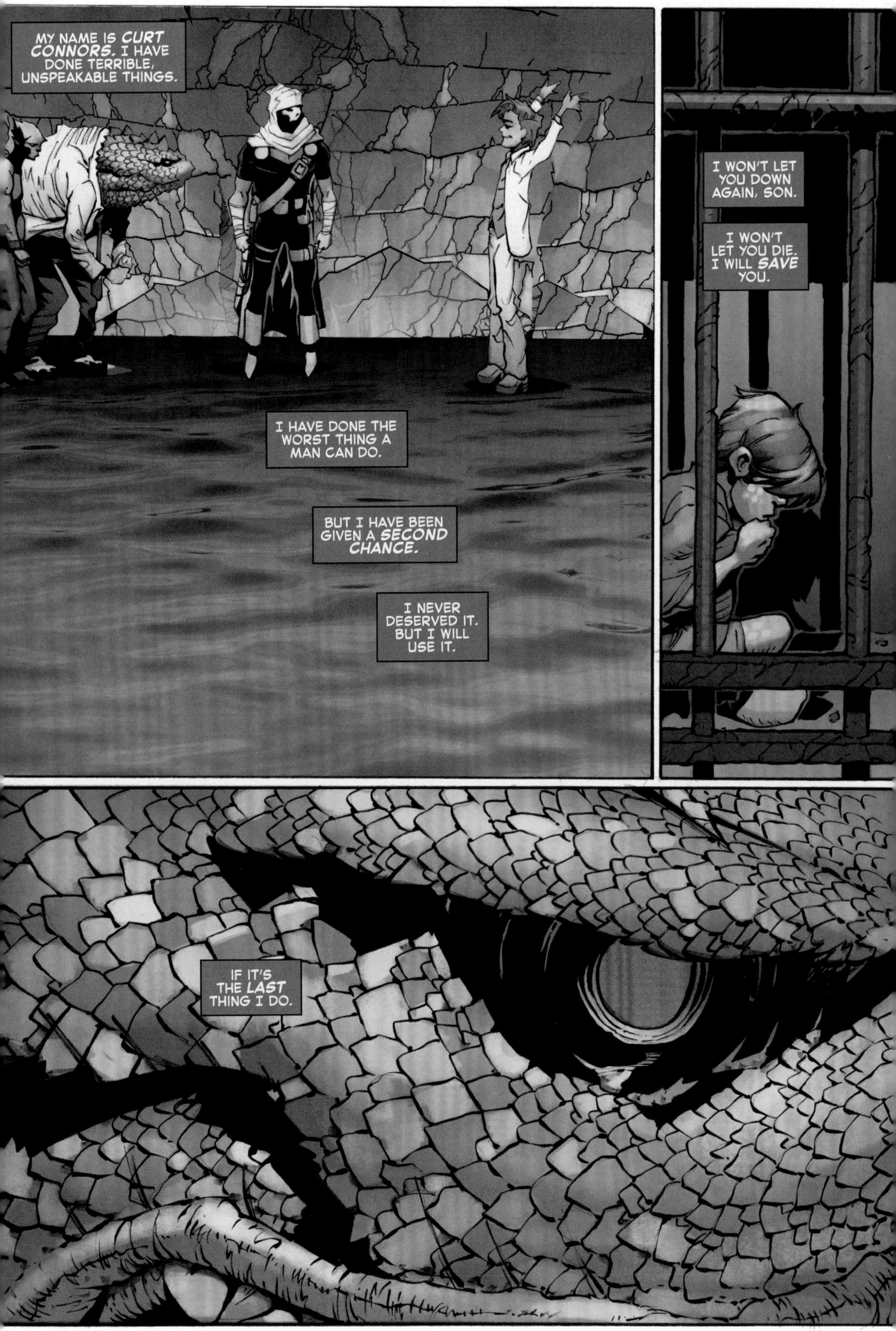

MY NAME IS CURT CONNORS. I HAVE DONE TERRIBLE, UNSPEAKABLE THINGS.
I HAVE DONE THE WORST THING A MAN CAN DO.
BUT I HAVE BEEN GIVEN A SECOND CHANCE.
I NEVER DESERVED IT. BUT I WILL USE IT.
I WON'T LET YOU DOWN AGAIN, SON.
I WON'T LET YOU DIE. I WILL SAVE YOU.
IF IT'S THE LAST THING I DO.

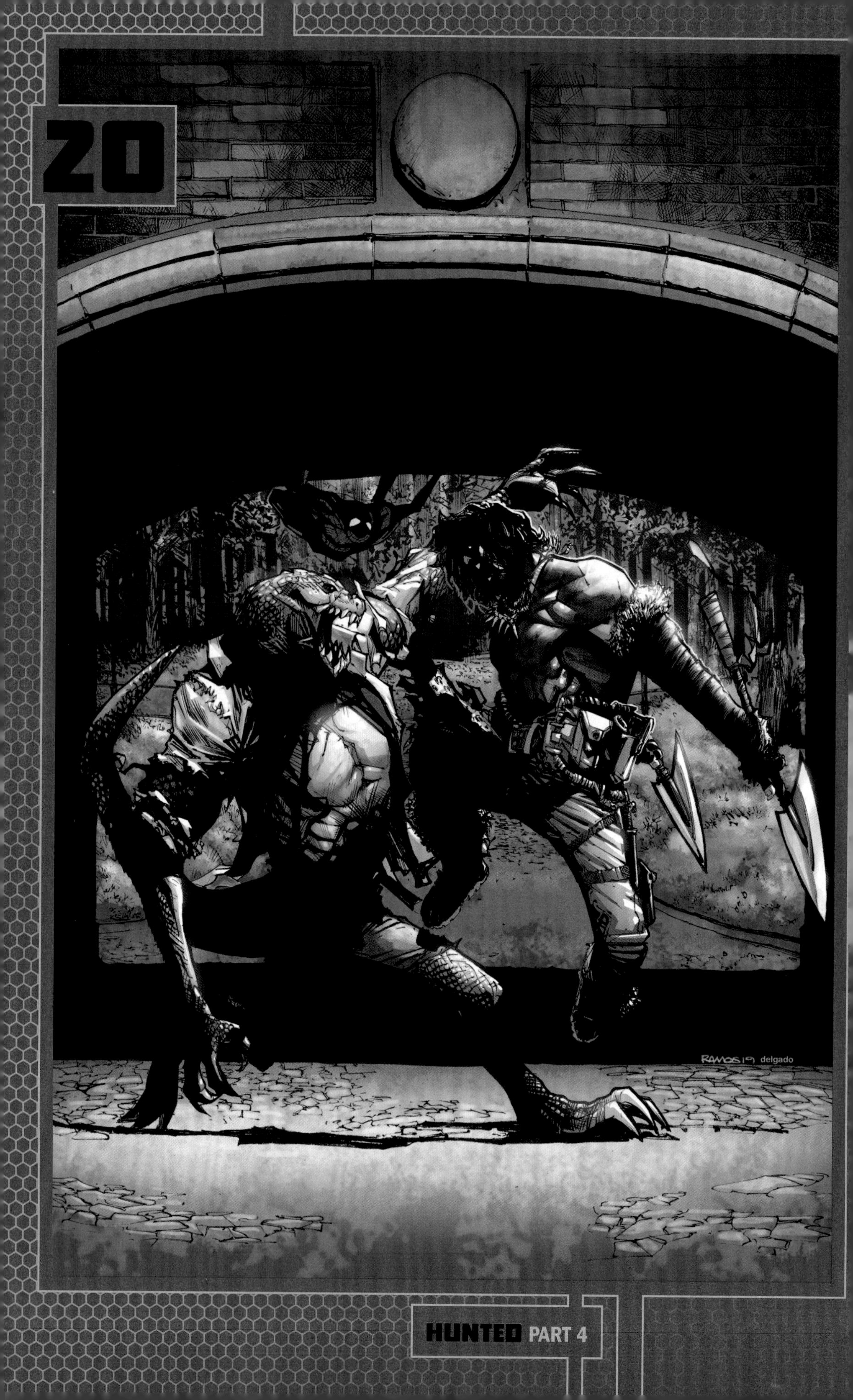
20
HUNTED PART 4

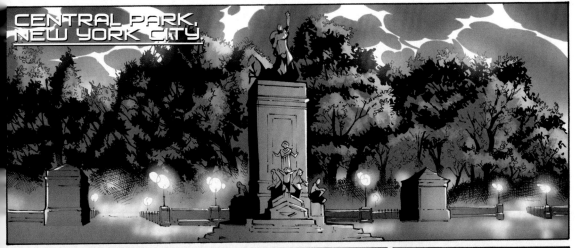

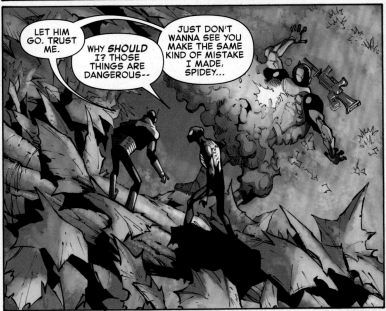

CENTRAL PARK, NEW YORK CITY.
LET HIM GO. TRUST ME.
WHY SHOULD I? THOSE THINGS ARE DANGEROUS--
JUST DON'T WANNA SEE YOU MAKE THE SAME KIND OF MISTAKE I MADE, SPIDEY...
I USED TO BE A GOOD GUY TOO, YOU KNOW.
OR AT LEAST I TRIED TO BE. GUESS I WAS NEVER REALLY CUT OUT FOR IT.
EVEN WHEN I WAS AN AVENGER, I FELT LIKE AN IMPOSTOR.
MAYBE THAT'S WHY ME AND TASKY HIT IT OFF SO WELL IN THE FIRST PLACE. FINALLY I'D MET SOMEBODY LOWER THAN ME. 'CAUSE NO MATTER WHAT I DID--
--IT WAS LIKE THERE WAS ALWAYS THIS THING INSIDE ME PULLING ME BACK, OUT OF THE LIGHT.
MAYBE THAT'S WHAT KRAVEN WAS TRYING TO TELL US, PUTTING THIS WHOLE SHEBANG TOGETHER. THAT NO MATTER HOW HARD WE TRY--

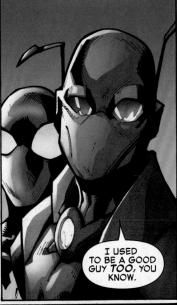

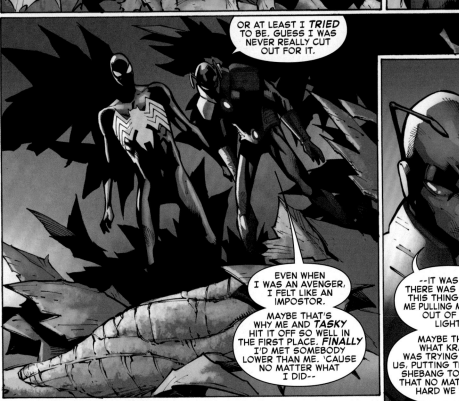

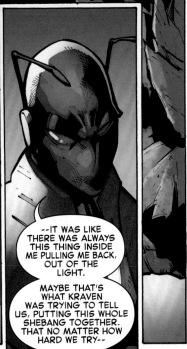

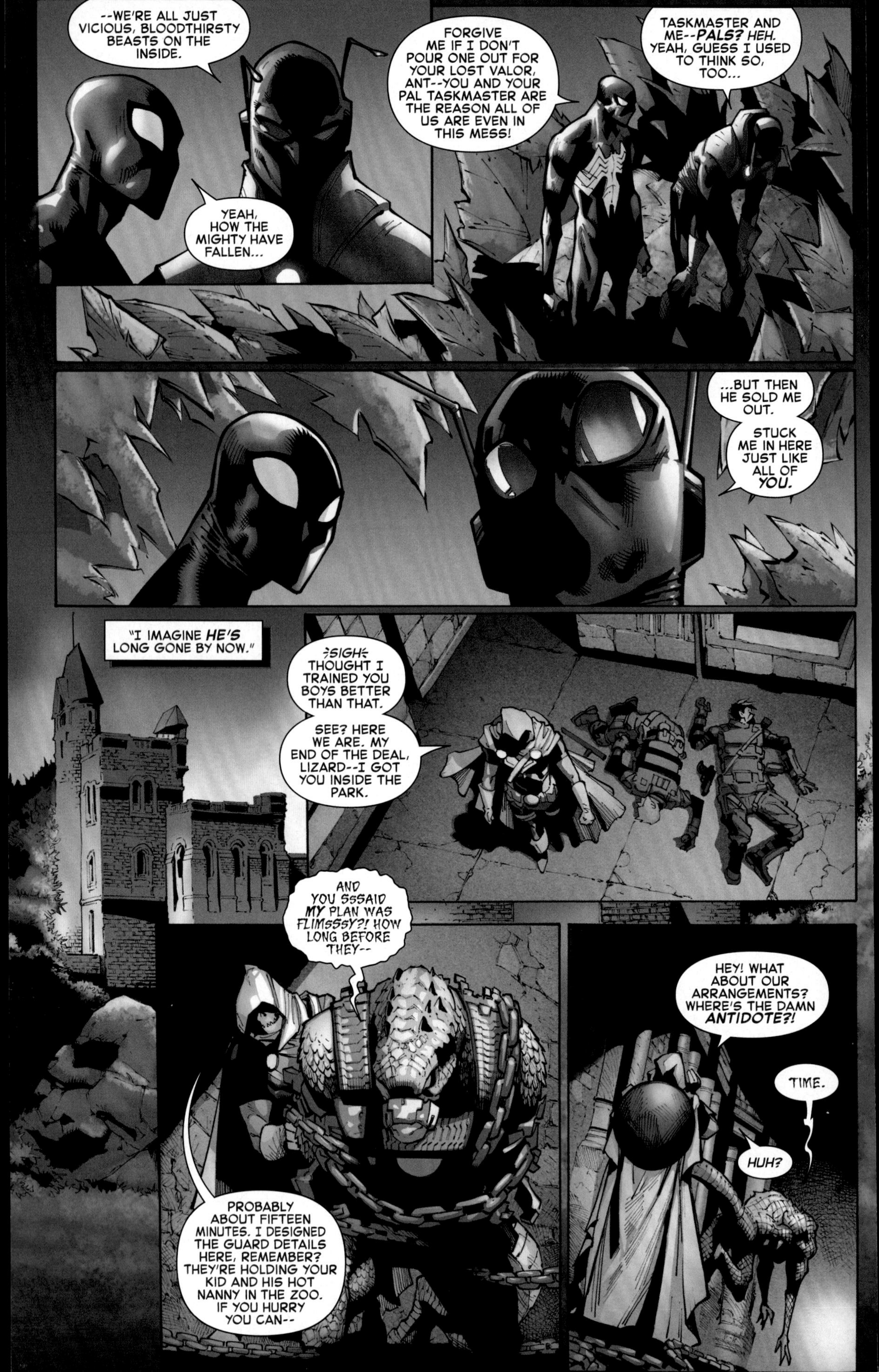
--WE'RE ALL JUST VICIOUS, BLOODTHIRSTY BEASTS ON THE INSIDE.
YEAH, HOW THE MIGHTY HAVE FALLEN...
FORGIVE ME IF I DON'T POUR ONE OUT FOR YOUR LOST VALOR, ANT--YOU AND YOUR PAL TASKMASTER ARE THE REASON ALL OF US ARE EVEN IN THIS MESS!
TASKMASTER AND ME--PALS? HEH. YEAH, GUESS I USED TO THINK SO, TOO...
...BUT THEN HE SOLD ME OUT.
STUCK ME IN HERE JUST LIKE ALL OF YOU.
"I IMAGINE HE'S LONG GONE BY NOW."
≠SIGH≠ THOUGHT I TRAINED YOU BOYS BETTER THAN THAT.
SEE? HERE WE ARE. MY END OF THE DEAL, LIZARD--I GOT YOU INSIDE THE PARK.
AND YOU SSSAID MY PLAN WAS FLIMSSSY?! HOW LONG BEFORE THEY--
PROBABLY ABOUT FIFTEEN MINUTES. I DESIGNED THE GUARD DETAILS HERE, REMEMBER? THEY'RE HOLDING YOUR KID AND HIS HOT NANNY IN THE ZOO. IF YOU HURRY YOU CAN--
HEY! WHAT ABOUT OUR ARRANGEMENTS? WHERE'S THE DAMN ANTIDOTE?!
TIME.
HUH?

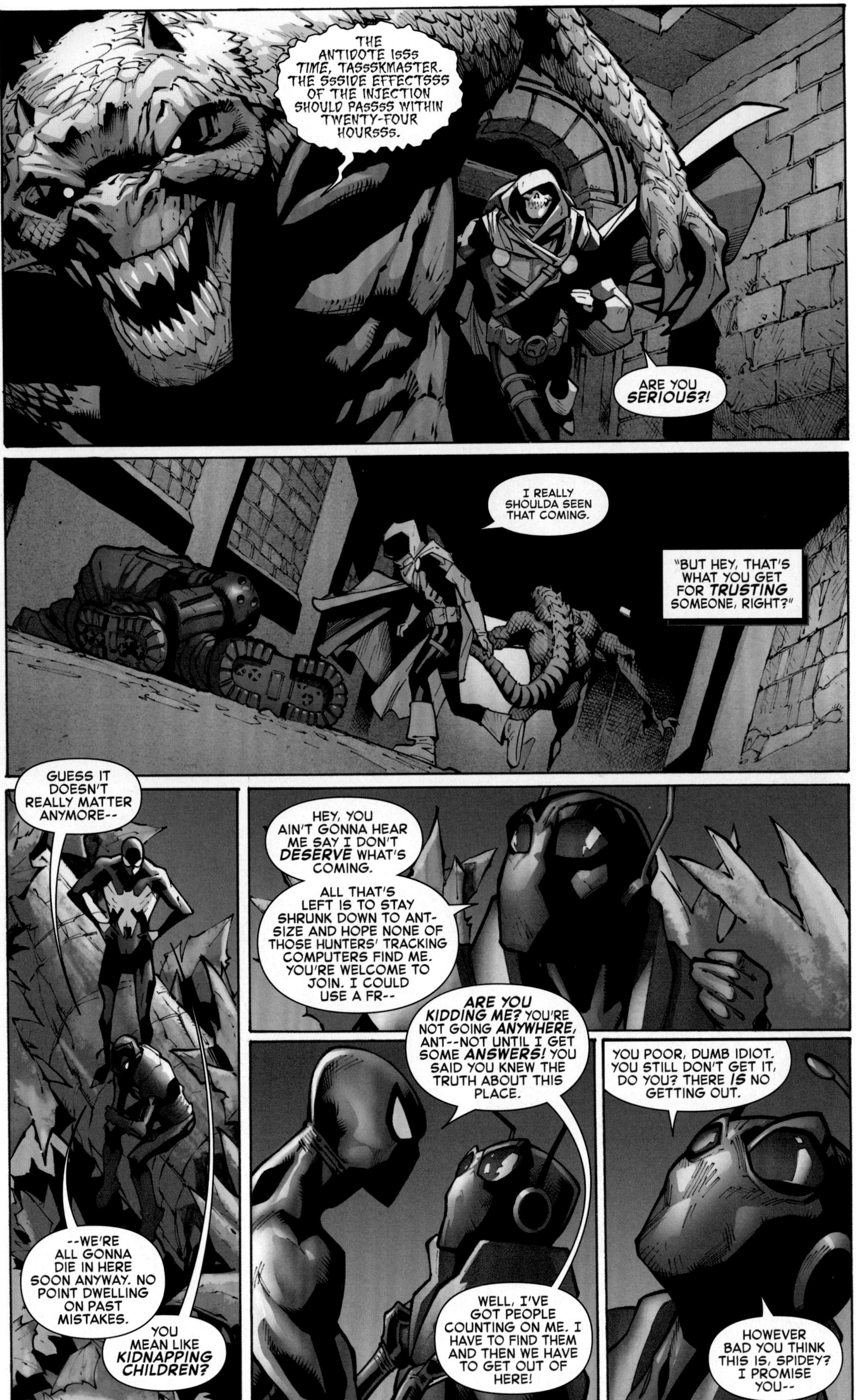
THE ANTIDOTE ISSS TIME, TASSSKMASTER. THE SSSIDE EFFECTSSS OF THE INJECTION SHOULD PASSSS WITHIN TWENTY-FOUR HOURSSS.
ARE YOU SERIOUS?!
I REALLY SHOULDA SEEN THAT COMING.
"BUT HEY, THAT'S WHAT YOU GET FOR TRUSTING SOMEONE, RIGHT?"
GUESS IT DOESN'T REALLY MATTER ANYMORE--
HEY, YOU AIN'T GONNA HEAR ME SAY I DON'T DESERVE WHAT'S COMING.
ALL THAT'S LEFT IS TO STAY SHRUNK DOWN TO ANT-SIZE AND HOPE NONE OF THOSE HUNTERS' TRACKING COMPUTERS FIND ME. YOU'RE WELCOME TO JOIN. I COULD USE A FR--
ARE YOU KIDDING ME? YOU'RE NOT GOING ANYWHERE, ANT--NOT UNTIL I GET SOME ANSWERS! YOU SAID YOU KNEW THE TRUTH ABOUT THIS PLACE.
--WE'RE ALL GONNA DIE IN HERE SOON ANYWAY. NO POINT DWELLING ON PAST MISTAKES.
YOU MEAN LIKE KIDNAPPING CHILDREN?
WELL, I'VE GOT PEOPLE COUNTING ON ME. I HAVE TO FIND THEM AND THEN WE HAVE TO GET OUT OF HERE!
YOU POOR, DUMB IDIOT. YOU STILL DON'T GET IT, DO YOU? THERE IS NO GETTING OUT.
HOWEVER BAD YOU THINK THIS IS, SPIDEY? I PROMISE YOU--

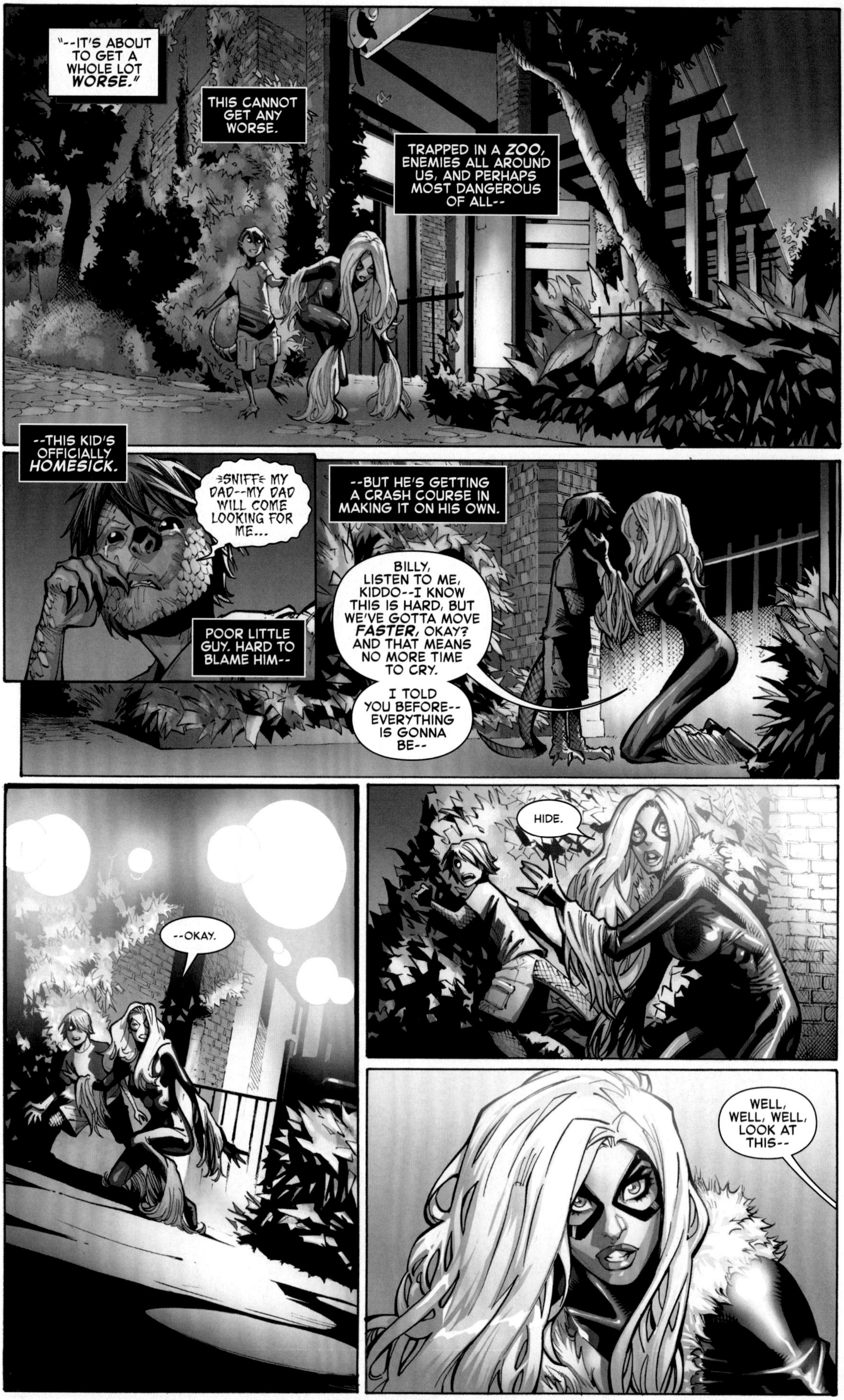

"--IT'S ABOUT TO GET A WHOLE LOT WORSE."
THIS CANNOT GET ANY WORSE.
TRAPPED IN A ZOO, ENEMIES ALL AROUND US, AND PERHAPS MOST DANGEROUS OF ALL--
--THIS KID'S OFFICIALLY HOMESICK.
SNIFF MY DAD--MY DAD WILL COME LOOKING FOR ME...
POOR LITTLE GUY. HARD TO BLAME HIM--
--BUT HE'S GETTING A CRASH COURSE IN MAKING IT ON HIS OWN.
BILLY, LISTEN TO ME, KIDDO--I KNOW THIS IS HARD, BUT WE'VE GOTTA MOVE FASTER, OKAY? AND THAT MEANS NO MORE TIME TO CRY.
I TOLD YOU BEFORE--EVERYTHING IS GONNA BE--
--OKAY.
HIDE.
WELL, WELL, WELL, LOOK AT THIS--

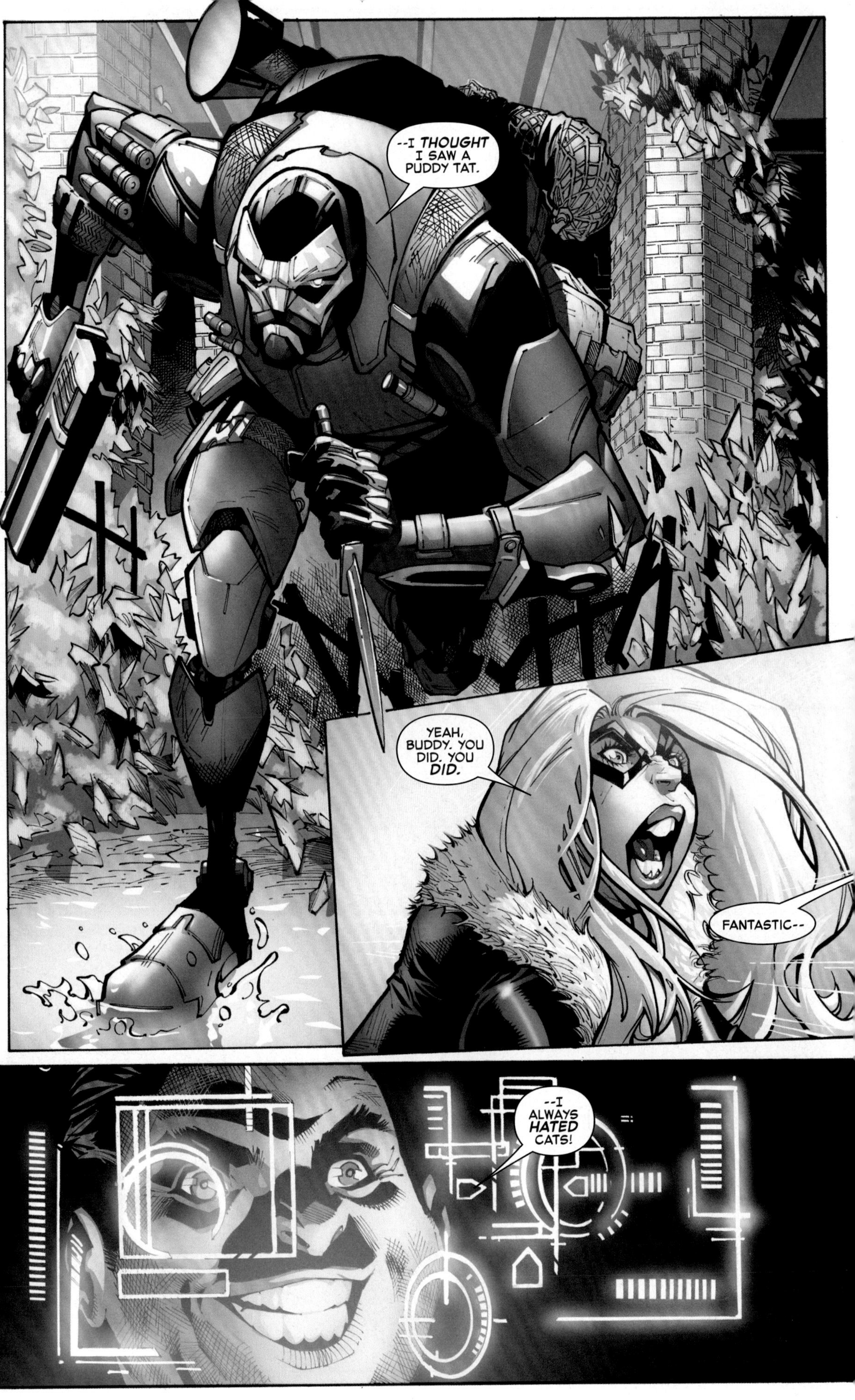
--I THOUGHT I SAW A PUDDY TAT.
YEAH, BUDDY. YOU DID. YOU DID.
FANTASTIC--
--I ALWAYS HATED CATS!

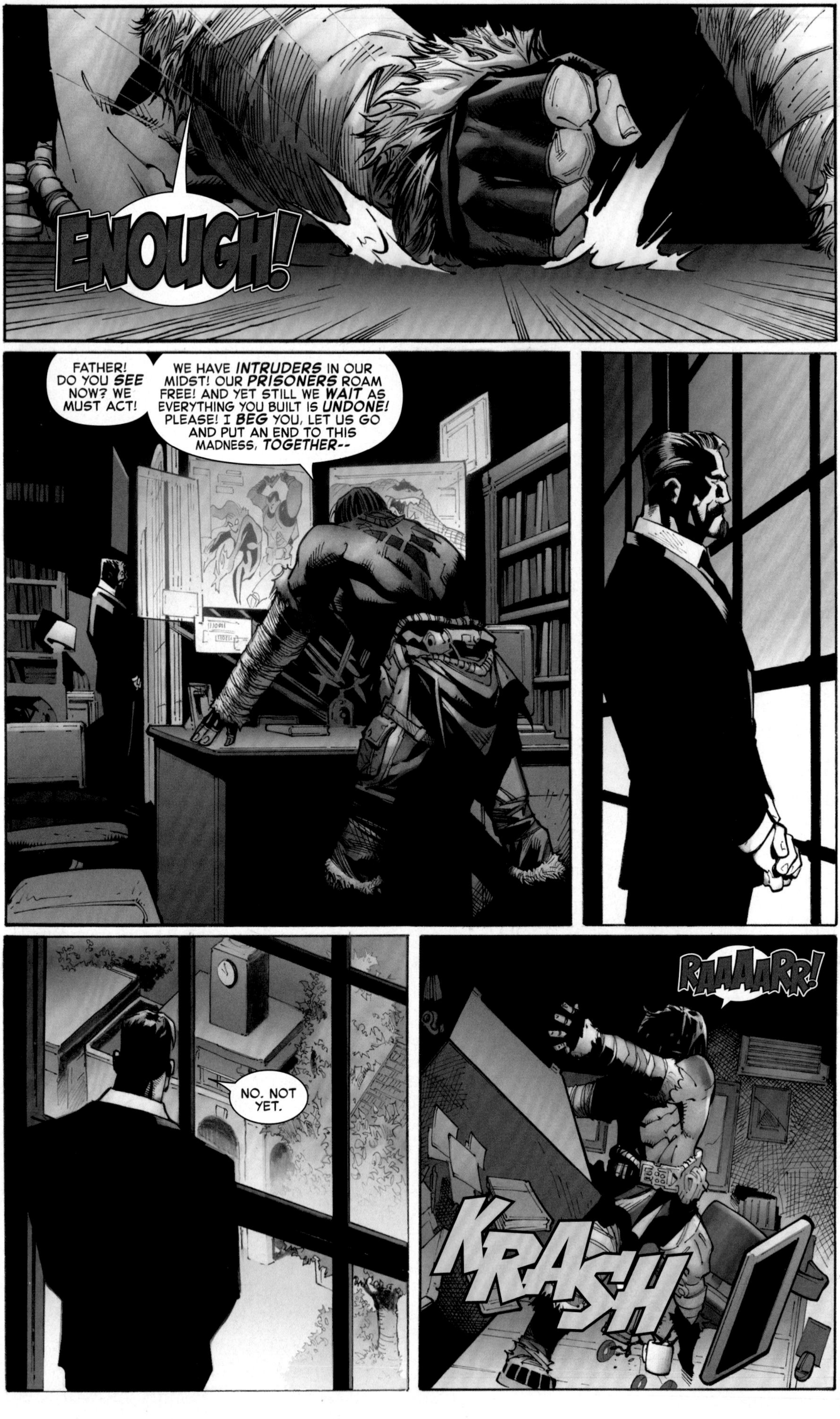
ENOUGH!
FATHER! DO YOU SEE NOW? WE MUST ACT!
WE HAVE INTRUDERS IN OUR MIDST! OUR PRISONERS ROAM FREE! AND YET STILL WE WAIT AS EVERYTHING YOU BUILT IS UNDONE! PLEASE! I BEG YOU, LET US GO AND PUT AN END TO THIS MADNESS, TOGETHER--
NO. NOT YET.
RAAAARR!
KRASH

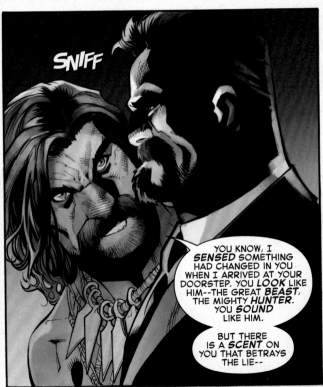

SNIFF

YOU KNOW, I **SENSED** SOMETHING HAD CHANGED IN YOU WHEN I ARRIVED AT YOUR DOORSTEP. YOU **LOOK** LIKE HIM--THE GREAT **BEAST**, THE MIGHTY **HUNTER**. YOU **SOUND** LIKE HIM.

BUT THERE IS A **SCENT** ON YOU THAT BETRAYS THE LIE--

ONE OF **FEAR**. OF **WEAKNESS**.

IT SICKENS ME.

I HAVE SPENT MY **ENTIRE LIFE** DREAMING OF OUR RULE TOGETHER, FATHER. BUT IF YOU NO LONGER HAVE THE **STRENGTH** TO DEFEND THE **KRAVINOFF NAME**, DON'T WORRY--

--I **WILL**.

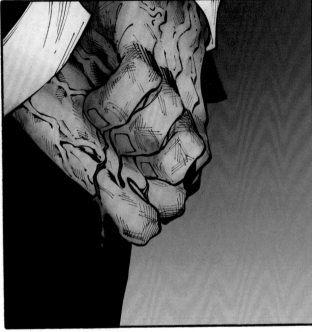

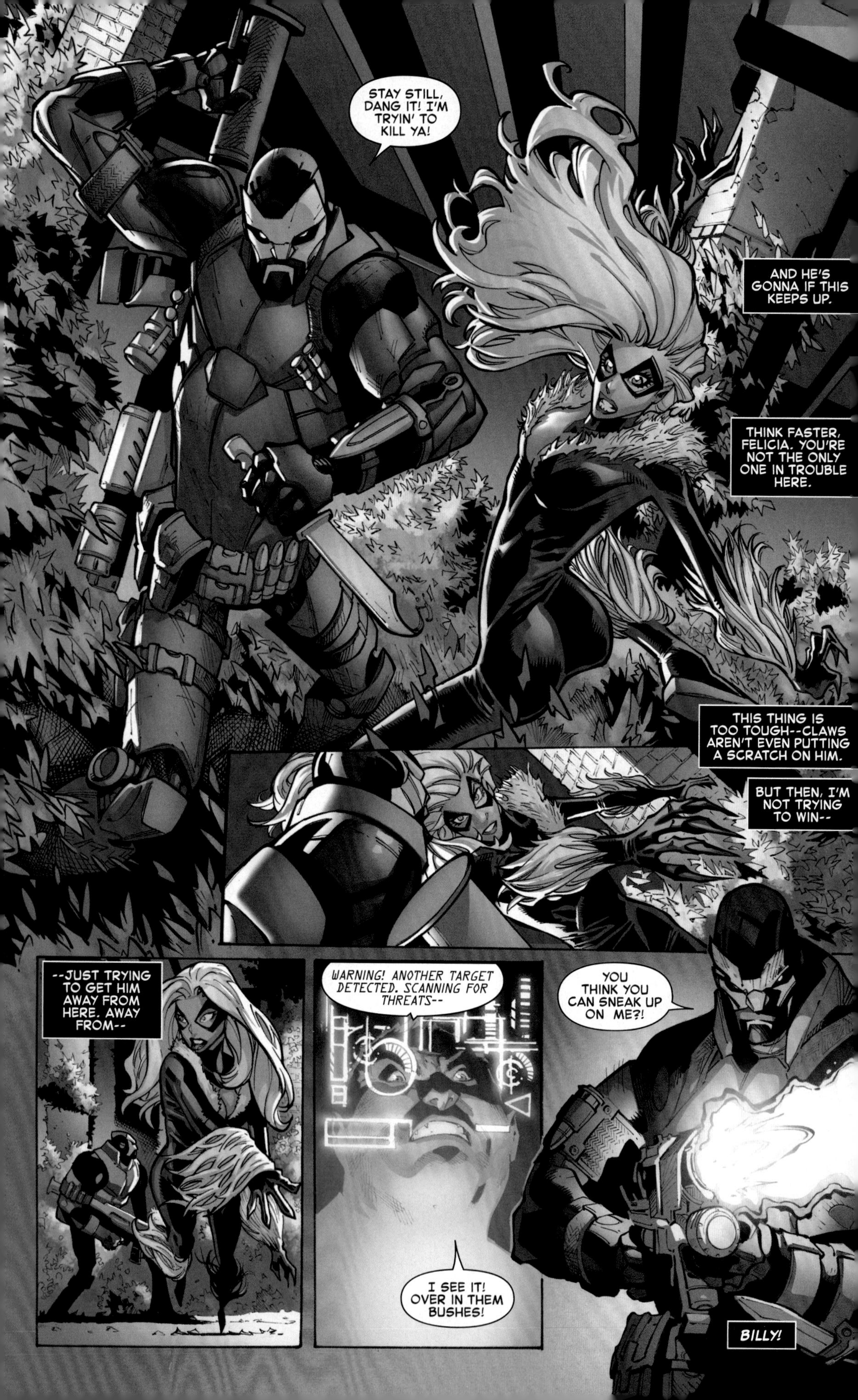
STAY STILL, DANG IT! I'M TRYIN' TO KILL YA!
AND HE'S GONNA IF THIS KEEPS UP.
THINK FASTER, FELICIA. YOU'RE NOT THE ONLY ONE IN TROUBLE HERE.
THIS THING IS TOO TOUGH--CLAWS AREN'T EVEN PUTTING A SCRATCH ON HIM.
BUT THEN, I'M NOT TRYING TO WIN--
--JUST TRYING TO GET HIM AWAY FROM HERE. AWAY FROM--
WARNING! ANOTHER TARGET DETECTED. SCANNING FOR THREATS--
I SEE IT! OVER IN THEM BUSHES!
YOU THINK YOU CAN SNEAK UP ON ME?!
BILLY!

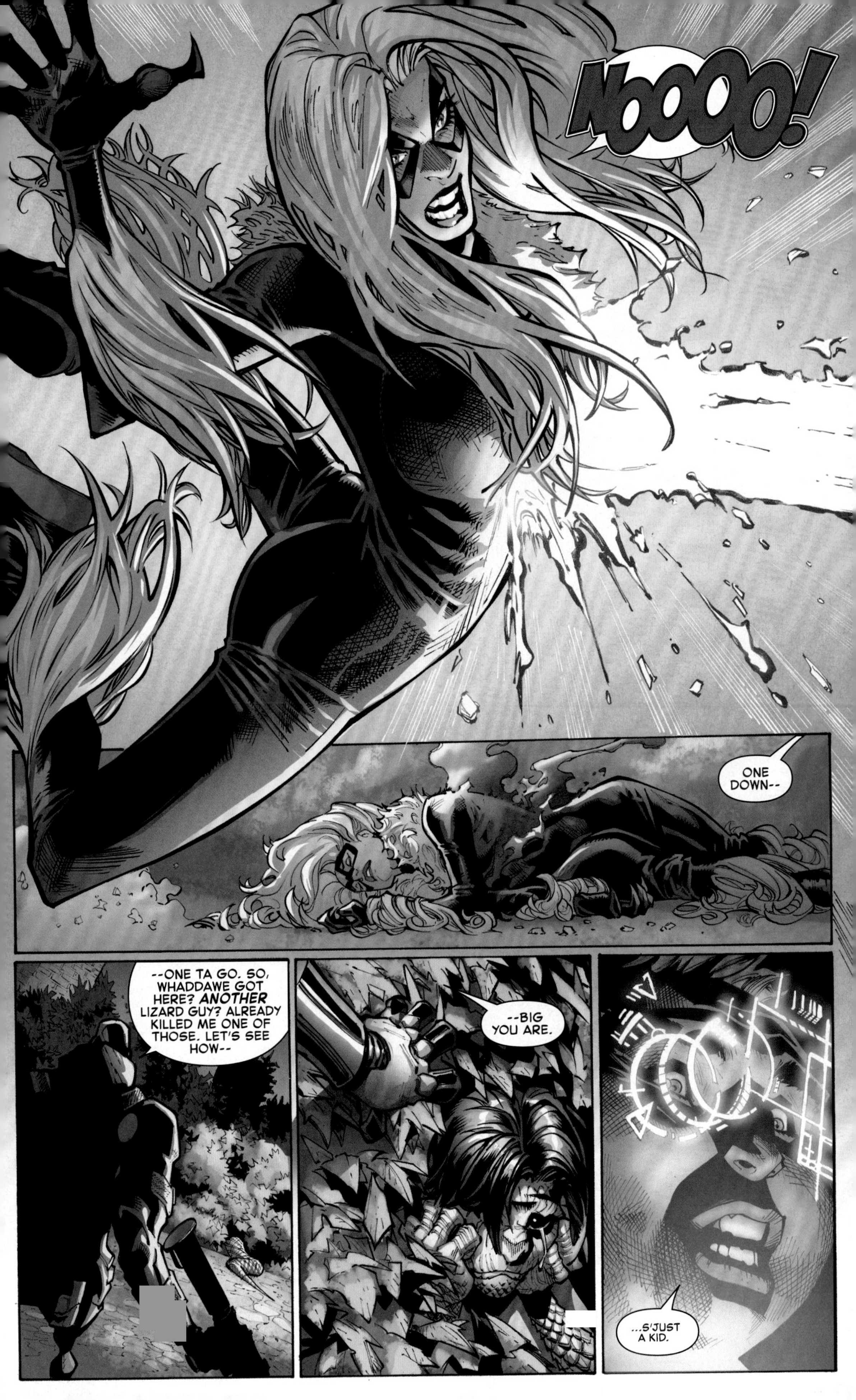
NOOOO!
ONE DOWN--
--ONE TA GO. SO, WHADDAWE GOT HERE? ANOTHER LIZARD GUY? ALREADY KILLED ME ONE OF THOSE. LET'S SEE HOW--
--BIG YOU ARE.
...S'JUST A KID.

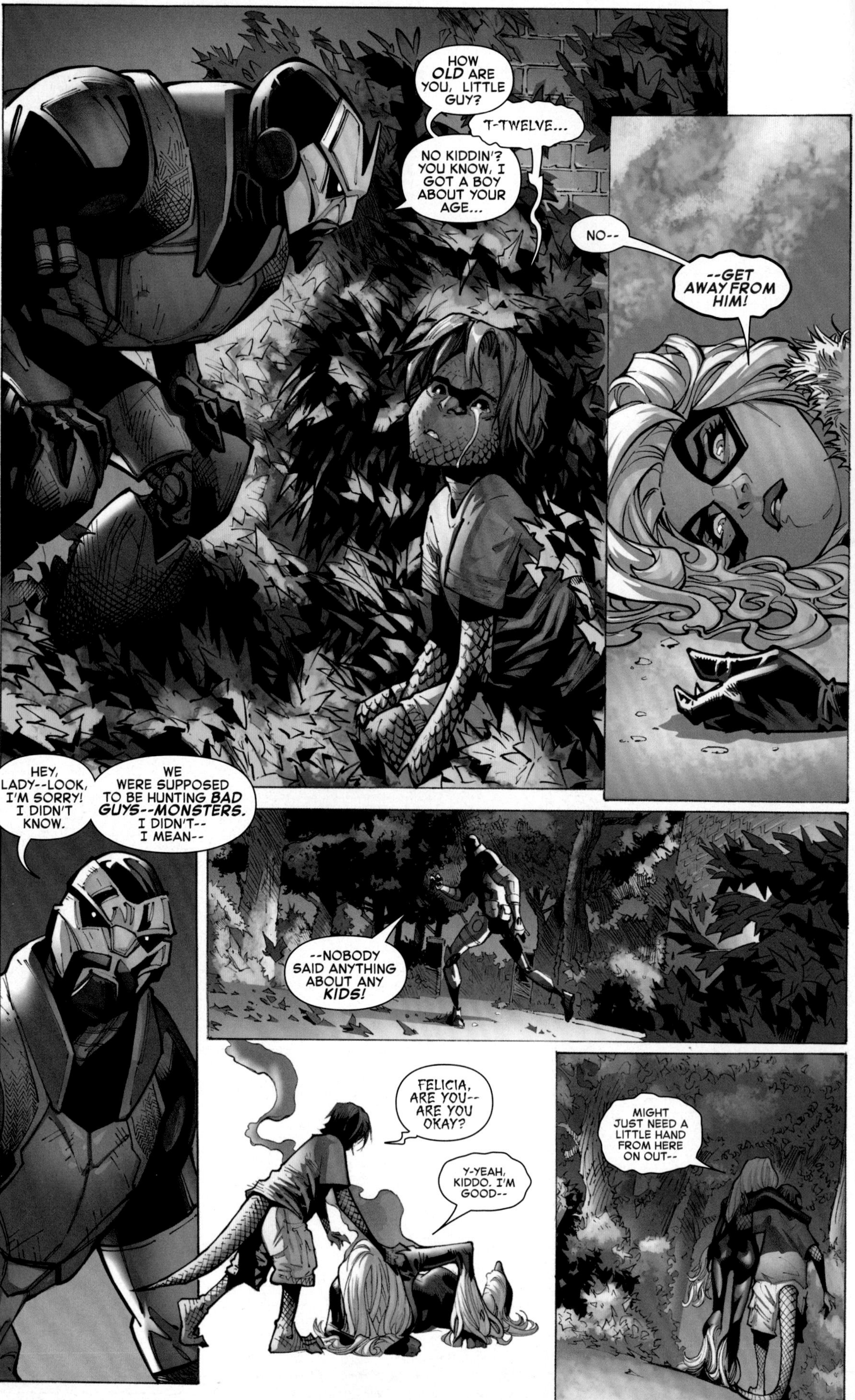
HOW OLD ARE YOU, LITTLE GUY?
T-TWELVE...
NO KIDDIN'? YOU KNOW, I GOT A BOY ABOUT YOUR AGE...
NO--
--GET AWAY FROM HIM!
HEY, LADY--LOOK, I'M SORRY! I DIDN'T KNOW.
WE WERE SUPPOSED TO BE HUNTING BAD GUYS--MONSTERS. I DIDN'T-- I MEAN--
--NOBODY SAID ANYTHING ABOUT ANY KIDS!
FELICIA, ARE YOU-- ARE YOU OKAY?
Y-YEAH, KIDDO. I'M GOOD--
MIGHT JUST NEED A LITTLE HAND FROM HERE ON OUT--

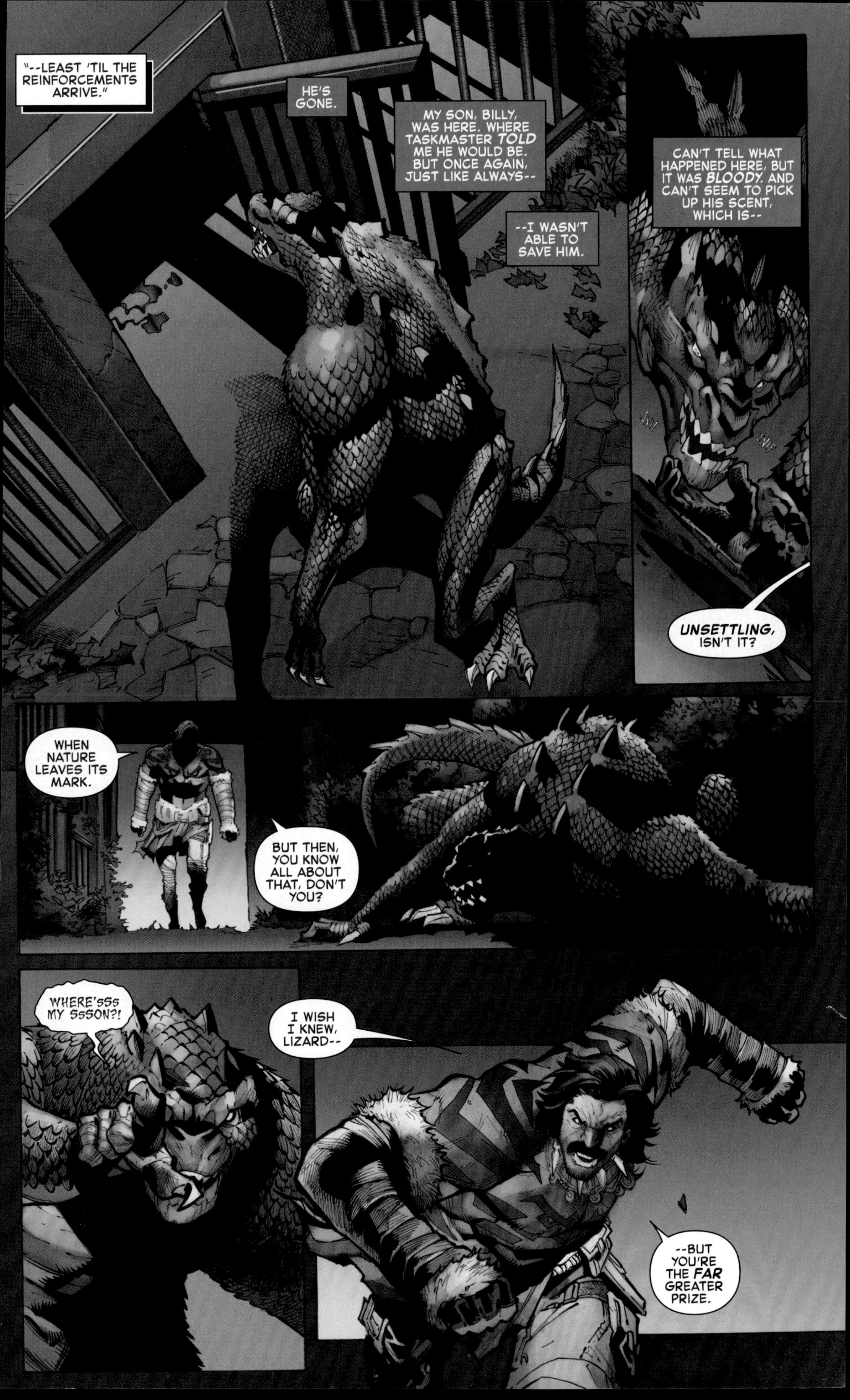
"--LEAST 'TIL THE REINFORCEMENTS ARRIVE."
HE'S GONE.
MY SON, BILLY, WAS HERE. WHERE TASKMASTER *TOLD* ME HE WOULD BE. BUT ONCE AGAIN, JUST LIKE ALWAYS--
--I WASN'T ABLE TO SAVE HIM.
CAN'T TELL WHAT HAPPENED HERE, BUT IT WAS *BLOODY.* AND CAN'T SEEM TO PICK UP HIS SCENT, WHICH IS--
SNIF
SNIF
UNSETTLING, ISN'T IT?
WHEN NATURE LEAVES ITS MARK.
BUT THEN, YOU KNOW ALL ABOUT THAT, DON'T YOU?
WHERE'SSS MY SSSON?!
I WISH I KNEW, LIZARD--
--BUT YOU'RE THE *FAR* GREATER PRIZE.

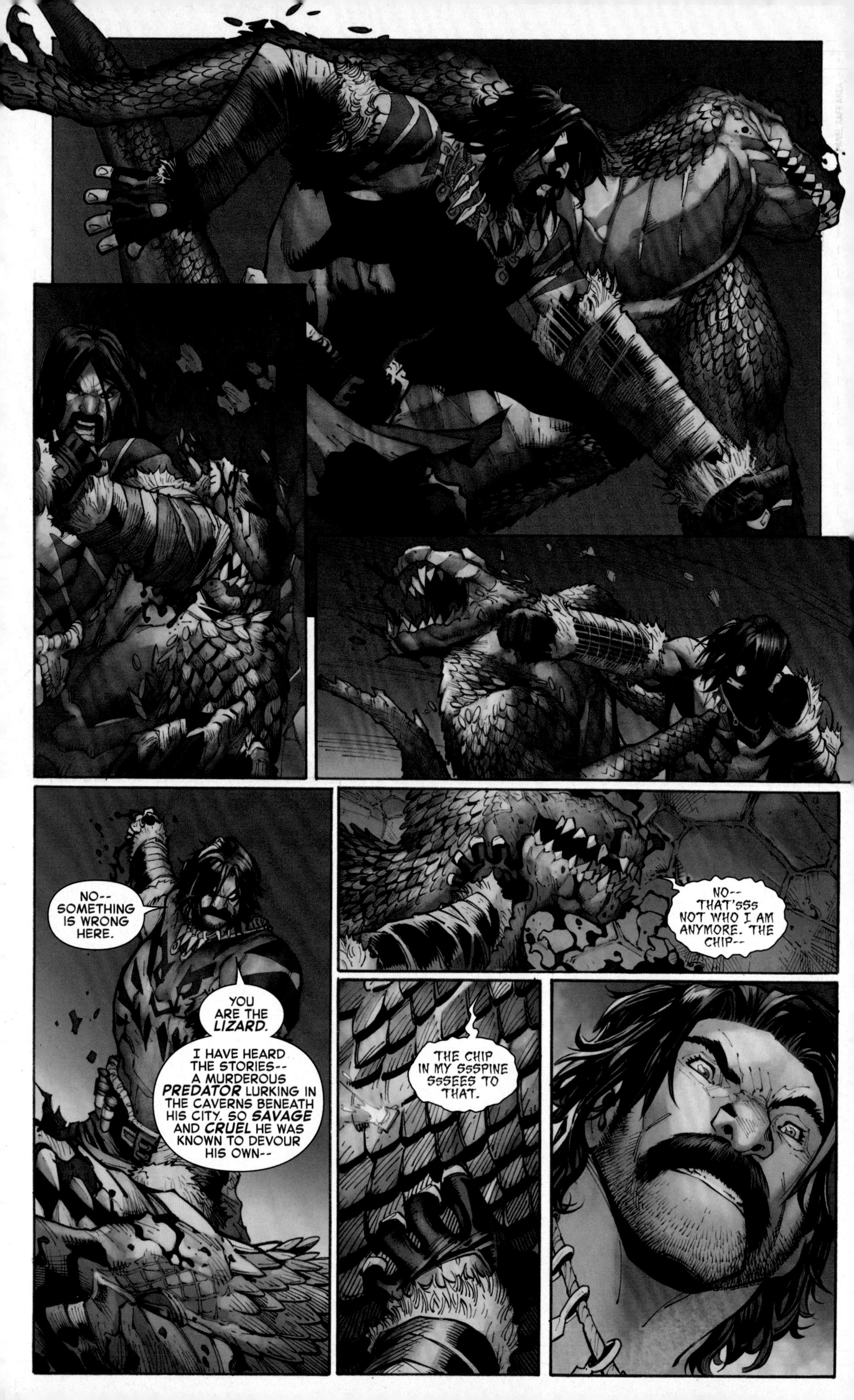
NO-- SOMETHING IS WRONG HERE.
NO-- THAT'SSS NOT WHO I AM ANYMORE. THE CHIP--
YOU ARE THE LIZARD.
I HAVE HEARD THE STORIES-- A MURDEROUS PREDATOR LURKING IN THE CAVERNS BENEATH HIS CITY. SO SAVAGE AND CRUEL HE WAS KNOWN TO DEVOUR HIS OWN--
THE CHIP IN MY SSSPINE SSSEES TO THAT.

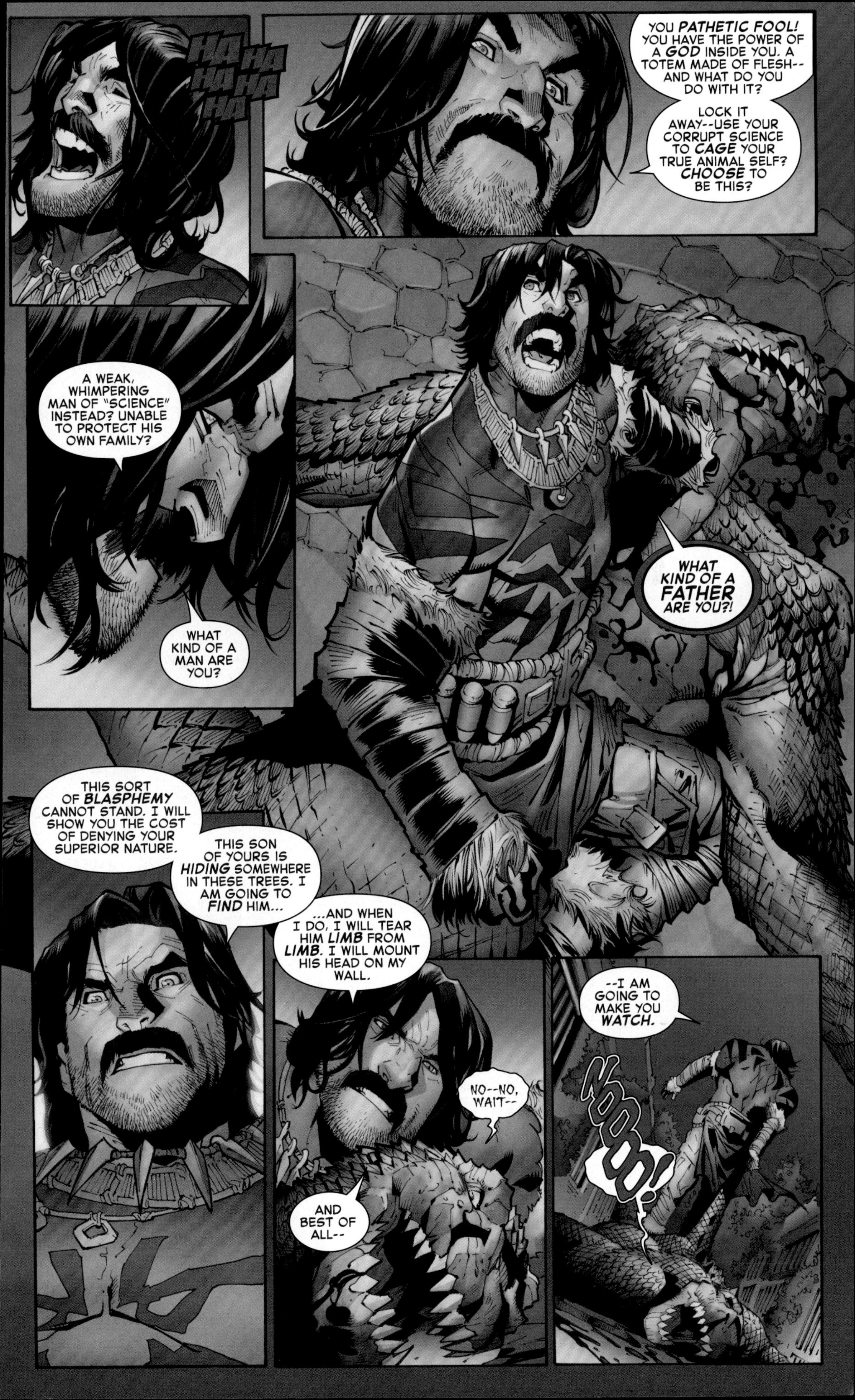
HA HA HA HA HA
YOU PATHETIC FOOL! YOU HAVE THE POWER OF A GOD INSIDE YOU. A TOTEM MADE OF FLESH--AND WHAT DO YOU DO WITH IT?
LOCK IT AWAY--USE YOUR CORRUPT SCIENCE TO CAGE YOUR TRUE ANIMAL SELF? CHOOSE TO BE THIS?
A WEAK, WHIMPERING MAN OF "SCIENCE" INSTEAD? UNABLE TO PROTECT HIS OWN FAMILY?
WHAT KIND OF A MAN ARE YOU?
WHAT KIND OF A FATHER ARE YOU?!
THIS SORT OF BLASPHEMY CANNOT STAND. I WILL SHOW YOU THE COST OF DENYING YOUR SUPERIOR NATURE.
THIS SON OF YOURS IS HIDING SOMEWHERE IN THESE TREES. I AM GOING TO FIND HIM...
...AND WHEN I DO, I WILL TEAR HIM LIMB FROM LIMB. I WILL MOUNT HIS HEAD ON MY WALL.
NO--NO, WAIT--
AND BEST OF ALL--
--I AM GOING TO MAKE YOU WATCH.
NOOOO!

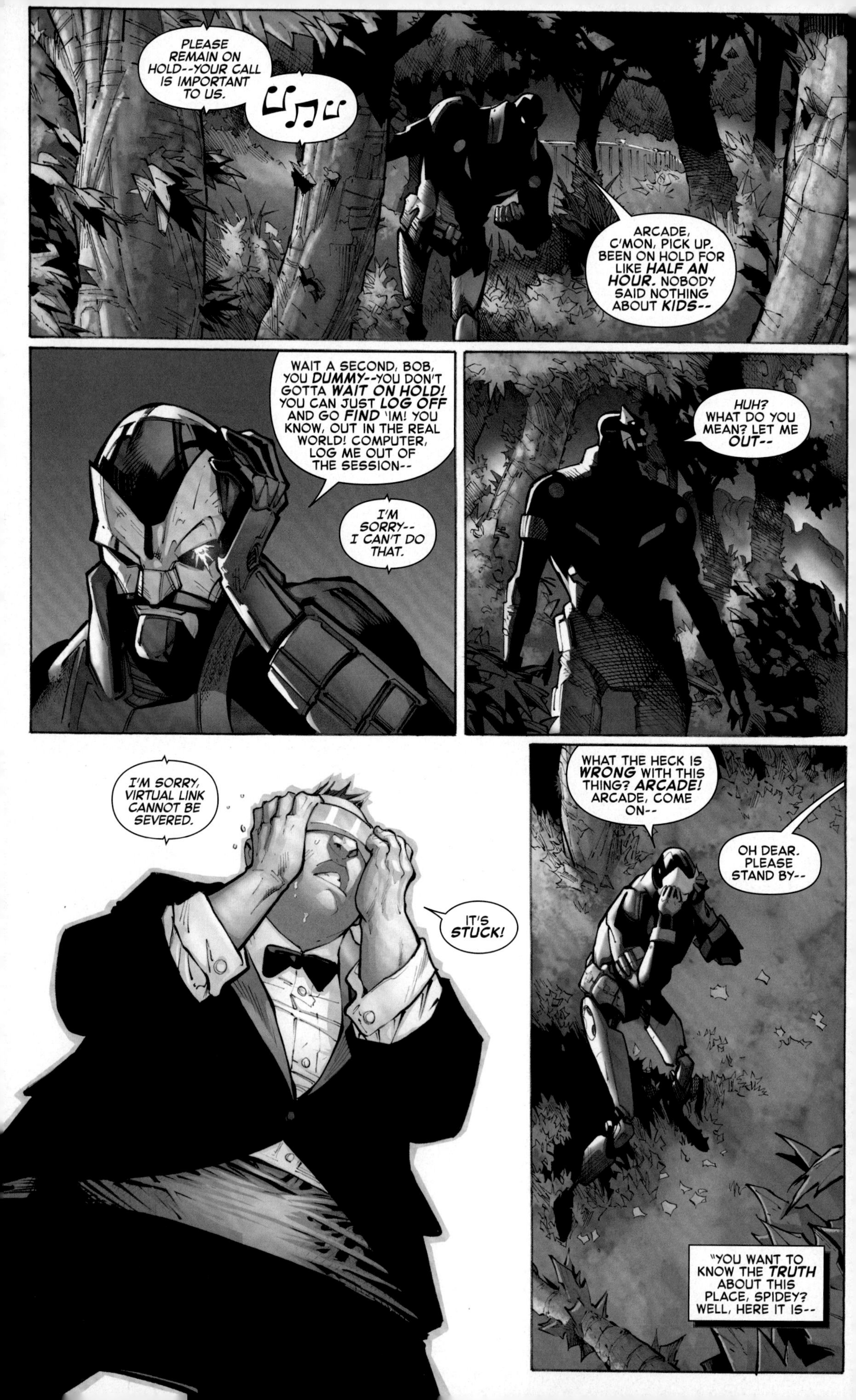
PLEASE REMAIN ON HOLD--YOUR CALL IS IMPORTANT TO US.
ARCADE, C'MON, PICK UP. BEEN ON HOLD FOR LIKE HALF AN HOUR. NOBODY SAID NOTHING ABOUT KIDS--
WAIT A SECOND, BOB, YOU DUMMY--YOU DON'T GOTTA WAIT ON HOLD! YOU CAN JUST LOG OFF AND GO FIND 'IM! YOU KNOW, OUT IN THE REAL WORLD! COMPUTER, LOG ME OUT OF THE SESSION--
I'M SORRY-- I CAN'T DO THAT.
HUH? WHAT DO YOU MEAN? LET ME OUT--
I'M SORRY, VIRTUAL LINK CANNOT BE SEVERED.
IT'S STUCK!
WHAT THE HECK IS WRONG WITH THIS THING? ARCADE! ARCADE, COME ON--
OH DEAR. PLEASE STAND BY--
"YOU WANT TO KNOW THE TRUTH ABOUT THIS PLACE, SPIDEY? WELL, HERE IT IS--

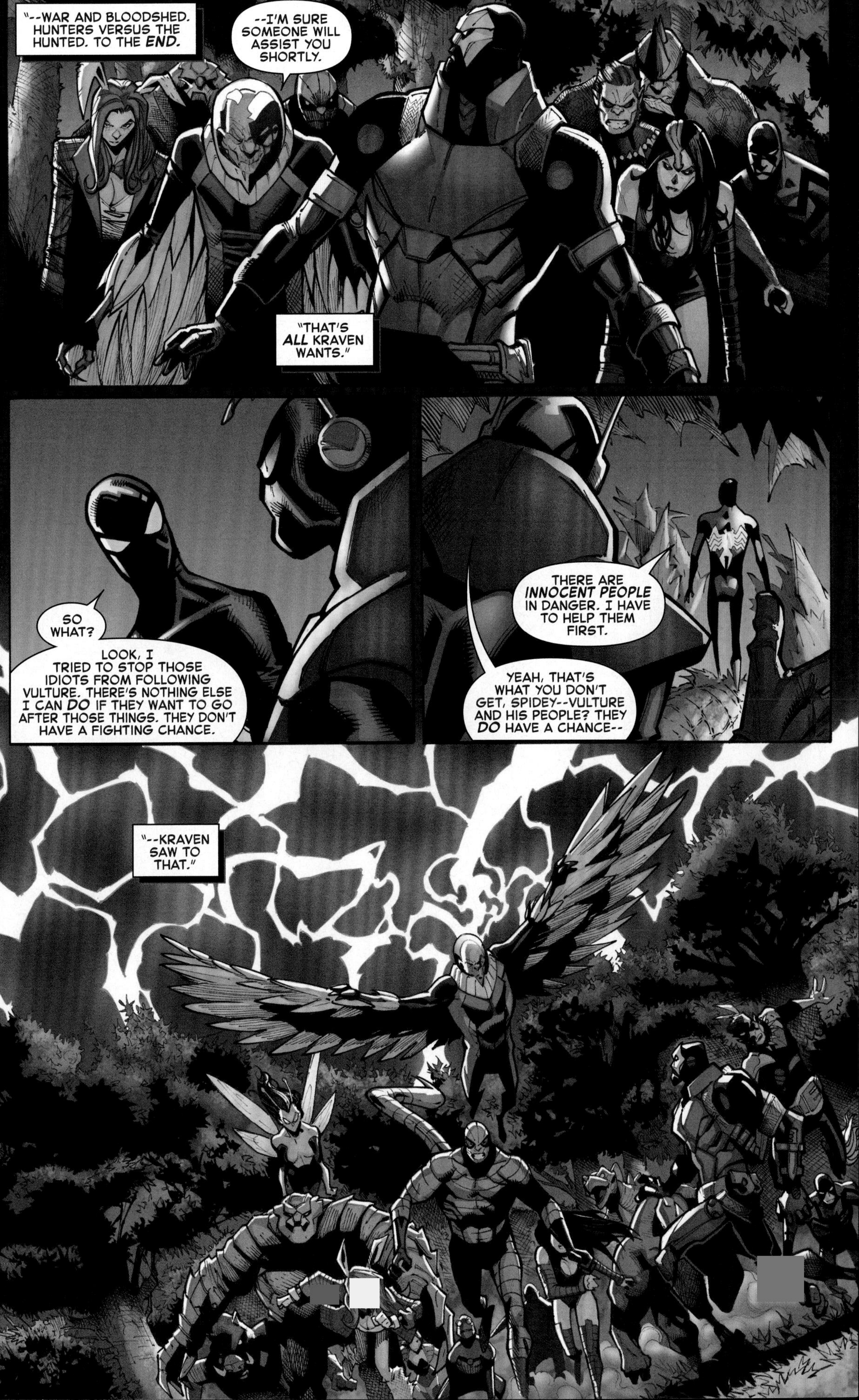
"--WAR AND BLOODSHED. HUNTERS VERSUS THE HUNTED. TO THE END.
--I'M SURE SOMEONE WILL ASSIST YOU SHORTLY.
"THAT'S ALL KRAVEN WANTS."
SO WHAT?
LOOK, I TRIED TO STOP THOSE IDIOTS FROM FOLLOWING VULTURE. THERE'S NOTHING ELSE I CAN DO IF THEY WANT TO GO AFTER THOSE THINGS. THEY DON'T HAVE A FIGHTING CHANCE.
THERE ARE INNOCENT PEOPLE IN DANGER. I HAVE TO HELP THEM FIRST.
YEAH, THAT'S WHAT YOU DON'T GET, SPIDEY--VULTURE AND HIS PEOPLE? THEY DO HAVE A CHANCE--
"--KRAVEN SAW TO THAT."

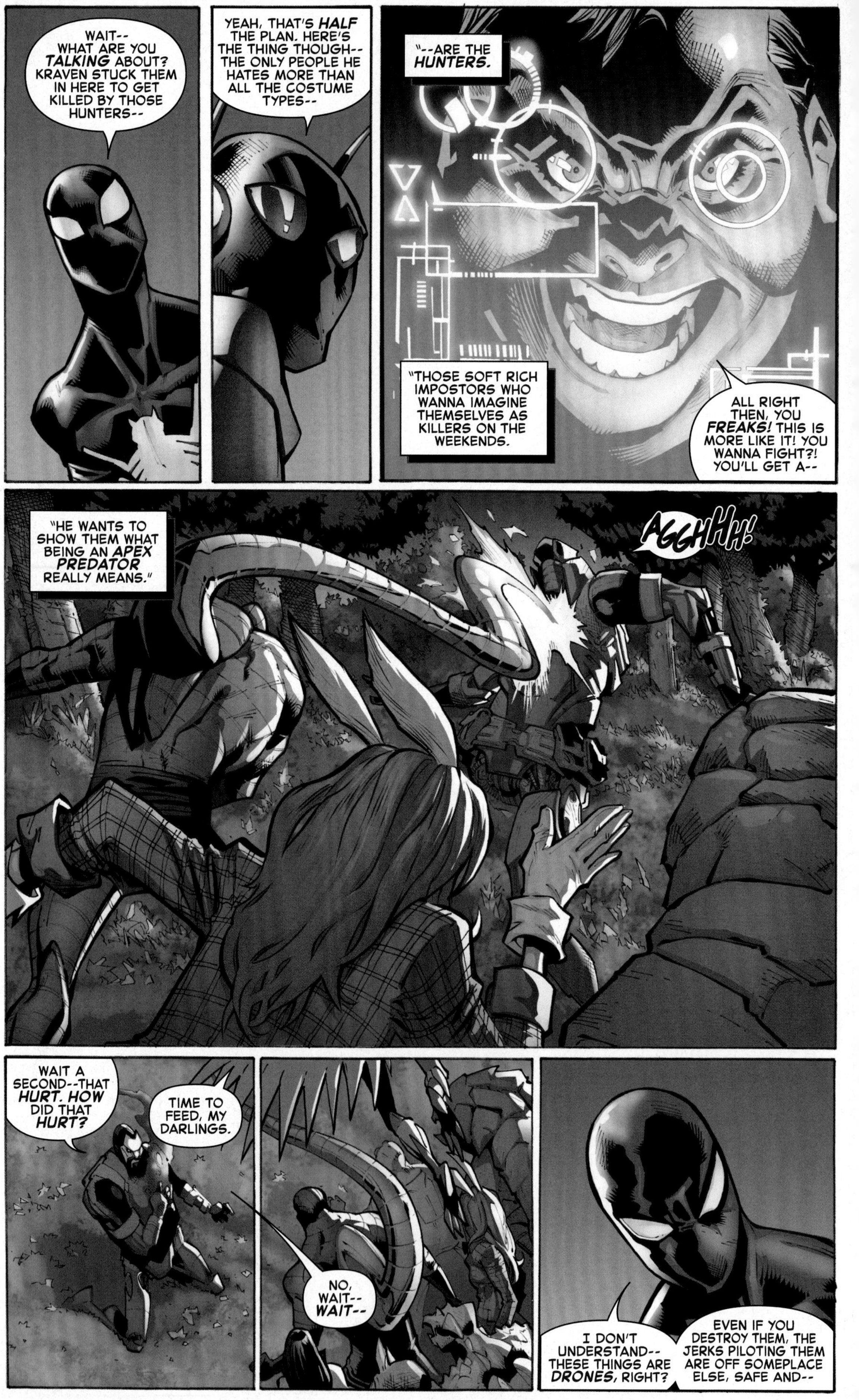
WAIT-- WHAT ARE YOU TALKING ABOUT? KRAVEN STUCK THEM IN HERE TO GET KILLED BY THOSE HUNTERS--
YEAH, THAT'S HALF THE PLAN. HERE'S THE THING THOUGH-- THE ONLY PEOPLE HE HATES MORE THAN ALL THE COSTUME TYPES--
"--ARE THE HUNTERS.
"THOSE SOFT RICH IMPOSTORS WHO WANNA IMAGINE THEMSELVES AS KILLERS ON THE WEEKENDS.
ALL RIGHT THEN, YOU FREAKS! THIS IS MORE LIKE IT! YOU WANNA FIGHT?! YOU'LL GET A--
"HE WANTS TO SHOW THEM WHAT BEING AN APEX PREDATOR REALLY MEANS."
AGGHHH!
WAIT A SECOND--THAT HURT. HOW DID THAT HURT?
TIME TO FEED, MY DARLINGS.
NO, WAIT-- WAIT--
I DON'T UNDERSTAND-- THESE THINGS ARE DRONES, RIGHT?
EVEN IF YOU DESTROY THEM, THE JERKS PILOTING THEM ARE OFF SOMEPLACE ELSE, SAFE AND--

"WRONG. THESE GUYS THINK THEY'RE **SAFE**. THINK THEY'RE **INDESTRUCTIBLE**.

"BUT KRAVEN WANTS THEM TO LEARN THE DANGERS OF THE HUNT THE **HARD WAY**.

"TEACH 'EM THAT CHASING DOWN DANGEROUS BEASTS MEANS THE TABLES CAN TURN FAST.

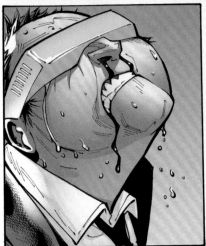

"THE VR VISORS THEY'RE WEARING BACK OFF-SITE, THEY'RE WIRED RIGHT INTO THEIR **BRAINS**. BUNCHA SCIENCE, BUT BASICALLY--

"DIE IN HERE...

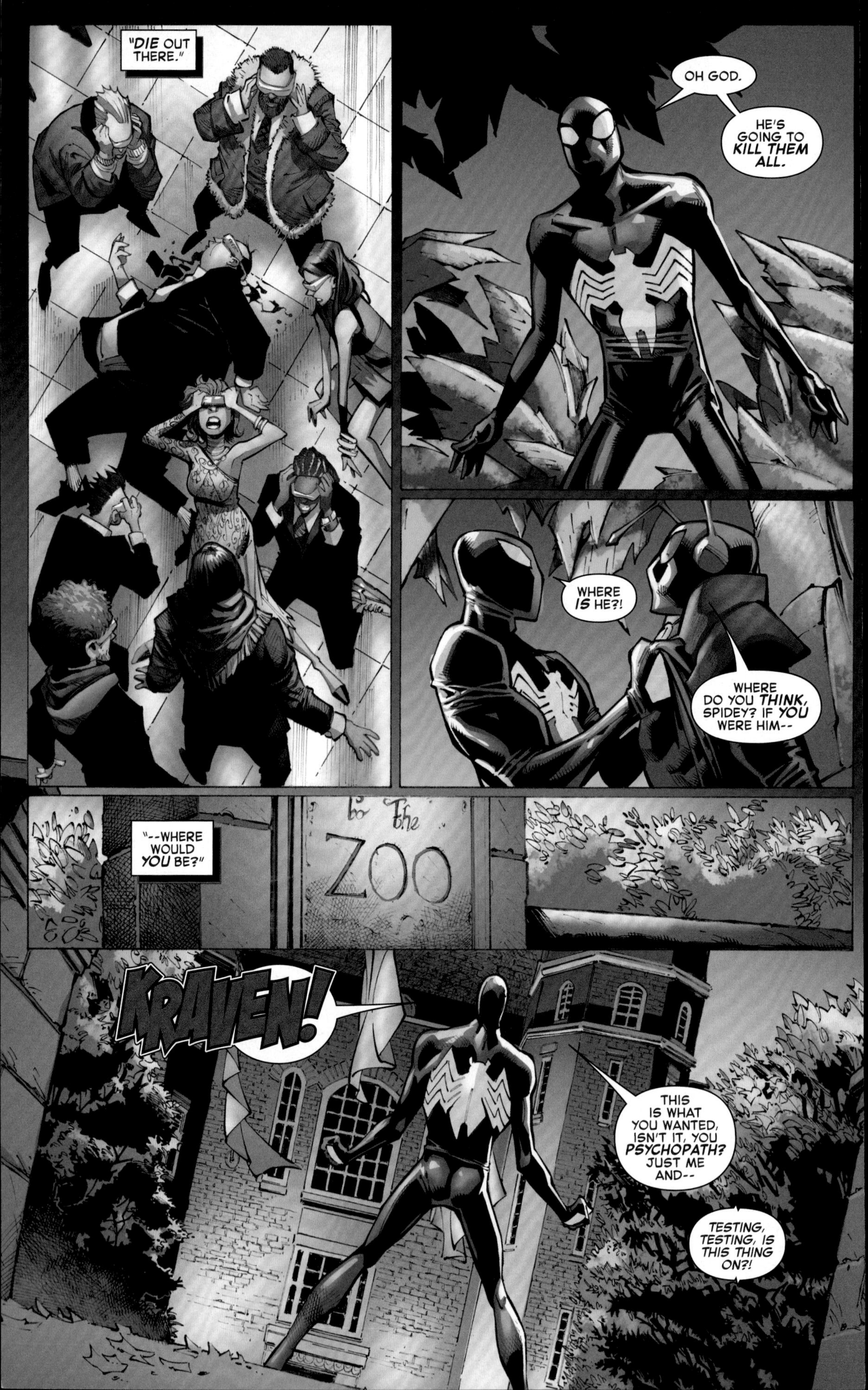
"DIE OUT THERE."
OH GOD.
HE'S GOING TO KILL THEM ALL.
WHERE IS HE?!
WHERE DO YOU THINK, SPIDEY? IF YOU WERE HIM--
"--WHERE WOULD YOU BE?"
to The ZOO
KRAVEN!
THIS IS WHAT YOU WANTED, ISN'T IT, YOU PSYCHOPATH? JUST ME AND--
TESTING, TESTING, IS THIS THING ON?!

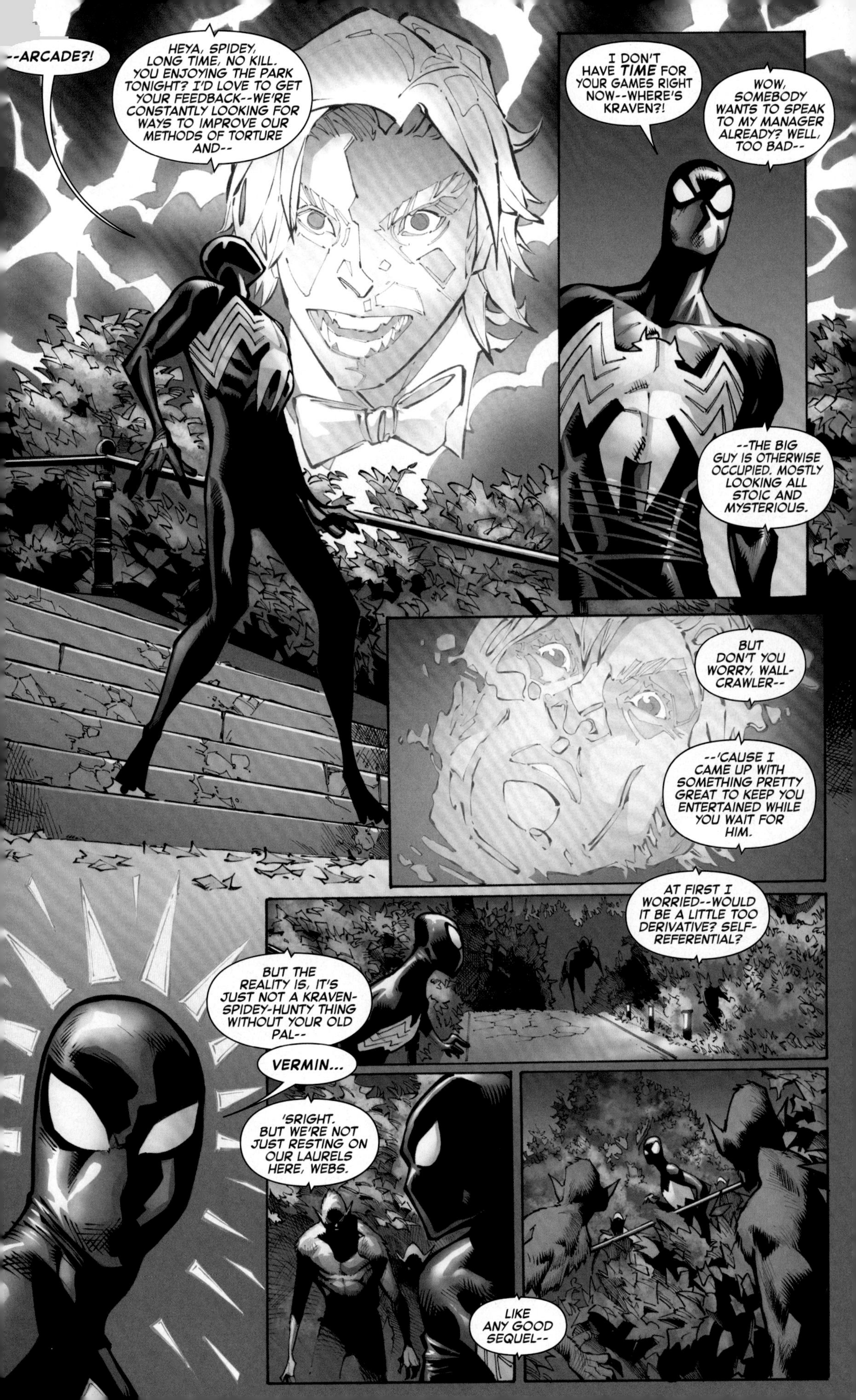

--ARCADE?!
HEYA, SPIDEY, LONG TIME, NO KILL. YOU ENJOYING THE PARK TONIGHT? I'D LOVE TO GET YOUR FEEDBACK--WE'RE CONSTANTLY LOOKING FOR WAYS TO IMPROVE OUR METHODS OF TORTURE AND--
I DON'T HAVE TIME FOR YOUR GAMES RIGHT NOW--WHERE'S KRAVEN?!
WOW, SOMEBODY WANTS TO SPEAK TO MY MANAGER ALREADY? WELL, TOO BAD--
--THE BIG GUY IS OTHERWISE OCCUPIED. MOSTLY LOOKING ALL STOIC AND MYSTERIOUS.
BUT DON'T YOU WORRY, WALL-CRAWLER--
--'CAUSE I CAME UP WITH SOMETHING PRETTY GREAT TO KEEP YOU ENTERTAINED WHILE YOU WAIT FOR HIM.
AT FIRST I WORRIED--WOULD IT BE A LITTLE TOO DERIVATIVE? SELF-REFERENTIAL?
BUT THE REALITY IS, IT'S JUST NOT A KRAVEN-SPIDEY-HUNTY THING WITHOUT YOUR OLD PAL--
VERMIN...
'SRIGHT. BUT WE'RE NOT JUST RESTING ON OUR LAURELS HERE, WEBS.
LIKE ANY GOOD SEQUEL--

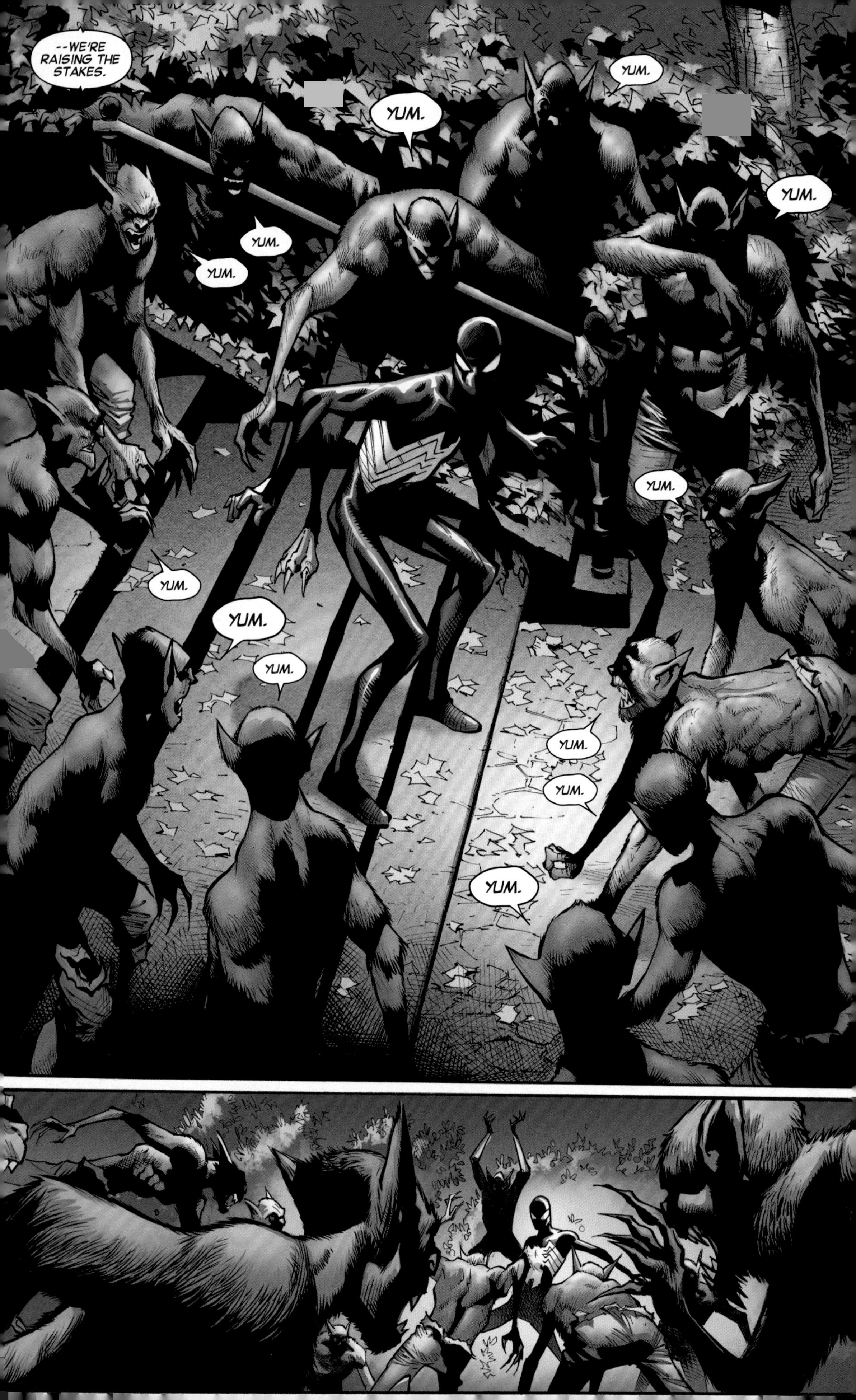
--WE'RE RAISING THE STAKES.
YUM.
YUM.
YUM.
YUM.
YUM.
YUM.
YUM.
YUM.
YUM.
YUM.
YUM.
YUM.
YUM.

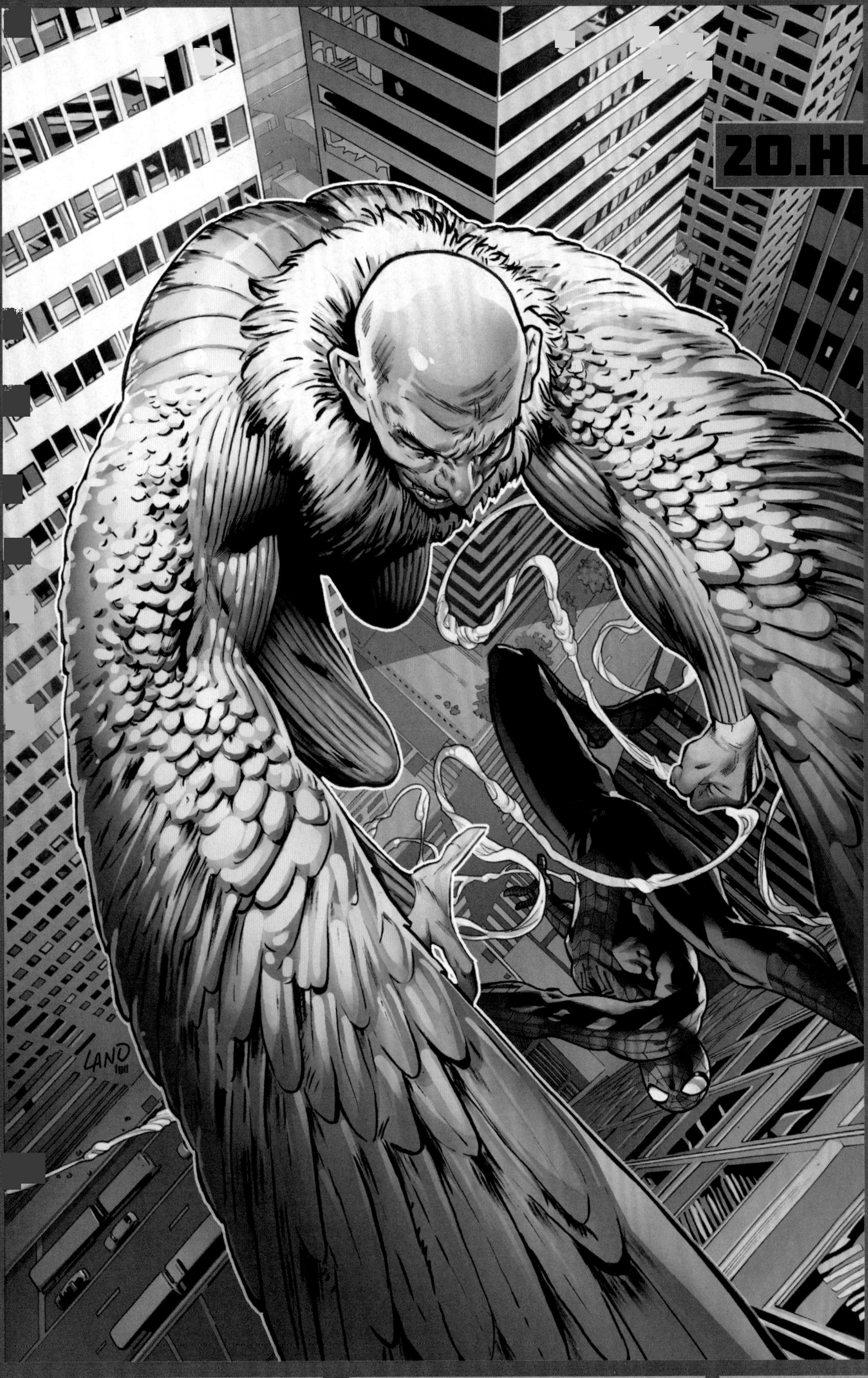
LAND

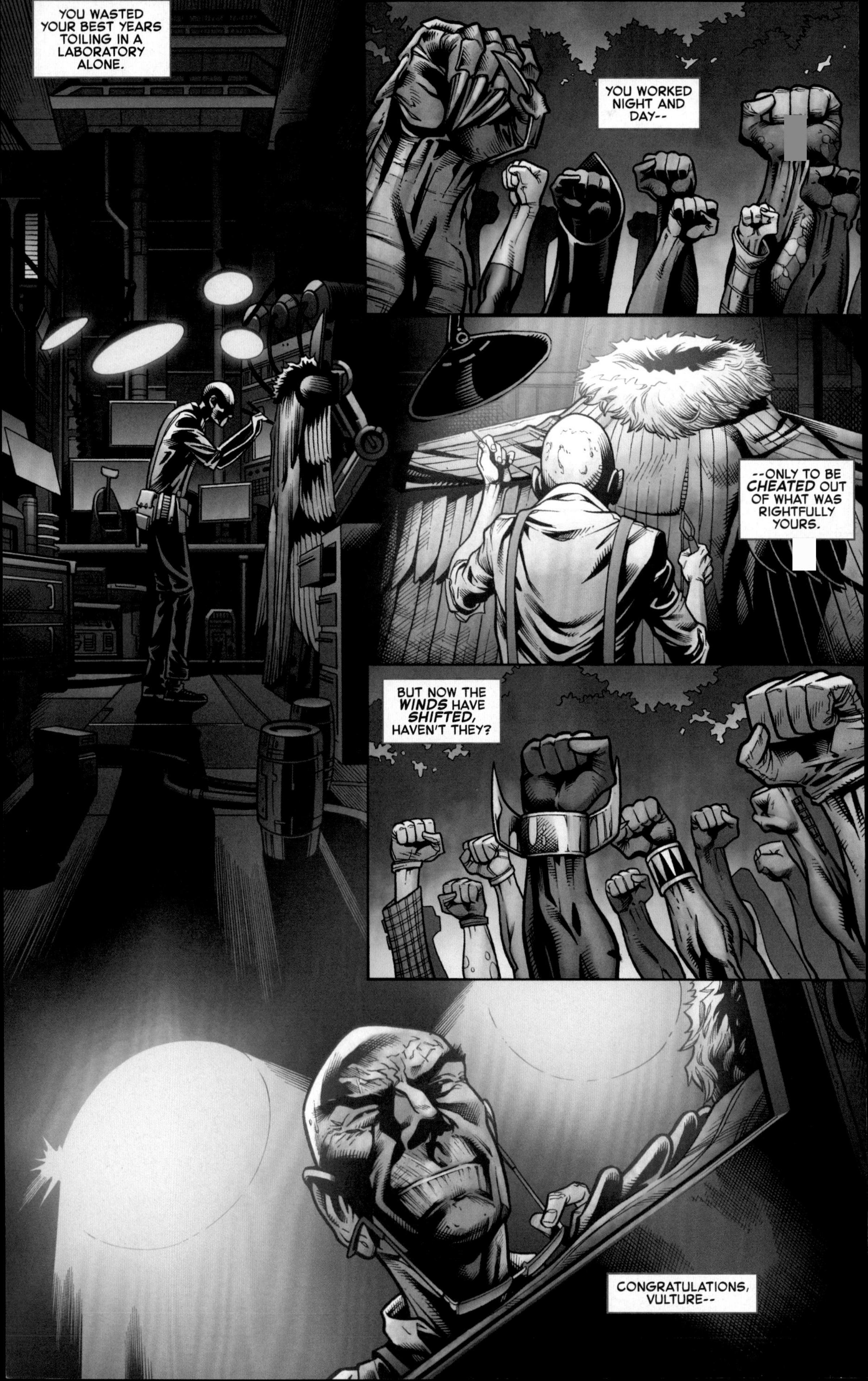
YOU WASTED YOUR BEST YEARS TOILING IN A LABORATORY ALONE.
YOU WORKED NIGHT AND DAY--
--ONLY TO BE CHEATED OUT OF WHAT WAS RIGHTFULLY YOURS.
BUT NOW THE WINDS HAVE SHIFTED, HAVEN'T THEY?
CONGRATULATIONS, VULTURE--

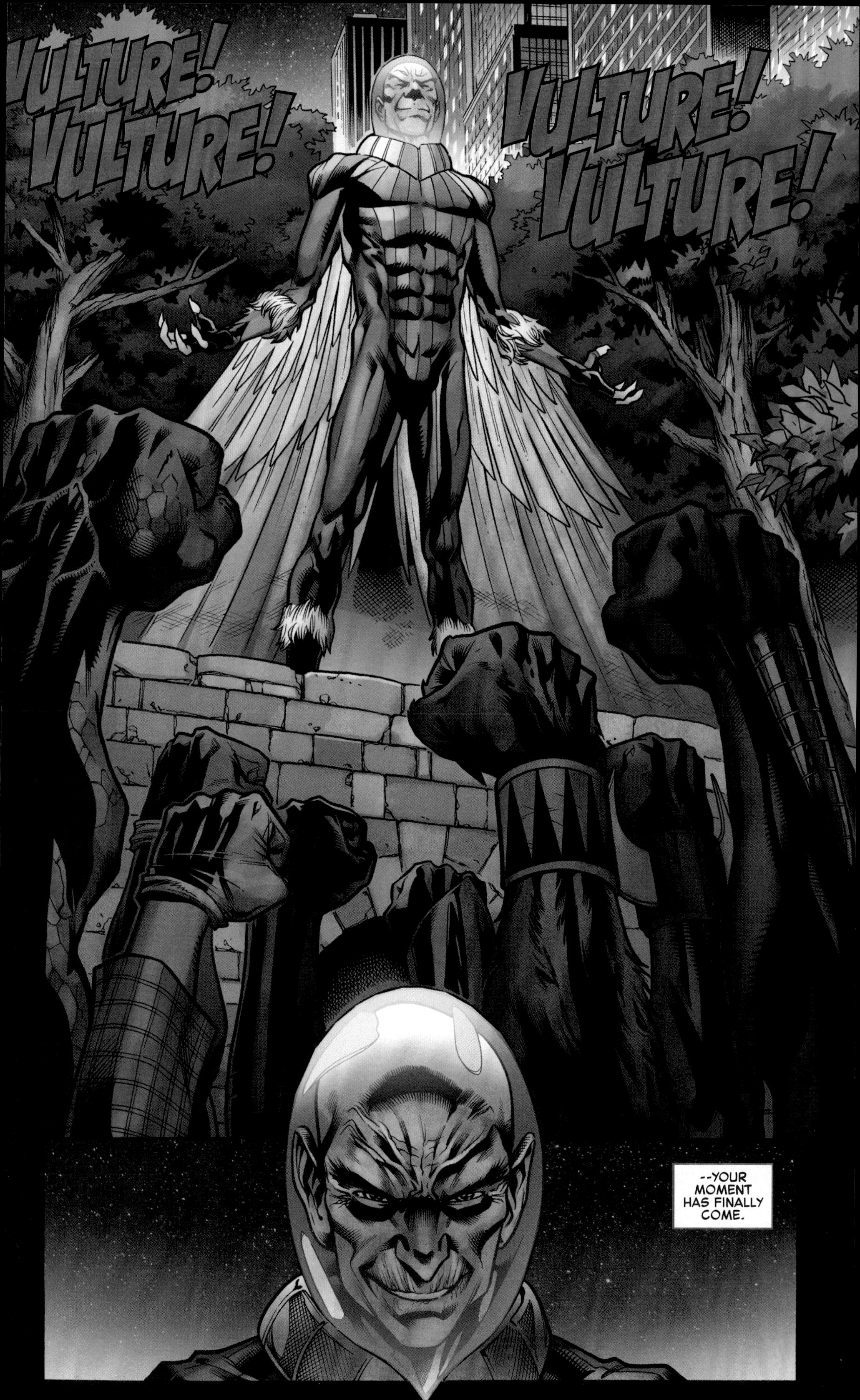
VULTURE! VULTURE!
VULTURE! VULTURE!
--YOUR MOMENT HAS FINALLY COME.

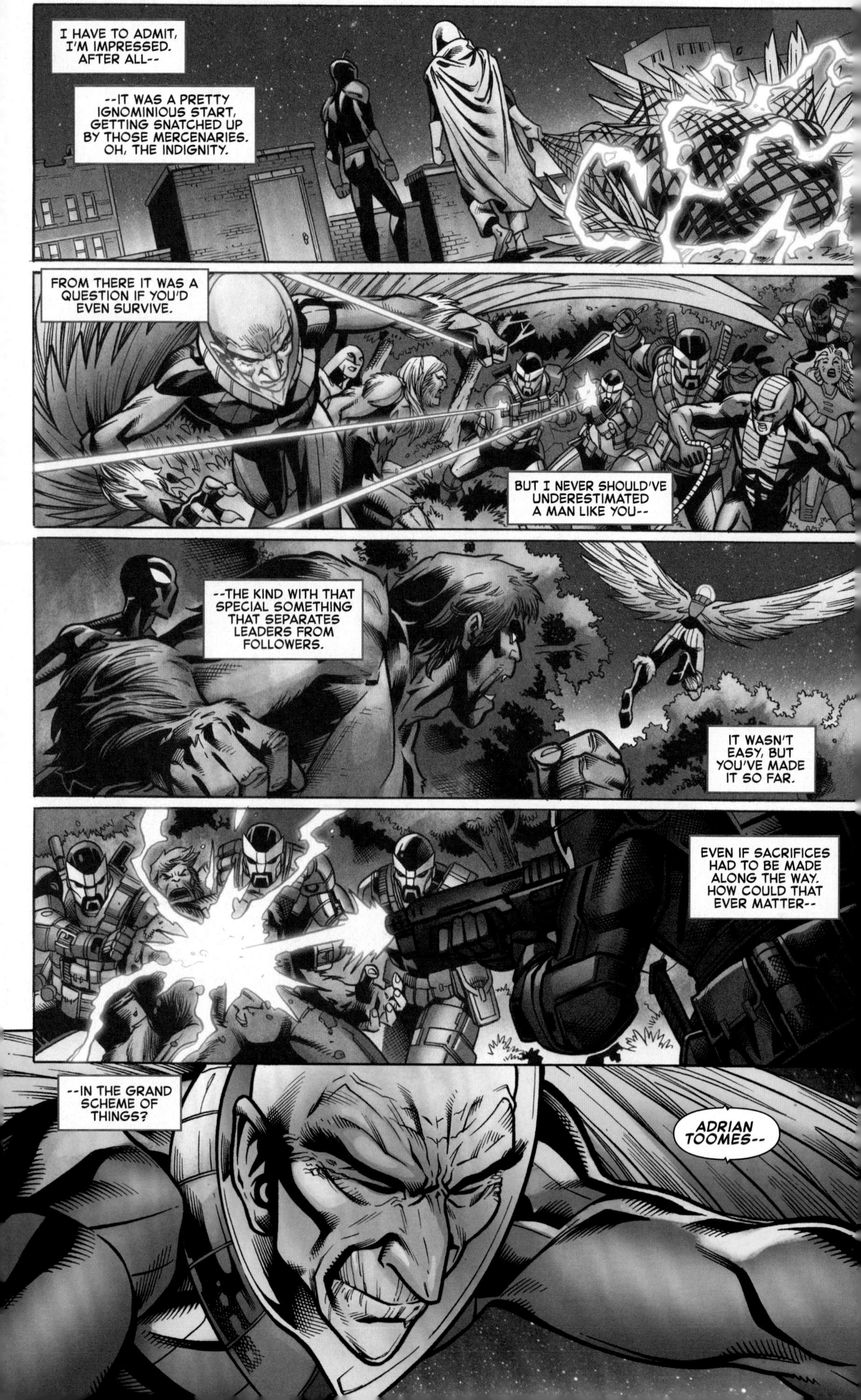
I HAVE TO ADMIT, I'M IMPRESSED. AFTER ALL--
--IT WAS A PRETTY IGNOMINIOUS START, GETTING SNATCHED UP BY THOSE MERCENARIES. OH, THE INDIGNITY.
FROM THERE IT WAS A QUESTION IF YOU'D EVEN SURVIVE.
BUT I NEVER SHOULD'VE UNDERESTIMATED A MAN LIKE YOU--
--THE KIND WITH THAT SPECIAL SOMETHING THAT SEPARATES LEADERS FROM FOLLOWERS.
IT WASN'T EASY, BUT YOU'VE MADE IT SO FAR.
EVEN IF SACRIFICES HAD TO BE MADE ALONG THE WAY. HOW COULD THAT EVER MATTER--
--IN THE GRAND SCHEME OF THINGS?
ADRIAN TOOMES--

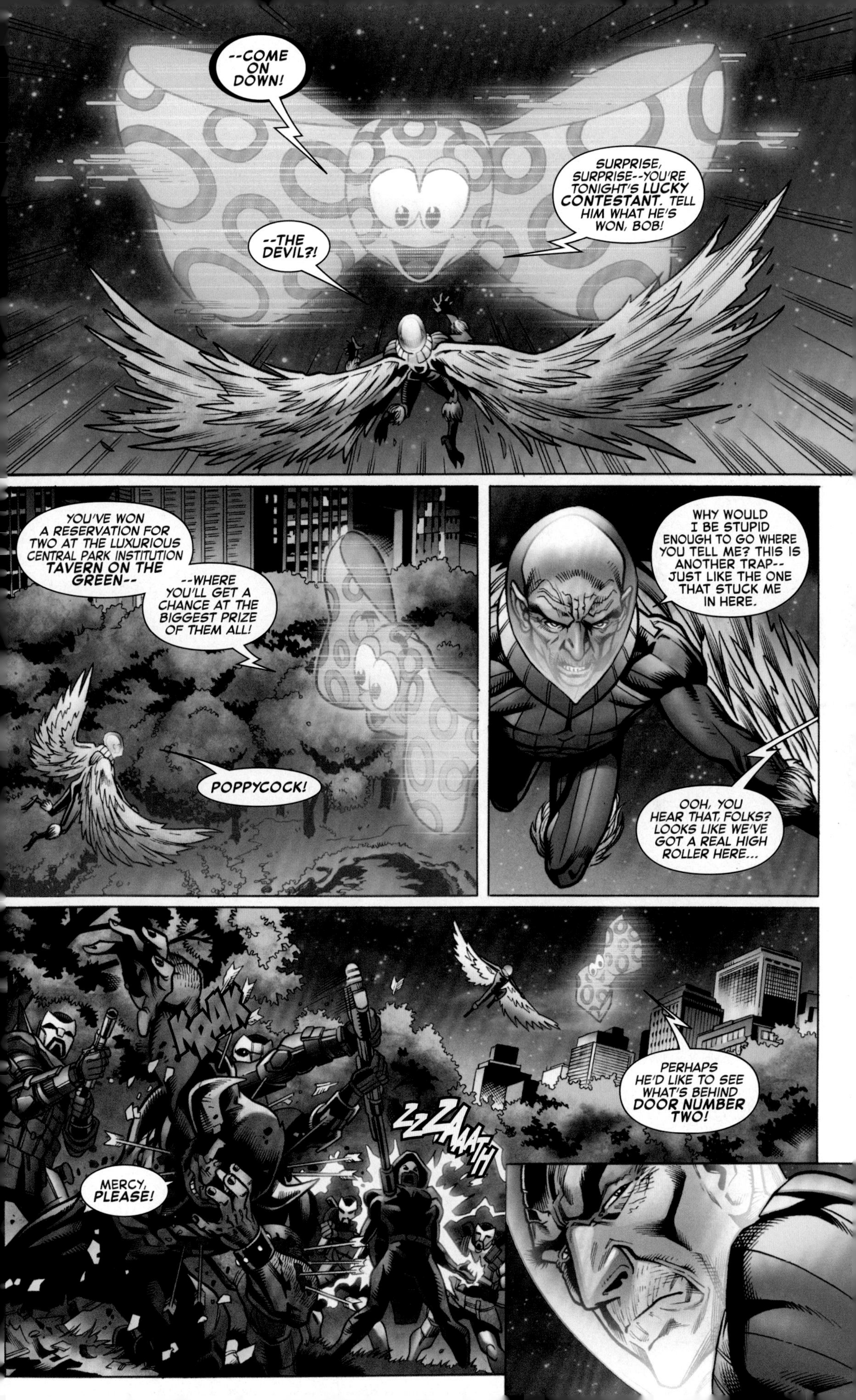

--COME ON DOWN!
SURPRISE, SURPRISE--YOU'RE TONIGHT'S LUCKY CONTESTANT. TELL HIM WHAT HE'S WON, BOB!
--THE DEVIL?!
YOU'VE WON A RESERVATION FOR TWO AT THE LUXURIOUS CENTRAL PARK INSTITUTION TAVERN ON THE GREEN--
--WHERE YOU'LL GET A CHANCE AT THE BIGGEST PRIZE OF THEM ALL!
POPPYCOCK!
WHY WOULD I BE STUPID ENOUGH TO GO WHERE YOU TELL ME? THIS IS ANOTHER TRAP-- JUST LIKE THE ONE THAT STUCK ME IN HERE.
OOH, YOU HEAR THAT, FOLKS? LOOKS LIKE WE'VE GOT A REAL HIGH ROLLER HERE...
KRAK
PERHAPS HE'D LIKE TO SEE WHAT'S BEHIND DOOR NUMBER TWO!
ZZZAAATH
MERCY, PLEASE!

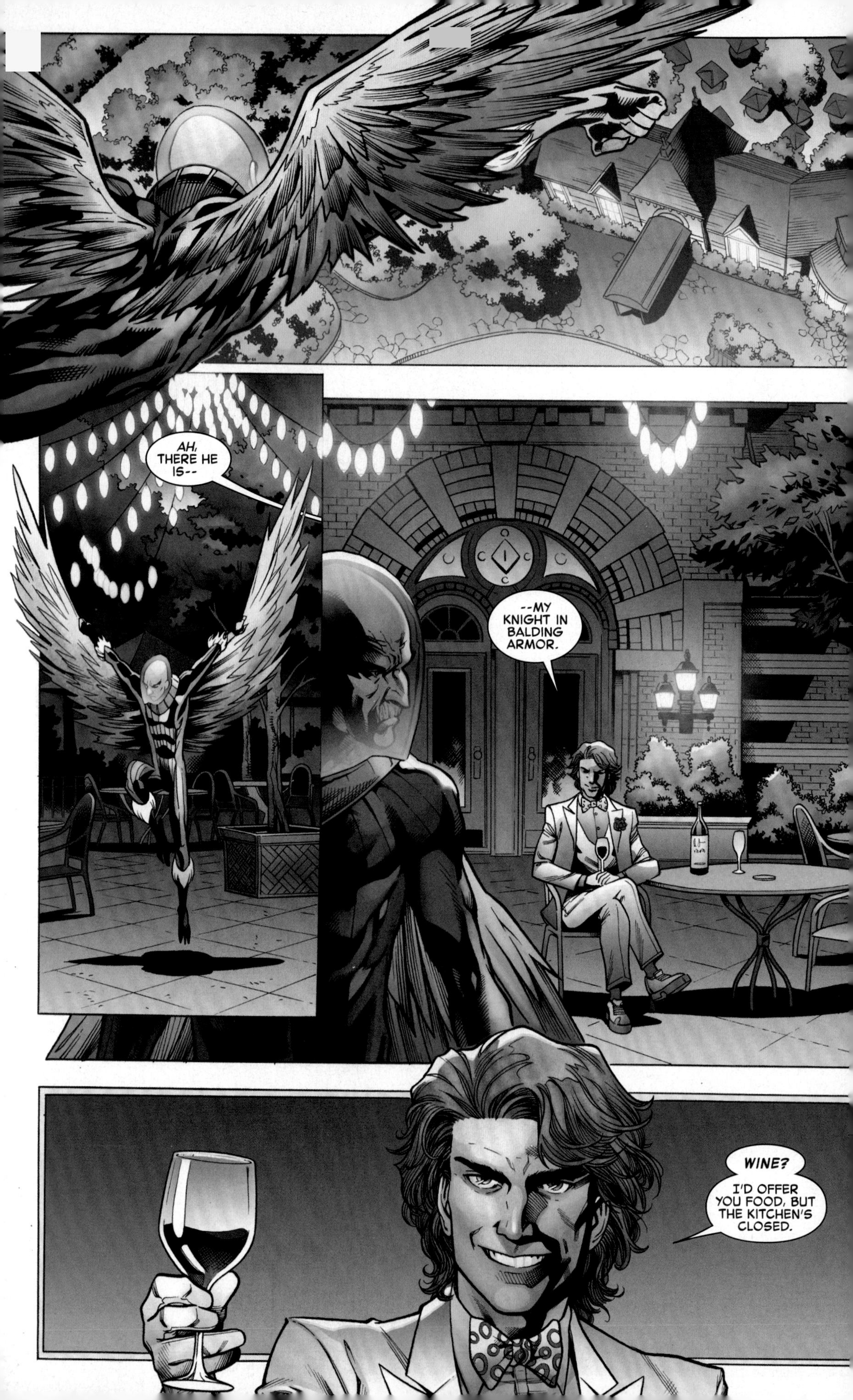
AH, THERE HE IS--
--MY KNIGHT IN BALDING ARMOR.
WINE?
I'D OFFER YOU FOOD, BUT THE KITCHEN'S CLOSED.

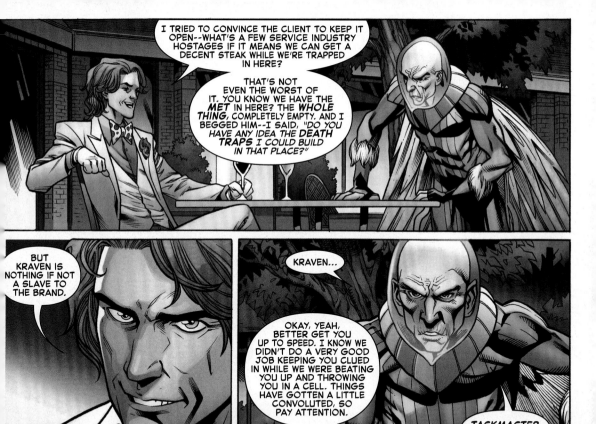

I TRIED TO CONVINCE THE CLIENT TO KEEP IT OPEN--WHAT'S A FEW SERVICE INDUSTRY HOSTAGES IF IT MEANS WE CAN GET A DECENT STEAK WHILE WE'RE TRAPPED IN HERE?

THAT'S NOT EVEN THE WORST OF IT. YOU KNOW WE HAVE THE *MET* IN HERE? THE *WHOLE THING,* COMPLETELY EMPTY. AND I BEGGED HIM--I SAID, "DO YOU HAVE ANY IDEA THE *DEATH TRAPS* I COULD BUILD IN THAT PLACE?"

BUT KRAVEN IS NOTHING IF NOT A SLAVE TO THE BRAND.

KRAVEN...

OKAY, YEAH, BETTER GET YOU UP TO SPEED. I KNOW WE DIDN'T DO A VERY GOOD JOB KEEPING YOU CLUED IN WHILE WE WERE BEATING YOU UP AND THROWING YOU IN A CELL. THINGS HAVE GOTTEN A LITTLE CONVOLUTED, SO PAY ATTENTION.

KRAVEN HIRED TWO MERCS--

TASKMASTER AND THE *BLACK ANT.*

S'RIGHT. KRAVEN HIRED TASKMASTER AND THE BLACK ANT TO *KIDNAP* YOU AND EVENTUALLY STICK YOU HERE IN CENTRAL PARK, UNDER A FORCE FIELD, WHERE YOU'RE BEING CHASED BY KILLER ROBOT DRONES PILOTED BY WEALTHY AND ALMOST IMPOSSIBLY RUDE TROPHY HUNTERS.

OKAY, MAYBE IT'S ACTUALLY PRETTY *STRAIGHT-FORWARD.*

HOW COULD KRAVEN--WE WERE *PARTNERS* ONCE! WE WERE IN THE *SINISTER SIX* TOGETHER! WHATEVER HAPPENED TO *LOYALTY?!*

YEAH, CAN'T BELIEVE THE GUY WHO CALLS HIMSELF "THE HUNTER" TURNED ON THE GUY IN A BIRD SUIT.

AND *YOU*--

I'LL *KILL* YOU FOR THIS!

WHOA, WHOA, DON'T BLAME *ME*--

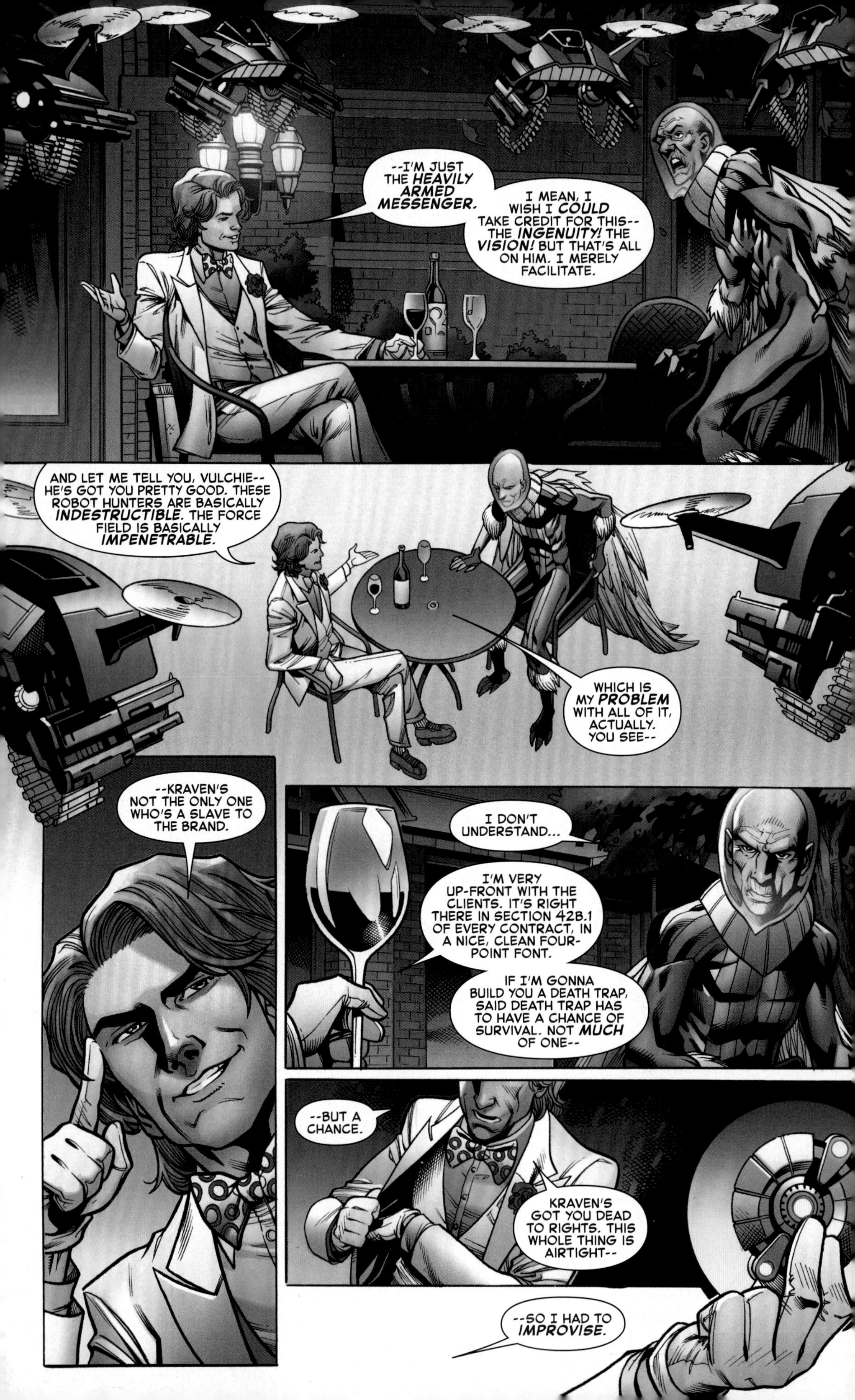

--I'M JUST THE HEAVILY ARMED MESSENGER.
I MEAN, I WISH I COULD TAKE CREDIT FOR THIS-- THE INGENUITY! THE VISION! BUT THAT'S ALL ON HIM. I MERELY FACILITATE.
AND LET ME TELL YOU, VULCHIE-- HE'S GOT YOU PRETTY GOOD. THESE ROBOT HUNTERS ARE BASICALLY INDESTRUCTIBLE. THE FORCE FIELD IS BASICALLY IMPENETRABLE.
WHICH IS MY PROBLEM WITH ALL OF IT, ACTUALLY. YOU SEE--
--KRAVEN'S NOT THE ONLY ONE WHO'S A SLAVE TO THE BRAND.
I DON'T UNDERSTAND...
I'M VERY UP-FRONT WITH THE CLIENTS. IT'S RIGHT THERE IN SECTION 42B.1 OF EVERY CONTRACT, IN A NICE, CLEAN FOUR-POINT FONT.
IF I'M GONNA BUILD YOU A DEATH TRAP, SAID DEATH TRAP HAS TO HAVE A CHANCE OF SURVIVAL. NOT MUCH OF ONE--
--BUT A CHANCE.
KRAVEN'S GOT YOU DEAD TO RIGHTS. THIS WHOLE THING IS AIRTIGHT--
--SO I HAD TO IMPROVISE.

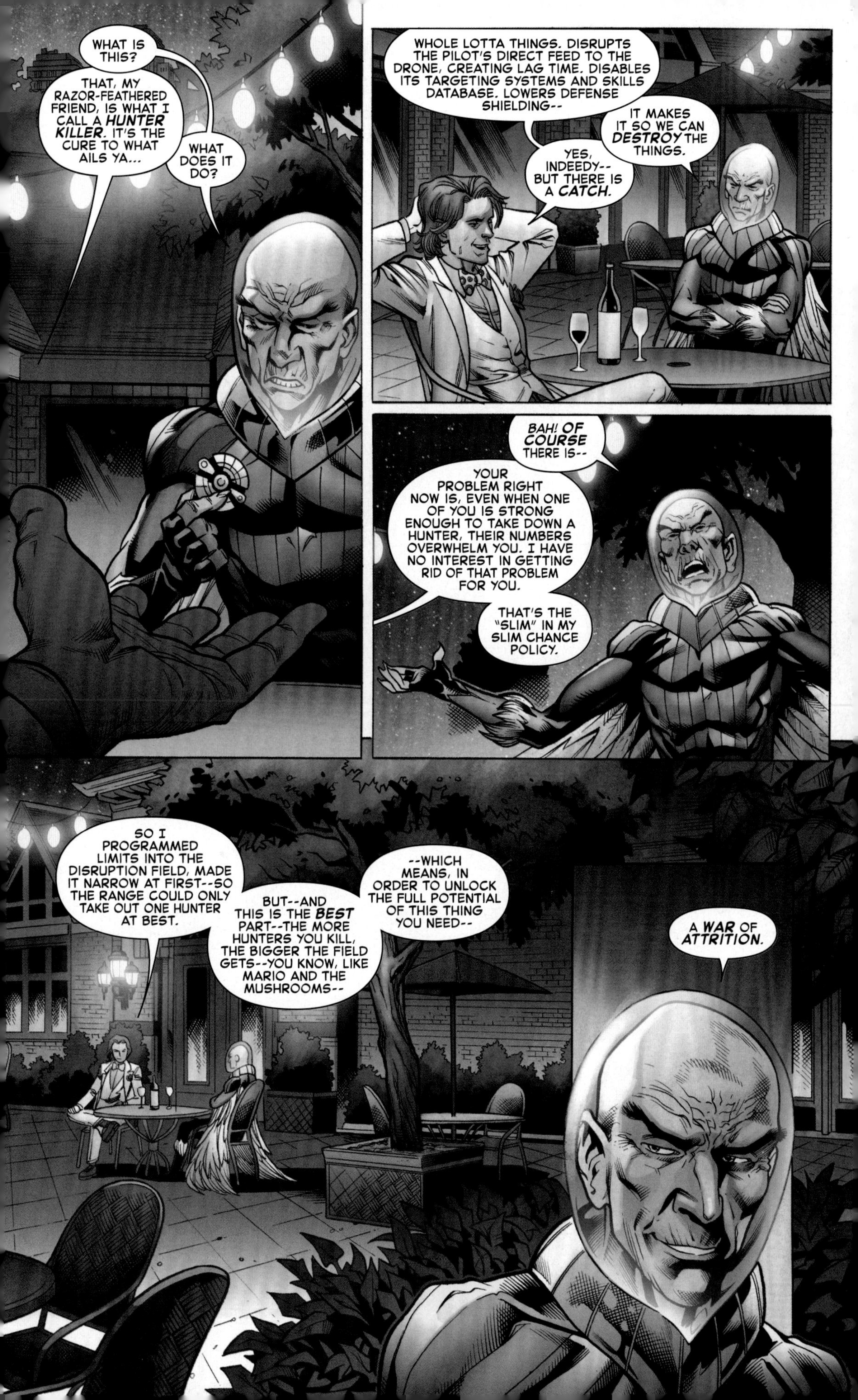

WHAT IS THIS?
THAT, MY RAZOR-FEATHERED FRIEND, IS WHAT I CALL A ***HUNTER KILLER.*** IT'S THE CURE TO WHAT AILS YA...
WHAT DOES IT DO?
WHOLE LOTTA THINGS. DISRUPTS THE PILOT'S DIRECT FEED TO THE DRONE, CREATING LAG TIME. DISABLES ITS TARGETING SYSTEMS AND SKILLS DATABASE. LOWERS DEFENSE SHIELDING--
IT MAKES IT SO WE CAN ***DESTROY*** THE THINGS.
YES, INDEEDY-- BUT THERE IS A ***CATCH.***
BAH! ***OF COURSE*** THERE IS--
YOUR PROBLEM RIGHT NOW IS, EVEN WHEN ONE OF YOU IS STRONG ENOUGH TO TAKE DOWN A HUNTER, THEIR NUMBERS OVERWHELM YOU. I HAVE NO INTEREST IN GETTING RID OF THAT PROBLEM FOR YOU.
THAT'S THE *"SLIM"* IN MY SLIM CHANCE POLICY.
SO I PROGRAMMED LIMITS INTO THE DISRUPTION FIELD, MADE IT NARROW AT FIRST--SO THE RANGE COULD ONLY TAKE OUT ONE HUNTER AT BEST.
BUT--AND THIS IS THE ***BEST*** PART--THE MORE HUNTERS YOU KILL, THE BIGGER THE FIELD GETS--YOU KNOW, LIKE MARIO AND THE MUSHROOMS--
--WHICH MEANS, IN ORDER TO UNLOCK THE FULL POTENTIAL OF THIS THING YOU NEED--
A ***WAR*** OF ***ATTRITION.***

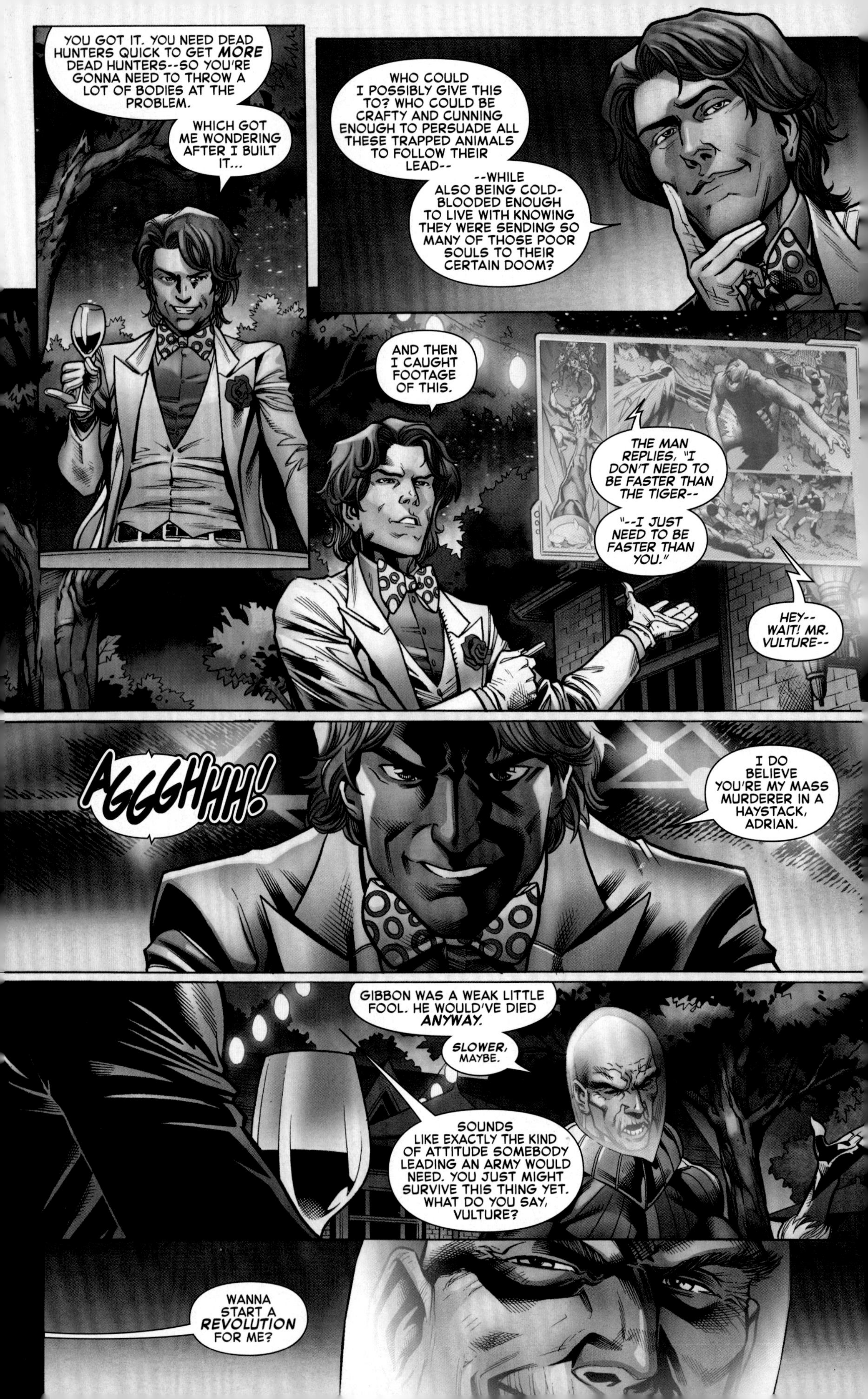
YOU GOT IT. YOU NEED DEAD HUNTERS QUICK TO GET MORE DEAD HUNTERS--SO YOU'RE GONNA NEED TO THROW A LOT OF BODIES AT THE PROBLEM.
WHICH GOT ME WONDERING AFTER I BUILT IT...
WHO COULD I POSSIBLY GIVE THIS TO? WHO COULD BE CRAFTY AND CUNNING ENOUGH TO PERSUADE ALL THESE TRAPPED ANIMALS TO FOLLOW THEIR LEAD--
--WHILE ALSO BEING COLD-BLOODED ENOUGH TO LIVE WITH KNOWING THEY WERE SENDING SO MANY OF THOSE POOR SOULS TO THEIR CERTAIN DOOM?
AND THEN I CAUGHT FOOTAGE OF THIS.
THE MAN REPLIES, "I DON'T NEED TO BE FASTER THAN THE TIGER--
"--I JUST NEED TO BE FASTER THAN YOU."
HEY-- WAIT! MR. VULTURE--
AGGGHHH!
I DO BELIEVE YOU'RE MY MASS MURDERER IN A HAYSTACK, ADRIAN.
GIBBON WAS A WEAK LITTLE FOOL. HE WOULD'VE DIED ANYWAY.
SLOWER, MAYBE.
SOUNDS LIKE EXACTLY THE KIND OF ATTITUDE SOMEBODY LEADING AN ARMY WOULD NEED. YOU JUST MIGHT SURVIVE THIS THING YET. WHAT DO YOU SAY, VULTURE?
WANNA START A REVOLUTION FOR ME?

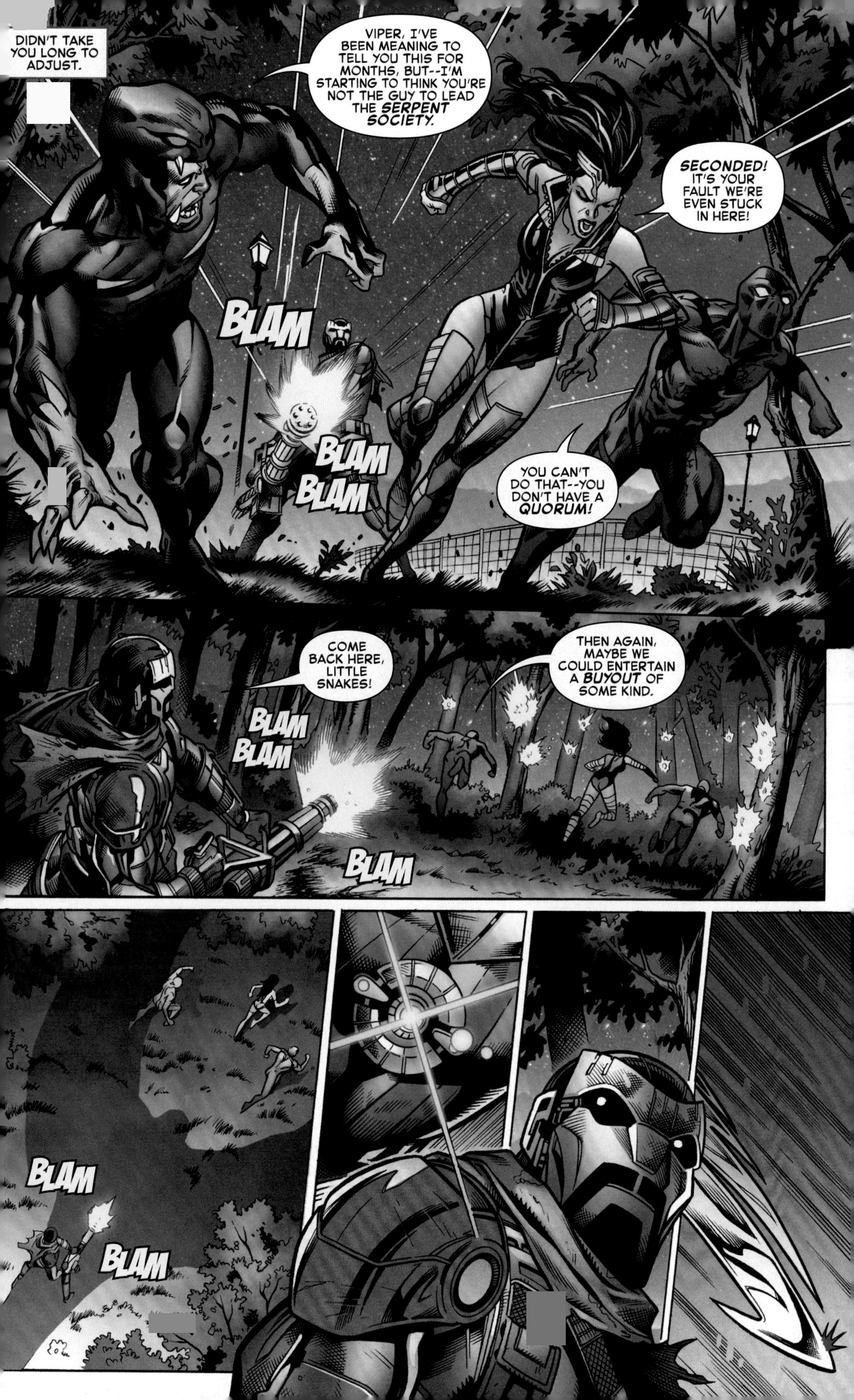
DIDN'T TAKE YOU LONG TO ADJUST.
VIPER, I'VE BEEN MEANING TO TELL YOU THIS FOR MONTHS, BUT--I'M STARTING TO THINK YOU'RE NOT THE GUY TO LEAD THE SERPENT SOCIETY.
SECONDED! IT'S YOUR FAULT WE'RE EVEN STUCK IN HERE!
BLAM
BLAM
BLAM
YOU CAN'T DO THAT--YOU DON'T HAVE A QUORUM!
COME BACK HERE, LITTLE SNAKES!
THEN AGAIN, MAYBE WE COULD ENTERTAIN A BUYOUT OF SOME KIND.
BLAM
BLAM
BLAM
BLAM
BLAM

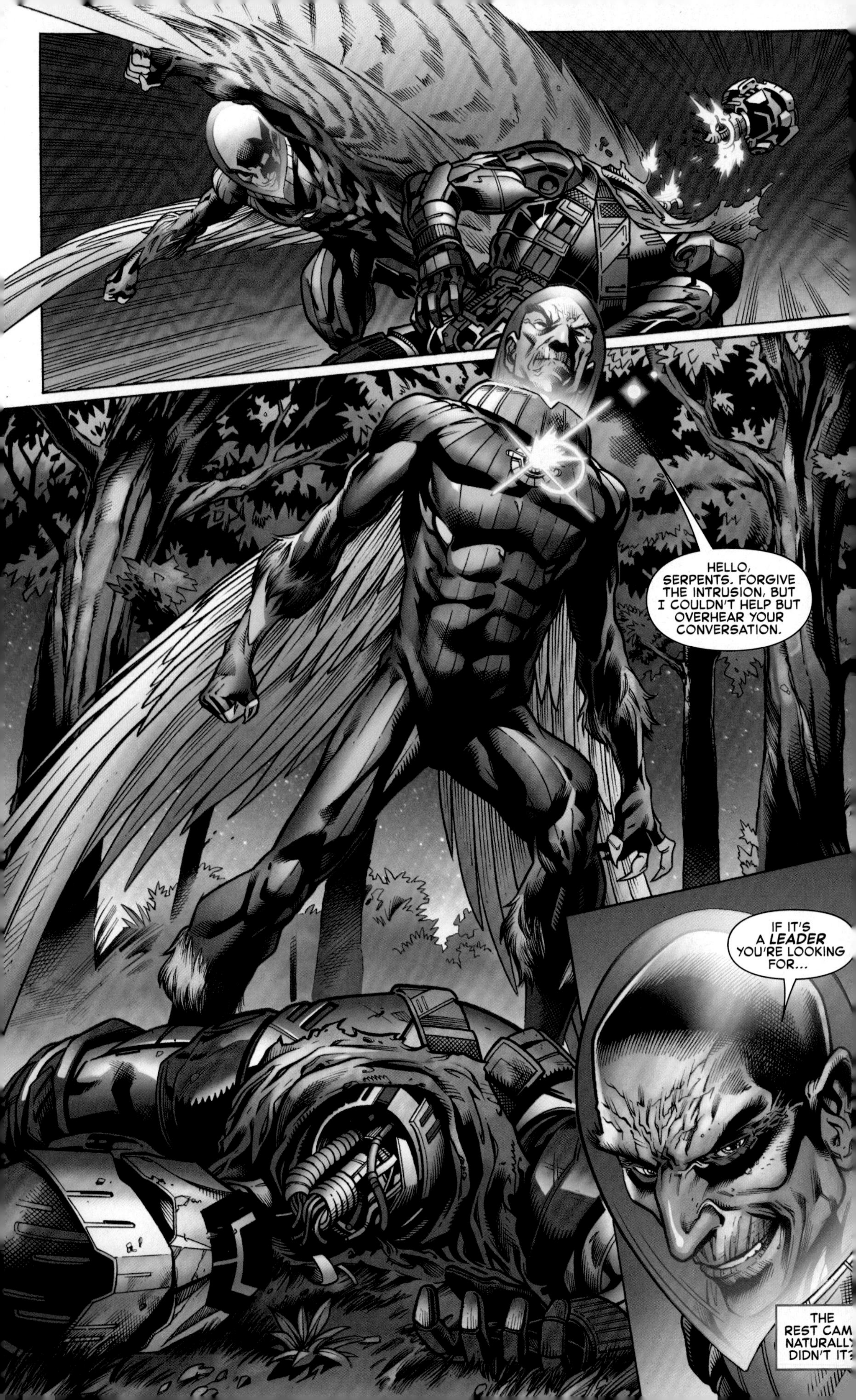

HELLO, SERPENTS. FORGIVE THE INTRUSION, BUT I COULDN'T HELP BUT OVERHEAR YOUR CONVERSATION.
IF IT'S A *LEADER* YOU'RE LOOKING FOR...
THE REST CAM NATURALLY DIDN'T IT?

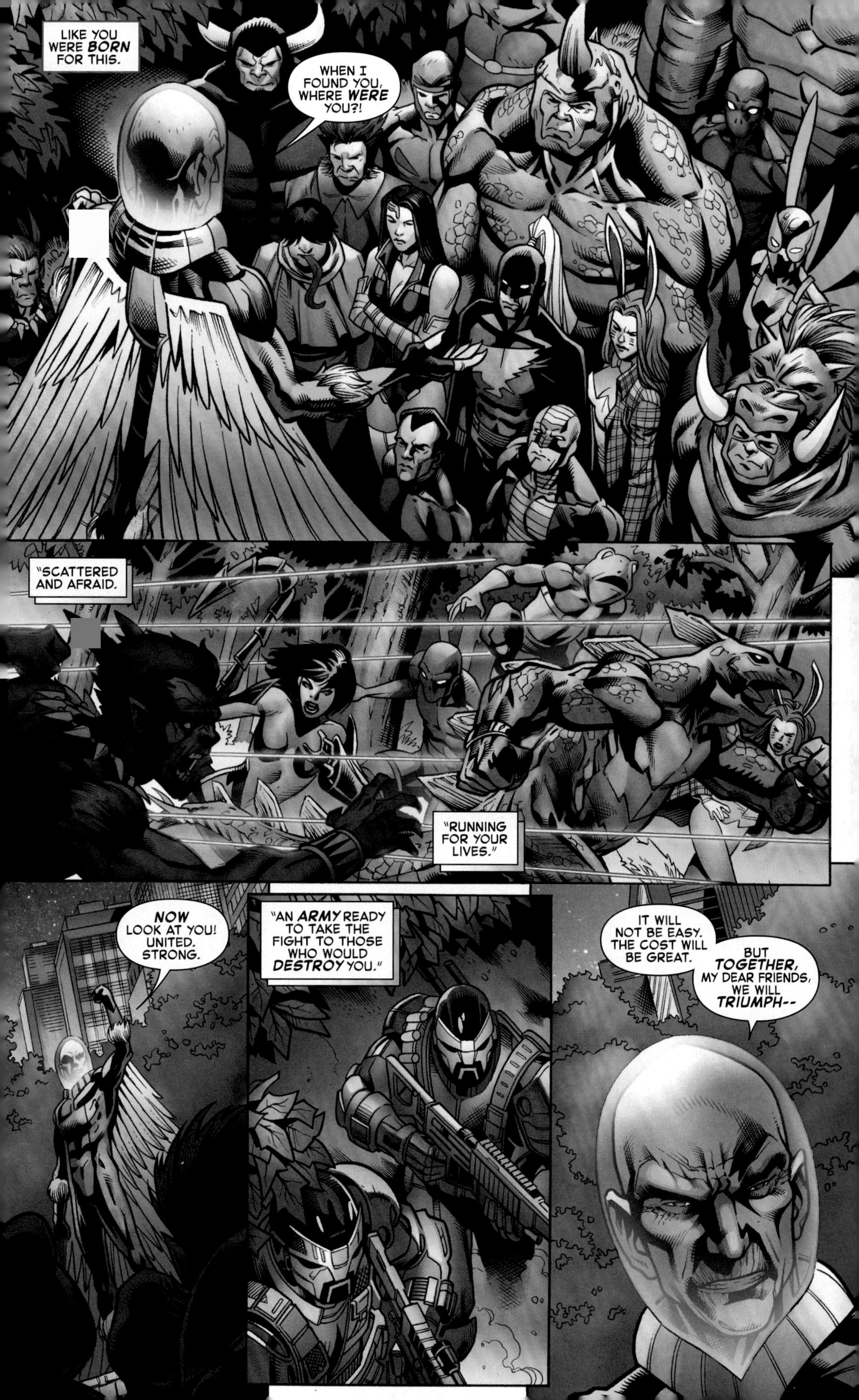
LIKE YOU WERE BORN FOR THIS.
WHEN I FOUND YOU, WHERE WERE YOU?!
"SCATTERED AND AFRAID.
"RUNNING FOR YOUR LIVES."
NOW LOOK AT YOU! UNITED. STRONG.
"AN ARMY READY TO TAKE THE FIGHT TO THOSE WHO WOULD DESTROY YOU."
IT WILL NOT BE EASY. THE COST WILL BE GREAT.
BUT TOGETHER, MY DEAR FRIENDS, WE WILL TRIUMPH--

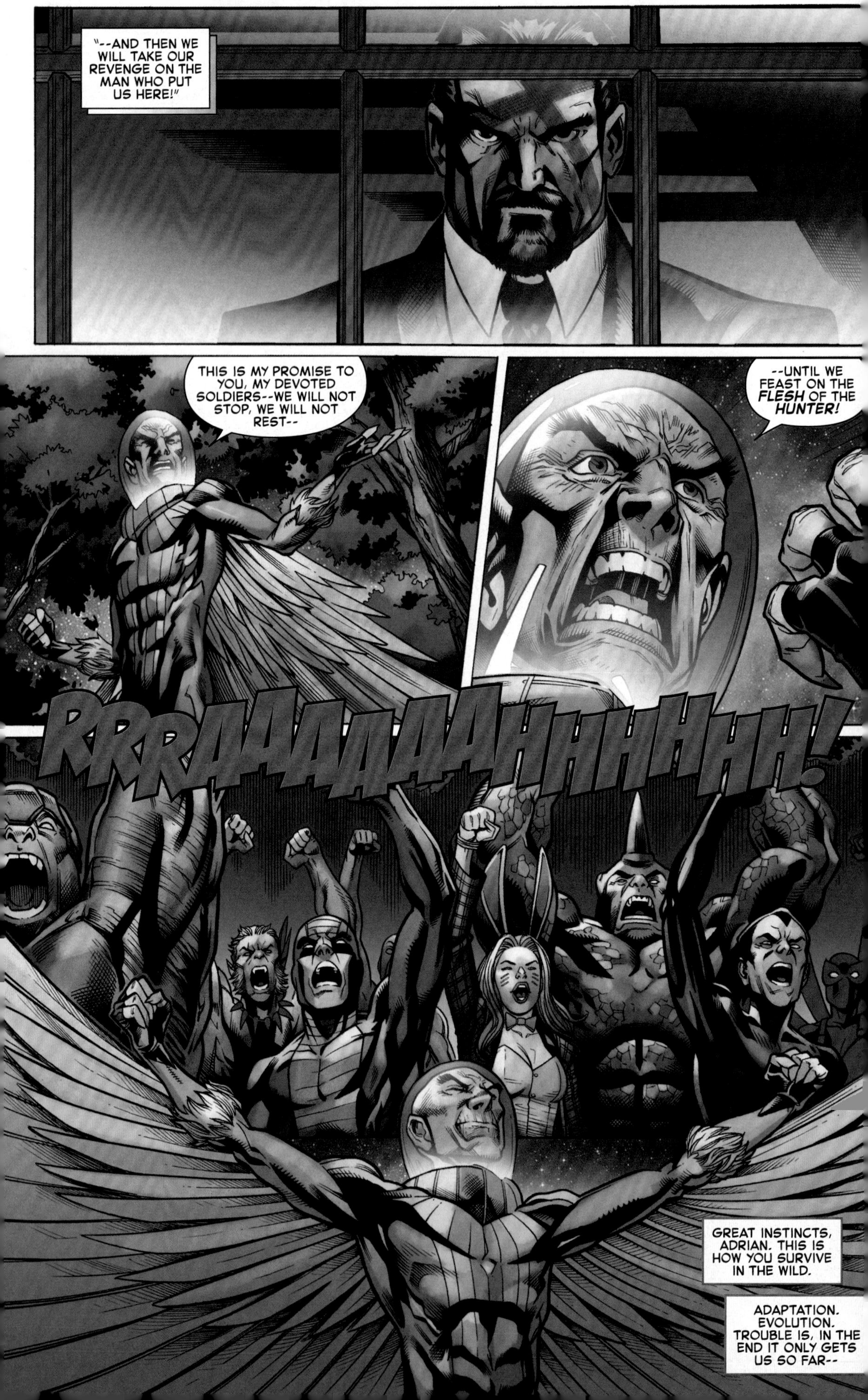
"--AND THEN WE WILL TAKE OUR REVENGE ON THE MAN WHO PUT US HERE!"
THIS IS MY PROMISE TO YOU, MY DEVOTED SOLDIERS--WE WILL NOT STOP, WE WILL NOT REST--
--UNTIL WE FEAST ON THE *FLESH* OF THE *HUNTER!*
RRRAAAAAAAHHHHHHH!
GREAT INSTINCTS, ADRIAN. THIS IS HOW YOU SURVIVE IN THE WILD.
ADAPTATION. EVOLUTION. TROUBLE IS, IN THE END IT ONLY GETS US SO FAR--

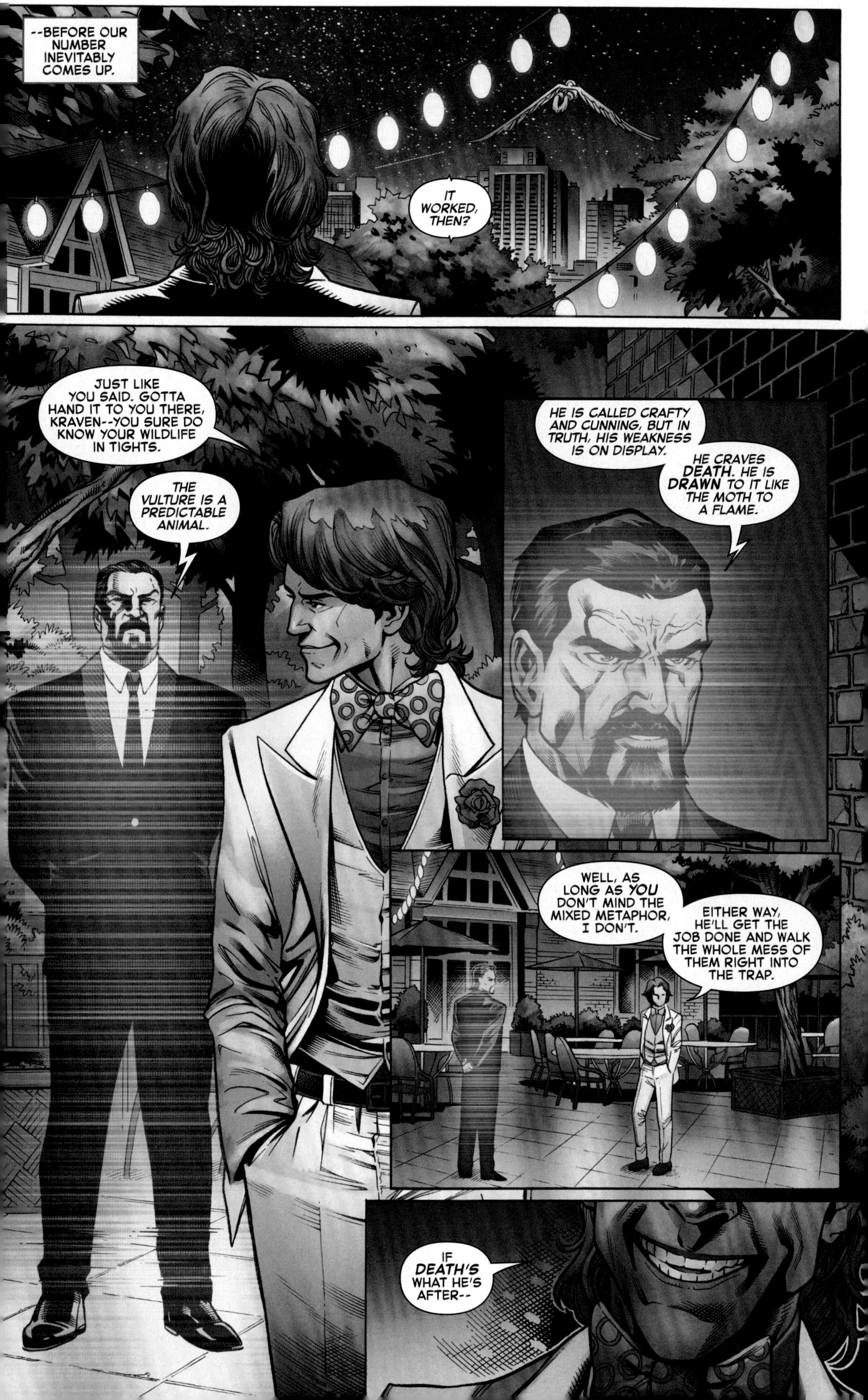
--BEFORE OUR NUMBER INEVITABLY COMES UP.
IT WORKED, THEN?
JUST LIKE YOU SAID. GOTTA HAND IT TO YOU THERE, KRAVEN--YOU SURE DO KNOW YOUR WILDLIFE IN TIGHTS.
THE VULTURE IS A PREDICTABLE ANIMAL.
HE IS CALLED CRAFTY AND CUNNING, BUT IN TRUTH, HIS WEAKNESS IS ON DISPLAY.
HE CRAVES DEATH. HE IS DRAWN TO IT LIKE THE MOTH TO A FLAME.
WELL, AS LONG AS YOU DON'T MIND THE MIXED METAPHOR, I DON'T.
EITHER WAY, HE'LL GET THE JOB DONE AND WALK THE WHOLE MESS OF THEM RIGHT INTO THE TRAP.
IF DEATH'S WHAT HE'S AFTER--

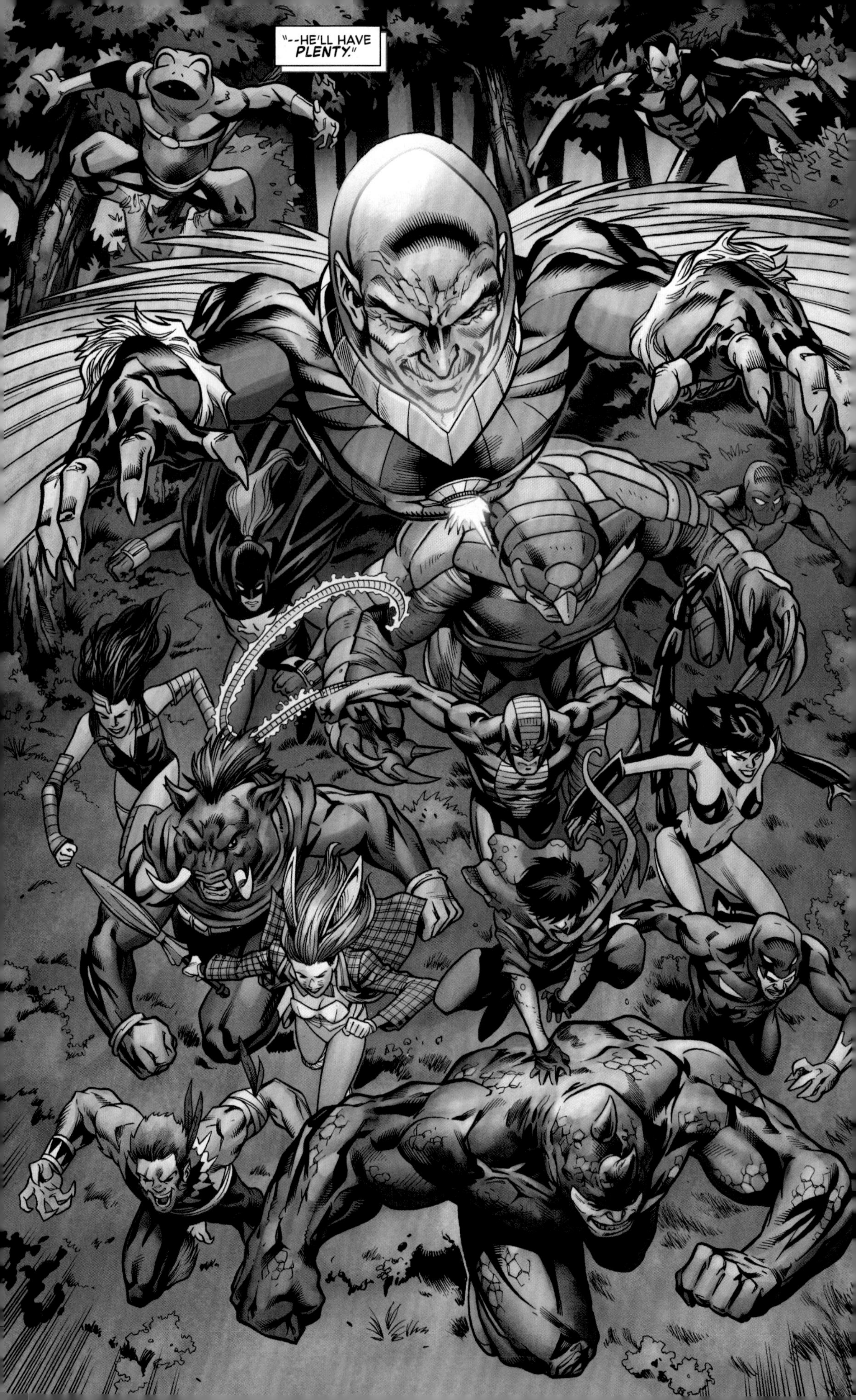
"--HE'LL HAVE PLENTY."

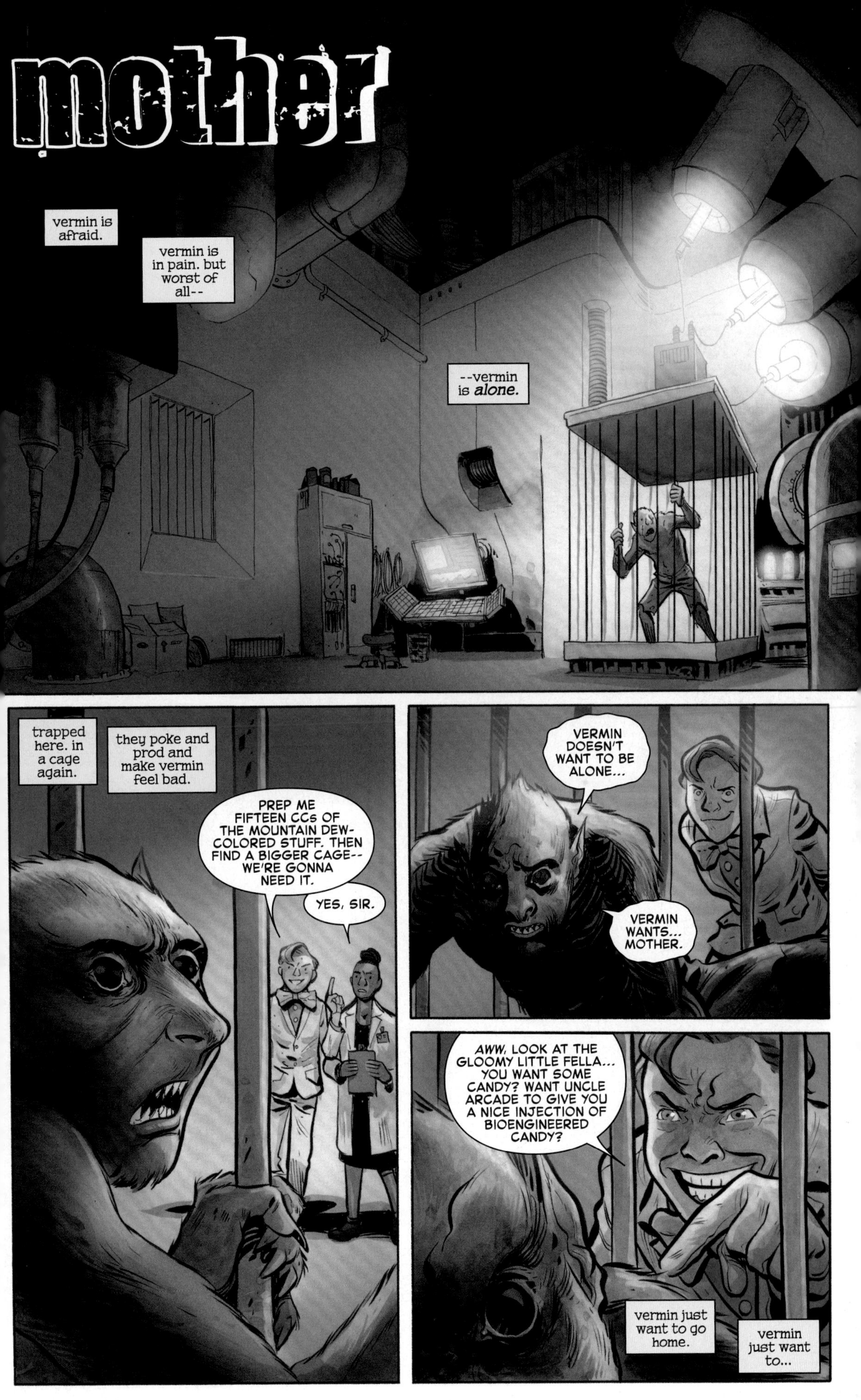
mother
vermin is afraid.
vermin is in pain. but worst of all--
--vermin is *alone.*
trapped here. in a cage again.
they poke and prod and make vermin feel bad.
PREP ME FIFTEEN CCs OF THE MOUNTAIN DEW-COLORED STUFF. THEN FIND A BIGGER CAGE-- WE'RE GONNA NEED IT.
YES, SIR.
VERMIN DOESN'T WANT TO BE ALONE...
VERMIN WANTS... MOTHER.
AWW, LOOK AT THE GLOOMY LITTLE FELLA... YOU WANT SOME CANDY? WANT UNCLE ARCADE TO GIVE YOU A NICE INJECTION OF BIOENGINEERED CANDY?
vermin just want to go home.
vermin just want to...

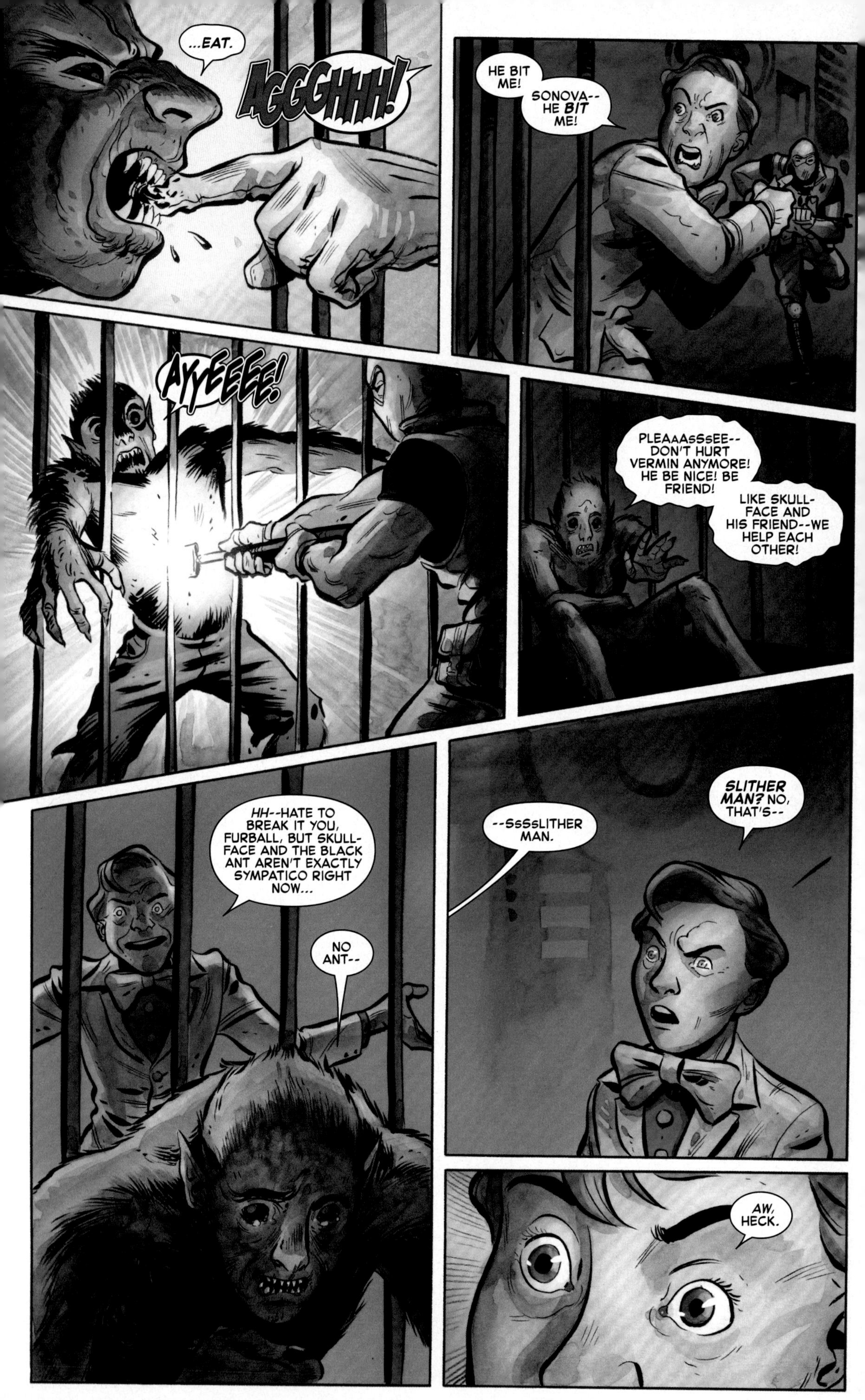

...EAT.
AGGGHHH!
HE BIT ME!
SONOVA-- HE BIT ME!
AYYEEEE!
PLEAAAsSsEE-- DON'T HURT VERMIN ANYMORE! HE BE NICE! BE FRIEND!
LIKE SKULL-FACE AND HIS FRIEND--WE HELP EACH OTHER!
HH--HATE TO BREAK IT YOU, FURBALL, BUT SKULL-FACE AND THE BLACK ANT AREN'T EXACTLY SYMPATICO RIGHT NOW...
NO ANT--
--SsSsLITHER MAN.
SLITHER MAN? NO, THAT'S--
AW, HECK.

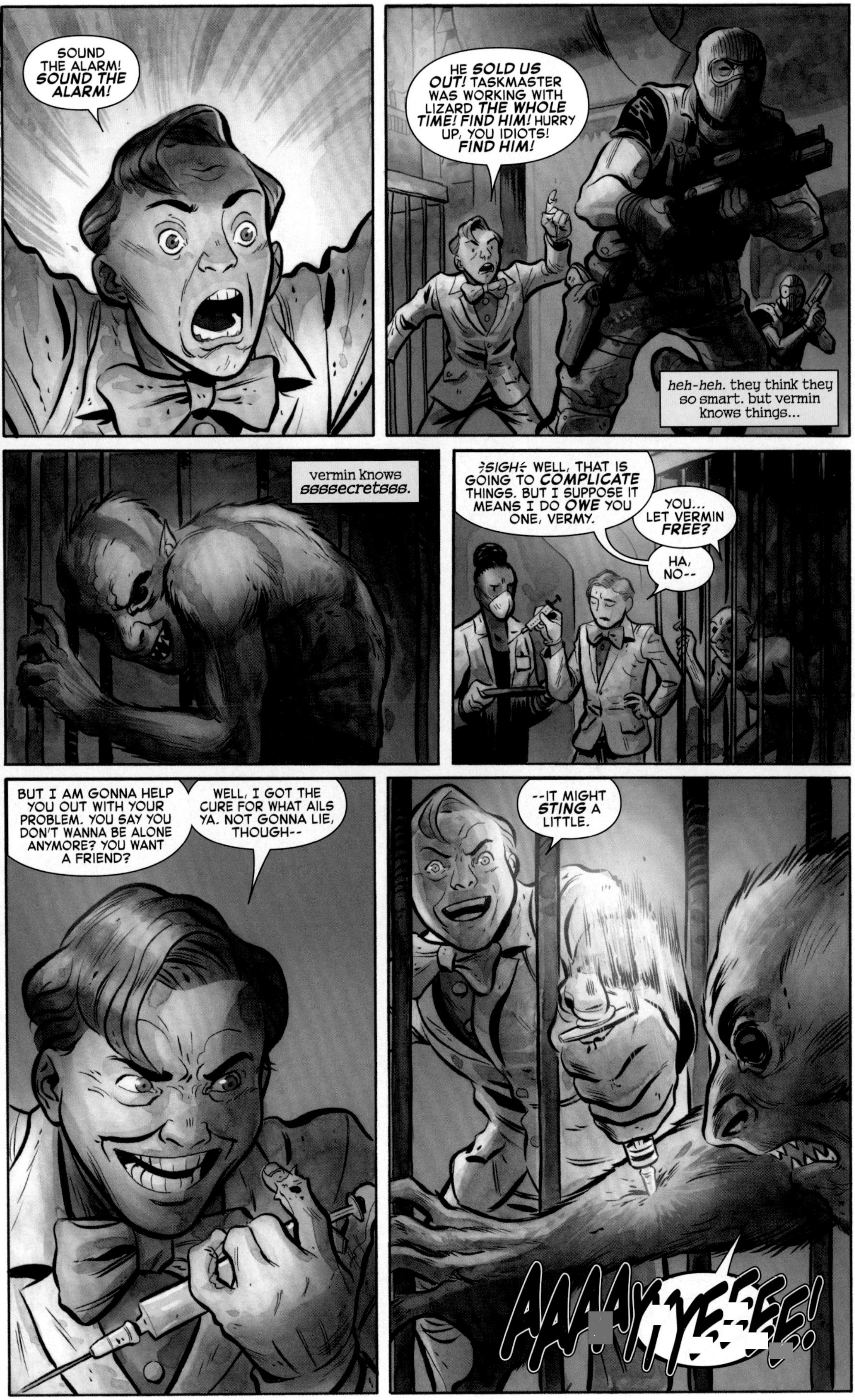
SOUND THE ALARM! SOUND THE ALARM!
HE SOLD US OUT! TASKMASTER WAS WORKING WITH LIZARD THE WHOLE TIME! FIND HIM! HURRY UP, YOU IDIOTS! FIND HIM!
heh-heh. they think they so smart. but vermin knows things...
vermin knows sssssecretsss.
≈SIGH≈ WELL, THAT IS GOING TO COMPLICATE THINGS. BUT I SUPPOSE IT MEANS I DO OWE YOU ONE, VERMY.
YOU... LET VERMIN FREE?
HA, NO--
BUT I AM GONNA HELP YOU OUT WITH YOUR PROBLEM. YOU SAY YOU DON'T WANNA BE ALONE ANYMORE? YOU WANT A FRIEND?
WELL, I GOT THE CURE FOR WHAT AILS YA. NOT GONNA LIE, THOUGH--
--IT MIGHT STING A LITTLE.
AAAAYYEEEE!

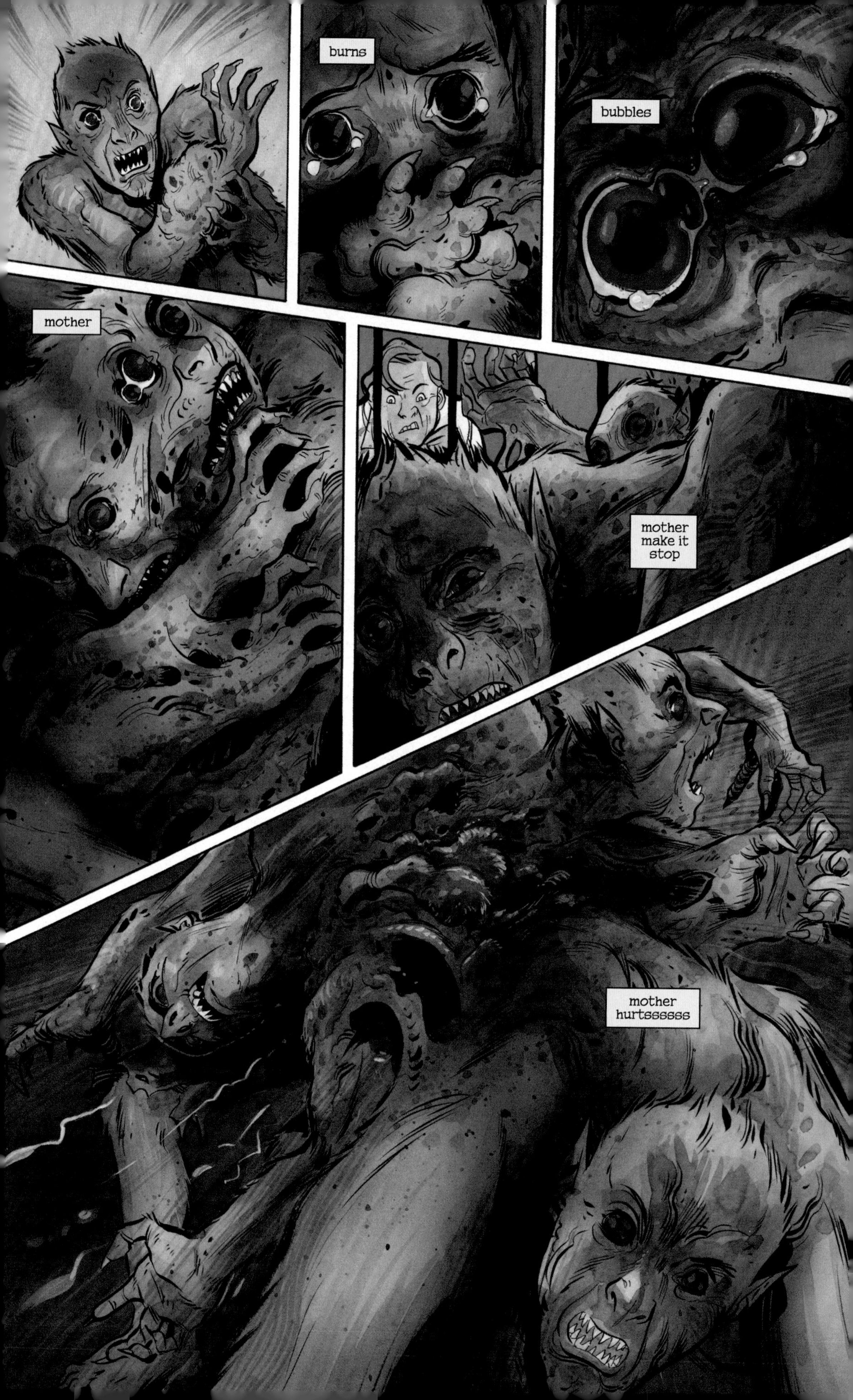
burns
bubbles
mother
mother
make it
stop
mother
hurtssssss

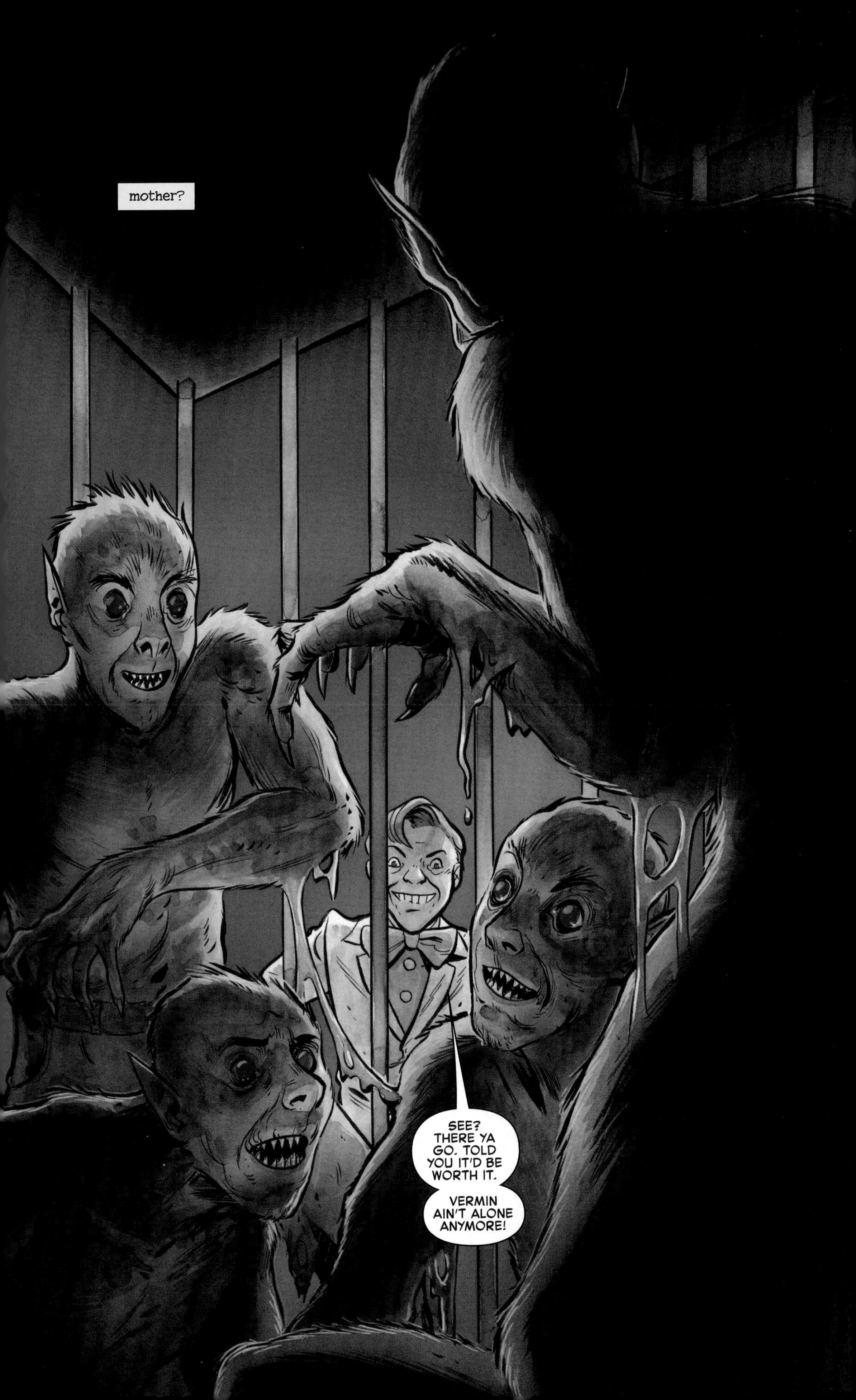
mother?
SEE? THERE YA GO. TOLD YOU IT'D BE WORTH IT.
VERMIN AIN'T ALONE ANYMORE!

21

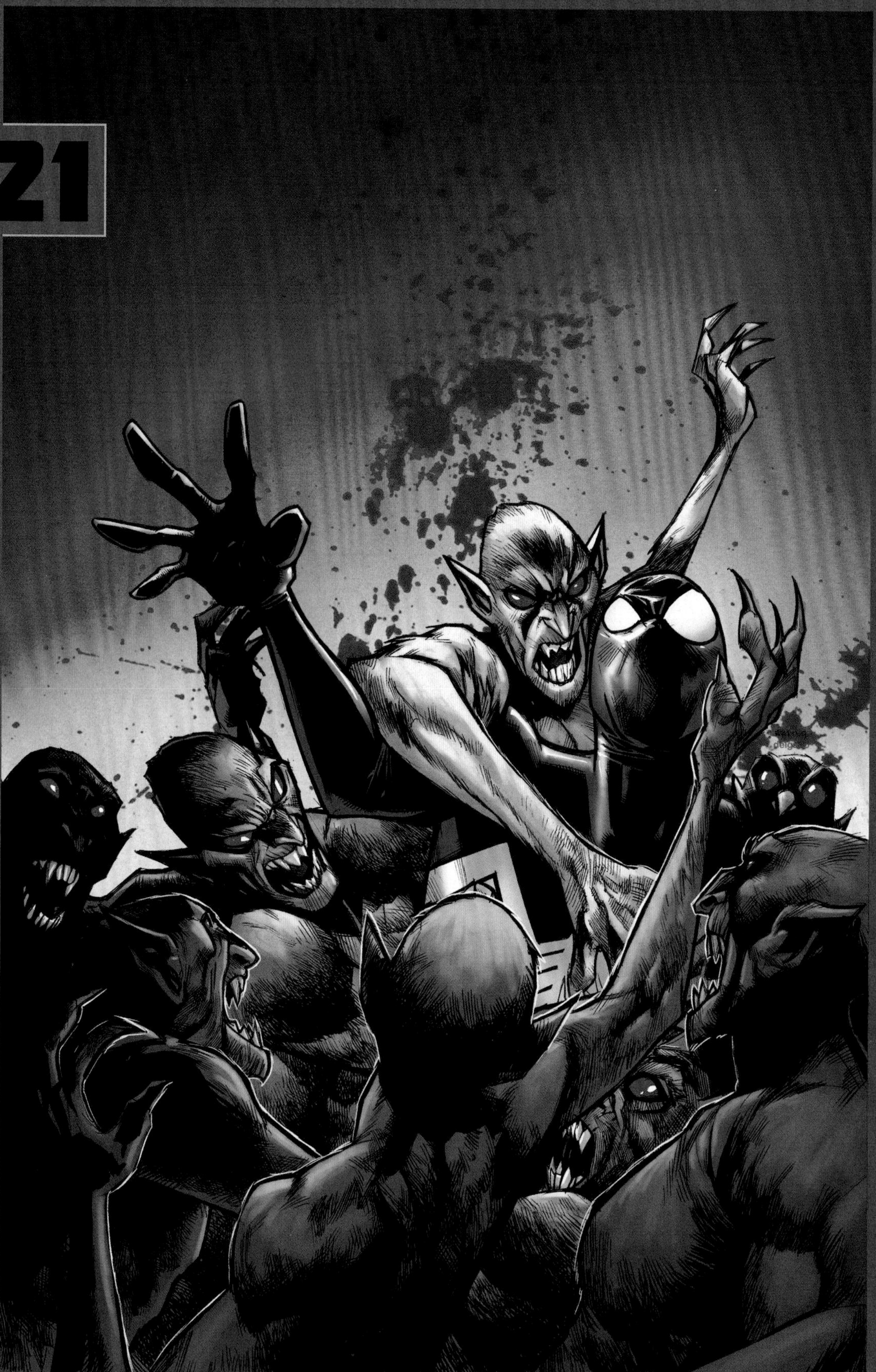

HUNTED PART 5

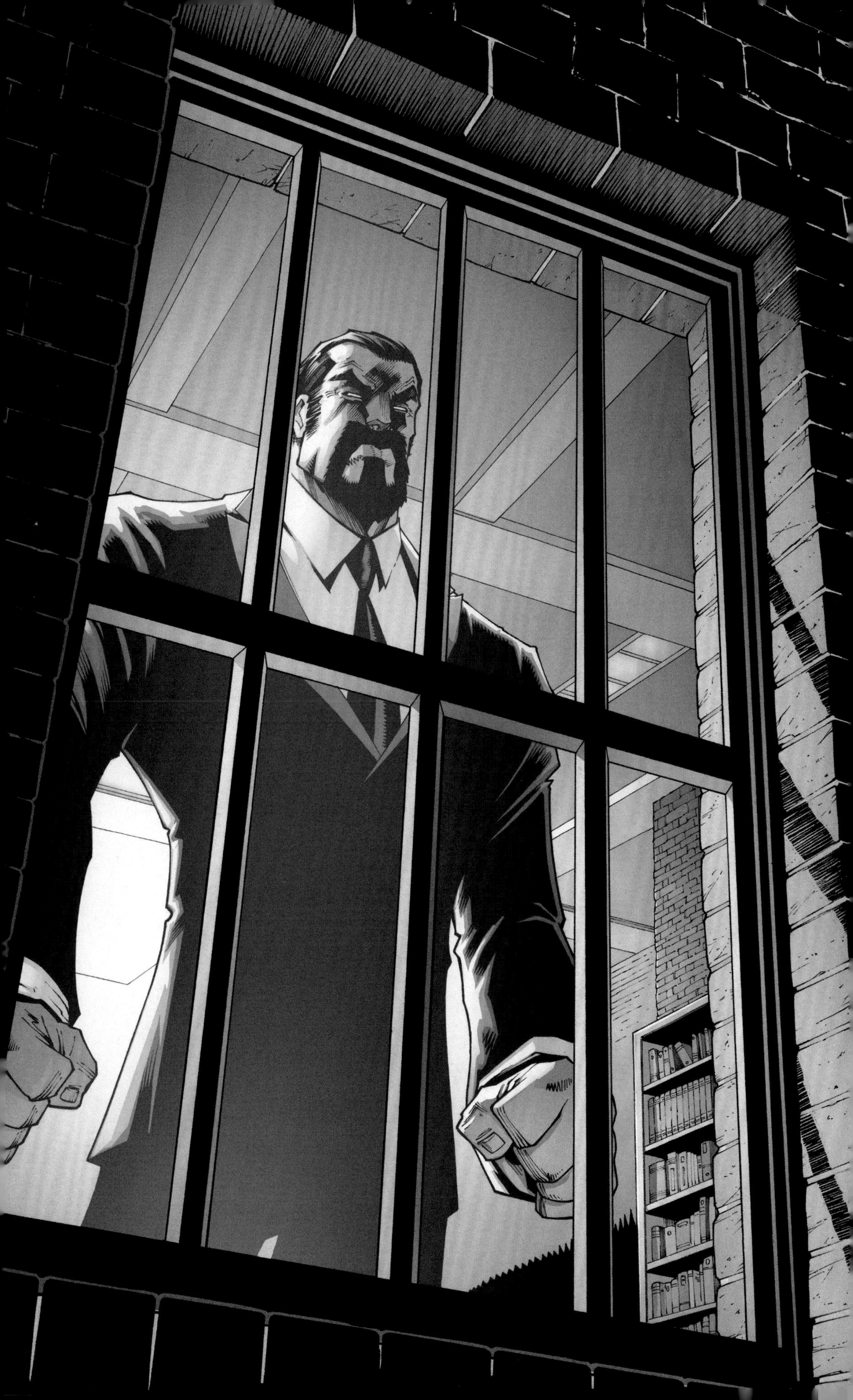

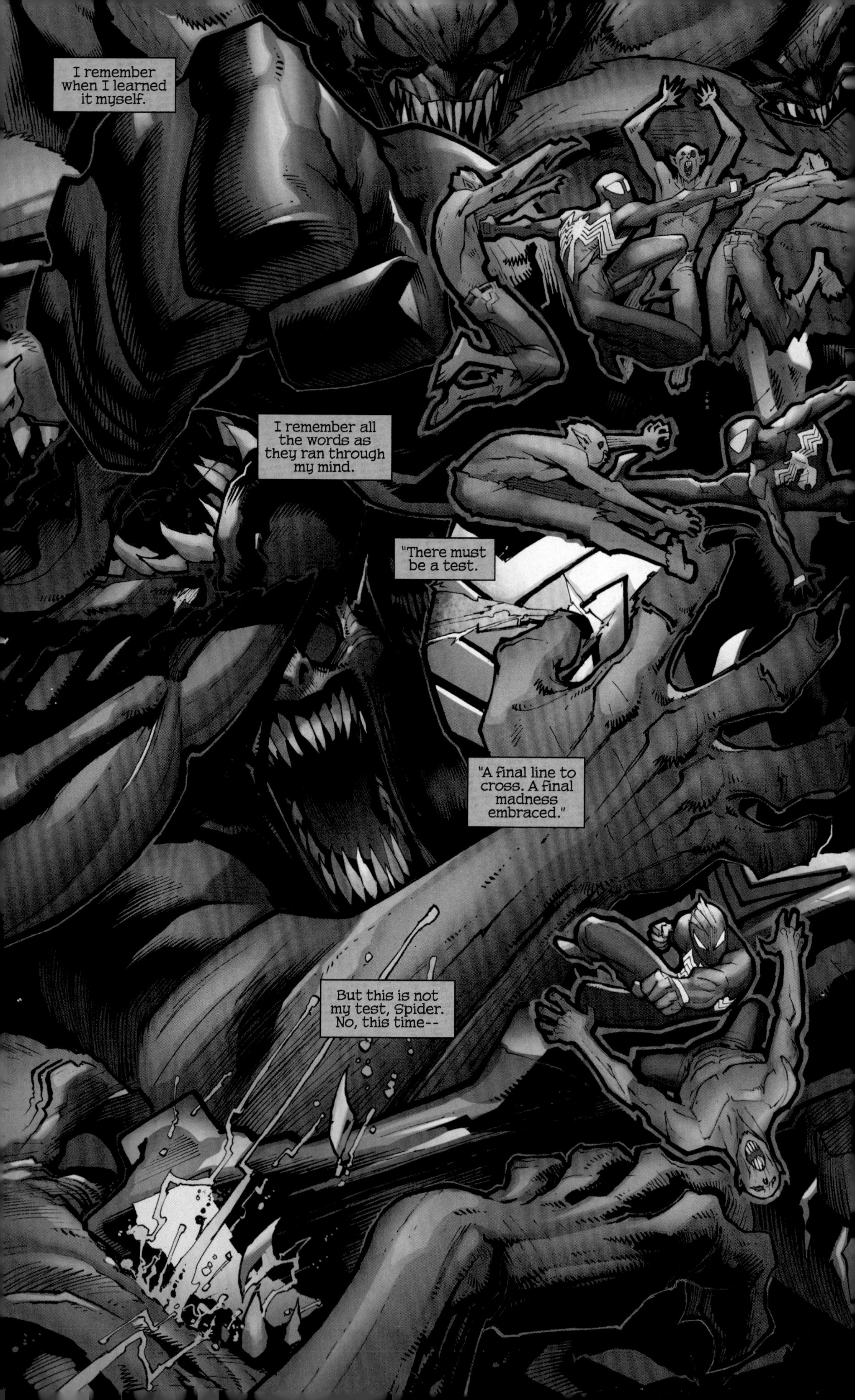
I remember when I learned it myself.
I remember all the words as they ran through my mind.
"There must be a test.
"A final line to cross. A final madness embraced."
But this is not my test, Spider. No, this time--

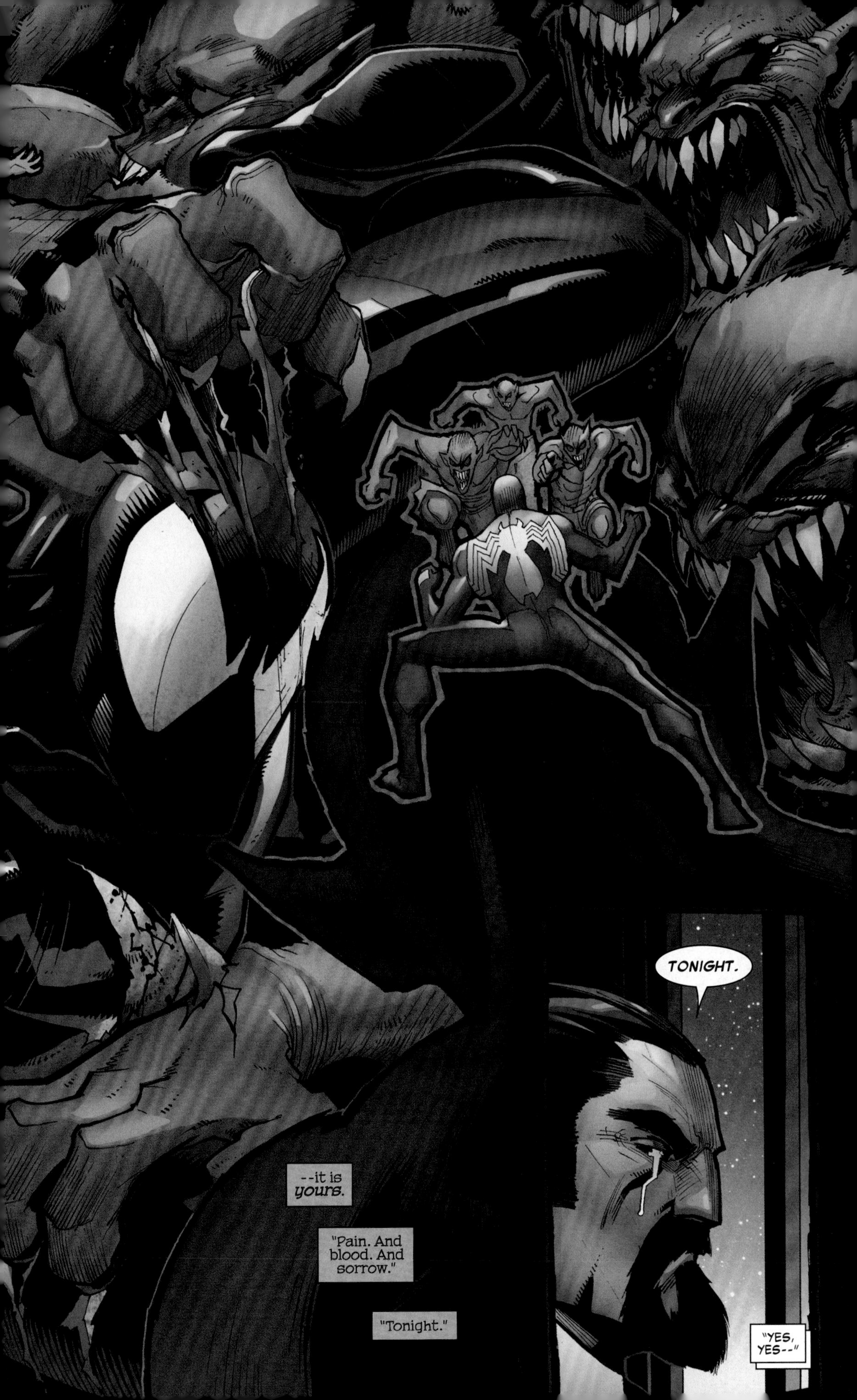

TONIGHT.
--it is yours.
"Pain. And blood. And sorrow."
"Tonight."
"YES, YES--"

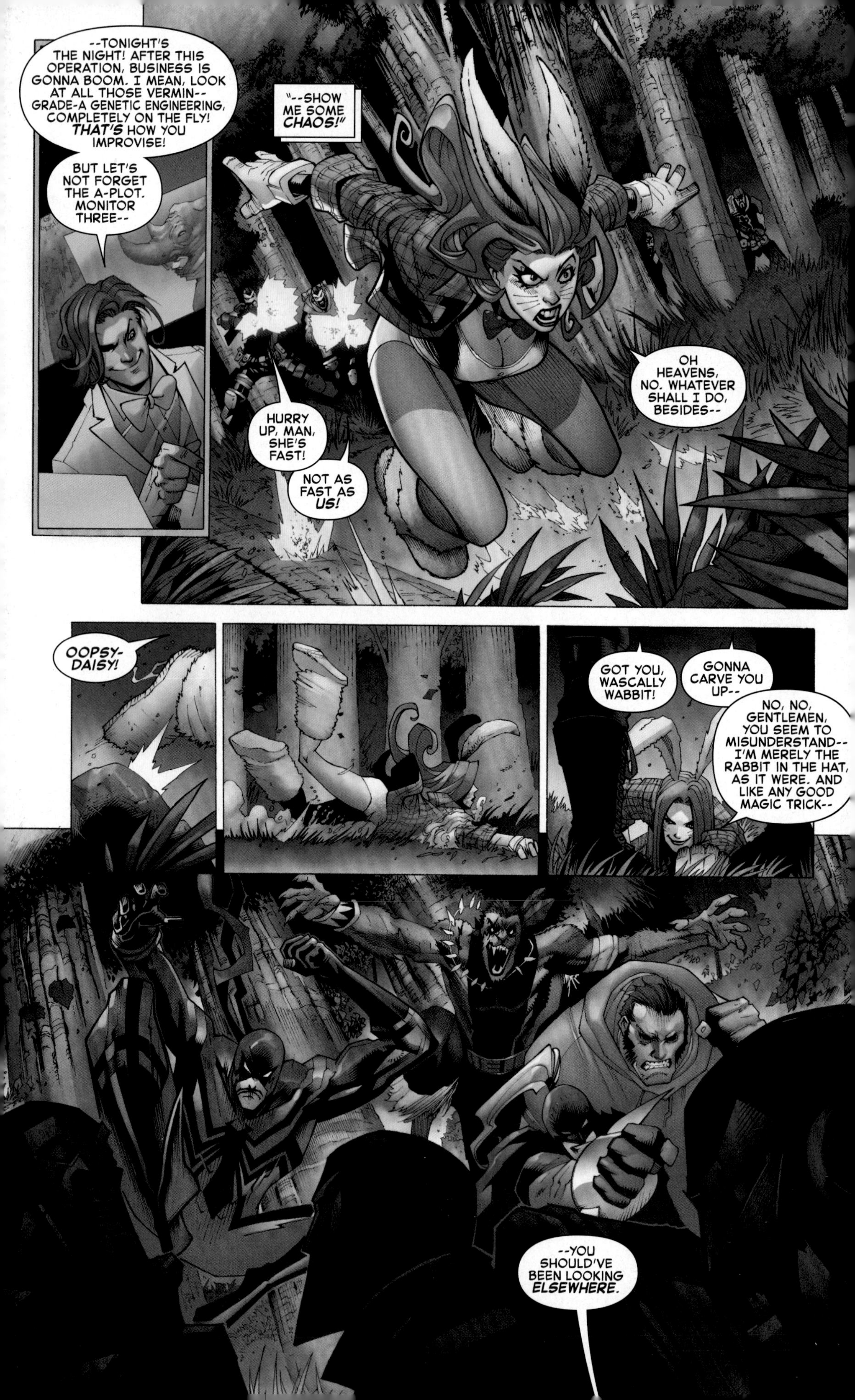
--TONIGHT'S THE NIGHT! AFTER THIS OPERATION, BUSINESS IS GONNA BOOM. I MEAN, LOOK AT ALL THOSE VERMIN-- GRADE-A GENETIC ENGINEERING, COMPLETELY ON THE FLY! THAT'S HOW YOU IMPROVISE!
BUT LET'S NOT FORGET THE A-PLOT. MONITOR THREE--
"--SHOW ME SOME CHAOS!"
HURRY UP, MAN, SHE'S FAST!
NOT AS FAST AS US!
OH HEAVENS, NO. WHATEVER SHALL I DO, BESIDES--
OOPSY-DAISY!
GOT YOU, WASCALLY WABBIT!
GONNA CARVE YOU UP--
NO, NO, GENTLEMEN, YOU SEEM TO MISUNDERSTAND-- I'M MERELY THE RABBIT IN THE HAT, AS IT WERE. AND LIKE ANY GOOD MAGIC TRICK--
--YOU SHOULD'VE BEEN LOOKING ELSEWHERE.

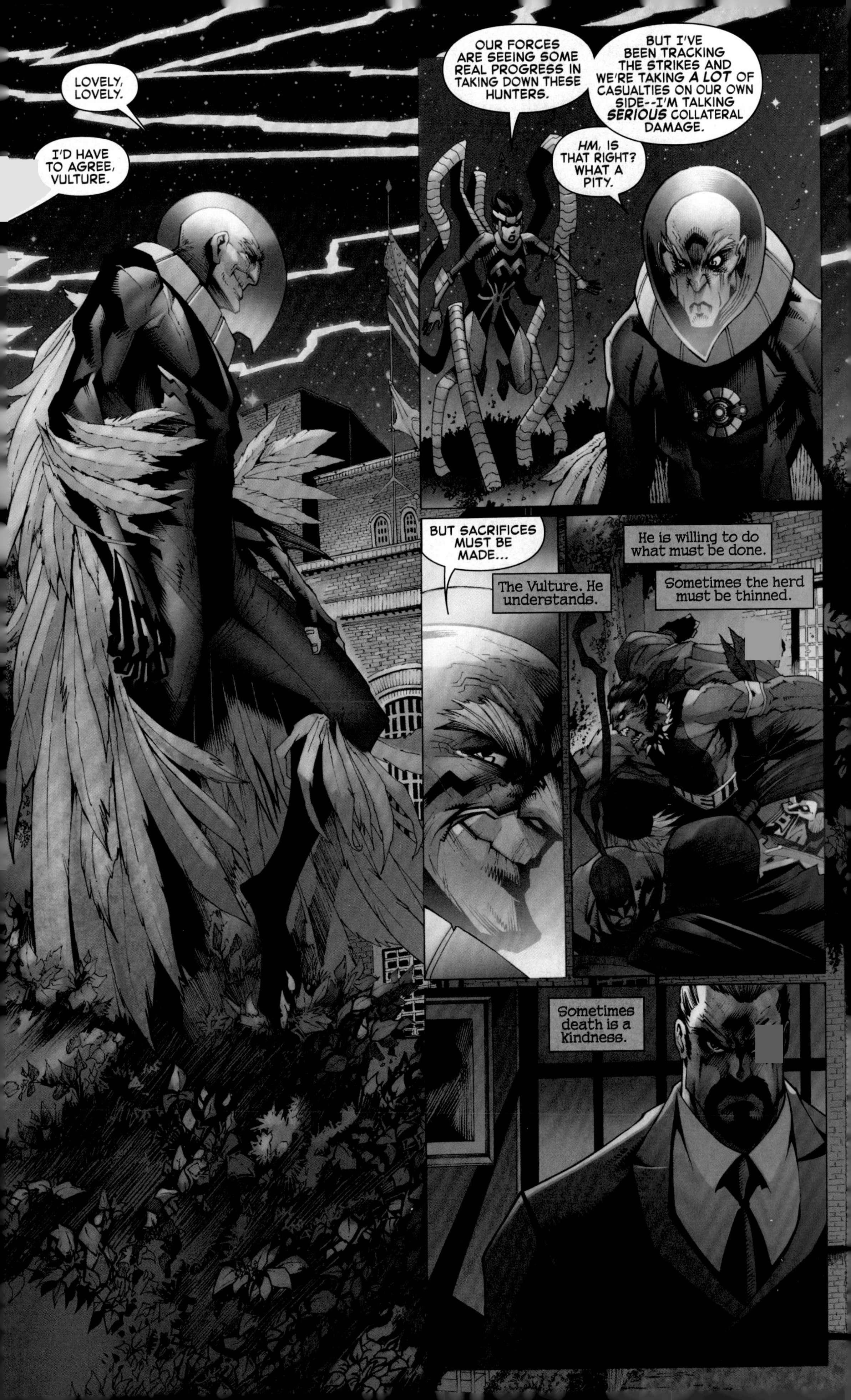

LOVELY, LOVELY.
I'D HAVE TO AGREE, VULTURE.
OUR FORCES ARE SEEING SOME REAL PROGRESS IN TAKING DOWN THESE HUNTERS.
BUT I'VE BEEN TRACKING THE STRIKES AND WE'RE TAKING A LOT OF CASUALTIES ON OUR OWN SIDE--I'M TALKING SERIOUS COLLATERAL DAMAGE.
HM, IS THAT RIGHT? WHAT A PITY.
BUT SACRIFICES MUST BE MADE...
The Vulture. He understands.
He is willing to do what must be done.
Sometimes the herd must be thinned.
Sometimes death is a kindness.

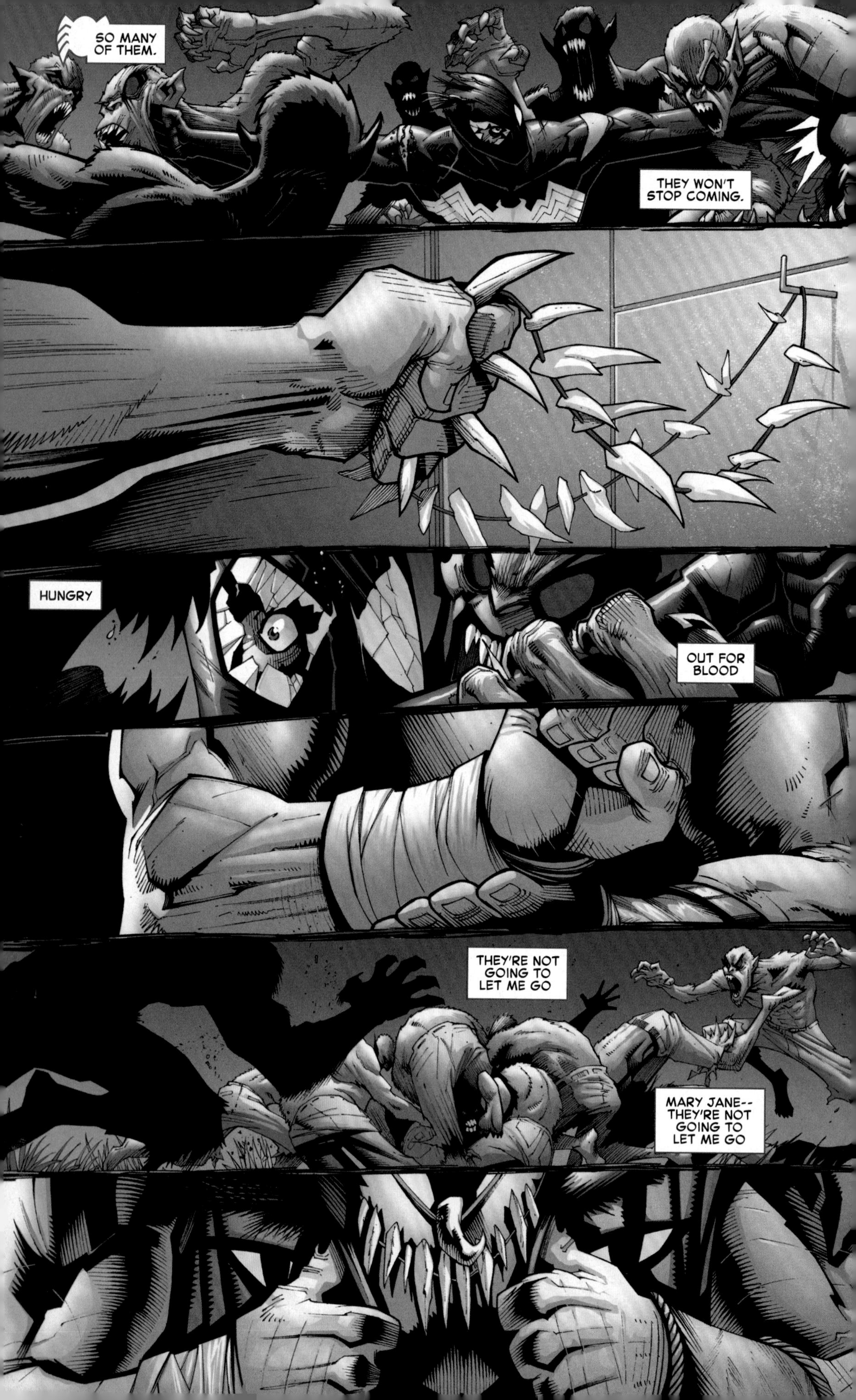
SO MANY OF THEM.
THEY WON'T STOP COMING.
HUNGRY
OUT FOR BLOOD
THEY'RE NOT GOING TO LET ME GO
MARY JANE-- THEY'RE NOT GOING TO LET ME GO

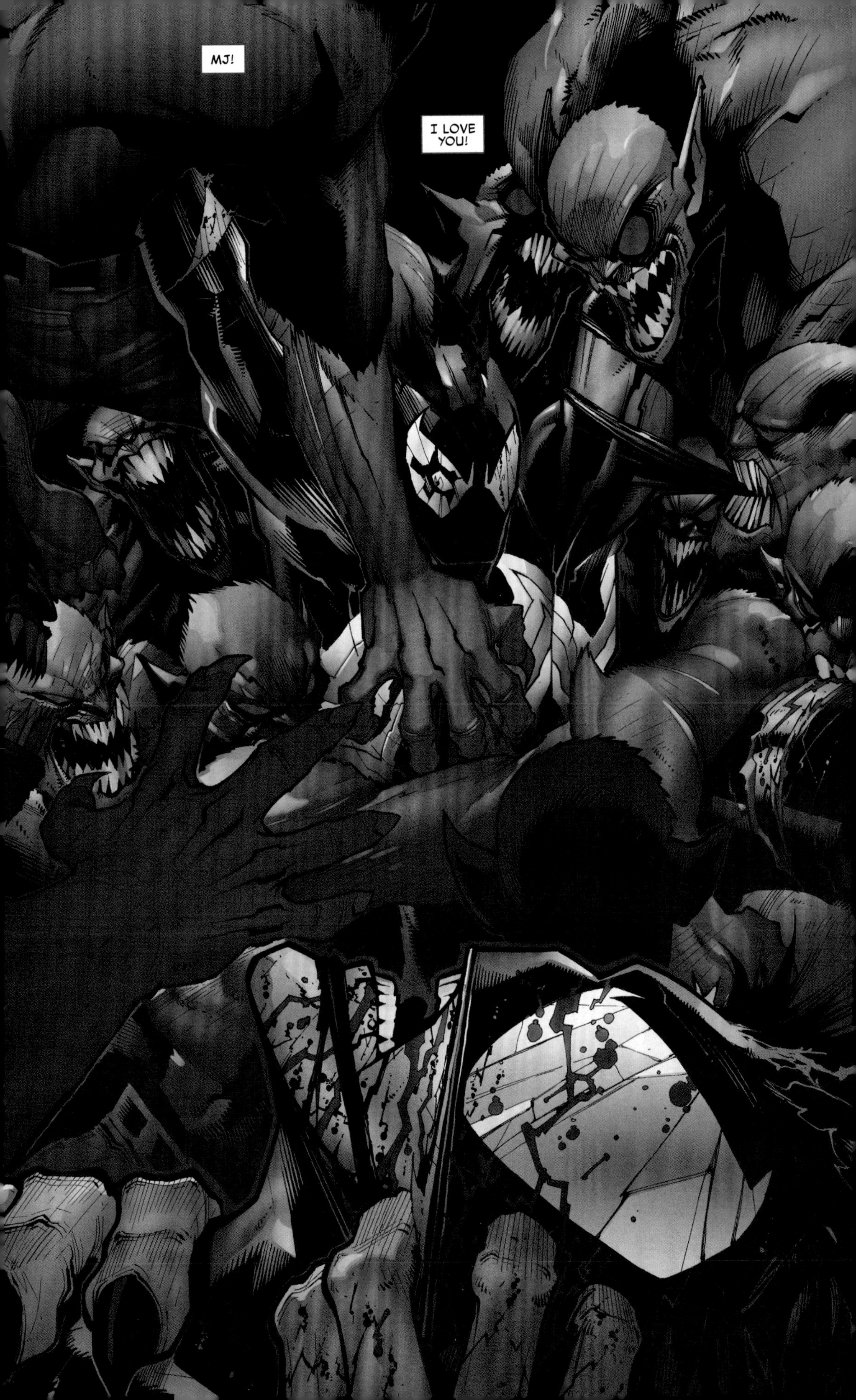
MJ!
I LOVE YOU!

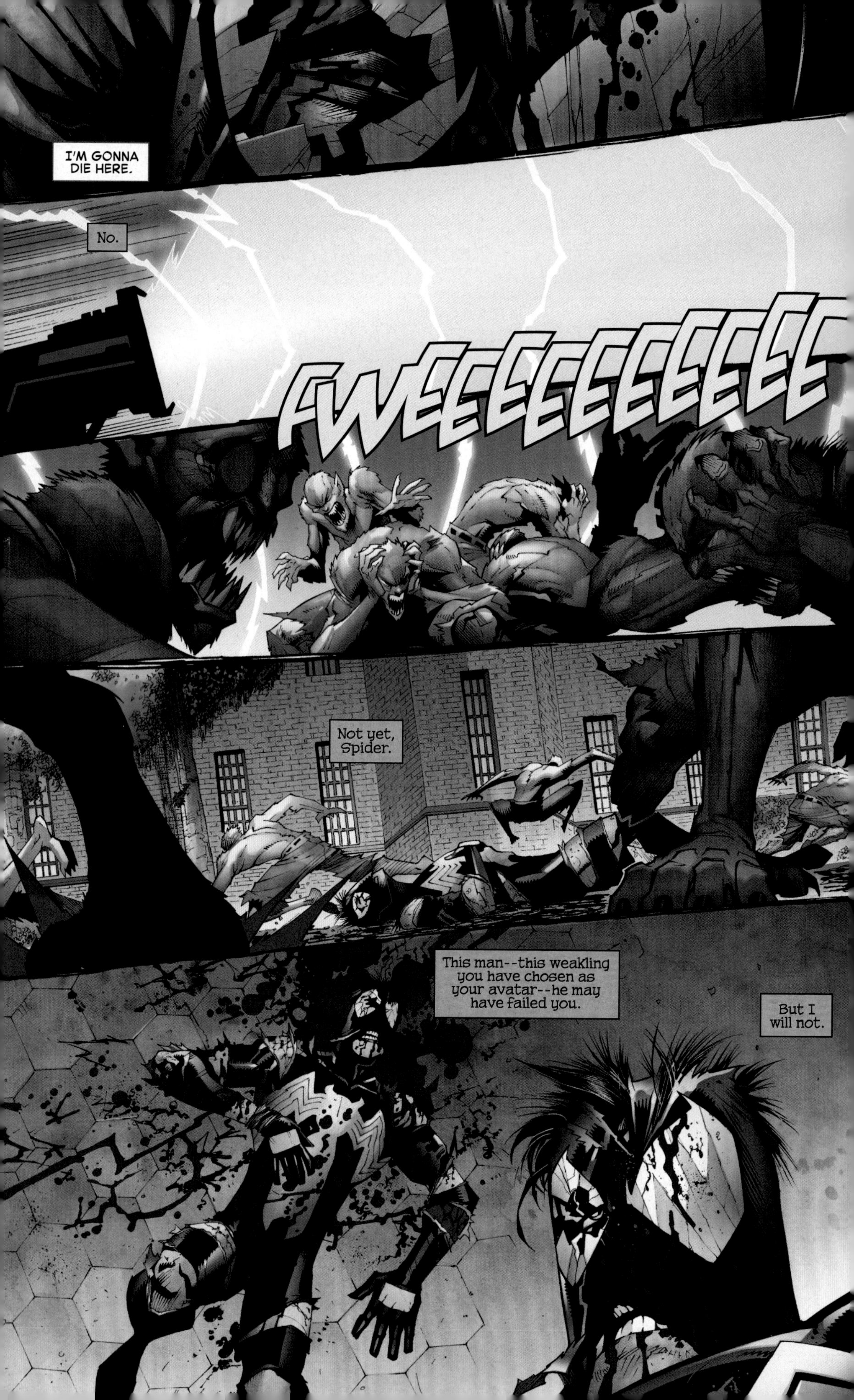
I'M GONNA DIE HERE.
No.
FWEEEEEEEEEEE
Not yet, Spider.
This man--this weakling you have chosen as your avatar--he may have failed you.
But I will not.

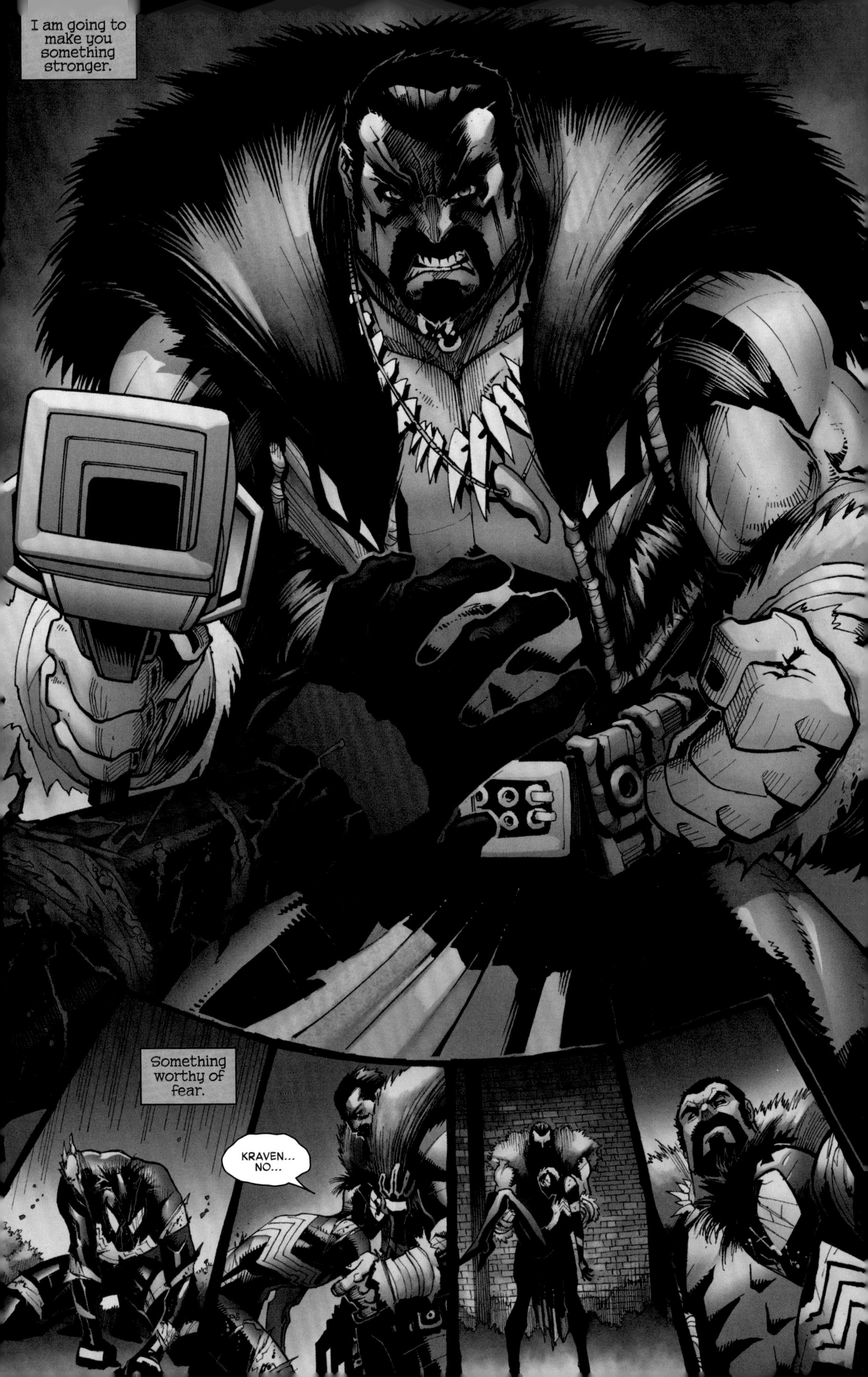
I am going to make you something stronger.
Something worthy of fear.
KRAVEN... NO...

WARM.

WHITE.

PEACEFUL.

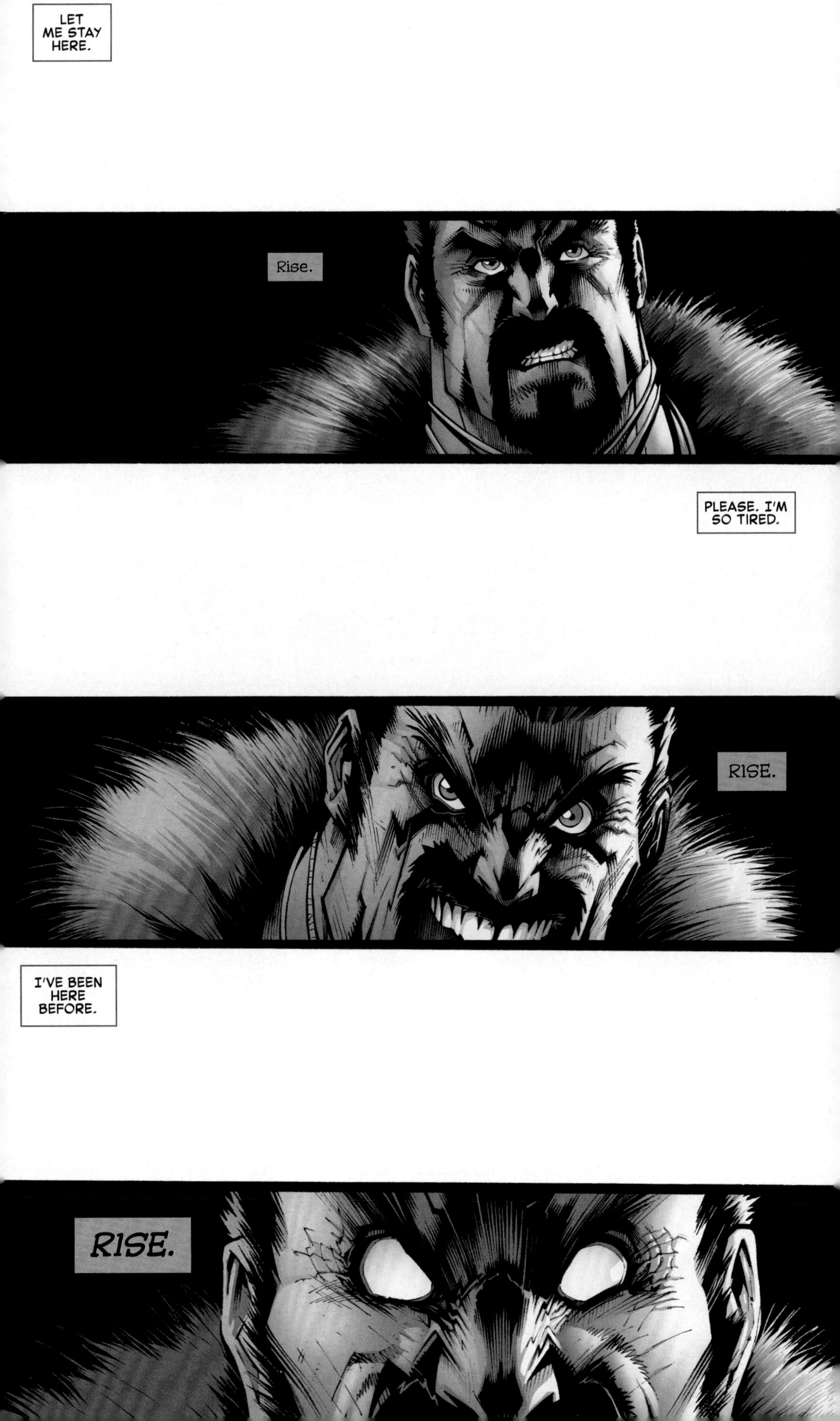
LET ME STAY HERE.
Rise.
PLEASE. I'M SO TIRED.
RISE.
I'VE BEEN HERE BEFORE.
RISE.

OHHH...

WHERE AM I? WHAT--WHAT HAPPENED?

I THOUGHT I WAS *GONE*--THAT I WAS FINALLY--HOW AM I BETTER? HOW DID--

KRAVEN'S HERBS AND POTIONS. I CAN FEEL THEM ON ME. STILL *TASTE* THEM. ENOUGH TO BRING ME BACK--

--AND IN A FRESH COSTUME, *AGAIN*. WHAT DOES HE HAVE, AN *ENDLESS SUPPLY* OF THESE THINGS? CREEPY. BUT EVEN WITH WHATEVER HE GAVE ME--

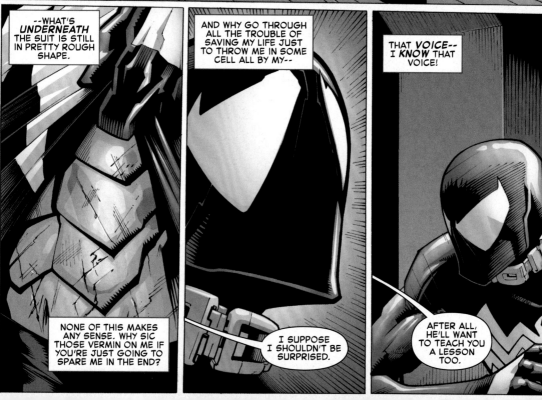

--WHAT'S *UNDERNEATH* THE SUIT IS STILL IN PRETTY ROUGH SHAPE.

NONE OF THIS MAKES ANY SENSE. WHY SIC THOSE VERMIN ON ME IF YOU'RE JUST GOING TO SPARE ME IN THE END?

AND WHY GO THROUGH ALL THE TROUBLE OF SAVING MY LIFE JUST TO THROW ME IN SOME CELL ALL BY MY--

I SUPPOSE I SHOULDN'T BE SURPRISED.

THAT *VOICE*-- I *KNOW* THAT VOICE!

AFTER ALL, HE'LL WANT TO TEACH YOU A LESSON TOO.

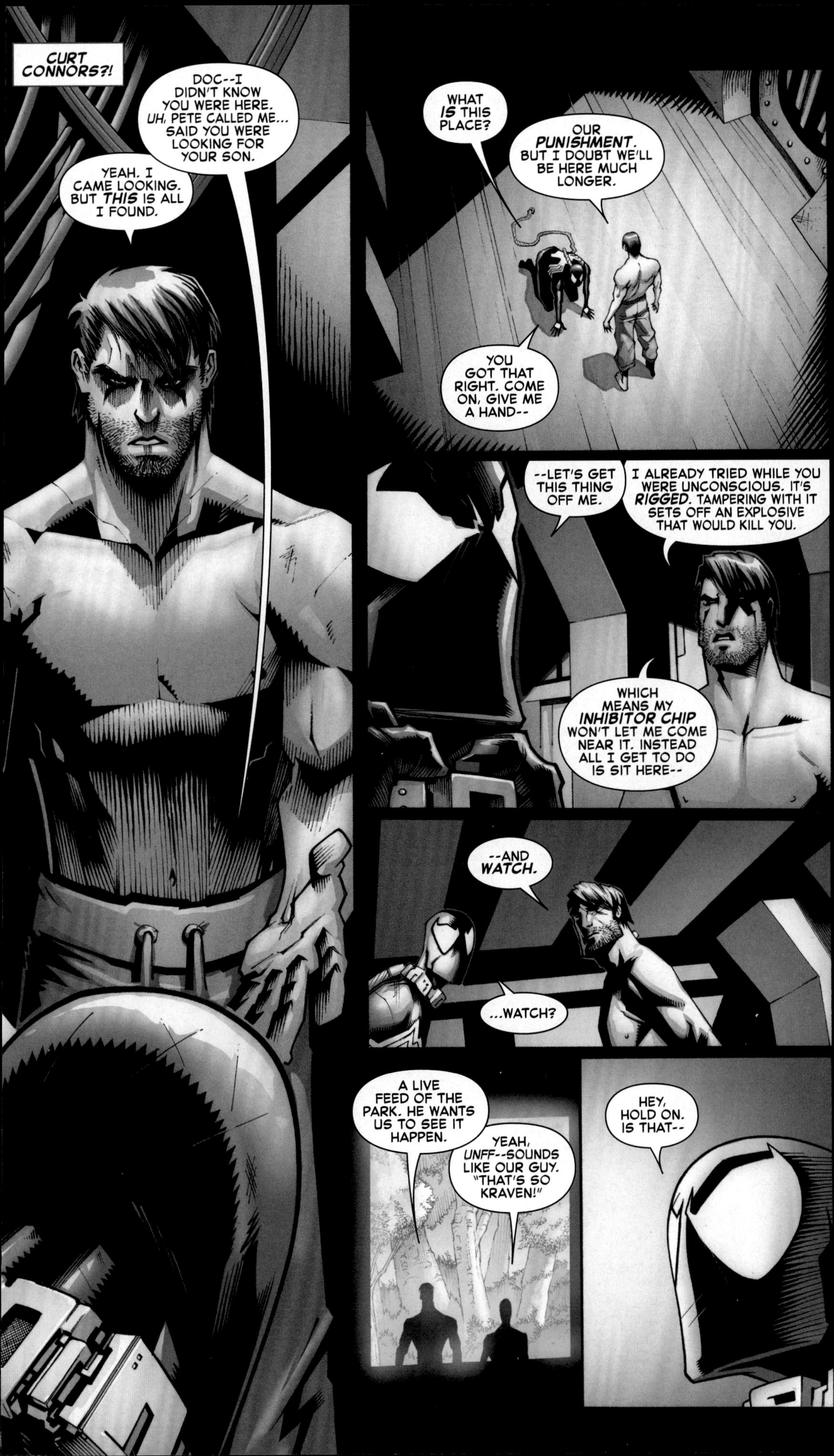
CURT CONNORS?!
DOC--I DIDN'T KNOW YOU WERE HERE. UH, PETE CALLED ME... SAID YOU WERE LOOKING FOR YOUR SON.
YEAH. I CAME LOOKING. BUT THIS IS ALL I FOUND.
WHAT IS THIS PLACE?
OUR PUNISHMENT. BUT I DOUBT WE'LL BE HERE MUCH LONGER.
YOU GOT THAT RIGHT. COME ON, GIVE ME A HAND--
--LET'S GET THIS THING OFF ME.
I ALREADY TRIED WHILE YOU WERE UNCONSCIOUS. IT'S RIGGED. TAMPERING WITH IT SETS OFF AN EXPLOSIVE THAT WOULD KILL YOU.
WHICH MEANS MY INHIBITOR CHIP WON'T LET ME COME NEAR IT. INSTEAD ALL I GET TO DO IS SIT HERE--
--AND WATCH.
...WATCH?
A LIVE FEED OF THE PARK. HE WANTS US TO SEE IT HAPPEN.
YEAH, UNFF--SOUNDS LIKE OUR GUY. "THAT'S SO KRAVEN!"
HEY, HOLD ON. IS THAT--

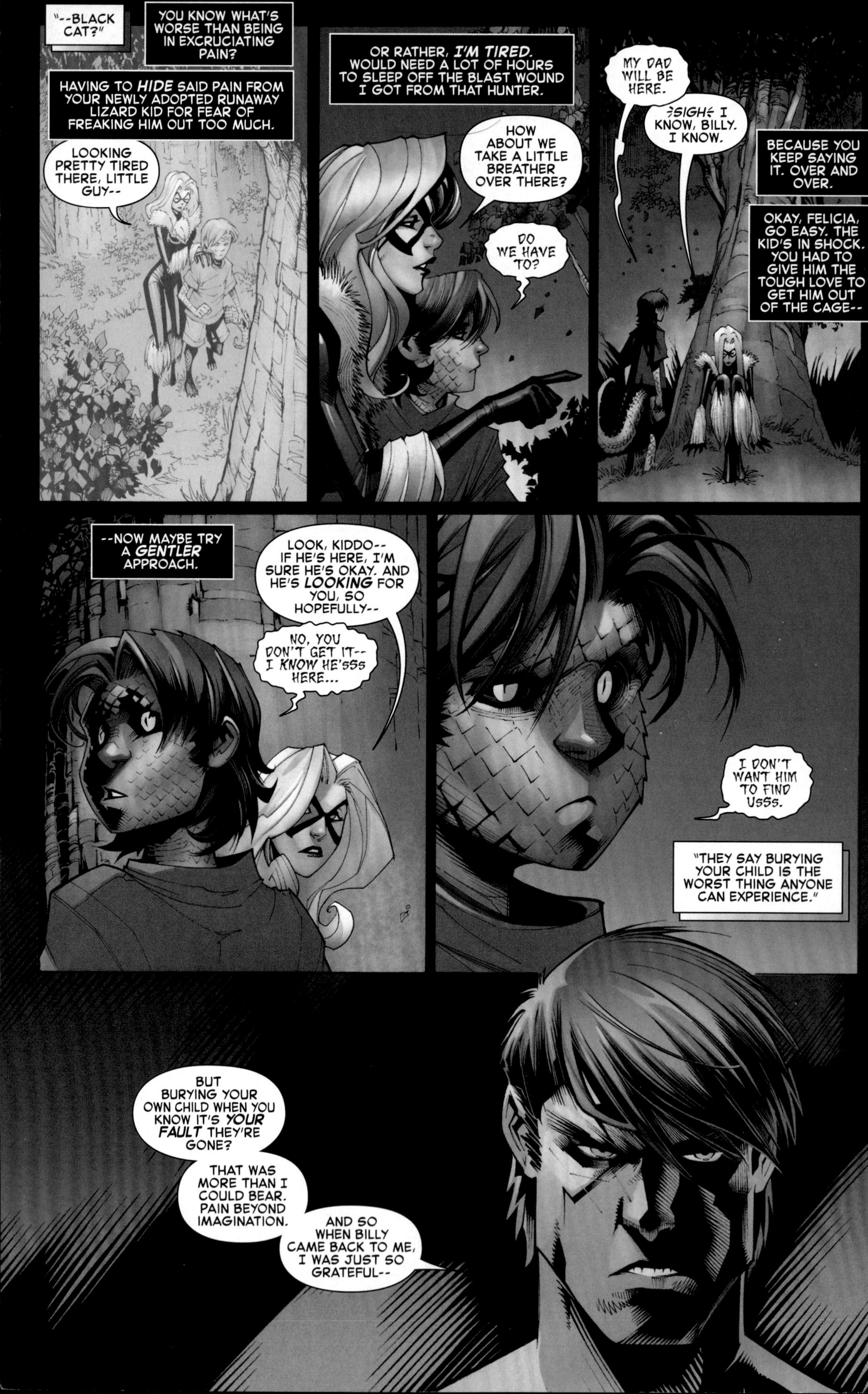
"--BLACK CAT?"
YOU KNOW WHAT'S WORSE THAN BEING IN EXCRUCIATING PAIN?
HAVING TO HIDE SAID PAIN FROM YOUR NEWLY ADOPTED RUNAWAY LIZARD KID FOR FEAR OF FREAKING HIM OUT TOO MUCH.
LOOKING PRETTY TIRED THERE, LITTLE GUY--
OR RATHER, I'M TIRED. WOULD NEED A LOT OF HOURS TO SLEEP OFF THE BLAST WOUND I GOT FROM THAT HUNTER.
HOW ABOUT WE TAKE A LITTLE BREATHER OVER THERE?
DO WE HAVE TO?
MY DAD WILL BE HERE.
SIGH I KNOW, BILLY. I KNOW.
BECAUSE YOU KEEP SAYING IT. OVER AND OVER.
OKAY, FELICIA, GO EASY. THE KID'S IN SHOCK. YOU HAD TO GIVE HIM THE TOUGH LOVE TO GET HIM OUT OF THE CAGE--
--NOW MAYBE TRY A GENTLER APPROACH.
LOOK, KIDDO-- IF HE'S HERE, I'M SURE HE'S OKAY. AND HE'S LOOKING FOR YOU, SO HOPEFULLY--
NO, YOU DON'T GET IT-- I KNOW HE'SSS HERE...
I DON'T WANT HIM TO FIND USSS.
"THEY SAY BURYING YOUR CHILD IS THE WORST THING ANYONE CAN EXPERIENCE."
BUT BURYING YOUR OWN CHILD WHEN YOU KNOW IT'S YOUR FAULT THEY'RE GONE?
THAT WAS MORE THAN I COULD BEAR. PAIN BEYOND IMAGINATION.
AND SO WHEN BILLY CAME BACK TO ME, I WAS JUST SO GRATEFUL--

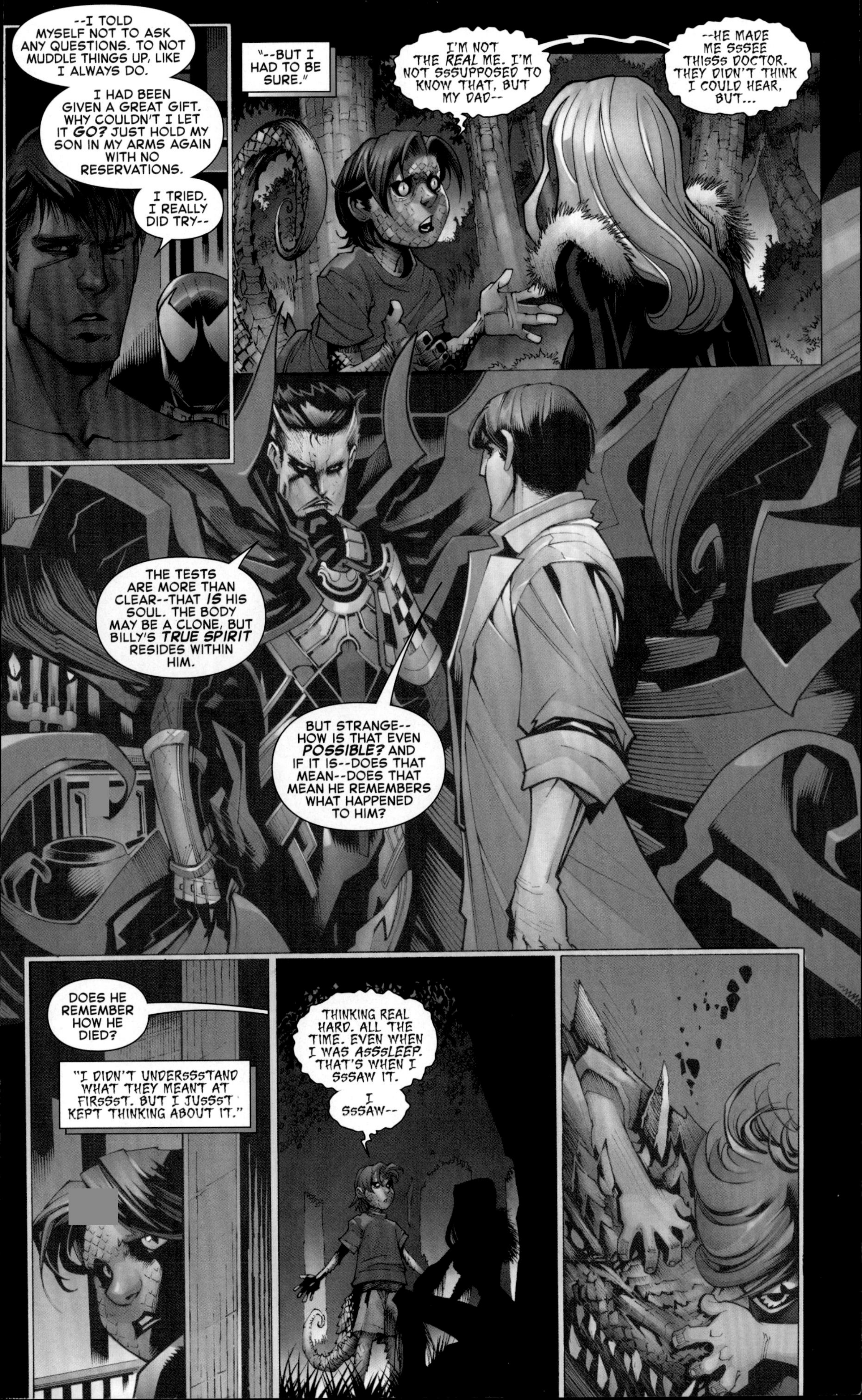
--I TOLD MYSELF NOT TO ASK ANY QUESTIONS. TO NOT MUDDLE THINGS UP, LIKE I ALWAYS DO.
I HAD BEEN GIVEN A GREAT GIFT. WHY COULDN'T I LET IT GO? JUST HOLD MY SON IN MY ARMS AGAIN WITH NO RESERVATIONS.
I TRIED. I REALLY DID TRY--
"--BUT I HAD TO BE SURE."
I'M NOT THE REAL ME. I'M NOT SSSUPPOSED TO KNOW THAT, BUT MY DAD--
--HE MADE ME SSSEE THISSS DOCTOR. THEY DIDN'T THINK I COULD HEAR, BUT...
THE TESTS ARE MORE THAN CLEAR--THAT IS HIS SOUL. THE BODY MAY BE A CLONE, BUT BILLY'S TRUE SPIRIT RESIDES WITHIN HIM.
BUT STRANGE-- HOW IS THAT EVEN POSSIBLE? AND IF IT IS--DOES THAT MEAN--DOES THAT MEAN HE REMEMBERS WHAT HAPPENED TO HIM?
DOES HE REMEMBER HOW HE DIED?
"I DIDN'T UNDERSSSTAND WHAT THEY MEANT AT FIRSSST. BUT I JUSSST KEPT THINKING ABOUT IT."
THINKING REAL HARD. ALL THE TIME. EVEN WHEN I WAS ASSSLEEP. THAT'S WHEN I SSSAW IT.
I SSSAW--

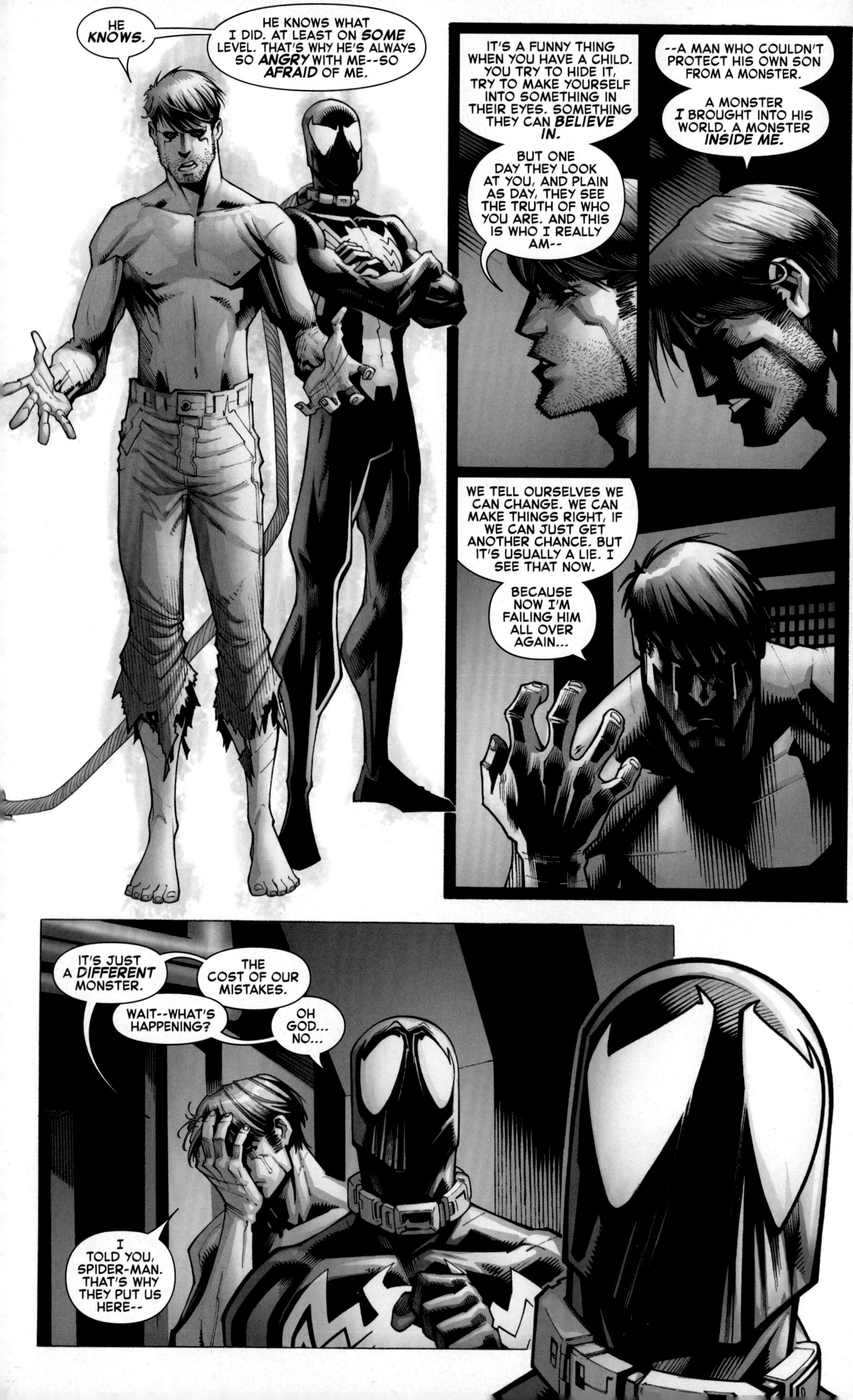
HE KNOWS.
HE KNOWS WHAT I DID. AT LEAST ON SOME LEVEL. THAT'S WHY HE'S ALWAYS SO ANGRY WITH ME--SO AFRAID OF ME.
IT'S A FUNNY THING WHEN YOU HAVE A CHILD. YOU TRY TO HIDE IT, TRY TO MAKE YOURSELF INTO SOMETHING IN THEIR EYES. SOMETHING THEY CAN BELIEVE IN.
BUT ONE DAY THEY LOOK AT YOU, AND PLAIN AS DAY, THEY SEE THE TRUTH OF WHO YOU ARE. AND THIS IS WHO I REALLY AM--
--A MAN WHO COULDN'T PROTECT HIS OWN SON FROM A MONSTER.
A MONSTER I BROUGHT INTO HIS WORLD. A MONSTER INSIDE ME.
WE TELL OURSELVES WE CAN CHANGE. WE CAN MAKE THINGS RIGHT, IF WE CAN JUST GET ANOTHER CHANCE. BUT IT'S USUALLY A LIE. I SEE THAT NOW.
BECAUSE NOW I'M FAILING HIM ALL OVER AGAIN...
IT'S JUST A DIFFERENT MONSTER.
THE COST OF OUR MISTAKES.
WAIT--WHAT'S HAPPENING?
OH GOD... NO...
I TOLD YOU, SPIDER-MAN. THAT'S WHY THEY PUT US HERE--

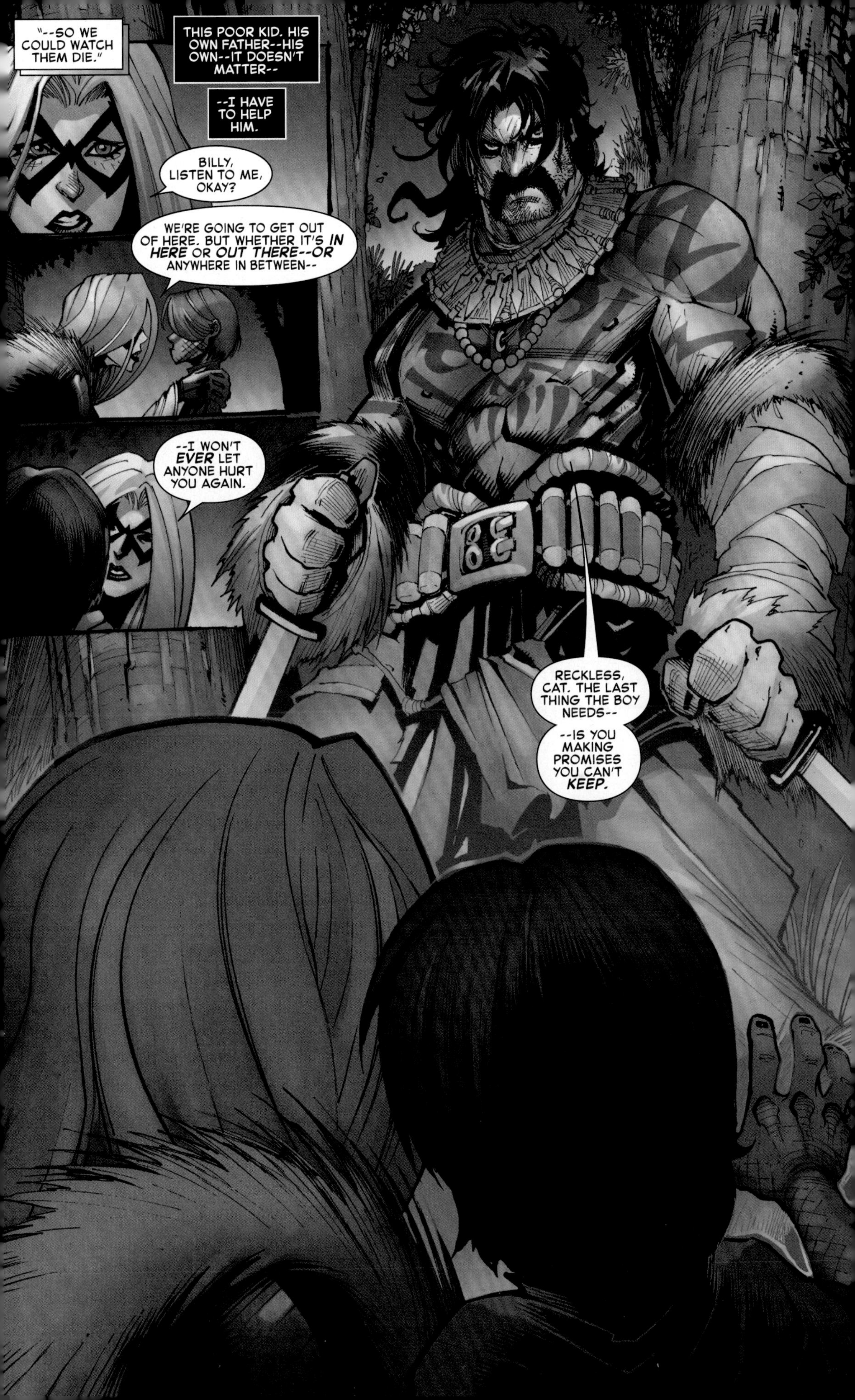
"--SO WE COULD WATCH THEM DIE."
THIS POOR KID. HIS OWN FATHER--HIS OWN--IT DOESN'T MATTER--
--I HAVE TO HELP HIM.
BILLY, LISTEN TO ME, OKAY?
WE'RE GOING TO GET OUT OF HERE. BUT WHETHER IT'S *IN HERE* OR *OUT THERE--OR* ANYWHERE IN BETWEEN--
--I WON'T *EVER* LET ANYONE HURT YOU AGAIN.
RECKLESS, CAT. THE LAST THING THE BOY NEEDS--
--IS YOU MAKING PROMISES YOU CAN'T *KEEP.*

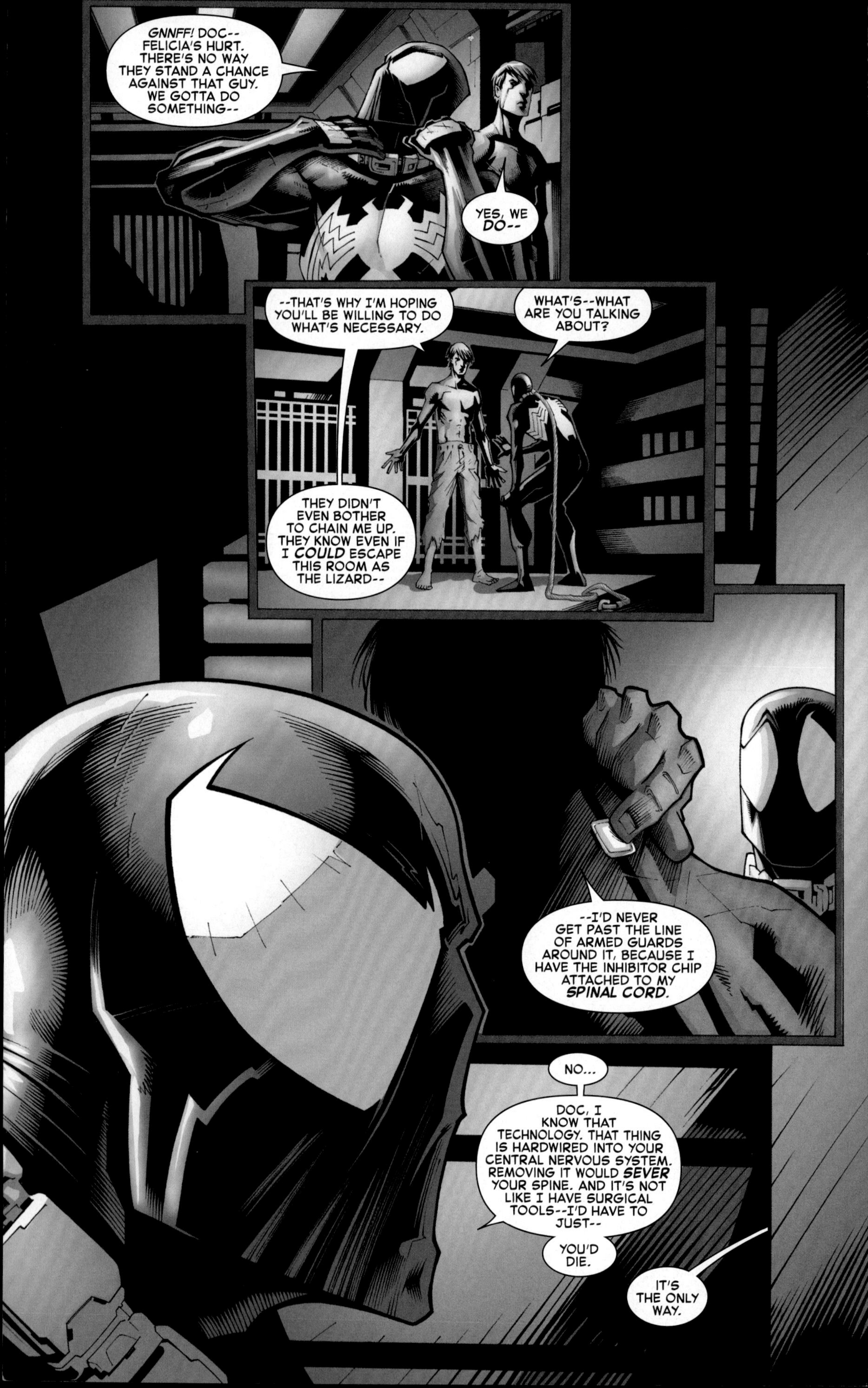
GNNFF! DOC-- FELICIA'S HURT. THERE'S NO WAY THEY STAND A CHANCE AGAINST THAT GUY. WE GOTTA DO SOMETHING--
YES, WE DO--
--THAT'S WHY I'M HOPING YOU'LL BE WILLING TO DO WHAT'S NECESSARY.
WHAT'S--WHAT ARE YOU TALKING ABOUT?
THEY DIDN'T EVEN BOTHER TO CHAIN ME UP. THEY KNOW EVEN IF I COULD ESCAPE THIS ROOM AS THE LIZARD--
--I'D NEVER GET PAST THE LINE OF ARMED GUARDS AROUND IT, BECAUSE I HAVE THE INHIBITOR CHIP ATTACHED TO MY SPINAL CORD.
NO...
DOC, I KNOW THAT TECHNOLOGY. THAT THING IS HARDWIRED INTO YOUR CENTRAL NERVOUS SYSTEM. REMOVING IT WOULD SEVER YOUR SPINE. AND IT'S NOT LIKE I HAVE SURGICAL TOOLS--I'D HAVE TO JUST--
YOU'D DIE.
IT'S THE ONLY WAY.

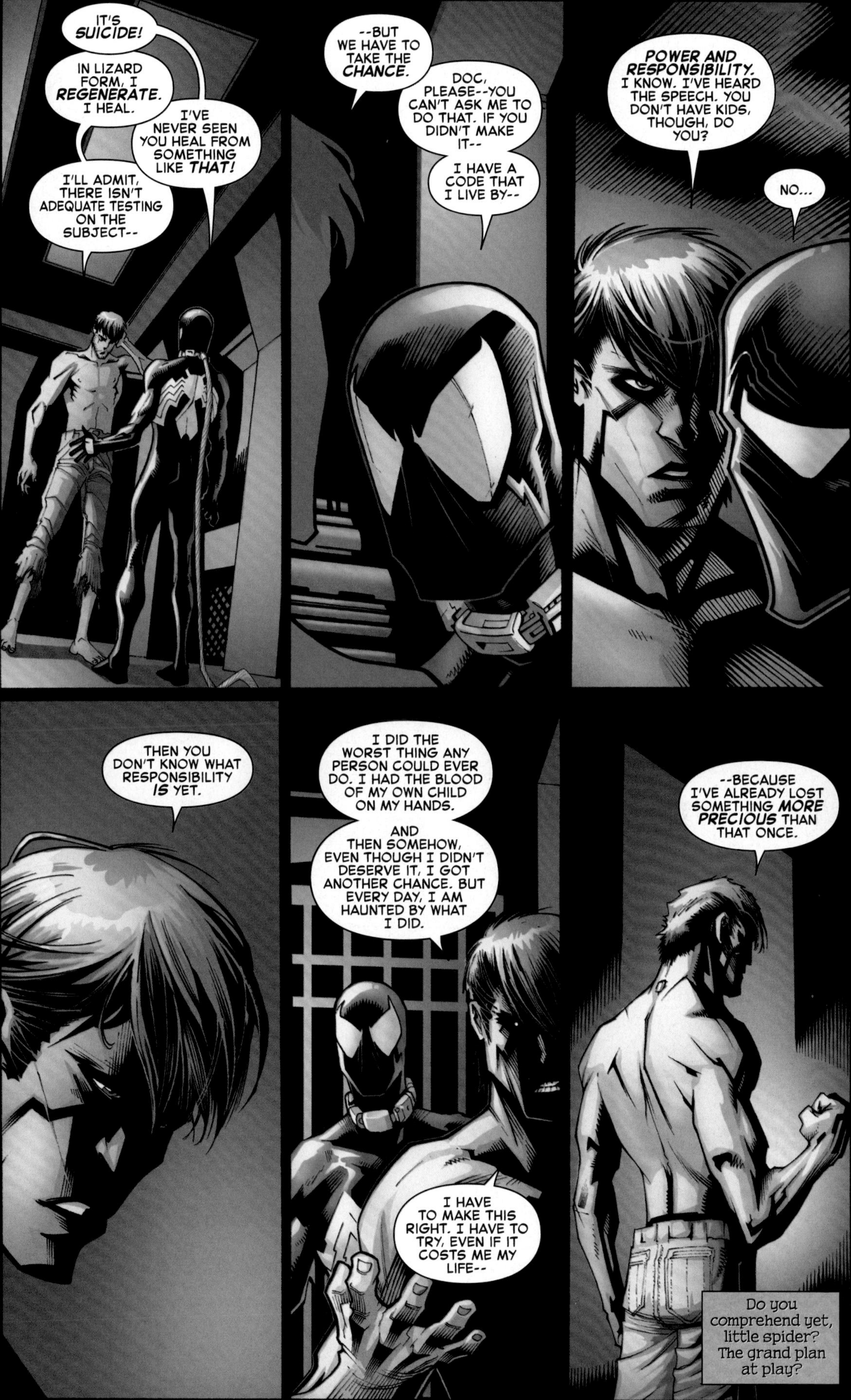
IT'S SUICIDE!
IN LIZARD FORM, I REGENERATE. I HEAL.
I'VE NEVER SEEN YOU HEAL FROM SOMETHING LIKE THAT!
I'LL ADMIT, THERE ISN'T ADEQUATE TESTING ON THE SUBJECT--
--BUT WE HAVE TO TAKE THE CHANCE.
DOC, PLEASE--YOU CAN'T ASK ME TO DO THAT. IF YOU DIDN'T MAKE IT--
I HAVE A CODE THAT I LIVE BY--
POWER AND RESPONSIBILITY. I KNOW. I'VE HEARD THE SPEECH. YOU DON'T HAVE KIDS, THOUGH, DO YOU?
NO...
THEN YOU DON'T KNOW WHAT RESPONSIBILITY IS YET.
I DID THE WORST THING ANY PERSON COULD EVER DO. I HAD THE BLOOD OF MY OWN CHILD ON MY HANDS.
AND THEN SOMEHOW, EVEN THOUGH I DIDN'T DESERVE IT, I GOT ANOTHER CHANCE. BUT EVERY DAY, I AM HAUNTED BY WHAT I DID.
I HAVE TO MAKE THIS RIGHT. I HAVE TO TRY, EVEN IF IT COSTS ME MY LIFE--
--BECAUSE I'VE ALREADY LOST SOMETHING MORE PRECIOUS THAN THAT ONCE.
Do you comprehend yet, little spider? The grand plan at play?

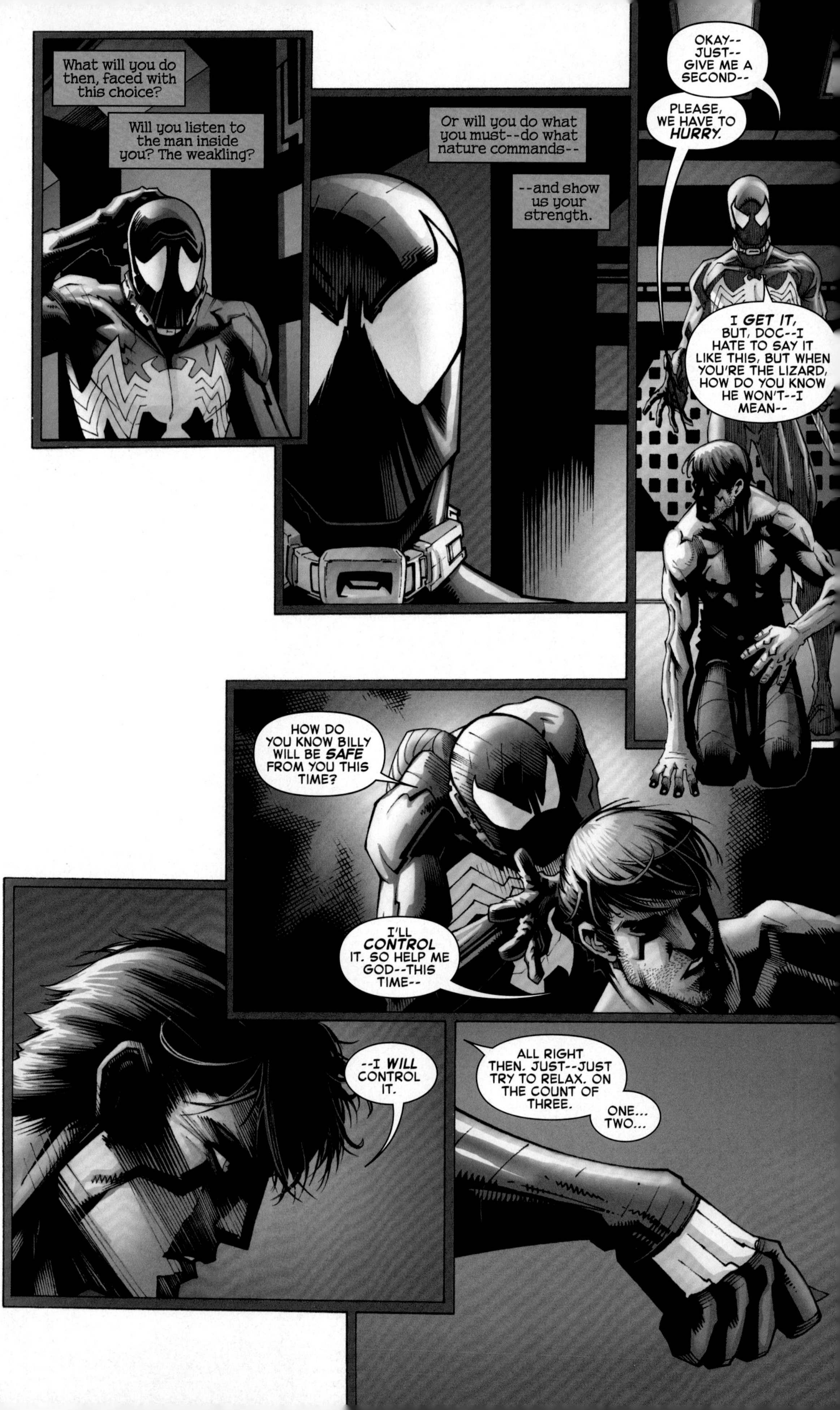
What will you do then, faced with this choice?
Will you listen to the man inside you? The weakling?
Or will you do what you must--do what nature commands--
--and show us your strength.
OKAY-- JUST-- GIVE ME A SECOND--
PLEASE, WE HAVE TO HURRY.
I GET IT, BUT, DOC--I HATE TO SAY IT LIKE THIS, BUT WHEN YOU'RE THE LIZARD, HOW DO YOU KNOW HE WON'T--I MEAN--
HOW DO YOU KNOW BILLY WILL BE SAFE FROM YOU THIS TIME?
I'LL CONTROL IT. SO HELP ME GOD--THIS TIME--
--I WILL CONTROL IT.
ALL RIGHT THEN. JUST--JUST TRY TO RELAX. ON THE COUNT OF THREE.
ONE... TWO...

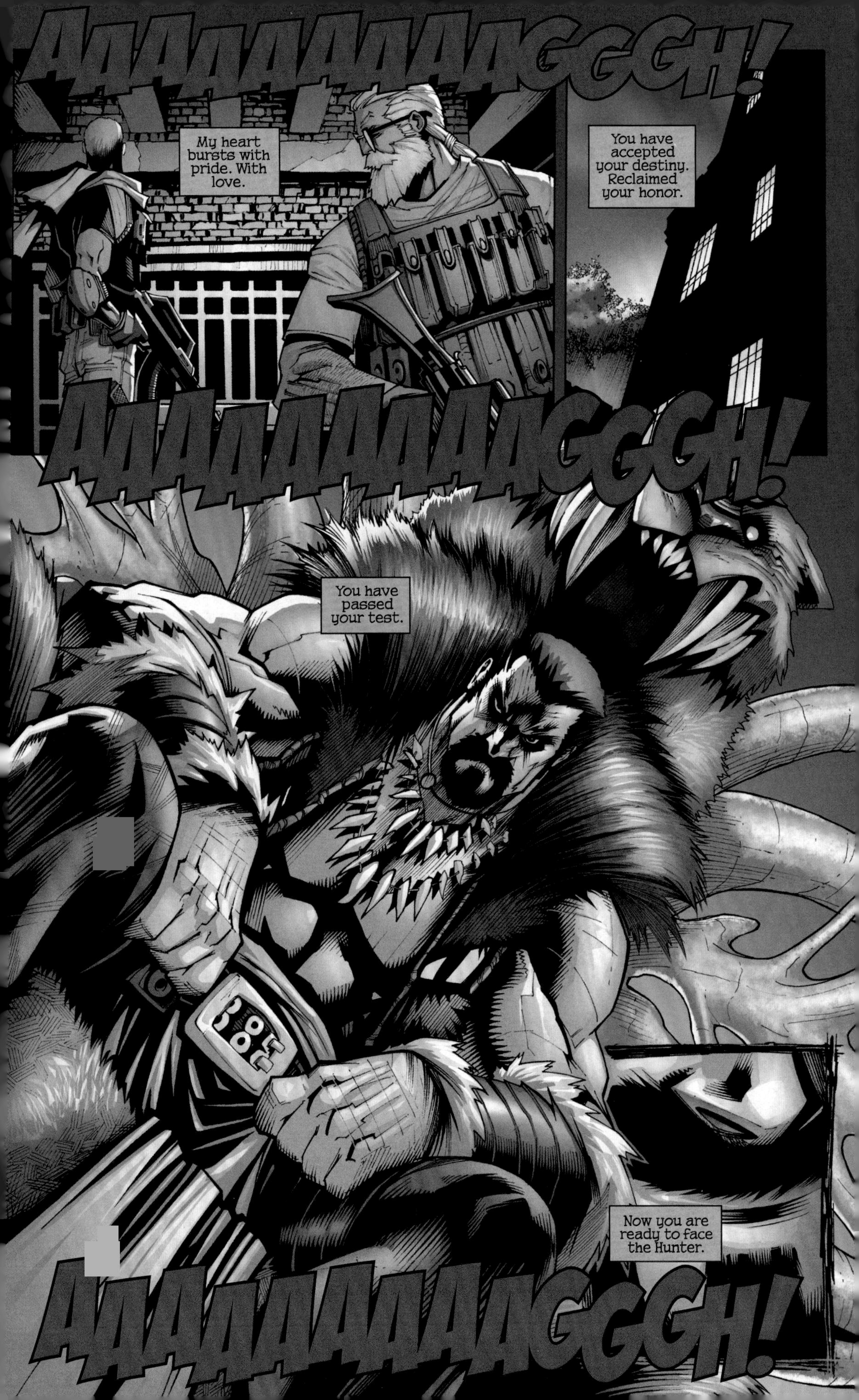
AAAAAAAAAGGGH!
My heart bursts with pride. With love.
You have accepted your destiny. Reclaimed your honor.
AAAAAAAAAGGGH!
You have passed your test.
Now you are ready to face the Hunter.
AAAAAAAAAGGGH!

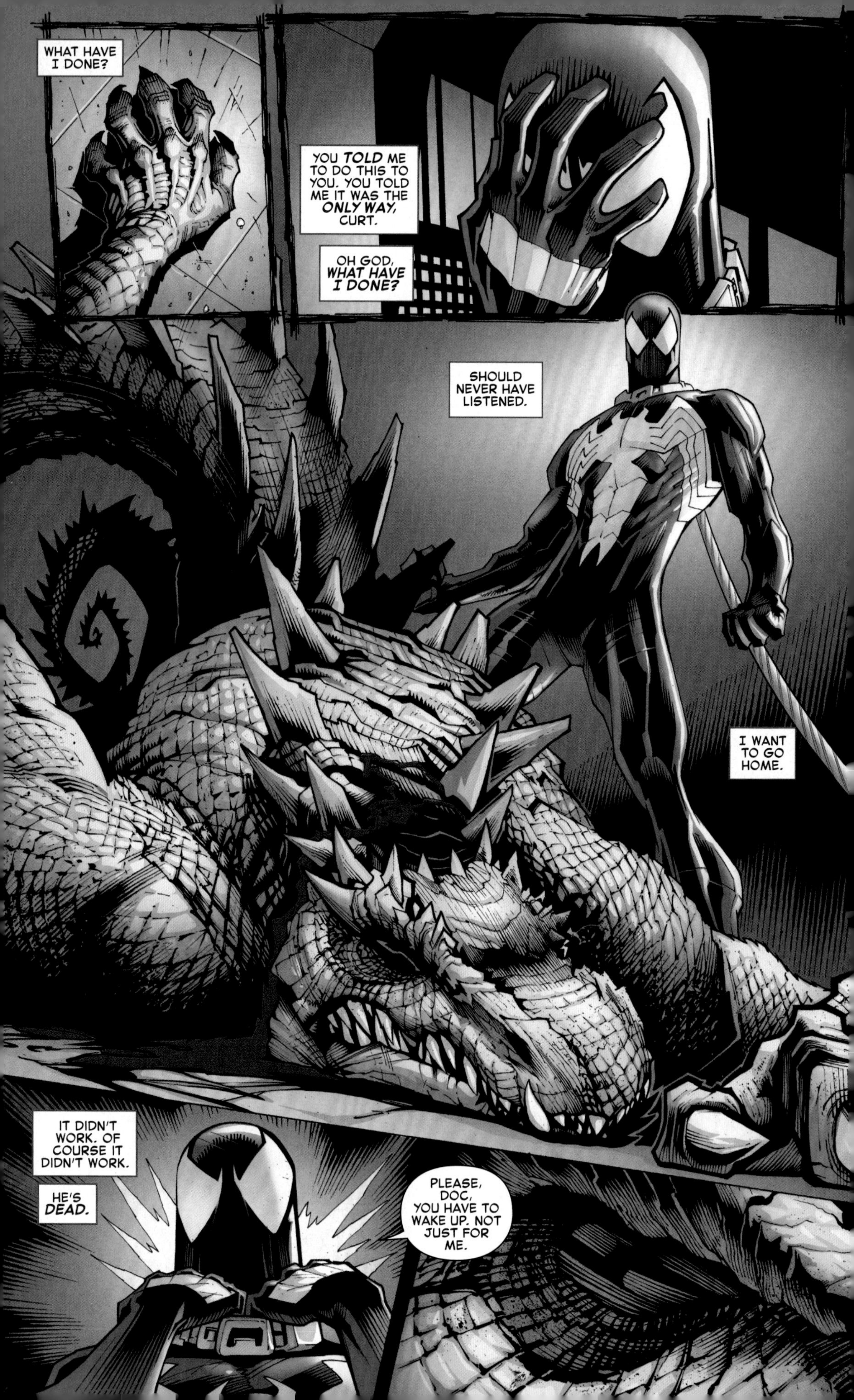
WHAT HAVE I DONE?
YOU ***TOLD*** ME TO DO THIS TO YOU. YOU TOLD ME IT WAS THE ***ONLY WAY,*** CURT.
OH GOD, ***WHAT HAVE I DONE?***
SHOULD NEVER HAVE LISTENED.
I WANT TO GO HOME.
IT DIDN'T WORK. OF COURSE IT DIDN'T WORK.
HE'S ***DEAD.***
PLEASE, DOC, YOU HAVE TO WAKE UP. NOT JUST FOR ME.

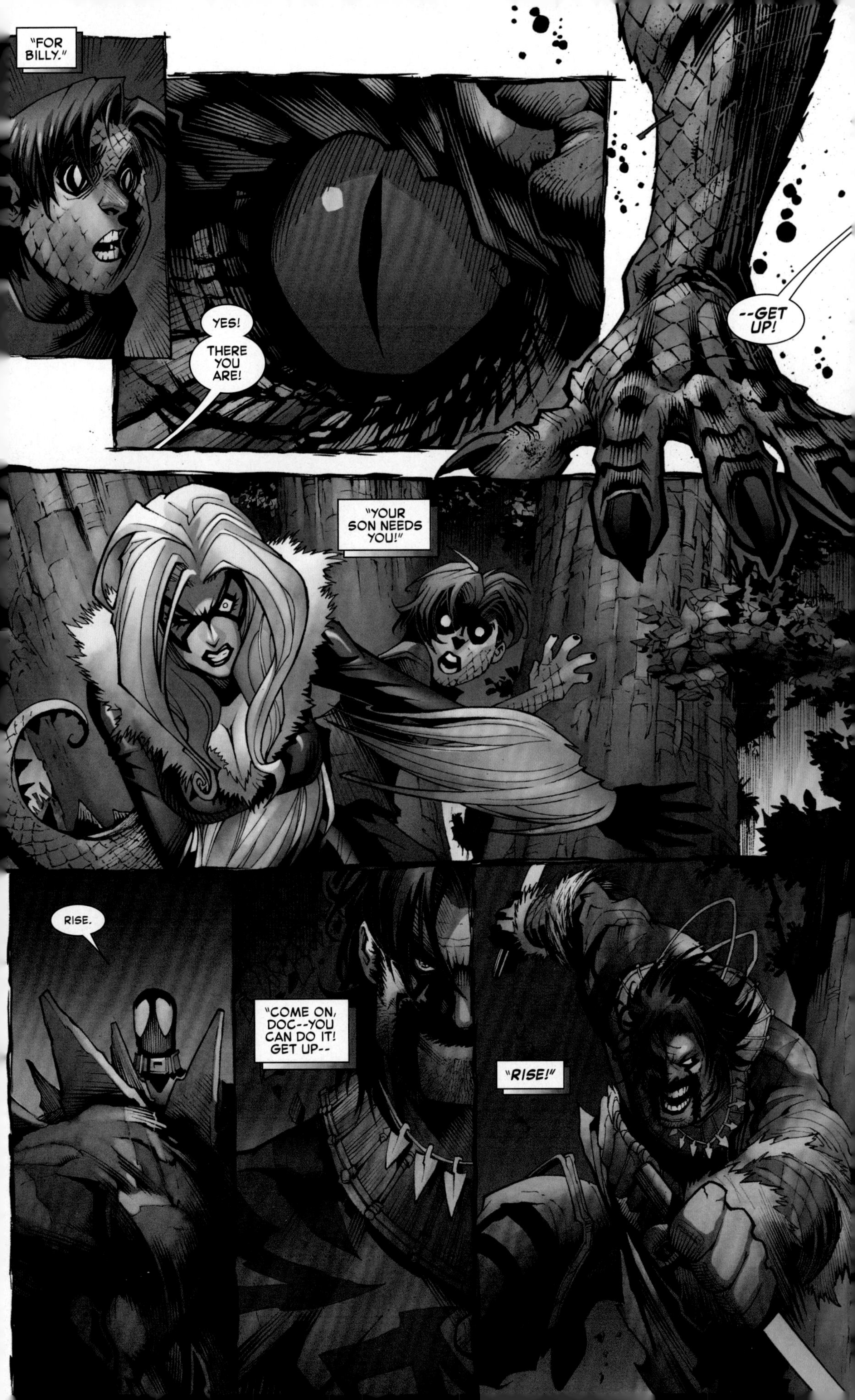

"FOR BILLY."
YES!
THERE YOU ARE!
--GET UP!
"YOUR SON NEEDS YOU!"
RISE.
"COME ON, DOC--YOU CAN DO IT! GET UP--
"RISE!"

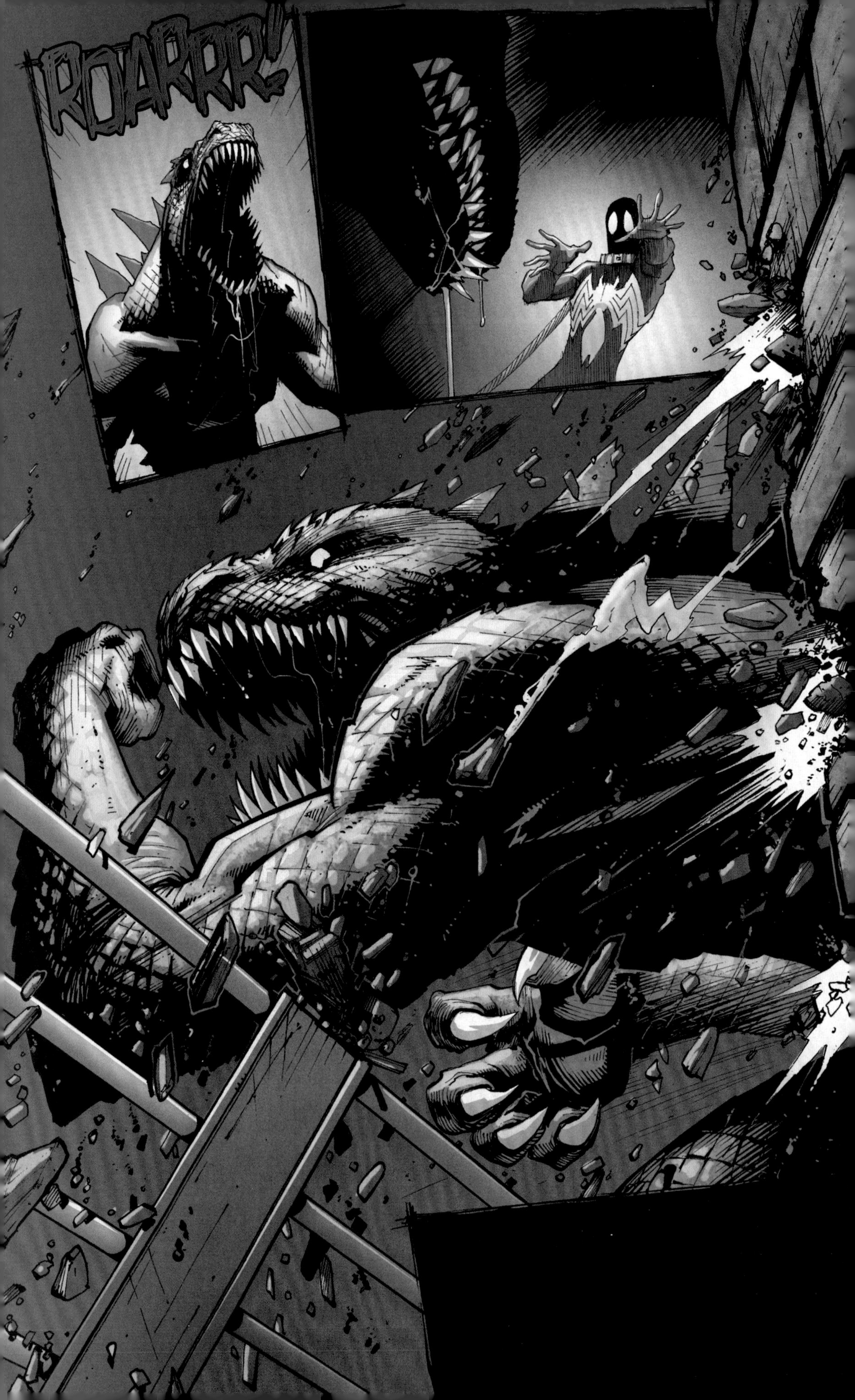
ROARRR!!

22

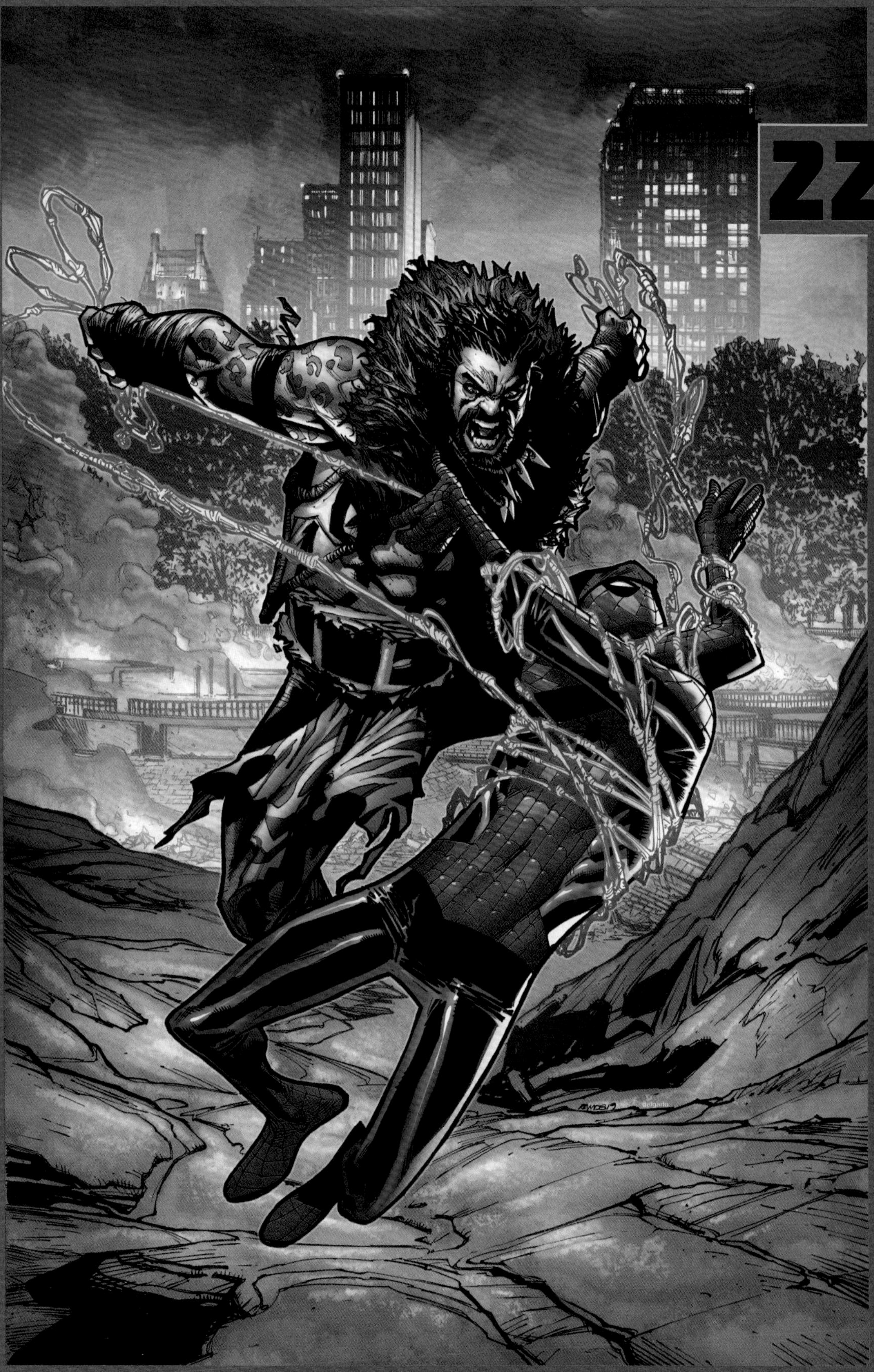

HUNTED PART 6

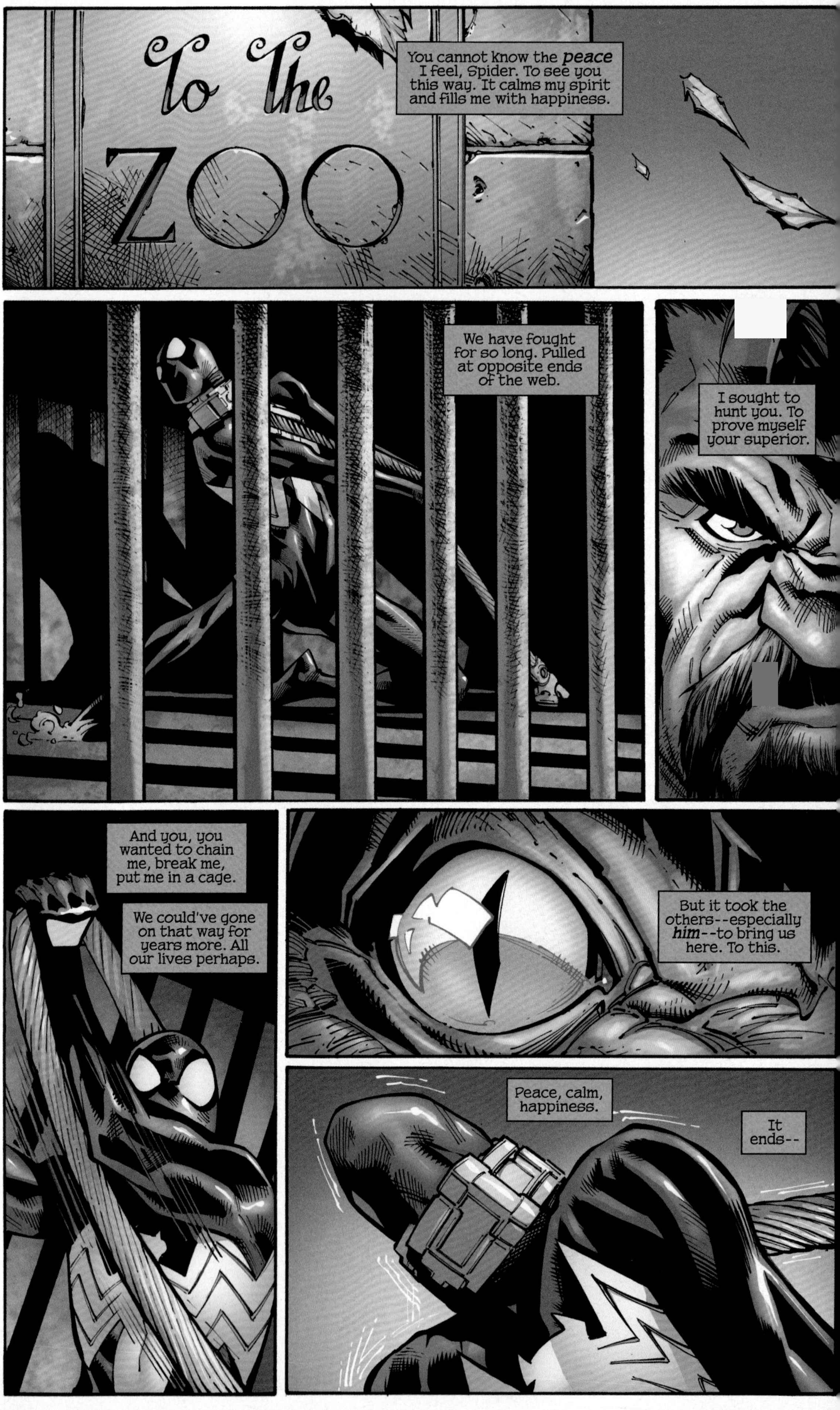
To The
ZOO
You cannot know the *peace* I feel, Spider. To see you this way. It calms my spirit and fills me with happiness.
We have fought for so long. Pulled at opposite ends of the web.
I sought to hunt you. To prove myself your superior.
And you, you wanted to chain me, break me, put me in a cage.
We could've gone on that way for years more. All our lives perhaps.
But it took the others--especially *him*--to bring us here. To this.
Peace, calm, happiness.
It ends--

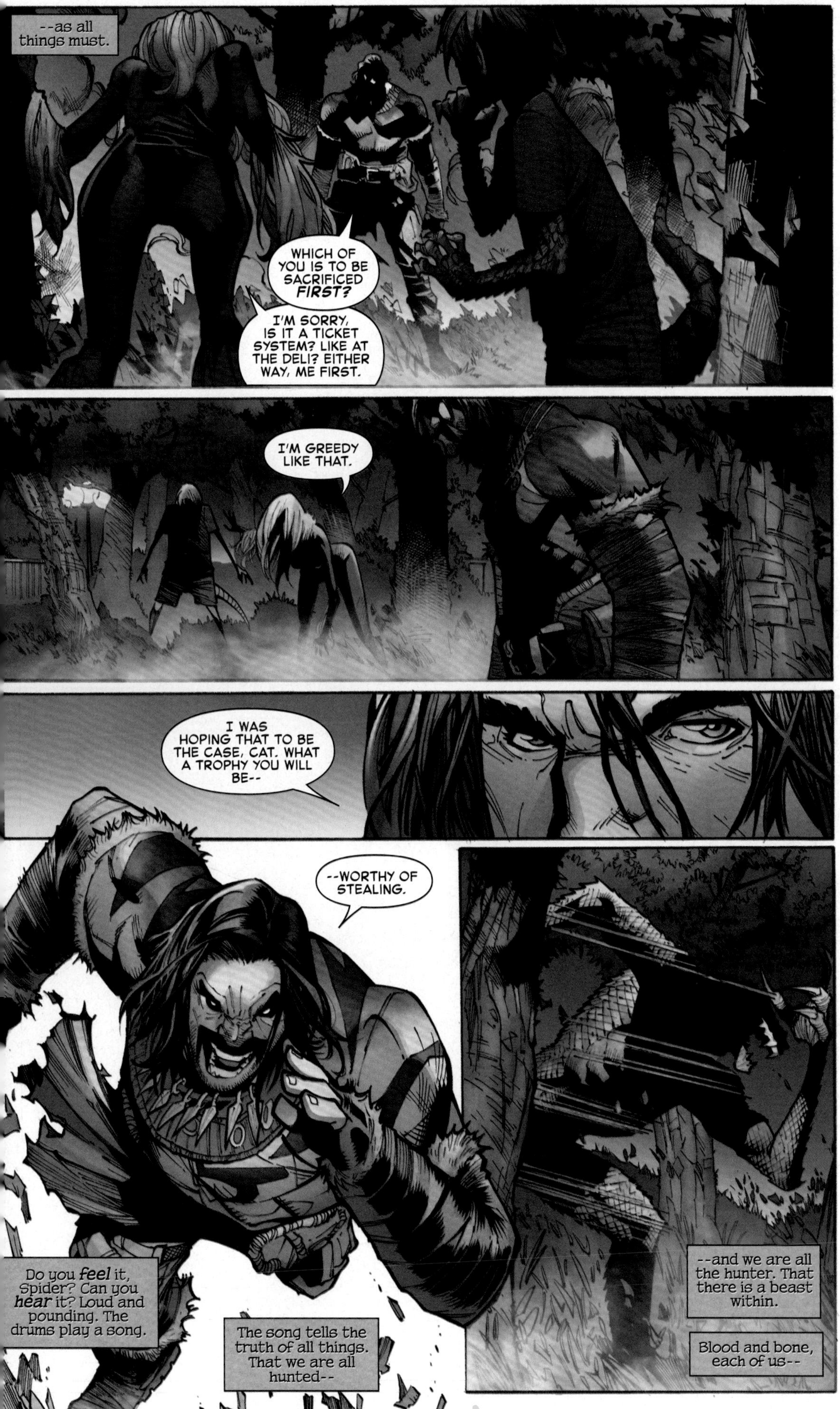
--as all things must.
WHICH OF YOU IS TO BE SACRIFICED FIRST?
I'M SORRY, IS IT A TICKET SYSTEM? LIKE AT THE DELI? EITHER WAY, ME FIRST.
I'M GREEDY LIKE THAT.
I WAS HOPING THAT TO BE THE CASE, CAT. WHAT A TROPHY YOU WILL BE--
--WORTHY OF STEALING.
Do you feel it, Spider? Can you hear it? Loud and pounding. The drums play a song.
The song tells the truth of all things. That we are all hunted--
--and we are all the hunter. That there is a beast within.
Blood and bone, each of us--

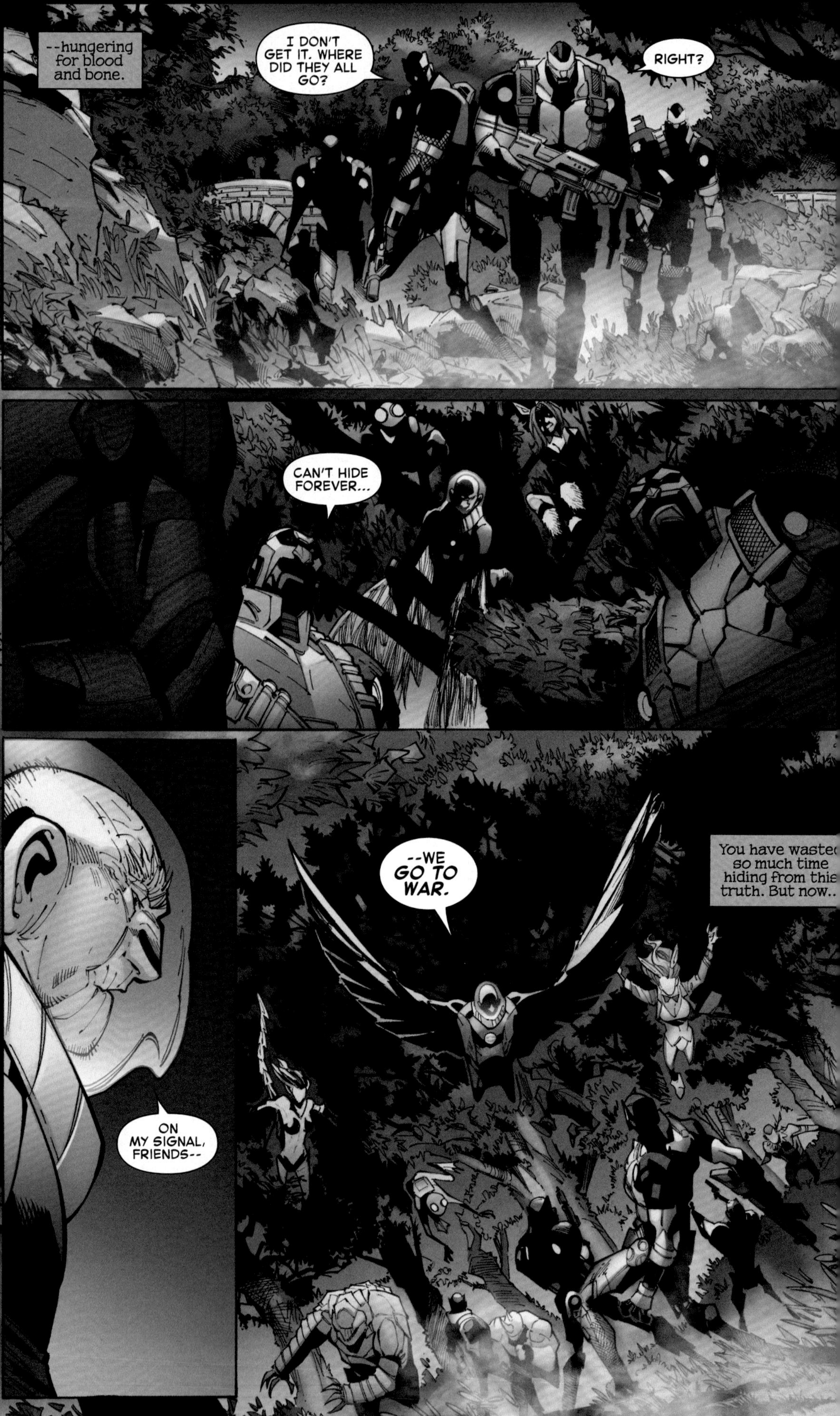
--hungering for blood and bone.
I DON'T GET IT. WHERE DID THEY ALL GO?
RIGHT?
CAN'T HIDE FOREVER...
You have wasted so much time hiding from this truth. But now...
ON MY SIGNAL, FRIENDS--
--WE GO TO WAR.

...now I will set you free.

FREE!

TSSSH

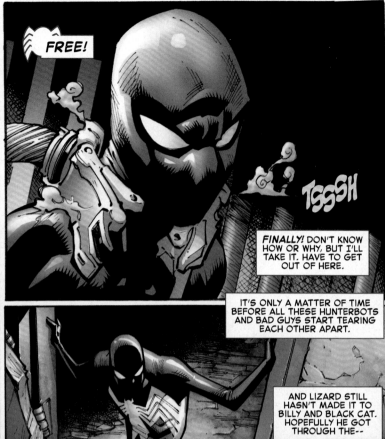

FINALLY! DON'T KNOW HOW OR WHY, BUT I'LL TAKE IT. HAVE TO GET OUT OF HERE.

IT'S ONLY A MATTER OF TIME BEFORE ALL THESE HUNTERBOTS AND BAD GUYS START TEARING EACH OTHER APART.

AND LIZARD STILL HASN'T MADE IT TO BILLY AND BLACK CAT. HOPEFULLY HE GOT THROUGH THE--

--GUARDS.

NO... DEAD. THEY'RE ALL DEAD. HE KILLED THEM. HE SAID HE COULD CONTROL IT! HE SAID--

THIS IS MY FAULT. I LET HIM LOOSE. I DID THIS. AND NOW HE'S ON HIS WAY TO--OH NO--BILLY! I HAVE TO--

NOT AN EASY SIGHT, IS IT? BUT THEN--

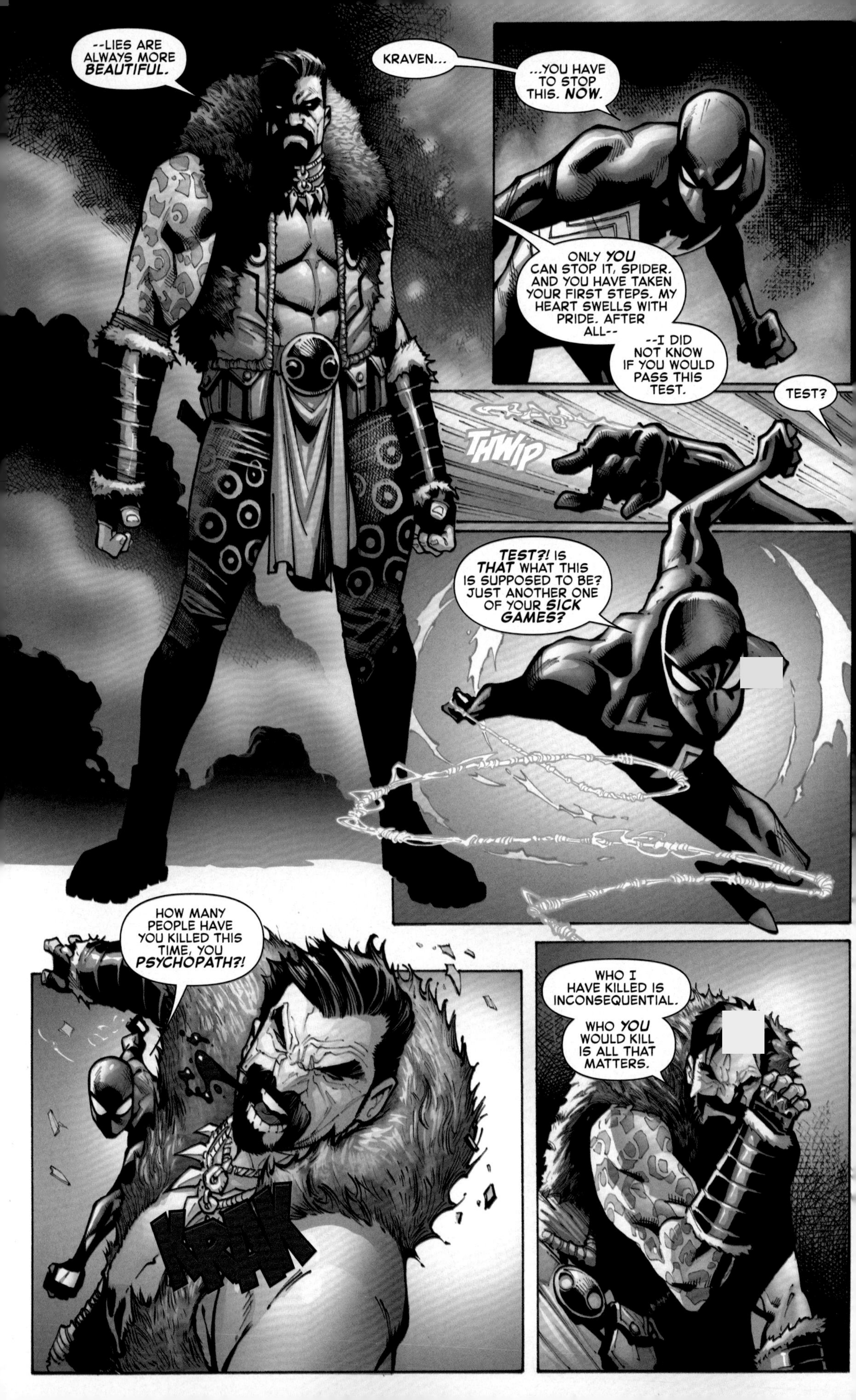
--LIES ARE ALWAYS MORE BEAUTIFUL.
KRAVEN...
...YOU HAVE TO STOP THIS. NOW.
ONLY YOU CAN STOP IT, SPIDER. AND YOU HAVE TAKEN YOUR FIRST STEPS. MY HEART SWELLS WITH PRIDE. AFTER ALL--
--I DID NOT KNOW IF YOU WOULD PASS THIS TEST.
TEST?
THWIP
TEST?! IS THAT WHAT THIS IS SUPPOSED TO BE? JUST ANOTHER ONE OF YOUR SICK GAMES?
HOW MANY PEOPLE HAVE YOU KILLED THIS TIME, YOU PSYCHOPATH?!
WHO I HAVE KILLED IS INCONSEQUENTIAL.
WHO YOU WOULD KILL IS ALL THAT MATTERS.

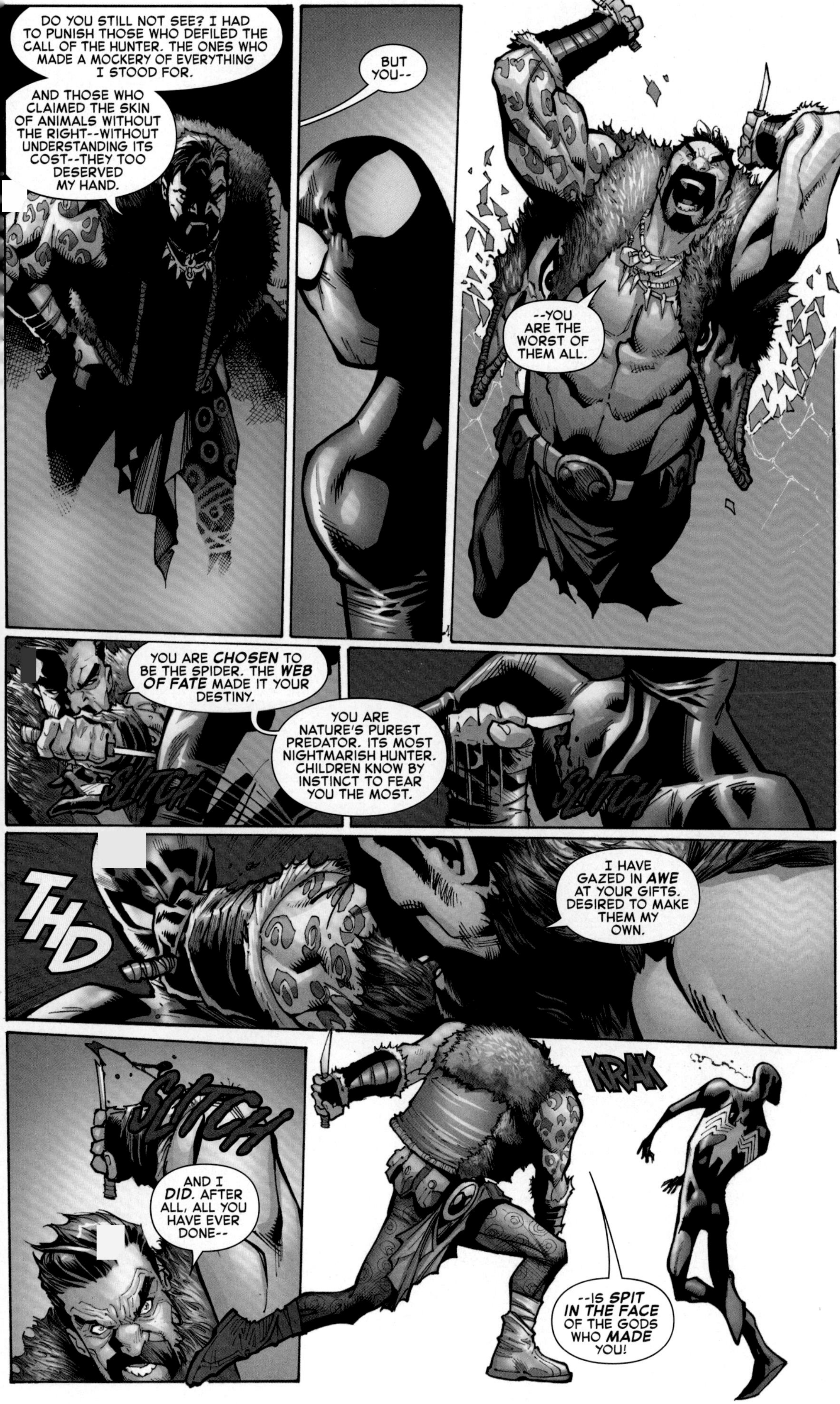

DO YOU STILL NOT SEE? I HAD TO PUNISH THOSE WHO DEFILED THE CALL OF THE HUNTER. THE ONES WHO MADE A MOCKERY OF EVERYTHING I STOOD FOR.
AND THOSE WHO CLAIMED THE SKIN OF ANIMALS WITHOUT THE RIGHT--WITHOUT UNDERSTANDING ITS COST--THEY TOO DESERVED MY HAND.
BUT YOU--
--YOU ARE THE WORST OF THEM ALL.
YOU ARE *CHOSEN* TO BE THE SPIDER. THE *WEB OF FATE* MADE IT YOUR DESTINY.
SLTCH
YOU ARE NATURE'S PUREST PREDATOR. ITS MOST NIGHTMARISH HUNTER. CHILDREN KNOW BY INSTINCT TO FEAR YOU THE MOST.
SLTCH
THD
I HAVE GAZED IN *AWE* AT YOUR GIFTS. DESIRED TO MAKE THEM MY OWN.
SLTCH
AND I *DID.* AFTER ALL, ALL YOU HAVE EVER DONE--
KRAK
--IS *SPIT IN THE FACE* OF THE GODS WHO *MADE* YOU!

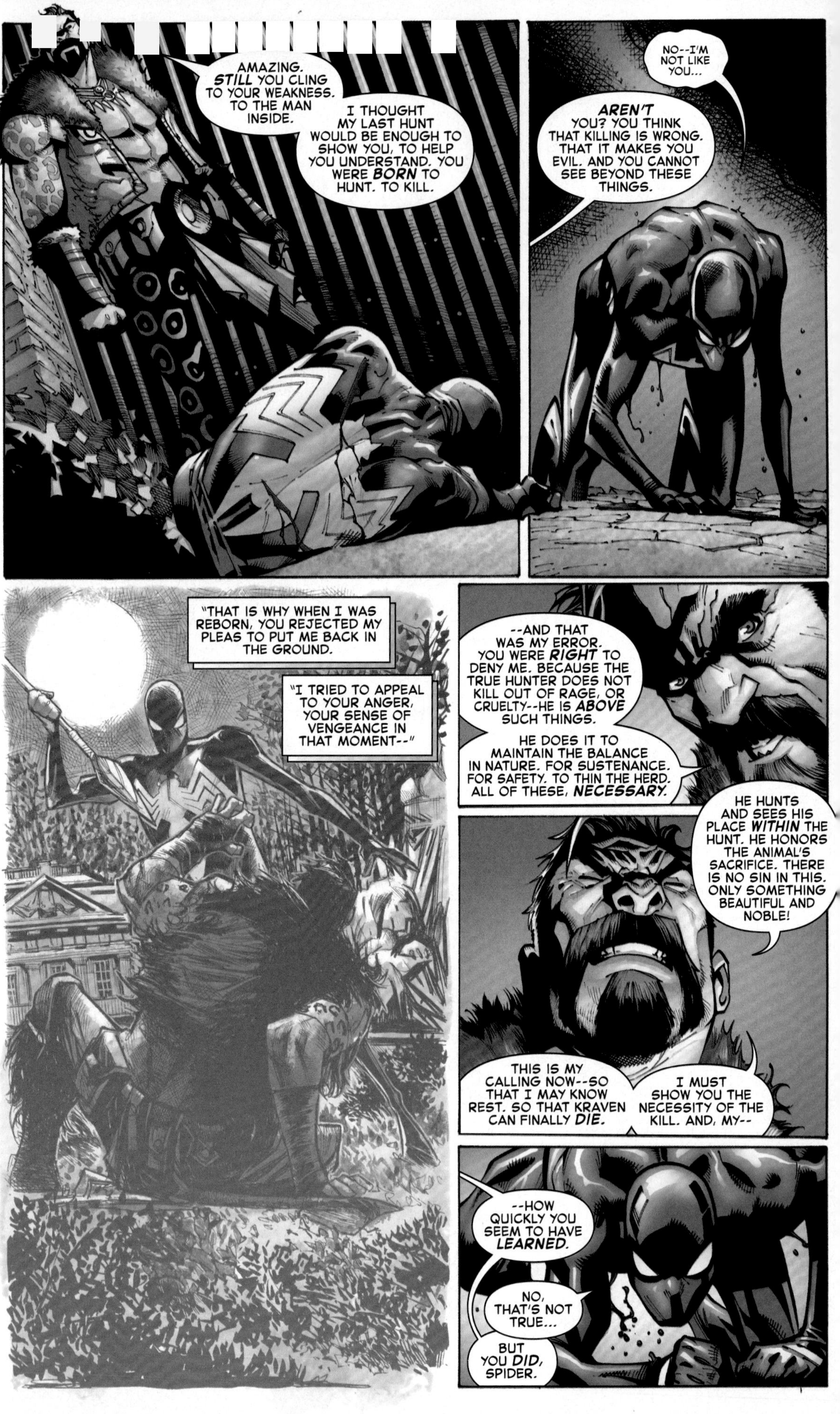

AMAZING. STILL YOU CLING TO YOUR WEAKNESS. TO THE MAN INSIDE.
I THOUGHT MY LAST HUNT WOULD BE ENOUGH TO SHOW YOU, TO HELP YOU UNDERSTAND. YOU WERE BORN TO HUNT. TO KILL.
NO--I'M NOT LIKE YOU...
AREN'T YOU? YOU THINK THAT KILLING IS WRONG. THAT IT MAKES YOU EVIL. AND YOU CANNOT SEE BEYOND THESE THINGS.
"THAT IS WHY WHEN I WAS REBORN, YOU REJECTED MY PLEAS TO PUT ME BACK IN THE GROUND.
"I TRIED TO APPEAL TO YOUR ANGER, YOUR SENSE OF VENGEANCE IN THAT MOMENT--"
--AND THAT WAS MY ERROR. YOU WERE RIGHT TO DENY ME. BECAUSE THE TRUE HUNTER DOES NOT KILL OUT OF RAGE, OR CRUELTY--HE IS ABOVE SUCH THINGS.
HE DOES IT TO MAINTAIN THE BALANCE IN NATURE. FOR SUSTENANCE. FOR SAFETY. TO THIN THE HERD. ALL OF THESE, NECESSARY.
HE HUNTS AND SEES HIS PLACE WITHIN THE HUNT. HE HONORS THE ANIMAL'S SACRIFICE. THERE IS NO SIN IN THIS. ONLY SOMETHING BEAUTIFUL AND NOBLE!
THIS IS MY CALLING NOW--SO THAT I MAY KNOW REST. SO THAT KRAVEN CAN FINALLY DIE.
I MUST SHOW YOU THE NECESSITY OF THE KILL. AND, MY--
--HOW QUICKLY YOU SEEM TO HAVE LEARNED.
NO, THAT'S NOT TRUE...
BUT YOU DID, SPIDER.

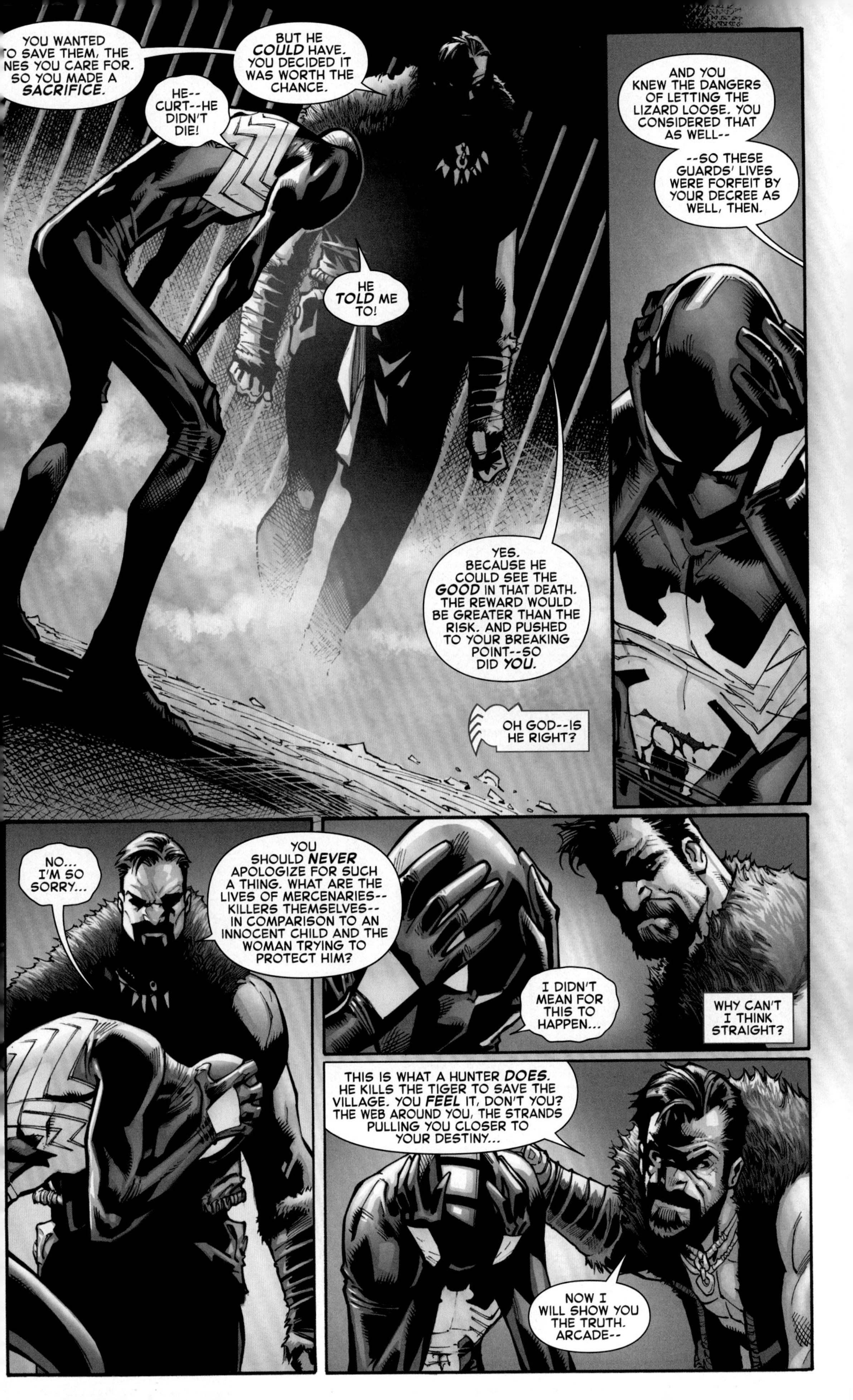
YOU WANTED TO SAVE THEM, THE ONES YOU CARE FOR. SO YOU MADE A SACRIFICE.
HE--CURT--HE DIDN'T DIE!
BUT HE COULD HAVE. YOU DECIDED IT WAS WORTH THE CHANCE.
AND YOU KNEW THE DANGERS OF LETTING THE LIZARD LOOSE. YOU CONSIDERED THAT AS WELL--
--SO THESE GUARDS' LIVES WERE FORFEIT BY YOUR DECREE AS WELL, THEN.
HE TOLD ME TO!
YES. BECAUSE HE COULD SEE THE GOOD IN THAT DEATH. THE REWARD WOULD BE GREATER THAN THE RISK. AND PUSHED TO YOUR BREAKING POINT--SO DID YOU.
OH GOD--IS HE RIGHT?
NO... I'M SO SORRY...
YOU SHOULD NEVER APOLOGIZE FOR SUCH A THING. WHAT ARE THE LIVES OF MERCENARIES--KILLERS THEMSELVES--IN COMPARISON TO AN INNOCENT CHILD AND THE WOMAN TRYING TO PROTECT HIM?
I DIDN'T MEAN FOR THIS TO HAPPEN...
WHY CAN'T I THINK STRAIGHT?
THIS IS WHAT A HUNTER DOES. HE KILLS THE TIGER TO SAVE THE VILLAGE. YOU FEEL IT, DON'T YOU? THE WEB AROUND YOU, THE STRANDS PULLING YOU CLOSER TO YOUR DESTINY...
NOW I WILL SHOW YOU THE TRUTH. ARCADE--

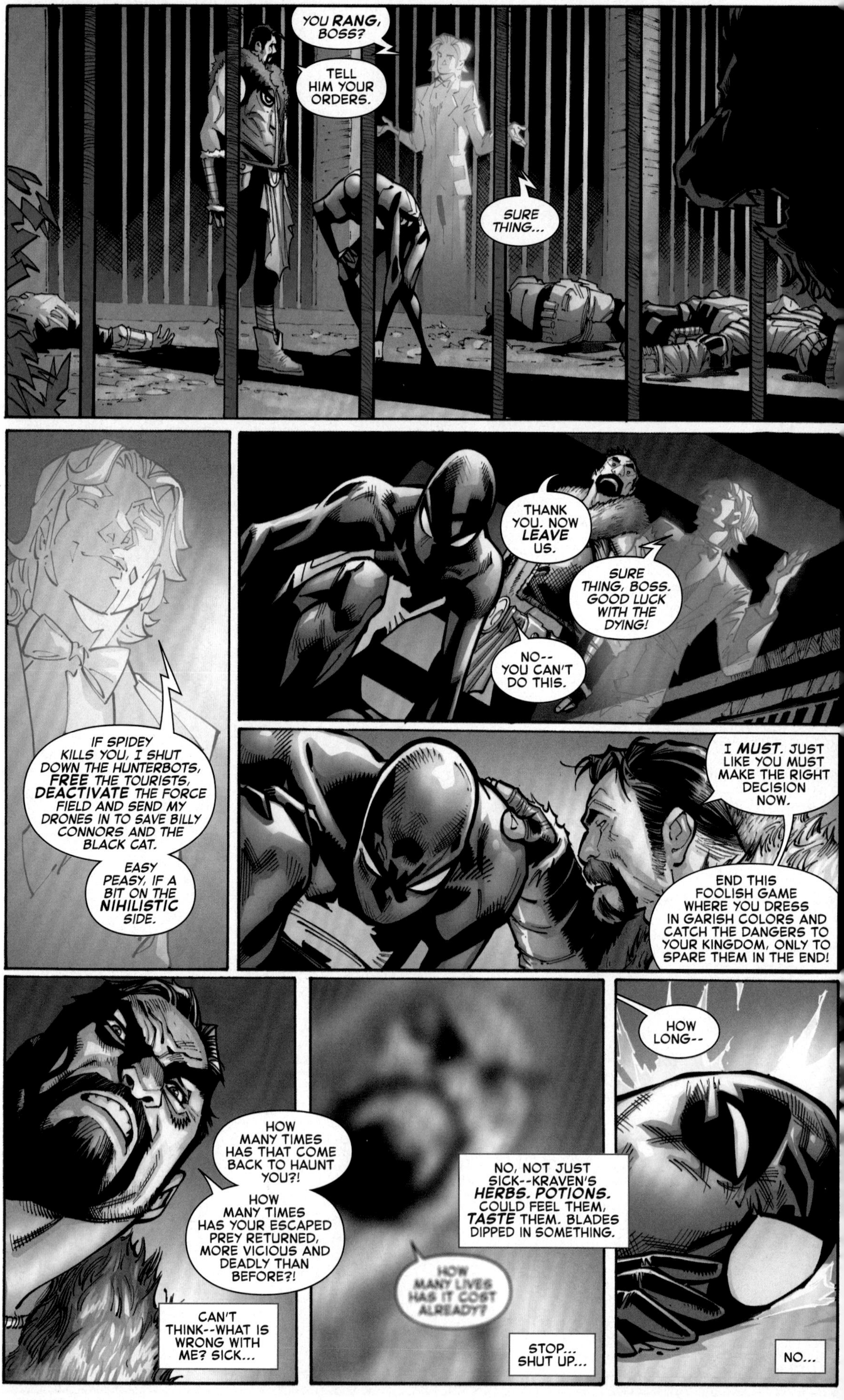
YOU RANG, BOSS?
TELL HIM YOUR ORDERS.
SURE THING...
IF SPIDEY KILLS YOU, I SHUT DOWN THE HUNTERBOTS, FREE THE TOURISTS, DEACTIVATE THE FORCE FIELD AND SEND MY DRONES IN TO SAVE BILLY CONNORS AND THE BLACK CAT.
EASY PEASY, IF A BIT ON THE NIHILISTIC SIDE.
THANK YOU. NOW LEAVE US.
SURE THING, BOSS. GOOD LUCK WITH THE DYING!
NO-- YOU CAN'T DO THIS.
I MUST. JUST LIKE YOU MUST MAKE THE RIGHT DECISION NOW.
END THIS FOOLISH GAME WHERE YOU DRESS IN GARISH COLORS AND CATCH THE DANGERS TO YOUR KINGDOM, ONLY TO SPARE THEM IN THE END!
HOW MANY TIMES HAS THAT COME BACK TO HAUNT YOU?!
HOW MANY TIMES HAS YOUR ESCAPED PREY RETURNED, MORE VICIOUS AND DEADLY THAN BEFORE?!
CAN'T THINK--WHAT IS WRONG WITH ME? SICK...
NO, NOT JUST SICK--KRAVEN'S HERBS. POTIONS. COULD FEEL THEM, TASTE THEM. BLADES DIPPED IN SOMETHING.
HOW MANY LIVES HAS IT COST ALREADY?
STOP... SHUT UP...
HOW LONG--
NO...

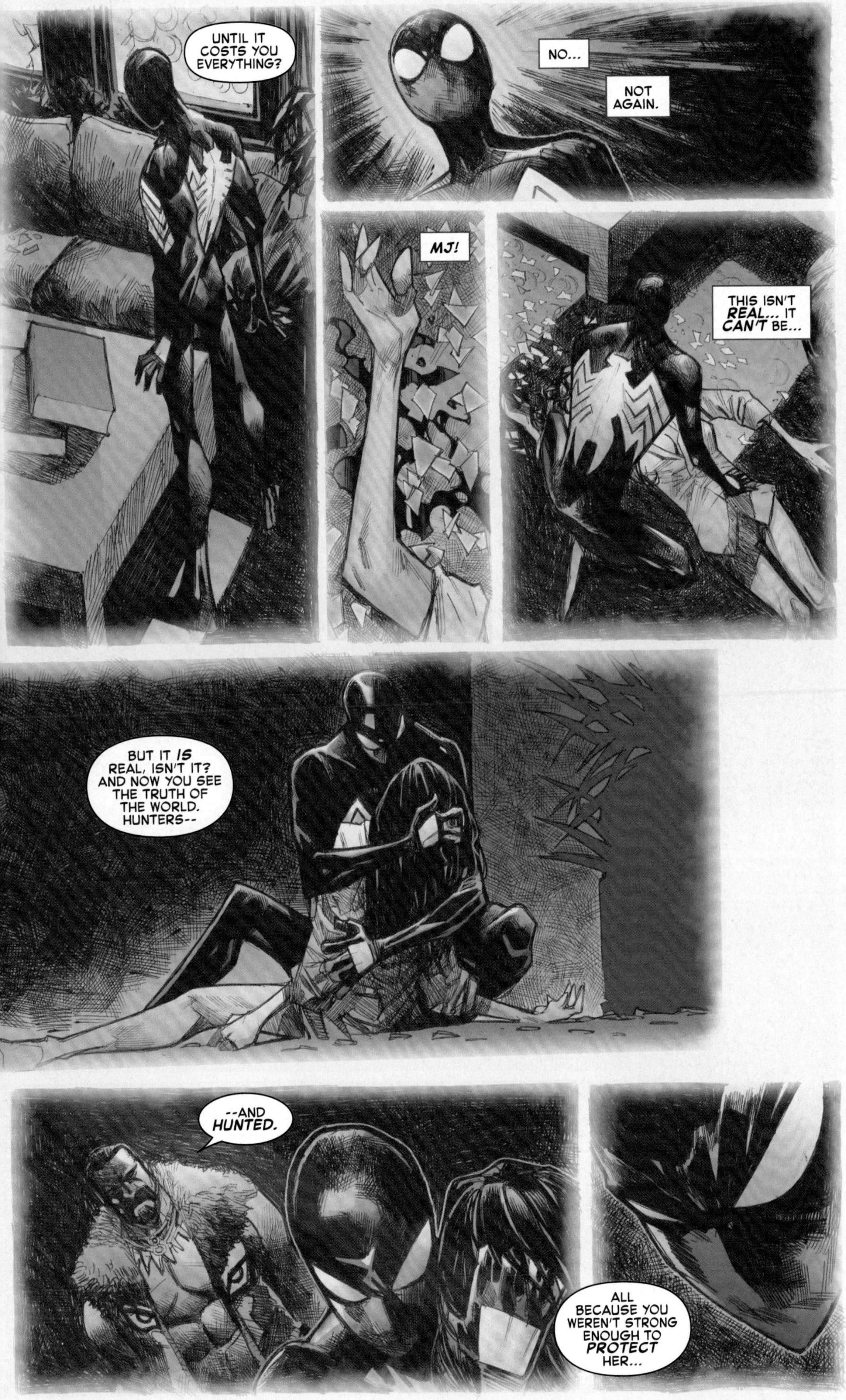
UNTIL IT COSTS YOU EVERYTHING?
NO...
NOT AGAIN.
MJ!
THIS ISN'T REAL... IT CAN'T BE...
BUT IT IS REAL, ISN'T IT? AND NOW YOU SEE THE TRUTH OF THE WORLD. HUNTERS--
--AND HUNTED.
ALL BECAUSE YOU WEREN'T STRONG ENOUGH TO PROTECT HER...

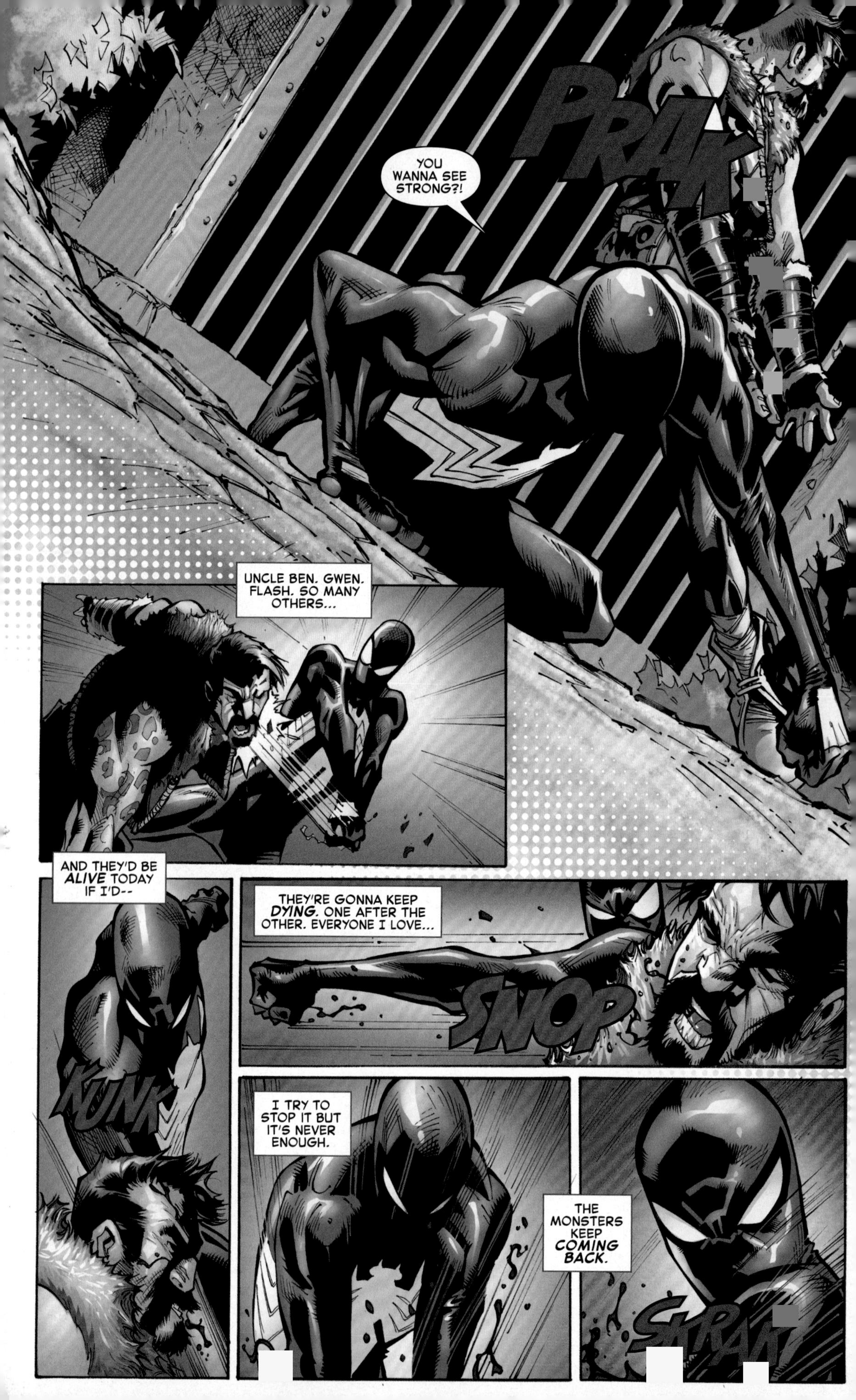
PRAK
YOU WANNA SEE STRONG?!
UNCLE BEN. GWEN. FLASH. SO MANY OTHERS...
AND THEY'D BE *ALIVE* TODAY IF I'D--
KUNK
THEY'RE GONNA KEEP *DYING*. ONE AFTER THE OTHER. EVERYONE I LOVE...
SNOP
I TRY TO STOP IT BUT IT'S NEVER ENOUGH.
THE MONSTERS KEEP *COMING BACK*.
SKRAK

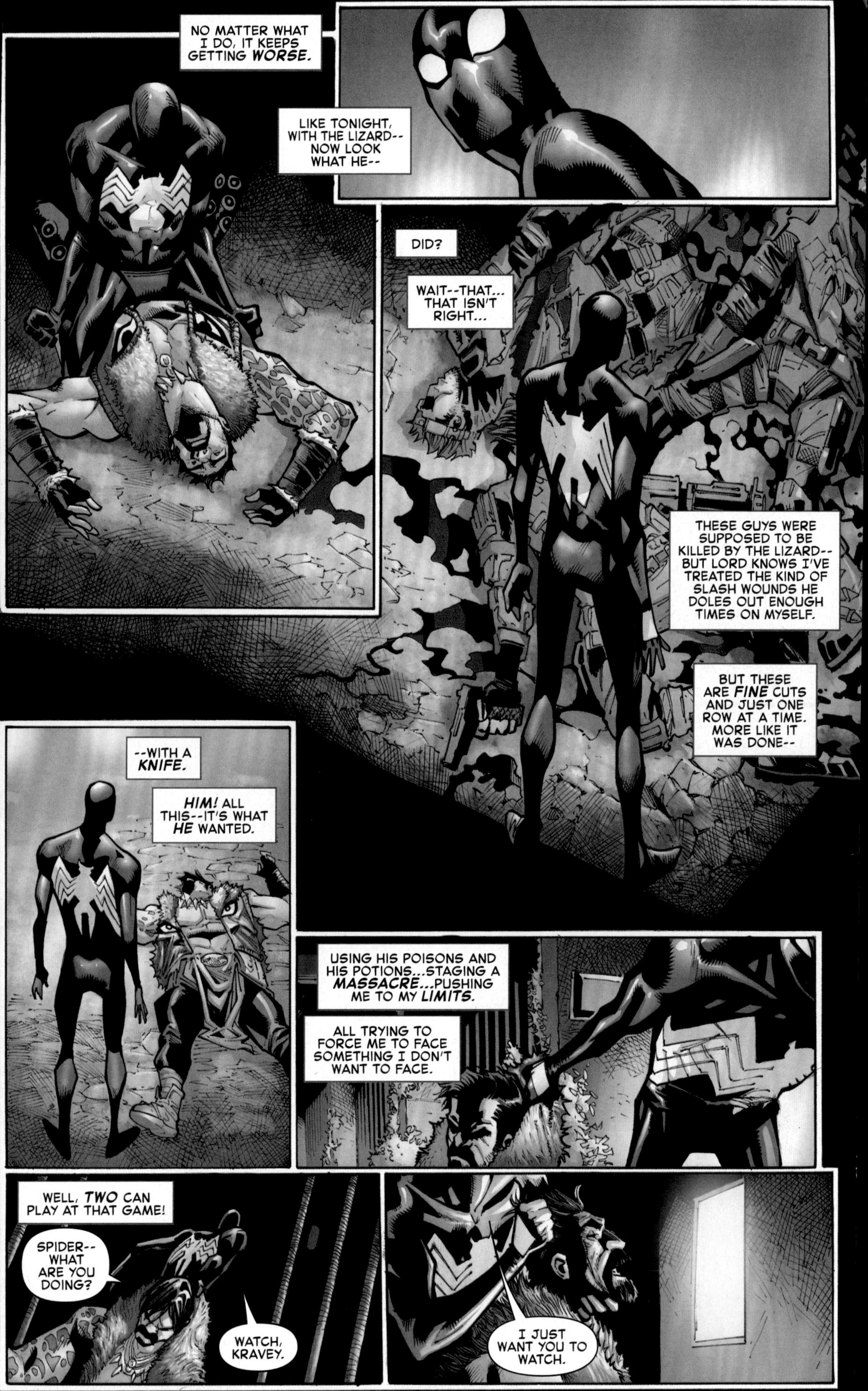
NO MATTER WHAT I DO, IT KEEPS GETTING WORSE.
LIKE TONIGHT, WITH THE LIZARD-- NOW LOOK WHAT HE--
DID?
WAIT--THAT... THAT ISN'T RIGHT...
THESE GUYS WERE SUPPOSED TO BE KILLED BY THE LIZARD-- BUT LORD KNOWS I'VE TREATED THE KIND OF SLASH WOUNDS HE DOLES OUT ENOUGH TIMES ON MYSELF.
BUT THESE ARE FINE CUTS AND JUST ONE ROW AT A TIME. MORE LIKE IT WAS DONE--
--WITH A KNIFE.
HIM! ALL THIS--IT'S WHAT HE WANTED.
USING HIS POISONS AND HIS POTIONS...STAGING A MASSACRE...PUSHING ME TO MY LIMITS.
ALL TRYING TO FORCE ME TO FACE SOMETHING I DON'T WANT TO FACE.
WELL, TWO CAN PLAY AT THAT GAME!
SPIDER-- WHAT ARE YOU DOING?
WATCH, KRAVEY.
I JUST WANT YOU TO WATCH.

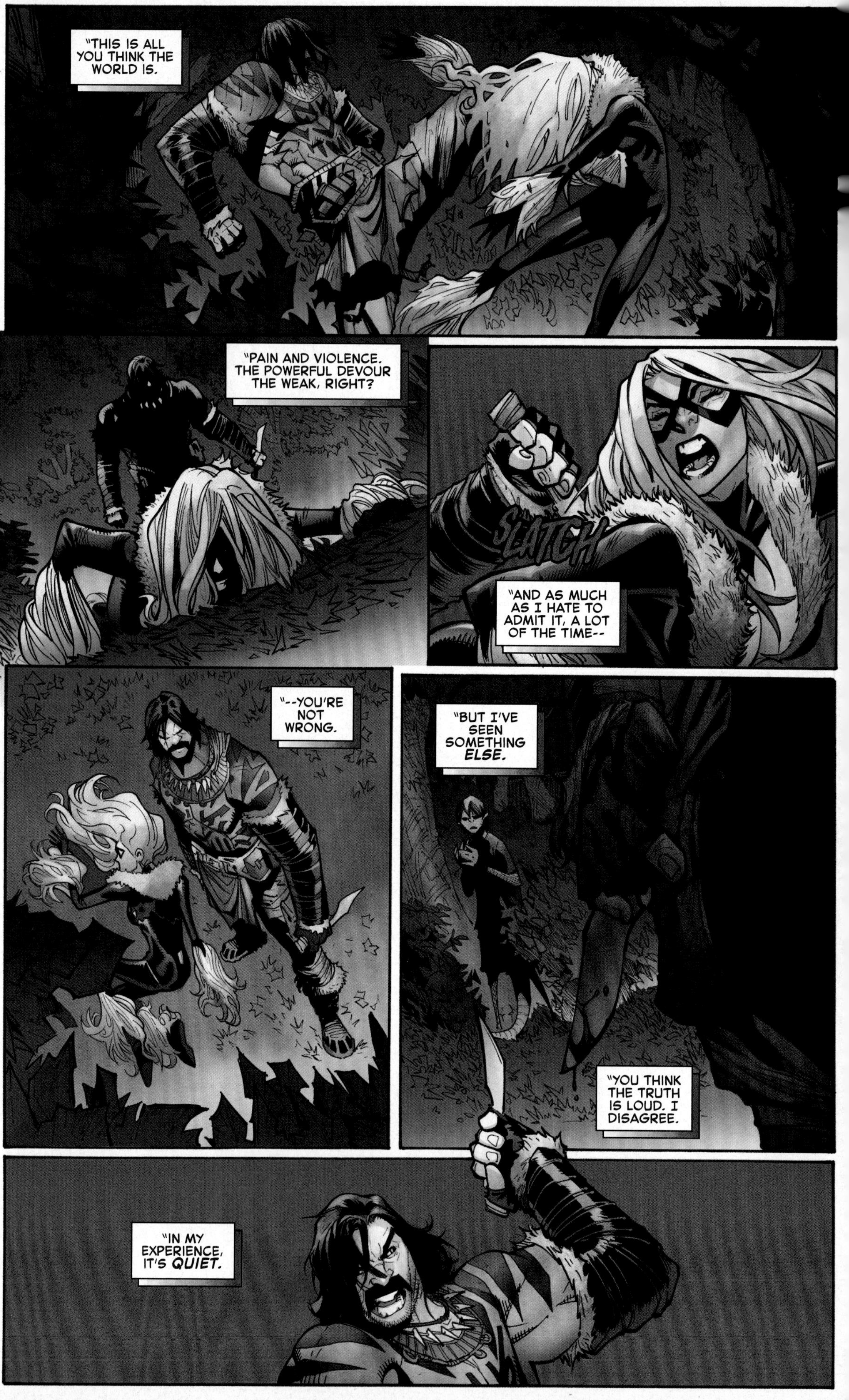

"THIS IS ALL YOU THINK THE WORLD IS.
"PAIN AND VIOLENCE. THE POWERFUL DEVOUR THE WEAK, RIGHT?
SLATCH
"AND AS MUCH AS I HATE TO ADMIT IT, A LOT OF THE TIME--
"--YOU'RE NOT WRONG.
"BUT I'VE SEEN SOMETHING *ELSE.*
"YOU THINK THE TRUTH IS LOUD. I DISAGREE.
"IN MY EXPERIENCE, IT'S *QUIET.*

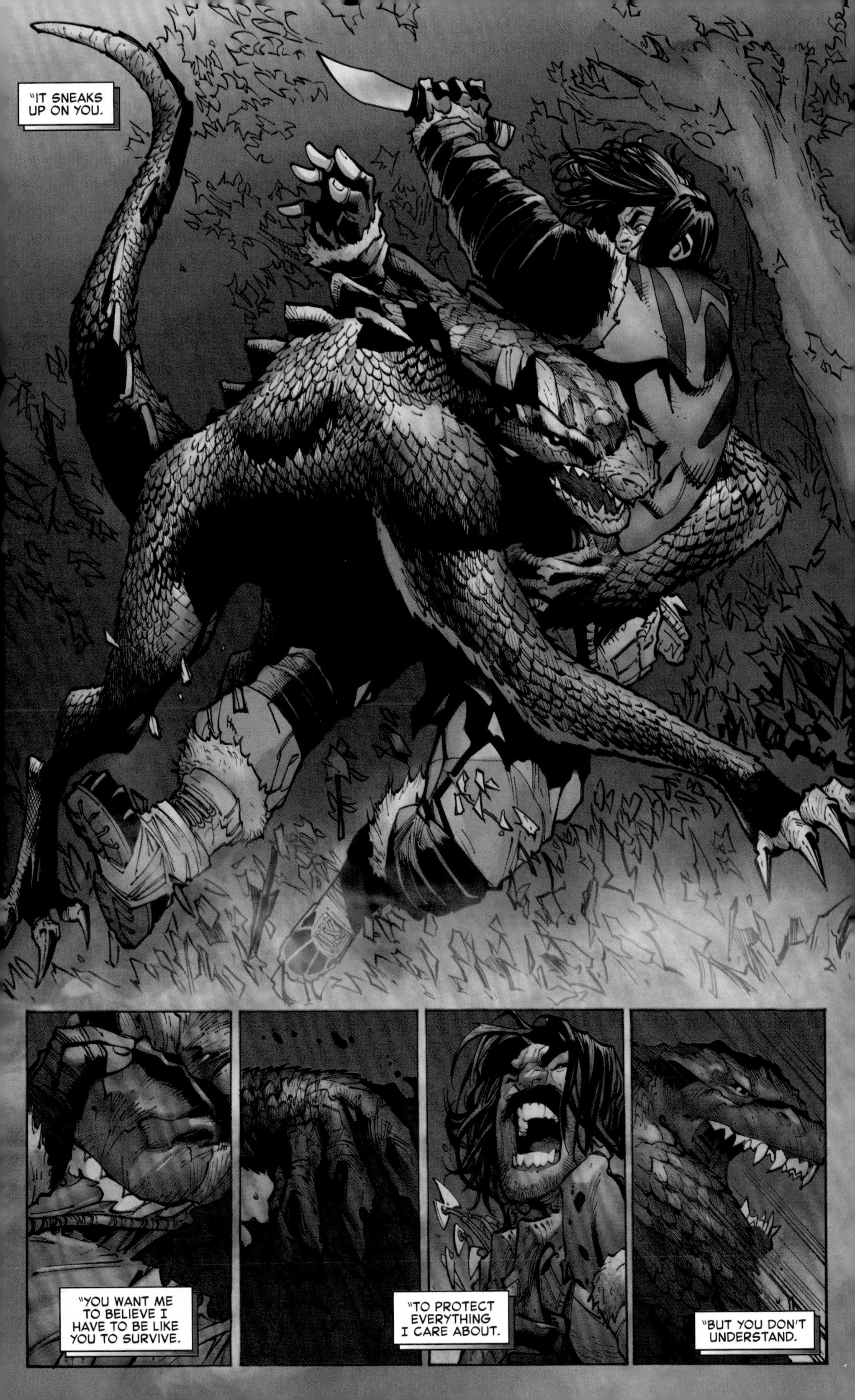
"IT SNEAKS UP ON YOU.
"YOU WANT ME TO BELIEVE I HAVE TO BE LIKE YOU TO SURVIVE.
"TO PROTECT EVERYTHING I CARE ABOUT.
"BUT YOU DON'T UNDERSTAND.

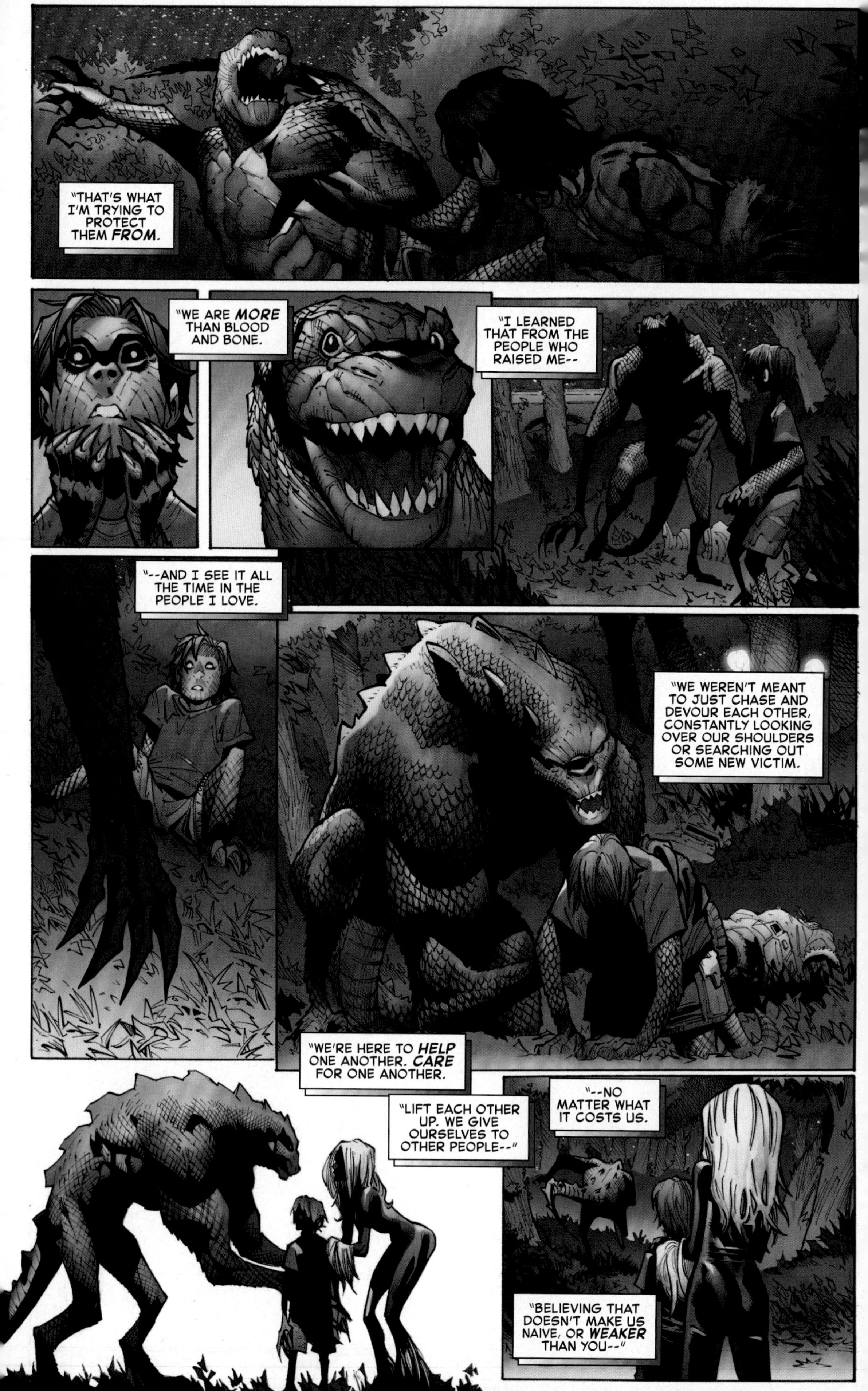
"THAT'S WHAT I'M TRYING TO PROTECT THEM FROM.
"WE ARE MORE THAN BLOOD AND BONE.
"I LEARNED THAT FROM THE PEOPLE WHO RAISED ME--
"--AND I SEE IT ALL THE TIME IN THE PEOPLE I LOVE.
"WE WEREN'T MEANT TO JUST CHASE AND DEVOUR EACH OTHER, CONSTANTLY LOOKING OVER OUR SHOULDERS OR SEARCHING OUT SOME NEW VICTIM.
"WE'RE HERE TO HELP ONE ANOTHER. CARE FOR ONE ANOTHER.
"LIFT EACH OTHER UP. WE GIVE OURSELVES TO OTHER PEOPLE--"
"--NO MATTER WHAT IT COSTS US.
"BELIEVING THAT DOESN'T MAKE US NAIVE, OR WEAKER THAN YOU--"

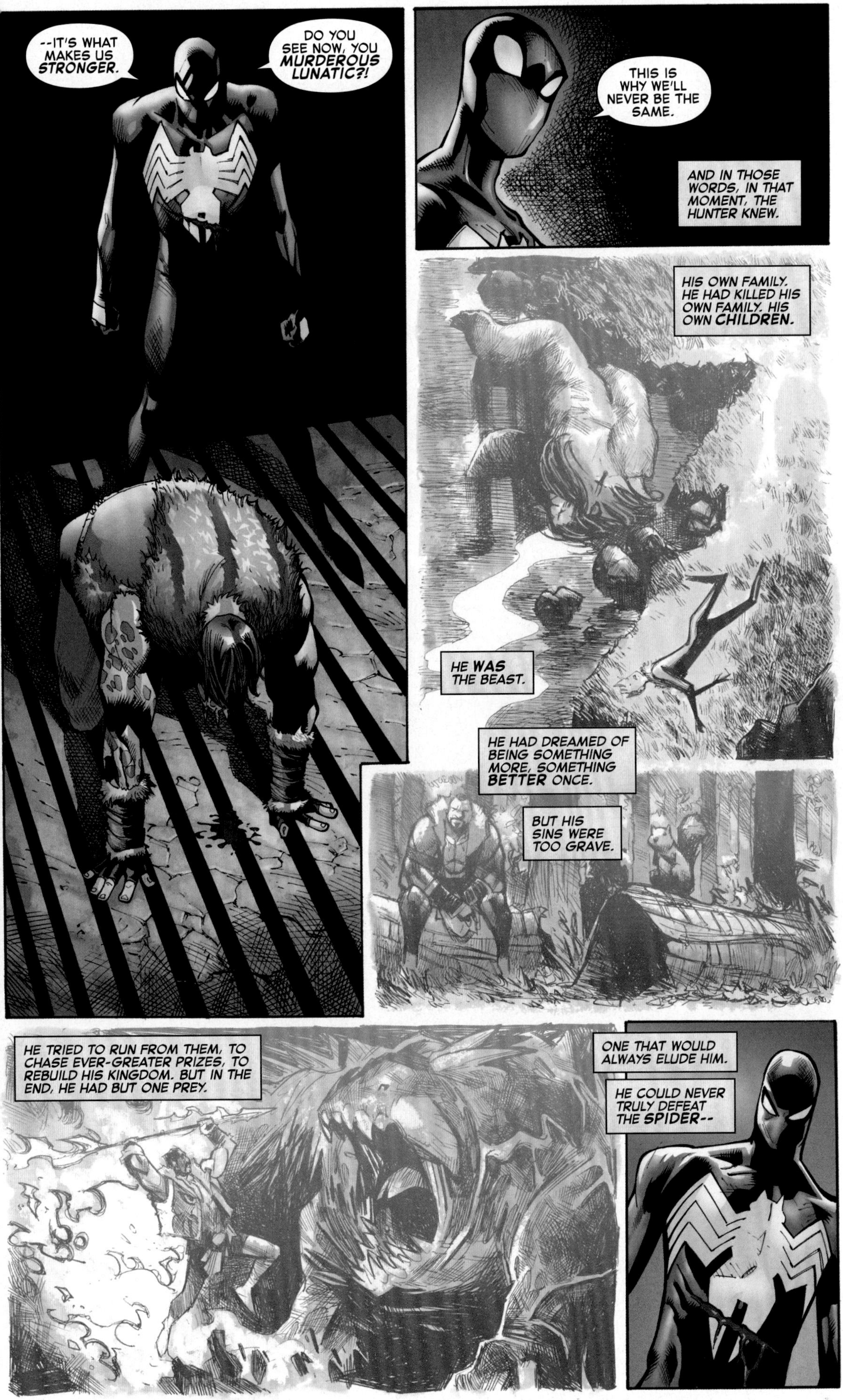

--IT'S WHAT MAKES US STRONGER.
DO YOU SEE NOW, YOU MURDEROUS LUNATIC?!
THIS IS WHY WE'LL NEVER BE THE SAME.
AND IN THOSE WORDS, IN THAT MOMENT, THE HUNTER KNEW.
HIS OWN FAMILY. HE HAD KILLED HIS OWN FAMILY. HIS OWN CHILDREN.
HE WAS THE BEAST.
HE HAD DREAMED OF BEING SOMETHING MORE, SOMETHING BETTER ONCE.
BUT HIS SINS WERE TOO GRAVE.
HE TRIED TO RUN FROM THEM, TO CHASE EVER-GREATER PRIZES, TO REBUILD HIS KINGDOM. BUT IN THE END, HE HAD BUT ONE PREY.
ONE THAT WOULD ALWAYS ELUDE HIM.
HE COULD NEVER TRULY DEFEAT THE SPIDER--

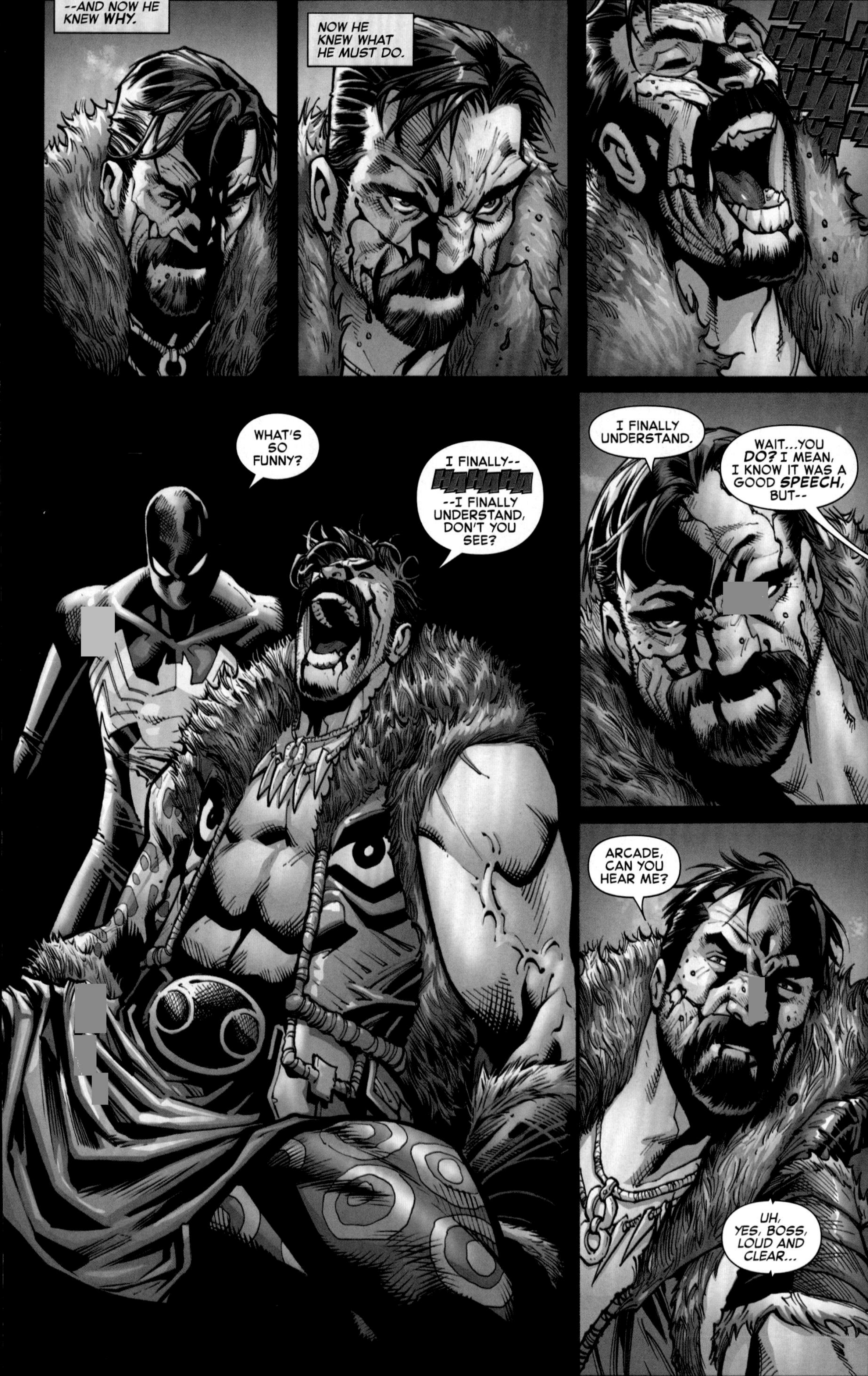
--AND NOW HE KNEW WHY.
NOW HE KNEW WHAT HE MUST DO.
WHAT'S SO FUNNY?
I FINALLY--
HAHAHA
--I FINALLY UNDERSTAND, DON'T YOU SEE?
I FINALLY UNDERSTAND.
WAIT...YOU DO? I MEAN, I KNOW IT WAS A GOOD SPEECH, BUT--
ARCADE, CAN YOU HEAR ME?
UH, YES, BOSS, LOUD AND CLEAR...

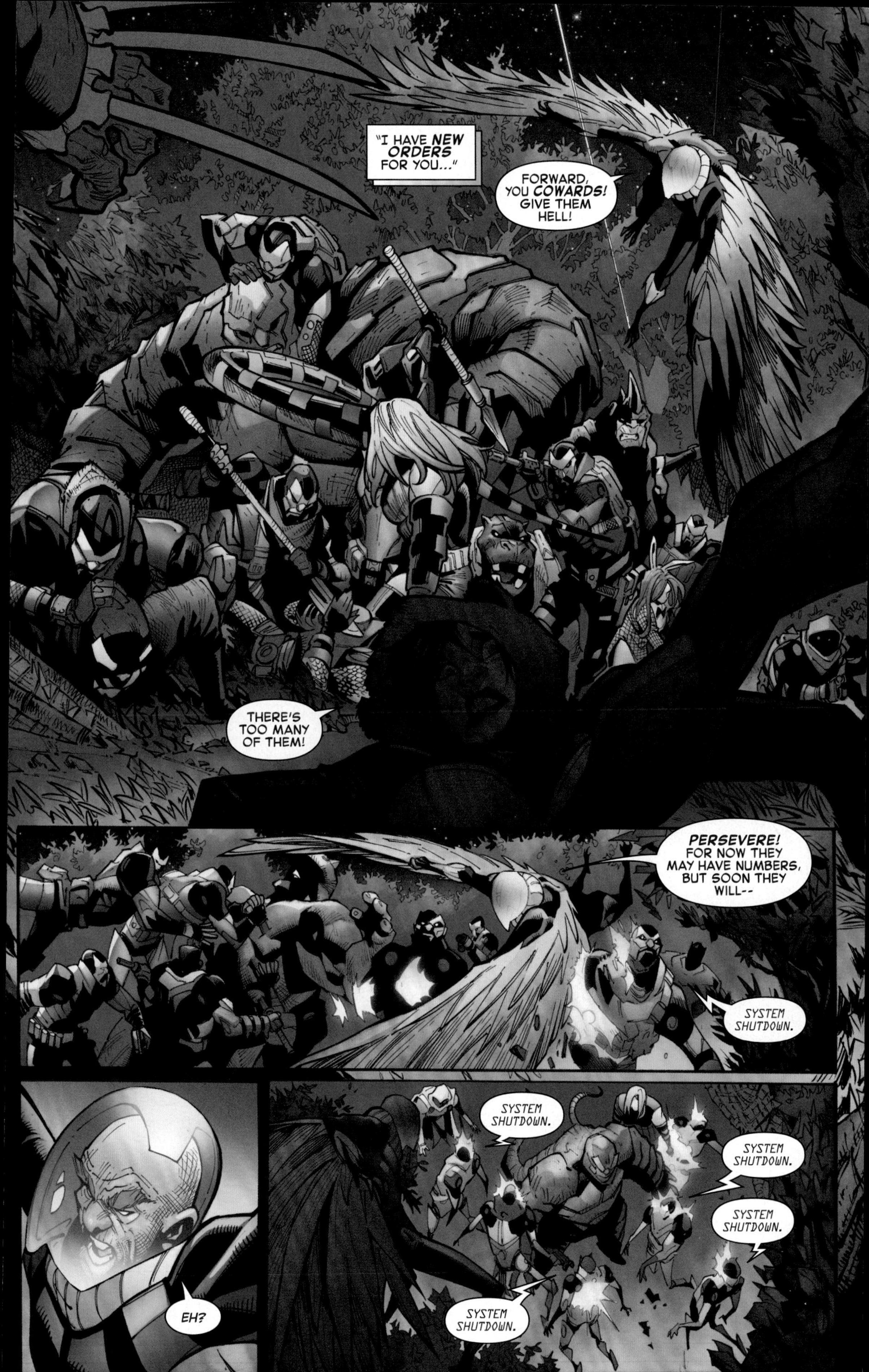
"I HAVE NEW ORDERS FOR YOU..."
FORWARD, YOU COWARDS! GIVE THEM HELL!
THERE'S TOO MANY OF THEM!
PERSEVERE! FOR NOW THEY MAY HAVE NUMBERS, BUT SOON THEY WILL--
SYSTEM SHUTDOWN.
EH?
SYSTEM SHUTDOWN.
SYSTEM SHUTDOWN.
SYSTEM SHUTDOWN.
SYSTEM SHUTDOWN.

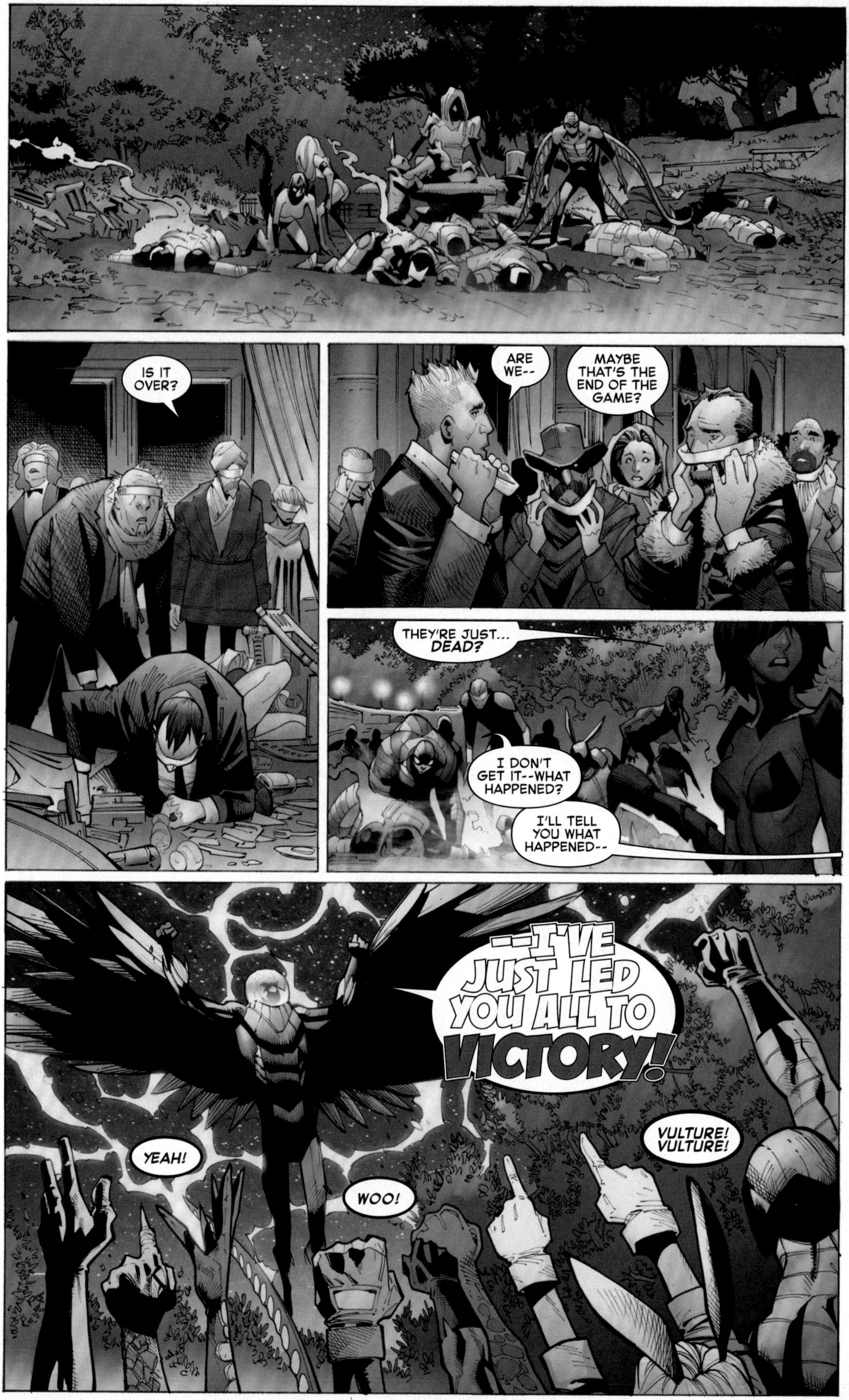

IS IT OVER?
ARE WE--
MAYBE THAT'S THE END OF THE GAME?
THEY'RE JUST... DEAD?
I DON'T GET IT--WHAT HAPPENED?
I'LL TELL YOU WHAT HAPPENED--
--I'VE JUST LED YOU ALL TO VICTORY!
YEAH!
WOO!
VULTURE! VULTURE!

WHAT--
WHAT DID
YOU JUST
DO?

SEVERED THE LINK BETWEEN HUNTER AND MAN. THERE WILL BE NO MORE BLOODSHED IN THE FIELDS OR THE BALLROOM TONIGHT.

AND-- THE *FORCE FIELD?*

WILL BE DOWN BY THE TIME YOU REACH THE OUTSIDE.

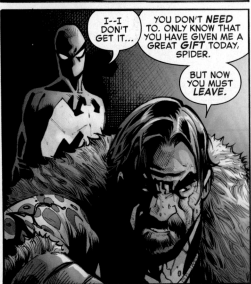

I--I DON'T GET IT...

YOU DON'T *NEED* TO. ONLY KNOW THAT YOU HAVE GIVEN ME A GREAT *GIFT* TODAY, SPIDER.

BUT NOW YOU MUST *LEAVE.*

WHAT? I'M NOT JUST GONNA LET YOU GO--

WHY NOT? I AM NO LONGER A THREAT. SAVE THOSE YOU CARE FOR.

SAVE WHAT YOU SAW IN YOUR VISIONS.

NO...

I AM A MAN OF MY WORD. I MADE YOU A *PROMISE* ONCE, AND I KEPT IT FOR THE REST OF THAT LIFE. DO YOU RECALL?

"I WILL *NEVER* HUNT AGAIN."

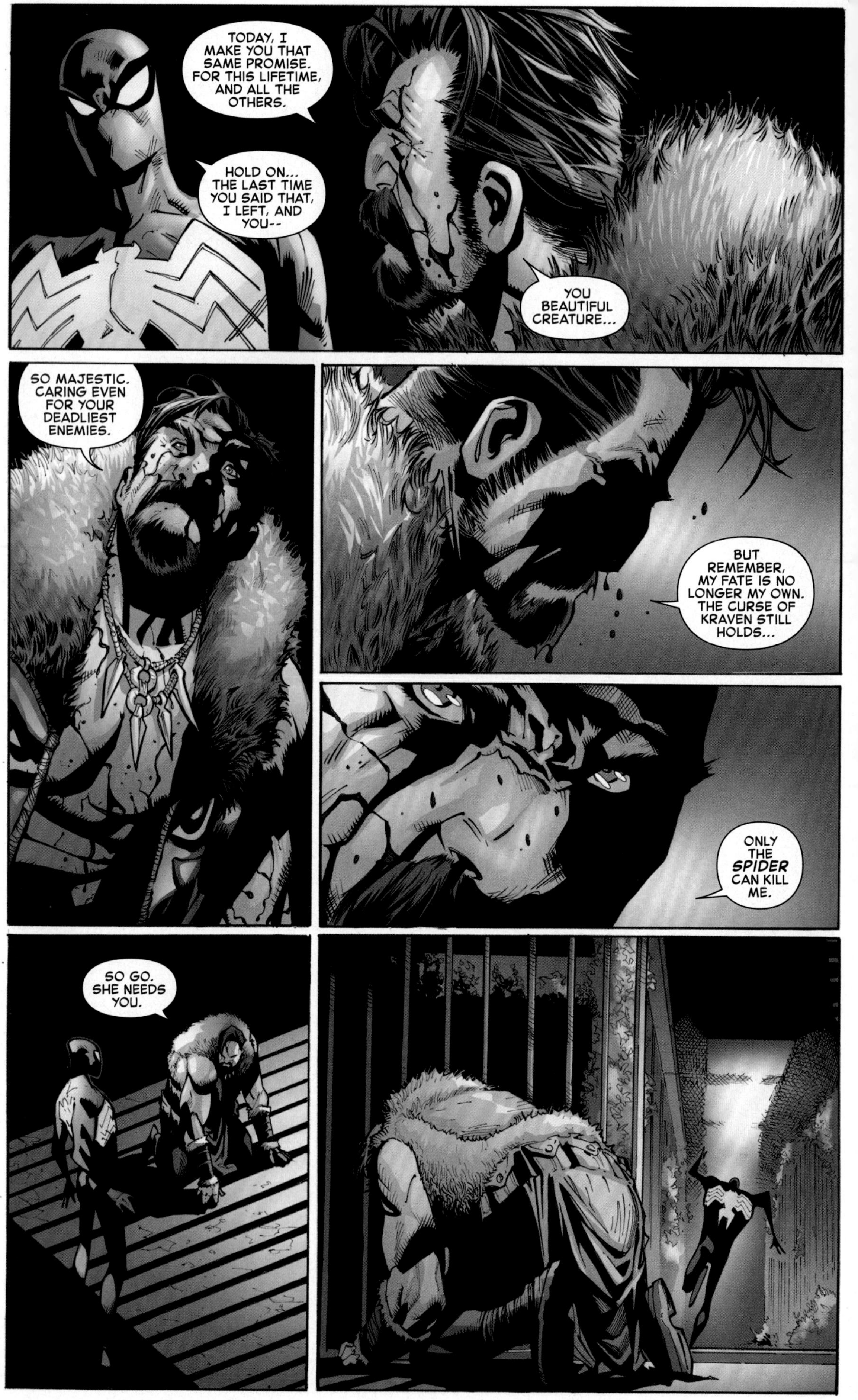
TODAY, I MAKE YOU THAT SAME PROMISE. FOR THIS LIFETIME, AND ALL THE OTHERS.
HOLD ON... THE LAST TIME YOU SAID THAT, I LEFT, AND YOU--
YOU BEAUTIFUL CREATURE...
SO MAJESTIC. CARING EVEN FOR YOUR DEADLIEST ENEMIES.
BUT REMEMBER, MY FATE IS NO LONGER MY OWN. THE CURSE OF KRAVEN STILL HOLDS...
ONLY THE *SPIDER* CAN KILL ME.
SO GO. SHE NEEDS YOU.

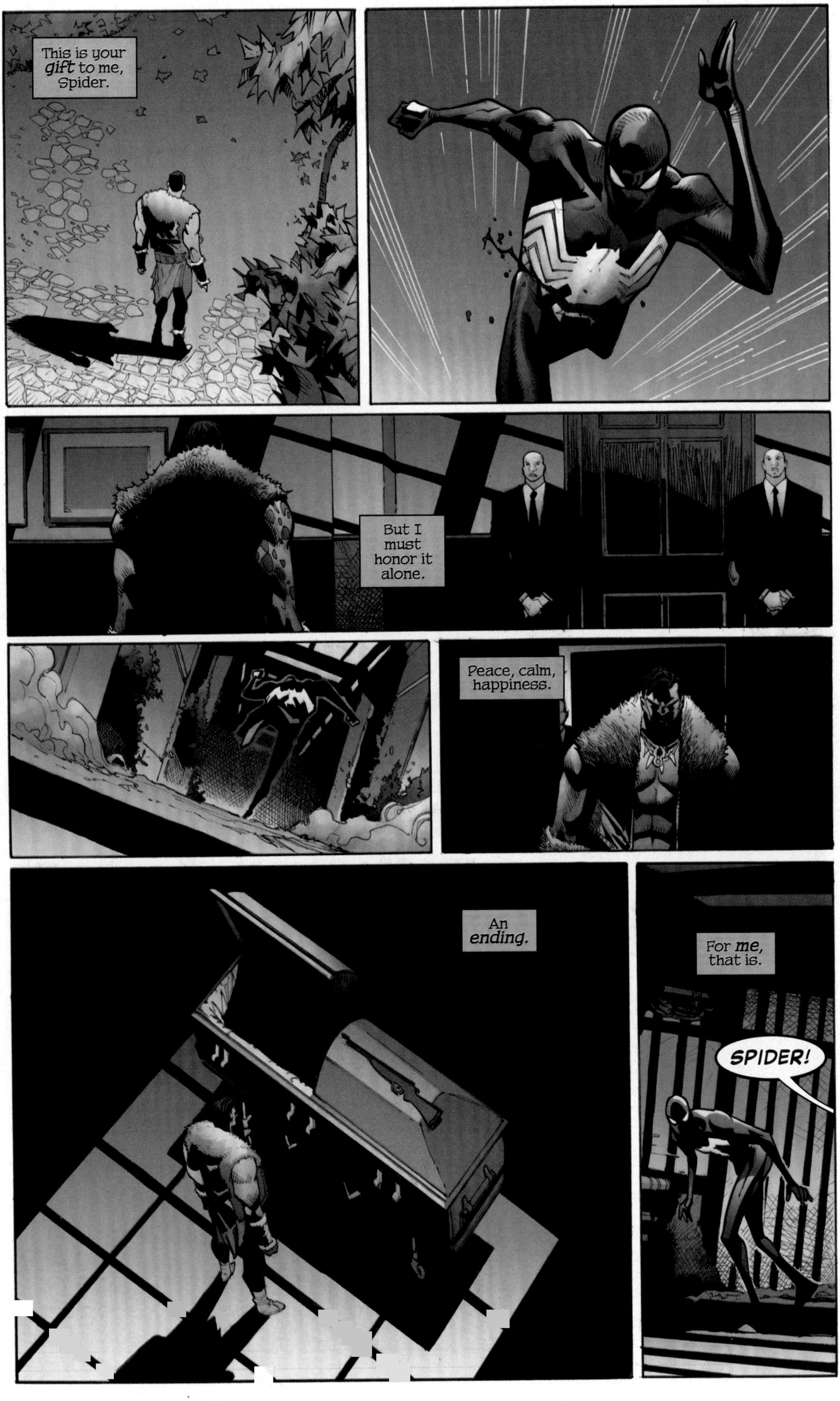
This is your *gift* to me, Spider.
But I must honor it alone.
Peace, calm, happiness.
An *ending.*
For *me,* that is.
SPIDER!

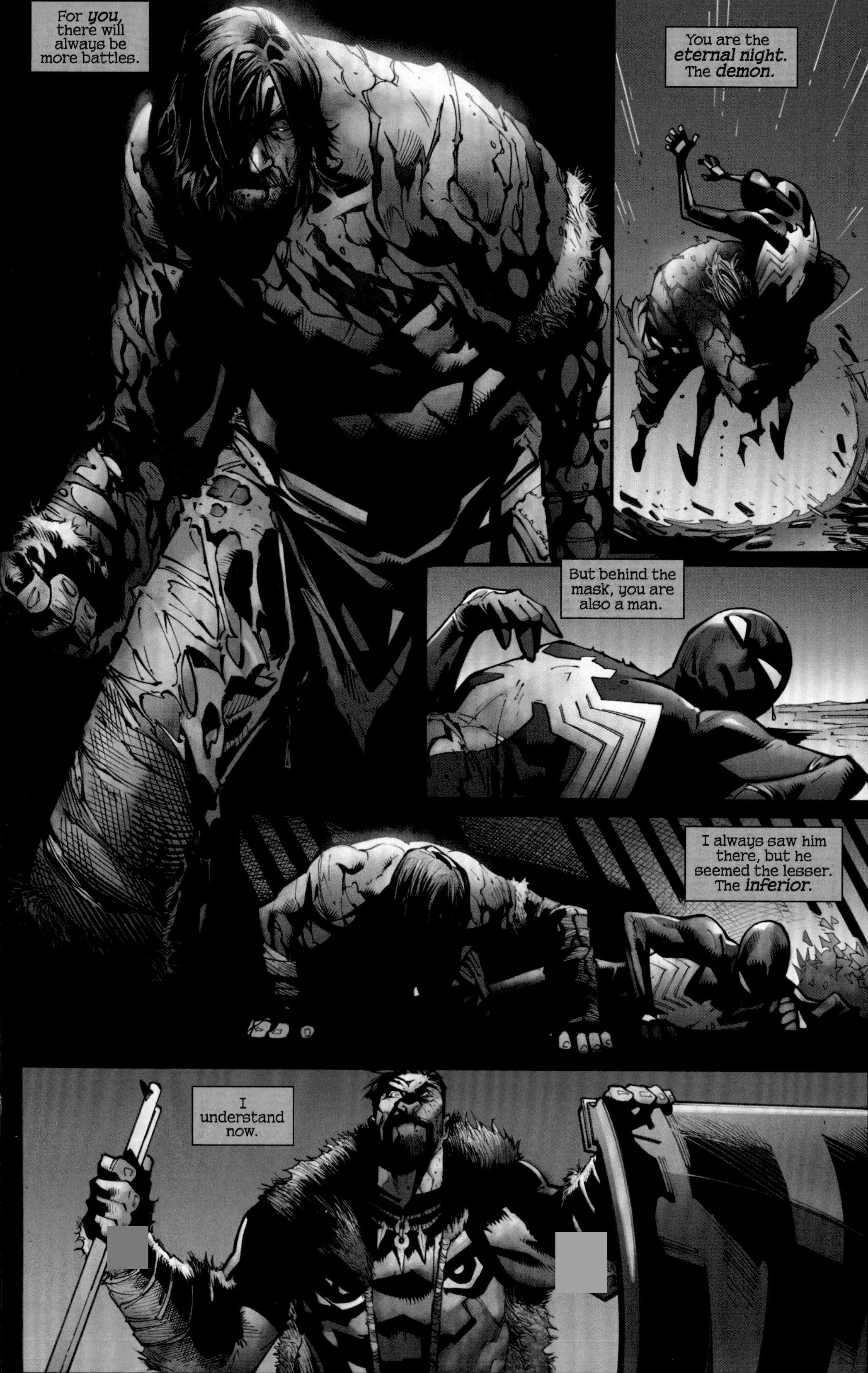
For *you*, there will always be more battles.
You are the *eternal night*. The *demon*.
But behind the mask, you are also a man.
I always saw him there, but he seemed the lesser. The *inferior*.
I understand now.

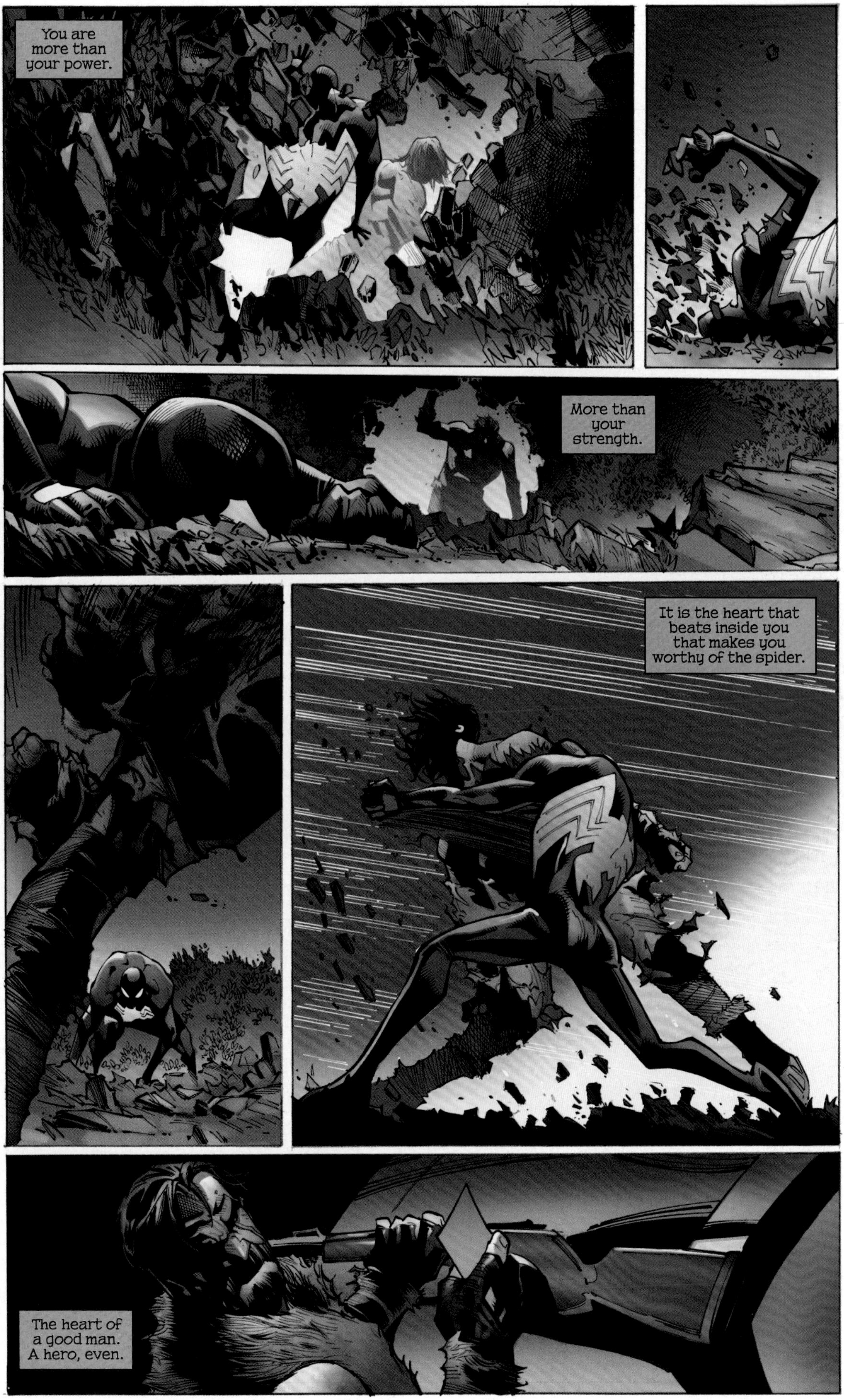
You are more than your power.
More than your strength.
It is the heart that beats inside you that makes you worthy of the spider.
The heart of a good man. A hero, even.

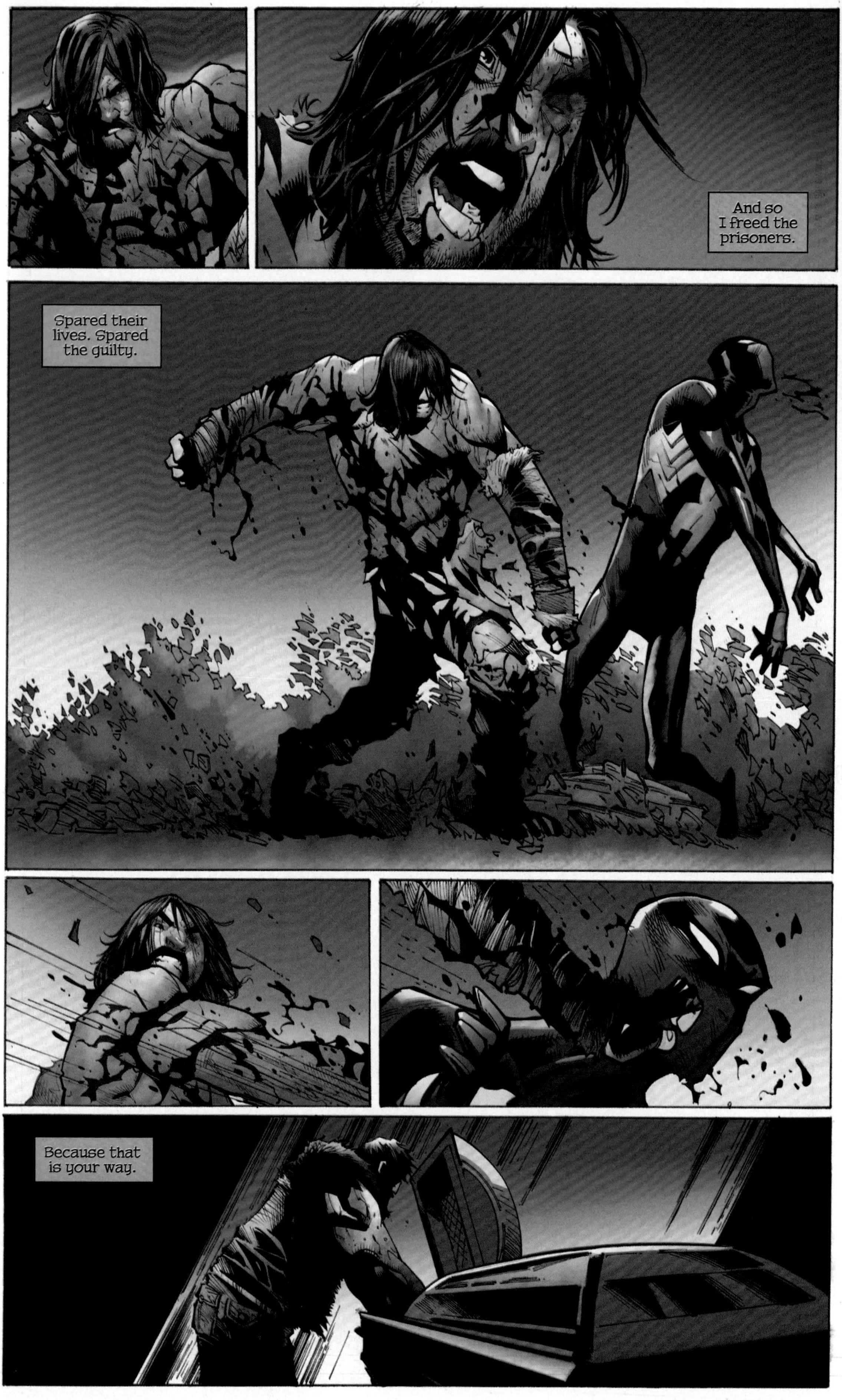
And so I freed the prisoners.
Spared their lives. Spared the guilty.
Because that is your way.

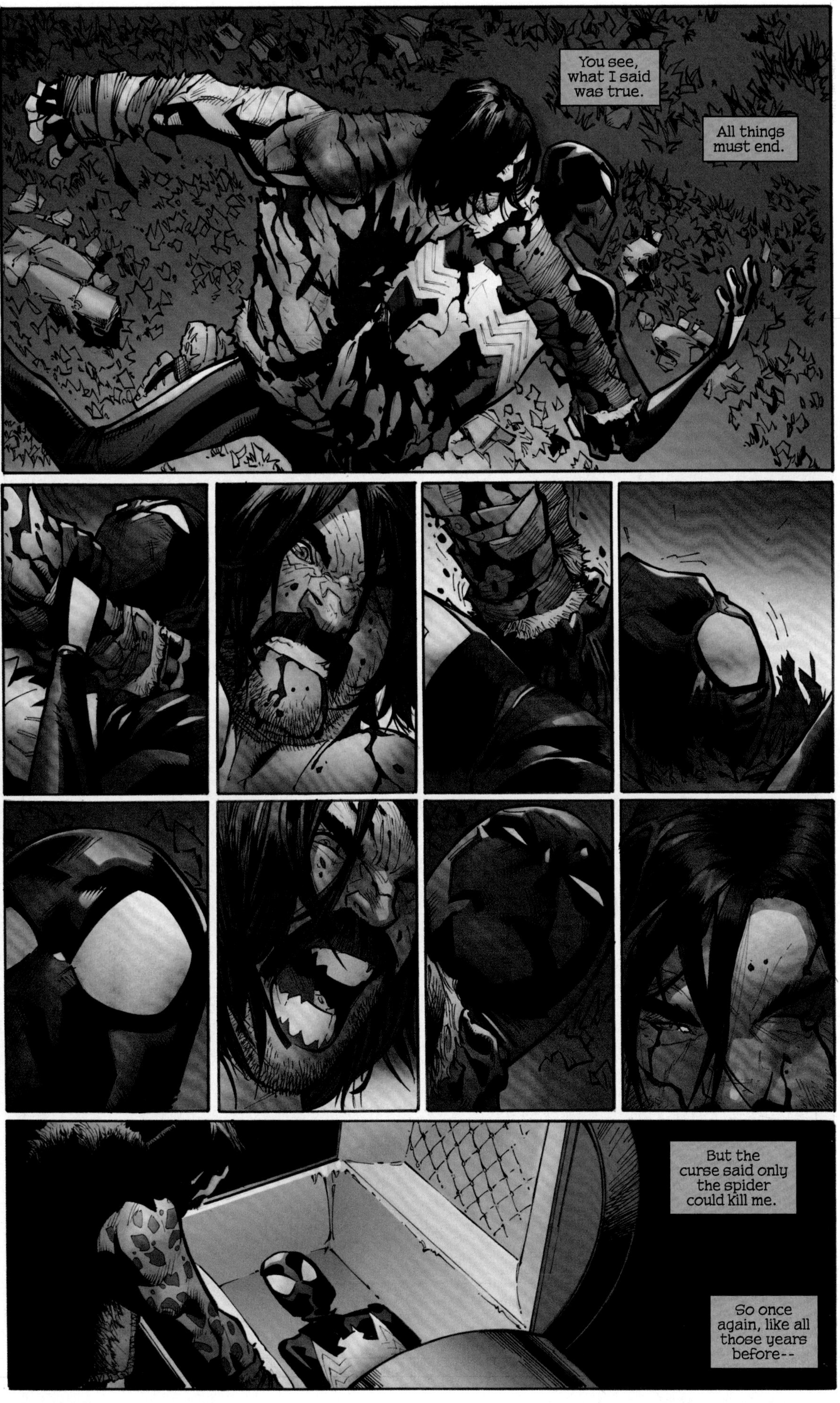

You see, what I said was true.
All things must end.
But the curse said only the spider could kill me.
So once again, like all those years before--

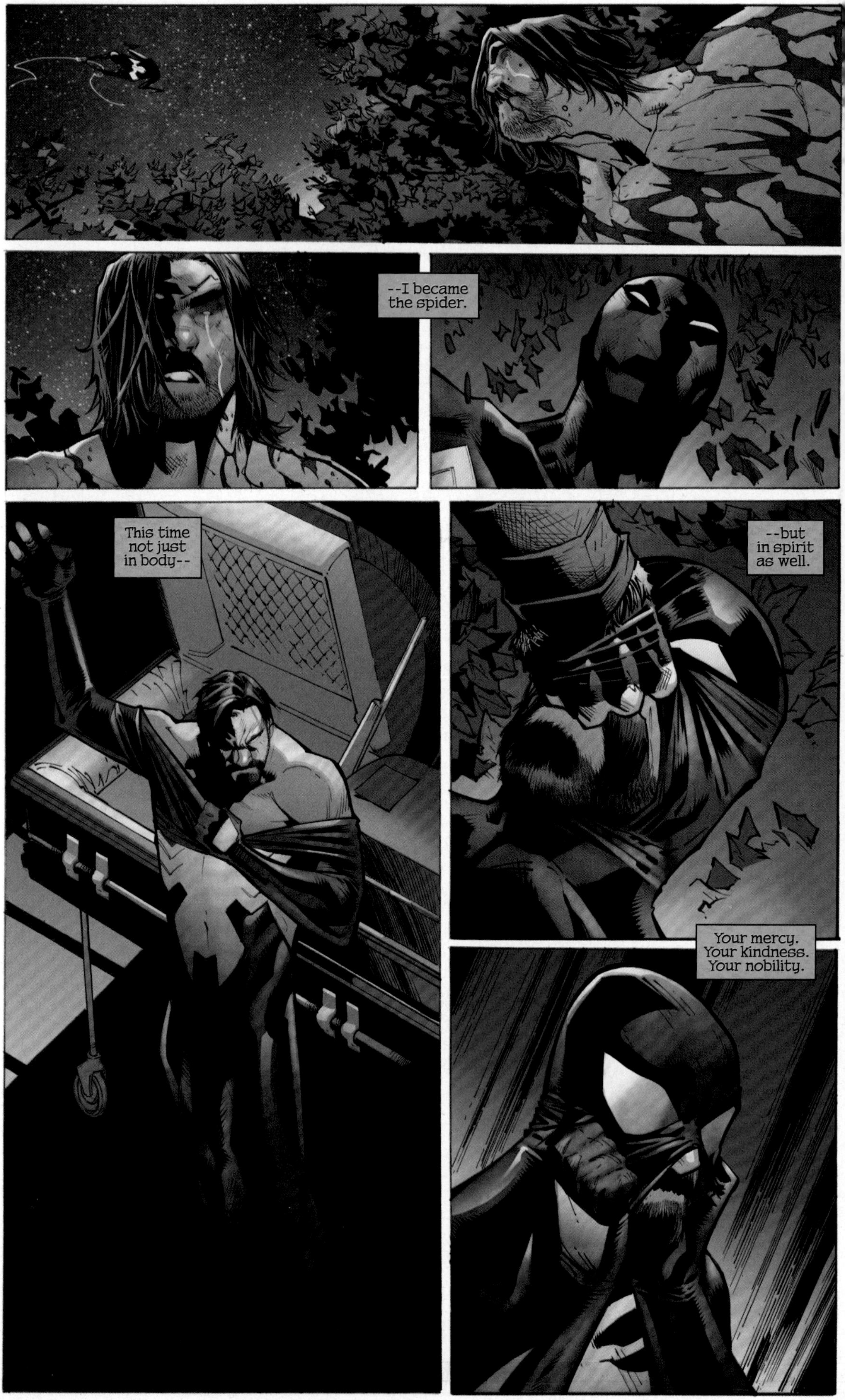
--I became the spider.
This time not just in body--
--but in spirit as well.
Your mercy. Your kindness. Your nobility.

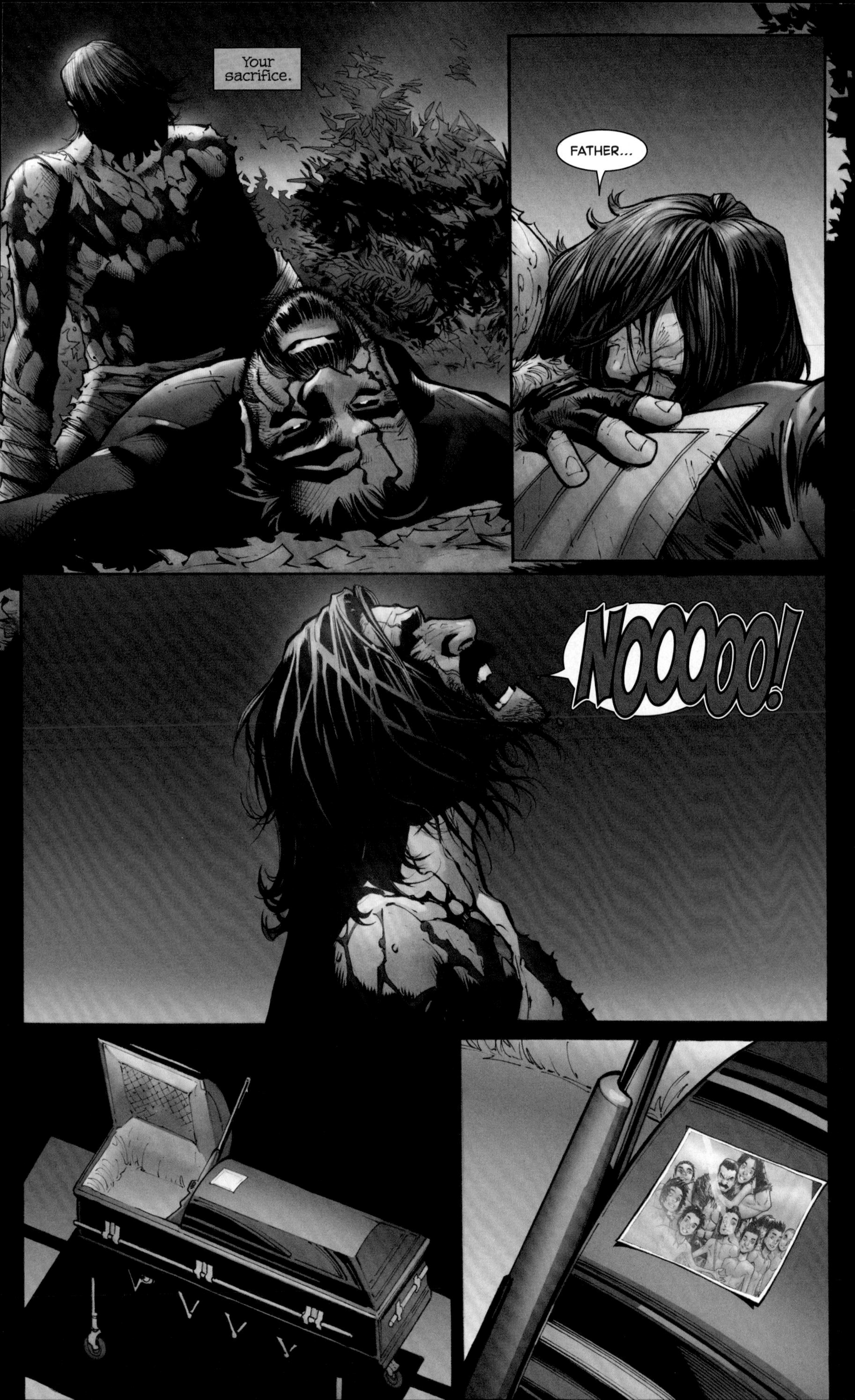
Your sacrifice.
FATHER...
NOOOOO!

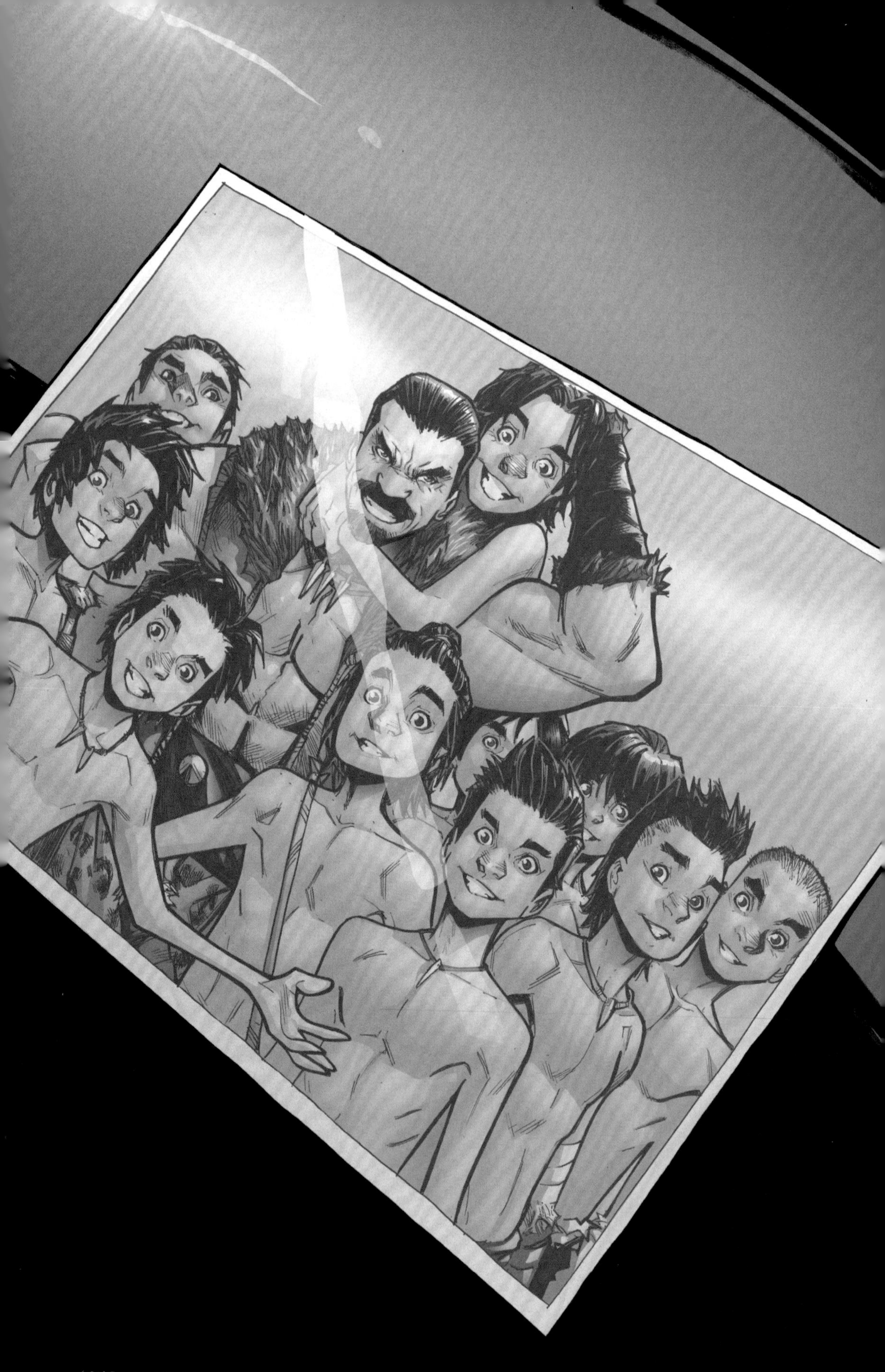

COMO SIEMPRE, FUE UN PLACER TRABAJAR CON USTEDES... NICK, KAT, MR. SPENCER, VICTOR Y EDGAR ... GRACIAS.

23

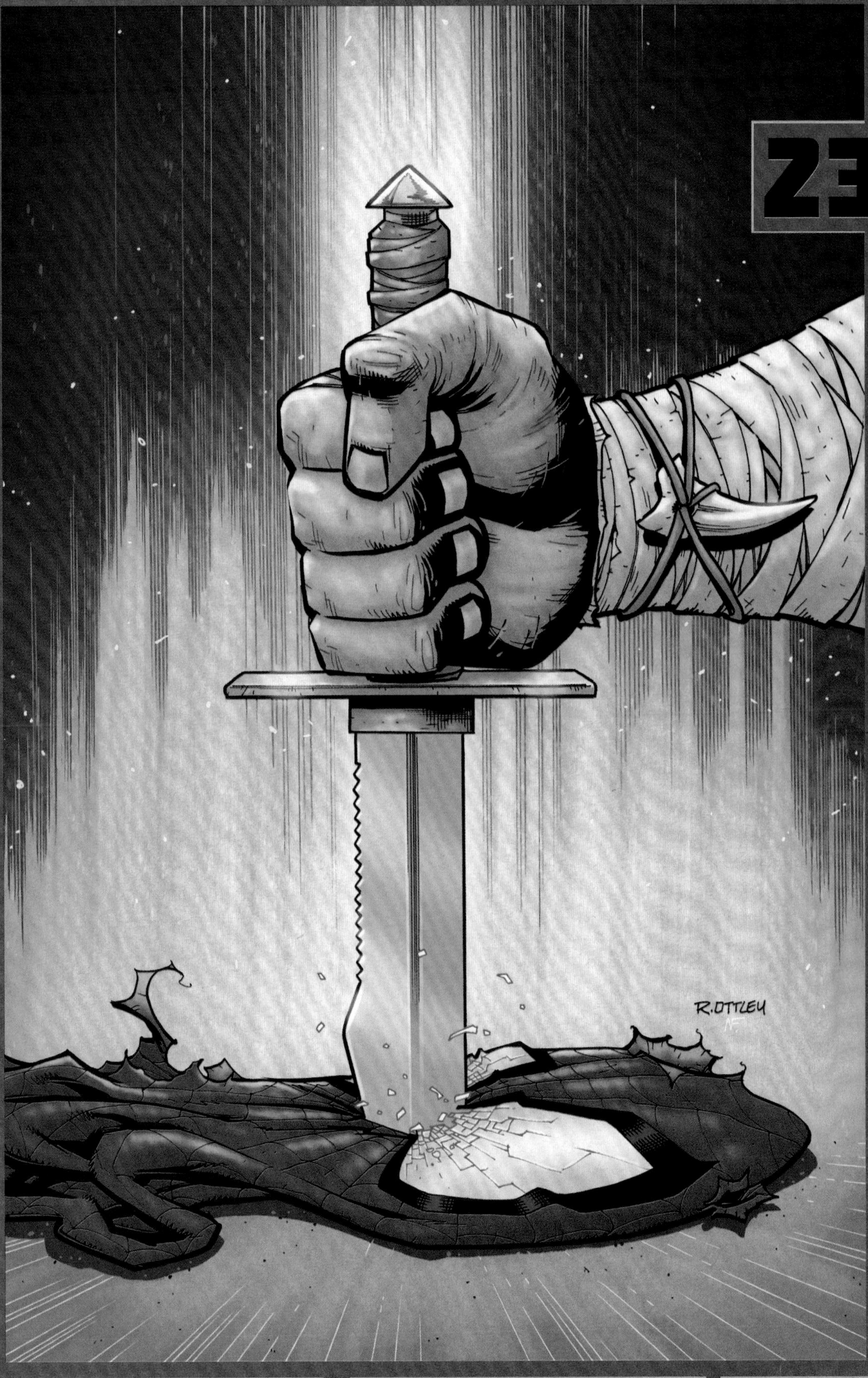
R.OTTLEY

HUNTED EPILOGUE

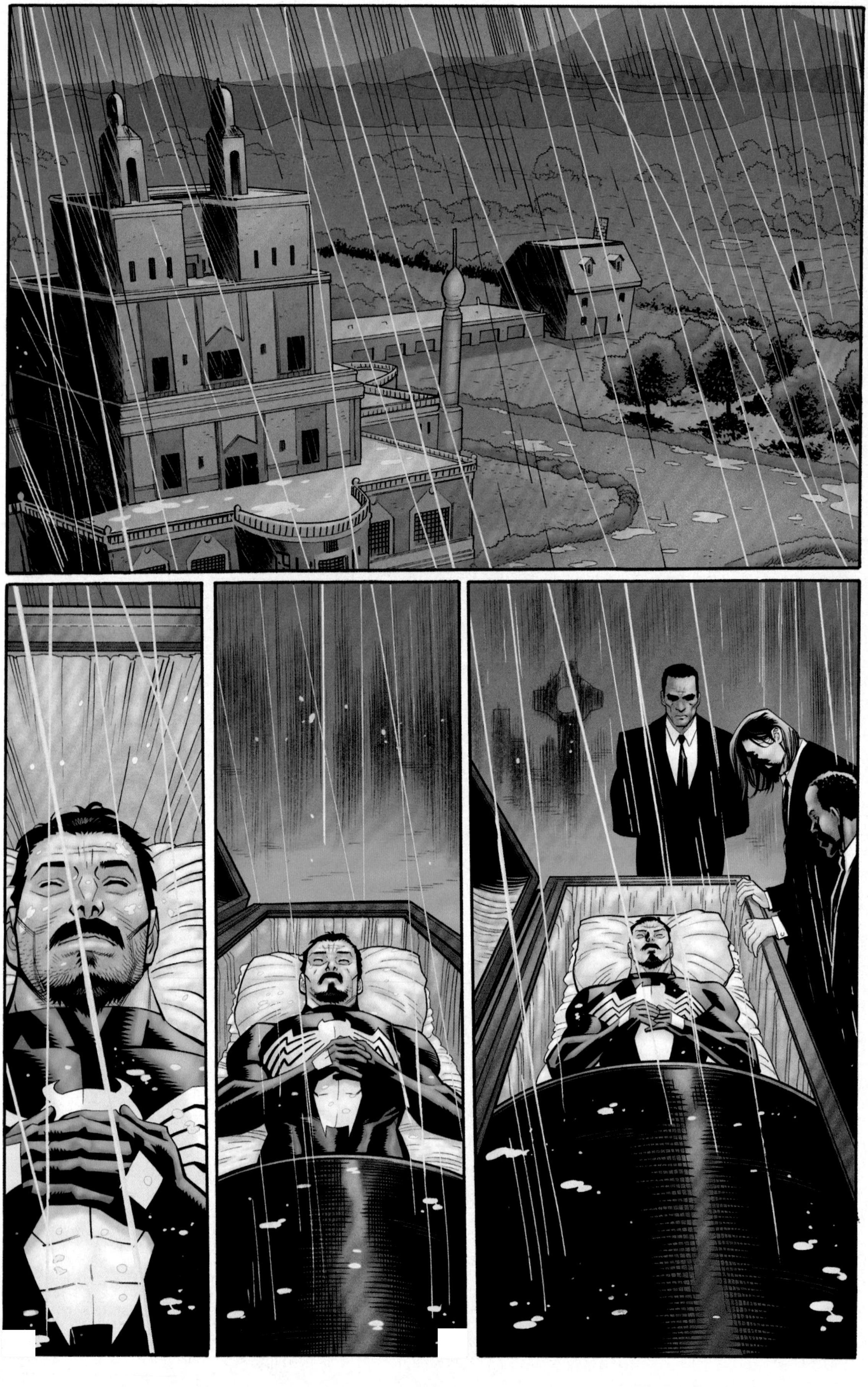

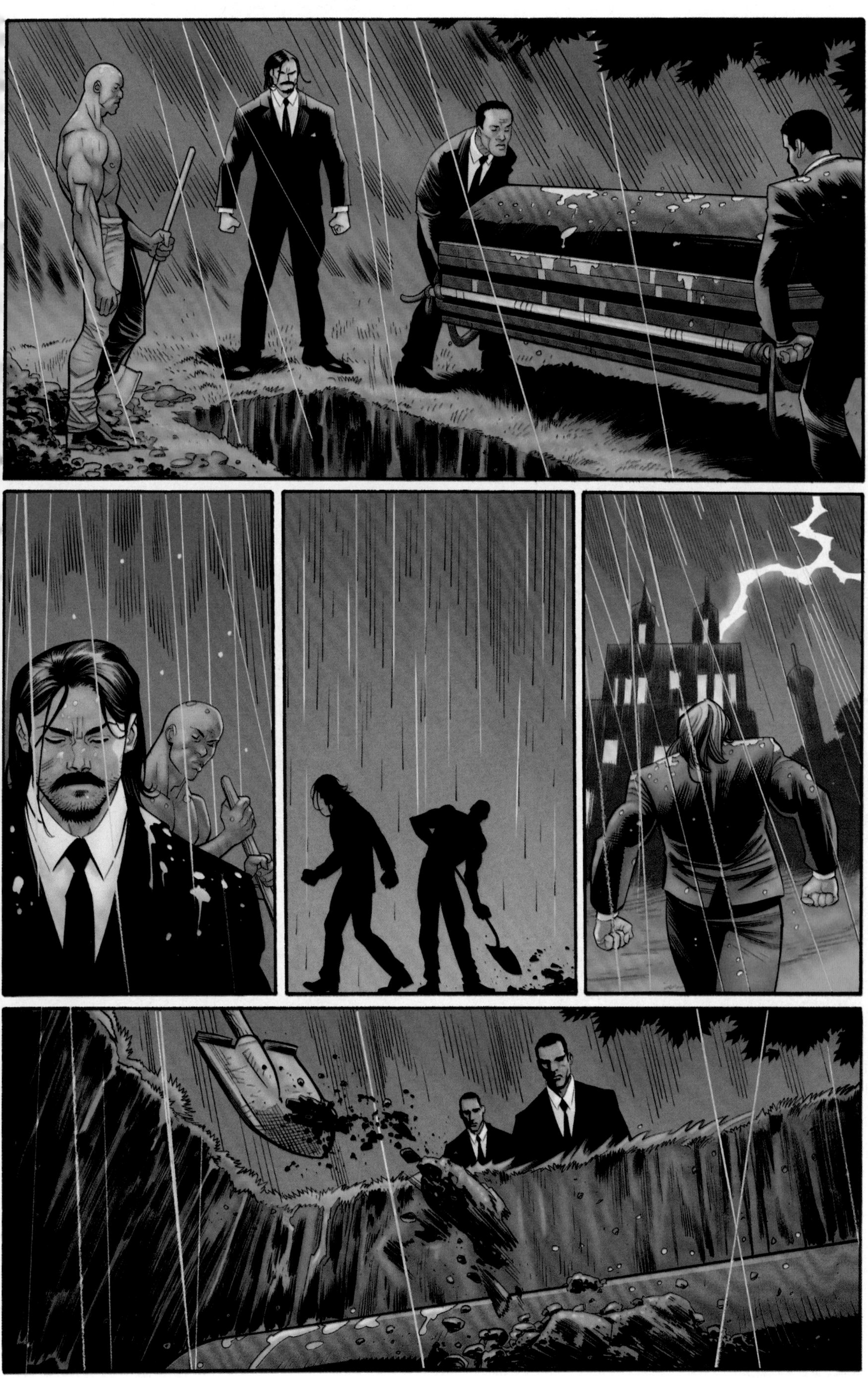

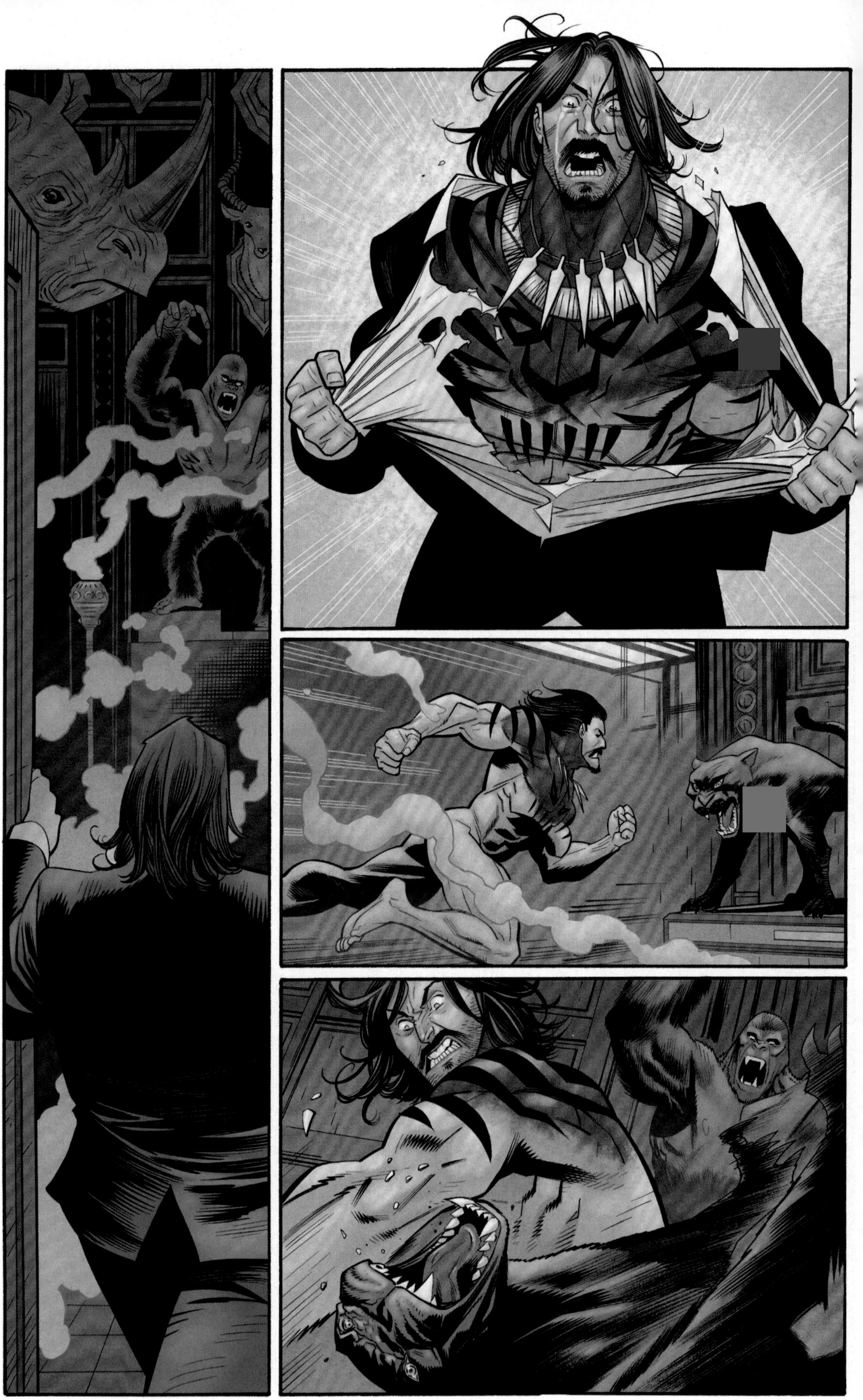

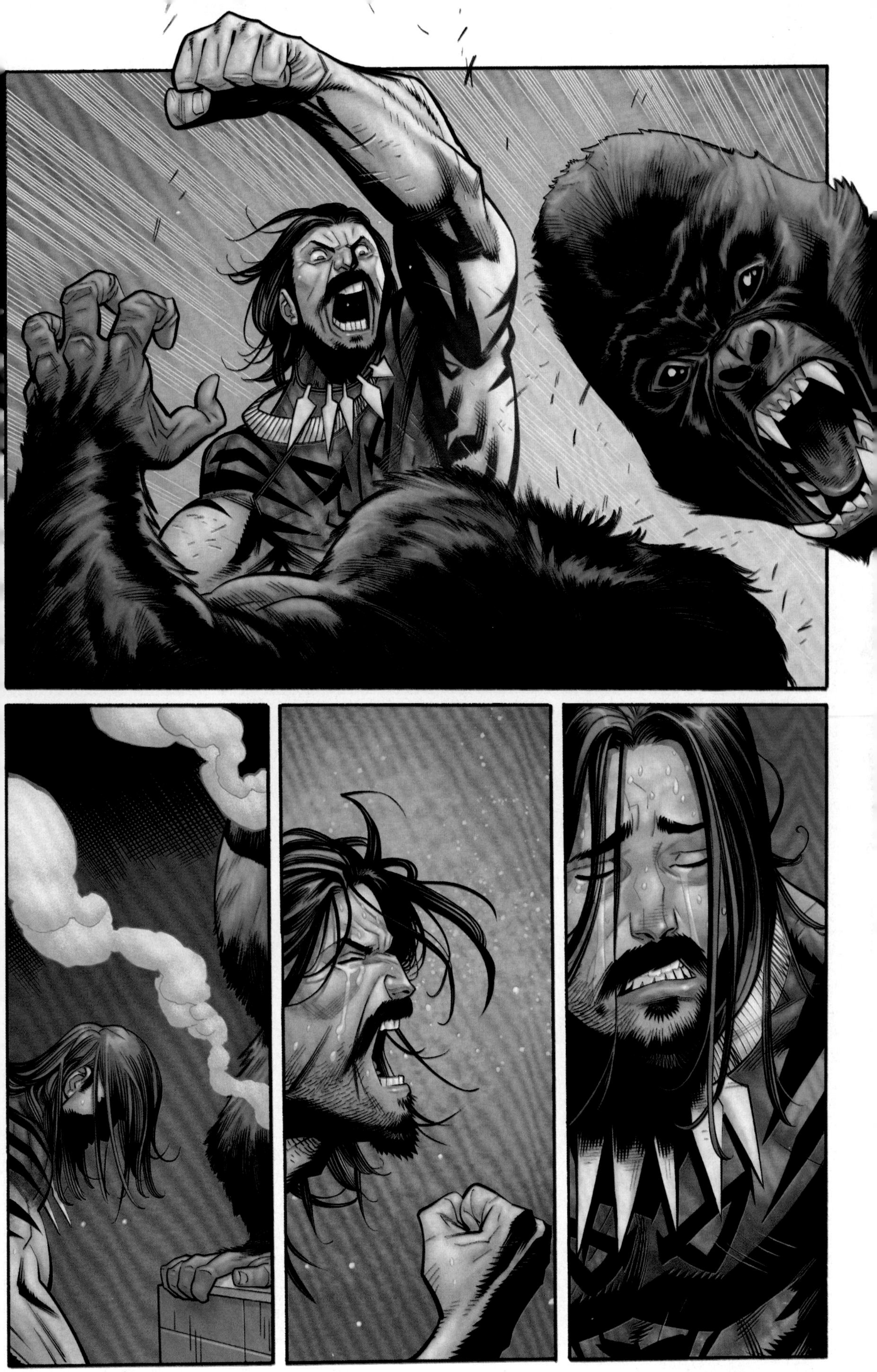

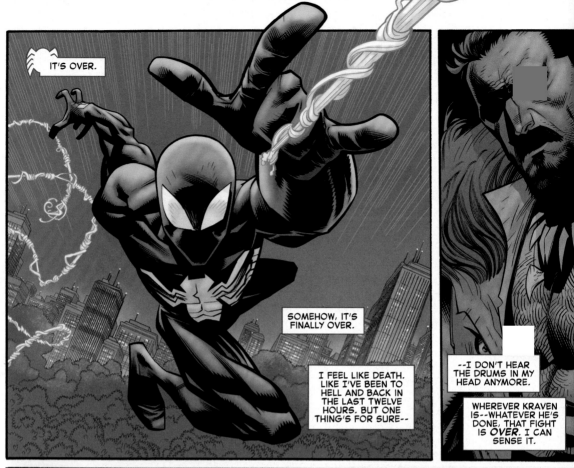

IT'S OVER.

SOMEHOW, IT'S FINALLY OVER.

I FEEL LIKE DEATH. LIKE I'VE BEEN TO HELL AND BACK IN THE LAST TWELVE HOURS. BUT ONE THING'S FOR SURE--

--I DON'T HEAR THE DRUMS IN MY HEAD ANYMORE.

WHEREVER KRAVEN IS--WHATEVER HE'S DONE, THAT FIGHT IS *OVER*. I CAN SENSE IT.

DOESN'T MEAN THE *WORST* IS ENTIRELY OVER, THOUGH.

THE FORCE FIELD HE PUT AROUND CENTRAL PARK HAS COME DOWN.

BUT THAT MEANS AN ARMY OF COSTUMED CRIMINALS HAS BEEN SET FREE IN THE MIDDLE OF MANHATTAN.

TOO MANY FOR ME, OR NEW YORK'S FINEST, TO HANDLE. LUCKILY--

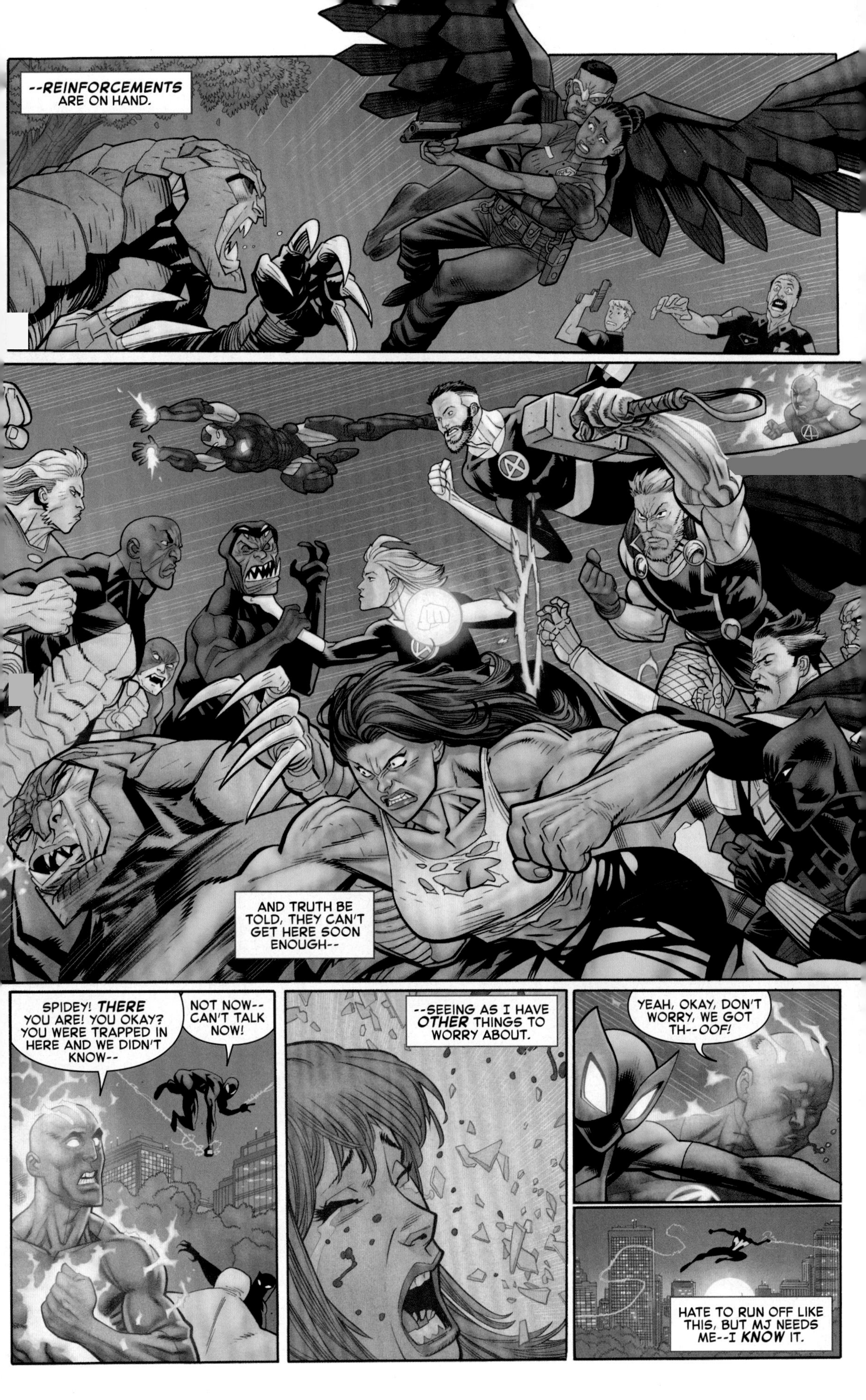
--REINFORCEMENTS ARE ON HAND.
AND TRUTH BE TOLD, THEY CAN'T GET HERE SOON ENOUGH--
SPIDEY! THERE YOU ARE! YOU OKAY? YOU WERE TRAPPED IN HERE AND WE DIDN'T KNOW--
NOT NOW-- CAN'T TALK NOW!
--SEEING AS I HAVE OTHER THINGS TO WORRY ABOUT.
YEAH, OKAY, DON'T WORRY, WE GOT TH--OOF!
HATE TO RUN OFF LIKE THIS, BUT MJ NEEDS ME--I KNOW IT.

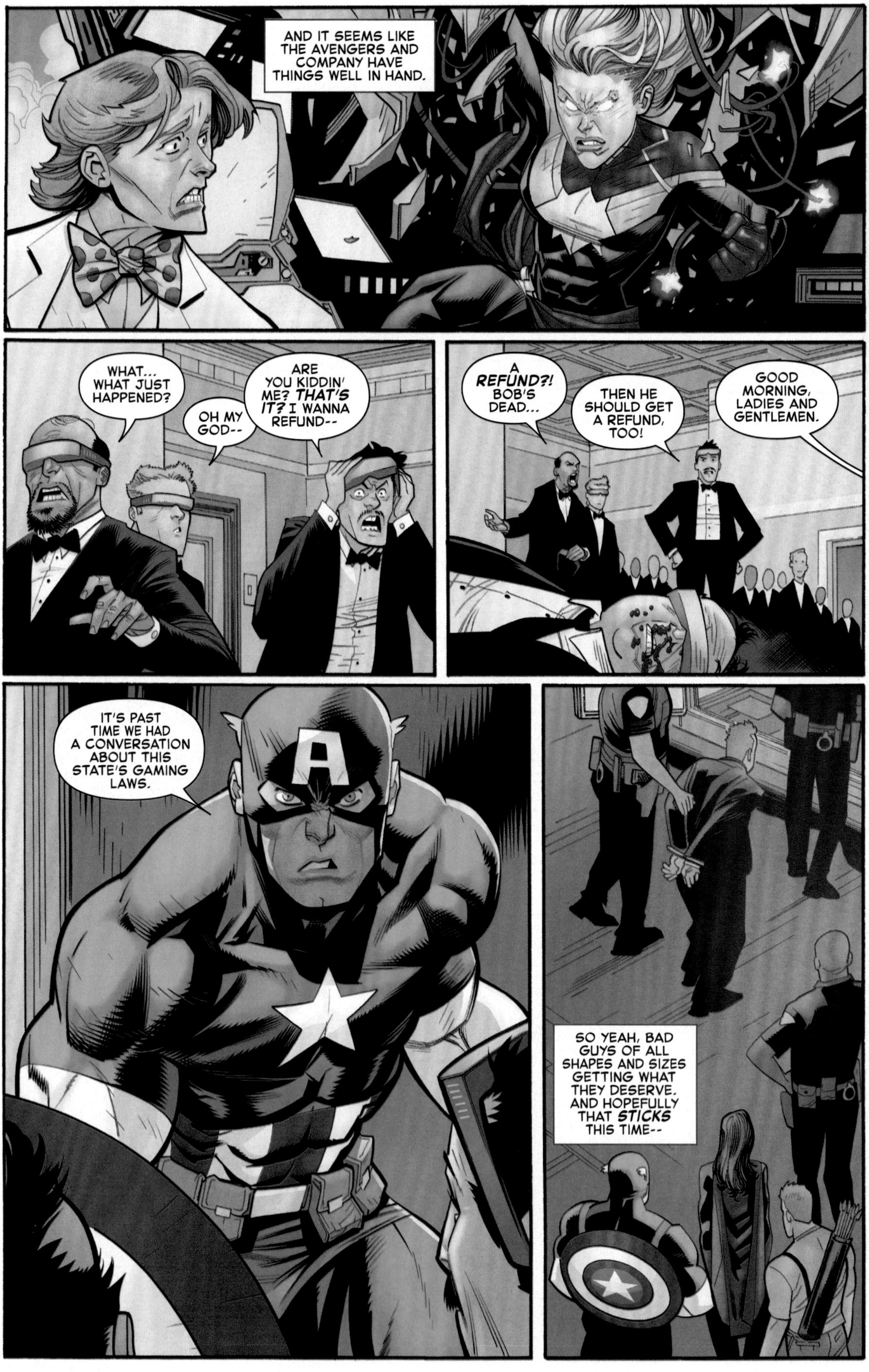
AND IT SEEMS LIKE THE AVENGERS AND COMPANY HAVE THINGS WELL IN HAND.
WHAT... WHAT JUST HAPPENED?
OH MY GOD--
ARE YOU KIDDIN' ME? THAT'S IT? I WANNA REFUND--
A REFUND?! BOB'S DEAD...
THEN HE SHOULD GET A REFUND, TOO!
GOOD MORNING, LADIES AND GENTLEMEN.
IT'S PAST TIME WE HAD A CONVERSATION ABOUT THIS STATE'S GAMING LAWS.
SO YEAH, BAD GUYS OF ALL SHAPES AND SIZES GETTING WHAT THEY DESERVE. AND HOPEFULLY THAT STICKS THIS TIME--

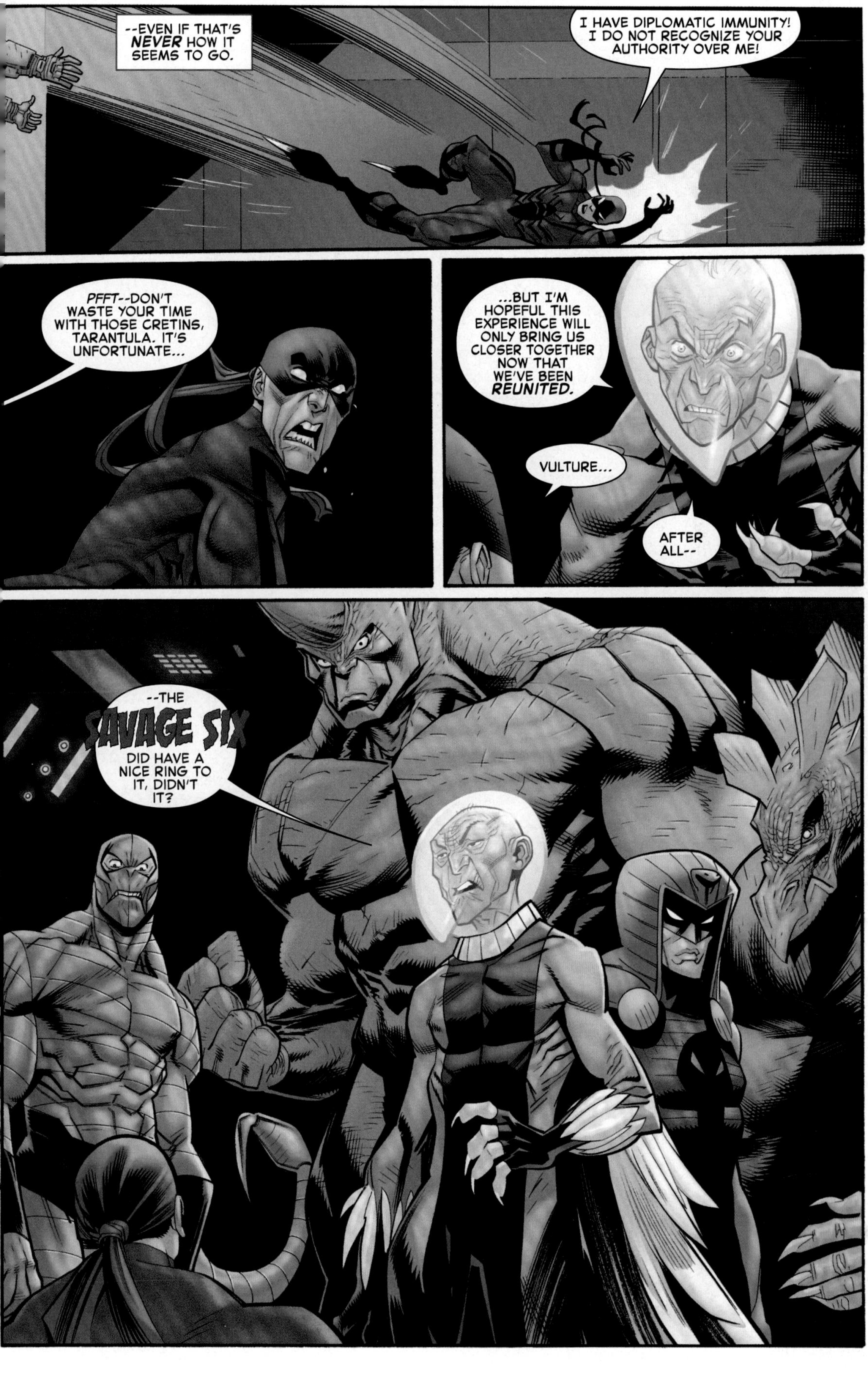
--EVEN IF THAT'S NEVER HOW IT SEEMS TO GO.
I HAVE DIPLOMATIC IMMUNITY! I DO NOT RECOGNIZE YOUR AUTHORITY OVER ME!
PFFT--DON'T WASTE YOUR TIME WITH THOSE CRETINS, TARANTULA. IT'S UNFORTUNATE...
...BUT I'M HOPEFUL THIS EXPERIENCE WILL ONLY BRING US CLOSER TOGETHER NOW THAT WE'VE BEEN REUNITED.
VULTURE...
AFTER ALL--
--THE SAVAGE SIX DID HAVE A NICE RING TO IT, DIDN'T IT?

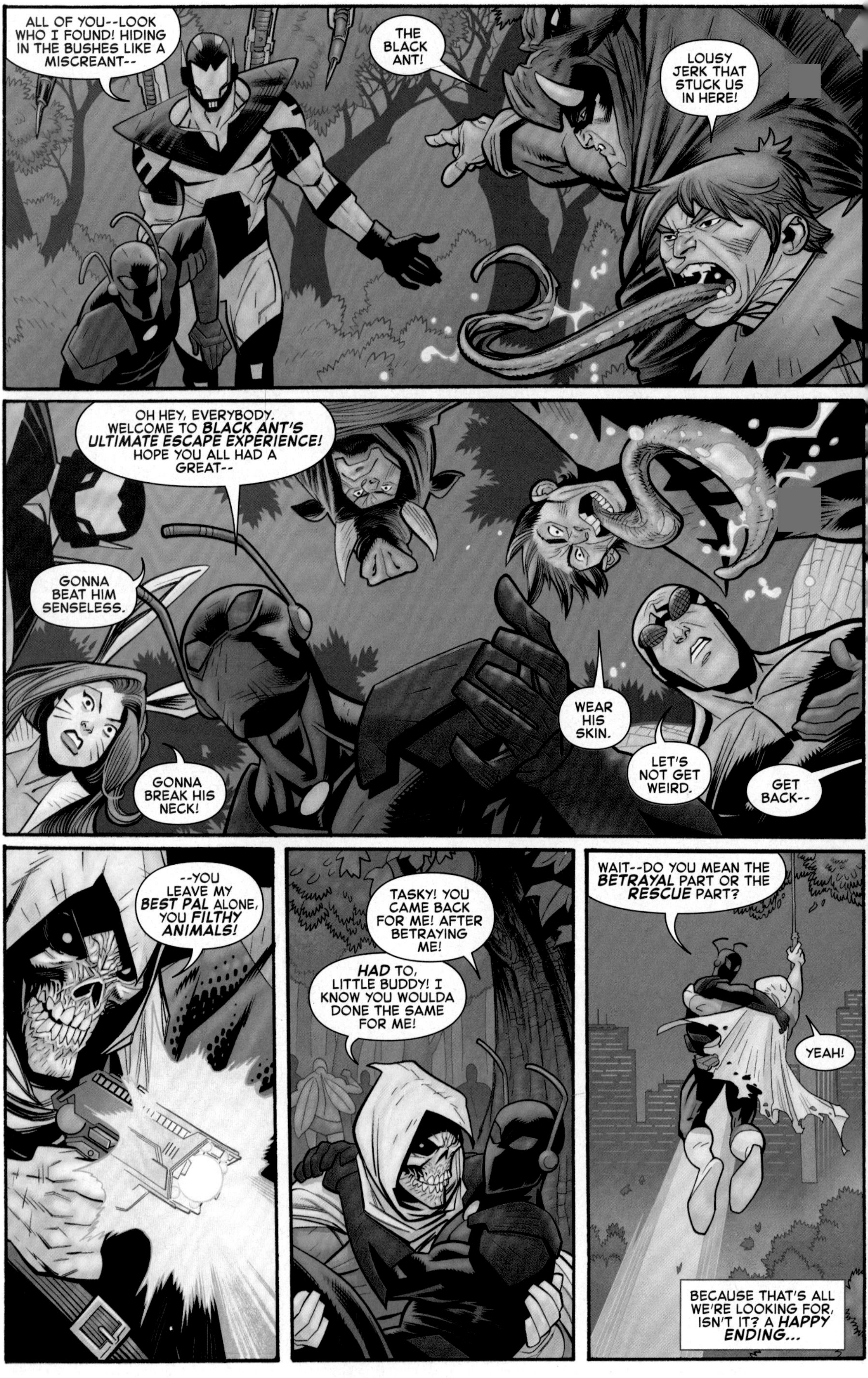
ALL OF YOU--LOOK WHO I FOUND! HIDING IN THE BUSHES LIKE A MISCREANT--
THE BLACK ANT!
LOUSY JERK THAT STUCK US IN HERE!
OH HEY, EVERYBODY. WELCOME TO BLACK ANT'S ULTIMATE ESCAPE EXPERIENCE! HOPE YOU ALL HAD A GREAT--
GONNA BEAT HIM SENSELESS.
GONNA BREAK HIS NECK!
WEAR HIS SKIN.
LET'S NOT GET WEIRD.
GET BACK--
--YOU LEAVE MY BEST PAL ALONE, YOU FILTHY ANIMALS!
TASKY! YOU CAME BACK FOR ME! AFTER BETRAYING ME!
HAD TO, LITTLE BUDDY! I KNOW YOU WOULDA DONE THE SAME FOR ME!
WAIT--DO YOU MEAN THE BETRAYAL PART OR THE RESCUE PART?
YEAH!
BECAUSE THAT'S ALL WE'RE LOOKING FOR, ISN'T IT? A HAPPY ENDING...

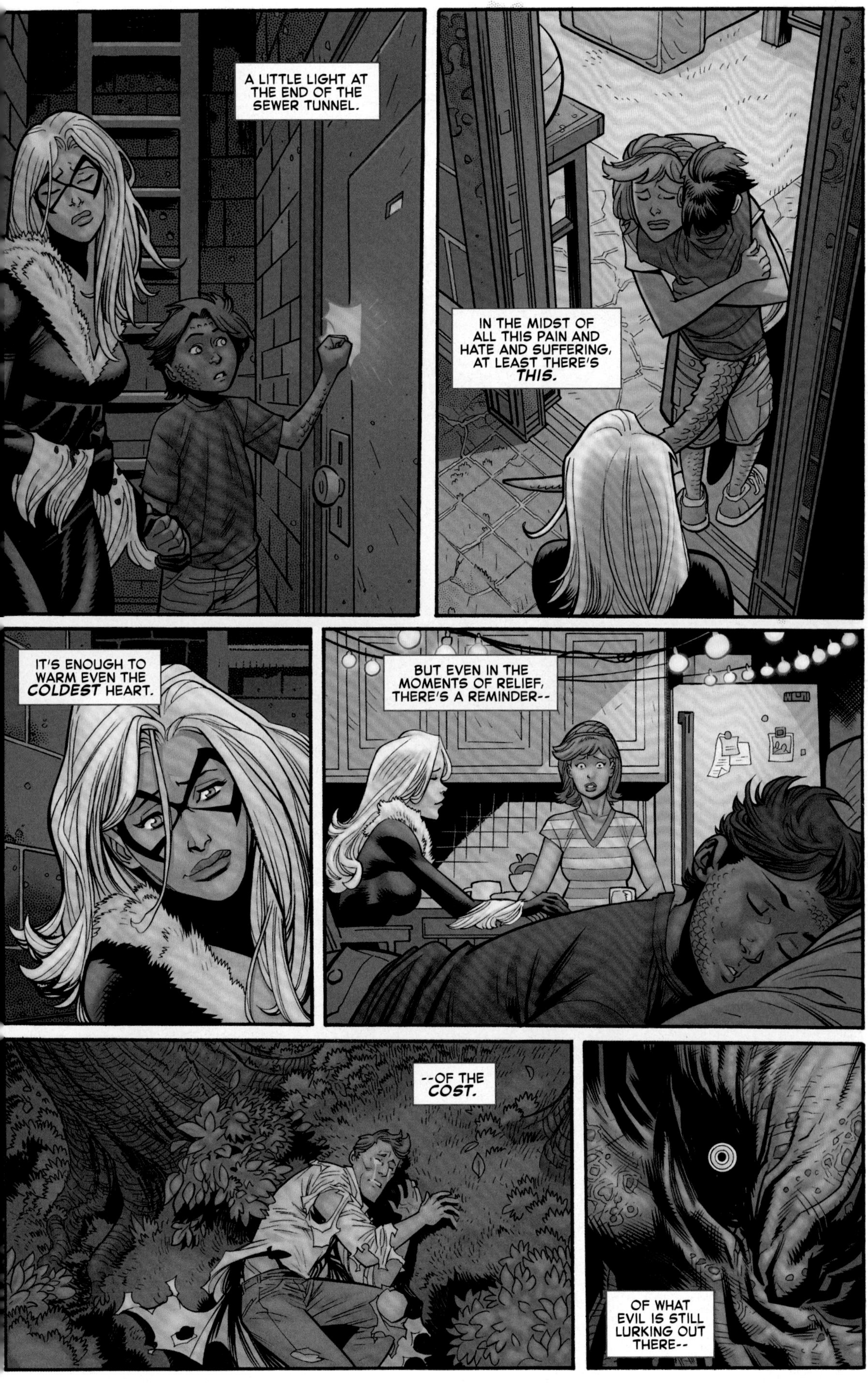
A LITTLE LIGHT AT THE END OF THE SEWER TUNNEL.
IN THE MIDST OF ALL THIS PAIN AND HATE AND SUFFERING, AT LEAST THERE'S *THIS.*
IT'S ENOUGH TO WARM EVEN THE *COLDEST* HEART.
BUT EVEN IN THE MOMENTS OF RELIEF, THERE'S A REMINDER--
--OF THE *COST.*
OF WHAT EVIL IS STILL LURKING OUT THERE--

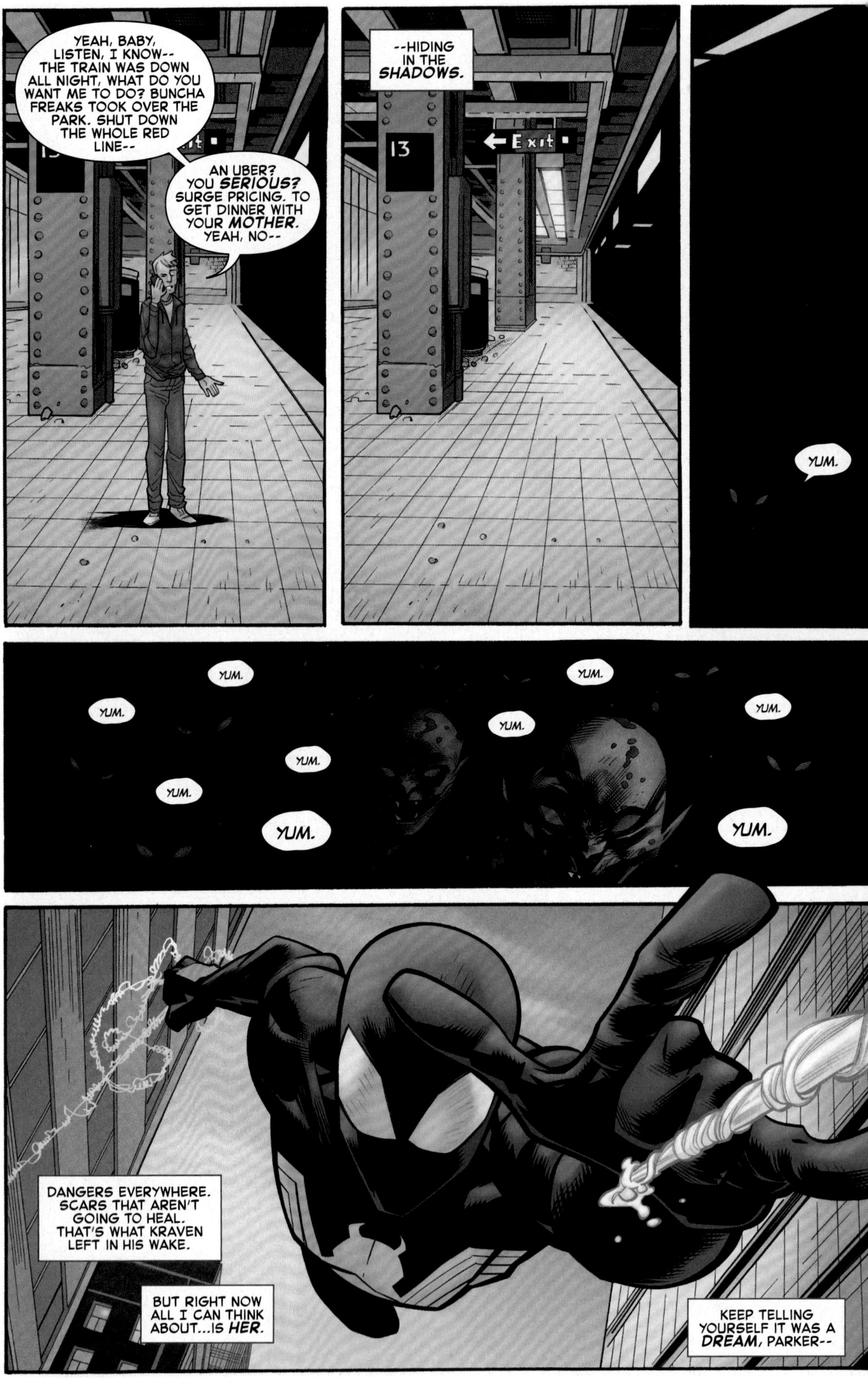
YEAH, BABY, LISTEN, I KNOW-- THE TRAIN WAS DOWN ALL NIGHT, WHAT DO YOU WANT ME TO DO? BUNCHA FREAKS TOOK OVER THE PARK. SHUT DOWN THE WHOLE RED LINE--
AN UBER? YOU SERIOUS? SURGE PRICING. TO GET DINNER WITH YOUR MOTHER. YEAH, NO--
--HIDING IN THE SHADOWS.
13
← Exit
YUM.
YUM.
YUM.
YUM.
YUM.
YUM.
YUM.
YUM.
YUM.
YUM.
DANGERS EVERYWHERE. SCARS THAT AREN'T GOING TO HEAL. THAT'S WHAT KRAVEN LEFT IN HIS WAKE.
BUT RIGHT NOW ALL I CAN THINK ABOUT...IS HER.
KEEP TELLING YOURSELF IT WAS A DREAM, PARKER--

JUST A DRUG-INDUCED HALLUCINATION MEANT TO TIP YOU OVER THE EDGE AND MAKE YOU A *KILLER.*

BUT IT FELT-- IT FELT--

REAL. AND NOW THAT I'M HERE, I KNOW--

--IT WASN'T ALL A LIE.

MJ'S APARTMENT-- THE WINDOW! IT'S JUST LIKE--

OH GOD.

I'M STILL DREAMING, AREN'T I?

I HAVE TO BE.

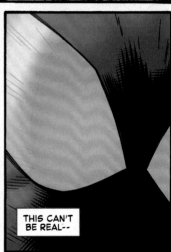

THIS CAN'T BE REAL--

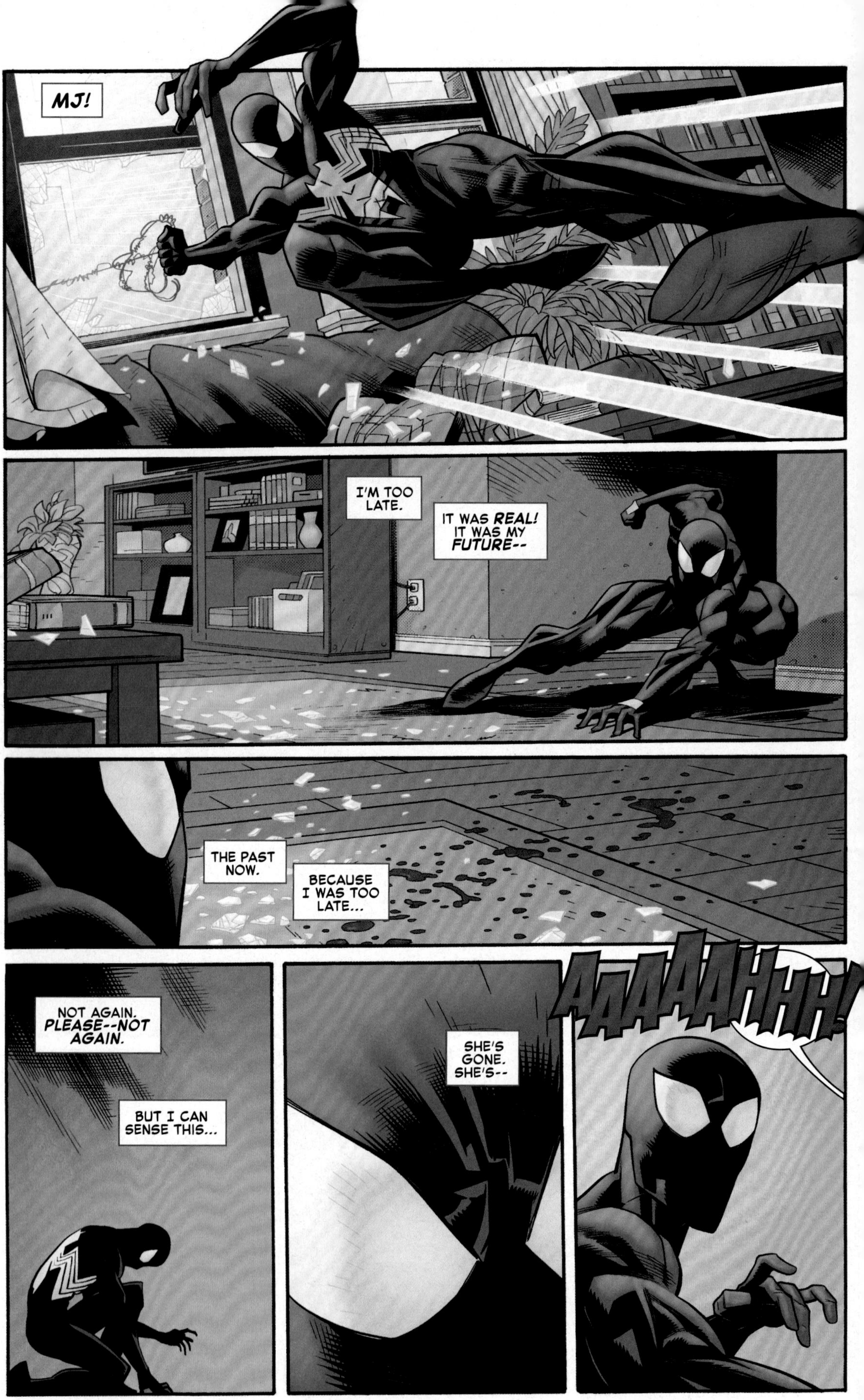
MJ!
I'M TOO LATE.
IT WAS REAL! IT WAS MY FUTURE--
THE PAST NOW.
BECAUSE I WAS TOO LATE...
NOT AGAIN. PLEASE--NOT AGAIN.
BUT I CAN SENSE THIS...
SHE'S GONE. SHE'S--
AAAAAAHHHH!

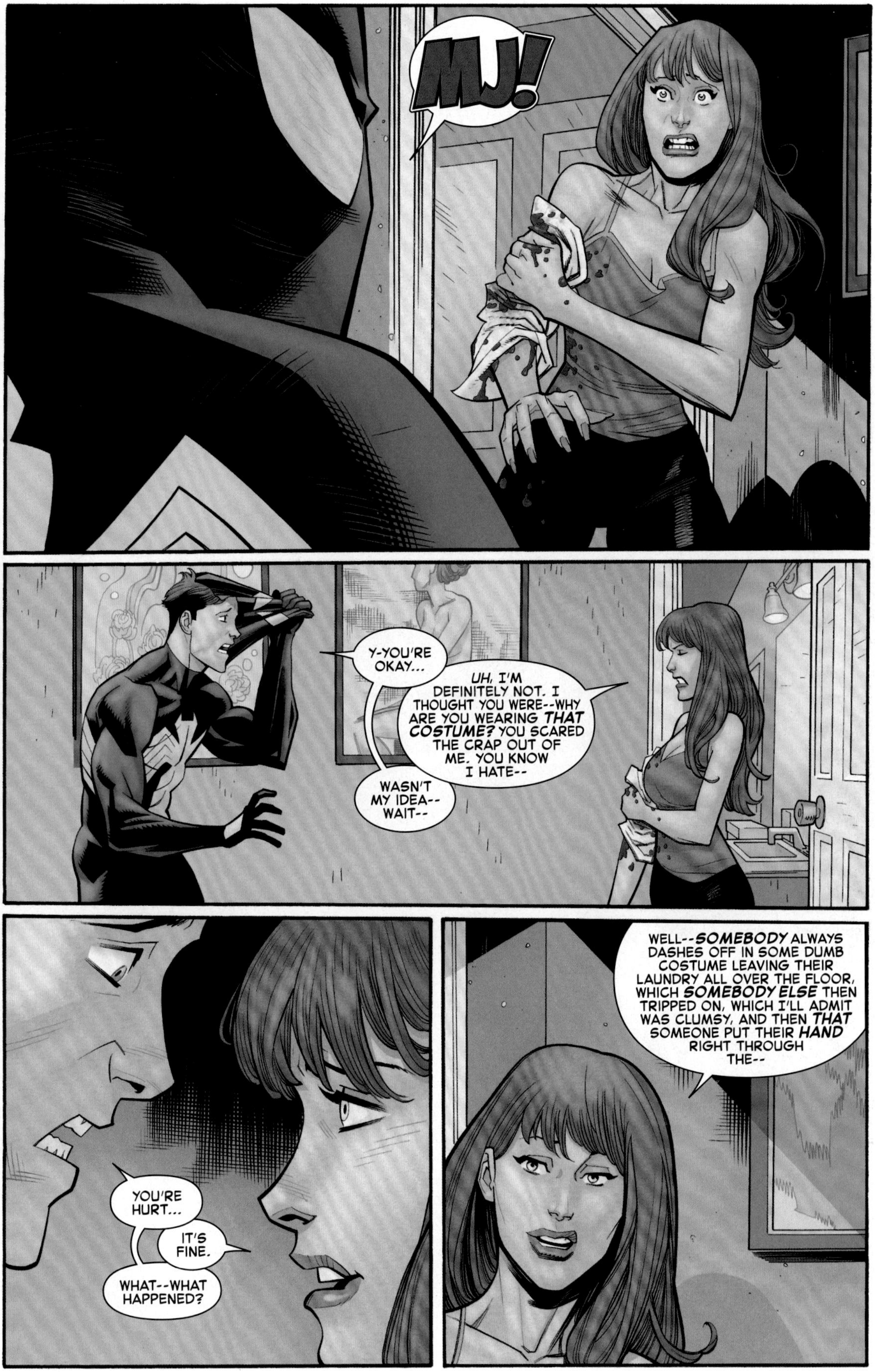
MJ!
Y-YOU'RE OKAY...
UH, I'M DEFINITELY NOT. I THOUGHT YOU WERE--WHY ARE YOU WEARING THAT COSTUME? YOU SCARED THE CRAP OUT OF ME. YOU KNOW I HATE--
WASN'T MY IDEA-- WAIT--
YOU'RE HURT...
IT'S FINE.
WHAT--WHAT HAPPENED?
WELL--SOMEBODY ALWAYS DASHES OFF IN SOME DUMB COSTUME LEAVING THEIR LAUNDRY ALL OVER THE FLOOR, WHICH SOMEBODY ELSE THEN TRIPPED ON, WHICH I'LL ADMIT WAS CLUMSY, AND THEN THAT SOMEONE PUT THEIR HAND RIGHT THROUGH THE--

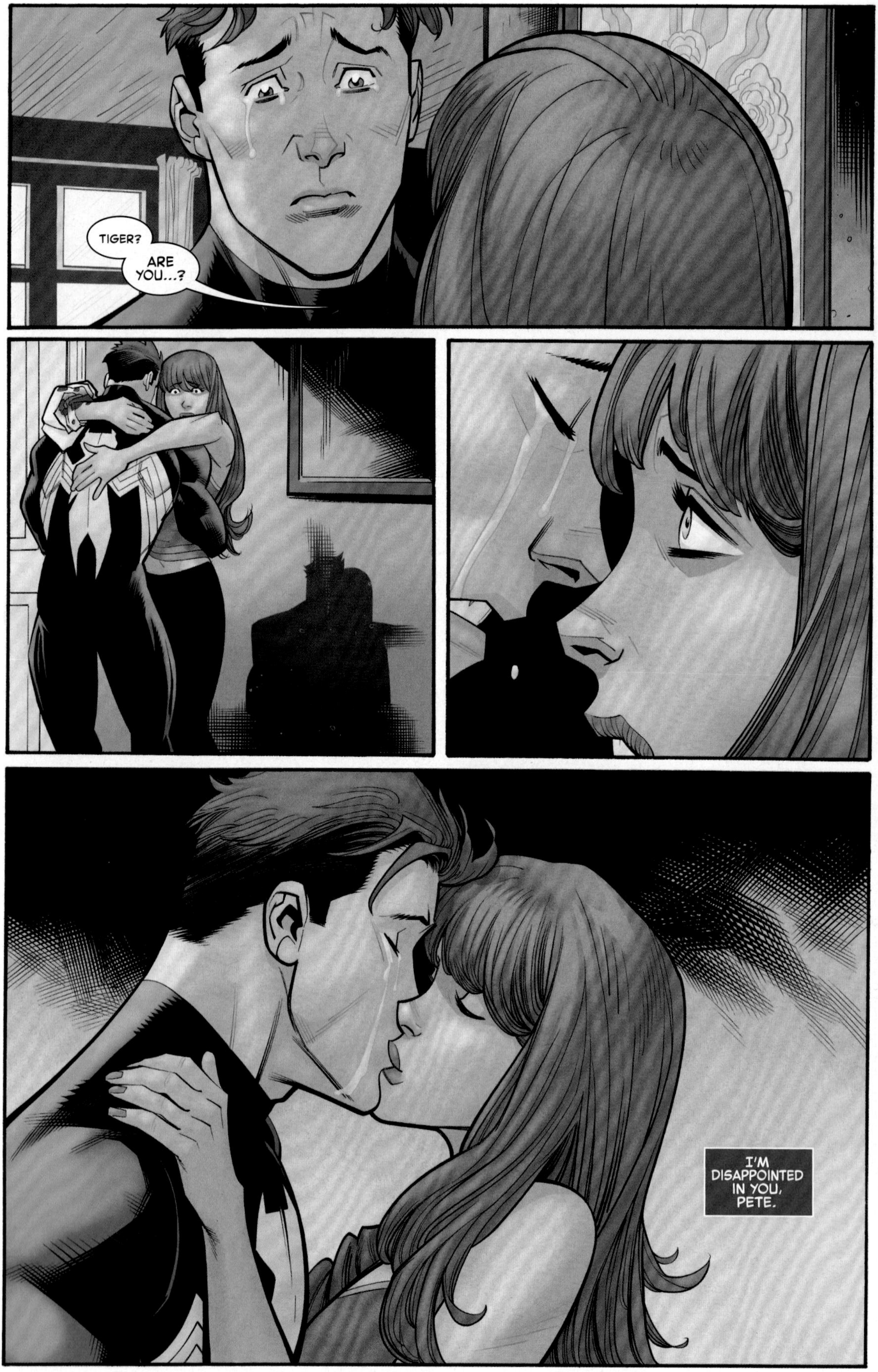
TIGER?
ARE YOU...?
I'M DISAPPOINTED IN YOU, PETE.

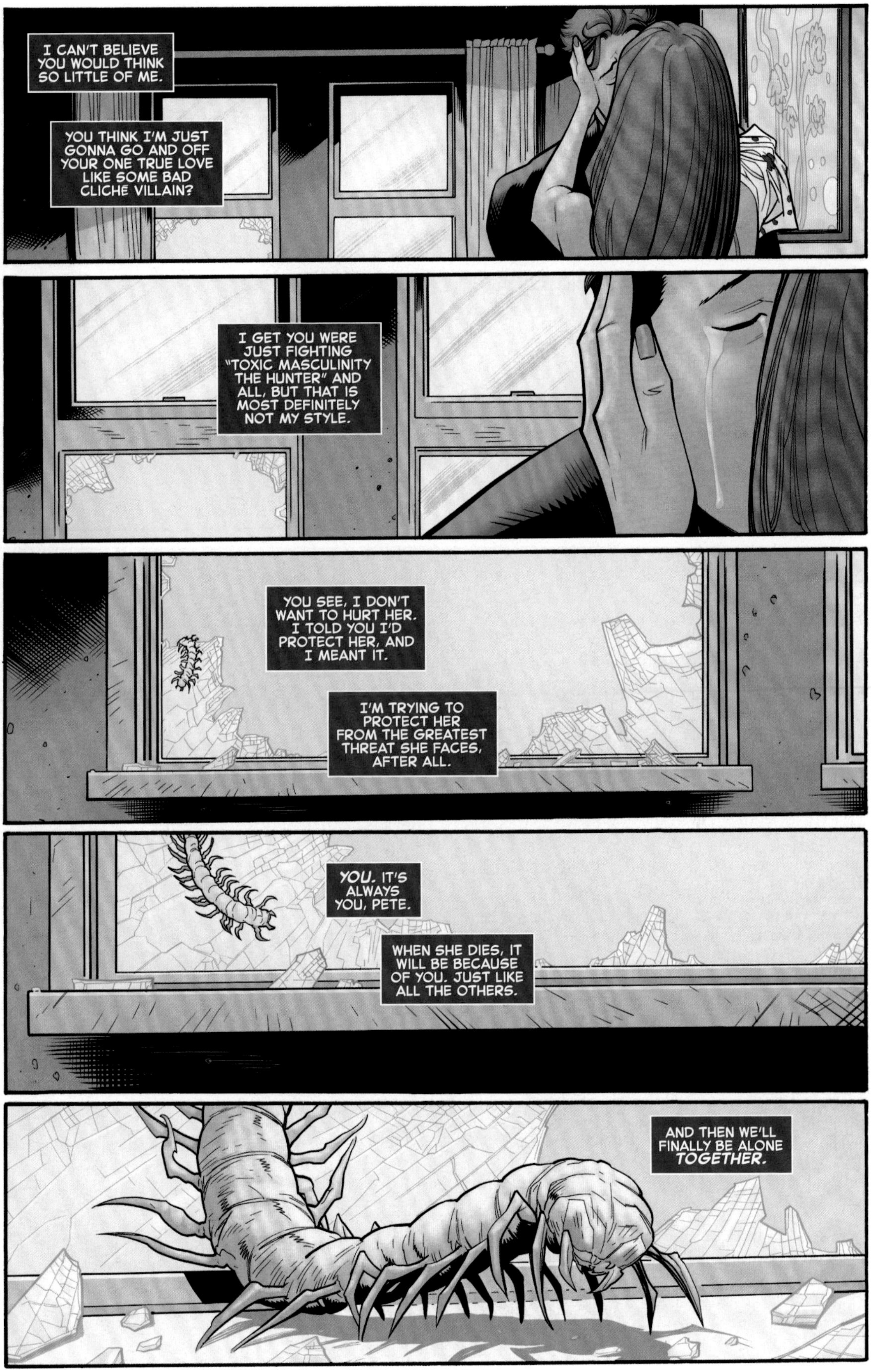

I CAN'T BELIEVE YOU WOULD THINK SO LITTLE OF ME.
YOU THINK I'M JUST GONNA GO AND OFF YOUR ONE TRUE LOVE LIKE SOME BAD CLICHE VILLAIN?
I GET YOU WERE JUST FIGHTING "TOXIC MASCULINITY THE HUNTER" AND ALL, BUT THAT IS MOST DEFINITELY NOT MY STYLE.
YOU SEE, I DON'T WANT TO HURT HER. I TOLD YOU I'D PROTECT HER, AND I MEANT IT.
I'M TRYING TO PROTECT HER FROM THE GREATEST THREAT SHE FACES, AFTER ALL.
YOU. IT'S ALWAYS YOU, PETE.
WHEN SHE DIES, IT WILL BE BECAUSE OF YOU. JUST LIKE ALL THE OTHERS.
AND THEN WE'LL FINALLY BE ALONE *TOGETHER.*

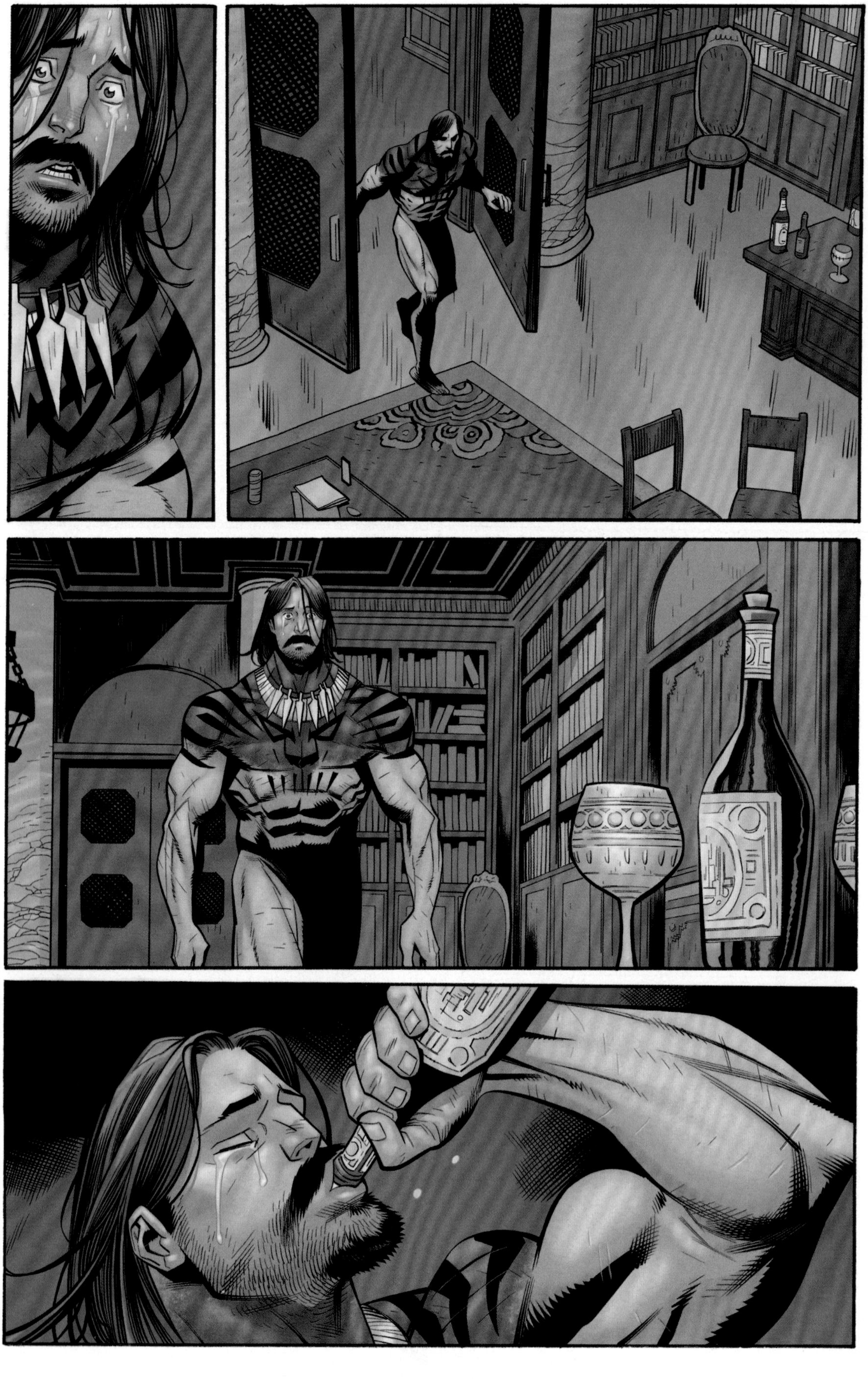

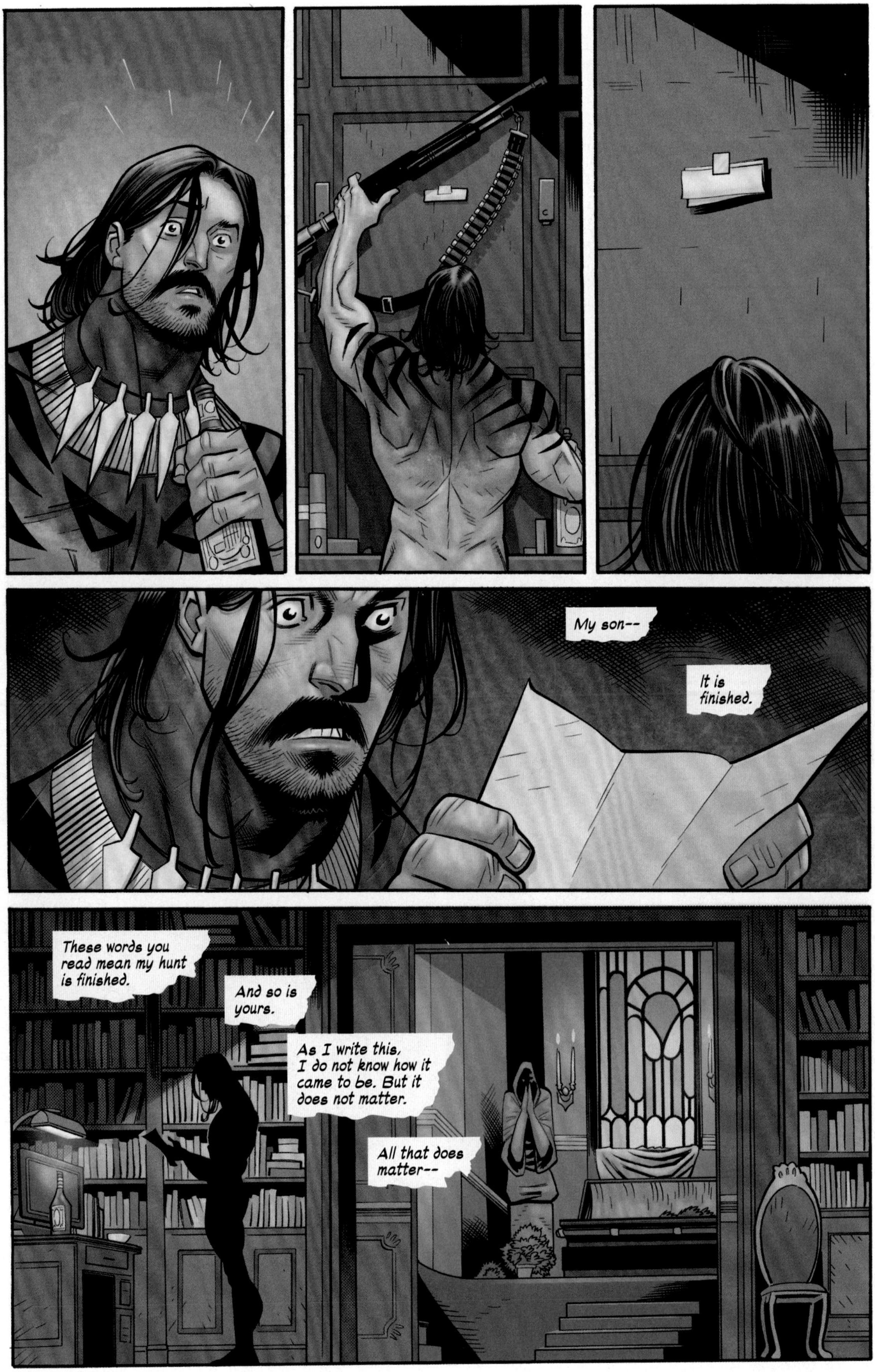

My son--
It is finished.
These words you read mean my hunt is finished.
And so is yours.
As I write this, I do not know how it came to be. But it does not matter.
All that does matter--

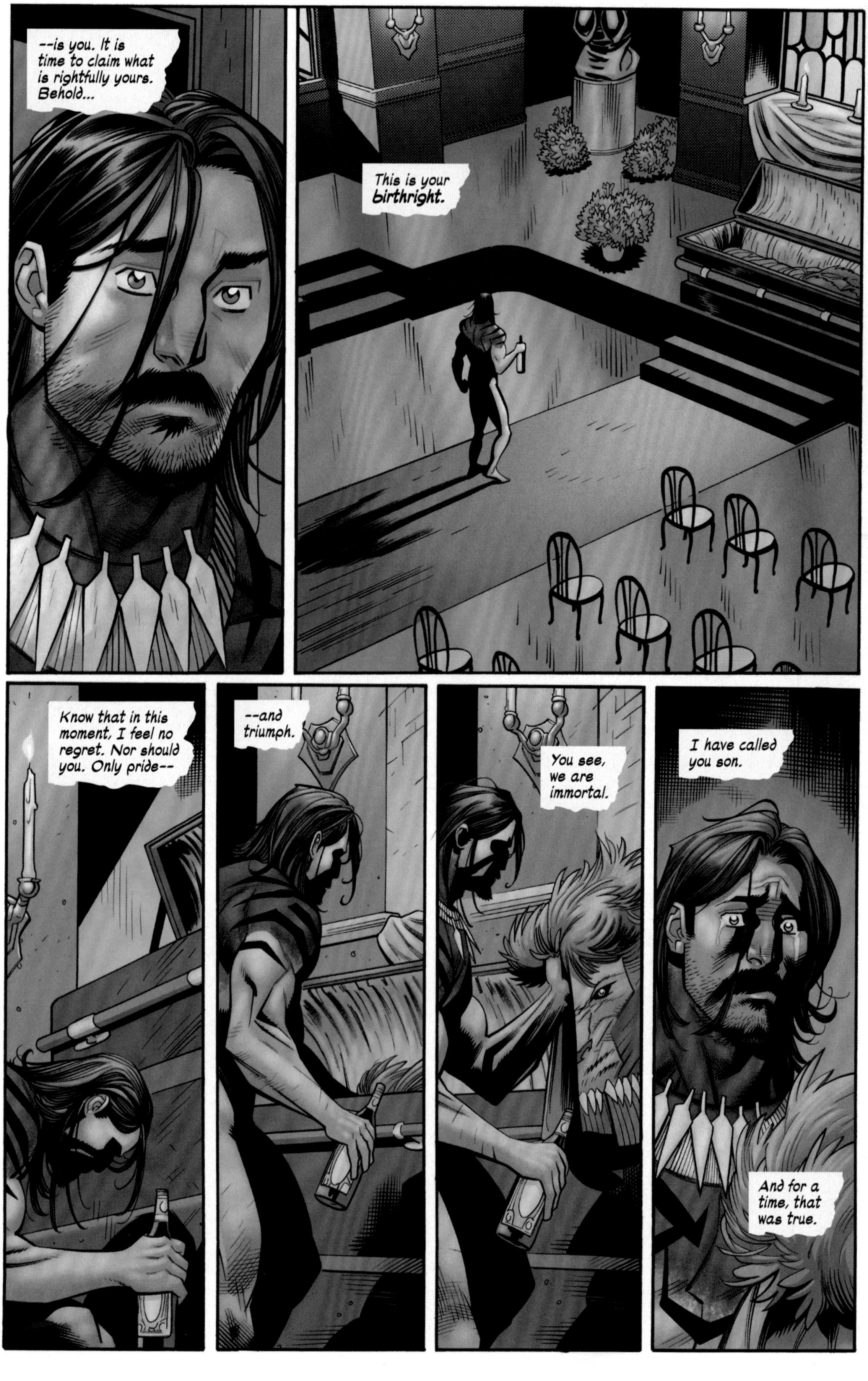
--is you. It is time to claim what is rightfully yours. Behold...
This is your birthright.
Know that in this moment, I feel no regret. Nor should you. Only pride--
--and triumph.
You see, we are immortal.
I have called you son.
And for a time, that was true.

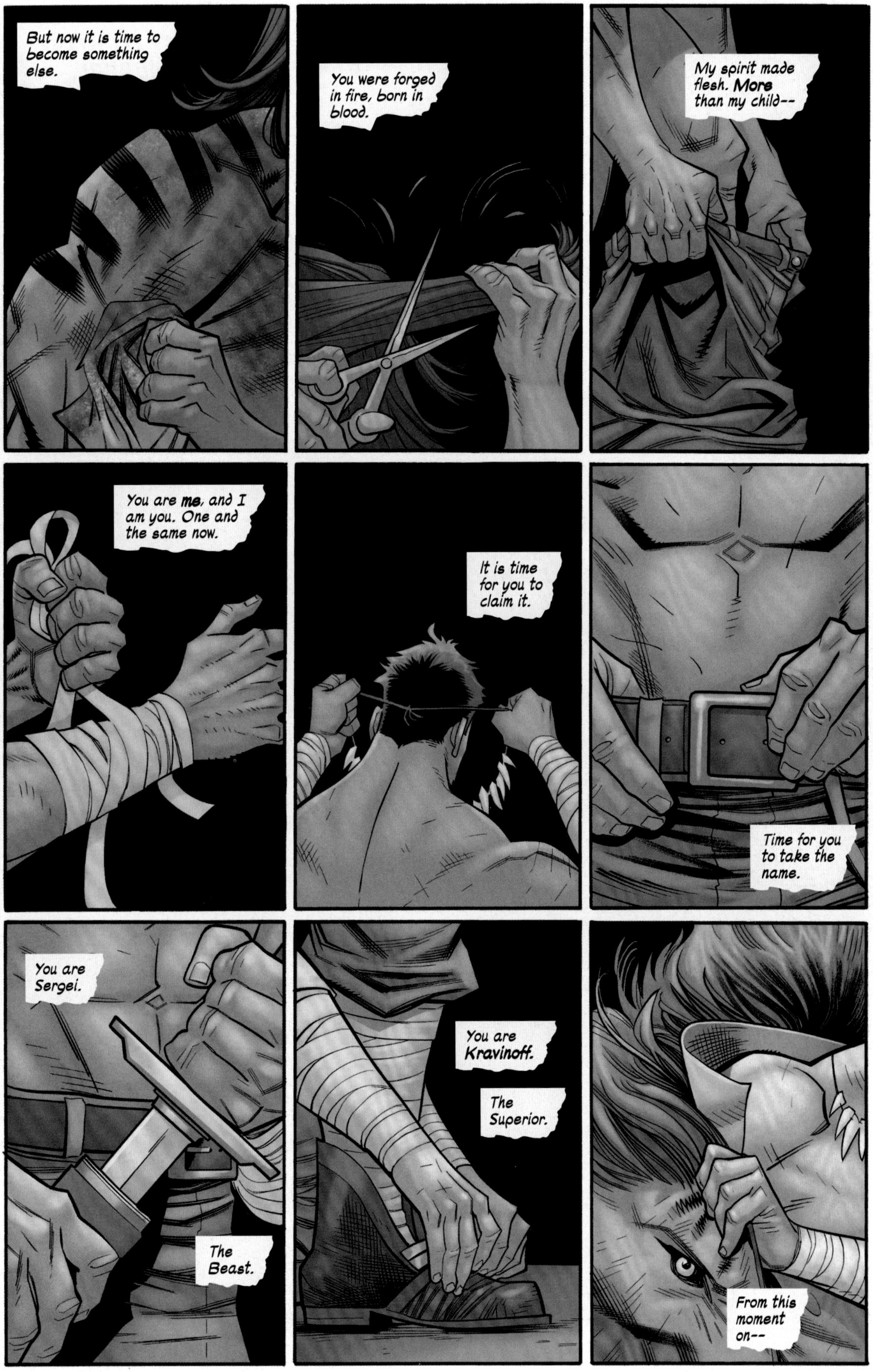
But now it is time to become something else.
You were forged in fire, born in blood.
My spirit made flesh. More than my child--
You are me, and I am you. One and the same now.
It is time for you to claim it.
Time for you to take the name.
You are Sergei.
The Beast.
You are Kravinoff.
The Superior.
From this moment on--

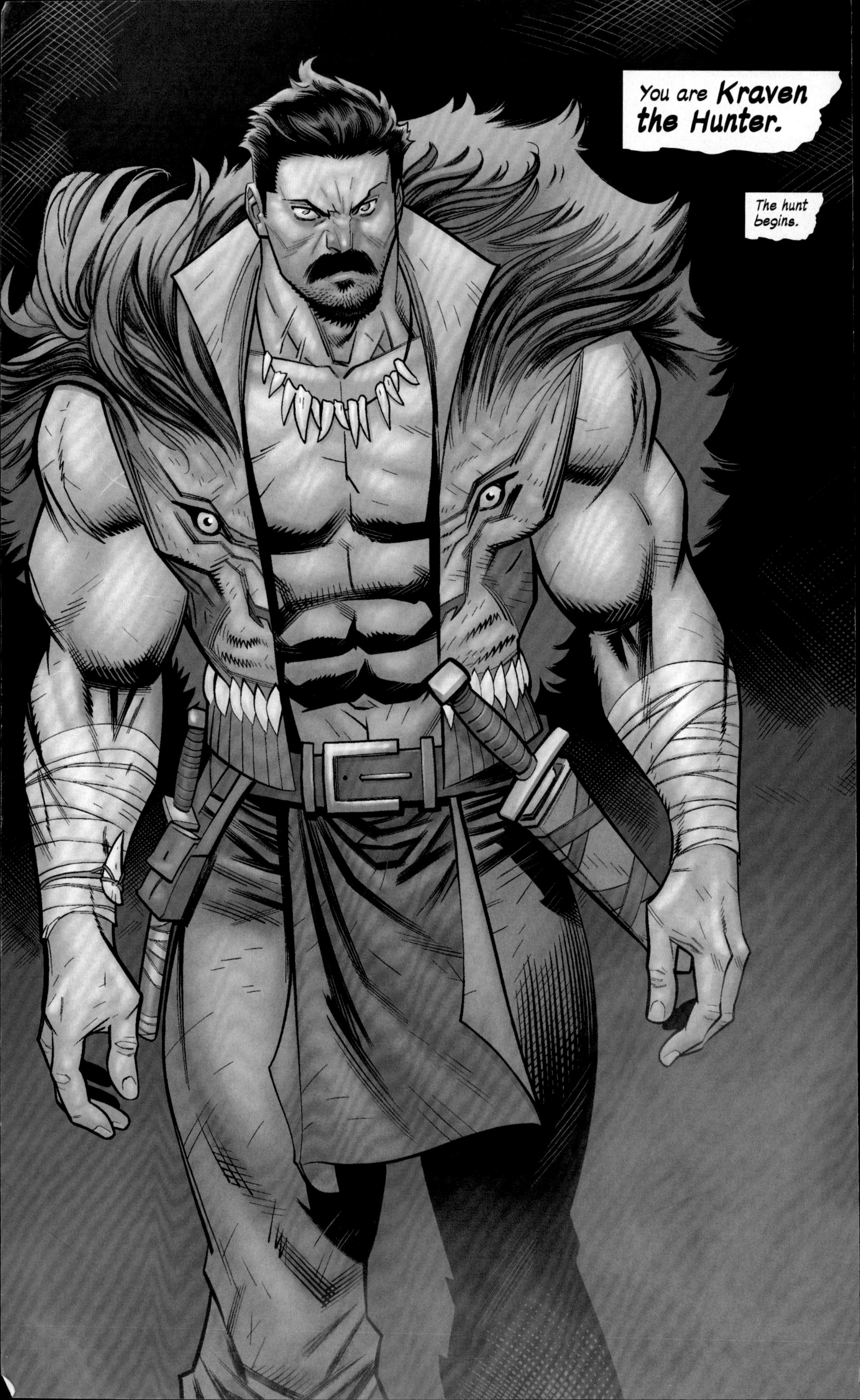
You are Kraven the Hunter.
The hunt begins.

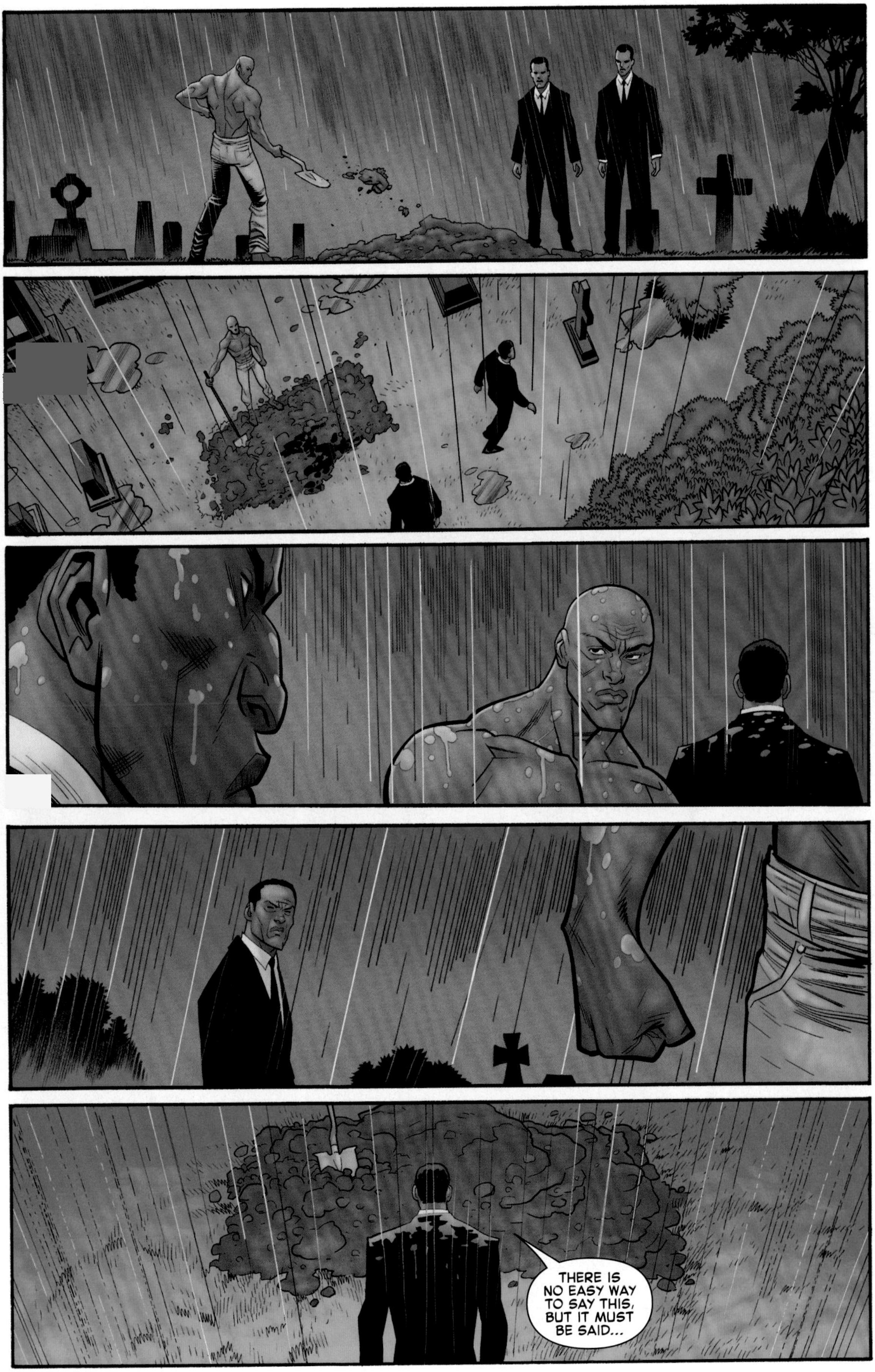
THERE IS NO EASY WAY TO SAY THIS, BUT IT MUST BE SAID...

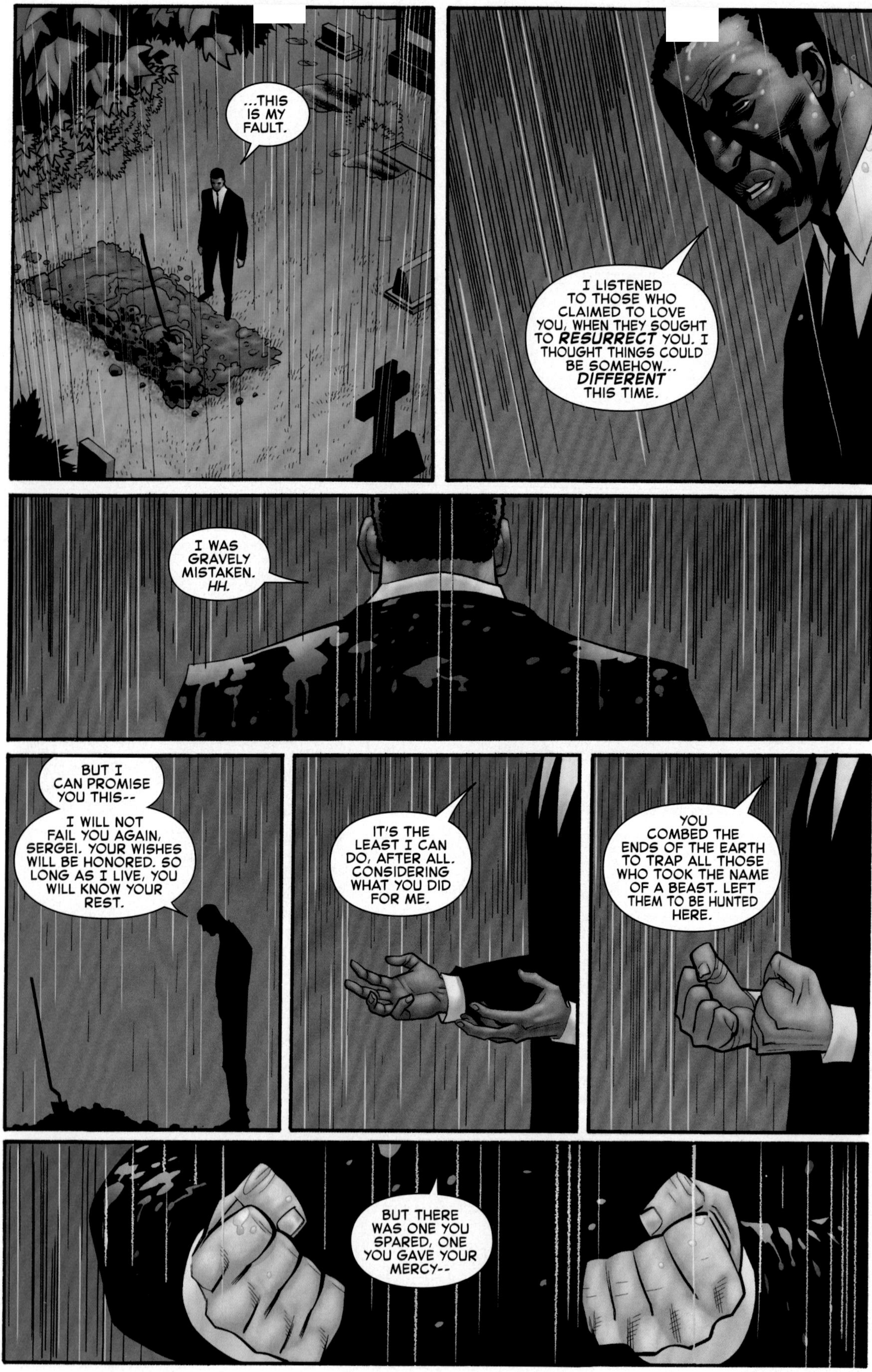
...THIS IS MY FAULT.
I LISTENED TO THOSE WHO CLAIMED TO LOVE YOU, WHEN THEY SOUGHT TO *RESURRECT* YOU. I THOUGHT THINGS COULD BE SOMEHOW... *DIFFERENT* THIS TIME.
I WAS GRAVELY MISTAKEN. *HH.*
BUT I CAN PROMISE YOU THIS--
I WILL NOT FAIL YOU AGAIN, SERGEI. YOUR WISHES WILL BE HONORED. SO LONG AS I LIVE, YOU WILL KNOW YOUR REST.
IT'S THE LEAST I CAN DO, AFTER ALL. CONSIDERING WHAT YOU DID FOR ME.
YOU COMBED THE ENDS OF THE EARTH TO TRAP ALL THOSE WHO TOOK THE NAME OF A BEAST. LEFT THEM TO BE HUNTED HERE.
BUT THERE WAS ONE YOU SPARED, ONE YOU GAVE YOUR MERCY--

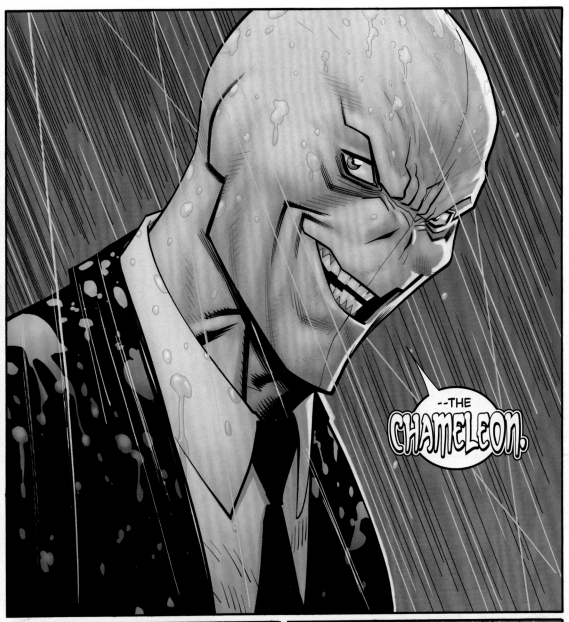

--THE CHAMELEON.

SLEEP WELL, BROTHER. YOU NEEDN'T WORRY. THIS WORLD IS NO LONGER YOUR BURDEN.

BESIDES, THERE WON'T BE MUCH OF IT LEFT SOON...

NOT BY THE TIME I'VE FINISHED.

TO BE CONTINUED...

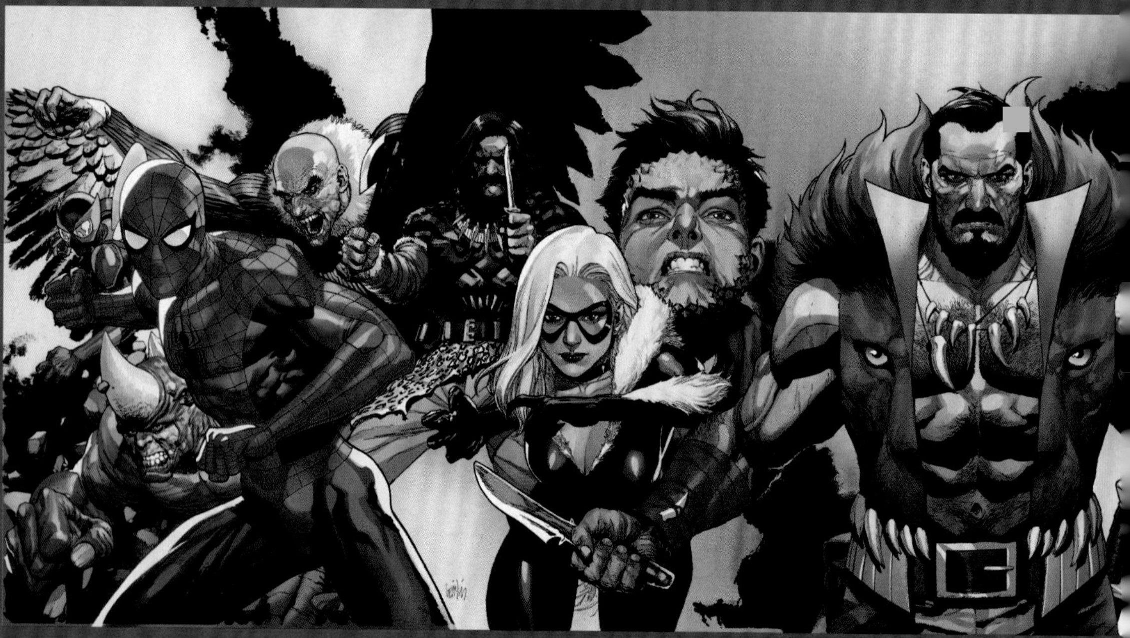

#17-22 CONNECTING VARIANTS BY LEINIL FRANCIS YU & SUNNY GHO

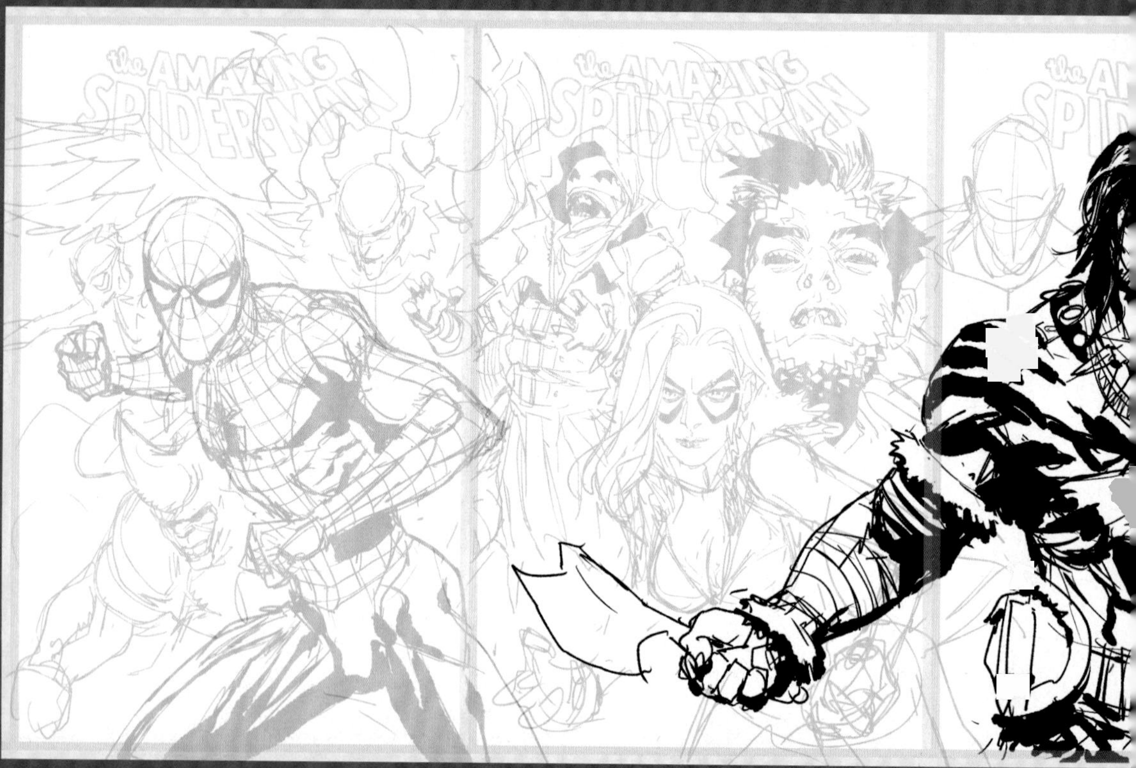
the AMAZING SPIDER-MAN
the AMAZING SPIDER-MAN

ORIGINAL CONCEPT SKETCH BY LEINIL FRANCIS YU

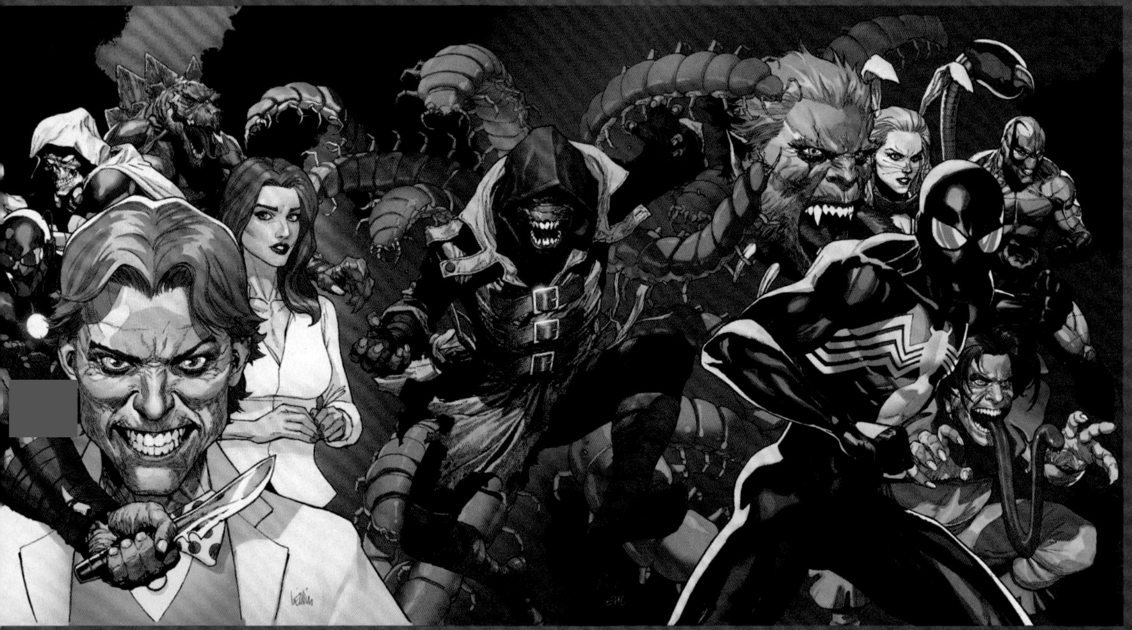

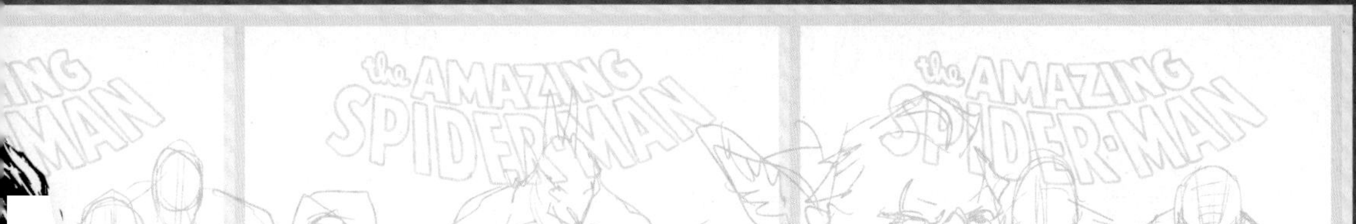

the AMAZING SPIDER-MAN
the AMAZING SPIDER-MAN

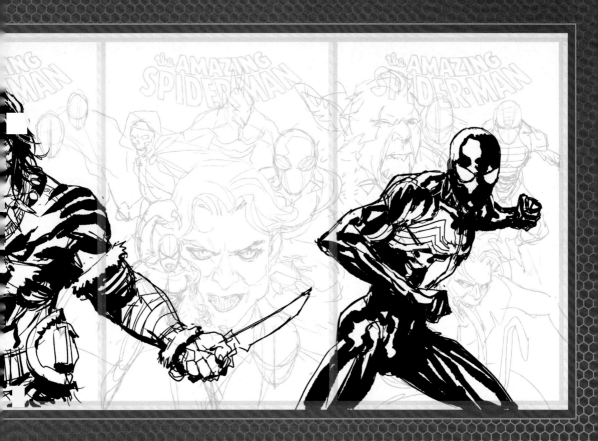

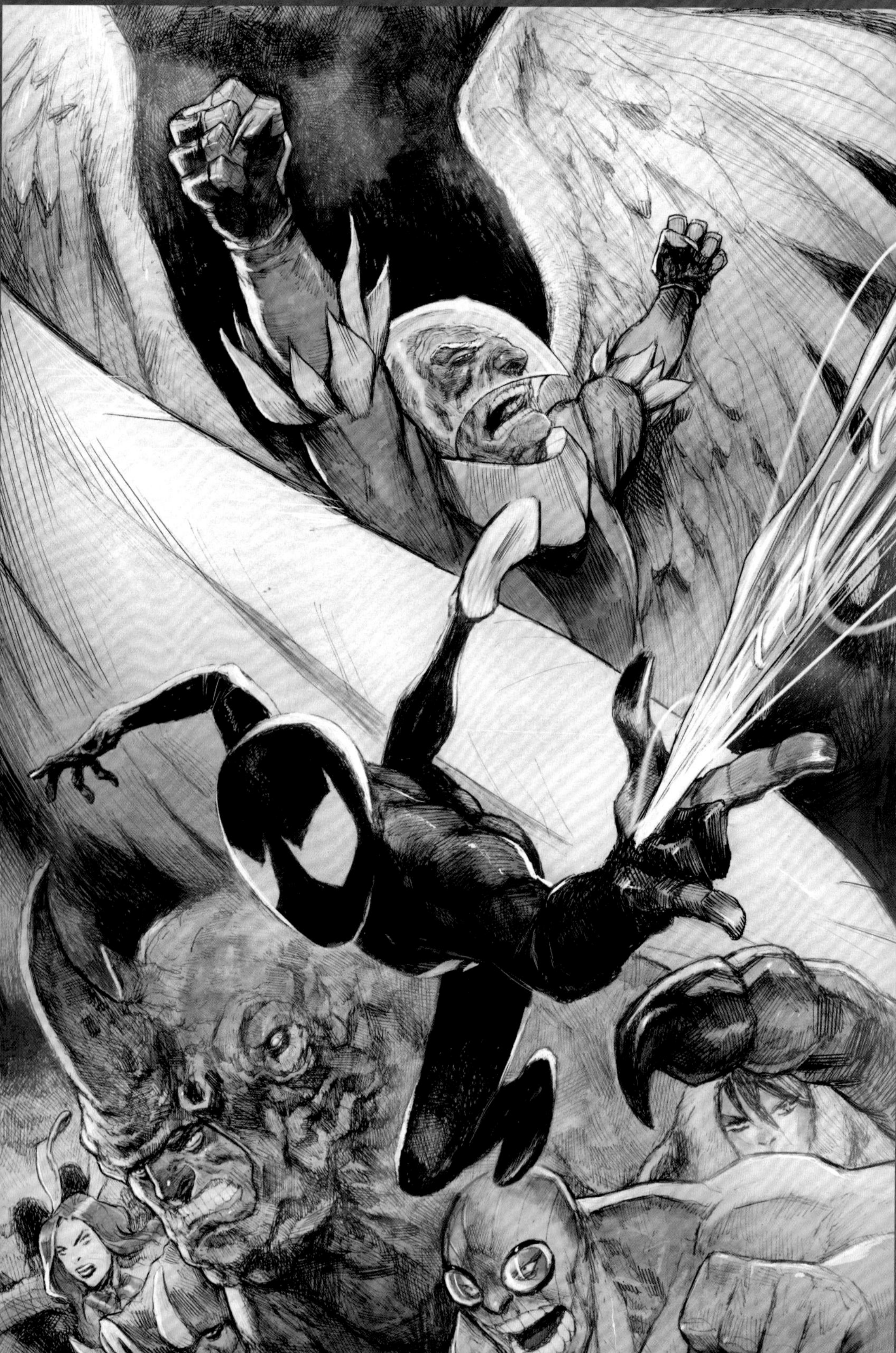

#19 VARIANT BY NIKO HENRICHON

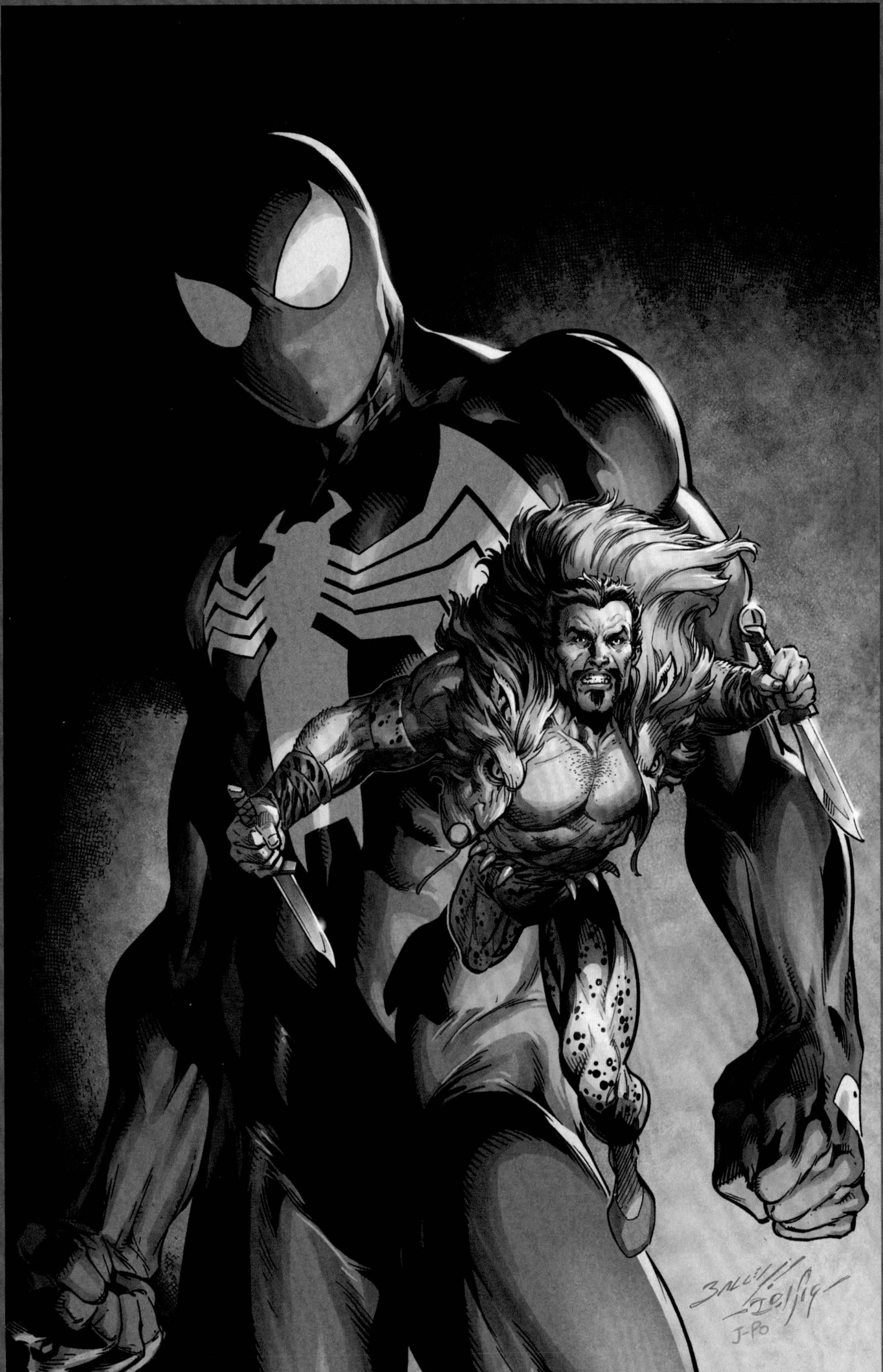

#20 VARIANT BY MARK BAGLEY, JOHN DELL & JUSTIN PONSOR

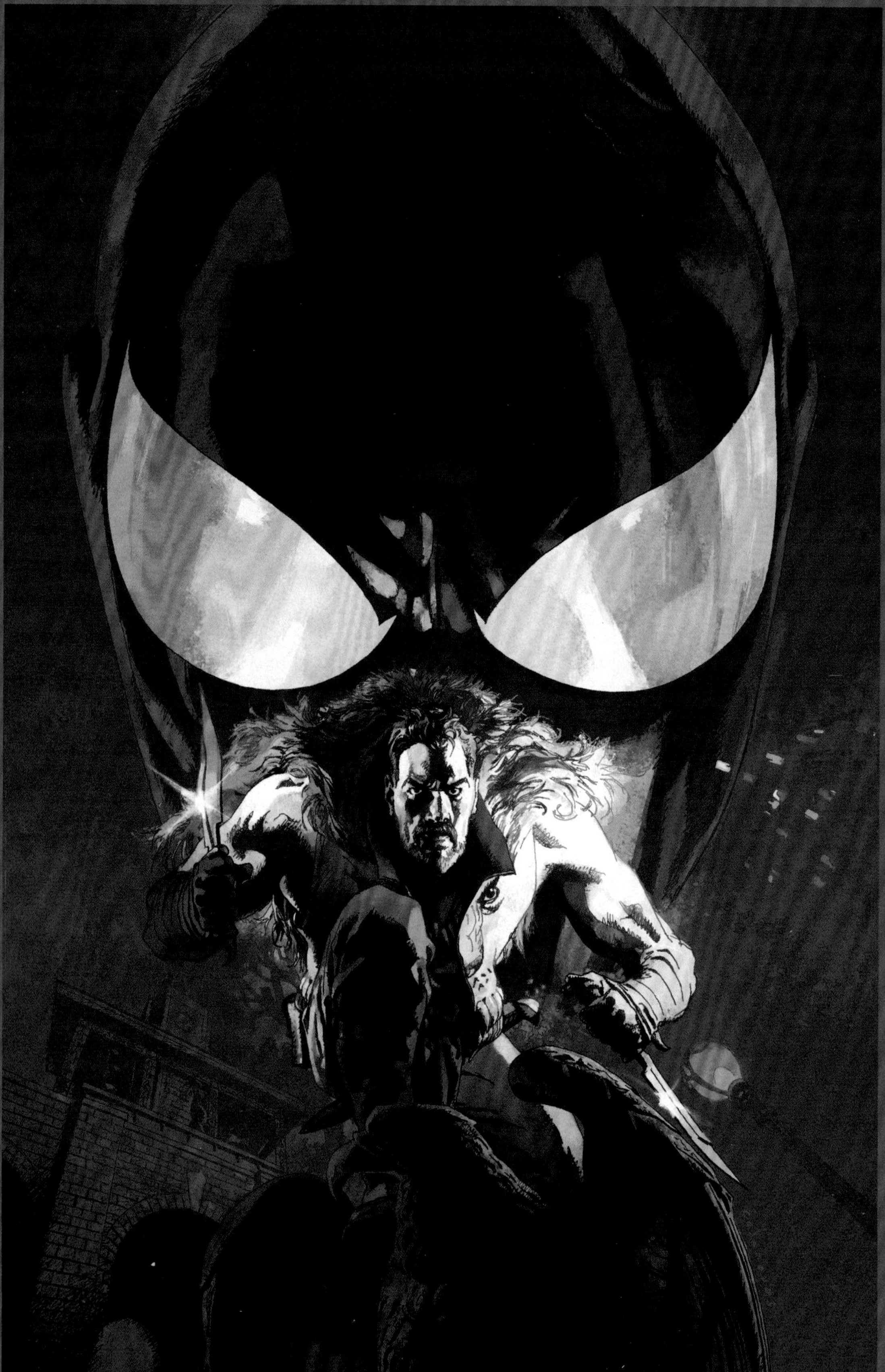

#21 VARIANT BY CASANOVAS

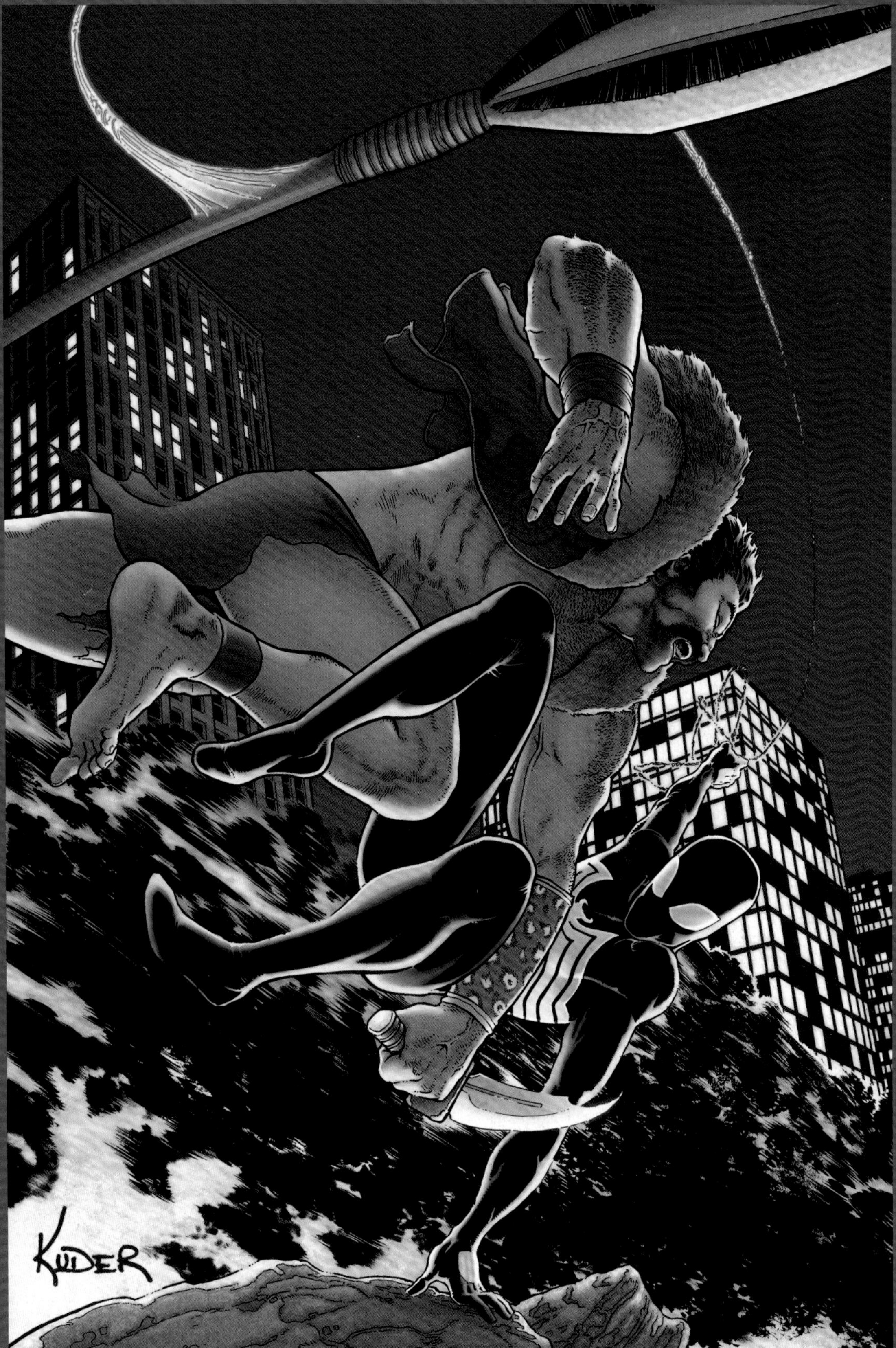
KUDER

#22 VARIANT BY AARON KUDER & MORRY HOLLOWELL

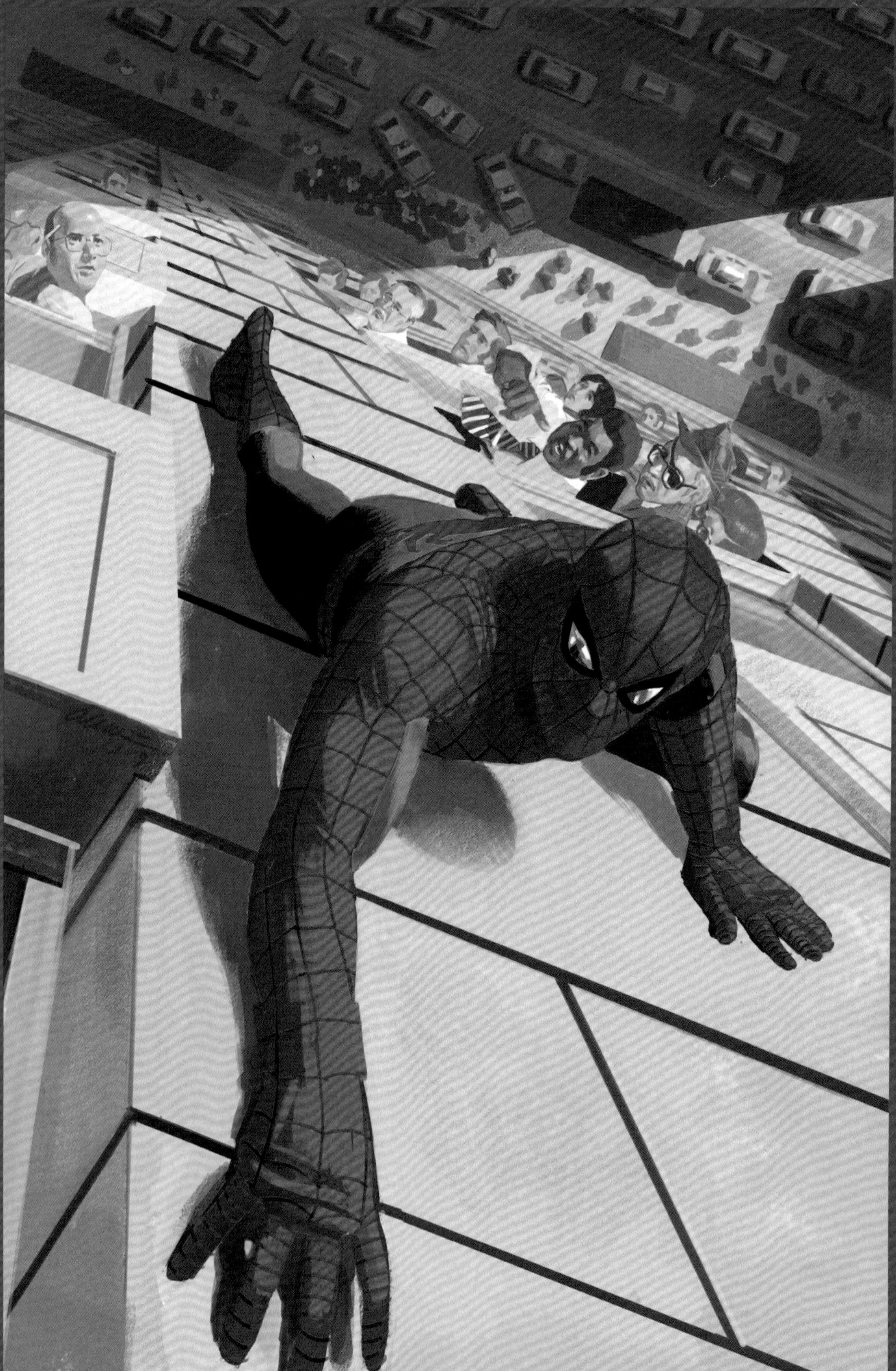

#23 MARVELS 25TH TRIBUTE VARIANT BY DANIEL ACUÑA

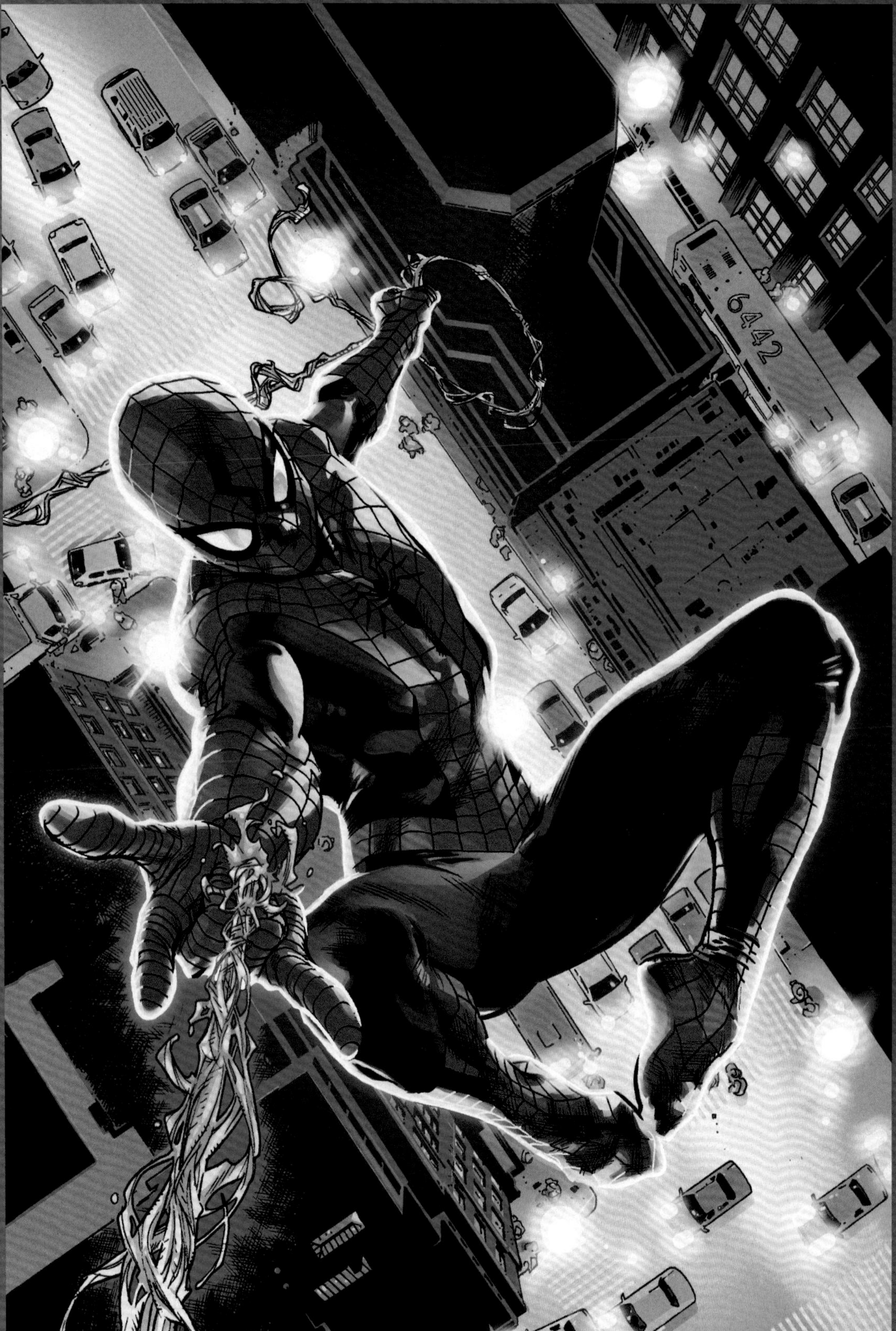
6442

#23 SPIDER-MAN VARIANT BY STUART IMMONEN

#21 COVER ART BY HUMBERTO RAMOS

#22 COVER ART BY HUMBERTO RAMOS